ESSENTIALS OF MANAGEMENT

8e

Andrew J. DuBrin

Professor Emeritus of Management
College of Business
Rochester Institute of Technology

SOUTH-WESTERN
CENGAGE Learning™

Australia • Brazil • Japan • Korea • Mexico • Singapore • Spain • United Kingdom • United States

SOUTH-WESTERN
CENGAGE Learning

Essentials of Management, 8th Edition
Andrew J. DuBrin

VP/Editorial Director: Jack W. Calhoun

VP/Editor-in-Chief: Melissa Acuna

Sr. Marketing Communications Manager: Jim Overly

Acquisitions Editor: Joe Sabatino

Developmental Editor: Michael J. Guendelsberger

Editorial Assistant: Ruth Belanger

Marketing Coordinator: Sara Rose

Marketing Manager: Clint Kernen

Content Project Manager: Lysa Oeters

Sr. Manufacturing Coordinator: Doug Wilke

Production Service: Integra

Art Director: Stacy Shirley

Cover Image: Getty Images/Conceptulize

Library of Congress Control Number: 2007936898
ISBN-13: 978-0-324-35389-1
ISBN-10: 0-324-35389-8

Instructor's Edition ISBN 13: 978-0-324-58394-6
Instructor's Edition ISBN 10: 0-324-358394-X

South-Western Cengage Learning
5191 Natorp Boulevard
Mason, OH 45040
USA

Cengage Learning products are represented in Canada by Nelson Education, Ltd.

For your course and learning solutions, visit **academic.cengage.com**

Purchase any of our products at your local college store or at our preferred online store **www.ichapters.com**

Printed in Canada
1 2 3 4 5 11 10 09 08

Preface

Essentials of Management is written for newcomers to the field of management and for experienced managers seeking updated information and a review of the fundamentals. It is also written for the many professionals and technical people who work closely with managers and who take their turn at performing some management work. An example would be the member of a cross-functional team who is expected to have the perspective of a general manager.

Based on extensive research about curriculum needs, the design of *Essentials of Management* addresses itself to the needs of introductory management courses and supervision courses offered in educational and work settings. Earlier editions of the text were used in the study of management in colleges and universities, as well as in career schools in such diverse programs as hospitality and tourism management, and nursing. The book can also be used as a basic resource for management courses that rely heavily on lecture notes, PowerPoint presentations, and DVDs or videos rather than an encyclopedia-like text.

Comments recently made by Jack and Suzy Welch support the intent and relevance of this text in both the present and previous editions. (Jack Welch was the long-time chairman and CEO of GE and Suzy Welch is a former *Harvard Business Review* editor.) Jack and Suzy Welch write,

> *In the past two years, we've visited 35 B-schools around the world and have been repeatedly surprised by how little classroom attention is paid to hiring, motivating, team-building, and firing. Instead B-schools seem far more invested in teaching brainiac concepts—disruptive technologies, complexity modeling, and the like. Those may be useful, particularly if you join a consulting firm, but real managers need to know how to get the most out of people.*
>
> (*Business Week*, December 11, 2006, p. 112.)

ASSUMPTIONS UNDERLYING THE BOOK

The approach to synthesizing knowledge for this book is based on the following five assumptions:

1. A strong demand exists for practical and valid information about solutions to managerial problems. The information found in this text reflects the author's orientation toward translating research findings, theory, and experience into a form useful to both the student and the practitioner.

2. Managers and professionals need both interpersonal and analytical skills to meet their day-to-day responsibilities. Although this book concentrates on managing people, it also provides ample information about such topics as decision making, job design, organization structure, information technology, cost cutting, and inventory management.
3. The study of management should emphasize a variety of large, medium, and small work settings, as well as profit and not-for-profit organizations. Many students of management, for example, intend to become small-business owners. Examples and cases in this book therefore reflect diverse work settings, including retail and service firms.
4. Introductory management textbooks tend to become unrealistically comprehensive. Many introductory texts today are more than 800 pages long. Such texts overwhelm students who attempt to assimilate this knowledge in a single quarter or semester. The goal with *Essentials of Management* was to develop a text that realistically—in terms of time and amount of information—introduces the study of management. Also, this text is not merely a condensation of a larger text, but a concise and comprehensive treatment of management since the first edition.

FRAMEWORK OF THE BOOK

The first three chapters present an introduction to management. Chapter 1, "The Manager's Job," explains the nature of managerial work with a particular emphasis on managerial roles and tasks. Chapter 2, "International Management and Cultural Diversity," describes how managers and professionals work in a multicultural environment. Chapter 3, "Ethics and Social Responsibility," examines the moral aspects of management.

The next three chapters address the subject of planning. Chapter 4, "Essentials of Planning," presents a general framework for planning—the activity underlying almost any purposeful action taken by a manager. Chapter 5, "Problem Solving and Decision Making," explores the basics of decision making, with an emphasis on creativity and other behavioral aspects. Chapter 6, "Quantitative Techniques for Planning and Decision Making," describes several adjuncts to planning and decision making, such as break-even analysis, PERT, and production-scheduling methods used for both manufacturing and services.

Chapters 7–9 focus on organizing, culture, and staffing. Chapter 7, "Job Design and Work Schedules," explains how jobs are laid out and work schedules arranged to enhance productivity and customer satisfaction. Chapter 8, "Organization Structure, Culture, and Change," explains how work is organized from the standpoint of the organization, how culture profoundly influences an organization, and how to cope with and capitalize on change. Chapter 9, "Staffing and Human Resource Management," explains the methods by which people are brought into the organization, trained, and evaluated.

The following three chapters, on leading, deal directly with the manager's role in influencing group members. Chapter 10, "Leadership," focuses on different approaches to leadership available to a manager and on the personal characteristics associated with leadership effectiveness. Chapter 11, "Motivation," describes what managers can do to increase or sustain employee effort toward achieving work goals. Chapter 12, "Communication," deals with the complex problems of accurately sending and receiving messages. Chapter 13, "Teams, Groups, and Teamwork," explains the nature of teams and how managers can foster group members' working together cooperatively. Chapter 14, "Information Technology and e-Commerce," describes how information technology, including the Internet and e-commerce, influences the manager's job,

The next two chapters, on controlling, each deal with an important part of keeping performance in line with expectations. Chapter 15, "Essentials of Control," presents an overview of measuring and controlling performance, and also describes how managers work with a variety of financial measures to monitor performance. Chapter 16, "Managing Ineffective Performers," describes current approaches to dealing with substandard performers, with an emphasis on elevating performance.

The final chapter in the text, Chapter 17, "Enhancing Personal Productivity and Managing Stress," describes how personal effectiveness can be increased by developing better work habits and time management skills and keeping stress under control. A major theme of the chapter is that good work habits help prevent and manage stress.

PEDAGOGICAL FEATURES

Essentials of Management is designed to aid both students and instructors in expanding their interest in and knowledge of management. The book contains the following features:

- Learning objectives coordinate the contents of each chapter. They preview the major topics and are integrated into the text by indicating which major topics relate to the objectives. The end-of-chapter Summary of Key Points, based on the chapter learning objectives, pulls together the central ideas in each chapter.
- An opening case example illustrates a major topic to be covered in the chapter.
- The Management in Action feature presents a portrait of how specific individuals or organizations practice an aspect of management covered in the chapter.
- Concrete, real-world examples with which the reader can readily identify are found throughout the text. Some examples are original, while others relate research information from magazines, newspapers, and journals.
- Exhibits, which include figures, tables, and self-assessment quizzes, aid in the comprehension of information in the text.
- Key terms and phrases highlight the management vocabulary introduced in each chapter with definitions that appear in the margin.

- Questions at the end of each chapter assist learning by encouraging the reader to review and reflect on the chapter objectives.
- Skill-building exercises, including Internet activities, appear at the end of each chapter.
- Self-assessment quizzes appear throughout the text, designed to help students think through their standing on important dimensions of behavior that influence managerial and professional work.
- Case problems, also located at the end of each chapter, can be used to synthesize the chapter concepts and simulate the practice of management.
- Video selections are cued to places in the text where they have particular applicability.

NEW TO THE EIGHTH EDITION

A number of significant changes and additions have been incorporated into this edition. A brief listing of these changes here is followed by a more detailed look.

- All 17 chapters contain new information where appropriate, and many older research findings and several topics of lesser interest today have been deleted.
- Twenty-six of the 34 end-of-chapter cases are new, and the Chapter 1 case about JetBlue has been updated.
- All the chapter-opening cases are new.
- All but one of the Management in Action boxes are new. The old Management in Action story about Wal-Mart has been updated.
- Four of the Internet skill-building activities are new. We attempt to avoid pointing students toward Web sites that will be closed before the student attempts to open them.
- Six of the skill-building exercises are new.

Visit the Web Site

The Web site address for *Essentials of Management*, Eighth Edition, is http://www.thomsonedu.com/management/dubrin.

New Topics Added to the Text

- C-level managers—a new term to identify top-level managers (Chapter 1)
- Evidence-based management (Chapter 1)
- New survey of attitude toward ethics among American workers (Chapter 3)
- Survey of questionable workplace behavior as reported by employees (Chapter 3)
- Business scandals as ethical violations including click fraud and backdating stock options at Silicon Valley companies (Chapter 3)
- An explanation of the framework for planning using the challenge Harley-Davidson faces in dealing with an aging customer base (Chapter 4)

- Obtaining input for strategy through *crowdcasting* (Chapter 4)
- Description of levels of strategy, competitive forces, and types of strategies (Chapter 4)
- Decision-making styles (Chapter 5)
- A list of the world's most innovative companies, including why they are considered so innovative (Chapter 5)
- Data-driven management (Chapter 6)
- The four dimensions and subdimensions of job design (Chapter 7)
- Musculoskeletal disorders including carpal tunnel syndrome (Chapter 7)
- Job design and high-performance work systems (Chapter 7)
- High-performance jobs through adjusting worker resources (Chapter 7)
- Homeshoring as a new type of outsourcing (Chapter 8)
- A table of the unique features of various organization structures (Chapter 8)
- How workers learn the organizational culture (Chapter 8)
- Managing and sustaining the organization culture (Chapter 8)
- The DICE framework for successful change management (Chapter 8)
- Human resource management and business strategy (Chapter 9)
- Job embeddedness theory of turnover (Chapter 9)
- Exhibit on sources of external hires (Chapter 9)
- Stack-ranking as the basis for distributing raises and bonuses (Chapter 9)
- The role of labor unions in human resource management (Chapter 9)
- Self-leadership and empowerment (Chapter 10)
- The new version of the Leadership Grid® (Chapter 10)
- Situational Leadership®II (the new version of the situational leadership model) (Chapter 10)
- The leader as a coach (Chapter 10)
- Cross-cultural differences in needs and suitable recognition awards (Chapter 11)
- Table about how to succeed in management by walking around (Chapter 12)
- Networks created by leaders (Chapter 12)
- Organizational learning as part of communication in organizations (Chapter 12)
- An exhibit about a sampler of current business buzzwords (Chapter 12)
- Political correctness as part of organizational politics (Chapter 12)
- Description of task forces (Chapter 13)
- e-leadership (providing leadership when work is mediated by information technology) (Chapter 14)
- Exhibit on how to make an outstanding Web site (Chapter 14)
- Work streamlining by means of information technology (Chapter 14)
- Pro forma earnings (Chapter 15)
- Diagram of measuring unit costs with activity-based costing (Chapter 15)

- Poor organizational citizenship behavior as a potential cause of poor performance (Chapter 16)
- A compensation structure that encourages deviant behavior as a potential cause of poor performance (Chapter 16)
- Anger management program as an intervention for poor performers (Chapter 16)
- Uncivil workers as another type of difficult person (Chapter 16)
- Working smarter, not harder (Chapter 17)
- Hindrance stressors versus challenge stressors (Chapter 17)

New Skill-Building Exercises

Every chapter contains two skill-building exercises, with seven new exercises added to the eighth edition, as follows:

- Managerial Skills of Athletic Coaches (Chapter 1)
- The Enormous Omelet Sandwich of Burger King as an ethical decision-making problem (Chapter 3)
- Choose an Effective Domain Name (Chapter 5)
- Comparing Organization Structures (Chapter 8)
- Practicing Your Active Listening Skills (Chapter 12)
- Cross-Cultural Communication Skills (Chapter 12)
- Housing for the Homeless (Chapter 13)

New Internet Skill-Building Exercises

Every chapter contains an Internet-based skill-building exercise designed to connect students to Web sites that will boost their knowledge of management topics and issues. Five new skill builders are:

- Worst Jobs Trophy (Chapter 7)
- Analyzing a Motivational Program (Chapter 11)
- The Communication Component of Jobs (Chapter 12)
- Productivity of Teams and Groups (Chapter 13)
- E-Commerce Fraud (Chapter 14)

Self-Quizzes

Not only will students enjoy taking the self-quizzes, they will also learn about their strengths and areas for improvement in the process. Your students will benefit from taking the following:

- My Managerial Role Analysis (Chapter 1)
- Cross-Cultural Skills and Attitudes (Chapter 2)
- The Ethical Reasoning Inventory (Chapter 3)
- How Involved Are You? (Chapter 7)

- Understanding Your Bureaucratic Orientation (Chapter 8)
- Behaviors and Attitudes of a Trustworthy Leader (Chapter 10)
- What Style of Leader Are You? (Chapter 10)
- My Approach to Motivating Others (Chapter 11)
- The Positive Organizational Politics Questionnaire (Chapter 12)
- Team Skills (Chapter 13)
- The Self-Sabotage Questionnaire (Chapter 16)
- Procrastination Tendencies (Chapter 17)
- The Stress Questionnaire (Chapter 17)

Brand-New Action Inserts

Students will find one or two Management in Action inserts in every chapter. All inserts are completely new or an update of an insert from the seventh edition. A complete list follows:

- Ronald A. Williams, the Multifaceted Aetna Executive (Chapter 1)
- High Tech Firms Turn to Indian Cultural Training to Boost Performance (Chapter 2)
- McDonald's Corp. Wins *Black Enterprise* Diversity Award (Chapter 2)
- Updating and expansion of Wal-Mart Managers Take the High Road and the Low Road (Chapter 3)
- Pepsi Thinks Outside the Cola Wars (Chapter 4)
- Thirteen of the Greatest Management Decisions Ever Made (Chapter 5)
- The Innovation lab at Fisher-Price (Chapter 5)
- Data-Driven Decision Making at Hewlett-Packard (Chapter 6)
- Supervisor at a Toyota Supplier Talks about JIT (Chapter 6)
- Steve Hance, Best Buy Employee Relations Manager Works from Wherever He Wants (Chapter 7)
- Overhauling the GE Culture (Chapter 8)
- Pinpointing Talent with IBM (Chapter 9)
- The Job Audition at Southwest Airlines (Chapter 9)
- The Enthusiastic Aylwin B. Lewis of Sears Holding Company (Chapter 10)
- Worker motivation at Nucor (Chapter 11)
- Google Encourages Office Graffiti (Chapter 12)
- The Three-Minute Huddle at UPS (Chapter 12)
- Hypertherm Chief Executive Organizes for Teamwork (Chapter 13)
- Using e-Commerce to Turn Surplus Steel into Gold (Chapter 14)
- Analyzing Unprofitable Customers (Chapter 15)
- Updating of the State of Tennessee Employee Assistance Program (Chapter 16)
- Cummins Inc. Searches to Jettison Unnecessary Work (Chapter 17)

New End-of-Chapter Cases

Twenty-six of the cases in the seventh edition are new and one is updated as follows:

- The Hands-On CEO of JetBlue is updated (Chapter 1)
- The Management Trainee Blues (Chapter 1)
- Cardone Industries Feels the Heat from China (Chapter 2)
- Medtronic Is So Kind to Doctors (Chapter 3)
- Is It Fair that Anyone Owns the Rights to Asthmahelp.com? (Chapter 3)
- Zales Jewelers Flops at the High End (Chapter 4)
- What Should Dell Do Next? (Chapter 4)
- The Sticky Priced Condo (Chapter 5)
- Staple's Annual Creativity Contest (Chapter 5)
- Just-In-Time Worries at the University of Utah Hospital (Chapter 6)
- The Sub Shop Blues (Chapter 7)
- Reshaping Microsoft (Chapter 8)
- Sparking Change at Coke (Chapter 8)
- Can Boomer Road Warriors Really Solve Our Problems? (Chapter 9)
- The Scrutinized Job Candidates (Chapter 9)
- Tough as Nails at Home Depot (Chapter 10)
- VW Gets a Turnaround Artist (Chapter 10)
- Motivating the Staff at HROutsource (Chapter 11)
- We Need More Engagement Around Here (Chapter 11)
- Do We Need This Blogger? (Chapter 12)
- The Adam Aircraft Work Group/Team (Chapter 13)
- Home Rehab Day at Tymco (Chapter 13)
- Tesco PLC Mines Data to Combat Wal-Mart (Chapter 14)
- Down the Tubes at utube (Chapter 14)
- Microsoft Counts Calories for Employees (Chapter 15)
- Coach Fred Zweiger (Chapter 16)
- Hard Charger Turned Soccer Mom (Chapter 17)

INSTRUCTIONAL RESOURCES

Essentials of Management is accompanied by comprehensive instructional support materials.

- *Instructor's Manual with Test Bank and Transparency Masters.* The instructor's manual provides resources to increase the teaching and learning value of *Essentials of Management.* The Manual contains "Chapter Outline and Lecture Notes," which is of particular value to instructors whose time budget does not allow for extensive class preparation.

For each chapter, the Manual provides a statement of purpose and scope, outline and lecture notes, lecture topics, comments on the end-of-chapter questions and activities, responses to case questions, an experiential activity, and an examination. The examination contains 25 multiple-choice questions, 25 true/false questions, and 3 essay questions. A set of transparency masters that duplicates key figures in the text is included in the manual.

- *Examview.* The examinations presented in the Manual are also available on disk with the test generator program, *Examview.* This versatile software package allows instructors to create new questions and edit or delete existing questions from the test bank.
- *Study Guide. The Study Guide* that accompanies the eighth edition of *Essentials of Management* is a real asset to students. For each text chapter, the *Study Guide* includes an overview, the objectives and key terms, an expanded study outline, and review questions—matching, multiple-choice, true/false, and fill-in. Each chapter also contains an application exercise that requires use of the concepts presented in the text chapter.
- *PowerPoint Slides.* A set of 150 professionally prepared PowerPoint slides accompanies the text. This slide package is designed for easy classroom use and includes reproductions of many of the exhibits found in the text.

A NOTE TO THE STUDENT

The information in the general preface is important for students as well as instructors. Here I offer additional comments that will enable you to increase the personal payoffs from studying management. My message can be organized around several key points.

- *Management is not simply common sense.* The number one trap for students in studying management is to assume that the material is easy to master because many of the terms and ideas are familiar. For example, just because you have heard the word *teamwork* many times, it does not automatically follow that you are familiar with specific field-tested ideas for enhancing teamwork.
- *Managerial skills are vital.* The information in the course for which you are studying this text and in the text itself are vital in today's world. People with formal managerial job titles such as *supervisor, team leader, department head,* or *vice president* are obviously expected to possess managerial skills. But many other people in jobs without managerial titles also benefit from managerial skills. Among them are people with titles such as *administrative assistant, customer-service representative,* and *inventory-control specialist.*
- *The combination of managerial, interpersonal, and technical skills leads to outstanding career success.* A recurring myth is that it is better to study "technical" or "hard" subjects than management because the pay is better. In reality, the people in business making the higher salaries and other compensation are those who combine technical skills with managerial and

interpersonal skills. Executives and business owners, for example, can earn incomes rivaled only by leading professional athletes and entertainment personalities.

- *Studying management, however, has its biggest payoff in the long run.* Entry-level management positions are in short supply. Management is a basic life process. To run a major corporation, manage a restaurant or a hair salon, organize a company picnic, plan a wedding, or run a good household, management skills are an asset. We all have some knowledge of management, but formally studying management can multiply one's effectiveness.

Take advantage of the many study aids in this text and the *Study Guide.* You will enhance your learning of management by concentrating on such learning aids as the chapter objectives, summaries, discussion questions, self-quizzes, skill-development exercises, and the glossary. Carefully studying a glossary is an effective way of building a vocabulary in a new field, Studying the glossary will also serve as a reminder of important topics. Activities such as the cases, discussion questions, and skill-building exercises facilitate learning by creating the opportunity to think through the information. Thinking through information, in turn, leads to better comprehension and long-term retention of information. The *Study Guide* will provide excellent review and preparation for examinations.

ACKNOWLEDGMENTS

Any project as complex as this text requires a team of dedicated and talented people to see that it gets completed effectively. Many reviewers made valuable comments during the development of this new edition as well as the previous seven editions of the text. I appreciate the helpful suggestions of the following colleagues:

Thelma Anderson
Montana State University–Northern
Zay Lynn Bailey
SUNY—Brockport
Tom Birkenhead
Lane Community College
Genie Black
Arkansas Tech University
Thomas M. Bock
Baruch College
Brenda Britt
Fayetteville Technical Community College
Murray Brunton
Central Ohio Technical College
Michel Cardinale
Palomar College
Gary Clark
North Harris College
Jose L. Curzet
Florida National College
Rex Cutshall
Vincennes University
Robert DeDominic
Montana Tech University
Robert Desman
Kennesaw State College

Kenneth Dreifus
Pace University
Ben Dunn
York Technical College
Debra Farley
Ozark College
Thomas Fiock
Southern Illinois University at Carbondale
Dan Geeding
Xavier University
Shirley Gilmore
Iowa State University
Philip C. Grant
Hussen College
Randall Greenwell
John Wood Community College
David R. Grimmett
Austin Peay State University
Robert Halliman
Austin Peay State University
Paul Hegele
Elgin Community College
Thomas Heslin
Indiana University
Peter Hess
Western New England College
Nathan Himelstein
Essex County College
Kim T. Hinrichs
Minnesota State University—Mankato
Judith A. Horrath
Lehigh Corbon Community College
Lawrence H. Jaffe
Rutgers University
Steven Jennings
Highland Community College
B. R. Kirkland
Tarleton State University
Margaret S. Maguire
SUNY—Oneonta
Patrician Manninen
North Shore Community College
Noel Matthews
Front Range Community College
Christopher J. Morris
Adirondack Community College
Ilona Motsiff
Trinity College of Vermont
David W. Murphy
University of Kentucky
Robert D. Nale
Coastal Carolina University
Christopher P. Neck
Virginia Tech
Ronald W. Olive
New Hampshire Technical College
George M. Padilla
New Mexico State University—Almogordo
J. E. Pearson
Dabney S. Lancaster Community College
Joseph Platts
Miami-Dade Community College
Larry S. Potter
University of Maine—Presque Isle
Thomas Quirk
Webster University
Jane Rada
Western Wisconsin Technical College
James Riley
Oklahoma Junior College
Robert Scully
Barry University
William Searle
Asnuntuck Community Technical College
William Shepard
New Hampshire Technical College
Howard R. Stanger
Canisius College

Lynn Suksdorf
Salt Lake Community College
John J. Sullivan
Montreat College
Gary Tilley
Surry Community College
Bernard Weinrich
St. Louis Community College
Blaine Weller
Baker College
Mara Winick
University of Redlands
Alex Wittig
North Metro Technical College
Marybeth Kardatzke Zipperer
Montgomery College

Thanks also to the members of the Thomson South-Western Marketing and Management Team who worked with me on this edition: Executive Editor, Joe Sabatino; Developmental Editor, Michael Guendelsberger; Production Editor, Starratt Alexander; Designer, Stacy Shirley; Senior Marketing Coordinator, Sarah Rose; and Editorial Assistant, Ruth Belanger. Writing without loved ones would be a lonely task. My thanks therefore go to my family, Drew, Rosie, Clare, Douglas, Gizella, Camila, Sofia, Melanie, and Will.

Andrew J. DuBrin

ABOUT THE AUTHOR

Andrew J. DuBrin is Professor Emeritus of Management in the College of Business at the Rochester Institute of Technology, where he has taught courses and conducted research in management, organizational behavior, leadership, and career management. He also gives presentations at other colleges, career schools, and universities. He has also served as department chairman and team leader in previous years. He received his Ph.D. in Industrial Psychology from Michigan State University. DuBrin has business experience in human resource management and consults with organizations and individuals. His specialties include career management leadership and management development. DuBrin is an established author of both textbooks and trade books, and he also contributes to professional journals, magazines, newspapers, and online media. He has written textbooks on management, leadership, organizational behavior, and human relations. His trade books cover many current issues, including charisma, team play, office politics, overcoming career self-sabotage, and coaching and mentoring.

Brief Contents

Contents

chapter 1

The Manager's Job

Objectives

After studying this chapter and doing the exercises, you should be able to:

1. Explain the term *manager*, and identify different types of managers.
2. Describe the process of management, including the functions of management.
3. Describe the various managerial roles.
4. Identify the basic managerial skills and understand how they can be developed.
5. Describe how managers have to synthesize five mind-sets to accomplish their work.
6. Identify the major developments in the evolution of management thought.

Muhammad Yunus is the founder of Grameen Bank that offers tiny loans to third-world entrepreneurs. He isn't just building a healthy stock of karma—he's inventing a new model for global investment. A former economics professor, Yunus had a eureka moment during a trip to a Bangladesh village, when he discovered that a loan of just 22 cents was enough to help a poor bamboo craftswoman start her own independent business.

That prompted him to found the Grameen Bank in the troubled country, and he later set about connecting an international network of investors to would-be entrepreneurs who need small-time investments. Grameen has since lent more than $5 billion, at interest rates as high as 20 percent. As a bank, it's even become completely self-financing.

Yunus says, "When we started giving out tiny loans which later became known as the Grameen Bank, we never imagined that one day we would be reaching hundreds of thousands, let alone give million borrowers. With tiny loans, financial services and technology, we help the poor, mostly women, start self-sustaining businesses to escape poverty. Our global network of microfinance partners has already reached 2.2 million families in 22 countries."

manager
A person responsible for the work performance of group members.

The Norwegian Nobel Committee decided to award the Nobel Peace Prize for 2006 in two equal parts, to Muhammad Yunus and Grameen Bank for their efforts to create economic and social development from below.[1]

The story about the bank manager illustrates, among other ideas, that a manager makes things happen. Without Yunus's insight into the need for a bank to lend money to poor people in Bangladesh, the Grameen Bank would never have happened. At the same time, Yunus carried out the all-important managerial contribution of pulling together the resources necessary to launch the bank and keep it running.

WHO IS A MANAGER?

Learning Objective 1

Explain the term *manager*, and identify different types of managers.

A **manager** is a person responsible for the work performance of group members. A manager holds the formal authority to commit organizational resources, even if the approval of others is required. For example, the manager of a Jackson-Hewitt income tax and financial service outlet has the authority to order the repainting of the reception area. The income tax and financial services specialists reporting to that manager, however, do not have that authority.

PLAY VIDEO

THE MANAGER'S JOB

Go to academic.cengage.com/management/dubrin and view the video. As you watch, think about how historical forces influence the practice of management. What are the benefits of going to employees for solutions? What are the drawbacks?

The concepts of manager and managing are intertwined. The term **management** in this book refers to the process of using organizational resources to achieve organizational objectives through the functions of planning, organizing and staffing, leading, and controlling. These functions represent the broad framework for this book and will be described later. In addition to being a process, the term *management* is also used as a label for a specific discipline, for the people who manage, and for a career choice.

Levels of Management

Another way of understanding the nature of a manager's job is to examine the three levels of management shown in Exhibit 1-1. The pyramid in this figure illustrates progressively fewer employees at each higher managerial level. The largest number of people is at the bottom organizational level. (Note that the term *organizational level* is sometimes more precise than the term *managerial level*, particularly at the bottom organizational level, which has no managers.)

management
The process of using organizational resources to achieve organizational objectives through planning, organizing and staffing, leading, and controlling.

Top-Level Managers

Most people who enter the field of management aspire to become **top-level managers**—managers at the top one or two levels in an organization.

1 "The 50 Who Matter Now: Meet the Executives, Entrepreneurs, and Cutting-Edge Innovators Who are Setting Today's Business Agenda," *Business 2.0*, July 2006, p. 89; http://www.grameenfoundation.org.

exhibit 1-1 **Managerial Levels and Sample Job Titles**

Many job titles can be found at each level of management.

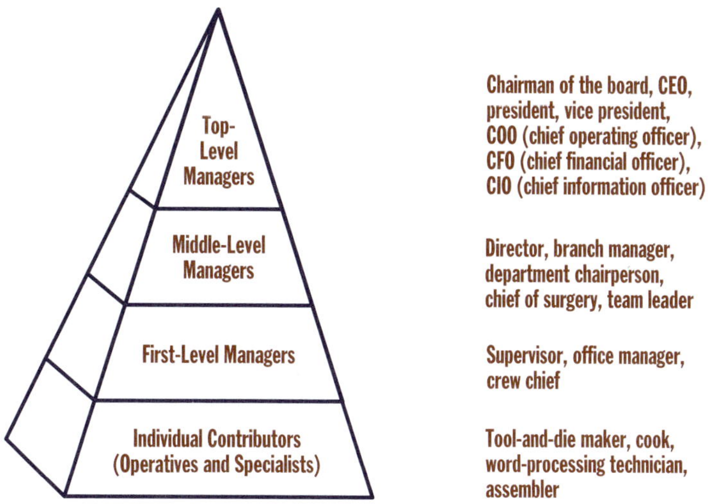

Note: Some individual contributors, such as financial analysts and administrative assistants, report directly to top-level managers or middle managers.

C-level manager is a recent term to describe a top-level manager because these managers usually have *chief* in their title, such as *chief operating officer*. Top-level managers are empowered to make major decisions affecting the present and future of the firm. Only a top-level manager, for example, would have the authority to purchase another company, initiate a new product line, or hire hundreds of employees. Top-level managers are the people who give the organization its general direction; they decide where it is going and how it will get there. The terms *executive, top-level manager,* and *c-level manager* can be used interchangeably.

top-level managers Managers at the top one or two levels in an organization.

c-level manager A recent term to describe top-level managers because they usually have *chief* in their title.

Middle-Level Managers

Middle-level managers are managers who are neither executives nor first-level supervisors, but who serve as a link between the two groups. Middle-level managers conduct most of the coordination activities within the firm, and they are responsible for implementing programs and policies formulated by top-level management. The jobs of middle-level managers vary substantially in terms of responsibility and income. A branch manager in a large firm might be responsible for more than 100 workers. In contrast, a general supervisor in a small manufacturing firm might have 20 people reporting to him or her. Other important tasks for many middle-level managers include helping the company undertake profitable new ventures and finding creative ways to reach goals. The number and proportion of middle managers had declined in the past two decades, but the number of middle managers has begun to increase recently. Middle-level managers play a major role in operating an organization, and therefore continue to be in demand.

middle-level managers Managers who are neither executives nor first-level supervisors, but who serve as a link between the two groups.

First-Level Managers

first-level managers Managers who supervise operatives (also known as first-line managers or supervisors).

Managers who supervise operatives are referred to as **first-level managers,** first-line managers, or supervisors. Historically, first-level managers were promoted from production or clerical positions into supervisory positions. Rarely did they have formal education beyond high school. A dramatic shift has taken place in recent years, however. Many of today's first-level managers are career school graduates and four-year college graduates, who are familiar with modern management techniques. The current emphasis on productivity and cost control has elevated the status of many supervisors.

To understand the work performed by first-level managers, reflect back on your first job. Like most employees in entry-level positions, you probably reported to a first-level manager. Such a manager might be supervisor of newspaper carriers, dining room manager, service station manager, maintenance supervisor, or department manager in a retail store. Supervisors help shape the attitudes of new employees toward the firm. Newcomers who like and respect their first-level manager tend to stay with the firm longer. Conversely, new workers who dislike and disrespect their first supervisor tend to leave the firm early.

TYPES OF MANAGERS

The functions performed by managers can also be understood by describing different types of management jobs. The management jobs discussed here are functional and general managers, administrators, entrepreneurs and small-business owners, and team leaders. (The distinction between line and staff managers will be described in Chapter 8 about organization structure.)

Functional and General Managers

Another way of classifying managers is to distinguish between those who manage people who do one type of specialized work and those who manage people who engage in different specialties. *Functional managers* supervise the work of employees engaged in specialized activities, such as accounting, engineering, information systems, food preparation, marketing, and sales. A functional manager is a manager of specialists and of their support team, such as office assistants.

General managers are responsible for the work of several different groups that perform a variety of functions. The job title "plant general manager" offers insight into the meaning of general management. Reporting to the plant general manager are various departments engaged in both specialized and generalized work, such as manufacturing, engineering, labor relations, quality control, safety, and information systems. Company presidents are general managers. Branch managers also are general managers if employees from different disciplines report to them. The responsibilities and tasks of a general manager highlight many of the topics contained in the study of management. These tasks will therefore be introduced at various places in this book.

Administrators

An *administrator* is typically a manager who works in a public (government) or nonprofit organization rather than in a business firm. Among these managerial positions are hospital administrator and housing administrator. Managers in all types of educational institutions are referred to as administrators. The fact that individual contributors in nonprofit organizations are sometimes referred to as administrators often causes confusion. An employee is not an administrator in the managerial sense unless he or she supervises others.

entrepreneur
A person who founds and operates an innovative business.

small-business owner
An individual who owns and operates a small business.

Entrepreneurs and Small-Business Owners

Millions of students and employees dream of turning an exciting idea into a successful business. Many people think, "If Michael Dell started Dell computers from his dormitory room and he is the wealthiest man in Texas today, why can't I do something similar?" Success stories such as Dell's kindle the entrepreneurial spirit. By a strict definition, an **entrepreneur** is a person who founds and operates an innovative business.

Researcher Michael H. Morris defines entrepreneurship along three dimensions: innovativeness, risk taking, and proactiveness. Each of these dimensions or aspects can occur in different degrees. Entrepreneurs vary in how innovative they are, how much risk they take, and how proactive (initiative taking) they are.[2] After the entrepreneur develops the business into something bigger than he or she can handle alone or without the help of a few people, that person becomes a general manager.

Similar to an entrepreneur, the owner and operator of a small business becomes a manager when the firm grows to include several employees. **Small-business owners** typically invest considerable emotional and physical energy into their firms. Note that entrepreneurs are (or start as) small-business owners, but that the reverse is not necessarily true. You need an innovative idea to be an entrepreneur. Simply running a franchise that sells sub sandwiches does not make a person an entrepreneur, according to the definition presented here. Also, an entrepreneur may found a business that becomes so big it is no longer a small business.

A major characteristic of both entrepreneurs and small-business owners is their passion for the work. These types of managers will usually have a single-minded drive to solve a problem. A case in point is a green-roofing company founded by Kelly Luckett and Mike Crowell. The business partners recognized that covering a roof with plants is environmentally friendly, but is traditionally expensive and difficult to implement. So Luckett and Crowell created Green Leaf Blocks—aluminum trays containing soil and plants. The blocks are designed to last 65 years with no maintenance because the plants resist drought and require no irrigation. Furthermore, the blocks increase roof life up to 200 percent and lower heating and cooling costs.[3]

---

2 Michael H. Morris, *Entrepreneurial Intensity: Sustainable Advantages for Individuals, Organizations, and Societies* (Westport, CT: Quorum Books, 1998).

3 Sara Wilson, "Reaching New Heights," *Entrepreneur*, July 2006, p. 55.

Team Leaders

team leader
A manager who coordinates the work of a small group of people, while acting as a facilitator and catalyst.

A major development in types of managerial positions during the last 20 years is the emergence of the **team leader.** A manager in such a position coordinates the work of a small group of people, while acting as a facilitator or catalyst. Team leaders are found at several organizational levels, and are sometimes referred to as project managers, program managers, process managers, and task force leaders. Note that the term *team* could also refer to an executive team, yet a top executive almost never carries the title *team leader*. You will be reading about team leaders throughout this text.

All of the managerial jobs described above vary considerably on the demands placed on the job holder. All workers carrying the job title *chief executive officer* may perform similar work, yet the position may be much more demanding and stressful in a particular organization.[4] Imagine being the CEO of an American auto parts manufacturer that is facing extinction because of overseas competition. His or her job is more demanding than that of the CEO of a company like Binney & Smith, the subsidiary of Hallmark Cards, which produces Crayola crayons among other popular products. With over 3 billion crayons produced each year, and a fan base in the millions, Binney & Smith is not threatened with extinction. So at least the CEO can enjoy his or her golf outings while the auto parts CEO worries about losing customers and laying off employees.

THE PROCESS OF MANAGEMENT

Learning Objective 2
Describe the process of management including the functions of management.

A helpful approach to understanding what managers do is to regard their work as a process. A process is a series of actions that achieves something—making a profit or providing a service, for example. To achieve an objective, the manager uses resources and carries out four major managerial functions. These functions are planning, organizing and staffing, leading, and controlling. Exhibit 1-2 illustrates the process of management.

Resources Used by Managers

Managers use resources to accomplish their purposes, just as a carpenter uses resources to build a terrace. A manager's resources can be divided into four types: human, financial, physical, and informational.

Human resources are the people needed to get the job done. Managers' goals influence which employees they choose. A manager might set the goal of delivering automotive supplies and tools to auto and truck manufacturers. Among the human resources he or she chooses are manufacturing technicians, sales representatives, information technology specialists, and a network of dealers.

4 Donald C. Hambrick, Sydney Finkelstein, and Ann C. Mooney, "Executive Job Demands: New Insights for Explaining Strategic Decisions and Leader Behavior," *Academy of Management Review*, July 2005, pp. 472–491.

exhibit 1-2 The Process of Management

The manager uses resources and carries out functions to achieve goals.

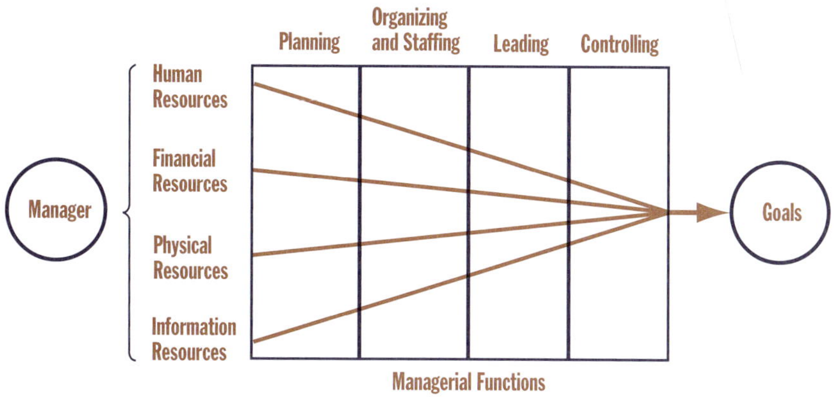

Source: Ricky W. Griffin, Management, 4e, Copyright (c) 1993 by Houghton Mifflin Co., p. 6. Used with permission.

Financial resources are the money the manager and the organization use to reach organizational goals. The financial resources of a business organization are profits and investments from stockholders. A business must occasionally borrow cash to meet payroll or to pay for supplies. The financial resources of community agencies come from tax revenues, charitable contributions, and government grants.

Physical resources are a firm's tangible goods and real estate, including raw materials, office space, production facilities, office equipment, and vehicles. Vendors supply many of the physical resources needed to achieve organizational goals.

Information resources are the data that the manager and the organization use to get the job done. For example, to supply leads to the firm's sales representatives, the sales manager of an office-supply company reads local business newspapers to learn about new firms in town. These newspapers are information resources. Jeffrey R. Immelt, the chairman and CEO of General Electric Corp., surfs the Internet regularly to learn about developments in the industry, thus using the Internet as an information resource.

The Four Managerial Functions

Exhibit 1-2 shows the four major resources in the context of the management process. To accomplish goals, the manager performs four managerial functions. These functions are planning, organizing and staffing, leading, and controlling.

Planning

Planning involves setting goals and figuring out ways of reaching them. Planning, considered the central function of management, pervades everything a manager does. In planning, a manager looks to the future, saying, "Here is what we want to achieve, and here is how we are going to do it." Decision making is usually a component of planning, because choices have to be made in the process of finalizing plans. The importance of planning expands as it contributes heavily to performing the other management functions. For example, managers must make plans to do an effective job of staffing the organization. Planning is also part of marketing. For example, cereal maker Kellogg Corp. established plans to diversify further into the snack-food business to reach its goal of expanding market share.

Organizing and Staffing

Organizing is the process of making sure the necessary human and physical resources are available to carry out a plan and achieve organizational goals. Organizing also involves assigning activities, dividing work into specific jobs and tasks, and specifying who has the authority to accomplish certain tasks. Another major aspect of organizing is grouping activities into departments or some other logical subdivision. The staffing function ensures the availability of necessary human resources to achieve organizational goals. Hiring people for jobs is a typical staffing activity. Staffing is such a major activity that it is sometimes classified as a function separate from organizing.

Leading

Leading means influencing others to achieve organizational objectives. As a consequence, it involves energizing, directing, persuading others, and creating a vision. Leadership involves dozens of interpersonal processes: motivating, communicating, coaching, and showing group members how they can reach their goals. Leadership is such a key component of managerial work that management is sometimes seen as accomplishing results through people. The leadership aspect of management focuses on inspiring people and bringing about change, whereas the other three functions focus more on maintaining a stable system.

Although leadership deals heavily with persuasion and inspiration, the leader also executes the visions and other ideas for change he or she formulates. As explained by business executive Larry Bossidy and consultant Ram Charan, visionaries often fail because they do not translate their strategies (master plans) into results.[5] Also, it has been said that *execution* has become an important new buzzword in business because leaders in the past placed too much emphasis on spinning grand visions without really taking care of business.

Controlling

Controlling generally involves comparing actual performance to a predetermined standard. Any significant difference between actual and desired performance would prompt a manager to take corrective action. He or she might, for example, increase advertising to boost lower-than-anticipated sales.

A secondary aspect of controlling is determining whether the original plan needs revision, given the realities of the day. The controlling function

5 Larry Bossidy and Ram Charan, *The Discipline of Getting Things Done* (New York: Crown, 2002).

sometimes causes a manager to return to the planning function temporarily to fine-tune the original plan. Gateway Inc. at one point opened a large number of retail stores to enhance the sale of Gateway products. The stores, however, proved to be unprofitable, so Gateway closed the stores and absorbed the losses. (Gateway is now a division of Acer.)

One important way in which the jobs of managers differ is in the relative amounts of time spent on planning, organizing and staffing, leading, and controlling. Executives ordinarily spend much more time on strategic (high-level and long-range) planning than do middle- or first-level managers. Lower-level managers are more involved with day-by-day and other short-range planning. Also, lower-level managers spend the most time in face-to-face leadership such as coaching and disciplining workers. This is true because entry-level workers are likely to need more assistance than those workers who have advanced higher in the organization.

THE SEVENTEEN MANAGERIAL ROLES

Learning Objective 3

Describe the various managerial roles.

To further understand the manager's job, it is worthwhile to examine the various roles managers play. A **role**, in the business context, is an expected set of activities or behaviors stemming from a job. Henry Mintzberg conducted several landmark studies of managerial roles.[6] Other researchers extended his findings.[7] In the sections that follow, the roles delineated by these researchers are associated with the major managerial functions to which they most closely pertain. (Roles and functions are closely related. They are both activities carried out by people.) The description of the 17 roles should help you appreciate the richness and complexity of managerial work, and also serve as a generic job description for a manager's position. These roles are described next and listed in Exhibit 1-3.

Planning

Two managerial roles—strategic planner and operational planner—relate to the planning function.

1. *Strategic Planner.* Top-level managers engage in strategic planning, usually assisted by input from others throughout the organization. Specific activities in this role include (a) setting a direction for the organization, (b) helping the firm deal with the external environment, and (c) developing corporate policies.
2. *Operational Planner.* Operational plans relate to the day-to-day operation of a company or unit. Two such activities are (a) formulating operating budgets and (b) developing work schedules for the unit supervised.

role
An expected set of activities or behaviors stemming from a job.

6 This research is reported in Henry Mintzberg, *The Nature of Managerial Work* (New York: Harper & Row, 1973).

7 Kenneth Graham Jr. and William L. Mihal, *The CMI Managerial Job Analysis Inventory* (Rochester, NY: Rochester Institute of Technology, 1987); Jeffrey S. Shippman, Erich Prien, and Gary L. Hughes, "The Content of Management Work: Formation of Task and Job Skill Composite Classifications," *Journal of Business and Psychology*, Spring 1991, pp. 325–354.

exhibit 1-3 The Seventeen Managerial Roles

Planning

1. Strategic planner
2. Operational planner

Organizing and Staffing

3. Organizer
4. Liaison
5. Staffing coordinator
6. Resource allocator
7. Task delegator

Leading

8. Figurehead
9. Spokesperson
10. Negotiator
11. Motivator and coach
12. Team builder
13. Team player
14. Technical problem solver
15. Entrepreneur

Controlling

16. Monitor
17. Disturbance handler

Middle-level managers are heavily involved in operational planning; first-level managers are involved to a lesser extent.

Organizing and Staffing

Five roles that relate to the organizing and staffing function are organizer, liaison, staffing coordinator, resource allocator, and task delegator.

3. *Organizer.* As a pure organizer, the manager emerges in activities such as (a) designing the jobs of group members; (b) clarifying group members' assignments; (c) explaining organizational policies, rules, and procedures; and (d) establishing policies, rules, and procedures to coordinate the flow of work and information within the unit.
4. *Liaison.* The purpose of the liaison role is to develop and maintain a network of work-related contacts with people. To achieve this end, the manager (a) cultivates relationships with clients or customers; (b) maintains relationships with suppliers, customers, and other persons or groups important to the unit or organization; (c) joins boards, organizations, or public service clubs that might provide useful, work-related contacts; and (d) cultivates and maintains a personal network of in-house contacts through visits, telephone calls, e-mail, and participation in company-sponsored events.
5. *Staffing Coordinator.* In the staffing role, the manager tries to make sure that competent people fill positions. Specific activities include (a) recruiting and hiring staff; (b) explaining to group members how their work performance will be evaluated; (c) formally evaluating group members' overall job performance; (d) compensating group members within the limits of organizational policy; (e) ensuring that group members are

properly trained; (f) promoting group members or recommending them for promotion; and (g) terminating or demoting group members.

6. *Resource Allocator.* An important part of a manager's job is to divide resources in the manner that best helps the organization. Specific activities to this end include (a) authorizing the use of physical resources (facilities, furnishings, and equipment); (b) authorizing the expenditure of financial resources; and (c) discontinuing the use of unnecessary, inappropriate, or ineffective equipment or services.
7. *Task Delegator.* A standard part of any manager's job is assigning tasks to group members. Among these task-delegation activities are (a) assigning projects or tasks to group members; (b) clarifying priorities and performance standards for task completion; and (c) ensuring that group members are properly committed to effective task performance.

Leading

Eight identified managerial roles relate to the leadership function. These roles are motivator and coach, figurehead, spokesperson, negotiator, team builder, team player, technical problem solver, and entrepreneur.

8. *Motivator and Coach.* An effective manager takes time to motivate and coach group members. Specific behaviors in this role include (a) informally recognizing employee achievements; (b) offering encouragement and reassurance, thereby showing active concern about the professional growth of group members; (c) providing feedback about both effective and ineffective performance; and (d) giving group members advice on steps to improve their performance.
9. *Figurehead.* Figurehead managers, particularly high-ranking ones, spend some of their time engaging in ceremonial activities or acting as a figurehead. Such activities include (a) entertaining clients or customers as an official representative of the organization, (b) serving as an official representative of the organization at gatherings outside the organization, and (c) escorting official visitors.
10. *Spokesperson.* When a manager acts as a spokesperson, the emphasis is on answering inquiries and formally reporting to individuals and groups outside the manager's organizational unit. As a spokesperson, the manager keeps five groups of people informed about the unit's activities, plans, and capabilities. These groups are (a) upper-level management, (b) clients and customers, (c) other important outsiders (such as labor unions), (d) professional colleagues, and (e) the general public. Usually, top-level managers take responsibility for keeping outside groups informed.
11. *Negotiator.* Part of almost any manager's job is trying to make deals with others for needed resources. Three specific negotiating activities are (a) bargaining with supervisors for funds, facilities, equipment, or other forms of support; (b) bargaining with other units in the organization for the use of staff, facilities, and other forms of support; and (c) bargaining with suppliers and vendors about services, schedules, and delivery times.

12. *Team Builder.* A key aspect of a manager's role is to build an effective team. Activities contributing to this role include (a) ensuring that group members are recognized for their accomplishments (by issuing letters of appreciation, for example); (b) initiating activities that contribute to group morale, such as giving parties and sponsoring sports teams; and (c) holding periodic staff meetings to encourage group members to talk about their accomplishments, problems, and concerns.
13. *Team Player.* Three behaviors of the team player are (a) displaying appropriate personal conduct, (b) cooperating with other units in the organization, and (c) displaying loyalty to superiors by fully supporting their plans and decisions.
14. *Technical Problem Solver.* It is particularly important for first- and middle-level managers to help group members solve technical problems. Two such specific activities related to problem solving are (a) serving as a technical expert or advisor and (b) performing individual contributor tasks, such as making sales calls or fixing software problems on a regular basis. The managers most in demand today are those who combine leadership skill with a technical or business specialty.
15. *Entrepreneur.* Managers who work in large organizations have some responsibility for suggesting innovative ideas or furthering the business aspects of the firm. Three entrepreneurial role activities are (a) reading trade publications and professional journals and searching the Internet to keep up-to-date; (b) talking with customers or others in the organization to keep abreast of changing needs and requirements; and (c) getting involved in activities outside the unit that could result in performance improvements within the manager's unit. These activities might include visiting other firms, attending professional meetings or trade shows, and participating in educational programs.

Controlling

The monitor role fits the controlling function precisely, because the term *monitoring* is often used as a synonym for *controlling*. The role of disturbance handler is categorized under controlling because it involves changing an unacceptable condition to an acceptable stable condition.

16. *Monitor.* The activities of a monitor are (a) developing systems that measure or monitor the unit's overall performance, (b) using management information systems to measure productivity and cost, (c) talking with group members about progress on assigned tasks, and (d) overseeing the use of equipment and facilities (for example, vehicles and office space) to ensure that they are properly used and maintained.
17. *Disturbance Handler.* Four typical activities of a disturbance handler are (a) participating in grievance resolution within the unit (working out a problem with a labor union, for example); (b) resolving complaints from customers, other units, and superiors; (c) resolving conflicts among group members; and (d) resolving problems about work flow and information exchange with other units. Disturbance handling might also be considered a leadership role.

The accompanying Management in Action illustrates how the leader of a well-known company is engaged in the various functions and roles of management.

management in action

Ronald A. Williams, the Multifaceted Aetna Executive

When Ronald A. Williams joined Aetna Inc., the nation's largest health insurance provider, in 2001, the company was on life support. The Hartford, Connecticut, company had strained relationships with physicians and hospitals and suffered significant losses. CEO and president Williams has reconstructed Aetna with surgical precision. He restructured corporate divisions and created an environment that fosters productivity. Williams' focus on customer satisfaction through a combination of technological upgrades and back-to-basics values has boosted Aetna's share price by roughly 600 percent.

His performance earned him the nickname "The Turnaround King," and he is largely viewed as one of the most brilliant corporate strategists in the healthcare industry. The 57-year-old was recognized as one of *Black Enterprise*'s "75 Most Powerful African Americans in Corporate America in 2005." "He's a better operational leader than anybody I've ever seen," says Jeff Weiss, founder and director of CCI healthcare executive summits. "His memory, command of the details, and understanding the complexity, is amazing."

These characteristics have earned Williams unwavering loyalty from Aetna employees. "People will walk through walls for him," offers Weiss. "The amount of work he gets out of people is ungodly. He gets tens of thousands of people to put out 120 percent, and Ron does it by the quality of his thinking and the integrity of his actions."

Shared Vision, Different Styles

Williams and chairman and CEO John Rowe of Aetna shared the same vision for what an HMO could become: an organization that would influence the quality of healthcare. The two, however, had wildly different management styles and personalities.

In outlining their differences, Rowe explains, "If we are going to visit a customer, all I need is a one-page-summary of our relationship and the current major issues. Hand it to me in the back seat of the car on the way back from the airport to see the customer. Ron wants a report that's this thick, about everything, the customer's company and the industry, etc."

The chemistry worked. When Williams joined the firm in 2001 as the new chief of health operations, there were concerns about a hostile takeover, and the company suffered net losses of $279.6 million. "This was a company that looked like at one point that it might even go bankrupt," explains an industry analyst. "It was really the low ebb of the company's 125-year history."

Part of Williams' turnaround strategy focused on targeting different customer segments and developing new products within various lines of business. He strengthened the dental company that had been losing market share for years. He also invested millions in the pharmacy business, opting to manage it internally rather than partner with a pharmaceutical company. Williams stopped outsourcing behavioral health services—which includes wellness and mind/body treatments—and brought the unit back in-house.

A technology buff, Williams has applied new systems to advance strategic initiatives, such as centralizing patient data using a patented set of computer algorithms. For example, the system can identify incompatible prescriptions for a patient who may be seeing several different doctors.

(Continued)

management in action (Continued)

Ronald A. Williams, the Multifaceted Aetna Executive

Leading by Example

Williams, who holds a degree in psychology from Roosevelt University and a master's degree from MIT Sloan School of Management, grew up on the South Side of Chicago. His mother, now deceased, was a part-time manicurist. His father worked as a parking-lot attendant, bus driver, and transition union trustee. Both parents instilled in him strong values that remain part of his personal and professional code.

One of his most difficult decisions at Aetna was cutting more than 10,000 jobs. "The result was that we became a healthier organization," he says. Elease E. Wright, senior vice president of human resources at Aetna, says Williams' understanding of people greatly improved the corporate culture. Adds Mark T. Bertoloni, executive vice president of regional businesses, "It was a very poisonous environment before. It had gone from internal sniping, politics, and self-promotion to one of a real team environment focused on getting things done."

Walking through Aetna, one finds Williams' guiding principles displayed on its walls: "Deliver bad news early and personally." "Own your plan and, quick, proactively, act on variances," "Attack the issue, not the person," and "Assume positive intent." They're not just mantras. They represent key elements of the company's operational model. Most employees know them by heart. Williams lives by them.

To give employees a better understanding of the competitive landscape and how Aetna earns and spends money, Williams introduced a business literacy program. He also conducts a series of quarterly managers' meetings, regular site visits, and town hall meetings. "We spend a lot of time educating employees about the condition of the business, what our plans were, and their roles in helping us to be successful," he says. "It's really to create an environment in which people know its OK to ask the difficult, tough questions."

Challenges of Being Chairman

As Williams moves into the chairman's seat, some believe letting go of the reins will be difficult. He is undoubtedly a micromanager, involved in every minute detail of running the company. "At heart, he's an engineer and mechanic and now he's a pilot," quips Bertolini. "He shouldn't be screwing around with the engine."

Rowe believes that "the Ron years are going to be marked by true industry leadership," and a continued emphasis on customer service.

Questions

1. Identify several of the management roles that Ronald A. Williams is carrying out.
2. In what ways does Williams appear to be a professional manager (someone who applies formal knowledge about management to his or her job).

Source: Excerpted from Sonia Alleyne, "The Turnaround King," *Black Enterprise*, September 2006, pp. 96–102.

Managerial Roles Currently Emphasized

Managerial work has shifted substantially away from the controller and director role to that of motivator and coach, facilitator, and supporter. As reflected in the position of team leader, many managers today deemphasize formal authority and rank. Instead, they work as partners with team members to jointly achieve results. Managers today emphasize horizontal relationships and deemphasize vertical (top-down) relationships. We encourage you not to think that traditional (old) managers are evil, while new managers are good.

Exhibit 1-4 gives you the opportunity to relate managerial roles to yourself, even if you are not presently working as a manager.

exhibit 1-4 My Managerial Role Analysis

Here is an opportunity for you to think through your current level of skill or potential ability to carry out successfully the 17 managerial roles already described. Each role will be listed with a few-word reminder of one of its key aspects. Check next to each role whether it is an activity you could carry out now, or something for which you will need more experience and preparation. For those activities you check as "capable of doing it now," jot down an example of your success in this area. For example, a person who checked "capable of doing it now" for Role 5, staffing coordinator, might have written, "I recruited three part-time servers to work in the restaurant where I worked as an assistant manager."

Few readers of this book will have had experience in carrying out most of these roles. So relate the specific roles to any management experience you may have had, including full-time work, part-time work, volunteer work, clubs, committees, and sports.

Managerial Role	Capable of Doing It Now	Need Preparation and Experience
1. Strategic planner (Set direction for others based on external environment.)	_______	_______
2. Operational planner (Plan for running the organization or the unit.)	_______	_______
3. Organizer (Design jobs for group members and clarify assignments.)	_______	_______
4. Liaison (Develop and maintain network of work-related contacts.)	_______	_______
5. Staffing coordinator (Recruit, hire, train, evaluate, and fire group members.)	_______	_______
6. Resource allocator (Divide resources to help get job done.)	_______	_______
7. Task delegator (Assign tasks to group members.)	_______	_______
8. Figurehead (Engage in ceremonial activities, and represent the group to outsiders.)	_______	_______
9. Spokesperson (Answer inquiries and report information about the group to outsiders.)	_______	_______
10. Negotiator (Make deals with others for needed resources.)	_______	_______
11. Motivator and coach (Recognize achievements, encourage, give feedback and advice.)	_______	_______
12. Team builder (Contribute to group morale, hold meetings to encourage members to talk about accomplishments and concerns.)	_______	_______
13. Team player (Correct conduct, cooperate with others, and be loyal.)	_______	_______
14. Technical problem solver (Help group members solve technical problems; perform individual contributor tasks.)	_______	_______
15. Entrepreneur (Suggest innovative ideas and further business activity of the group; search for new undertakings for the group.)	_______	_______
16. Monitor (Measure performance and productivity, and review progress on tasks.)	_______	_______
17. Disturbance handler (Resolve problems and complaints.)	_______	_______

Interpretation: The more of the 17 roles you are ready to perform, the more ready you are to function as a manager or to perform managerial work. Your study of management will facilitate carrying out more of these roles effectively.

The Influence of Management Level on Managerial Roles

A manager's level of responsibility influences which roles he or she is likely to engage in most frequently. Information about the influence of level on roles comes from research conducted with 228 managers in a variety of private-sector service firms (such as banks and insurance companies) and manufacturing firms. The roles studied were basically those described in this chapter. One clear-cut finding was that, at the higher levels of management, four roles were the most important: liaison, spokesperson, figurehead, and strategic planner. Another finding was that the role of leader is critical at the first level of management.[8] Although the study in question is 25 years old, it is consistent with current management practice. For example, in organizations of today first-level managers are expected to be effective leaders who motivate and coach subordinates.

FIVE KEY MANAGERIAL SKILLS

Learning Objective 4

Identify the basic managerial skills and understand how they can be developed.

To be effective, managers need to possess technical, interpersonal, conceptual, diagnostic, and political skills. The sections that follow will first define these skills and then comment on how they are developed. Whatever the level of management, a manager needs a combination of all five skills.

Technical Skill

Technical skill involves an understanding of and proficiency in a specific activity that involves methods, processes, procedures, or techniques. Technical skills include the ability to prepare a budget, lay out a production schedule, prepare a spreadsheet analysis, and demonstrate a piece of electronic equipment. Intricate knowledge of the business, such as developing a marketing campaign for a product can also be regarded as a technical skill. Technical skills are frequently referred to as *hard skills*. A well-developed technical skill can facilitate the rise into management. For example, Bill Gates of Microsoft Corp. launched his career by being a competent programmer.

Interpersonal Skill

Interpersonal (or human relations) skill is a manager's ability to work effectively as a team member and to build cooperative effort in the unit. Communication skills are an important component of interpersonal skills. They form the basis for sending and receiving messages on the job. Although interpersonal skills are often referred to as *soft skills*, it does not mean these skills are easy to learn or insignificant. Interpersonal skills are more important than technical skills in getting to the top and providing leadership to people. Many managers at all levels ultimately fail because

8 Cynthia M. Pavett and Alan W. Lau, "Managerial Work: The Influence of Hierarchical Level and Functional Specialty," *Academy of Management Journal*, March 1983, pp. 170–177.

their interpersonal skills do not match the demands of the job. For example, some managers intimidate, bully, and swear at group members. In the process, they develop such a poor reputation that it may lead to their being replaced. Have you ever worked for a manager who was so rude and insensitive that he or she damaged morale and productivity?

An important subset of interpersonal skills for managers is **multiculturalism**, or the ability to work effectively and conduct business with people from different cultures. Closely related is the importance of bilingualism for managers as well as other workers. Being able to converse in a second language represents an important asset in today's global and multicultural work environment.

multiculturalism The ability to work effectively and conduct business with people from different cultures.

Conceptual Skill

Conceptual skill is the ability to see the organization as a total entity. It includes recognizing how the various units of the organization depend on one another and how changes in any one part affect all the others. It also includes visualizing the relationship of the individual business to the industry; the community; and the political, social, and economic forces of the nation as a whole. For top-level management, conceptual skill is a priority because executive managers have the most contact with the outside world.

The late Peter Drucker emphasized that the only comparative advantage of the developed countries is in the number of knowledge workers (people who work primarily with concepts). Educated workers in underdeveloped countries are just as smart as those in developed countries, but their numbers are smaller. According to Drucker and many other authorities, the need for knowledge workers and conceptual knowledge will continue to grow.[9]

Diagnostic Skill

Managers are frequently called on to investigate a problem and then to decide on and implement a remedy. Diagnostic skill often requires other skills, because managers need to use technical, human, conceptual, or political skills to solve the problems they diagnose. Much of the potential excitement in a manager's job centers on getting to the root of problems and recommending solutions. An office supervisor, for example, might attempt to understand why productivity has not increased in his office despite the installation of the latest office technology.

Political Skill

An important part of being effective is the ability to obtain power and prevent others from taking it away. Managers use political skill to acquire the power necessary to reach objectives. Other political skills include establishing the right connections and impressing the right people. Furthermore, managers high in political skill possess an astute understanding of people, along with a fundamental belief that they can control the outcomes of their interactions

9 Peter F. Drucker, "The Future Has Already Happened," *Harvard Business Review*, September–October 1997, p. 22.

with people. This feeling of mastery often reduces the stress associated with interacting with people.[10]

Political skill should be regarded as a supplement to job competence and the other basic skills. Managers who overemphasize political skill at the expense of doing work of substance focus too much on pleasing company insiders and advancing their own careers. Too much time invested in office politics takes time away from dealing with customer problems and improving productivity.

DEVELOPMENT OF MANAGERIAL SKILLS

This text is based on the assumption that managerial skills can be learned. Education for management begins in school and continues in the form of training and development programs throughout a career. Examples of such programs include a seminar about how to be an effective leader or a workshop about e-commerce.

Developing most managerial skills is more complex than developing structured skills such as computing a return on investment ratio or transferring images from a camcorder to a projector. Nevertheless, you can develop managerial skills by studying this text and doing the exercises, which follow a general learning model:

1. *Conceptual knowledge and behavioral guidelines.* Each chapter in this text presents useful information about the practice of management, including step-by-step procedures for a method of group decision making called the nominal group technique.
2. *Conceptual knowledge demonstrated by examples.* Brief descriptions of managers and professionals in action, including small-business owners, are presented throughout the text.
3. *Skill-development exercises.* The text provides an opportunity for practice and personalization through cases and self-assessment exercises. Self-quizzes are included because they are an effective method of helping you personalize the information.
4. *Feedback on skill utilization, or performance, from others.* Feedback exercises appear at several places in the text. Implementing some of these managerial skills outside of the classroom will provide additional opportunities for feedback.
5. *Frequent practice of what you have learned, including making adjustments from the feedback.* Soft skills as well as technical skills must be practiced frequently to develop expertise. If you also make the adjustments that feedback has suggested, the level of expertise is likely to be higher. Suppose you wanted to develop the managerial skill of giving praise and recognition to others.

10 Pamela L. Perrewé et al., "Political Skill: An Antidote for Workplace Stressors," *Academy of Management Executive*, August 2000, p. 120.

Not everybody is naturally good at giving praise and recognition so you would have to practice frequently. If several people told you that your praise was too heavy, you might diminish the amount of praise you were heaping upon others.

Experience is obviously important in developing management skills. Yet experience is likely to be more valuable if it is enhanced with education. Take an analogy to soccer. A person learning soccer might read and watch on DVD or video the proper way to kick a soccer ball. With this education behind her she now kicks the ball with the side of her foot instead of toe first. She becomes a competent kicker by combining education and experience. People often make such statements as, "You can't learn to be a manager (or leader) from a book." However, you can learn managerial concepts from a book, or lecture, and then apply them. People who move vertically in their careers usually have both education and experience in management techniques.

A key reason for continuing to develop managerial skills is that the manager's job is more demanding than ever, and the workplace keeps changing. A manager is likely to work in an intense, pressure-filled environment requiring many skills. Companies forced to keep up with competition are driving the demand for managers with updated skills. Rapid changes, such as developing an e-commerce presence, require managers to continually develop new skills.[11]

THE MANAGER AS AN INTEGRATOR OF FIVE MIND-SETS

Learning Objective 5

Describe how managers have to synthesize five mind-sets to accomplish their work.

Our final set of information about the manager's job is based on current information. Based on their extensive work in an international program of executive education, Jonathan Gosling and Henry Mintzberg believe that managers need to synthesize different mind-sets or perspectives at the same time. Each mind-set is associated with one of the five key tasks of managers.[12] The five tasks, and their associated mind-sets (or perspectives) are described next, and outlined in Exhibit 1-5.

1. *Managing Self: The Reflective Mind-set.* Managers need to stop and think about what they are doing, so they can understand the meaning of their actions. For example, a manager might ponder *why* a particular Web site promotion was so successful, so Web sites for other purposes might have the same winning ingredient. A reflex reaction to stem high turnover might be to increase wages, yet reflection might reveal that employees are leaving because many of the supervisors lack effective leadership skills.

11 "Managers Face Greater Demands," *Knight Ridder*, July 30, 2000.

12 Jonathan Gosling and Henry Mintzberg, "The Five Minds of a Manager," *Harvard Business Review*, November 2003, pp. 54–63.

exhibit 1-5 Managing by Integrating Five Mind-sets

Source: Figure based on information in Jonathan Gosling and Henry Mintzberg, "The Five Minds of a Manager," *Harvard Business Review*, November 2003, pp. 56–63.

2. *Managing Organizations: The Analytical Mind-set.* A manager cannot get organized without analysis, particularly in a large company. The type of analysis suggested is much like the reflection mentioned in managing self. The manager has to go beyond the superficial data to understand the values underlying certain events. A company office in a small town might achieve wonders after organizing into teams. The superficial analysis is that teamwork enhances productivity. A deeper analysis reveals that small-town people value collaborating with each other because many of them are relatives and friends. The teams might be less effective in a large urban environment in which people lack off-the-job ties to each other.
3. *Managing Context: The Worldly Mind-set.* An effective manager understands the context, or culture and environment, in which decisions are to be made and actions taken. The manager must visit countries and cultures to understand how and why products are used, and how and why certain human resource policies might work or not work. A manager from the United States, for example, might visit Mumbai and learn firsthand that Indian workers do not particularly like the American practice of empowerment. The reason is that Indians have a high respect for authority, and expect the boss to make the important decisions.
4. *Managing Relationships: The Collaborative Mind-set.* The effective manager must manage relationships between and among people. The manager must help people collaborate with each other, and create conditions and attitudes

whereby people want to get tasks accomplished. A major way of collaborating with people is to work closely with people, listen to them, and to share a vision of what must be accomplished. For example, the manager might describe the dream of the company becoming number one it its field, and then encourage workers to figure out how they might contribute to this dream.

5. *Managing Change: The Action Mind-set.* The effective manager makes changes when necessary, such as enabling customers to bank online. However, the effective manager also manages change by recognizing that continuity is also important—such as giving customers an opportunity to cash checks and interact face-to-face with tellers about financial transactions.

According to Gosling and Mintzberg, the successful manager weaves the five mind-sets together to achieve the best result in a given situation. The manager might analyze, then act, and if that does not work well, he or she reflects on what might have gone wrong. A manager might conclude, "Too many of our employees are involved in auto accidents on the way home." He or she might then initiate a program of reminding employees through posters and meetings about the importance of auto safety. The accident rate does not diminish, so the manager gives some serious thought as to what might be causing the high accident rate. The manager hypothesizes that too much job stress is causing the employees to lose concentration while driving. So the manager now begins to investigate job stress as a cause of accidents. Finally, a program of stress management combined with reducing stressful events on the job reduces the accident toll. For the organization to be effective, most of the managers must weave their five mind-sets together.

THE EVOLUTION OF MANAGEMENT THOUGHT

Management as a practice has an almost unlimited history. Visualize a group of prehistoric people attempting to develop a device that would help transport heavy objects. Given a modern label, the caveperson suggesting this development is the head of product research and development. The project of building the curious new circular device was turned over to a group of people who had hands-on access to raw material. Because the developers of the wheel did not constitute a business enterprise, they handed over the technology of the wheel to all interested parties. Also, in prehistoric times, patents were not available.

Learning Objective 6

Identify the major developments in the evolution of management thought.

Management as a formal study, in comparison to a practice, began in the 1700s as part of the Industrial Revolution. Here we take a brief historical look at management, covering both historical developments and various approaches to understanding it. The anchor points to our discussion are as follows:

1. Classical approach (scientific management and administrative management)
2. The behavioral approach
3. Quantitative approaches to management

scientific management The application of scientific methods to increase individual workers' productivity.

4. The systems perspective
5. The contingency approach
6. The information technology approach and beyond.

All of these approaches are mentioned here, but also appear in later sections of the book. For example, the study of leadership and motivation stems from both the classical and behavioral approaches. The historical approaches laid the foundation for understanding and practicing management.

Classical Approach to Management

The study of management became more systematized and formal as a by-product of the Industrial Revolution that took place from the 1700s through the 1900s. Approaches to managing work and people needed to be developed to manage all the new factories that were a central part of the Industrial Revolution. The classical approach to management encompasses scientific management and administrative management.

The focus of **scientific management** was on the application of scientific methods to increase individual workers' productivity. An example would be assembling a washing machine with the least number of wasted motions and steps. Frederick W. Taylor, considered the father of scientific management, was an engineer by background. He used scientific analysis and experiments to increase worker output. Other key contributors to scientific management were Henry Gantt and Frank and Lillian Gilbreth. (Gantt charts for scheduling activities are still used today.)

Administrative management was concerned primarily with how organizations should be managed and structured. The French businessman Henri Fayol and the German scholar Max Weber were the main contributors to administrative management. Based on his practical experience, Fayol developed 14 management principles through which management engaged in planning, organizing, commanding, coordinating, and controlling. Two examples of his principles are (1) *unity of command*—for any tasks, each worker should receive orders from only one supervisor, and (2) *esprit de corps*—promoting team spirit builds harmony and creates organizational unity. Weber proposed an ideal form of bureaucracy to improve upon inefficient forms of organization that included using favoritism to promote workers.[13] Among Weber's recommendations were to break each job down into simple, routine, and well-defined tasks.

administrative management The use of management principles in the structuring and managing of an organization.

Alfred D. Chandler, Jr., the Harvard University business historian, was a key figure in promoting the importance of the classical approach to management. He championed the study of modern bureaucratic administration, and influenced the thinking of executives about organizing large business firms. Many of the insights Chandler developed were based on the individual histories he gathered of Du Pont, General Motors, Standard Oil

13 "Theory of Social and Economic Organization: Max Weber," in *Business: The Ultimate Resource* (Cambridge, MA: Perseus Publishing, 2002), p. 950.

(now Exxon), and Sears, Roebuck & Co. The time period he chose for studying these organizations was between 1850 and 1920, and the most comprehensive version of his conclusions about major business firms was published in *Strategy and Structure* in 1962.

Chandler's book demonstrates the essential link between a company's strategy (master plan) and its structure (layout or division of work). His famous thesis is that a firm's structure is determined or chosen by its strategy—and unless structure follows strategy, inefficiency results. In other words, what a firm wants to accomplish determines how the company is organized. Chandler's insights contributed to the decentralization of many modern organizations.[14]

Consider today's Colgate-Palmolive Company, whose strategy might be stated as responding to the personal-care needs of people and animals throughout the world. To achieve this lofty goal, the company is divided into four mammoth divisions: Oral Care, Personal Care, Home Care, and Pet Nutrition. Each division is subdivided into products groups of its own, such as Personal Care including Men's Antiperspirant and Deodorant, Women's Antiperspirant and Deodorant, Body Wash, and Liquid Hand Soap. If Colgate-Palmolive were not organized by divisions, the company would consist of major groups such as manufacturing, engineering, research and development, finance, and information systems.

The core of management knowledge lies within the classical school. As its key contributions, it studies management from the framework of planning, organizing, leading, and controlling—the framework chosen in this text. The classical school provides a systematic way of managing people and work that has proven useful over time and represents its major strength. Its major limitation is that it sometimes ignores differences among people and situations. For example, some of the classical principles for developing an organization are not well suited to fast-changing situations.

The Behavioral Approach

The **behavioral approach to management** emphasizes improving management through the psychological makeup of people. In contrast to the largely technical emphasis of scientific management, a common theme of the behavioral approach focuses on the need to understand people. The behavioral approach is sometimes referred to as the human resources approach because of the focus on making optimum use of workers in a positive way, such as making jobs motivational. One hope of the behavioral approach was to reduce some of the labor–management conflict so prevalent under the classical approach to management. The behavioral approach has profoundly influenced management, and a portion of this book is based on behavioral theory. Typical behavior and human resource topics include leadership, motivation, communication, teamwork, and conflict.

behavioral approach to management
An approach to management that emphasizes improving management through an understanding of the psychological makeup of people.

14 Alfred Chandler, *Strategy and Structure* (New York: Doubleday, 1962); Albert Chandler, "Strategy and Structure: Albert Chandler," in *Business: The Ultimate Resource* (Cambridge, MA: Perseus Publishing, 2002), p. 950.

The most direct origins of the behavioral approach are set in the 1930s through the 1950s. Yet earlier scholars, such as Robert Owen and Mary Parker Follett, also wrote about the importance of the human element. Working in the textile industry in Scotland in the early 1800s, Owen criticized fellow managers for failing to understand the human element in the mills. He contended that showing concern for workers resulted in greater profitability while at the same time reducing hardship for workers. Owen reported that efforts to pay careful attention to the human element often resulted in a 50 percent return on his investment.[15]

Follett focused her attention on the importance of groups in managing people. Although she published her works during the period of scientific management, Follett did not share Taylor's view that organizations should be framed around the work of individuals. In contrast, she argued that groups were the basis on which organizations should be formed. Follett explained that to enhance productivity and morale, managers should coordinate and aid the efforts of work groups.[16]

Three cornerstones of the behavioral approach are the Hawthorne studies, Theory X and Theory Y, and Maslow's need hierarchy. These developments contributed directly to managers' understanding of the importance of human relations on the job. Yet again, practicing managers have probably always known about the importance of human relations. The prehistoric person who developed the wheel probably received a congratulatory pat on the back from another member of the tribe!

The Hawthorne Studies

The purpose of the first study conducted at the Hawthorne plant of Western Electric (an AT&T subsidiary located in Cicero, Illinois) was to determine the effects of changes in lighting on productivity.[17] In this study, workers were divided into an experimental group and a control group. Lighting conditions for the experimental group varied in intensity from 24 to 46 to 70 foot-candles. The lighting for the control group remained constant.

As expected, the experimental group's output increased with each increase in light intensity. But unexpectedly, the performance of the control group also changed. The production of the control group increased at about the same rate as that of the experimental group. Later, the lighting in the experimental group's area was reduced. The group's output continued to increase, as did that of the control group. A decline in the productivity of the control group finally did occur, but only when the intensity of the light was roughly the same as moonlight. Clearly, the researchers reasoned, something other than illumination caused the changes in productivity.

An experiment was then conducted in the relay-assembly test room over a period of six years, with similar results. In this case, relationships among rest, fatigue, and productivity were examined. First, normal productivity

---

15 Robert Owen, *A New View of Society* (New York: E. Bliss and F. White, 1825), p. 57.

16 Mary Parker Follett, *The New State: Group Organization of the Solution of Popular Government* (New York: Longmans Green, 1918), p. 28.

17 E. J. Roethlisberger and W. J. Dickson, *Management and the Worker* (Cambridge, MA: Harvard University Press, 1939).

was established with no formal rest periods, and a 48-hour week. Rest periods of varying length and frequency were then introduced. Productivity increased as the frequency and length of rest periods increased. Finally, the original conditions were reinstated. The return to the original conditions, however, did not result in the expected productivity drop. Instead, productivity remained at the same high level.

hawthorne effect The phenomenon in which people behave differently in response to perceived attention from evaluators.

One interpretation of these results was that the workers involved in the experiment enjoyed being the center of attention. Workers reacted positively because management cared about them. The phenomenon is referred to as the **Hawthorne effect.** It is the tendency of people to behave differently when they receive attention because they respond to the demands of the situation. In a work setting, employees perform better when they are part of any program, whether or not that program is valuable. Another useful lesson learned from the Hawthorne studies is that effective communication with workers is critical to managerial success.

Theory X and Theory Y of Douglas McGregor

A widely quoted development of the behavioral approach is Douglas McGregor's analysis of the assumptions managers make about human nature.[18] Theory X is a set of traditional assumptions about people. Managers who hold these assumptions are pessimistic about workers' capabilities. They believe that workers dislike work, seek to avoid responsibility, are not ambitious, and must be supervised closely. McGregor urged managers to challenge these assumptions about human nature because they are untrue in most circumstances.

Theory Y, the alternative, poses an optimistic set of assumptions. These assumptions include the idea that people do accept responsibility, can exercise self-control, possess the capacity to innovate, and consider work to be as natural as rest or play. McGregor argued that these assumptions accurately describe human nature in far more situations than most managers believe. He therefore proposed that these assumptions should guide managerial practice.

Maslow's Need Hierarchy

Most readers are already familiar with the need hierarchy developed by psychologist Abraham Maslow. This topic will be presented in Chapter 11 in discussions about motivation. Maslow suggested that humans are motivated by efforts to satisfy a hierarchy of needs, ranging from basic needs to those for self-actualization, or reaching one's potential. The need hierarchy prompted managers to think about ways of satisfying a wide range of worker needs to keep them motivated.

The primary strength of the behavior (or human resources) approach is that it encourages managers to take into account the human element. Many valuable methods of motivating employees are based on behavioral research. The primary weakness of the behavioral approach is that it sometimes leads

18 Douglas McGregor, *The Human Side of Enterprise* (New York: McGraw-Hill, 1960), pp. 33–57.

quantitative approach to management A perspective on management that emphasizes use of a group of methods in managerial decision making, based on the scientific method.

systems perspective A way of viewing aspects of an organization as an interrelated system.

to an oversimplified view of managing people. Managers sometimes adopt one behavioral theory and ignore other relevant information. For example, several theories of motivation pay too little attention to the importance of money in people's thinking.

Quantitative Approaches to Management

The **quantitative approach to management** is a perspective on management that emphasizes the use of a group of methods in managerial decision making, based on the scientific method. Today, the quantitative approach is often referred to as management science or operations research (OR). Frequently used quantitative tools and techniques include statistics, linear programming, network analysis, decision trees, and computer simulations. These tools and techniques can be used when making decisions regarding inventory control, plant-site locations, quality control, and a range of other decisions where objective information is important. Several quantitative approaches to decision making are found in Chapter 6 (quantitative techniques for planning and decision making).

Frederick Taylor's work provided the foundation for the quantitative approach to management. However, the impetus for the modern-day quantitative approach was the formation of OR teams to solve a range of problems faced by the Allied forces during World War II. Examples of the problems considered by the OR team included the bombing of enemy targets, the effective conduct of submarine warfare, and the efficient movement of troops from one location to another. Following World War II, many industrial applications were found for quantitative approaches to management. The approach was facilitated by the increasing use of computers. A representative problem tackled by a quantitative approach to management would be to estimate the effect of a change in the price of a product on the product's market share.

The primary strength of the quantitative approach to management is that it enables managers to solve complex problems that cannot be solved by common sense alone. For example, management science techniques are used to make forecasts that take into account hundreds of factors simultaneously. A weakness of management science is that the answers it produces are often less precise than they appear. Although quantitative approaches use precise methods, much of the data is based on human estimates, which can be unreliable.

The Systems Perspective

The **systems perspective** is a way of viewing problems more than it is a specific approach to management. It is based on the concept that an organization is a system, or an entity of interrelated parts. If you adjust one part of the system, other parts will be affected automatically. For example, suppose you offer low compensation to job candidates. According to the systems approach, your action will influence your product quality. The "low-quality" employees who are willing to accept low wages will produce low-quality goods. Exhibit 1-2, which showed the process of management, reflected a systems viewpoint.

Another aspect of systems theory is to regard the organization as an open system, one that interacts with the environment. As illustrated in Exhibit 1-6, the organization transforms inputs into outputs and supplies them to the outside world. If these outputs are perceived as valuable, the organization will survive and prosper. The feedback loop indicates that the acceptance of outputs by society gives the organization new inputs for revitalization and expansion. Managers can benefit from this diagram by recognizing that whatever work they undertake should contribute something of value to external customers and clients.

Two other influential concepts from the systems perspective are entropy and synergy. **Entropy** is the tendency of a system to run down and die if it does not receive fresh inputs from its environment. As indicated in Exhibit 1-6, the organization must continually receive inputs from the outside world to make sure it stays in tune with, or ahead of, the environment. **Synergy** means that the whole is greater than the sum of the parts. When the various parts of an organization work together, they can produce much more than they could working independently. For example, a few years ago product developers at Motorola Corp. thought about building a stylish new mobile (cell) phone called the Razr. The developers consulted immediately with manufacturing, engineering, purchasing, and dealers to discuss the feasibility of their idea. Working together, the units of the organization produced a highly successful product launch in a tightly competitive market.

entropy
A concept of the systems approach to management that states that an organization will die without continuous input from the outside environment.

synergy
A concept of the systems approach to management that states that the whole organization working together will produce more than the parts working independently.

The Contingency Approach

The **contingency approach to management** emphasizes that there is no single best way to manage people or work in every situation. A method that leads to high productivity or morale under one set of circumstances may not achieve the same results in another. The contingency approach is derived from the study of leadership and organization structures. With respect to leadership, psychologists developed detailed explanations of which style of leadership would work best in which situation. An example would be for the manager to give more leeway to competent group members. Also, the study of organization structure suggests that some structures work better in

contingency approach to management
A perspective on management that emphasizes that no single way to manage people or work is best in every situation. It encourages managers to study individual and situational differences before deciding on a course of action.

exhibit 1-6 A Systems View of Organization

A systems perspective keeps the manager focused on the external environment.

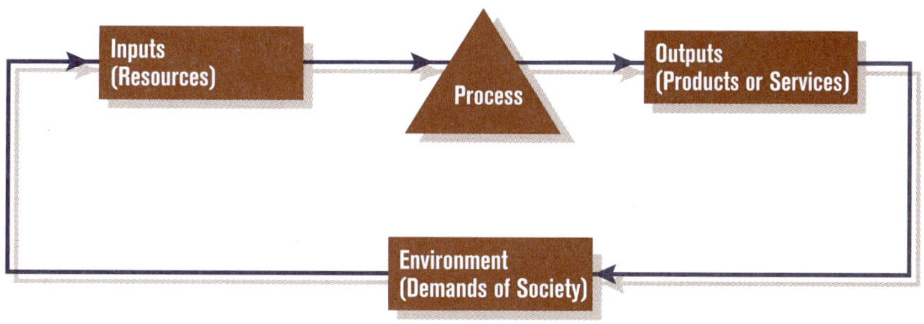

different environments, such as a team structure being best for a rapidly changing environment. Common sense also contributes heavily to the contingency approach. Experienced managers know that not all people and situations respond identically to identical situations. The contingency approach is emphasized throughout this book.

The strength of the contingency approach is that it encourages managers to examine individual and situational differences before deciding on a course of action. Its major problem is that it is often used as an excuse for not acquiring formal knowledge about management. If management depends on the situation, why study management theory? The answer is because a formal study of management helps a manager decide which factors are relevant in a given situation.

The Information Technology Era and Beyond

The information technology era had relatively modest beginnings in the 1950s with the use of electronic data processing to take over the manual processing of large batches of data and numbers. By the late 1980s, the impact of information technology and the Internet began to influence how managers manage work and people. A report by two economists concluded that the impact of the Internet on business is similar to the impact of electricity at the beginning of the twentieth century.[19] Can you visualize what it must have been like to work in an office or factory without electricity?

The impact of information technology and the Internet on the work of managers is so vast that it receives separate attention in Chapter 14. Information technology modified managerial work in the following ways:

- Managers often communicate with people, even sending layoff notices, by e-mail rather than by telephone or in person. Managers send and receive messages more frequently than in the past because they are in frequent contact with the office through their BlackBerry and other brands of personal digital assistants.
- Many managers organize their sales and marketing efforts differently by using the Internet to conduct most transactions. Similarly, much purchasing of supplies and materials is conducted through the Internet.
- Managers run their organizations more democratically because through e-mail they receive input from so many workers at different levels in the organization.

Be careful not to dismiss the evolution of management thought with historical information that is no longer relevant. Practicing managers can use all six major developments in management thought. An astute manager selects information from the various schools of thought to achieve good results in a given situation. Visualize Ronald Williams making Aetna more efficient and effective. He relied on the classical school of management in

19 Martin Brooks and Zakhi Wahhaj, Is the Internet Better Than Electricity? Goldman Sachs report cited in Gary Hamel, "Inside the Revolution—Edison's Curse," *Fortune*, March 5, 2001, p. 176.

restructuring company divisions. At the same time his site visits and town hall meetings to communicate with employees reflect the behavioral approach to management.

evidence-based management An approach to management whereby managers translate principles based on best evidence into management practices.

The history of management is being written each year in the sense that the practice of management continues to evolve. As you study this book and listen to associated lectures you will learn about the new era in management, such as more emphasis on employee empowerment, outsourcing, and helping employees manage stress. An example of a leading-edge approach to management is **evidence-based management** whereby managers translate principles based on best evidence into organizational practices.[20] Quite often the best evidence is empirical (based on experience) and recent, yet old principles can still be useful. The alternative to evidence-based management is to rely heavily on common sense and adopting practices used by other companies whether or not they fit a particular situation. Many of the principles and suggestions presented throughout this text would help a manager practice evidence-based management. The following anecdote will help you develop the flavor of the approach:

> *The executive director of a healthcare system with twenty rural clinics notes that their performance differs tremendously across the array of metrics (measures) used. This variability has nothing to do with patient mix or employee characteristics. After interviewing clinic members who complain about the sheer numbers of metrics for which they are accountable (200+ monthly, comparing each clinic to the 19 others), the director recalls a psychological principle: human decision makers can only process a limited amount of information at any one time.*
>
> *With input from clinic staff, a redesigned feedback system takes shape. The new system uses three performance categories—care quality, cost, and employee satisfaction—and provides a summary measure for each of the three. Over the next year, through provision of feedback in a more interpretable form, the health system's performance improves across the board, with low-performing units showing the greatest improvement.*

In this example, a *principle* (human beings can translate only a limited amount of information) is translated into *practice* (provide feedback on a small set of critical performance indicators using terms people readily understand).[21] Evidence-based management is not yet widely practiced, but taking the study of management seriously will have moved managers and organizations toward basing their practices and decisions on valid evidence. The results are likely to be higher productivity and employee morale.

---

20 Denis M. Rousseau, "Presidential Address: Is There Such a Thing As 'Evidence-Based Management'?" *The Academy of Management Review*, April 2006, pp. 256–269; Jeffrey Pfeffer and Robert I. Sutton, "Evidence-Based Management," *Harvard Business Review*, January 2006, pp. 62–74.

21 Rousseau, "Presidential Address," p. 256.

SUMMARY OF Key Points

To facilitate your study and review of this and the remaining chapters, the summaries are organized around the learning objectives.

1 Explain what the term *manager* means, and identify different types of managers.

A manager is a person responsible for work performance of other people. Management is the process of using organizational resources to achieve specific objectives through the functions of planning, organizing and staffing, leading, and controlling. Organizational levels consist of top-level managers, middle-level managers, first-level managers, and individual contributors. Categories of managers include functional managers (who deal with specialties within the firm) and general managers, administrators (typically managers in nonprofit firms), entrepreneurs (those who start innovative businesses), small-business owners, and team leaders.

2 Describe the process of management, including the functions of management.

To accomplish organizational goals, managers use resources and carry out the basic management functions. Resources are divided into four categories: human, financial, physical, and informational. The four managerial functions are planning, organizing, organization and staffing, leading, and controlling.

3 Describe the various managerial roles.

The work of a manager can be divided into 17 roles that relate to the four major functions. Planning roles include strategic planner and operational planner. Organizing and staffing calls for the organizer, liaison, staffing coordinator, resource allocator, and task delegator roles. Leading roles include figurehead, spokesperson, negotiator, motivator and coach, team builder, team player, technical problem solver, and entrepreneur. Controlling involves the monitor and disturbance handling roles. Managerial work has shifted substantially away from the controller and director role to that of coach, facilitator, and supporter. Top-level managers occupy more external roles than do lower-ranking managers.

4 Identify the basic managerial skills and understand how they can be developed.

Managers need interpersonal, conceptual, diagnostic, and political skills to accomplish their jobs. An effective way of developing managerial skills is to follow a general learning model. The model involves conceptual knowledge, behavioral guidelines, following examples, skill-development exercises, feedback, and frequent practice. Management skills are also acquired through a combination of education and experience.

5 Describe how managers have to synthesize five mind-sets to accomplish their work.

Another perspective on the manager's job is that managers need to synthesize five different mind-sets or perspectives at the same time. The tasks and associated mind-sets are as follows: managing self (the reflective mind-set); managing organizations (the analytical mind-set); managing context (the worldly mind-set); managing relationships (the collaborative mind-set); and managing change (the action mind-set).

6 Identify the major developments in the evolution of management thought.

Management practice has an almost unlimited history, whereas the formal study of management began as part of the Industrial Revolution. The major developments in management thought and the history of management are (1) the classical approach (scientific management and administrative management); (2) the behavioral or human resources approach; (3) quantitative approaches to management; (4) the systems approach; (5) the contingency approach; and (6) the information technology era.

Management thought continues to evolve. A leading-edge trend is evidence-based management in which managers base their decisions and practices on principles derived from good evidence. The best practices of managers today include elements of the six major developments in management thought.

KEY TERMS AND PHRASES

Manager, 2
Management, 2
Top-level managers, 2
C-level manager, 3
Middle-level managers, 3
First-level managers, 4
Entrepreneur, 5
Small-business owner, 5
Team leader, 6
Role, 9
Multiculturalism, 17
Scientific management, 22
Administrative management, 22
Behavioral approach to management, 23
Hawthorne effect, 25
Quantitative approach to management, 26
Systems perspective, 26
Entropy, 27
Synergy, 27
Contingency approach to management, 27
Evidence-based management, 29

QUESTIONS

Here, as in other chapters, groups or individuals can analyze the questions and cases. We strongly recommend using some small-group discussion to enhance learning.

1. In addition to a paid job, where else might a person develop managerial experience?
2. In recent years, many employers seek out technically trained job candidates who also have studied management. What advantages do you think employers see in a technical person studying management?
3. Why do large companies encourage many of their employees to "think like entrepreneurs"?
4. If managing really involves synthesizing five tasks, is it still important for managers to understand separate tasks such as budgeting, marketing, and making use of information technology?
5. During weather emergencies, such as a severe ice storm, some companies send out an alert that only "essential" employees should report to work. Explain why managers should or should not stay home on such emergency days.
6. Why might evidence-based management make an organization more competitive?
7. Why is "management" regarded by some people as an essential life skill?

SKILL-BUILDING EXERCISE 1-A: Identifying Managerial Roles

Interview a manager at any level in any organization, including a retail store or restaurant. Determine which of the 17 managerial roles the manager you interview thinks apply to his or her job. Find out which one or two roles the manager thinks are the most important. Be ready to discuss your findings in class. You can often gain insight into which roles the manager emphasizes, by asking about challenges the manager faces. For example, when asked about the biggest challenges in her job, a restaurant manager might say, "Turnover is a bear. It's so hard to find good servers who stick around for at least a year." The manager's comments indicate the organizing function.

SKILL-BUILDING EXERCISE 1-B: Managerial Skills of Athletic Coaches

The key managerial skills described in this chapter apply to managers in all fields. To help visualize these skills in action, individually or as a group, identify these skills as used by a coach during the next week. Perhaps you can watch a coach in person, on television, or read a newspaper report. Find a good example for each of the five skills, and jot down the basis for your answer. To help point you in the right direction, consider the following example a student might furnish: "Last night I was watching a college basketball game on television. The score was tied with ten seconds to go, and a timeout was called. With the five players in the game in a huddle, the coach got out his clipboard, and diagrammed a play using Xs, Os, and a marker. The play worked, and the team won in the final second. I would say the coach was using technical skill because he dug into the details of how to win."

For which skills was it easiest to find an example? For which skill was it the most difficult? What conclusions can you draw about the managerial skills of athletic coaches?

Technical Skill ____________________

Interpersonal Skill ____________________

Conceptual Skill ____________________

Diagnostic Skill ____________________

Political Skill ____________________

INTERNET SKILL-BUILDING EXERCISE: Hard Skills and Soft Skills for Managers

As explained in the chapter section Five Key Managerial Skills, managers need a combination of hard skills and soft skills to be effective. However, it is not so easy to find a specific list of both types of skills, and perhaps what constitutes an effective combination of these skills. Use one or two of your favorite search engines to compose a list of at least five hard skills and five soft skills that will help you in your managerial career. A starting point in your search might be to enter into your search engine the phrase "hard skills and soft skills for managers." You will most likely have to dig further to get the information you need to complete this assignment.

Case Problem 1-A

The Hands-On CEO of JetBlue

The first thing you notice when getting on board is the new-car smell. "No wonder," says the flight attendant, hearing your remark. She points to a metal plaque on the doorway rim that says the Airbus A320 was delivered one month ago. Other notable features are the free cable on your personal video screen, and the leather seats. Flight attendants are trained on how to give service with a retro flair. All attendants have to learn how to strut proudly, as if there were an imaginary string between their chin and belly button.

Just as discontent with airlines was mounting in 2000, JetBlue Airlines came into being with a new attitude, new planes, and a new concept of service. What perfect takeoff timing for a carrier that is trying to bring pleasure and even style back to flying. JetBlue is low-price and all-coach, like Southwest Airlines, yet hip and sassy, like Virgin Atlantic. In the air, JetBlue offers the plush seats and satellite TV; on the ground it offers hyperefficiency and candor about delays.

JetBlue has been achieving an impressive profit picture. In June 2001, the company became the most ambitious start-up in U.S. aviation history when it ordered 320 jetliners to accompany 68 planes on the way and 15 in service. By 2006, JetBlue had taken delivery of its hundredth aircraft.

Credit CEO David Neeleman, who founded the firm at age 41, for piloting JetBlue past the early disasters that typically befall fledgling carriers. For starters, Neeleman raised $160 million from investors—almost triple what other new airline entrants have managed to obtain. The hefty sum is insurance against any unforeseen cash crunch.

Consumers are usually concerned about the safety issue with "new" airlines that fly 25-year-old planes. JetBlue flies only factory-fresh, state of-the-art A320s. Neeleman has fitted each with 162 seats—versus the A320's 180-seat maximum. Flyers are ecstatic about the so-called JetBlue experience. It begins with pricing, which is competitive and doesn't torture consumers with requirements like Saturday-night stays. JetBlue is attracting business travelers, the industry's most valuable passengers and the source of up to 50 percent of its profits. Neeleman believes that airlines have to make a personal connection with their passengers in order to survive.

A JetBlue spokesperson said, "We see our customers as the same ones who can afford more but shop at Target because their stuff is hip but inexpensive." That kind of thinking drove decisions like JetBlue's choice of leather seats instead of less expensive cloth. "It's a nicer look, a better feel," says Neeleman, in full salesman mode.

Neeleman obsesses over keeping employees happy, and with good reason. Airline watchers say JetBlue's ability to stay union-free is critical to its survival as a low-cost carrier. The industry's labor-relations record is weak. "But if there is anyone who realizes the importance of treating their employees right, it's the management team at JetBlue," says airline analyst Holly Hegeman. All employees, even the CEO, pitch in for cleanup duty. After they land the plane, the pilots exit the cockpit to help pick up the debris.

Neeleman is obsessed with controlling costs. Flying only one type of aircraft holds down training and maintenance expenses. With all workers chipping in to help clean the jets even before they have landed, turnaround times average just 35 minutes, as fast as industry leader Southwest. Despite the emphasis on cost control, JetBlue has some costs other airlines have avoided. For example, it has configured its planes with emergency equipment such as life rafts and beacons for flying over water, thus allowing its flights to swing out over the ocean to avoid congestion on crowded East Coast routes.

On September 21, 2005 JetBlue Flight 292 in Los Angeles narrowly escaped a crash when its front landing gear stuck sideways, so the plane had to land while metal scraped the runway instead of the wheels rolling in their intended manner. The day after the mishap Neeleman released a statement acknowledging the problem, and thanking everyone concerned for their assistance and emotional support. Neeleman's public statement included these words:

> *The crew of Flight 292 has asked use to communicate their appreciation to the 140 customers on board for their cooperation, and they are also grateful for the messages of support sent to JetBlue by thousands of people. The crew looks forward to returning to their families and loved ones, and to their normal lives as quickly as possible.*

Case Problem 1-A

Neeleman notes that despite heavy competition, JetBlue's profit margins are the highest in the industry. He attributes part of the company's success to selecting the right people, which is especially important because an airline is a people business. "We have a saying at JetBlue that you're either serving a customer or serving someone who is serving a customer."

An example of the selection process at JetBlue was an applicant pilot who was furious about being rejected. The pilot telephoned Neeleman and explained that he had 15,000 hours of flying experience. Neeleman then spoke to the interviewer, who said that she asked the pilot, "You've flown for 15,000 hours, tell us one thing that you've done besides just sitting there and flying the airplane." He couldn't come up with a single example. He retorted, "What do you mean by that? I'm a pilot, and that's what I do." The interviewer explained that the pilot was not somebody JetBlue wants in the company.

To manage the company JetBlue, Neeleman emphasizes the quality of supervisors. The company has one supervisor for every 80 employees. Neeleman tells the supervisors, "You can know 80 people. You can know who they're married to, you can know who their kids are, and what their challenges are." In this way JetBlue employees know there is a personal touch to the company.

Neeleman expresses his business philosophy on the company Web site in these words: "Although we have many changes on the horizon, one thing that won't change is the customer service you can expect at JetBlue. Every single JetBlue crewmember is dedicated to making sure your flight on JetBlue is the very best you'll ever take."

JetBlue had an embarrassing problem that began with a Valentine's Day ice storm at the John F. Kennedy International Airport in New York City. The problem ballooned into 1,000 canceled flights and hundreds of passengers trapped for hours in idled planes that soon became unsanitary. Neeleman apologized to the public, followed up by a "customers' bill of rights" that promises vouchers to passengers whose flights are delayed or canceled by problems that JetBlue could have rectified. The value of the vouchers ranges from $25 to the full price of the airline ticket.

Five months after the JFK embarrassment, Neeleman resigned as CEO, but remained on as non-executive chairman of the airline he founded. Dave Barger, chief operating officer, and long-time second-in-command was appointed as the new chief executive.

Discussion Questions

1. In what way did Neeleman demonstrate an understanding of the behavioral approach to management?
2. Even though this text has mentioned leadership only briefly so far, in what way was Neeleman a *hands-on leader* (one who gets directly involved in the details of an operation)?
3. How else might Neeleman and his successor make use of management knowledge to improve the chances of JetBlue Airlines staying successful?
4. Why should passengers being trapped for hours in an idled plane be considered a management problem?

Source: Sally B. Donnelly, "Blue Skies: Is Jet Blue the Next Great Airline—Or Just a Little Too Good to Be True?" *Time*, July 30, 2001, pp. 24–27; Eric Gillin, "JetBlue Soars Past Profit Targets," *TheStreet.com*, July 25, 2002; (http://www.thestreet.com/pf/tech/earnings/10034305.html); "Jet Blue: Flying Higher?" "Statement by JetBlue CEO David Neeleman Regarding Flight 292, http://www.primezone.com, September 29, 2005; September 19, 2003; "Welcome from Our CEO," http://www.jetblue.com, September 17, 2006; "Jet Blue Cancels Flights in Storm Under New Policy," Reuters, February 27, 2007; Al Lewis, "Troubles Put JetBlue CEO in Pilot's Seat," http://www.denverpost.com, February 24, 2007.

Case Problem 1-B

The Management Trainee Blues

Sara Fenton was excited about having been recruited into the restaurant manager training program at a national restaurant chain. As an assistant manager to Johnny Sanchez, she would perform a variety of managerial duties at a busy restaurant in suburban Cleveland, Ohio. If she performed well in her responsibilities for two years, she would be assigned to manage her own restaurant within the chain.

Before shifting into her job as assistant manager, first Sara had to spend six weeks on the wait staff. "This assignment was a natural for me because I had worked part-time as a server for several years in high school and college," Sara said. "Working in the dining room was also a good way to learn more about the restaurant where I would be an assistant manager." After performing well as a server, and earning wonderful tips, Sara was appointed to the assistant manager position as promised.

Influenced by a workshop in time management Sara took at school, she decided to maintain a log of her activities as manager. Among the entries were as follows:

September 2: Bill, one of the wait staff, sent me an e-mail saying that he could not work today because his uncle shot himself in a hunting accident, and Bill had to wait at the hospital. What a mess, because we are shorthanded in the dining room this busy Labor Day weekend anyway.

September 6: Jen, one of the best servers on the staff said she needs a week off to take care of a personal problem. After 25 years of marriage, her mother and father announced their plans and Jen just can't take the emotional pain. It will be tough replacing Jen until she returns.

September 25: Chuck, a member of the wait staff, accidentally spilled hot coffee on one of the customers. The customer demanded to see the manager, so I tried to take care of the problem. The man was irate, and talked about suing the restaurant. I tried to calm him down, and offered to pay for his meal as well as for dry cleaning his trousers. I don't know the final outcome of this problem, but it looks ugly.

October 5: Johnny informs me that the restaurant chain is concerned that some of the spinach it bought this week contained E. coli bacteria. We are getting rid of all the spinach we can find in the restaurant, but some of the salads we served the last few days may have been contaminated. Johnny wants me to investigate. Does he think I'm a chemist and detective as well as a management trainee?

Sara is scheduled to meet with Johnny Sanchez later this week to discuss her impressions of her work as the assistant restaurant manager. Sara reflected, "What can I say that is positive? The type of problems I'm dealing with so far don't seem like the job of a real manager. I wonder if I've chosen the right field? These day-by-day headaches are a lot to cope with."

Discussion Questions

1. Advise Sara on whether she is really learning some valuable lessons as a potential manager.
2. What should Sara tell Johnny on her review of her experiences?
3. Which managerial roles has Sara been carrying out as indicated by her activity log?

chapter 2

International Management and Cultural Diversity

Arte Nathan earned his international stripes without moving to a foreign land. Nathan, the top human resources officer at Wynn Resorts in Las Vegas, did so by visiting China a dozen times in the past few years. He was helping to plan the recruitment and hiring of 5,000 staffers for the company's Macau casino-resort. The project exposed him to innovative hiring ideas that he hopes to import. His Macau performance "has been terrific," says CEO Steve Wynn.

Nathan knew little about China before his initial visit. He and his Las Vegas colleagues spent a year learning to do business there from well-established foreign players. They assisted local managers chosen to run the Macau complex. In staffing the 600-room resort, he recalls, Wynn Resorts had to adapt a lot of things to fit the Chinese culture. For example, about 93 percent of the Macau applications came online. Yet few Chinese jobseekers wanted to follow up by e-mail. They preferred to arrange interviews via cell phone text messages.

"It didn't dawn on me before that many young American adults communicate the same way," Nathan admits. "It was like slapping yourself on the forehead." He's now experimenting with text messaging for U.S. recruiting.

The Macau project also made Nathan recognize the importance of earning applicants' respect through a series of personal

Objectives

After studying this chapter and doing the exercises, you should be able to:

1. Appreciate the importance of multinational corporations and outsourcing in international business.
2. Recognize the importance of sensitivity to cultural differences in international enterprise.
3. Identify major challenges facing the global managerial worker.
4. Explain various methods of entry into world markets.
5. Pinpoint success factors in the global marketplace, and several positive and negative aspects of globalization.
6. Describe the scope of diversity, the competitive advantage, and potential problems of a culturally diverse workforce.
7. Summarize organizational practices to encourage diversity.

interactions and job interviews, taking time to build a strong rapport. "This is a good thing for all cultures that may improve retention broadly," he says. As it did in China, Wynn Resorts will soon audition prospective U.S. dealers—forging a firmer bond by testing their skills in a work-like environment.

Hiring Macau hourly employees consumed a year longer than Nathan preferred but faster than expected. He posted milestones on a corporate Web site to keep senior management abreast of the project's progress.[1]

The story about the human resources officer from the resort company illustrates how working with people from another culture can be a broadening experience as well as a learning one. Some ideas and practices from other countries can be imported to improve the local workplace. In this chapter we describe major aspects of the international and culturally diverse environment facing managers. Among the topics covered are methods of entry into the global marketplace, success factors in globalization, and the advantages and disadvantages of going global. We also highlight cultural diversity, including its competitive advantage and the skills required to become a multicultural manager. Globalization and cultural diversity are such major forces in the workplace that they receive some attention throughout our study of management.

INTERNATIONAL MANAGEMENT

Learning Objective 1

Appreciate the importance of multinational corporations and outsourcing in international business.

The internationalization (or global integration) of business and management exerts an important influence on the manager's job. Approximately 10 to 15 percent of all jobs in the United States are dependent upon trade with other countries. Another way of understanding the impact of global integration is to recognize that many complex manufactured products are built with components from several countries. The mix of components can sometimes confuse the national identity of a product, with automobiles being a prime example. The Ford Mustang, identified as an American vehicle, is manufactured in Michigan and Ontario and contains 65 percent U.S. and Canadian parts. The Toyota Sienna XLE, identified as a Japanese vehicle, is manufactured in Indiana and contains 90 percent U.S. and Canadian parts.[2]

The internationalization of management is part of the entire world becoming more global, representing challenges for workers at every level. These economic trends were highlighted in the well-known book by Thomas Friedman, *The World is Flat: A Brief History of the 21st Century*.[3] Friedman

1 Joann S. Lublin, "Global Experience Doesn't Have to Mean Going to Live Overseas," *The Wall Street Journal*, August 29, 2006, p. B1.

2 Jathon Sapsford and Norihiko Shirouzu, "Mom, Apple Pie and ... Toyota?" *The Wall Street Journal*, May 11, 2006, pp. B1–B2.

3 Thomas L. Friedman, *The World is Flat: A Brief History of the Twenty-First Century* (New York: Farrar, Strauss and Giroux, 2005).

PLAY VIDEO

INTERNATIONAL MANAGEMENT AND CULTURAL DIVERSITY

Go to academic.cengage.com/management/dubrin and view the video. In what ways can domestic and international businesses take advantage of the Internet's global nature? What are some strategies that Yahoo! Use to remain in a top slot amongst international competitors?

explains that the world—and the playing field—have become flattened as countries, companies, and individuals compete because barriers to competition have been lowered. For example, a financial analyst in Bangalore, India, can perform the work of a financial analyst in Columbus, Ohio, at a lower wage rate. A counterforce to the global economy is that jobs involving personal contacts and relationships are less subject to competition from another country.

As business becomes more global, the manager must adapt to the challenges of working with organizations and people from other countries. Keeping time zone differences clearly in mind and converting back and forth between the metric and decimal (American) system is a challenge for many people.

The Multinational Corporation

The heart of international trade is the **multinational corporation (MNC)**, a firm with units in two or more countries in addition to its own. An MNC has headquarters in one country and subsidiaries in others. However, it is more than a collection of subsidiaries that carry out decisions made at headquarters. A multinational corporation sometimes hires people from its country of origin (expatriates) for key positions in facilities in other countries. At other times, the MNC will hire citizens of the country in which the division is located (host-country nationals) for key positions. Most of the best-known companies are MNCs, including PepsiCo, IBM, and Daimler/Chrysler among hundreds of others.

multinational corporation (MNC) A firm with operating units in two or more countries in addition to its own.

transnational corporation A special type of MNC that operates worldwide without having one national headquarters.

The **transnational corporation** is a special type of MNC that operates worldwide without having one national headquarters. The transnational executive thinks in terms of the entire world, rather than looking upon operations in other countries as being "foreign operations." Components of the company located in different part of the world sometimes provide continuous service as the workers from different time zones begin their contribution when work ends in another time zone. Tokyo-based Trend Micro, a specialist in combating computer viruses, is a highly developed transnational company. A recent thrust of the company is to address the mounting threat imposed by *botnets* (networks of compromised machines that can be remotely controlled by an attacker). Trend Micro is able to respond quickly because it spreads the top executives, engineers, and support staff around the world to enhance its response to new virus threats. The main virus response center is in the Philippines, yet six other labs are spread out from Munich to Tokyo. "With the Internet, viruses became global. To fight them, we had to become a global company," says Chairman Steve Chang, a Taiwanese who launched the company.[4]

4 Quoted in Steve Hamm, "Borders Are So 20th Century," *Business Week*, September 22, 2003, p. 68; "Trend Micro Takes Unprecedented Approach to Eliminating Botnet with the Unveiling of InterCloud Security Service," http://www.trendmicro.com, September 29, 2006, p. 1.

Two key issues in international business and management are government agreements about trade, and outsourcing, or "offshoring." Both issues have been highly challenging for many companies, workers, and countries.

Trade Agreements Among Countries

Trade agreements are important for understanding international management because these agreements facilitate business in exporting, importing, and building goods in other countries. Also, the agreements have trigged considerable controversy often leading to anti–trade-agreement demonstrations.

The North American Free Trade Agreement (NAFTA)

NAFTA establishes liberal trading relationships among the United States, Canada, and Mexico. The pact also calls for the gradual removal of tariffs and other trade barriers on most goods produced and sold in the United States. NAFTA became effective in Canada, Mexico, and the United States as of January 1, 1994. The agreement creates a giant trading zone extending from the Arctic Ocean to the Gulf of Mexico. NAFTA forms the world's second largest free trade zone, bringing together 420 million consumers in the three countries. The largest free trade zone is the European Union.

Many companies benefit from NAFTA because of better access to the two other countries in the pact. Consequently, U.S. trade with Mexico and Canada has increased dramatically. Many U.S. companies have expanded sales of industrial and consumer products to Canada and Mexico. These products include computers, videos and DVDs, and machine tools. As a result of NAFTA, Canadian and Mexican firms have sold more products to the United States. More Canadian and Mexican beer now flows in the United States, as well as the sale of electronic products and furniture. Much of the surge in the Mexican auto industry can be attributed to the substantial drop in tariffs between the United States and Mexico. (Mexico assembles autos for the U.S. market.)

Large American manufacturers benefited from NAFTA as they slashed production costs and boosted profits by opening factories in Mexico, where workers are paid about $3 an hour. In addition to auto manufacturers, computer and electronic companies have used Mexico as a platform for fast, inexpensive, and flexible production facilities.[5]

A number of critics perceive NAFTA to be a miserable failure. Many labor union representatives argue that NAFTA threatens jobs of American workers. By the tenth anniversary of NAFTA, approximately 880,000 U.S. workers had been displaced. Many Mexican farm workers lost out economically when subsidies and important quotas were lifted. Illegal immigration to the United States surged as millions of rural Mexican citizens left Mexican farms in search of opportunity.

Other concerns are that free trade has widened the gap between the rich and the poor (many middle-class jobs have disappeared), and that national sovereignty has been superceded in terms of the environment, worker rights,

5 Dawn Hilbertson and Jonathan H. Higuera, "At 10, NAFTA is a Mixed Bag," *Gannett News Service*, June 23, 2003; Robert E. Scott, "The High Price of 'Free' Trade," *Economic Policy Institute* (http://www.epinet.org), November 17, 2003.

and economic security. Critics of NAFTA point out that the agreement does not maintain labor or environmental standards. Another reason NAFTA has been termed a miserable failure is that the promise of better living and working conditions on the 1,950-mile U.S.–Mexico border is still unfulfilled. Many residents live in the streets, and even those with housing must still haul water for drinking, bathing, and washing clothes.[6]

Styled after NAFTA, The Central American Free Trade Agreement, or CAFTA, is being implemented on a slower pace than planned, with El Salvador being the first country to participate, followed by the Dominican Republic. Nicaragua, Honduras, Guatemala, and Costa Rica are expected to follow. Only governments that the United States Trade Representative certifies have made necessary changes to their laws are permitted to become part of CAFTA. These laws involve such matters as intellectual property rights and meat inspection.

The ultimate hope of proponents of the agreement is a 34-nation Free Trade Agreement covering all countries in the Western Hemisphere except Cuba. Critics of the proposed agreements contend that thousands of textile and apparel jobs will be lost in the United States. Another major concern about CAFTA is that there is a lack of enforceable worker rights protection in the agreement.[7]

The European Union (EU)

The European Union is a 27-nation alliance that virtually turns member countries into a single marketplace for ideas, goods, services, and investment strategies. The EU was a 15-nation alliance for many years, but continues to incorporate new nations, and has become the world's largest economic entity. The EU trades with member nations, the United States and Canada, and other countries throughout the world. In addition, Japanese firms are now investing extensively in Europe. An example of the unity created among nations is the Schengen Agreement. The agreement ended passport control and customs check at many borders, creating a single space where EU citizens can travel, work, and invest. A major step for the European Union is its monetary union in which 11 countries traded their national money for currency called the Euro. The Euro fluctuates in value, but in 2007 was about 37 percent higher in value than the U.S. dollar.

The World Trade Organization (WTO)

The World Trade Organization liberalizes trade among many nations throughout the world. The idea is to lower trade barriers, thereby facilitating international trade, with the ultimate goal of moving the world toward free trade and open markets. According to the *most favored nation* clause, each member country is supposed to grant all other member countries the most favorable treatment it grants any country with respect to imports and exports. As a result, all countries are supposed to make trade with other member countries quite easy.

---

6 Lisa J. Adams, "NAFTA's Impact, Future Unclear After 10 Years," Associated Press, January 1, 2004; Diana Washington Valdez, "Promised NAFTA Improvements Have Yet to Happen," http://www.elpasotimes.com/news, June 23, 2003.

7 Tom Ricker and Burke Stansbury, "Cafta Chronicles: Strong-Arming Central America, Mocking Democracy," *Multinational Monitor*, Volume 27, Number 1, January/February 2006, pp. 1–7; "A New Trade Deal Moves Ahead," Associated Press, December 18, 2003.

The WTO now has about 150 member countries, which accounts for about 95 percent of world trade. Lower trade barriers eliminate the artificially high prices consumers previously paid for imported goods. A continuing problem for the WTO is the distrust of developing countries that claim they are bullied by rich countries. Instead the developing countries want trade agreements that will help poor nations also. Another concern is that the WTO exerts too much authority, such as ruling that the EU law banning hormone-treated beef is illegal.[8]

One issue in facilitating trade is that global trade liberalization leads to continuous job cuts and downward pressures on wages in industrialized nations. The concern about global trade contributing to worker exploitation is so strong that riots frequently take place outside the meetings of the WTO. Rioters regularly pelt security workers with rocks and smash the windows of American-owned stores, or U.S. franchises abroad. McDonald's restaurants are a frequent target because McDonald's symbolizes American trade overseas.

The counterargument to objections to overseas trade is that free trade, in the long run, creates more job opportunities by making it possible to export more freely. For example, the United States has more recycled paper than it needs. At the same time, China and other developing countries, such as India, are building paper plants but have a shortage of forests. As a result, these countries are big purchasers of cellulose fiber. Big Moe's paper recycling plant in South Jersey is one such beneficiary of the overseas demand for waste paper. The value of exported waste paper (the type you put in your "blue box") has increased from about $12 million per month in 1997 to $125 million per month in 2006.[9]

A related argument is that when companies shift manufacturing to low-wage countries, the companies can remain more cost competitive. As a consequence of globalizing production, the companies stay in business and keep more domestic workers employed.

Global Outsourcing as Part of International Trade

The trade agreements described above have made it much easier for companies to have manufacturing and many services performed in other countries. In general, **outsourcing** refers to the practice of hiring an individual or another company outside the organization to perform work. Here we are concerned with global outsourcing, frequently referred to as **offshoring**. We will visit outsourcing again in Chapter 8, as part of the discussion of organization structure.

outsourcing The practice of hiring an individual or another company outside the organization to perform work.

offshoring Global outsourcing.

Outsourcing continues to grow in scope, thereby increasing trade among countries. The number of industries immune to outsourcing is shrinking. A case in point is the U.S. construction industry, particularly because construction is thought to be a local or regional activity. The façade of a huge library in Salt Lake City, Utah, was assembled entirely from concrete panels cast in Mexico. Instead of pouring concrete forms on-site, a Mexico City firm cast 2,000 individual panels, then shipped them 2,350 miles north on mammoth flatbed trucks. Each panel was delivered in order of its assembly, and on time.[10]

8 "World Trade Organization," http://www.globalexchange.org, accessed September 29, 2006.
9 Bob Fernandez, "Scrap Paper, Made in U.S.A.," *Inquirer* (http://www.philly.com), September 10, 2006.
10 Joel Millman, "Blueprint for Outsourcing," *The Wall Street Journal*, March 3, 2004, p. B1.

A major force behind global outsourcing is the pressure discount retailers such as Wal-Mart, Target, and Dollar General exert on manufacturers to keep their prices low. Visualize a mermaid doll being sold for $1.00 at a discount store in the United States. The distributor of these dolls has to rely on an extremely low-priced manufacturer to be able to sell the doll to the retailer for about 50 cents. So, the doll is made in China where the cost of production is extremely low. A specific example of offshoring as a survival tactic is Wahl Clipper Corp., the last home-grown family manufacturer in Sterling, Illinois. Most of the other manufacturers have either shut down or shriveled in recent years because of the pressure of big-box retailers for rock-bottom prices. Nearly all the low-priced items such as nose-hair clippers and curling irons are shipped from China. Although a few higher-end products, such as the Wahl Clipper, are still made in Illinois, some components are made in China to reduce costs. "I think pricing pressure is probably the single biggest dynamic that is pushing people to go to China," says Greg Wahl, chief executive of Wahl and grandson of the founder.[11]

Sending so much manufacturing and service work (such as computer programming and call centers) continues to create heated controversy. Many Americans believe that offshoring is responsible for the permanent loss of jobs in the United States, as well as slow job creation. Yet, increased productivity through information technology has created the vast majority of the lost jobs.[12] Another problem tied with global outsourcing is that American employers can offer low wages to domestic employees because their work could be sent offshore. The counterargument is that sending jobs overseas can create new demand for the lower-priced goods, ultimately leading to new jobs in the United States. Consumer electronics is a germane example. In the United States and Canada, people consume an enormous amount of electronic products, such as cell phones, video games, and laptop computers made overseas. As a result, many retail stores and jobs are created as well as technicians to service all the equipment. If these products were manufactured domestically, their high price might limit demand.

The arguments in favor of global outsourcing are part of the argument for free trade. Slashing costs of production through offshoring can help a company become more competitive, and win new orders. An example is the Paper Converting Machine Company (PCMC) in Green Bay, Wisconsin. Part of the parent company's turnaround strategy for PCMC was to shift some design work to its 160-engineer center in Chennai, India. By having U.S. and Indian designers collaborate around the clock, the company was able to slash development costs and time and win orders—and keep production in Green Bay. The same strategy boosted profits at many other midsize U.S. machinery makers the parent company bought. "We can compete and create great American jobs," vows CEO Robert Chapman. "But not without offshoring."[13]

---

11 Timothy Aeppell, "Savior or Villain: With Manufacturing Headed Overseas, Former 'Hardware Capital' Embraces Its Future: Wal-Mart," *The Wall Street Journal,* February 24, 2006, p. B1.

12 "Where Are the Jobs?" *Business Week,* March 22, 2004, p. 37.

13 Pete Engardio, "The Future of Outsourcing: How It's Transforming Whole Industries and the Way We Work," *Business Week,* January 30, 2006, p. 50.

Sensitivity to Cultural Differences

The guiding principle for people involved in international enterprise is sensitivity to cultural differences. **Cultural sensitivity** is awareness of local and national customs and their importance in effective interpersonal relationships. Ignoring the customs of other people creates a communications block that can impede business and create ill will. For example, Americans tend to be impatient to close a deal while businesspeople in many other cultures prefer to build a relationship slowly before consummating an agreement. Exhibit 2-1 presents a sampling of cultural differences that can affect business.

Learning Objective 2

Recognize the importance of sensitivity to cultural differences in international trade.

Cultural sensitivity can also take the form of adapting your behavior to meet the requirements of people from another culture. A frequent challenge in international business is speaking slowly enough in your own language, so workers for whom your language is not their native tongue can understand you readily. To not adapt your rate of speech can be a sign of cultural insensitivity, as illustrated by the behavior of William Amelio. He is the American CEO of Lenovo, the China-based technology company that acquired the IBM PC business. The Chinese are stressed by having to speak English, the official language of Lenovo. Amelio speaks so rapidly that the language barrier is intensified. "We have to ask him several times to slow down," says George He, the chief technology officer at Lenovo. "He just doesn't stop."[14]

Cultural sensitivity is also important because it helps a person become a **multicultural worker**. Such an individual is convinced that all cultures are equally good, and enjoys learning about other cultures. Multicultural workers are usually people who have been exposed to more than one culture in childhood. A person from another culture is likely to accept a multicultural person. A recent theoretical analysis concludes that multiculturalism is the virtue of being open to others.[15] The multicultural worker is open to people who harbor different beliefs and customs.

Being culturally sensitive and multicultural is important because it is challenging to manage employees with dissimilar backgrounds and cultures, yet attaining business goals while adapting to these differences. According to the research of Development Dimensions International, *how* a manager manages people in different cultures can influence results. One potential area for culture conflict occurs between East and West. In Japan, communication about change tends to be more subtle and indirect than in the United States. Japanese managers often use consensus-building techniques to bring about acceptance of change before executing the change. An American manager in Japan might fall back on his or her natural pattern of being much more authoritarian and direct as a way of bringing about change.[16]

cultural sensitivity
Awareness of local and national customs and their importance in effective interpersonal relationships.

multicultural worker
An individual who is aware of and values other cultures.

Candidates for foreign assignments generally receive training in the language and customs of the country they will work in. The accompanying Management in Action provides more information about the business use of cultural training. Intercultural training exercises include playing the roles

14 Michael Schuman, "Lenovo's Global Gambit," *Time*, October 2006, p. G19.

15 Blaine J. Fowers and Barbara J. Davidov, "The Virtue of Multiculturalism," *American Psychologist*, September 2006, pp. 581–594.

16 Dianne Nilsen, Brenda Kowske, and Kshanika Anthony, "Managing Globally," *HR Magazine*, August 2005, pp. 111–115.

exhibit 2-1 Cultural Mistakes to Avoid in Selected Regions and Countries

EUROPE

Great Britain
- Asking personal questions. The British protect their privacy.
- Thinking that a businessperson from England is unenthusiastic when he or she says, "Not bad at all." English people understate positive emotion.
- Gossiping about royalty

France
- Expecting to complete work during the French two-hour lunch.
- Attempting to conduct significant business during August—les vacances (vacation time).

Italy
- Eating too much pasta, as it is not the main course.
- Handing out business cards freely. Italians use them infrequently.

Spain
- Expecting punctuality. Your appointments will usually arrive 20 to 30 minutes late.
- Making the American sign of "okay" with your thumb and forefinger. In Spain (and many other countries) this is vulgar.

Scandinavia (Denmark, Sweden, Norway)
- Being overly rank conscious. Scandinavians pay relatively little attention to a person's place in the hierarchy.

ASIA

All Asian countries
- Pressuring an Asian job applicant or employee to brag about his or her accomplishments. Asians feel self-conscious when boasting about individual accomplishments, and prefer to let the record speak for itself. In addition, they prefer to talk about group rather than individual accomplishment.

Japan
- Shaking hands or hugging Japanese (as well as other Asians) in public. Japanese consider the practices to be offensive.
- Not interpreting "We'll consider it" as a no when spoken by a Japanese businessperson. Japanese negotiators mean no when they say, "We'll consider it."
- Not giving small gifts to Japanese when conducting business. Japanese are offended by not receiving these gifts.

China
- Using black borders on stationary and business cards. Black is associated with death.
- Giving small gifts to Chinese when conducting business. Chinese are offended by these gifts.

Korea
- Saying "no." Koreans feel it is important to have visitors leave with good feelings.

India
- Telling Indians you prefer not to eat with your hands. If the Indians are not using cutlery when eating, they expect you to do likewise.

MEXICO AND LATIN AMERICA

Mexico
- Flying into a Mexican city in the morning and expecting to close a deal by lunch. Mexicans build business relationships slowly

Brazil
- Attempting to impress Brazilians by speaking a few words of Spanish. Portuguese is the official language of Brazil.

Most of Latin America
- Wearing elegant and expensive jewelry during a business meeting. Most Latin Americans think people should appear more conservative during a business meeting.

Note: A cultural mistake for Americans to avoid when conducting business in most countries outside the United States and Canada is to insist on getting down to new business quickly. North Americans in small towns also like to build a relationship before getting down to business.

of businesspeople from a different culture. International workers are also sensitized to cultural mistakes to avoid, as shown in Exhibit 2-1.

A large-scale research study has demonstrated that personality factors as well as cultural understanding contribute to the effectiveness of expatriate (sent to another country) managers. The participants in the study included a diverse sample of expatriates in Hong Kong as well as expatriate managers from Japan and Korea working throughout the world. Substantial individual differences were found in terms of performing well in another country, including getting the job done and adjusting well to the new culture. In terms of personality factors, expatriates who function better than others are emotionally stable,

management in action

High-Tech Firms Turn to Indian Cultural Training to Boost Performance

One August day, Intel software manager Connie Martin arrived for work and received a new identity. She was handed some fake rupees and a nametag that read "Rekha Gupta," and was told that she now hailed from a northern Indian trading family. For the next eight hours, she hit the books, studying the subtle dietary differences between Jainism and Hinduism, Indian political history, and Bollywood movies. At the end of the day, she was given a test on it all, which she aced. "I can even tell you how things changed under British rule in the 1800s," she says.

A North Carolina native, Martin is a graduate of "Working with India," an optional training class that Intel began offering to employees in 2002. With an estimated 400,000 Indian nationals in Silicon Valley—and roughly a third of the 65,000 new H-1B visas issued by the United States annually allocated for Indians—companies such as Adaptec, AMD, Intuit, and Rockwell Automation have also held similar sessions during the past year. "Indian cultural training is at the top of the radar screen right now," says Lisa Spivey, director of business development at Meridian Resources, an intercultural training company.

The biggest problems addressed by the classes are communication breakdowns around conflict. Sometimes Indian employees "make promises they can't keep to maintain harmony, but then they'll run into problems at the end of a project," says Ashok Mathur, an associate at Charis Intercultural.

That's what happened at Adaptec, a Milpitas, California, maker of memory hardware, where managers requested Indian cultural training after a major chip-manufacturing project ran more than a month late. "My gut feeling was that our Indian engineers didn't understand the sense of urgency," says David Sommers, Adaptec's vice president for engineering. After employees received intercultural training, including lessons on communication style ("yes" doesn't always mean yes), Adaptec's next chip came in on schedule. "Things became more predictable, with fewer problems that I could attribute to cultural differences," Sommers says.

Questions

1. Why would American workers need to learn about Indian culture to get along better with Indians working in the United States?
2. How did American workers learning more about the Indian culture lead to prompter project completions?

Source: Rachel Rosmarin, "Mountain View Masala: High-tech Firms are Turning to Indian Cultural Training to Boost Performance," *Business 2.0,* March 2005, pp. 54–56.

extraverted (outgoing), and open to new experiences. Several cross-cultural competencies are also important. Being able to focus on the task to be done as well as the attitudes and feelings of people is important, and so is not being ethnocentric. (Ethnocentrism is the belief that the ways of one's culture is the best way of doing things.[17]) Although the previous findings might not be surprising, they make a contribution to management knowledge because the findings stem from research with hundreds of managers in dozens of countries.

CHALLENGES FACING THE GLOBAL MANAGERIAL WORKER

Learning Objective 3
Identify major challenges facing the global managerial worker.

Managerial workers on assignment in other countries, as well as domestic managers working on international dealings, face a variety of challenges. Rising to these challenges can be the difference between success and failure. Among the heaviest challenges are developing global leadership skills, economic crises, balance of trade problems, human rights violations, culture shock, differences in negotiating style, and piracy (see Exhibit 2-2).

Developing Global Leadership Skills

global leadership skills
The ability to effectively lead people of other cultures.

Managerial workers occupying leadership positions need to develop **global leadership skills**, the ability to effectively lead people from other cultures. Having such skills is a combination of cultural sensitivity and leadership skills in general. An attitude of welcoming other cultures is perhaps more important than overseas experience itself in becoming an

exhibit 2-2 Challenges Facing the Global Managerial Worker

Global managerial workers have to juggle many different challenges.

17 Margaret A. Shaffer et al., "You Can Take It With You: Individual Differences and Expatriate Effectiveness," *Journal of Applied Psychology*, January 2006, pp. 109–125.

effective global leader. The global leader manages across distance, countries, and cultures. To be effective as a global leader, the manager must inspire others, such as getting workers in another country excited about the future of the multinational corporation. Good interpersonal relationships are required, as they are of all leaders. Also similar to leaders in general, the global leader must show good initiative and be oriented toward success.[18]

Another aspect of global leadership skills is to understand how well management principles from one's own culture transfer to another. The point about understanding cultural differences as part of cultural sensitivity made above is a variation on the same theme. A specific example is supply-chain management. According to Kim Tae Woo, a management advisor from South Korea, most Western companies are quite willing to switch parts suppliers to cut costs. Switching suppliers is a tougher sell in Japan, where executives frequently have long-term or personal relationships with key people at their suppliers.[19]

The nature of what constitutes global leadership skills is a vast topic, yet consider this example: You are the manager of a unit of a company that expects employees to give utmost attention to meeting customer deadlines, even if it means working 70 hours per week. In your group are several workers from overseas who are from a culture that gives family life much higher priority than work life, so workers are not disposed to work more than 37 and one-half hours per week. During crunch time, it is your job to cultivate the overseas worker to become more work oriented.

Currency Fluctuations

A frequent challenge to the international manager is adjusting business practices in response to changes in the value of currencies in the home country and elsewhere. If the currency of a country suddenly *gains* in value, it may be difficult to export products made in that country. However, when a country's currency *weakens* versus the currency of other countries, it is easier to export goods because the goods are significantly less expensive and competitive in other countries. The weakening of the U.S. dollar during the 2000s made it more difficult for U.S. citizens to purchase foreign goods. For example, the U.S. dollar fell to about 72 cents against the euro (€) in 2007. (A handbag for 100€ would cost $138 U.S. In contrast a handbag priced at $100 U.S. would cost 72€.) So Europeans would find U.S. handbags to be a relative bargain.

In overview, a falling U.S. dollar invigorates the market for U.S. exports, and helps close the trade gap. The weaker dollar makes foreign goods more expensive in the United States, and gives domestic companies more leeway to raise their prices. However, as described later, the United States remains a much bigger importer than exporter of goods. It is often argued that one

---

18 Maxine Dalton, Chris Ernst, Jennifer Deal, and Jean Leslie, *Success for the New Global Manager: How to Work Across Distances, Countries, and Cultures* (San Francisco: Jossey-Bass, 2002).

19 Phred Dvorak, "Making U.S. Management Ideas Work Elsewhere," *The Wall Street Journal*, May 22, 2006, p. B3.

balance of trade The difference between exports and imports in both goods and services.

of the reasons China can export so freely to the United States is that the Chinese government keeps the yuan (the Chinese currency) at an artificially low rate, approximately 8.28 per dollar.[20]

Currency fluctuations are of obvious concern for workers in marketing. Yet, managers in manufacturing and in services must also be concerned. For example, the manufacturing manager might be forced to find ways to lower the manufacturing cost of a produce to compete better against imports—as in the opening story about the hair clippers. As a country's currency rises in value, exporting companies must become more and more efficient to lower costs.

Balance of Trade Problems

A concern at the broadest level to an international manager is a country's **balance of trade**, the difference between exports and imports in both goods and services. Many people believe that it is to a country's advantage to export more than it imports. Yet in 2006, the total international deficit in goods and services for the United States was $763.6 billion. For goods, the deficit was $823.6 billion, the highest on record. For services, the surplus was $60.0 billion. It marked the fifth consecutive year that that America's trade deficit established a record.

The trade deficit can be attributed to many factors, such as the preference for Americans to purchase lower-priced goods and to take vacations in foreign countries rather than the United States, as well as deficit spending by the U.S. government. The sharp increase in the price of imported petroleum products has also contributed to the deficit. Exhibit 2-3 presents some interesting facts about the trade deficit.

An individual manager might want to contribute to the national economy by exporting more than importing. In an effort to accomplish this goal, the manager might have to find ways to cut costs on products or services offered for export. An alternative would be to design products or services so attractive they would sell well despite their relatively high price in foreign markets. Examples include American movies, the iPod, and Harley-Davidson motorcycles.

A concern about the U.S. trade deficit is that it contributes to the loss of domestic manufacturing jobs, with 3.5 million jobs lost since mid-2000 as U.S. companies shifted production to nations that pay lower wages. "Such a huge trade gap undercuts domestic manufacturing and destroys good U.S. jobs," said Richard Trumka, secretary-treasurer of the AFL-CIO. "America's gargantuan trade deficit is a weight around American workers' necks that is pulling them into a cycle of debt, bankruptcy and low-wage service jobs."[21] Yet free traders contend that American consumers benefit from the flood of imports from low-cost producers by being able to purchase goods at low prices.[22] For example, electric alarm clocks made in China retail for about $4.00 at discount stores in the United States.

---

20 Peter S. Goodman and Paul Blustein, "China's Export Engine," http://www.washingtonpost.com, September 13, 2006.

21 Martin Crutsinger, "U.S. Trade Deficit Reaches New High: Record Imports Widen Gap to $725.8B in 2005," The Associated Press, February 11, 2006.

22 David Armstrong, "U.S. Racks Up Record Trade Deficit in '05," *Chronicle* (http://www.sfgate.com), February 11, 2006.

exhibit 2-3 U.S. International Trade in Goods and Services Highlights

Goods and Services Deficit Increases in May 2007

The Nation's international deficit in goods and services increased to $60.0 billion in May from $58.7 billion (revised) in April, as imports increased more than exports.

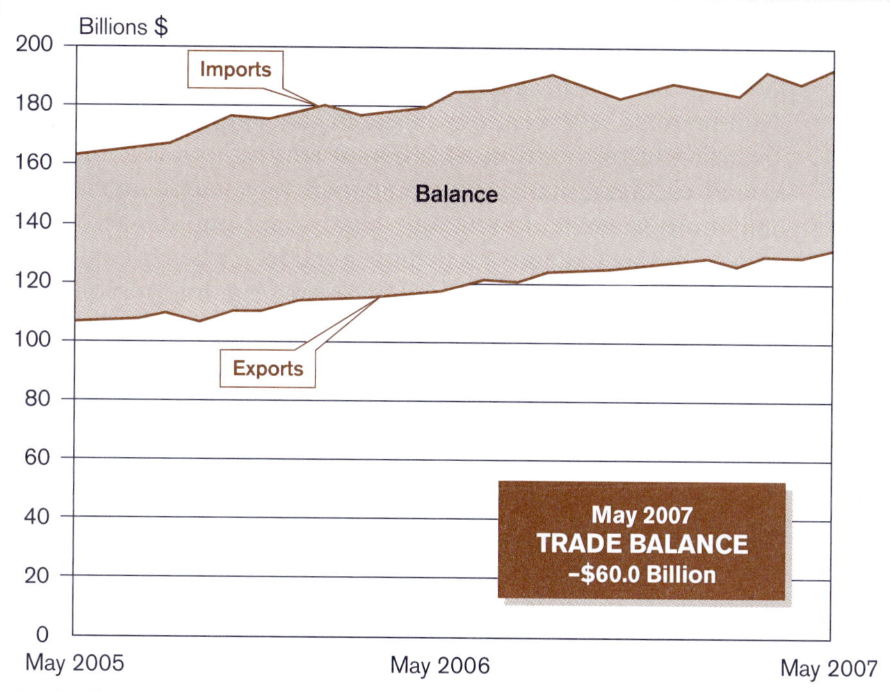

Goods and Services

- Exports increased to $132.0 billion in May from $129.2 billion in April. Goods were $93.3 billion in May, up from $90.9 billion in April, and services were $38.7 billion in May, up from $38.2 billion in April.
- Imports increased to $192.1 billion in May from $187.8 billion in April. Goods were $162.3 billion in May, up from $158.3 billion in April, and services were $29.8 billion in May, up from $29.6 billion in April.
- For goods, the deficit was $69.0 billion in May, up from $67.3 billion in April. For services, the surplus was $9.0 billion in May, up from $8.7 billion in April.

Goods by Geographic Area (Not Seasonally Adjusted)

- The goods deficit with Canada decreased from $5.8 billion in April to $5.2 billion in May. Exports increased $1.6 billion (primarily civilian aircraft, automotive parts and accessories, and fuel oil) to $21.8 billion, while imports increased $1.0 billion (primarily petroleum products, fish and shellfish, and automotive parts and accessories) to $27.0 billion.
- The goods deficit with China increased from $19.4 billion in April to $20.0 billion in May. Exports increased $0.5 billion (primarily semiconductors and civilian aircraft) to $5.3 billion, while imports increased $1.1 billion (primarily apparel and household goods) to $25.3 billion.
- The goods deficit with Mexico increased from $5.2 billion in April to $5.9 billion in May. Exports increased $1.1 billion (primarily automotive parts and accessories and electric apparatus) to $12.1 billion, while imports increased $1.7 billion (primarily crude oil, automotive parts and accessories and electric apparatus) to $17.9 billion.

Source: http://www.census.gov/indicator/www/ustrade.html.

Human Rights Violations and Corruption

International managers face potential ethical problems when their customers and suppliers reside in countries where human rights are violated. Should a U.S. rug distributor purchase carpets from a supplier that employs ten-year-old children who work 11 hours a day for the equivalent of $4 U.S.? Should a U.S. shoe manufacturer buy components from a country that uses political prisoners as free labor? Ethical issues require careful thought, especially when they are not always clear-cut. To a child in an underdeveloped country, receiving $4 per day can mean the difference between malnutrition and adequate food.

The subject of human rights violations is complicated and touchy. Multinational corporations based in the United States are often accused of profiting from the fruits of labor of employees exploited in less-developed countries. Also, many U.S. companies hire undocumented aliens at below minimum wage, and maintain substandard and dangerous working conditions. The United States sets high standards when it comes to human rights in other countries. Yet, according to Amnesty International, these standards are sometimes violated, such as torturing suspected terrorists.[23]

Another ethical and legal problem the international manager faces is dealing with corruption by foreign officials. To conduct business in some countries, a string of officials demand payments to facilitate allowing foreigners to conduct business or speed approval of an operating license. The same countries often engage in corruption with their own citizens, with Mexico being a leading example. For example, Luis Alfonso Sanchez Contreras was in the process of establishing a pasta restaurant in Mexico, when local officials solicited an under-the-table payment of $1,350 to speed approval of his business operating license. He refused to pay and did not receive his license. Mexican officials have estimated that as much as 9 percent of Mexico's gross domestic product goes for corruption, more than the nation invests in educational and defense combined. However, the United States is not immune to corruption as evidenced by the billions in waste and fraud surrounding federal payouts from Hurricane Katrina.[24]

Culture Shock

culture shock
A group of physical and psychological symptoms that may develop when a person is abruptly placed in a foreign culture.

Many managers and professionals on overseas assignments face **culture shock**. The condition refers to a group of physical and psychological symptoms that may develop when a person is abruptly placed in a foreign culture. Among them are excessive hand washing and concern for sanitation, fear of physical contact with others, fear of being mugged, and strong feelings of homesickness.[25] Another potential contributor to culture shock is that the expatriate may work in one time zone while contacts in company headquarters work in a time zone with a time difference of six or more hours. As a

23 "USA: Congress Rubber Stamps Torture and Other Abuses," Amnesty International Press Release, http://www.amnesty.org, September 29, 2006.

24 Marla Dickerson, "The Bite of Corruption," *The Los Angeles Times* (http://www.latimes.com), August 6, 2006.

25 Harry C. Triandis, *Culture Shock and Social Behavior* (New York: McGraw-Hill, 1994), p. 263.

result, the expatriate is often expected to answer e-mails and respond to phone calls during his or her typical evening or sleeping hours. For example, a person from headquarters in Los Angeles might place an urgent telephone call at 5 p.m. his time to a worker in London whose time is 3 a.m. Frequent disruptions to personal life of this nature contribute to making the international assignment uncomfortable for the expatriate.

As an expatriate working in Amsterdam, Holland, said, "People never remember what time zone you're in. I decided that I was going to make my own schedule. I wanted to be available to our European clients and have meetings in Europe, but I didn't want to be in a position where I missed the West Coast." Her own schedule involved working from noon to 8:30 p.m. on Mondays and Fridays.[26] On other workdays, she works from 9 a.m. to noon, then restarts at 5 p.m. and stays until late in the evening.

Differences in Negotiating Style

A recurring challenge in other countries, as indicated in Exhibit 2-1, is that the international managerial worker may have to use a different negotiation style. A do-or-die attitude is often self-defeating. American negotiators, for example, often find that they must be more patient, use a team approach, and avoid being too informal. Patience is a major factor in negotiating outside the United States. Asian negotiators are willing to spend many days negotiating a deal. Much of their negotiating activity seems to be ceremonial (including elaborate dining) and unrelated to the task. This protracted process can frustrate many Americans. Although members of another culture spend a long time working a deal, they may still take a tough stance, such as insisting on a reasonable profit.

An experiment conducted by Jeanne Brett and Tetsushi Okumura provides more evidence about the challenges of cross-cultural negotiation. The researchers demonstrated that people negotiating with others from their own culture were more likely to achieve mutual gains, as when Americans negotiated with Americans or Japanese negotiated with Japanese. Mutual gains were less likely when negotiating across cultures—when Americans negotiated with Japanese.[27]

Piracy of Intellectual Property Rights and Other Merchandise

In international business, considerable revenue is lost when firms in other countries illegally copy and sell products. Furthermore, these imitations (or "knock-offs") might be sold in the domestic market as well, depriving the firm of additional revenue. Managers must address the reality of unauthorized third-party sales of imitations of their product. Products widely reproduced illegally include fine watches, perfume, videos and CDs, clothing with high-status brand names, and software. The movie industry is another major victim of piracy, with unauthorized copies of films sometimes surfacing even before the formal release date of a film.

---

26 Mary Kissel, "The Jungle: Focus on Recruitment, Pay and Getting Ahead," *The Wall Street Journal*, January 25, 2005, p. B6.

27 Jeanne Brett and Tetsushi Okumura, "Inter- and Intracultural Negotiations: U.S. and Japanese Negotiators," *Academy of Management Journal*, October 1998, pp. 495–510.

The global cost of software piracy was estimated to be $34 billion in 2005, according to a study commissioned by the Business Software Alliance. The study also found that one out of three copies of personal computing software installed in 2005 was pirated. The United States had a piracy rate of 21 percent, the lowest of any country, followed by New Zealand, Austria, and Finland. China, Russia, and India have seen a decline of two points in their piracy rates versus the previous year.[28] Microsoft is working hard to reduce software piracy. One tactic was to make China part of an effort to improve communications with government worldwide. Part of the Microsoft message was that stronger intellectual property protection would help China build its own economy in addition to protecting foreign developers of technology products.[29]

METHODS OF ENTRY INTO WORLD MARKETS

Learning Objective 4

Explain various methods of entry into world markets.

Firms enter the global market in several different ways, and new approaches continue to evolve. At one time a small firm relied on importer-exporters or distributors to enter the world market. Now many home-based businesses sell worldwide through an established Web site. Two broad purposes of foreign commerce are to enhance sales, and to produce goods and services. A physical presence in another country might enhance sales, and goods and services might be produced less expensively in another country such as a call center located overseas. The reference to *markets*, however, implies that the company is looking to sell goods and services in another country rather than manufacture in or provide services from the new location.

The initial entry mode used to penetrate a foreign market must be chosen carefully because of its potential effects on the success of the venture. Another factor is the difficulty in changing the mode without considerable loss of time and money. Six methods of entry into world markets are described next.

1. *Exporting.* Goods produced in one country are then sold for direct use or resale to one or more companies in foreign countries. Many small firms specialize in helping companies gain entry into foreign markets through exporting. An overseas distributor can be quite helpful, but one must be chosen carefully to determine compatibility and perhaps the integrity of the proposed partner.
2. *Licensing and franchising.* Companies operating in foreign countries are authorized to produce and market products or services with specific territories on a fee basis. A franchise arrangement, such as a U.S. citizen operating a Subway store in Madrid, Spain, would fit this category.
3. *Local assembly and packaging.* In this arrangement, components rather than finished products are shipped to company-owned facilities in other countries. There assembly is completed and the goods are marketed. Trade regulations sometimes require that a large product, such as a computer

28 Candace Lombardi, "Study: Software Piracy Costs U.S. $24B," http://www.zdnet.com, May 24, 2006.

29 Jason Dean and Ron Guth, "How Microsoft, Boeing Manage Business in China," *The Wall Street Journal*, April 17, 2006, p. A4.

server or an automobile, be assembled locally rather than shipped from the exporting country as a finished product.

4. *Strategic alliance and joint ventures.* Instead of merging formally with a firm of mutual interest, a company in one country pools resources with one or more foreign companies. A major reason for the willingness of so many firms to form alliances is the enormous expense and effort necessary for a single organization to accomplish a full range of business activities. In a joint venture, the companies in alliance produce, warehouse, transport, and market products. A joint venture is thus a special type of strategic alliance. Profits or losses from these operations are shared in some predetermined proportion. Many digital products, including digital cameras, result from strategic alliances and joint ventures. Alliances are becoming more frequent with consumer vehicles. For example, Volkswagen AG and Chrysler are collaborating on a VW minivan to be assembled in Windsor, Ontario, or near St. Louis for the North American market in 2008. Dodge and Chrysler will provide the platform, and VW will be responsible for the interior and exterior designs.[30]
5. *Direct foreign investment.* The most advanced stage of multinational business activity takes place when a company in one country produces and markets products through wholly owned facilities in foreign countries. Toyota Motor Co. and Ford Motor Co., two well-known multinational corporations, conduct business in this manner. A positive perspective on direct foreign investment is that the multinational corporation exports jobs to other countries, such as the substantial manufacturing facilities of Honda, Toyota, Hyundai, and Mercedes-Benz in the United States. These overseas companies have helped turn the United States into the center of a global industry. Foreign players are said to have reinvigorated the U.S. auto industry. A merger of business firms from different countries is a similar way of gaining entry into the international market place, such as Ford merging with Land Rover and Jaguar.
6. *Global start-up.* A **global start-up** is a small firm that comes into existence by serving an international market. By so doing, the firm circumvents the previous methods. Logitech Inc., the leading manufacturer of the computer mouse, is one of the most successful global start-ups. A Swiss and two Italians who wanted to have an international company from the start founded the company in 1982. Logitech began with headquarters, manufacturing, and engineering in California and Switzerland and then established facilities in Taiwan and Ireland. Founders of global start-ups have one key characteristic in common: some international experience before going global.[31] Selling through the Internet facilitates creating a global start-up because customers can be reached directly without a distributor. However, trade restrictions such as paying tariffs and obtaining approval from the foreign government usually apply.

global start-up
A small firm that comes into existence by serving an international market.

30 Tony Van Alphen, "VW, Chrysler Team Up On Van," *The Toronto Star* (http://www.thestar.com), January 6, 2006.
31 Benjamin M. Oviatt and Patricia Phillips McDougal, "Global Start-Ups: Entrepreneurs on a Worldwide Stage," *The Academy of Management Executive*, May 1995, p. 30.

Of the methods of entry into the global marketplace, exporting offers the least protection for the company doing business in another country. Multinational firms run the risk that the firm in the other country may drop its affiliation and sell the product on its own. The affiliate thus becomes a competitor. To avoid this risk, direct foreign investment is recommended as the best way to protect the company's competitive advantage. The advantage is protected because the manager of a foreign subsidiary can control its operation.

SUCCESS FACTORS IN THE GLOBAL MARKETPLACE

Learning Objective 5

Pinpoint success factors in the global marketplace, and several positive and negative aspects of globalization.

Success in international business stems from the same factors that lead to success at home. The ultimate reason for the success of any product or service is its ability to satisfy customer needs. Additional strategies and tactics, however, are required for success in the global marketplace. It is important to recognize that internationalization of business is not always successful. Most of these strategies and tactics logically extend the topics discussed previously in this chapter.

Think Globally, Act Locally

A competitive enterprise combines global scale and world-class technology with deep roots in local markets. Local representatives of the firm behave as though their primary mission is to serve the local customer. Multinational corporations implementing a local market focus face the challenge of adapting a product to local trends and preferences. Often the differences are subtle, and require a careful study of the local market. For example, the direct seller of cosmetics, Mary Kay, has adapted its products to Chinese culture, which perceives smooth white skin as the essence of beauty, said Paul Mak, president of Mary Kay China. As a result, sunless tanners or bronzers are not distributed in China. Instead Mary Kay markets skin whiteners, and is developing a line of botanical lotions that include traditional Chinese herbs.[32]

Part of acting locally is close familiarity with the local scene. U.S. companies with established maquiladoras have discovered the importance of this principle. For example, a unique aspect of Mexican law comes into play when an officially recognized labor union declares a strike. All employees, including managers, must leave the building, and red and black flags are hung at entrances to the plant. Furthermore, employees receive full pay for all the time they are out on a legal strike.

Recruit and Select Talented Nationals and Domestic Workers

A major success factor in building a business in another country is to hire talented citizens of that country to fill important positions. After the host-company nationals are hired, they must be taught the culture of the parent company. By teaching the overseas managers the values and traditions of the firm, those managers can better achieve corporate objectives. Networking

32 Julia Glick, "China Market Helps Mary Kay Stay in the Pink," Associated Press, August 6, 2006.

with contacts in the other country is important. One way to network would be to make a list of other companies from your country already established in your destination country. These people might include bankers, lawyers, suppliers, and distributors.

Staffing in other countries may require a modification of U.S. ideas about good candidates. An international human resources manager observes that "One of the most common mistakes companies make when hiring and recruiting employees in China is to judge candidates based on U.S. perceptions and criteria. Chinese employees often have different ways of communicating their interests and skills during an interview, and they consider it unbecoming to place too much emphasis on their skills and experience." An interviewer not familiar with this mind-set could miss hiring an excellent candidate.[33]

Employees in the home country also have to be of high caliber to compete well in the international arena. A leading example is the Global Engine Manufacturing Alliance (GEMA) plant in Dundee, Michigan, thought to be the workforce model for the future of U.S. auto making. Workers are trained in a wide array of subjects, including how to assemble an engine and the study of mathematical formulas designed to teach problem-solving skills. Hourly employees at GEMA are highly educated relative to other workers in their job category, and rotate jobs to provide for more flexibility. Mark Dunning, senior manager of human resources, sums up the company's staffing strategy in these words: "The time and money spent on finding good employees at GEMA are considerable, but so is the payoff in terms of workforce creativity. The amount of time from problem to solution is shorter than I have even seen it in my 17 years at Chrysler."[34]

Hire or Develop Multicultural Workers

A contributing factor to success in global markets is to hire multicultural workers. Multiculturalism enhances acceptance of a firm by overseas personnel and customers. Included in multiculturalism is the ability to speak the language of the target (or host) country. Even though English is the official language of business and technology, overseas employees should develop the right foreign language skill. Being able to listen to and understand foreign customers speaking in their native language about their requirements may reveal nuances that would be missed by having them speak in English. Showing that one has made an effort to learn the native language can earn big dividends with employees, customers, prospective customers, bankers, and government officials. To be impressive, however, it is important to go beyond the most basic skill level.

To help workers and their family members become multicultural, many companies offer cultural training. Joerg Schmitz, a global management training expert, shares an illuminating example of the impact of culture on an employee's job performance: "The U.S. culture is extraordinarily task

---

33 Mary E. Medland, "Setting Up Overseas," *HR Magazine*, January 2004, p. 72.

34 Jessica Marquez, "Streamlined Model," *Workforce Management*, July 17, 2006, pp. 1, 20, 22. The quote is from page 22.

oriented. Northern Europe is perhaps the closest to the type of task orientation you'll find in the United States. But about every other country in the world is relationship oriented."[35] Expatriates must understand this observation as they work hard to build rapport and gain credibility with business colleagues in other cultures.

Research and Assess Potential Markets

Another basic success strategy in international markets is to acquire valid information about the firm's target market. Trade statistics usually provide a good starting point. If the company manufactures long-lasting light bulbs, it must find out where such bulbs sell the best. Basic trade data are often available at foreign embassies, banks with international operations, and departments of commerce. Wal-Mart invests enormous energy and money into researching which overseas markets—and consumer reaction—would fit its retailing model. In general, the planning has worked well. For example, Wal-Mart has been highly successful in Mexico and Canada, and has stayed out of Paris. The company, however, stumbled in Germany and eventually sold its stores in that country.

The Advantages and Disadvantages of Globalization

Many managers and scholars believe that globalization of business is both inevitable and highly desirable. Yet for other managers, business owners, and individual workers, the internationalization of the workplace has created more problems than opportunities. Many of the advantages and disadvantages of globalization depend upon an individual's vantage point. An executive in an MNC might receive a generous bonus because shifting a call center to India saves the company $5 million per year in labor costs. As a consequence she welcomes globalization. The middle-aged call center supervisor who lost his enjoyable, well-paying job and is now a greeter at a discount department store would view globalization more negatively. Exhibit 2-4 outlines the major pros and cons of globalization.

exhibit 2-4 The Pros and Cons of Globalization

Advantages

- By sending jobs overseas, a country such as the United States is better able to compete globally, thus saving jobs in the long run. A company frequently cannot get the contracts it needs to survive if it cannot reduce prices, so offshoring becomes a necessity.
- Productivity grows more quickly when countries produce goods and services in which they have a

Disadvantages

- Millions of Americans have lost jobs due to imports or production shifts abroad. Most find lower-paying jobs. One-quarter of laid-off workers are still job-hunting three years later. Most of the jobs sent overseas from the United States are permanent losses. Many service and professional jobs, such as financial analysis and design engineering, are now sent to other countries.

35 Andrea C. Poe, "Selection Savvy," *HR Magazine*, April 2002, p. 78.

comparative advantage. Living standards go up faster. Productivity in high-wage companies also increases because they are forced to reduce the cost of production to survive worldwide competition.

- Global integration helps reduce worldwide poverty. At the same time, economic growth around the world contributes to economic stability and peace because impoverished people are more likely to revolt and attack wealthier people and institutions.
- Global competition and inexpensive imports set a ceiling on prices, so inflation is less likely to be too high.
- When one country buys goods from and sends jobs to another country, the second country is better able to purchase goods from the first country. For example, India furnishes its call centers for U.S. firms with U.S. computers and software.
- An open economy spurs innovation with fresh ideas from abroad. Innovation at home receives a boost because the domestic company has to become more specialized and creative to compete against international rivals.
- When research and development jobs are moved overseas, products reach the market faster because work can be done 24/7 as scientists and engineers in one part of the world pass off their project at the end of the day to research workers just waking up overseas.
- Workers become broader in their outlook and profit from the opportunity to become multicultural, including foreign travel.
- With many jobs shipped overseas, talent is freed up within the United States, which can be re-skilled and used elsewhere in a tight labor market. At the same time, many people whose jobs are outsourced, or fear being outsourced, start small enterprises of their own, helping to revitalize the economy.
- It is possible for an American company, such as online store Fair Indigo, to promote fair trade around the world by choosing foreign vendors who pay beyond the minimum wage, and also offer workers bonuses and medical benefits.
- Millions of others fear losing their jobs, especially at those companies operating under competitive pressure. Workers are forced to compete against foreign workers in countries like Pakistan and Malaysia, where workers are paid on average one-tenth as their American counterparts.
- To stay competitive in a global economy, many companies reduce wages, close plants rather than have a unionized workforce, reduce health and retirement benefits, and eliminate some pension plans.
- Profits and executive salaries increase while workers toil in overseas sweatshops. Many of these workers are vulnerable to human rights violations.
- National pride is hurt as many Americans lament, "Nothing is 'made in the USA' any longer. We used to be such a great country." At the same time, many American consumers resent call center workers from 6,000 miles away responding to their requests for information and service. Many Americans have a difficult time understanding workers who speak English with a foreign accent.

Source: Brian Blackstone, "Fed Chairman Expects Globalization to Enhance Living Standards," *The Wall Street Journal*, August 26–27, 2006, p. A3; Bob Tedeschi, "A Click on Clothes to Support Fair Trade," *The New York Times* (http://www.nytimes.com), September 25, 2006; David Crane, "There's No Realistic Alternative to Globalization," *Toronto Star*, February 28, 2004 (also http://www.thestar.com); Douglas A. Irwin, "Outsourcing Is Good for America," *The Wall Street Journal*, January 28, 2004, p. A16.

THE SCOPE, COMPETITIVE ADVANTAGE, AND POTENTIAL PROBLEMS OF MANAGING DIVERSITY

Learning Objective 6

Describe the scope of diversity, and the competitive advantage and potential problems of a culturally diverse workforce.

The globalization of business means that the managerial workers must be able to deal effectively with people from other countries. At the same time it is important to deal effectively with different cultural groups within one's own country and company. Both the international and domestic workforces are diverse. In the present context, **diversity** refers to a mixture of people with different group identities within the same work environment. Workplace diversity is not prized simply because it is pleasant to have different groups working next to each other, but because these groups must work *together* as a team to serve a variety of customers, and to generate a wide variety of useful ideas.[36] The term *diversity* includes two subtypes, demographic and cultural.

Demographic diversity refers to the mix of group characteristics of the organization's workforce. Demographic characteristics include such factors as age, sex, religion, physical status, and sexual orientation. *Cultural diversity* refers to the mix of cultures and subcultures to which the organization's workforce belongs. Among these cultures are the Hispanic culture, the deaf culture, the Muslim culture, the Jewish culture, the Native American culture, and the Inuit (Eskimo) culture. It is possible for people with the same demographic characteristics not to share the same cultural characteristics. A deaf person who went to school with hearing people, whose parents are hearing, and most of whose friends can hear, may be deaf from a demographic standpoint, yet the person does not identify with the deaf culture. Following common practice, in this text the term *diversity* is used to reflect both demographic and cultural diversity.

Here and in the next section, we study diversity in the workplace from five perspectives: (1) the scope of diversity, (2) its competitive advantage, (3) potential disadvantages, and (4) organizational practices for capitalizing on diversity, and (5) an analysis of how the English language is used to unify people in business. Before reading further, take the self-quiz about cross-cultural skills and attitudes presented in Exhibit 2-5.

The Scope of Diversity

Improving cross-cultural relations includes appreciating the true meaning of diversity. To appreciate diversity, a person must go beyond tolerating and treating people from different racial and ethnic groups fairly. Valuing diversity means to respect and enjoy a wide range of cultural and individual differences. To be diverse is to be different in some measurable way. Although the diversity factor is measurable in a scientific sense, it may not be visible on the surface. Upon meeting a team member, it may not be apparent that the person is diverse from the standpoint of being dyslexic, color-blind, gay, lesbian, or vegetarian. However, all these factors are measurable.

diversity
A mixture of people with different group identities within the same work environment.

36 Jennifer Schramm, "Acting Affirmatively," *HR Magazine*, September 2003, p. 192.

exhibit 2-5 Cross-Cultural Skills and Attitudes

Various employers and cross-cultural experts believe the following skills and attitudes are important for relating effectively to coworkers in a culturally diverse environment.

	Applies To Me Now	Not There Yet
1. I have spent some time in another country.	______	______
2. At least one of my friends is deaf, blind, or uses a wheelchair.	______	______
3. I know how much at least two foreign currencies are worth in comparison to the money of my country	______	______
4. I can read in a language other than my native tongue.	______	______
5. I can speak in a language other than my native tongue.	______	______
6. I can write in a language other than my own.	______	______
7. I can understand people speaking in a language other than my own.	______	______
8. I use my second language regularly.	______	______
9. My friends include people of races different from my own.	______	______
10. My friends include people of different ages.	______	______
11. I feel (or would feel) comfortable having friends with a sexual orientation different from mine.	______	______
12. My attitude is that although another culture may be different from mine, that culture is equally good.	______	______
13. I would be willing to (or already do) hang art from various countries in my home.	______	______
14. I would accept (or have already accepted) a work assignment of more than several months in another country.	______	______
15. I have a passport.	______	______

Interpretation: If you answered "Applies to Me Now" to ten or more of the questions, you most likely function well in a multicultural work environment. If you answered "Not There Yet" to ten or more of the questions, you need to develop more cross-cultural awareness and skills to work effectively in a multicultural work environment. You will notice that being bilingual gives you at least five points on this quiz.

Source: Several of the statements are based on Ruthann Dirks and Janet Buzzard, "What CEOs Expect of Employees Hired for International Work," *Business Education Forum*, April 1997, pp. 3–7; Gunnar Beeth, "Multicultural Managers Wanted," *Management Review*, May 1997, pp. 17–21.

As just implied, some people are more visibly diverse than others because of physical features or disabilities. Yet the diversity umbrella is supposed to include everybody in an organization. The goal of a diverse organization, then, is for persons of all cultural backgrounds to achieve their full potential, not restrained by group identification, such as sex, nationality, or race.[37]

37 Joan Crockett, "Winning Competitive Advantage Through a Diverse Workforce," *HRfocus*, May 1999, p. 9.

The Competitive Advantage of Diversity

Encouraging diversity within an organization helps an organization achieve social responsibility goals. Also, diversity brings a competitive advantage to a firm. Before diversity can offer a competitive advantage to a firm, it must be woven into the fabric of the organization. This stands in contrast to simply having a "diversity program" offered on rare occasions by the human resources department. Instead, the human resource efforts toward accomplishing diversity become part of organizational strategy. The potential competitive (or bottom-line) benefits of cultural diversity, as revealed by research and observations, are described next:

1. *Managing diversity well offers a marketing advantage, including increased sales and profits.* A representational workforce facilitates reaching a multicultural market. Allstate Insurance Company invests considerable effort into being a culturally diverse business firm. More than coincidentally, Allstate is now recognized as the nation's leading insurer of African Americans and Hispanics. The "Rainbow Team" of American Airlines in one year brought in $192 million in revenue by targeting the gay community.[38]
2. *Effective management of diversity can reduce costs.* More effective management of diversity may increase job satisfaction of diverse groups, thus decreasing turnover and absenteeism and their associated costs. A diverse organization that welcomes and fosters the growth of a wide variety of employees will retain more of its minority and multicultural employees. A study of 250,000 crew members from 3,400 quick-service restaurants indicated that diversity helps reduce turnover. A tendency was noted for crew workers to more likely quit when they were the only member of their demographic group within the crew, such as being the only Asian/Pacific Islander.[39] Effective management of diversity can also help avoid costly lawsuits over discrimination based on age, race, or sex.
3. *Companies with a favorable record in managing diversity are at a distinct advantage in recruiting talented people.* Those companies with a favorable reputation for welcoming diversity attract the strongest job candidates among women and racial and ethnic minorities. A shortage of workers gives extra impetus to diversity. During a tight labor market, companies cannot afford to be seen as not welcoming any particular group.
4. *Workforce diversity can provide a company with useful ideas for favorable publicity and advertising.* A culturally diverse workforce, or advertising agency, can help a firm place itself in a favorable light to targeted cultural groups. During Kwanzaa, the late-December holiday celebrated by many African Americans, McDonald's Corp. has run ads aimed at showing its understanding of and respect for African Americans' sense of family and community. For such ads to be effective, however, the company must also

---

38 Cliff Edwards, "Coming Out in Corporate America," *Business Week*, December 15, 2003, p. 65.

39 Joshua M. Sacco and Neal Schmitt, "A Dynamic Multilevel Model of Demographic Diversity and Misfit Effects," *Journal of Applied Psychology*, March 2005, pp. 203–231.

have a customer-contact workforce that is culturally diverse. Otherwise the ads would lack credibility.

5. *Workforce diversity, including using the services of a culturally diverse advertising agency, can help reduce cultural bloopers and hidden biases.* Companies still make the occasional advertising bloopers that might offend a particular consumer group, leading to lost sales or potential. For example, an extra pair of eyes helped PNC bank avoid what could have been a painful error. A PNC branch employee noticed that the brochures for low-income people showed far more photos of people of color than did brochures developed for higher-income customers. The employee contacted the worker responsible for developing the brochures, who quickly pulled the materials and developed more inclusive replacements.[40]
6. *Workforce heterogeneity may also offer a company a creativity advantage.* Creative solutions to problems are more likely when a diverse group attacks a problem due to the variety of perspectives that contribute to creative alternatives. For example, if a company is going to launch products that fit the needs of young people, it is best to include young people in generating ideas for these products.

The implication for managers is that diversity initiatives should be explained in terms of tangible business purposes to achieve the best results. Yet managers must also recognize that diversity within the organization can also create problems.

Potential Problems Associated with Diversity

In addition to understanding the competitive advantages of diversity within an organization, a brief look at some of the potential problems is also helpful. Cultural diversity initiatives are usually successful in assembling heterogeneous groups, but the group members do not necessarily work harmoniously. The potential for conflict is high. In general, if the demographically different work group members are supportive toward each other, the benefits of group diversity, such as more creative problem solving, will be forthcoming. Group members must also share knowledge with each other for the heterogeneous groups to be successful. Another problem is that diverse groups may be less cohesive than those with less diverse composition.

Denny's restaurant presents a case history of how a diverse workforce does not inevitably contribute to increased business. In the early 1990s, Denny's settled anti-discrimination lawsuits by African American customers. By 2000, the company was considered a positive model of diversity, being named the Fortune No. 1 company for minorities based on Denny's investing millions on a wide range of diversity initiatives. Denny's management is proud to be such a culturally diverse and socially responsible company, but has yet to see any positive financial results. CEO Nelson Marchioli says, "If you think diversity is going to sell one more pancake, you're crazy."[41]

---

40 Indra Lahiri, "Avoid Bloopers in Multicultural Marketing," http://www.workforcedevelopmentgroup.com/news_seven.html.
41 Irwin Speizer, "Diversity on the Menu," *Workforce Management*, November 2004, pp. 41–45. The quote is from page 42.

ORGANIZATIONAL PRACTICES TO ENCOURAGE DIVERSITY

Learning Objective 7

Summarize organizational practices to encourage diversity.

The combined forces of the spirit of the times and the advantages of valuing diversity spark management initiatives to manage diversity well. Three representative practices that enhance diversity management are (1) corporate policies about diversity, (2) the establishment of employee network groups, and (3) diversity training.

Corporate Policies Favoring Diversity

Many companies formulate policies that encourage and foster diversity. A typical policy is "We are committed to recruiting, selecting, training, and promoting individuals based solely on their capabilities and performance. To accomplish this goal, we value all differences among our workforce." To create a culturally and demographically diverse organization, some companies monitor recruitment and promotions to assure that diverse people are promoted into key jobs. After they are promoted, the minority group members are eligible to be coached by an external consultant in terms of becoming a successful leader—as is frequently done with majority group members.

MGM Mirage, the hotel, entertainment, and gambling giant, is a leading example of a corporate policy favoring diversity. The company's Bellagio resort unit runs a nine-month executive mentoring program designed to prepare high-potential minority employees in management positions for advancement into the executive level.[42]

The accompanying management-in-action insert describes a company with a household name that has been cited for promoting, and retaining, minority group members. (Being a member of a minority group is but one dimension of diversity.)

management in action

McDonald's Corp. Wins Black Enterprise Diversity Award

McDonald's is the leading global quick-service restaurant with more than 30,000 restaurants in 119 countries. The creator of the Big Mac scored highly in all four diversity categories developed by *Black Enterprise* magazine: supplier diversity, senior management, employee base, and board of directors. A *strength* in any category indicates the company ranked among the top 20 respondents. McDonald's was most impressive in employee diversity. More than one-half of McDonald's staff—from crew members to the COO—belong to an ethnic minority group.

42 Janet Perez, "A Fresh Deck: Publicly Traded MGM Mirage Begins Dealing Diversity," *Hispanic Business*, January/February 2006, p. 62.

> *"It was 1994 when I joined the McDonald's family as a regional manager in our Sacramento region," says Ralph Alvarez, who is now president of McDonald's North America. "I believed then, and I know now, the culture of McDonald's is unique and one where diversity is part of the organizational fabric."*

McDonald's is primarily an operations company, therefore the majority of employees are in restaurant operations. However, the company prides itself on having diversity throughout its senior management ranks. Don Thomson, executive vice president and chief operations officer of McDonald's USA, and William Lamar Jr., chief marketing officer of McDonald's USA, both made the *Black Enterprise* "75 Most Powerful Blacks in Corporate America List."

> *"I have been part of planning sessions that focus on understanding the dimensions of diversity in our customers and the importan of having a workforce that represents these very important values and beliefs," says Harris, who began her career at the company 29 years ago as an administrative assistant in the legal department. "I personally experienced numerous promotions and increasing responsibilities. I have had the opportunity to view and participate in the demonstrated commitment to diversity."*

McDonald's has been recognized as a top company for people with disabilities as well as the best employer for Asians, African American women, and Hispanics. Harris says she doesn't take their record for granted. "We focus on doing the smart things for our employees like our efficacy-based diversity education classes, diverse communities, and recognizing and celebrating accomplishments. It's no secret that minorities are more likely to join an organization where they see themselves represented across the business at all levels."

An analysis by *Black Enterprise* also rates McDonald's as one of the ten best in marketing diversity, with a rank of five. Marketing diversity reflects how companies spend their marketing and advertising dollars in outreach efforts to the black community. Such diversity also includes which companies are hiring African American and other ethnic minorities to craft brand images, create messages, and deliver those messages and images to the consumers, who are vitally important to their survival and growth. Another factor was the extent to which the company used black-owned media to carry the message.

Questions

1. Based on whatever first-hand evidence you have, to what extent do you think McDonald's is culturally diverse?
2. What is Alvarez referring to when he says that diversity is part of the organizational fabric at McDonald's Corp.?
3. To what extent do you think *Black Enterprise* magazine is being discriminatory toward majorities in making its diversity awards?

Source: Sakina P. Spruell, "McDonald's Corp." In "The 30 Best Companies for Diversity," *Black Enterprise*, July 2005, p. 120; Sonia Alleyne, "The 40 Best Companies for Diversity," *Black Enterprise*, July 2006, p. 106.

Employee Network Groups

A company approach to recognizing cultural differences is to permit and encourage employees to form **employee network groups**. The network group is composed of employees throughout the company who affiliate on the basis of group characteristics such as race, ethnicity, gender, sexual orientation, or physical ability status. Group members typically have similar interests, and look to groups as a way of sharing information about succeeding in the organization. Although some human resource specialists are concerned that network groups can lead to divisiveness, others believe they play a positive role.

employee network group
A group composed of employees throughout the company who affiliate on the basis of group characteristics such as race, ethnicity, gender, sexual orientation, or physical ability status.

diversity training Training that attempts to bring about workplace harmony by teaching people how to get along better with diverse work associates

The Latino Employee Network at Frito-Lay, the snack food division of PepsiCo, illustrates how such a network group can contribute to the bottom line. The Latino group proved invaluable during the development of Doritos Guacamole Flavored Tortilla Chips. Network members, called Adelante, gave management feedback on the taste and packaging to help ensure that the product would have authenticity in the Latino community. The guacamole-flavored Doritos became one of the most successful new-product launches in the company's history, with sales of more than $100 million in its first year. PepsiCo management notes that the Doritos experience is one example of how the company leverages diversity to drive business results.[43]

Diversity Training

Cultural training, as described in the section about international business, aims to help workers understand people from another culture. **Diversity training** has a slightly different purpose. It attempts to bring about workplace harmony by teaching people how to get along better with diverse work associates. Quite often the program is aimed at minimizing open expressions of racism and sexism. All forms of diversity training center on increasing people's awareness of and empathy for people who are different from themselves.

Diversity training sessions focus on the ways that men and women, or people of different races, reflect different values, attitudes, and cultural background. These sessions can vary from several hours to several days. Sometimes the program is confrontational, sometimes not.

An essential part of relating more effectively to diverse groups is to empathize with their point of view. To help training participants develop empathy, representatives of various groups explain their feelings related to workplace issues. During one of these training sessions, a Chinese woman said she wished people would not act so shocked when she is assertive about her demands. She claimed that many people she meets at work expect her to fit the stereotype of the polite, compliant Chinese woman.

Many other exercises are used in diversity training. In one exercise, a nationality is mentioned, such as Italian. All group members then describe what comes to mind when the nationality "Italian" is mentioned. Later, the group discusses how their stereotypes help and hinder diversity. Another type of diversity training focuses on cross-generational diversity, or relating effectively to workers much older or younger than you. Wendy's International Inc., with the help of a consultant, has developed training programs that raise awareness of generational issues. Allen Larson, director of management resources, says, "Since generational cohorts help form people's attitudes toward work, employees of different generations who must work together may find that their work styles conflict with those of coworkers."[44]

---

43 Robert Rodriguez, "Diversity Finds Its Place," *HR Magazine*, August 2006, pp. 57–58.

44 Joanne M. Glenn, "Wendy's International, Inc.—Managing Cross-Generational Diversity," *Business Education Forum*, February 2000, p. 16.

A study demonstrated that diversity training is the most likely to lead to more promotions for women and minorities when it is combined with a person or committee to oversee diversity, and to ensure direct accountability for results.[45] Nevertheless, diversity training can still make a contribution in terms of better understanding among diverse workers.

The English Language as a Force for Unity

Although differences among people are important to business firms around the world, international workers have to communicate effectively with each other. To compete globally, more and more European businesses are making English their official language. In this way, workers of different European nationalities can communicate with each other. In many Asian countries also, English is widely used in business. The majority of managerial, professional, technical, and support positions in Europe require a good command of English.

One reason English maintains the edge as the official language of business in so many countries is that English grammar is less complex than that of many other languages. The Internet, and information technology in general, with its heavy emphasis on English, is another force for making English the language of business. A cartoon in *Fortune* summarizes the heavy presence of English in the e-world. Two men wearing business suits and carrying briefcases are talking to each other with the Eiffel Tower in the background. One man says to the other, "Oui, j'adore [French for 'Yes, I love'] e-commerce start-ups!"[46]

Although English may have emerged as the official language of business, the successful international manager needs to be multicultural. Furthermore, if business associates throughout the world are fluent in their native tongue as well as English, command of a second language remains an asset for North Americans. Also, for certain purposes it can be helpful for American companies to communicate with workers in their native language. One such situation is advising workers of dangerous situations on construction sites and on oil rigs. Also, some employers are providing banking, health care, and retirement information in Spanish to help Hispanic workers become more knowledgeable about money matters.[47] The perceptive manager knows when being bicultural and bilingual is helpful.

---

45 Research synthesized in Lisa Takeuchi Cullen, "The Diversity Delusion," *Time*, May 7, 2007, p. 74.
46 Justin Fox, "The Triumph of English," *Fortune*, September 18, 2000, pp. 209–212.
47 Kathryn Tyler, "Financial Fluency," *HR Magazine*, July 2006, pp. 76–81.

SUMMARY OF Key Points

1 Appreciate the importance of multinational corporations in international business.

Multinational corporations (MNCs) are the heart of international business. The continued growth of the MNC has been facilitated by the North American Free Trade Agreement, the World Trade Organization, and the European Union. Concern has been expressed that free trade agreements have shrunk the number of middle-class jobs in the United States, and leads to downward pressures on wages in industrialized nations. Sending work offshore, or outsourcing, has become a key part of international trade.

2 Recognize the importance of sensitivity to cultural differences in international enterprise.

The guiding principle for people involved in international enterprise is sensitivity to cultural differences. Cultural sensitivity can take the form of adapting your behavior (such as speaking more slowly) to meet the requirements of people from another culture. Candidates for foreign assignments generally receive training in the language and customs of the country in which they will work. Another approach to developing cross-cultural sensitivity is to learn cultural mistakes to avoid in the region in which you will be working.

3 Identify major challenges facing the global managerial worker.

Challenges facing global managerial workers include developing global leadership skills, currency fluctuations, balance of trade problems, human rights violations and corruption, culture shock, differences in negotiating style, and piracy of intellectual property rights and other merchandise.

4 Explain various methods of entry into world markets.

Firms enter global markets via the following methods: exporting, licensing and franchising, local assembly and packaging, strategic alliance and joint ventures, direct foreign investment, and global start-up.

5 Pinpoint success factors in the global marketplace, and several positive and negative aspects of globalization.

Success factors for the global marketplace include (a) think globally, act locally, (b) recruit talented nationals and domestic workers, (c) hire or develop multicultural workers, and (d) research and assess local markets. Many of the advantages and disadvantages of globalization depend upon an individual's point of view. For example, profits may increase at the cost of many workers' jobs.

6 Describe the scope of diversity and the competitive advantage and potential problems of a culturally diverse workforce.

To be diverse is to be different in some measurable, but not necessarily visible way. The diversity umbrella is supposed to encompass everybody in the organization. Diversity often brings a competitive advantage to a firm, including the following: marketing advantage, lowered costs due to turnover and absenteeism, improved recruitment, useful ideas for publicity and advertising, a reduction of cultural bloopers and hidden biases, and a creativity advantage. A potential problem is that diverse group members may not get along well with each other, and sometimes diversity does not translate into profits.

7 Summarize organizational practices to encourage diversity.

Three representative practices that enhance diversity management are corporate policies about diversity, the establishment of employee network groups, and diversity training.

KEY TERMS AND PHRASES

Multinational corporation (MNC), 38
Transnational corporation, 38
Outsourcing, 41
Offshoring, 41
Cultural sensitivity, 43
Multicultural worker, 43
Global leadership skills, 46
Balance of trade, 48
Culture shock, 50
Global start-up, 53
Diversity, 58
Employee network groups, 63
Diversity training, 64

QUESTIONS

1. To reduce the trade deficit, and to slow the outsourcing (or "offshoring") of U.S. jobs, many people encourage Americans to insist on purchasing consumer goods made in the United States. What are the advantages and disadvantages of a buy-American policy?
2. Identify a profit-making enterprise that does not have to be bothered with international trade, and for whom international competition is not a threat.
3. What can you do in your career to help reduce the threat that your job will be outsourced to another country?
4. How can a management team justify dealing with a subcontractor based in a country in which human rights are being widely violated?
5. What steps can you take, starting this week, to ready yourself to become a multicultural worker?
6. Suppose an African American couple opens a restaurant that serves African cuisine, hoping to appeal mostly to people of African descent. The restaurant is a big success, yet the couple finds that about 50 percent of its clientele is Caucasian or Asian. Should the restaurant owners then hire several Caucasians and Asians so the employee mix will match the customer mix?
7. What do you see as two advantages and disadvantages of employee network groups to both the individual and the organization?

SKILL-BUILDING EXERCISE 2-A: Coping with Cultural Values and Traditions

The purpose of this exercise is to develop sensitivity to how cultural values and traditions create problems for people from other countries. Find three fellow students, coworkers, friends, or acquaintances from another country who are willing to be interviewed for about ten minutes on the subject of adapting to a new culture. An alternative is to interview people from a far-away region in the same country, such as interviewing somebody from New York City if you are taking this course in Salt Lake City. Dig for answers to the following questions:

1. Which cultural values in this (the country or region in which you are taking this course) country (or regions) do you find the most unusual?
2. In what way are these values unusual?
3. What adaptations have you had to make to cope with these values?
4. Which cultural traditions in this country (or region) do you find the most unusual?
5. In what ways are these values unusual?
6. What adaptations have you had to cope with these traditions?

Be prepared to have a class discussion of your findings and conclusions. Identify any lesson you have learned that will help you be more effective as a multicultural worker.

SKILL-BUILDING EXERCISE 2-B: Evaluating a Multicultural Digital Assistant

You and several of your classmates are part of a task force to help develop the multicultural skills of your workforce. You have been placed on this assignment because your transnational corporation conducts business in 17 different countries, with a total of six different languages. Today you are asked to evaluate the feasibility of a digital device to enhance the multicultural and foreign language skills of your workforce. The product description is as follows:

> *Next time you find yourself linguistically challenged, whip out the* ***Universal Translator UT 106 from Ectaco Inc.*** *Here's how it works: Simply speak the desired phrase into the unit's built-in microphone. The palm-size machine uses speech-to-speech technology to translate the phrase into one of six languages. Then the translator talks back, providing the correct pronunciation via a built-in speaker. Easy to use, the unit can store 2,000 sentences in French, German, Italian, Portuguese, Russian, and Spanish. And you can go to the Web and download additional phrases. Bravo! The Universal Translator UT 106 retails for about $200. Visit Ectaco on the Web (http://www.ectaco.com).*

Discuss the merits of the Universal Translator for helping your workforce become more multicultural, and reach a conclusion about equipping your international workers with the Translator. As part of your evaluation, visit the company Web site. See whether you can obtain a demonstration that can be played through the speakers connected to your computer and monitor.

INTERNET SKILL-BUILDING EXERCISE: Becoming Multicultural

A useful way of developing skills in a second language and learning more about another culture is to create a homepage written in your target language. Or, simply make the foreign language site a favorite or bookmark. In this way, each time you go the Internet on your own computer, your cover page will contain fresh information in the language you want to develop.

To get started, use a search engine that offers choices in several languages. Enter a key word like "newspaper" or "current events" in the search probe. Once you find a suitable choice, enter the edit function for "Favorites" or "Bookmarks" and insert that newspaper as your home page or cover page. For example, imagine that French were your choice, your search might have brought you to http://www.france2.fr, or http://www.cyberpresse.ca. These Web sites keep you abreast of French (or Canadian) international news, sports, and cultural events—written in French. Another example is to find a Spanish-language version of a U.S. newspaper such as found on http://www.elpasotimes.com. Now every time you access the Internet, you can spend five minutes becoming multicultural. You can save a lot of travel costs and time using the Internet to help you become multicultural.

Case Problem 2-A

Cardone Industries Feels the Heat from China

Salsa music blares from a factory boom box as Akouvi Tokoni grabs a used Honda Civic distributor from a milk crate. The 32-year-old immigrant from Togo checks the metal casting to make sure that it can be rebuilt to the correct specifications. Satisfied that it can be, she inserts bushings and seals, sprays the part with compressed air, and screws in wire harnesses before passing the partially built distributor to a coworker. By the end of Tokoni's shift, Cardone Industries Inc. will convert more than 1,500 used distributors into good-as-new parts ready to ship to wholesalers, repair shops, and auto dealers across the country.

The Company, the Work, and Compensation

Cardone is Philadelphia's largest factory employer, with 4,200 workers in five local plants. The company is also the country's largest rebuilder of auto parts, turning out more than 12 million parts a year. Now, Cardone faces a fight to survive as a Philadelphia manufacturer.

Remanufacturing is hard, physical work. It requires lifting awkward metal car parts, and scrubbing, machining, moving, and packaging them in boxes. At Plant 13, dozens of Cardone employees in safety glasses and blue shirts bend over large round magnifying glasses attached to workbenches, prying at printed circuit boards. At one workstation, a computer-controlled hammer gently pounds a circuit board, simulating a car traveling a bumpy road and testing a finished board for weak solder joints before shipment.

In developing the rebuilt printed-circuit boards, the company's reverse engineering department analyzed the 1,500 or so resistors, electronic connectors, diodes, and computer chips that could fail on a typical board on a General Motors vehicle. It found that 240 of them are likely candidates to fail. Instead of hunting for a single faulty electronic part when it rebuilds the board, the company saves time and money be replacing only those 240, says remanufacturing vice president Robert P. Spuler.

Spuler feels the pressure every day to be more efficient. "There is a breaking point for every product, and right now that breaking point is coming from China," he says, looking at a line of workstations where steering components were being packed for shipment.

In addition to starting wages of $7 to $8 an hour and a 401 (k) retirement plan, Cardone employees get healthcare coverage, paid vacations and profit sharing. They can boost their wages to as high as $15 an hour by learning new skills.

Competing against China

Competition from China has Cardone so rattled that its chief executive is reaching out for help, both in Philadelphia and Washington. "I want to do my best to keep as many jobs here as I can for as long as I can," says Michael Cardone Jr., the son of the company's founder. At the same time, he says, "I still have to be competitive."

But Cardone Industries is fighting a flood of Chinese imports that are so cheap that they undercut the parts the company rebuilds after salvaging used parts from service stations, auto dealerships, and junkyards. To maintain market share against the Chinese influx, Cardone Industries has cut prices across its product lines by 16 percent in the last five years. Cardone slashed the prices of its water pumps by 22 percent. Another product under siege, drive axles, has declined in price by about 60 percent in the last decade. The cuts come at a time of dramatic increases in energy costs and double-digit hikes in healthcare costs.

Trying to become more efficient, Cardone last year relocated a Philadelphia line that rebuilds drive-axle components to a new, 250-employee plant in Matamoros, Mexico, and says that marginally profitable product lines could head south. The company has even turned to China to make some parts, creating a line of new products called Cardone Select.

Cardone, which competes with local auto-part rebuilders throughout the nation, began preparing for the Chinese several years ago. It adopted Toyota's efficient manufacturing practices and expanded its product line to 43 categories and 25,000 separate items. The company also moved into more complex products. Along with parts made of steel or plastic castings, Cardone rebuilds electronics that control vehicles.

It has ramped up productivity and broadened its product line, but this hasn't stopped the financial slide. "We've squeezed as much out of the Philadelphia operations as we can," says George Zauflik, vice president

Case Problem 2-A

for government relations. "We're at the point that something has to shift here."

One of the initiatives to survive that Cardone Industries is taking is to work with the Automotive Parts Remanufacturing Association. The company is promoting the idea of federal tax credits for remanufactured products. Cardone and other rebuilders argue that they keep parts out of landfills and conserve raw materials and energy by recycling metal, aluminum, and plastics. In rebuilding, the parts don't have to be melted and recast, and they don't have to be transported many times to China to be processed.

Vincent Dougherty, director of Mayor Street's Business Action Team, says that Cardone's situation "is troubling, but not necessarily something we can control, given the local economy. We want to be as supportive as we can."

Meanwhile, Jason Hilts, president of the Brownville Economic Development Council in Texas, wants Cardone to relocate more of its Philadelphia lines to his area on the U.S.–Mexican border. The area has lost factory jobs to China and is courting new companies to fill the gap.

Discussion Questions

1. What do you recommend that Cardone Industries do to compete more successfully with auto parts rebuilders in China?
2. What are several advantages and disadvantages associated with relocating more lines of the company to the U.S.–Mexican border?
3. What do you think of the possibilities of the company either shutting down or selling the business, perhaps to a Chinese company?

Source: Excerpted from Bob Fernandez, "Local Firm Faces Fight to Survive," http://www.philly.com, May 28, 2006; http://www.cardone.com.

Case Problem 2-B

What to Do About Louie?

Louie is the manager of a Mighty Muffler Brake service center in the Great Lakes Region of the United States. Mighty Muffler Brake offers a wide range of services for vehicles, including muffler and exhaust system replacement, brake systems, oil change, lubrication, tune-ups, and state inspections. Louie's branch is located close to a busy highway, yet stores and residential neighborhoods are also close by. His store is among the chain's highest volume and most profitable units. The fact that Louie's Mighty Muffler Brake is located in a region that heavily salts the streets and highways during periods of snow and ice contributes to the steady influx of business at Louie's store.

Management at Mighty Muffler Brake is pleased with the financial management of Louie's store, yet complaints have surfaced about aspects of his relationships with employees and customers. Emma, the human resources and marketing manager for the company, was recently poring over the results from customer satisfaction cards mailed back to the company. She found that a few of the customer comments suggested that Louie might have made a few inappropriate comments, as reflected in these remarks:

> *You did a wonderful job in replacing my brakes, and fixing a rattle in my exhaust system. But the manager insulted me a little by suggesting that I talk over with my husband whether or not to get a new exhaust system now.*
>
> *I have no complaints about the repairs you did or the price you charged. However, you had better replace that manager of yours who is definitely out of touch with the times. My partner and I are proud of our gayness, so we don't attempt to hide occasional public displays of affection. When your manager saw me giving my patner a peck on the cheek he asked if we were from San Francisco.*
>
> *When I came to pick up my car, I had to wait two hours even though I was told the car would be ready by three in the afternoon. I also found some smudge marks on the beige leather seats. When I complained to the manager, he said, "Granny, watch your blood pressure. It's not good for a senior citizen to get too excited." I was never so insulted.*

Concerned about these comments, Emma scheduled a trip to Louie's store to investigate any possible problems he might be having in managing cultural diversity among employees. Emma explained to Louie that the home office likes to make periodic trips to the stores to see how well employee relations are going, and how well employees are working together. Louie responded, "Talk to anybody you want. I may joke a little with the boys and girls in the shop, but we all get along great."

In Emma's mind, her informal chats with workers at Louie's store suggested that employee relations were generally satisfactory, but she did find a few troublesome comments. A young African American noted that when he does something particularly well, or Louie agrees with him strongly, Louie gives him a "high-five." In contrast, Caucasian or Hispanic workers will receive a congratulatory handshake.

A woman brake technician said that Louie is a kind-hearted boss but that he is sometimes patronizing or insulting without realizing it. She volunteered this incident, "During breaks I sometimes enter the waiting room area because we have a vending machine up front that sells small bags of nuts and raisins that I particularly like. One day I was about to enter the waiting room, when Louie tells me to stay in the back. He said that there was a Hell's Angel-type guy waiting for his truck to be repaired, and he probably wouldn't appreciate it if he thought that a 'girl' was working on his truck. How could anybody be that sexist in today's world?"

Emma went back to the home office to discuss her findings with the CEO and the vice president of administration. Emma said that Louie is making a contribution to the firm, but that some changes needed to be made. The two other executives agreed that Louie should become a little more multicultural, but that they didn't want to upset him too much because he could easily join a competitor. Emma concluded, "So I guess we need to figure out what to do about Louie."

Discussion Questions

1. Does Louie have a problem, or are the people who made the negative comments about Louie just being too sensitive?

Case Problem 2-B

2. If you were the CEO of Mighty Muffler Brake, would the profitability of Louie's store influence your decision about approaching him about his ability to relate to culturally diverse people?
3. What improvements might Louie need to make to become a truly multicultural manager?
4. What activity would you recommend to help make Louie more culturally sensitive?

Ethics and Social Responsibility

Objectives

After studying this chapter and doing the exercises, you should be able to:

1 Identify the philosophical principles behind business ethics.

2 Explain how values relate to ethics.

3 Identify factors contributing to lax ethics, and common ethical temptations and violations.

4 Apply a guide to ethical decision making.

5 Describe the stakeholder viewpoint of social responsibility and corporate social performance.

6 Present an overview of social responsibility initiatives.

7 Summarize the benefits of ethical and socially responsible behavior, and how managers can create an environment that fosters such behavior.

Seeking to promote more healthy eating habits among children, Mickey Mouse and his Walt Disney Co. friends are changing their diets. Disney announced a companywide initiative to phase out the promotion of unhealthy foods to kids and eliminate artery-clogging trans fats from its theme-park menus and in promotions across its businesses. The Burbank, California, entertainment company said its characters and brands will be used only on child-focused products that meet certain guidelines in terms of calories, fat, saturated fat, and sugar. It also said its parks would promote more healthy options for kids.

"A company such as ours, with the reach we have, has a responsibility because of how much we can influence people's opinion and behavior," says Disney chief executive Robert Iger. He adds, "There's also a business opportunity here."

A challenge for Disney is determining what foods are unhealthy. "We're not declaring our guidelines to be absolute science," says Mr. Iger, the father of two young boys. "It would be wrong to take a holier-than-thou approach."[1]

The move by the Disney company to help prevent children from eating unhealthy foods that could contribute to cardiac problems and obesity can be considered socially responsible, or

---

1 Merissa Marr and Janet Adamy, "Disney Pulls Characters from Junk Food: Media Giant Announces Guidelines For Calorie, Fat, Sugar Content For Goods Using Its Brands in Ads," *The Wall Street Journal*, October 17, 2006, p. D1.

Looking out for the welfare of society. At the same time the Disney Co. hints at the subtle point that being socially responsible can also lead to increased profits for a company because of the favorable publicity. The purpose of this chapter is to explain the importance of and provide insights into ethics and social responsibility. To accomplish this purpose we present various aspects of ethics and social responsibility. We also present guidelines to help managerial workers make ethical decisions and to conduct socially responsible acts.

BUSINESS ETHICS

Learning Objective 1

Identify the philosophical principles behind business ethics.

Understanding and practicing good business ethics is an important part of a manager's job. **Ethics** is the study of moral obligation, or separating right from wrong. Although many unethical acts are illegal, others are legal and issues of legality vary by nation. An example of an illegal unethical act in the United States is giving a government official a kickback for placing a contract with a specific firm. An example of a legal, yet unethical, practice is making companies more profitable by eliminating their pension plans. A master of this approach is turnaround artist Robert S. Miller. As chief executive of Bethlehem Steel in 2002, Miller closed the pension plan, leaving a federal program to take care of the company's $3.7 billion in unfunded obligations to retirees. Several years later, at Delphi the auto parts maker spun off by General Motors, Miller succeeded in reducing health-care payments to retirees, and was working on ditching the pension plan. Again, nasty but legal if you are a retiree but an astute move if you are a stockholder.[2]

PLAY VIDEO

ETHICS AND SOCIAL RESPONSIBILITY

"Go to academic.cengage.com/management/dubrin and view the video. Who are BP's stakeholder's? How would each view BP's environmental practices?"

One of the many reasons ethics are important is that customers, suppliers, and employees prefer to deal with ethical companies. According to an LRN ethics study, corporate ethics have an impact on the company's ability to attract, retain, and ensure productivity. Specifically, among a sample of 834 U.S. workers, it was found that

- A majority of full-time workers say it is critical to work for a company that is ethical.
- More than one in three workers say they have left a job because of ethical misconduct by fellow employees or managers.
- Eighty-two percent of workers would be willing to receive less pay if they worked for an ethical company.
- Only 11 percent claim not to be negatively affected by unethical behavior in the workplace.[3]

ethics The study of moral obligation, or separating right from wrong.

2 Mary Williams Walsh, "Whoops! There Goes Another Pension Plan," *The New York Times* (http://www.nytimes.com), September 18, 2005.

3 "New Report Details Findings of LRN Ethics Study," http://www.lrn.com, August 14, 2006.

moral intensity The magnitude of an unethical act.

A useful perspective in understanding business ethics emphasizes **moral intensity**, or the magnitude of an unethical act.[4] When an unethical act is not of large consequence, a person might behave unethically without much thought. However, if the act is of large consequence, the person might refrain from unethical or illegal behavior. For example, a manager might plagiarize someone else's speech or make an unauthorized copy of software (both unethical and illegal acts). The same manager, however, might hesitate to dump toxins into a river or sexually harass a business intern.

Business ethics will be mentioned at various places in this text. Here we approach the subject from several perspectives: philosophical principles, values, contributing factors to ethical problems, common ethical problems, and a guide to ethical decision making. To better relate the study of ethics to you, take the self-quiz presented in Exhibit 3-1.

Philosophical Principles Underlying Business Ethics

A standard way of understanding ethical decision making is to know the philosophical basis for making these decisions. When attempting to decide what is right and wrong, managerial workers can focus on (1) consequences, (2) duties, obligations, and principles, or (3) integrity.[5]

Focus on Consequences and Pragmatism

When attempting to decide what is right or wrong, people can sometimes focus on the consequences of their decision or action. According to this criterion, if no one gets hurt, the decision is ethical. Focusing on consequences is often referred to as *utilitarianism*. The decision maker is concerned with the utility of the decision. What really counts is the net balance of good consequences over bad. An automotive body-shop manager, for example, might decide that using low-quality replacement fenders is ethically wrong because the fender will rust quickly. To focus on consequences, the decision maker would have to be aware of all the good and bad consequences of a given decision. The body-shop manager would have to estimate such factors as how angry customers would be whose cars were repaired with inferior parts, and how much negative publicity would result.

Closely related to focusing on consequences is *pragmatism*, the belief that there are no absolute principles or standards, no objective truth, and no objective reality. "Truth" is whatever works, or helps you attain the goals you want. Edwin A. Locke, professor of leadership and management at the University of Maryland, believes that pragmatism is the most prevalent ethical theory in use.[6] Unfortunately, being a pragmatist can land an executive in prison. An example is Jeffrey Skilling, the CEO of Enron, who encouraged employees to purchase more shares in the company although he

4 Thomas M. Jones, "Ethical Decision Making by Individuals in Organizations," *Academy of Management Review*, April 1991, p. 391.

5 Linda K. Treviño and Katherine A. Nelson, *Managing Business Ethics: Straight Talk About How to Do It Right* (New York: Wiley, 1995), pp. 66–70; O. C. Ferrell, John Fraedrich, and Linda Ferrell, *Business Ethics: Ethical Decision Making and Cases* (Boston: Houghton Mifflin Company, 2000), pp. 54–60.

6 Edwin A. Locke, "Business Ethics: A Way Out of the Morass," *Academy of Management Learning & Education*, September 2006, pp. 324–332.

exhibit 3-1 The Ethical Reasoning Inventory

Describe how much you agree with each of the following statements, using the following scale: disagree strongly (DS); disagree (D); neutral (N); agree (A); agree strongly (AS). Circle the answer that best fits your level of agreement.

	DS	D	N	A	AS
1. When applying for a job, I would cover up the fact that I had been fired from my most recent job.	5	4	3	2	1
2. Cheating just a few dollars in one's favor on an expense account is okay if the person needed the money.	5	4	3	2	1
3. Employees should inform on each other for wrongdoing.	1	2	3	4	5
4. It is acceptable to give approximate figures for expense account items when one does not have all the receipts.	5	4	3	2	1
5. I see no problem with conducting a little personal business, such as shopping online on company time.	5	4	3	2	1
6. A business owner has the right to take family members on a business trip and claim the cost as a business expense.	5	4	3	2	1
7. To make a sale, I would stretch the truth about a delivery date.	5	4	3	2	1
8. I would flirt with my boss just to get a bigger salary increase.	5	4	3	2	1
9. If I received $200 for doing some odd jobs, I would report it on my income tax returns.	1	2	3	4	5
10. I see no harm in taking home a few office supplies.	5	4	3	2	1
11. It is acceptable to read the e-mail and instant messages of coworkers even when not invited to do so.	5	4	3	2	1
12. It is unacceptable to call in sick to take a day off, even if only done once or twice a year.	1	2	3	4	5
13. I would accept a permanent, full-time job even if I knew I wanted the job for only six months.	5	4	3	2	1
14. I would check company policy before accepting an expensive gift from a supplier.	1	2	3	4	5
15. To be successful in business, a person usually has to ignore ethics.	5	4	3	2	1
16. If I were physically attracted to a job candidate, I would hire him or her over another better qualified candidate.	5	4	3	2	1
17. I tell the truth all the time on the job.	1	2	3	4	5
18. Software should never be copied, except as authorized by the publisher.	1	2	3	4	5
19. I would authorize accepting an office machine on a 30-day trial period, even if I knew I had no intention of making a purchase.	5	4	3	2	1
20. I would never accept credit for a coworker's ideas.	1	2	3	4	5

Scoring and interpretation: Add the numbers you have circled to obtain your score.

90–100	You are a strongly ethical person who may take a little ribbing from coworkers for being too straightlaced.
60–89	You show an average degree of ethical awareness, and therefore should become more sensitive to ethical issues.
41–59	Your ethics are underdeveloped, but you have at least some awareness of ethical issues. You need to raise your level of awareness about ethical issues.
20–40	Your ethical values are far below contemporary standards in business. Begin a serious study of business ethics.

knew Enron was headed toward bankruptcy. Skilling apparently thought that lying to employees was pragmatic.

Focus on the Rights of Individuals (Deontology)

Another approach to making an ethical decision is to examine one's duties in making the decision. The theories underlying this approach are referred to as *deontology*, from the Greek word *deon*, or duty. Deontology also refers to moral philosophies that center on the rights of individuals and the intentions associated with a particular behavior. A fundamental idea of deontology is that equal respect must be given to all persons. The deontological approach is based on universal principles based on moral philosophies such as honesty, fairness, justice, and respect for persons and property.

Rights, such as the rights for privacy and safety, are the key aspect of deontology. From a deontological perspective, the principles are more important than the consequences. If a given decision violates one of these universal principles, it is automatically unethical even if nobody gets hurt. An ethical body-shop manager might think, "It just isn't right to use replacement fenders that are not authorized by the automobile manufacturer. Whether or not these parts rust quickly is a secondary consideration."

Focus on Integrity (Virtue Ethics)

The third criterion for determining the ethics of behavior focuses on the character of the person involved in the decision or action. If the person in question has good character, and genuine motivation and intentions, he or she is behaving ethically. The ingredients making up character will often include the two other ethical criteria. One might judge a person to have good character if she or he follows the right principles and respects the rights of others.

The decision maker's environment, or community, helps define what integrity means. You might have more lenient ethical standards for a person selling you a speculative investment than you would for a bank vice president who accepted your cash deposit.

The virtue ethics of managers and professionals who belong to professional societies can be judged readily. Business-related professions having codes of ethics include accountants, purchasing managers, and certified financial planners. To the extent that the person abides by the tenets of the stated code, he or she is behaving ethically. An example of such a tenet would be for a financial planner to be explicit about any commissions gained from a client accepting the advice.

When faced with a complex ethical decision, you are best advised to incorporate all three philosophical approaches. You might think through the consequences of a decision, along with an analysis of duties, rights, principles, and intentions. Tim Berry, the president of Palo Alto Software in Eugene, Oregon, exemplifies a manager who believes that integrity contributes to his success. Part of his integrity is expressed in refusing to lie. "There were times I felt at a disadvantage with people who lacked integrity," he admits. "But I've found the truth always pays off in the long term, even if it hurts in the short term." Berry learned to appreciate the power of integrity while working as a consultant for Apple Computer, early in his career. He observed as other consultants made generous promises, only to back out or fail to deliver. Berry says that clients might be fooled temporarily, but dishonest consultants lost clients quickly.[7]

Learning Objective 2

Explain how values relate to ethics.

Values and Ethics

Values are closely related to ethics. Values can be considered clear statements of what is critically important. Ethics become the vehicle for converting values into actions, or doing the right thing. For example, a clean environment is a value, whereas not littering is practicing ethics. Many firms contend that they "put people before profits" (a value). If this assertion were true, a manager would avoid actions such as delaying payments to a vendor just to hold on to money longer, or firing a group member for having negotiated a deal that lost money.

A person's values also influence which kind of behaviors he or she believes are ethical. An executive who strongly values profits might not find it unethical to raise prices more than are needed to cover additional costs. Another executive who strongly values family life might suggest that the company invest money in an on-premises child-care center.

Values are important because the right values can lead to a competitive advantage. An example of a winning value is building relationships with customers. A major contributor to the success of Mary Kay is that associates are taught to build relationships with their direct customers and try extra hard to please them.

The concept of **ethically centered management** helps put some teeth into an abstract discussion of how values relate to ethics. Ethically centered management emphasizes that the high quality of an end product takes precedence over its scheduled completion. At the same time, it sets high quality standards for dealing with employees and managing production. The concept of ethically centered management is helpful in understanding what went wrong in the many serious accidents involving Ford Explorer sport utility vehicles (SUV) equipped with two different models of Firestone tires. The outer treads of the tires sometimes peeled off, causing the driver to lose control of the vehicle. By fall 2000, more than 1,100 incident reports and 57 lawsuits had been filed against Firestone.

ethically centered management An approach to management that emphasizes that the high quality of an end product takes precedence over its scheduled completion.

The first lawsuits were filed against Firestone involving tires on the Ford Explorer. Evaluations by Bridgestone/Firestone Inc. emphasize that it is the interaction (combined effect) of the Firestone tires with the Ford Explorer in particular that caused the tire failures and vehicle turnovers. Explorers had been involved in 16,000 rollover mishaps over a ten-year period since the vehicle was introduced, yet less than 10 percent of those accidents involved tread separation from the tire casing.

First reports of the tire failure surfaced in the press in Saudi Arabia in 1998. Ford responded in several months by approving a tire recall in Saudi Arabia. Within one year, Ford recalled tires in Thailand and Malaysia, prompting the

7 "Software Executive Puts Integrity First," *Executive Leadership*, April 2001, p. 3.

company to persuade Firestone to launch a study of why the failure was occurring. Soon Firestone recalled 6.6 million tires. In August of 2000, the National Highway Traffic Safety Association labeled 1.4 million more tires as defective. The number of fatalities associated with the tires rose to 88, and injuries to 250. Venezuela launched a criminal probe into an alleged cover-up by Ford and Firestone.

Firestone officials pointed out that the lower level of air pressure that Ford recommended for the tires—26 pounds per square inch (psi), compared with Firestone's suggested 30 psi—may have contributed to the tire separations. However, other explanations for the problems have been offered, such as poor quality control at the Decatur, Illinois, plant where many of the faulty tires were manufactured. A government investigator also charged that Firestone and Ford knew for several years that they had a serious problem, but decided to continue equipping the Ford Explorers with the faulty tires. If Firestone and Ford indeed glossed over the tread separation and vehicle rollover problems, management was far from being ethically centered.[8]

Contributing Factors to Ethical Problems

Learning Objective 3

Identify factors contributing to lax ethics, and common ethical temptations and violations.

Individuals, organizations, and society itself must share some of the blame for the prevalence or unethical behavior in the workplace. The survey results presented in Exhibit 3-2 illustrate that ethical problems remain a major concern in the workplace. Major contributors to unethical behavior are an *individual's greed and gluttony, or the desire to maximize self-gain at the expense of others.* Another major contributor to unethical behavior is an *organizational atmosphere that condones such behavior.* A group of case histories of unethical behavior in business detected the underlying theme of a management culture that fostered ethical misdoing—or at least permitted it to happen—even when the organization espoused a code of ethics. One such ethical lapse was hiring undocumented immigrant workers.[9]

The financial scandals at the now bankrupt Enron Corporation illustrate how a culture of lawless behavior and high–risk taking directly feeds unethical, and even criminal, behavior. One of the many scandals involved company officials hiding $25 billion in debt to help inflate the stock price so a handful of executives could sell their stock at a high price before declaring bankruptcy. Although Enron's culture supported risk-taking and entrepreneurial thinking and behavior, it also valued personal ambition over teamwork, youth over wisdom, and earnings growth no matter what the cost. The preoccupation with earnings, without a system of checks and balances, resulted in ethical lapses that led to the company's downfall.[10]

moral laxity
A slippage in moral behavior because other issues seem more important at the time.

A third cause of unethical behavior is ***moral laxity***, *a slippage in moral behavior because other issues seem more important at the time.* The implication is that the businessperson who behaves unethically has not carefully planned the immoral behavior but lets it occur by not exercising good

---

8 "Anatomy of a Recall," *Time*, September 11, 2000, pp. 28–32; Joann Muller, David Welch, and Jeff Green, "Would You Buy One?" *Business Week*, September 25, 2000, pp. 46–47.

9 Ann Pomeroy, "The Ethics Squeeze," *HR Magazine*, March 2006, p. 48.

10 John A. Byrne, "How to Fix Corporate Governance," *Business Week*, May 6, 2002, p. 78.

exhibit 3-2 Questionable Workplace Behavior as Reported by Employees

Despite a heightened emphasis on business ethics following scandals earlier this decade, a significant number of employees say they still witness questionable workplace behavior. Here is the percentage of employees who say they observed certain behaviors in the previous year, according to a survey of 3,015 workers by the Ethics Resource Center.

Abusive or intimidating behavior toward employees	21%
Lying to employees, customers, vendors, or public	19%
Violations of safety regulations	16%
Misreporting of actual time worked	16%
Race, sex, or other discrimination	12%
Theft	11%
Sexual harassment	9%

Source: Ethics Resource Center as reported in Erin White, "What Would You Do? Ethics Courses Get Context," *The Wall Street Journal*, June 12, 2006, p. B3.

judgment. For example, many deaths from fires in nightclubs result from management not paying careful enough attention to fire regulations, such as having adequate escape exits or fireproofing.

Unethical behavior is often triggered by *pressure from higher management to achieve goals*. Too much emphasis on meeting financial targets can push workers toward meeting financial targets in questionable ways. Visualize a chain of hearing centers for which management places difficult-to-attain sales goals on each unit. Some associates might be inclined to exaggerate the necessity for hearing aids for some potential customers who visit the center to find out if their hearing needs improvement.

Self-interest continues to be a factor that influences ethics. An experiment with 75 graduate business students showed that people are willing to misrepresent the truth if given an incentive. The students were enrolled in a negotiation class, and participated in a negotiation exercise. The negotiation involved dissolving a partnership formed by two people, with a conflict over trying to figure out the value of two products. Of the participants, 55 percent misrepresented their true estimates of the value of the product to an arbitrator. (The incentive is that the negotiator would receive a $100 prize instead of a $1 prize if the overestimate were accepted.)[11]

Yet another reason for unethical behavior is *unconscious biases that lead us to behave in unjust ways toward others*. More than two decades of psychological research indicates that most of us harbor unconscious biases that differ from our consciously held beliefs. The flawed judgments from these biases create ethical problems and can interfere with a manager's intention to recruit and retain high-level talent, among other problems. Suppose a

11 Ann E. Tenbrunsel, "Misrepresentation and Expectations of Misrepresentation in an Ethical Dilemma: The Role of Incentives and Temptation," *The Academy of Management Journal*, June 1998, pp. 330–339.

real-estate manager holds the common stereotype that women are more suited to real-estate sales because they are more home oriented, and more responsive to the needs of customers. When the manager is recruiting new agents he or she might unjustly exclude a qualified male for the position. If the male candidate is equally or better qualified than a given women candidate, the real-estate manager is behaving unethically.

It is difficult to overcome an unconscious bias because it is below the level of awareness. However, if you carefully analyze the decisions you have made recently, you might find a pattern of slightly unethical behavior.[12] For example, a worker might say, "Of the last six people I recommended to work for our company, all are the same nationality and race as mine. Have I been excluding other good candidates without meaning to do so?"

Perhaps the most pervasive reason for unethical behavior is *rationalization*, or making up a good excuse for poor ethics. In this context, a rationalization can be regarded as a mental strategy that enables employees, and other around them, to view their corrupt acts as justified.[13] Many of the reasons already presented for unethical behavior involve an element of rationalization, such as blaming the organizational culture for a personal misdeed.

The person who commits an unethical act might dismiss its significance by observing that other people in comparable positions are doing the same thing, such as cheating on an expense account. At the top of the organization, a CEO and CFO might team together to lie to outside analysts about accumulating debt and plunging sales with the rationalization that they are trying to save the company. Bernie Ebbers, the now imprisoned former top executive at MCI/Worldcom, was at the center of the biggest accounting fraud of all time. One of his courtroom pleas was that he was only trying to save the company and jobs.

Ethical Temptations and Violations

Certain ethical mistakes, including illegal actions, recur in the workplace. Familiarizing oneself with these behaviors can be helpful in managing the ethical behavior of others as well as monitoring one's own behavior. A list of commonly found ethical temptations and violations, including criminal acts, follows:[14]

1. *Stealing from employers and customers.* Employee theft costs U.S. and Canadian companies about $60 billion annually. Retail employees steal goods from their employers, and financial service employees steal money. Examples of theft from customers include airport baggage handlers who

12 Mahzarin R. Banaji, Max H. Bazerman, and Dolly Chugh, "How (Un)ethical Are You?" *Harvard Business Review*, December 2003, pp. 56–64.

13 Vikas Anand, Blake E. Ashforth, and Mahendra Joshi, "Business as Usual: The Acceptance and Perpetuation of Corruption in Organizations," *Academy of Management Executive*, November 2005, p. 9. Reprinted from 2004, Vol. 18, No. 3.

14 The first seven items on the list are from Treviño and Nelson, pp. 47–57; "Cyberethics: Teaching Internet Ethics," *Keying In*, November 2000, pp. 1, 3, 5–7; Matt Villano, "Sticky Fingers in the Supply Closet," *The New York Time* (http://www.nytimes.com), April 30, 2006; Diya Gullapalli, "After the Scandals: More Work, More Money," *The Wall Street Journal*, January 31, 2005, p. R6.

steal from passenger suitcases, and bank employees, stockbrokers, and attorneys who siphon money from customer accounts. In the current era, many examples have been uncovered of executives stealing money from companies, such as two former key executives at Tyco International having allegedly taken over $600 million in corporate funds for themselves, including using the money to purchase homes.

2. *Illegally copying software.* A rampant problem in the workplace is making unauthorized copies of software for either company or personal use. The penalties for violating software licensing agreements can be stiff, reaching over $500,000. Similarly, many employees make illegal copies of DVDs, videos, books, and magazine articles instead of purchasing these products.
3. *Treating people unfairly.* Being fair to people means equity, reciprocity, and impartiality. Fairness revolves around the issue of giving people equal rewards for accomplishing the same amount of work. The goal of human resource legislation is to make decisions about people based on their qualifications and performance—not on the basis of demographic factors such as gender, race, or age. A fair working environment is where performance is the only factor that counts (equity). Employer-employee expectations must be understood and met (reciprocity). Prejudice and bias must be eliminated (impartiality).
4. *Sexual harassment.* Sexual harassment involves making compliance with sexual favors a condition of employment, or creating a hostile, intimidating environment related to sexual topics. Harassment violates the law and is also an ethical issue because it is morally wrong and unfair. A study of about 750 women who worked for either a private firm or a university revealed that 65 percent had been sexually harassed at least once during the last 24 months. Furthermore, sexual harassment led to problems of psychological well-being such as dissatisfaction with work. After being harassed, women also tended to be absent and tardy more frequently.[15] A study of 35 teams in the food-service industry found that when sexual harassment is frequent within a team, cohesiveness and financial performance tended to be lower.[16]

   Sexual harassment is such a widespread problem that most employers take steps to prevent the problem. Exhibit 3-3 describes actions employers can take to protect themselves against harassment charges.
5. *Conflict of interest.* Part of being ethical is making business judgments only on the basis of the merits in a situation. Imagine that you are a supervisor who is romantically involved with a worker within the group. When it came time to assigning raises, it would be difficult for you to be objective. A **conflict of interest** occurs when your judgment or objectivity is compromised. Most of the major financial scandals in brokerage firms in recent years have stemmed from blatant conflicts of interest. An example would

conflict of interest
A situation that occurs when one's judgment or objective is compromised.

15 Kimberly T. Schneider, Suzanne Swan, and Louise F. Fitzgerald, "Job-Related and Psychological Effects of Sexual Harassment in the Workplace: Empirical Evidence from Two Organizations," *Journal of Applied Psychology*, June 1997, pp. 401–415.

16 Jana L. Raver and Michele J. Gelfand, "Beyond the Individual Victim: Linking Sexual Harassment, Team Processes and Team Performance," *Academy of Management Journal*, June 2005, pp. 387–400.

exhibit 3-3 A Corporate Tip Sheet on Sexual Harassment

The U.S. Supreme Court has given companies guidelines on how to protect themselves against sexual harassment charges. Most of these suggestions reflect actions that many companies already employ to prevent and control sexual harassment.

- Develop a zero-tolerance policy on harassment, and communicate it to employees.
- Ensure that victims can report abuses without fear of retaliation.
- Take reasonable care to prevent and promptly report any sexually harassing behavior.
- When defending against a charge of sexual harassment, show that an employee failed to use internal procedures for reporting abusive behavior.
- Publicize antiharassment policies aggressively and regularly—in handbooks, on posters, in training sessions, and in reminders in paychecks.
- Give supervisors and employees real-life examples of what could constitute offensive conduct.
- Ensure that workers do not face reprisals if they report offending behavior. Designate several managers to take these complaints so that employees do not have to report the problem to their supervisor, who may be the abuser.
- Train managers at all levels in sexual harassment issues.
- Provide guidelines to senior managers explaining how to conduct investigations that recognize the rights of all parties involved.
- Punishment against harassers should be swift and sure.

Source: Adapted from information in Susan B. Garland, "Finally, a Corporate Tip Sheet on Sexual Harassment," *Business Week*, July 13, 1998, p. 39; Jonathan A. Segal, "Prevent Now or Pay Later," *HR Magazine*, October 1998, pp. 145–149.

be a research analyst from an investment firm giving a recommendation to purchase a stock from a company who is an investment banking client of the analyst's firm. If the analyst makes "buy" recommendations about the company's stock, that company will more likely continue to be a lucrative client of the analyst's firm. The Sarbanes–Oxley Act of 2002 attempted to reduce many conflicts of interest in business, such as requiring that a company auditing a firm must not receive money for other services from that firm. Also, companies are required to assign certain consulting and auditing work to different firms. Sun Microsystems Inc., for example, hires all of the four major accounting firms for auditing, tax, and internal-control assignments.

6. *Accepting kickbacks and bribes for doing business with another company.* Also referred to as "payola" or "palm-greasing," accepting cash payments, special deals on stocks, and lavish gifts from industrial customers is a perennial temptation in business. Sending a manager and his or her family on a week's vacation after the manager closes a deal to make a huge purchase from the vendor is an example of a kickback. In the high-tech industry, kickbacks often take the form of managers being granted exclusive stock in companies with which their employers did business. The kickbacks also extend to stock analysts who are inclined to give favorable recommendations to companies who grant them stocks. Giving gifts to curry favor in business has long been standard practice in business, yet is unethical because it creates a conflict of interest described above.

7. *Divulging confidential information.* Other people can trust an ethical person not to divulge confidential information unless the welfare of others is at stake. The challenge of dealing with confidential information arises in many areas of business, including information about performance-evaluation results, compensation, personal problems of employees, disease status of employees, and coworker bankruptcies.
8. *Misuse of corporate resources.* A corporate resource is anything the company owns, including its name and reputation. Assume that a woman named Jennifer Yang worked as a financial consultant at Merrill Lynch. It would be unethical for her to establish a financial advisory service and put on her Web site "Jennifer Yang, financial consultant, Merrill Lynch." Using corporate resources can fall into the gray area, such as whether to borrow a notebook computer to prepare income taxes for a fee.

   An ethical temptation, particularly among top-level executives, is to misuse corporate resources in an extravagant, greedy manner. The temptation is greater for top executives because they have more control over resources. Examples of the greedy use of corporate resources include using the corporate jet for personal vacations for oneself, friends, and family members; paying for personal items with an expense account; and paying exorbitant consulting fees to friends and family members. (Observe that an ethical temptation is to be greedy about the use of resources, while at the same time being greedy can be a cause of ethical problems.)
9. *Corporate espionage.* A growing unethical practice is to collect competitive information to the extent that it constitutes spying on competitors. Among the common forms of spying are computer hacking, bribing present employees to turn over trade secrets, and prying information from relatives of workers with useful information. Another controversial practice is dumpster diving, or digging through the garbage of competitors or rivals to uncover trade secrets or derogatory information. Oracle Corp. is one of several well-known companies that publicly admitted to spying. Oracle chairman Larry Ellison hired detectives to dig up information on archrival Microsoft, including rifling through Microsoft dumpsters.[17] Outright stealing of information about rivals is obviously unethical. A less obvious form of espionage would be to leave your company, join a competitor, and then reveal key insider information about the first company to your new employer.
10. *Poor cyberethics.* The Internet creates new potential for unethical behavior, thereby making it important for all employees to resist the temptation of practicing poor cyberethics. One example of questionable ethics would be to send a giant e-mail file with a video containing your opinion about a nonwork-related issue to everyone in your company. As a consequence the servers would be blocked from conducting legitimate company business. An ethical breach of greater consequences would be to steal personal identities from job résumés

17 "Spy vs. Spy Is a High-Stakes Corporate Duel," Associated Press, July 1, 2000.

online. A scam in this area is to contact the author of a résumé claiming to be an employer. The scam artist then asks for additional personal information such as the person's social security number and bank account number. Exhibit 3-4 presents suggestions for practicing good cyberethics and netiquette. (Etiquette is related to ethics because gross etiquette, such as widely distributing racist or sexist jokes, borders on being unethical.)

Business Scandals as Ethical Violations

Major ethical and legal violations in business have taken place forever. The scandals that occurred in the early 2000s and mid-2000s led to a sharp decline in the trust of managers. Eight out of ten Americans polled in a nationwide survey said the accounting scandals, such as at Enron, dragged down trust in corporate executives.[18] The best-known scandals are associated with infamous executives. Yet scandals are also perpetuated by hundreds of players, including the Internet frauds of identity theft and work-at-home scams (such as making you an agent for transferring funds received from customers).

Among the financial and personal consequences of these scandals have been mammoth job losses, the wiping out of pension funds, huge investment losses by individuals, and the bankruptcy of vendors who supplied the companies that went bankrupt. Furthermore, the families of some of the unethical executives were badly hurt when the primary breadwinner consumed family resources on legal fees and then went to prison. People who worked for a scandalized company sometimes find it difficult to find work elsewhere.

exhibit 3-4 Netiquette Tips

- Observe the Golden Rule in cyberspace: Treat others as you would like to be treated.
- Act responsibly when sending e-mail, instant messages, or posting messages to a discussion group. Do not use language or photographs that are racist, sexist, or offensive.
- Respect the privacy of others. Do not read other individuals' e-mail or access their personal files without permission.
- Help maintain the security of your local system and the Internet by taking precautions when downloading files to avoid introducing a virus. Also, watch out for opening e-mail attachments from unknown sources. Do not engage in hacking. Protect your account number, password, and access codes.
- Respect intellectual property rights. Do not use or copy software you have not paid for. Give proper credit for other people's work—do not plagiarize work from the Internet.
- Observe the rules of your school or employer. Most schools and companies have Acceptable Use Policies that outline responsible behavior on the Internet.
- Conserve resources. Do not add to network congestion by downloading huge files, sending long-winded e-mail messages, or spamming.
- Protect your personal safety. Never give personal information, such as your phone number or address, to strangers on the Internet. Report any concerns to a network administrator.

Source: Adapted from "Netiquette Tips," *Keying In*, November 2000, p. 4.

18 Emma Blake, "Few Trust Corporate Managers, Survey Finds," *The Wall Street Journal*, November 25, 2003.

Another problem is that distrust of managers could lead to fewer talented people wanting to enter the field of business. At times scandals are embarrassing but do not have huge negative financial consequences. A small sampling of well-publicized scandals follows.

- *Click Fraud.* An individual or dozens of people click on Internet advertising solely to generate illegitimate revenue for the Web site carrying those ads. (Search engines charge the advertiser by the number of mouse clicks in response to their ad.) The people doing the clicking receive a small payment also. The major search engines such as Google and Yahoo! attempt to minimize click fraud, with the scandal usually focusing on a *parked Web site.* Nevertheless, a major search engine benefits from click fraud. In 2006, without admitting or denying wrongdoing, Google agreed to pay about $90 million as its share of an industry-wide lawsuit against clicks not from real or potential customers. A parked Web site usually has little or no content except for lists of Internet ads. Because Google and Yahoo! have distributed these ads to the parked sites, the scam artists receive a small cut of the money Google and Yahoo! receive from the advertiser. So the owner of the parked Web site might use live people or software to generate an enormous number of useless clicks on the Web sites of advertisers. About 10 percent to 15 percent of ad clicks are estimated to be fake.[19]
- *Enron Corporation.* One of the most famous business frauds of all time was the collapse of Enron Corporation in 2001. Jeffrey Skilling was the last Enron executive to be punished, being sent to prison for 24 years and four months. Accounting tricks and dishonest deals cost thousand of jobs, along with $60 billion in shareholder value, and more than $2 billion in employee pension assets. Dawn Powers Martin, a 22-year Enron employee summed up years of testimony in these words, "Mr. Skilling has proved to be a liar, a thief and a drunk, flaunting an attitude above the law. He has betrayed everyone who trusted him."[20] When Enron was on the rise, Skilling was considered to be a brilliant business strategist who had found new ways of making money for a corporation. He professed his innocence throughout the trial, and blamed market forces and bad press for the demise of Enron.
- *Tyco International.* Dennis Kozlowski, the former CEO of Tyco, and his chief financial officer, Mark Swartz, were convicted of first-degree larceny related to stealing $180 million directly from the company and making $430 million by manipulating Tyco stock value. Kozlowski was also accused of failing to pay more than $1 million in sales taxes on artwork by shipping it to an office in another state. Kozlowski and Swartz were sentenced to eight and one-third to 25 years in prison. The two were ordered to pay a total of $134 million in restitution, and were fined a combined total of $105 million. Kozlowski has become an icon for greed, gluttony, and avarice, including the company buying him an $18 million New York City duplex apartment. Kozlowski said he was not guilty of avoiding sales tax.

---

19 Brian Grow and Ben Elgin, "Click Fraud: The Dark Side of Online Advertising," *Business Week*, October 2, 2006, pp. 46–56.
20 Juan A. Lozano, "Former Enron CEO Gets 24 Years in Federal Prison," Associated Press, October 24, 2006.

- *Hewlett-Packard (HP).* A scandal with embarrassing rather than financial consequences took place at HP in relation to the investigation of leaks to the press from a board member. The investigation of the leaks received some supervision from Patricia C. Dunn, the company's chairwoman, along with its general counsel and a staff attorney. Most of the work was subcontracted to a network of private investigators who spied on HP directors and nine newspaper reporters. The investigators used shady and perhaps illegal methods to conduct their investigations and to gather phone records, including *pretexting.* The latter involves pretending to be a phone company customer by using the targeted individuals' Social Security numbers. Detectives tried to plant software in at least one journalist's computer so messages could be traced. The pretexting was investigated by California and federal authorities, including the FBI. Dunn and two other directors resigned, along with the chief ethics and compliance officer, who was charged with four felonies. California Attorney General Bill Lockyer said of the HP probes, "I don't have a settled idea yet whether it was illegal, but it certainly was colossally stupid." Later, a California State court dropped all charges against Dunn based somewhat on the sketchiness of privacy laws.[21]
- *Backdating Stock Options at Silicon Valley Companies.* One way of compensating managers and other employees is to grant them the opportunity to purchase stock at today's price some time in the future. If the price goes up, the recipient profits; if the price goes down, the recipient is not obliged to purchase the stock. In 2006, Apple Inc. executives as well as senior officers of many other Silicon Valley (high-tech area of California) companies were accused of sliding the stock-price date back to a time when the stock was lower than the true date of the option. In this way the company pretends the stock-option date was earlier than reality. Backdating usually involves accounting and disclosure violations, and can also constitute fraud. Apple said that CEO Steve Jobs was aware of the "favorable grant dates," but he didn't profit from them personally and he was not aware of the accounting implications.[22] Some critics doubt, however, that a micromanager like Jobs was not aware of substantial backdating at both Apple and Pixar, where he is also the CEO.[23]

A person reading this small sampling of unethical behavior of managers might wonder how wealthy, intelligent people could exercise such poor judgment. The answer lies partially in the explanations for unethical behavior presented earlier, with particular attention to greed, gluttony, and avarice. Also, a small proportion of senior officers believe they are entitled to extraordinary perks like penthouse apartments and stock options guaranteed to be profitable.

---

21 Quote from Rachel Conrad, "Snooping to Find Leader Backfires on HP Official," Associated Press, September 7, 2006.

22 Charles Forrelle and James Bandler, "As Companies Problem Backdating, More Top Officials Take a Fall," *The Wall Street Journal*, October 12, 2006; Holman W. Jenkins Jr., "A Typical Backdating Miscreant," *The Wall Street Journal*, October 11, 2006, p. A15.

23 Roger Perloff, "Is Jobs Really Cleared?" *Fortune*, January 22, 2007, p. 30.

Learning Objective 4

Apply a guide to ethical decision making.

A Guide to Ethical Decision Making

A practical way of improving ethical decision making is to run contemplated decisions through an ethics test when any doubt exists. The ethics test presented next was used at the Center for Business Ethics at Bentley College as part of corporate training programs. Decision makers are taught to ask themselves:[24]

1. *Is it right*? This question is based on the deontological theory of ethics that there are certain universally accepted guiding principles of rightness and wrongness, such as "thou shall not steal."
2. *Is it fair*? This question is based on the deontological theory of justice, implying that certain actions are inherently just or unjust. For example, it is unjust to fire a high-performing employee to make room for a less competent person who is a personal friend.
3. *Who gets hurt*? This question is based on the utilitarian notion of attempting to do the greatest good for the greatest number of people.
4. *Would you be comfortable if the details of your decision were reported on the front page of your local newspaper, on a popular Web site or blog, or through your company's e-mail system*? This question is based on the universalist principle of disclosure.
5. *Would you tell your child (or young relative) to do it*? This question is based on the deontological principle of reversibility, referring to reversing who carries out the decision.
6. *How does it smell*? This question is based on a person's intuition and common sense. For example, underpaying many accounts payable by a few dollars to save money would "smell" bad to a sensible person.

A decision that was obviously ethical, such as donating some managerial time for charitable organizations, would not need to be run through the six-question test. Neither would a blatantly illegal act, such as not paying employees for work performed. But the test is useful for decisions that are neither obviously ethical nor obviously unethical. Among such gray areas would be charging clients based on their ability to pay and developing a clone of a successful competitive product.

Another type of decision that often requires an ethical test is choosing between two rights (rather than right versus wrong).[25] Suppose a blind worker in the group has personal problems so great that her job performance suffers. She is offered counseling but does not follow through seriously. Other members of the team complain about the blind worker's performance because she is interfering with the group achieving its goals. If the manager dismisses the blind worker, she might suffer severe financial consequences. (She is the only wage earner in her family.) However, if she is retained the

24 James L. Bowditch and Anthony F. Buono, *A Primer on Organizational Behavior*, 5th ed. (New York: Wiley, 2001), p. 4.

25 Joseph L. Badaracco Jr., *Defining Moments: When Managers Must Choose Between Right and Wrong* (Boston: Harvard Business School Press, 1997).

group will suffer consequences of its own. The manager must now choose between two rights, or the lesser of two evils.

SOCIAL RESPONSIBILITY

Learning Objective 5

Describe the stakeholder viewpoint of social responsibility and corporate social performance.

Many people believe that firms have an obligation to be concerned about outside groups affected by an organization. **Corporate social responsibility** is the idea that firms have obligations to society beyond their economic obligations to owners or stockholders and also beyond those prescribed by law or contract. Both ethics and social responsibility relate to the goodness or morality of organizations. However, business ethics is a narrower concept that applies to the morality of an individual's decisions and behaviors. Corporate social responsibility is a broader concept that relates to an organization's impact on society, beyond doing what is ethical.[26] To behave in a socially responsible way, managers must be aware of how their actions influence the environment.

A continuing debate concerns what obligations companies have toward being socially responsible. The position advanced by a growing number of nongovernmental organizations is business firms should take action on issues ranging from pollution and global warming to AIDS, illiteracy, and poverty. The other position is that many investors want companies in which they invest to focus on the bottom line so they can maximize their returns.[27] In reality, these positions can be mutually supportive. Many socially responsible actions are the by-products of sensible business decisions. For instance, it is both socially responsible and profitable for a company to improve the language and math skills of entry-level workers, and invest in local schooling. Literate and numerate entry-level workers for some jobs may be in short supply, and employees who cannot follow written instructions and do basic math may be unproductive. Also, a business firm that is environmentally friendly might attract the type of workers who are talented enough to help the firm become more profitable.

A practical problem in practicing corporate social responsibility is that not all interested parties agree on what constitutes responsible behavior. Target stores might have many customers who believe that citizens have a constitutional right to defend themselves with handguns against intruders to their home. To this group of customers, a retailer selling handguns to the public would reflect corporate social responsibility. Another customer group might believe strongly in tight gun controls. To this group, Target not selling handguns to the public would reflect corporate social responsibility.

Corporate social responsibility The idea that firms have obligations to society beyond their economic obligations to owners or stockholders and also beyond those prescribed by law or contract.

This section will examine three aspects of social responsibility: (1) the stockholder versus stakeholder viewpoints of social responsibility, (2) corporate social performance, and (3) a sampling of social responsibility initiatives.

26 "Corporate Social Responsibility: Good Citizenship or Investor Rip-off?" *The Wall Street Journal*, January 9, 2006, p. R6.
27 Ibid.

Stockholder Versus Stakeholder Viewpoints

stockholder viewpoint The traditional perspective on social responsibility that a business organization is responsible only to its owners and stockholders.

The **stockholder viewpoint** of social responsibility is the traditional perspective. It holds that business firms are responsible only to their owners and stockholders. The job of managers is therefore to satisfy the financial interests of the stockholders. By so doing, says the stockholder view, the interests of society will be served in the long run. Socially irresponsible acts ultimately result in poor sales. According to the stockholder viewpoint, corporate social responsibility is therefore a by-product of profit seeking.

stakeholder viewpoint The viewpoint on social responsibility contending that firms must hold themselves responsible for the quality of life of the many groups affected by the firm's actions.

The **stakeholder viewpoint** of social responsibility contends that firms must hold themselves responsible for the quality of life of the many groups affected by the firm's actions. These interested parties, or stakeholders, include those groups composing the firm's general environment. Two categories of stakeholders exist. Internal stakeholders include owners, employees, and stockholders; external stakeholders include customers, labor unions, consumer groups, and financial institutions. The stakeholder viewpoint reflects the modern viewpoint of the corporation. Today, a company's assets are likely to be found in the employees who contribute their time and talents rather than in the stockholders who invest their money. Furthermore, the modern company should be a wealth-creating community whose members have certain rights. In this way the various stakeholders will be more willing to cooperate with each other.[28] Exhibit 3-5 depicts the stakeholder viewpoint of social responsibility.

Another way of framing the stakeholder perspective is that society grants authority to business leaders, shareholders, employees, and customers. Yet according to an iron law, in the long run those parties who do not use their power in an acceptable manner will lose that power. Under extreme misuse of power, the government might intervene, such as declaring a company to be an illegal monopoly. Microsoft has fought charges for years that it abused its power by bullying other companies into using its products, and not using competitors' products.

Many organizations regard their various stakeholders as partners in achieving success, rather than as adversaries. The organizations and the stakeholders work together for their mutual success. For example, Ford Motor Company owns 49 percent of the Hertz rental car company, which is also a major Ford customer. With Ford facing so many financial troubles in recent years, a mutual relationship of this type is essential. An example of a company partnership with a labor union is the establishment of joint committees on safety and other issues of concern to employees.

Part of understanding the stakeholder viewpoint is to recognize that not all stakeholders are the same. Instead, they can be differentiated along three dimensions. Some stakeholders are more powerful than others, such as the United Auto Workers (UAW) union being more powerful than a small group of protesters. Some stakeholders are more legitimate than others, such as the UAW, which is a well-established and legal entity.

28 Charles Handy, "What's Business For?" *Harvard Business Review*, December 2002, pp. 49–55. For an expansion on this point of view, see Stuart Cooper, *Corporate Social Performance: A Stakeholder Approach* (Burlington, VT: Ashgate, 2004).

exhibit 3-5

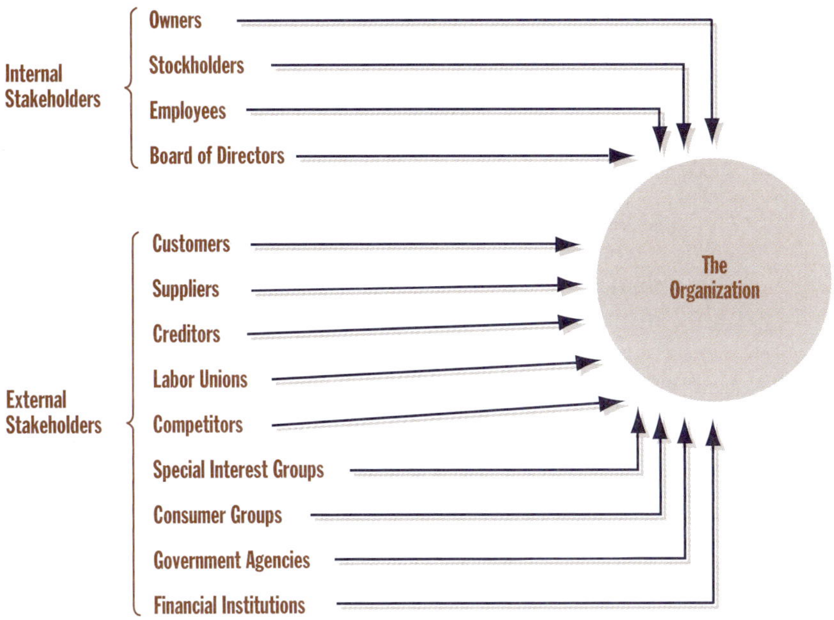

Some stakeholders are more urgent than others because they require immediate attention. A group of protesters chaining themselves to a company fence because they believe the company is polluting the soil would require immediate attention.[29]

Corporate Social Performance

Corporate social performance is the extent to which a firm responds to the demands of its stakeholders for behaving in a socially responsible manner. After stakeholders have been satisfied with the reporting of financial information, they may turn their attention to the behavior of the corporation as a good citizen in the community. One way of measuring social performance is to analyze the company's annual report in search of relevant statistical information. For example, you might look for data about contribution to charities, arts, education, and to pollution measures.

Another consequence of social performance is that a group of mutual funds purchase stocks only of companies the fund manager believes to have good social performance. At the same time the fund manager does not purchase the stocks of companies it believes to have poor social performance. Domini Social Investments is an example of such a socially responsible mutual fund. Fund manager Amy Domini screens out the

corporate social performance
The extent to which a firm responds to the demands of its stakeholders for behaving in a socially responsible manner.

29 Ronald K. Mitchell, Bradly R. Agle, and Dona J. Wood, "Toward a Theory of Stakeholder Identification and Salience: Defining the Principle of Who and What Really Counts," *Academy of Management Review*, October 1997, p. 869.

industries in disfavor with most advocates of social responsibility: alcohol, tobacco, weapons, gambling, and nuclear power. One of the primary indicators Domini uses in evaluating a company is a supportive environment for employees. Among these factors are "paying them fair wages and rewarding them for their contributions to the company, and providing a range of benefits that may save them money, enrich their lives, and advance their careers."[30]

Another approach to measuring corporate social performance is to observe how a company responds to social issues by examining programs in greater detail. The next section describes corporate activities in relation to a variety of social issues. However, first examine the corporate social performance of the world's largest employer, as outlined in the accompanying Management in Action.

management in action

Wal-Mart Managers Take the High Road and the Low Road

Wal-Mart Stores Inc. is the world's largest retailer and one of the best-known companies, with annual sales of over $315 billion and a payroll of 1.8 million employees worldwide, with 1.3 million U.S. employees—1 percent of the workforce. Every week, 176 million shoppers visit Wal-Mart's 6,500 stores in 15 countries. (All these figures trend upward each year.) Company management, as well as many employees and outside observers, perceive Wal-Mart to be a wonderful corporate citizen because of the jobs it creates, the suppliers it helps keep in business, its endless amount of site construction and real-estate purchases, and its corporate philanthropy. The many critics of Wal-Mart, however, regard the super-giant as an unethical and evil force that suppresses wages and health benefits and combats labor unions, and should be dismantled. Here we present a sampling of some of the evidence and opinion on the positive and negative aspects of Wal-Mart's ethics and social responsibility.

The Ethical and Socially Responsible Side of Wal-Mart

Wal-Mart is a great boon for low-income people in every location they serve. Customers can stretch their dollars, and afford things they could not with the mega-retailer. Wal-Mart has wrung tens of billions of dollars in cost efficiencies out of the retail supply chain, passing many of these savings on to shoppers. Wal-Mart's low prices save the average American household $2,300 per year. The company's low prices on generic drugs have forced other chain stores to follow suit.

The Unethical and Socially Irresponsible Side of Wal-Mart

Wal-Mart encourages its suppliers to rely on low-paid offshore workers so it can make large profits on its general merchandise, allowing it to give away toys at below cost. As a result, several toy stores, including FAO and Zany Brainy, have gone bankrupt. To remain a Wal-Mart supplier, many companies are forced to lay off employees and close U.S. plants in favor of sending production offshore.

30 Amy Domini, "Letter from the President," http://www.domini.com, July 31, 2006.

Wal-Mart is an excellent corporate citizen as evidenced by its quest to help build a green (environmentally friendly) environment. The company strives to be supplied 100 percent by renewable energy; to minimize waste; and to sell products that sustain resources and the environment. The chain encourages customers to purchase energy-saving light bulbs thereby helping to fight global warming. In response to Hurricane Katrina, Wal-Mart contributed $20 million in cash donations, 1,500 truckloads of free merchandise, food for 100,000 meals, and the promise of a job for each one of its displaced workers.

Wal-Mart has taken the initiative to help small businesses in the communities it serves. The Jobs and Opportunity Zones assist nearby small business enterprises, sponsor local training programs, and support the local chamber of commerce. Most of the company's charitable donations are made at the local level.

Wal-Mart provides one-stop shopping, including groceries, furniture, digital image and film processing, and pharmaceuticals, for individuals whose busy lives make it difficult to visit several stores during a shopping trip. Wal-Mart thereby saves consumers time, a precious resource for many.

Many consumers save by shopping at Wal-Mart as it enables them to purchase luxuries for themselves, such as more expensive cars, Starbucks coffee, and cable or satellite television. Wal-Mart continuously searches for ways to save customers money, such as starting the trend to eliminate the boxes in which individual containers of deodorant were packed.

The "Wal-Mart Effect" has suppressed inflation and rippled productivity gains through the economy year after year. (Wal-Mart's share of the economy is an estimated 2.4 percent.)

Wal-Mart encourages free trade because it forces suppliers to go offshore for its products, and Wal-Mart buys directly from many overseas suppliers.

Wal-Mart forces the companies it does business with to become more efficient and focused, leaner, and faster. The suppliers learn the art of continuous improvement. Wal-Mart is a poor corporate citizen because its presence leads to the deterioration of many small downtown areas. The company often abandons stores to pursue lower taxes in another county, leaving behind an ugly, limited-use big box building. Also, the presence of a Wal-Mart store cheapens the image of a city or village.

Wal-Mart keeps hundreds of thousands of employees in low-wage jobs and meager health benefits, making it difficult for them to move up the economic ladder. Wal-Mart pay practices depress wages beyond the retail sector. In 2006 the company scaled back health-care plans available to new employees, including much higher deductibles. The antiunion stance of the company has contributed to the low wages in retailing throughout North America.

Wal-Mart is so powerful that it is the third most pressing concern of U.S. businesses, after rising health-care costs and China. The company forces out of business many supermarket as well as other merchants. The failures of so many stores forces thousands of storeowners and employees out of work.

Wal-Mart faces a continuing stream of lawsuits for mistreating employees, including sex discrimination and forcing employees to work unpaid overtime. The company has been investigated for using illegal immigrants to clean its stores. (The cleaning subcontractor, not Wal-Mart, hired the illegal immigrants.)

Wal-Mart is a cultural gatekeeper by choosing which magazines, books, and music it will sell. Its preferences tend to be conservative, thus presenting a one-sided viewpoint to the public.

Many Wal-Mart suppliers face such a price squeeze that they are forced to produce goods of lower quality. As a mother told the *Denver Post*, "When you buy a kid a swimsuit that falls apart after they wear it, was it worth the $10?"

The smaller the Wal-Mart supplier, the more likely it will be forced into making damaging concessions—such as losing money on a popular product.

(Continued)

management in action (Continued)

Wal-Mart Managers Take the High Road and the Low Road

The Ethical and Socially Responsible Side of Wal-Mart

Wal-Mart provides stable employment for many members of the workforce who might not qualify for jobs in higher-end retail stores, or offices. Wal-Mart creates jobs for people who need them the most, and offers them mobility. About 70 percent of Wal-Mart managers worked their way up from the company frontlines.

The wages, benefits, and job security offered by Wal-Mart surpass those typically offered by smaller enterprises such as mom-and-pop stores, as well as many large retailers. Wal-Mart provides health insurance to more than 1 million associates and family members. Leadership at Wal-Mart advocates a higher federal minimum wage, thus championing the cause of low-paid workers.

Wal-Mart grocery stores are a boon for families of modest means. Food prices are low because the company does not have to pay union wages.

Wal-Mart continues to create a more flexible workforce that will meet the needs of its customers.

Wal-Mart welcomes diversity, as evidenced by it joining the corporate council of the National Gay and Lesbian Chamber of Commerce. The company conducts workshops for gay and lesbian business owners on how to become a Wal-Mart supplier.

The Unethical and Socially Irresponsible Side of Wal-Mart

A company that says something negative about Wal-Mart publicly may wind up in the Wal-Mart "penalty box"—punished, or even excluded from the store shelves.

Many Wal-Mart workers are so poorly paid they rely on Medicaid to pay many of their medical expenses. Pushing for a higher minimum wage is a self-serving attempt to enhance the buying power of its lowest-paid workers.

As Wal-Mart takes away business from traditional grocery chains, more and more union workers will lose their jobs paying decent wages.

Wal-Mart has capped wages for many employees, has increased the percent of part-time employees, and schedules more workers on nights and on weekends, making it difficult on families.

The American Family Association believes that Wal-Mart is shifting away from its "pro-family" stance. Pride at Work, a group that represents gay and lesbian workers, claims that the company is just taking on a shameless marketing opportunity.

Questions

1. If many of these charges about Wal-Mart being unethical and socially irresponsible are true, why does the company keep growing in size and profits?
2. Recommend several additional actions Wal-Mart might take to develop a better reputation for ethics and social responsibility.
3. Has the information just presented had any impact on your propensity to shop or *not* shop at Wal-Mart? Explain.

Source: Charles Fishman, "The Wal-Mart Effect and a Decent Society: Who Knew Shopping Was So Important?" *Academy of Management Perspectives*, August 2006, pp. 6–25; Fishman, "The Wal-Mart You Don't Know: Why Low Prices Have Such a High Cost," *Fast Company*, December 2003, pp. 68–80; Marc Gunther, "The Green Machine," *Fortune*, August 7, 2006, pp. 42–57; Kris Hudson and Gary McWilliams, "Seeking Growth in Urban Areas, Wal-Mart Gets Cold Shoulder," *The Wall Street Journal*, September 25, 2006, pp. A1, A8; Ylan Q. Mui and Amy Joyce, "Wal-Mart to Shrink Options for New Hires' Health Care," *Washington Post* (http://www.washingtonpost.com), September 27, 2006, p. D3; Abigail Goldman, "Wal-Mart Seeks

Unbiased Research—and Gets It," *Los Angeles Times*, November 3, 2005; Steven Greenhouse and Michael Barbara, "Wal-Mart's Shift Changes Irk Workers," *The New York Times* syndicated story, October 3, 2006; Abigail Goldman, "Wal-Mart Can't Seem to Win," *Chicago Tribune*, August 27, 2006; Holman W. Jenkins Jr., "Propaganda Clean-Up in Aisle Six," *The Wall Street Journal*, November 9, 2005, p. A17; http://www.walmartfacts.com/FactSheets/, accessed October 22, 2006.

Social Responsibility Initiatives

Learning Objective 6

Present an overview of social responsibility initiatives.

Creating opportunities for a diverse workforce, as described in Chapter 2, is an important social responsibility initiative. Here we describe positive corporate responses to other important social issues. A firm that takes initiatives in these areas can be considered socially responsible. The five social responsibility initiatives described here are: environmental protection, work/life programs, community redevelopment projects, acceptance of whistle blowers, and compassionate downsizing.

Environmental Protection

Many companies take the initiative to preserve the natural environment in a way that pleases environmental groups (e.g., Greenpeace). As a result, the company works in partnership with a group intent on such purposes as reducing carbon dioxide in the air, preserving forests, or protecting a species of fish or animal. Environmental protection is at present a major social responsibility initiative with business enterprises, large and small, investing money in preserving the environment. Another key aspect of environmental protection is to prevent pollution rather than control wastes after they have surfaced. For example, a company might eliminate the use of mercury in electrical switches and instead substitute a metal such as copper that is less toxic to the environment. The concern is that when the switch is discarded, the highly poisonous mercury could eventually work its way into the ground. Recycling also helps prevent pollution because recycled products are resources in use rather than resources decaying in dumps or land fills. A sampling of social responsibility initiatives centering on protecting the environment is presented next.[31]

- Virgin Group founder Richard Branson plans to invest an estimated $3 billion over a ten-year period in renewable energy projects and technologies that help reduce global warming. The money will be managed though an investment company called Virgin Fuels. (Observe that this initiative could be controversial because many people think that the concern about global warming has no scientific basis.)

31 The sources in order of use are: Tyler Hamilton, "Branson's $3B Pledge," *Toronto Star* (http://www.thestar.com), September 22, 2006; Laura Blue, "Let's Talk Trash," *Time*, October 9, 2006, p. A37; Lee Gomes, "Prodded by Consumers, The Computer Industry Slowly Grows Greener," *The Wall Street Journal*, June 14, 2006, p. B1; Richard Gibson, "Companies Opt for Paperless Route," *The Wall Street Journal*, September 27, 2006, p. B5A.

- Tom Szaky, age 24, is the CEO of TerraCycle, a plant-food manufacturer. The product is a ready-to-use organic plant-food spray fabricated from the excrement of worms fed on compost and packed in repurposed soda bottles. (Okay, it's not a glamour industry but it is green.) Furthermore, the company's furniture is manufactured from recycled trash. Szaky defines garbage as any commodity with a negative value—something you are willing to pay to get rid of.
- The computer industry in general is making a giant initiative to slow down energy consumption when using computers. CPUs are being designed to run cooler; LCD display screens use less than half as much power as the CRTs they replace. Also, modern operating systems interact with hardware to turn off disk drives or slow down microprocessors not in use at a given time. The power supply part of the computer is now designed to meet the federal Energy Star standard by being more efficient.
- Computershare Ltd, and Australian shareholder services company, has launched a campaign backed by one dozen U.S. companies to persuade more shareholders to switch to electronic versions of shareholder-related communications. As an incentive, shareholders are informed that a tree will be planted for everyone who goes the paperless route. The program is called eTree. McDonalds's has found that so far more than 6 percent of its 270,000 registered shareholders have switched to electronic reports. (Observe here that the "paperless" route often translates into people printing the information they need, so the savings in paper is not really so substantial.)

In addition to top-level management taking the initiative to protect the environment, companies often trigger many employees into thinking about environmental protection in ways such as carpooling, being a good recycler, and not littering.

Work/Life Programs

Organizations take a major social responsibility initiative when they establish programs that help employees balance the demands of work and personal life. The intent of a work-life program is to help employees lead a more balanced life, and be more satisfied and productive on the job. Exhibit 3-6 lists a variety of work/life programs. The most popular of these programs remains flextime, or flexible work schedules. (Chapter 7 describes flexible work schedules in more detail.) Flextime has grown in popularity because evidence suggests that it reduces turnover, improves morale, and helps recruit talent.

Community Redevelopment Projects

As a large-scale social responsibility initiative, business firms invest resources in helping rebuild distressed communities. Investing in a community is but one aspect of philanthropy, or charitable giving. Investment could mean constructing offices or factories in an impoverished section of town, or offering job training for residents from these areas. A specific goal of some community redevelopment projects is to replace a crime-ridden development with new housing that is associated with less crime and more community pride.

A notable example of community redevelopment is the Prudential Foundation established by Prudential Financial. The Foundation provides support to innovative direct-service programs that address the needs of the community in three areas: Ready to Learn, Ready to Work, and Ready to Live. Community housing development is included in the Ready to Work initiative that helps rebuild inner cities by investing money in ventures such as grocery stores, housing, and entertainment. The New Jersey Performing Arts Center is one of their investment projects. The Ready to Work program concentrates on initiatives that increase employment opportunities by strengthening job skills and opportunities, and promoting neighborhood development activities. Encouraging entrepreneurship is also emphasized. The program also aims to create decent, affordable housing by working in partnership with Community Housing Development Corporations and community development financial institutions.[32]

Despite the contribution of community redevelopment, this social responsibility initiative does have its drawbacks. Tenants may be forced out of their homes to make way for new development, which cannot accommodate all previous tenants.

Community redevelopment can also be done on a small scale by an enterprise investing in the community in which it is located, or "giving

exhibit 3-6 A Variety of Work/Life Programs

- Flexible work schedules
- Child-care resource and referral
- Part-time options
- Compressed workweek
- Telecommuting
- Job sharing among two or more employees
- Eldercare resource and referrals
- Eldercare case management and assessment
- Subsidy for emergency care for dependents
- "Family sick days" that permit employees to stay home and care for sick children or relatives
- Arrangements for school counselors to meet with parents on-site during regular working hours
- Electric breast pumps for mothers of young children who want to return to work and continue breast-feeding
- Maintenance worker on company payroll whom employees can hire for household tasks, by paying only for supplies
- Laundry service, including ironing, on company premises
- Concierge service in which company employee runs a variety of errands for employees
- Postal service
- Automatic teller machines
- On-site fitness centers, including massages at workplace

Note: During a business downturn, the least essential of these work/life programs are likely to be abandoned, such as massages at the desk, and maintenance workers for household tasks.

32 http://www.prudential.com, accessed October 26, 2006.

whistle blower An employee who discloses organizational wrongdoing to parties who can take action.

back." Robert F. McGraw, the owner of Longjian River Health Products, decided to help redevelop Longjian Village, a town in southwestern China where his New York State company has built a modern raw-materials processing center. His company financed the village's first waste management facility, donated 40 computers to the local school, and started a fund to ensure that schoolgirls have textbooks. In addition, Health Products employees tutor local children and work on construction projects.[33]

Acceptance of Whistle Blowers

A **whistle blower** is an employee who discloses organizational wrongdoing to parties who can take action. It was a whistle blower who began the process of exposing the scandalous financial practices at Enron Corp., such as hiding losses. Sherron Watkins, a vice president, wrote a one-page anonymous letter exposing unsound, if not dishonest, financial reporting. Enron had booked profits for two entities that had no assets. She dropped the letter off at company headquarters the next day. Also, the CEO had announced to employees that Enron's financial liquidity had never been stronger, while exercising his own $1.5 billion in stock options, just ahead of the company's announcement of a $618 million quarterly loss.[34] Watkins later became a public heroine and celebrity because of her role in exposing the Enron scandal.

In an unusual twist, the administrator of an employee hotline for making complaints about ethical and legal violations became a whistle blower herself. Christine Holtzman, of DaimlerChrysler AG, complained to the Securities and Exchange Commission that she was fired in 2003 after complaining about how the hotline was run. Holtzman alleges that corporate auditors suppressed several claims of theft and fraud that came through the hotline, and failed to investigate others. Another complaint was that corporate security officers attempted in several cases to identify hotline callers, and fired at least one. (Hotline calls are supposed to be anonymous.) DaimlerChrysler denied Holtzman's assertions in federal court.[35]

A whistle blower has to be patient because it usually takes years to resolve a claim, including an agonizing court procedure. Another problem is that whistle blowers are often ostracized and humiliated by the companies they hope to improve, by such means as no further promotions or poor performance evaluations. More than half the time, the pleas of whistle blowers are ignored. So it is important for leaders at all levels to create a comfortable climate for legitimate whistle blowing. The manager needs the insight to sort out the difference between a troublemaker and a true whistle blower. Careful investigation is required. Only an organization with a strong social conscience would embrace employees who inform the public about its misdeeds. Yet some companies are becoming more tolerant of employees who help keep the firm socially responsible by exposing actions that could harm society.

---

33 Chris Pentttila, "Give a Little," *Entrepreneurship*, May 2006, p. 89.

34 Erin McClam, "*Time* Names Whistleblowers Persons of Year," Associated Press, December 2002; "Former Enron Vice President Sherron Watkins on the Enron Collapse," *Academy of Management Executive*, November 2003, p. 119.

35 John R. Wilke, "Hotline Suit Pits Whistle-Blower, DaimlerChrysler," *The Wall Street Journal*, July 26, 2005, pp. A17, A23.

Compassionate Downsizing

downsizing The slimming down of operations to focus resources and boost profits or decrease expenses.

To remain competitive and provide shareholders with a suitable return on investment, about 80 percent of large organizations have undergone downsizing. **Downsizing** is the slimming down of operations to focus resources and boost profits or decrease expenses. Downsizings occur regularly worldwide among companies of all sizes, yet the size of layoffs is more substantial during business downturns. Laid-off employees obviously suffer from downsizing when they cannot readily find comparable employment or are forced to leave their communities. The community can also suffer substantially from mammoth downsizings. For example, the aftermath of the many cutbacks in the Michigan-based automotive industry has been substantial collateral damage. Retailers, restaurants, the housing market, charitable organizations, and community tax bases were all hurt as the state lost an estimated 158,000 manufacturing jobs between 2003 and 2008, according to a University of Michigan study.[36]

The focus here is on the social responsibility aspects of downsizing. Chapter 8 views downsizing as a strategy for improving organizational effectiveness. To begin, a company might challenge the need for downsizing. An ideal goal is to look to expand sales rather than downsize. Carlos Ghosn, the much-publicized CEO of both Nissan and Renault, prefers to introduce new models rather than downsize when an automotive company he manages faces financial difficulties. For example, in 2006 Ghosn established a goal of increasing annual vehicle sales by 800,000 during a three-year period—without resorting to job cuts.[37]

Quite often a company sees no way out of financial trouble other than downsizing. In these circumstances, compassionate downsizing would include the following considerations:

- Redeploy as many workers as possible by placing them in full-time or temporary jobs throughout the organization, where their skills and personality fit. Several companies have turned surplus workers into sales workers to generate new business for the firm. During one downturn in international sales at Lincoln Electric, 54 factory workers were redeployed as salespeople, who grossed $10 million in sales the first year. Workers are guaranteed a job, but as a trade-off get neither paid sick days nor holidays and pay their own health insurance.[38]
- Provide outplacement services to laid-off employees, thereby giving them professional assistance in finding a new position or redirecting their careers. (The vast majority of employers do provide outplacement services to laid-off workers.)

---

36 Study cited in Louis Aguilar, "Cutbacks to Ripple through Economy," *The Detroit News* (http://www.detnews.com), September 16, 2006.

37 David Pearson, Stephen Power, and Jathon Sapsford, "Ghosn Aims to Improve Renault Without Cutting Jobs," *The Wall Street Journal*, February 10, 2006, p. A3.

38 Marlene Piturro, "Alternatives to Downsizing," *Management Review*, October 1999, p. 38; Daniel Eisenberg, "Where People Are Never Let Go," *Time*, June 18, 2001, p. 40.

- Provide financial and emotional support to the downsized worker. Included here is treating employees with respect and dignity rather than escorting them out the door immediately after the downsizing announcement. Many companies already provide severance pay and extended health benefits to the laid-off workers. Financial assistance with retraining is also helpful.

BENEFITS DERIVED FROM ETHICS AND SOCIAL RESPONSIBILITY

Learning Objective 7

Summarize the benefits of ethical and socially responsible behavior, and how managers can create an environment that fosters such behavior.

Highly ethical behavior and socially responsible acts are not always free. Initiatives such as work/life programs and community redevelopment may not have an immediate return on investment. Here we look at evidence and opinions about the advantages of ethics and social responsibility.

Edwin A. Locke argues that virtuous behavior can be successfully applied by a business. He cites the example of BB&T, a banking company based in Winston-Salem, North Carolina, with close to $8 billion annual revenue that emphasizes virtues as the core of its value system. The company has shown steady growth for many years and has provided outstanding returns to shareholders. BB&T has also been consistently rated as one of the best companies, and has been scandal free.[39]

The relationship between profits and social responsibility works two ways in another perspective. More profitable firms can better afford to invest in social responsibility initiatives, and these initiatives in turn lead to more profits. Sandra A. Waddock and Samuel B. Graves conducted a large-scale study that supports the two-way conclusion. The researchers analyzed the relationship between corporate social performance and corporate financial performance for 469 firms, spanning 13 industries, for a two-year period. Many different measures of social and financial performance were used.

virtuous circle The relationship between social and financial performance where corporate social performance and corporate financial performance feed and reinforce each other.

Researchers found that levels of corporate social performance were influenced by prior financial success. This result suggests that financial success creates enough money left over to invest in corporate social performance. The study also found that good corporate social performance contributes to improved financial performance as measured by return on assets and return on sales. Waddock and Graves concluded that the relationship between social and financial performance may be a **virtuous circle**, meaning that corporate social performance and corporate financial performance feed and reinforce each other.[40]

39 Locke, "Business Ethics: A Way Out of the Morass," p. 332.

40 Sandra A. Waddock and Samuel B. Graves, "The Corporate Social Performance–Financial Performance Link," *Strategic Management Journal*, Spring 1997, pp. 303–319.

Being ethical also helps avoid the costs of paying huge fines for being unethical, including charges of discrimination and class action lawsuits because of improper financial reporting. Charges of age discrimination and sex discrimination are two leading sources of lawsuits against companies. Operating an illegal business can also be costly. Kazaa, a well-known file-sharing network and a once-popular source of illegal downloads paid heavily for its ethically and legally questionable activities. Kazaa's owner, Sharmon Networks, was ordered to pay the world's four major music companies more than $100 million and commit to going legitimate.[41]

Creating an Ethical and Socially Responsible Workplace

Establishing an ethical and socially responsible workplace is not simply a matter of luck and common sense. Top-level managers, assisted by other managers and professionals, can develop strategies and programs to enhance ethical and socially responsible attitudes and behavior. We turn now to a description of several of these initiatives.

Formal Mechanisms for Monitoring Ethics

The majority of companies with 500 or more employees have ethics programs of various types. Large organizations frequently set up ethics committees to help ensure ethical and socially responsible behavior. Committee members include a top management representative plus other managers throughout the organization. An ethics and social responsibility specialist from the human resources department might also join the group. The committee establishes policies about ethics and social responsibility, and may conduct an ethical audit of the firm's activities. In addition, committee members might review complaints about ethical violations.

The Lockheed Martin Corporation's ethics and compliance program has received much favorable publicity. A contributing factor to its formation was that in the mid-1980s the company had a series of ethics scandals in its role as a defense contractor to the U.S. government. (Among the problems was a product substitution not in agreement with the contract.) Elements of the Lockheed Martin program include the following:

- *Make ethics training mandatory.* Mandatory means for every employee, the CEO included.
- *Develop multiple channels for raising questions and voicing concerns.* These mechanisms include a toll-free hotline, a formal ethics office at the corporate level, and a culture that welcomes discussion of ethical issues.
- *Allow for voicing concerns anonymously.* Many employees fear reprisals if they identify ethical problems in their company.

41 Adam Pasick, "Kazaa Pays $100 Mln to Settle Lawsuits," *The Washington Post* (http://www.washingtonpost.com), July 27, 2006.

- *Act decisively on legitimate ethical problems reported by employees.* Demonstrate to employees that the company's commitment to good ethics is serious.[42]

The point of these suggestions is that they should be incorporated into a manager's way of thinking and behaving. To facilitate making use of these ideas, Lockheed Martin managers have ethics discussion with their direct reports annually. The same approach to thinking through ethical issues would apply to you. Being aware of laws and regulations about unethical behavior is not enough. An individual has to personalize ideas about unethical behavior. For example, Mark Hurd, the CEO at Hewlett-Packard, had probably read somewhere that spying on company directors is unethical but he did not incorporate such knowledge into his thinking and behavior. Now, HP has an enormous reputation problem to overcome.

Written Organizational Codes of Conduct

About 75 percent of large organizations use written ethical codes of conduct as guidelines for ethical and socially responsible behavior. Some general aspects of these codes require people to conduct themselves with integrity and candor. Here is a statement of this type from the Johnson & Johnson (medical and health supplies) code of ethics: "We believe our first responsibility is to the doctors, nurses, and patients, to mothers and fathers and all others who use our products and services. In meeting these needs everything we do must be of high quality."

Other aspects of the codes might be specific, such as indicating the maximum gift that can be accepted from a vendor. In many organizations, known code violators are disciplined.

Widespread Communication about Ethics and Social Responsibility

Extensive communication about the topic reinforces ethical and socially responsible behavior. Top management can speak widely about the competitive advantage of being ethical and socially responsible. Another effective method is to discuss ethical and social responsibility issues in small groups. In this way the issues stay fresh in the minds of workers. A few minutes of a team meeting might be invested in a topic such as "What can we do to help the homeless people who live in the streets surrounding our office?"

Leadership by Example and Ethical Role Models

A high-powered approach to enhancing ethics and social responsibility is for members of top management to behave in such a manner themselves. If people throughout the firm believe that behaving ethically is "in" and behaving unethically is "out," ethical behavior will prevail. Visualize a scenario in which key people in an investment-banking firm vote themselves a $3 million year-end bonus. Yet to save money, entry-level clerical workers earning $9 an hour are denied raises. Many employees might feel that top

---

42 Barbara Ley Toffler, "Five Ways to Jump-Start Your Company's Ethics," *Fast Company*, October 2003, p. 36; Erin White, "What Would You Do? Ethics Courses Get Context," *The Wall Street Journal*, June 12, 2006, p. B2.

management has a low sense of ethics, and therefore that being ethical and socially responsible is not important.

Leading by example is particularly useful in encouraging ethical behavior because it provides useful role models. Employees are often influenced by the people they work with everyday, such as a supervisor or team leader. In contrast, top executives are distant figures who the worker rarely observes directly. Role modeling an immediate manager might proceed in this manner: A worker observes a manager consistently treat others fairly (and not play favorites). In future dealings with people, the worker treats people fairly, modeling the behavior of his or her manager. An interview study with experienced managers pointed to four general categories of attitudes and behaviors that characterized their ethical role models: (1) everyday interpersonal behaviors such as taking responsibility for others, (2) high ethical expectations for oneself, (3) high ethical expectations for others, such as holding them ethically accountable, and (4) fairness in dealing with others, such as soliciting their input.[43]

One way of encouraging managers to demonstrate ethics through leading by example and being a good role model is to tie compensation to ethical behavior. A year after Jim McNerney was appointed as CEO of Boeing Co., he developed a plan to facilitate strong ethical behavior at the aerospace giant—a company that had major ethical problems in the past. Executive compensation would be tied in part to ethical leadership, McNerney included. The CEO said, "The message is that there is no compromise between doing things the right way and performance."[44]

Encouragement of Confrontation about Ethical Deviations

Unethical behavior may be minimized if every employee confronts anyone seen behaving unethically. For example, if you spotted someone making an unauthorized copy of software, you would ask the software pirate, "How would you like it if you owned a business and people stole from your company?" The same approach encourages workers to ask about the ethical implications of decisions made by others in the firm.

Training Programs in Ethics and Social Responsibility

About 70 percent of employers train managerial workers about ethics, with a steady increase in recent years.[45] Forms of training include messages about ethics from executives, classes on ethics at colleges, and exercises in ethics. Understanding the company's code of ethics is usually incorporated into the training. Knowledge or relevant legislation, such as antidiscrimination laws, is another key subject. A recent approach is to conduct ethics training through e-training (over the computer), and DVDs and videos about ethics, followed by small-group discussion with a manager often leading the discussion group.

---

43 Gary R. Weaver, Linda Klebe Treviño, and Bradley Agle, "'Somebody to Look Up To:' Ethical Role Models in Organizations," *Organizational Dynamics*, No. 4, 2005, pp. 313–330.

44 J. Lynn Lunsford, "Piloting Boeing's New Course," *The Wall Street Journal*, June 13, 2006, p. B1.

45 J. White, "What Would You Do?" *The Wall Street Journal*, June 12, 2006, p. B3.

Ethics training programs reinforce the idea that ethical and socially responsible behavior is both morally right and good for business. Discussing ethical issues combined with factual knowledge helps raise workers' level of awareness. Much of the content of this chapter reflects the type of information communicated in such programs. In addition, Skill-Building Exercise 3-A represents the type of activity included in ethical training programs in many companies.

A final word about ethics training is that top management must take it seriously. Gundars Kaupins, a management professor at Boise State University, observes, "Ethics training provides more legal protection only if there is management commitment to ethical decision-making."[46]

46 Quoted in Kathryn Tyler, "Do the Right Thing: Ethics Training Programs Help Employees Deal with Ethical Dilemmas," *HR Magazine*, February 2005, p. 102.

SUMMARY OF Key Points

1 Identify the philosophical principles behind business ethics.

When deciding on what is right and wrong, people can focus on consequences; duties, rights of individuals; or integrity. Focusing on consequences is called utilitarianism, because the decision maker is concerned with the utility of the decision. Examining the rights of individuals in making a decision is the deontological approach and is based on universal principles such as honesty and fairness. According to the integrity (or virtue) approach, if the decision maker has good character and genuine motivation and intentions, he or she is behaving ethically. Pragmatism (whatever works) is closely related to focusing on the consequences.

2 Explain how values relate to ethics.

Ethics becomes the vehicle for converting values into action, or doing the right thing. A firm's moral standards and values also influence which kind of behaviors managers believe are ethical. According to ethically centered management, the high quality of an end product takes precedence over meeting a delivery schedule. Catastrophes can result when management is not ethically centered.

3 Identify factors contributing to lax ethics, and common ethical temptations and violations.

Major contributors to unethical behavior are greed and gluttony, and an organizational atmosphere that condones unethical behavior. Other contributors are moral laxity (other issues seem more important at the time), and pressure from higher management to achieve goals. Incentives for being unethical, such as being rewarded for cutting back on quality, can contribute to low ethics, as can self-interest, and weak relationships among people. Unconscious biases can also lead us to behave unjustly toward others. Rationalization is perhaps the most pervasive reason for unethical behavior.

Recurring ethical temptations and violations, including criminal acts, include the following: stealing from employers and customers, illegally copying software, treating people unfairly, sexual harassment, conflict of interest, accepting kickbacks and bribes, divulging confidential information, misusing corporate resources. Two other problems are corporate espionage and poor cyberethics. Business scandals are ethical and legal violations that have created mammoth job losses, the wiping out of pension funds, high investment losses, and bankruptcy of some vendors of the bankrupt companies. Backdating of stock options is scandalous but has not brought down companies.

4 Apply a guide to ethical decision making.

When faced with an ethical dilemma, ask yourself: Is it right? Is it fair? Who gets hurt? Would you be comfortable with the deed exposed? Would you tell your child to do it? How does it smell?

5 Describe the stakeholder viewpoint of social responsibility and corporate social performance.

Social responsibility refers to a firm's obligations to society. Corporate consciousness expands this view by referring to values that guide and motivate individuals to act responsibly.

The stakeholder viewpoint of social responsibility contends that firms must hold themselves accountable for the quality of life of the many groups affected by the firm's actions. Corporate social performance is the extent to which a firm responds to the demands of its stakeholders for behaving in a socially responsible way. Wal-Mart makes an excellent case study of corporate social performance.

6 Present an overview of social responsibility initiatives.

Creating opportunities for a diverse workforce is a major social responsibility initiative. Also important are environmental management, work/life programs, community redevelopment projects, acceptance of whistle blowers, and compassionate downsizing.

7 Summarize the benefits of ethical and socially responsible behavior, and how managers can create an environment that fosters such behavior.

High ethics and social responsibility are related to good financial performance, according to research evidence and opinion. Also, more profitable firms can invest in good corporate social performance. Being ethical helps avoid big fines for being unethical, and ethical organizations attract more employees. Initiatives for creating an ethical and socially responsible workplace include (a) formal mechanisms for monitoring ethics, (b) written organizational codes of conduct, (c) communicating about the topic, (d) leadership by example and ethical role models, (e) confrontation about ethical deviations, and (f) training programs.

KEY TERMS AND PHRASES

Ethics, 74
Moral intensity, 75
Ethically centered management, 78
Moral laxity, 79
Conflict of interest, 82
Corporate social responsibility, 89
Stockholder viewpoint, 90
Stakeholder viewpoint, 90
Corporate social performance, 91
Whistle blower, 98
Downsizing, 99
Virtuous circle, 100

QUESTIONS

1. What is your reaction to the following statement made by many business graduates? "It may be nice to study ethics, but in the real world the only thing that counts is money."
2. Give examples of rights that you think every employee is entitled to.
3. The Vice Fund (http://www.vicefund.com) is a mutual fund that favors "products or services often considered socially irresponsible," including investments in tobacco, alcoholic beverages, gambling companies, as well as defense contractors. Discuss whether you would be willing to invest in this fund (it has above-average returns).
4. According to several religious and community leaders, companies can become more socially responsible by allowing homeless people to stay overnight in the office lobby. The need is particularly urgent when it is extremely cold outside. The companies are also urged to serve basic meals. What is your evaluation of the merits of making office lobbies shelters for the homeless during extreme weather conditions?
5. Suppose a person makes extensive use of work/life benefits offered by the company. How might using

these benefits frequently have a negative effect on his or her career?

6. Get together with a group of people and rank the occupations listed next in terms of your perception of their ethical reputation. The most ethical occupation receives a rank of one. (The list that follows is presented in random order.) Use the average rank of the group members if consensus is not reached.
   - —— Cosmetic (plastic) surgeon
   - —— Computer programmer
   - —— Business executive, major firm
   - —— Criminal lawyer
   - —— Veterinarian for domestic animals
   - —— Business school professor
   - —— Family court judge
   - —— Small-business owner
   - —— New-car sales representative
   - —— Stockbroker/financial consultant
7. Search the print media or the Internet for an example of an act of high social responsibility by a business firm. Explain why you think the actions taken by the firm reflect high social responsibility.

SKILL-BUILDING EXERCISE 3-A: Ethical Decision Making

Working in small groups, take the following two ethical dilemmas through the six steps for screening contemplated decisions. You might also want to use various ethical principles in helping you reach a decision.

Scenario 1: The Budget Furniture

You are the office manager at a company that does considerable business with the federal government. You put together a proposal for purchasing $20,000 of new furniture for the office, including desks, chairs, sofas, and filing cabinets. You have asked for several bids on the furniture, including investigating several business-to-business portals. You have identified a supplier whom you think offers the best combination of price and quality. You submit your proposal to your manager for final approval. He says, "I have studied your proposal, and I think we can do much better. Through our contacts with the government, we can purchase the same furniture for about $6,000 through Unicor. All their goods are manufactured with prison labor. The inmates are paid about $1.00 per hour, so a lot of the cost savings would go directly to us. Besides, these jobs keep the inmates out of trouble, and teach them valuable skills they can use in the future."

You begin to reflect, "Yes, Unicor furniture may be a bargain, but what about the honest furniture-company employees who are losing their jobs? Their employers cannot compete well with Unicor."

What do you do now? Do you fight for your proposal for spending $20,000 for furniture manufactured by workers not in the prison system? Or do you go along with the idea of purchasing from Unicor? Explain your position.

Scenario 2: The Enormous Omelet Sandwich

You and three other students are placed on an ethics task force at Burger King being asked to investigate the ethics of selling the Enormous Omelet Sandwich. The sandwich is composed of one sausage patty, two eggs, two American cheese slices, and three strips of bacon on a bun, and contains 730 calories and 47 grams of fat. The Enormous Omelet sells particularly well with males between 18 and 35. "Food police" outside the company claim that the Enormous Omelet is so loaded with fat and bad cholesterol that it could lead to heart disease. Yet the position of company management is that there are plenty of options on the Burger King menu for customers who want to make healthy choices. The Enormous Omelet Sandwich has been a major financial success for the restaurant chain. You and your teammates are asked to present top management with an evaluation of the ethics of continuing the Enormous Omelet Sandwich.

SKILL-BUILDING EXERCISE 3-B: Value-Based Business: Avoiding Conflicts by Discovering Your Corr Values

According to mediate.com, unbalanced values and unconscious habits are potentially harmful in business. You can avoid many ethical conflicts by discovering your core values and unconscious habits, and learning to make conscious decisions about how to react in difficult situations. Visit http://www.mediate.com, and register. You will then have the opportunity to answer questions, and receive information about minimizing ethical conflicts.

INTERNET SKILL-BUILDING EXERCISE: Ethical Product Promotion

Search the Internet for an advertisement or similar promotional information about a food supplement or beauty product, such as wrinkle remover. An example of such a product would be a bottle of pine-tree resin to help ward off colds. Note carefully whether the information is provided by the company or the individual that manufactures or sells the product, or by an objective third party. Give your opinion on the ethics of the person making the claim. For example, attempt to evaluate the honesty of the claims. Use the six-step guide to ethical decision making to help you in your ethical evaluation.

Case Problem 3-A

Medtronic is So Kind to Doctors

A prominent surgeon in Wisconsin was paid $400,000 a year by Medtronic for a consulting contract requiring him to work just eight days. Another doctor in Virginia received nearly $700,000 in consulting fees from Medtronic for the first nine months of 2005. These doctors work in a growing field, complex back surgery, and this makes them particularly valuable to the spinal-implant division of Medtronic. In recent years, the company has spent tens of millions of dollars on consulting contracts and other types of payment to them and numerous other prominent surgeons, according to papers filed as part of a whistle-blower lawsuit. The suit contends that some of these payments were made to attract or retain the doctors' business.

Medtronic, based in Minneapolis, is one of the country's largest medical-device makers with $10 billion in annual sales. The lawsuit, filed in the United States District Court in Memphis in 2004 and amended later, was brought by the whistle blower, a former Medtronic employee. The Justice Department, which has the right to intervene in the case but has not yet done so, is seeking to recover Medicare funds. According to legal filings, it proposes that Medtronic settle the matter by paying $40 million.

The suit, which was sealed until January 13, 2006, accuses Medtronic of giving spine surgeons "excessive remuneration, unlawful perquisites and bribes in other forms for purchasing goods and medical devices." The plaintiff, Jacqueline Kay Poteet, a senior manager for travel services for Medtronic until 2003, has also accused the company in a supplemental complaint of continuing these improper payments in 2004 and 2005. Her lawyer, Andrew R. Carr Jr., has objected to the proposed settlement as too low. Whistle blowers typically receive a share of any settlement.

All the doctors in the lawsuit who were reached for comment said that the payments to them were appropriate and fair compensation for work done for Medtronic. The company, which said it continues to cooperate fully with the government to resolve the case, declined to comment directly on the accusations, saying they remained the subject of litigation.

In a written response, a spokesman, Rob Clark, said, "We take these allegations very seriously and we do not tolerate conduct that is illegal or unethical." Consulting arrangements with doctors to improve devices, he said, "are critical in our view, to the delivery of state-of-the-art health care and are perfectly legal."

The internal Medtronic documents filed as part of the suit show that Medtronic spent at least $50 million on payments to doctors over some four years, through June 2005. The payments become illegal when they are linked to a doctor's use of a particular device and violate the federal law against kickbacks, which says that payments and other benefits cannot be provided to doctors if the payments are intended to induce them to use the company's products.

In addition to consulting fees and other payments, the lawsuit said, Medtronic played host at medical conferences where the "principal objective" was to "induce the physician through any financial means necessary" to use its devices. According to Medtronic documents, the company closely tracked the use of its devices by the doctors who attended the conferences, choosing some for "special attention."

Poteet, the whistle blower, worked for Medtronic until an injury forced her to leave in 2003. She was also involved in a legal dispute with Medtronic over her disability benefits; it has since been resolved. At Medtronic, she arranged trips for doctors to the company's conferences and became familiar with attempts to win the doctors' favor.

Because the devices are so profitable, the money being spent by Medtronic "is peanuts," said a former employee who still works in the industry and insisted on not being identified for fear of retaliation. Sales representatives earn generous commissions, so they will work hard to satisfy the doctors' demands, the employee said, adding, "You're going to make sure you do whatever he [or she] wants, whatever it is." The cost of the components involved in a typical fusion surgery for the lower back is around $13,000, and the overall U.S. market has grown to about $4 billion a year.

Case Problem 3-A

Medtronic's overtures to doctors often began when the surgeons were still in training, Poteet said. The company commonly paid doctors to attend any of 200 professional meetings a year. If the doctors wanted to go snorkeling or play golf, the sales representatives or Medtronic employees almost invariably paid the expense, she said. When the doctors visited Memphis, she said, Medtronic employees would take them to a local strip club, PlatinumPlus, disguising the expenses as an evening at the ballet.

A Medtronic lawyer, Todd N. Sheldon, raised concerns in 2003 about whether the company should pay to take doctors sailing or fishing, or ask for contributions, according to a company e-mail message that is part of the legal findings. "When we are sending scores of doctors to a nice resort like this under the guise of training and education on our products," he said, "I think we need to be more careful and stick to the limits of our rules as best we can."

Medtronic said it has been a leader in pursuing industry ethical guidelines that suggest that device companies provide only modest meals and receptions and not pay for costly leisure activities.

Discussion Questions

1. What conflict of interest for doctors appears to be involved in this case?
2. What conflict of interest for the whistle blower appears to be involved in this case?
3. So what's wrong with taking doctors to strip clubs for a little fun?
4. What do you recommend that Medtronic do about its approach to influencing doctors to use their spinal implants on patients?

Source: Reed Abelson, "Whistle-Blower Suit Says Device Maker Generously Rewards Doctors," http://www.nytimes.com, January 24, 2006.

Case Problem 3-B

Is it Fair that Anyone Owns the Rights to Asthmahelp.com?

The Web site http://www.flashgames.com has no staff, spends no money on marketing its name, offers no games. All it offers is a list of links to other game sites. Yet it earns revenue of more than $150,000 a year selling online ads. Flashgames.com is just one of thousands of Web sites that are cashing in on the online advertising boom in an unusual way—by piggybacking on the ad-sales efforts of giant search engines Google Inc. and Yahoo Inc.

These sites' ability to make lots of money for little investment is now attracting attention from big players. A group of investors led by former MySpace.com chairman Richard Rosenblatt has raised $120 million from investors to build a new company, Demand Media Inc., centered on generic domain names like these. The venture has already acquired 150,000 domain names—including flashgames.com—and plans to aggressively acquire more. But, conscious of the limitations of these bare-bones sites, it plans to add some low-cost content in hopes of making the business even stronger. "We will be taking billboards and turning them into content Web sites," says Rosenblatt.

Sites like flashgames.com used to be considered "cybersquatting," a long-standing Internet tactic where entrepreneurs register domain names either associated with a particular subject or a company and then sell the name for a quick profit. These new generation sites go a little further, reaping ad revenue. Demand Media says it will not buy trademarked domain names.

Owned until recently by two Australian entrepreneurs, flashgames.com draws people—about 250,000 per month—looking for a Web-based game that uses flash-animation technology. The links that the would-be gamers find on flashgames.com are actually paid ads placed by Google or Yahoo!, both of which sprinkle ad links all over the Web, paying the host sites a cut of the revenue they received when anyone clicks on one of their links. So when someone finds flashgmes.com, and then clicks on a link to another games site, flashgames.com gets paid.

Analysts estimate these types of sites, known as "domain parking," generate about 5 percent to 10 percent of search-engine revenue, putting the industry's annual revenue at about $600 million. "The profit margins are extraordinary," says RBC Capital Markets' Jordan Rohan. He predicts industry revenue could double to $1.2 billion in three years.

Given the sites' meager offerings, some in the industry worry that these domains may not have staying power. Even finding one of these sites is a matter of luck. Web surfers have to type its full name into the address line of a Web browser, although some browsers automatically add a dot-com to the end of something they type. But most parked domains don't generate enough traffic to show up at the top of search-engine rankings.

"This is grandma type of navigation," says Matt Bentley, chief strategy officer of Sedo.com LLC, a domain-name parking business. "It's probably not currently being done by a lot of sophisticated people."

A critic of the domain-game business commented, "How crazy has the world become? A handful of people are getting rich when people with poor Internet search skills type into their browser, phrases like *dogfood.com, helpwitharthritis.com, asthmahelp.com*, and *carloan.com*. What really drives me up the wall is that somebody is getting a cut when a person enters into the browser, *alzheimersdisease.com*."

Discussion Questions

1. What is your evaluation of the ethics of domain-name companies getting commissions when people insert ordinary names into their Internet browser?
2. What about the ethics of Google and Yahoo getting involved by paying ad revenues to the domain-name companies?
3. What possible links are there between domain-name companies and click fraud?

Source: All but the last paragraph are from Julia Angwin, "For These Sites, Their Best Asset Is a Good Name," *The Wall Street Journal,* May 1, 2006, p. B1.

chapter 4

Essentials of Planning

One recent wintry day, Dave Rozek prowled auction lots and city pounds in Chicago's South Side looking for big game: Cougars, Mustangs, Sables and Bobcats. "I don't see Impalas very much, so I like to buy them when I do," he said, eyes darting from side to side as he steered a 1998 Oldsmobile Intrigue past mounds of wrecked cars.

Schnitzer Steel Industries Inc. of Portland, Oregon, Rozek's employer, is one of the nation's largest steel recyclers. For years it simply bought old cars and mashed them along with steel girders, railcars and the tracks they rode on. In 2003, as demand from Asia's booming economies started creating metal shortages, Schnitzer switched tactics and started buying auto junkyards to better feed it recycling plants. Rozek, in turn, feeds the junkyards.

Schnitzer now operates about 50 yards in North America and plans to triple that number by the end of the decade mostly by purchasing existing junkyards. The move has transformed the old-line scrap hauler and modernized the auto-salvage industry. In Schnitzer's yards, you can find computerized modeling and ideas drawn from retailing such as bar codes, and discount coupons. The business also turned out to be surprisingly profitable.

"We felt we needed to be closer to our source of scrap," says Kelly Lang, Schnitzer's vice president for capital investment. In traditional junkyards, sedans and trucks are stacked on top of

Objectives

After studying this chapter and doing the exercises, you should be able to:

1 Summarize a general framework for planning and apply it to enhance your planning skills.

2 Describe the nature of business strategy.

3 Explain how business strategy is developed, including SWOT analysis.

4 Identify levels of business strategy, competitive forces, and types of business strategies.

5 Explain the use of operating plans, policies, procedures, and rules.

6 Present an overview of management by objectives.

each other in open dirt lots guarded by pit bulls. Grease monkeys yank the parts that buyers want. At some point, unwanted hulks go for scrap. At Schnitzer's Pick-n-Pull chain, customers armed with their own toolboxes select and wrench off auto parts, saving both the consumer and the company the cost of hiring high-priced mechanic labor. Cars and parts are carefully monitored and they're shipped to Schnitzer's crushers before costs such as storage rise too high.

Booming Hispanic immigration is bringing more customers—and their dismantling tools—to Schnitzer's door. International demand is surging, too, especially in Mexico. There is rising demand for U.S. wrecks from newly affluent motorists in Russia, Eastern Europe and Latin America, who want the cars either for parts to or drive anew.

Schnitzer has focused on one of the industry's fastest growing niches—self-service salvage yards. Pick-n-Pulls pride themselves on providing clean waiting rooms for wives and children who join dad on his parts search—nearly all customers are male. Traditional junk yards lack the computer power or organizational skill to track the vehicles. They frequently keep clunkers on the books—or on blocks—for months, waiting for a customer to monetize the asset. During that time, without a guaranteed buyer, the junk cars are essentially worthless. Schnitzer, by contrast, knows it will always have its scrap maw (steel recycler) as a guaranteed customer. [1]

The story about the successful chain of auto junk yards illustrates how strategic planning can catapult a business to success. Schnitzer and his executive team developed the niche of combining a modern car junk yard with a steel scrap business. The niche of Schnitzer Steel Industries is almost like having a restaurant and selling the scrap food to pig farmers! Finding a focus or developing a niche is one of the business strategies covered in this chapter. By virtue of planning, including using a basic strategy, businesspeople manage the future instead of being guided by fate.

Planning is important because it contributes heavily to success and gives you some control over the future. According to one analysis, the value of planning is in the process itself. By planning, you set aside your daily tasks and deadlines so you can enlarge your mental focus and see the bigger picture.[2] More specifically, planning often leads to improvement in productivity, quality, and financial results.

---

1 Adapted from Joel Millman and Paul Glader, "In Car Junkyards, Scrap Haulers Find a Surprise: Healthy Profits," *The Wall Street Journal*, March 21, 2006, pp. A1, A13.

2 "The Real Value of Planning," *Working Smart*, January 1995, p. 1.

The purpose of this chapter is to describe the planning function in such a way that you can use what you learn to plan more effectively as a manager or individual contributor. First the chapter looks at a framework for the application of planning. You will also learn about high-level, or strategic planning, including how strategy is developed and the types of strategy that result from strategic planning. We then describe operating plans, policies, procedures, and rules, and a widely used method for getting large numbers of people involved in implementing plans: management by objectives.

A GENERAL FRAMEWORK FOR PLANNING

Learning Objective 1

Summarize a general framework for planning and apply it to enhance your planning skills.

Planning is a complex and comprehensive process involving a series of overlapping and interrelated elements or stages, including strategic, tactical, and operational planning. **Strategic planning** establishes master plans that shape the destiny of the firm. An example of strategic planning is when the executive team at Harley-Davidson Inc. planned how to deal with the demographic shift of their customer base becoming much older. The strategic issue it faced was whether to change its iconic product line to win over young buyers.

PLAY VIDEO

ESSENTIALS OF PLANNING

"Go to academic.cengage.com/management/dubrin and view the video. How can Yahoo's competitors benefit from all the attention Yahoo has received in regarding its strategic alliances?"

A second type of planning is needed to support strategic planning, such as how to build motorcycles that fit the preferences of younger motorcyclists. **Tactical planning** translates strategic plans into specific goals and plans that are most relevant to a particular organizational unit. The tactical plans also provide details of how the company or business unit will compete within its chosen business area. Middle managers have the primary responsibility for formulating and executing tactical plans. These plans are based on marketplace realities when developed for a business. Conditions can change rapidly in competitive fields such as a Korean company suddenly developing a substantially lower-price sports bike. The scope of tactical plans is broader than operational plans (described next), but not as broad as that of strategic plans.

A third type of planning is aimed more at day-to-day operations or the nuts and bolts of doing business. **Operational planning** identifies the specific procedures and actions required at lower levels in the organization. If Harley-Davidson wants to revamp an assembly line to produce more sports bikes, operational plans would have to be drawn. In practice, the distinction between tactical planning and operational planning is not clear-cut. However, both tactical plans and operational plans must support the strategic plan such as revamping manufacturing and marketing to capture a larger group of young cyclists.

strategic planning A firm's overall master plan that shapes its destiny.

tactical planning Planning that translates a firm's strategic plans into specific goals by organizational unit.

The framework presented in Exhibit 4-1 summarizes the elements of planning. With slight modification the model could be applied to strategic, tactical, and operational planning. A planner must define the present situation, establish goals and objectives, and analyze the environment in

exhibit 4-1 **A Framework for Planning**

Planning at its best is a systematic process.

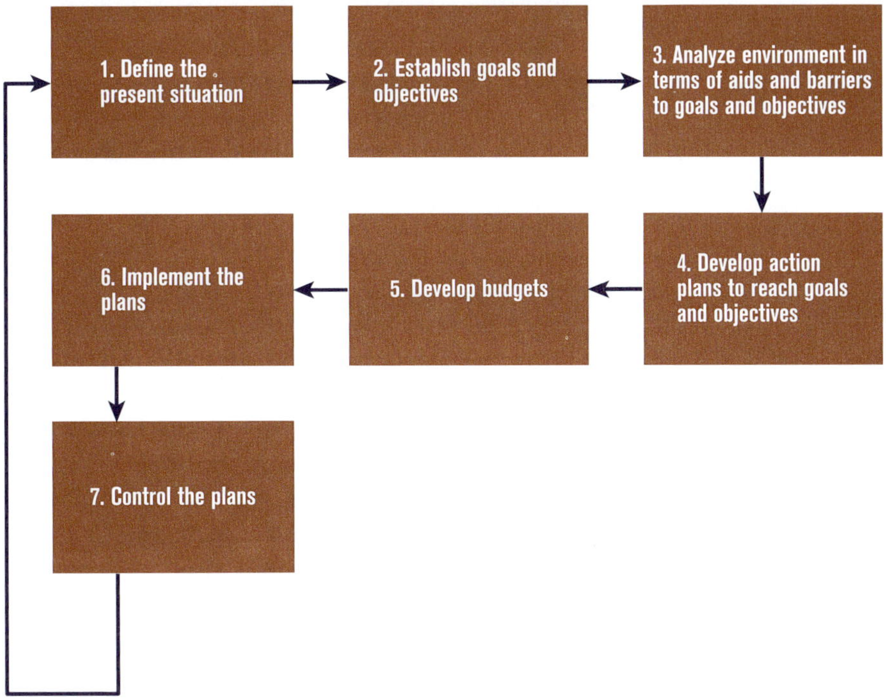

terms of aids and barriers to goals and objectives. The planner must also develop action plans to reach goals and objectives, develop budgets, implement the plans, and control the plans.

operational planning
Planning that requires specific procedures and actions at lower levels in an organization.

This chapter examines each element separately. In practice, however, several of these stages often overlap. For example, a manager might be implementing and controlling the same plan simultaneously. Also, the planning steps are not always followed in the order presented in Exhibit 4-1. Planners frequently start in the middle of the process, proceed forward, and then return to an earlier step. This change of sequence frequently happens because the planner discovers new information or because objectives change. Also, many managers set goals before first examining their current position.

To illustrate the general framework for planning we turn to Harley-Davidson, that is dealing with the planning challenge presented by its aging customer base. The challenge was expressed by Joe Mammolito, a tow-truck company owner from Dix Hills, N.Y., and Harley devotee for 30 years: “I have about 14 guys driving trucks for me. The younger guys ride sports bikes, the older fellows like a big bike. I think they should get guys in their 20s and 30s accustomed to riding Harleys. They need to get the younger guys accustomed to the name, the products, and the dealership network.”[3]

3 The facts about Harley-Davidson and the quotes are from Joseph Weber, "Harley Just Keeps on Cruisin'," *Business Week*, November 6, 2006, pp. 71–72.

Define the Present Situation

Knowing where you are is critical to establishing goals for change. Defining the present situation includes measuring success and examining internal capabilities and external threats. Harley-Davidson has had a long tradition of success. At one time the motorcycle had a youth-oriented counterculture mystique. By the mid-2000s, Harley had become a middle-aged nostalgia brand. Because of so many loyal customers, Harley had been able to turn small product improvements into sustained growth. Many Harley-Davidson customers own multiple—sometimes even 12—Harley motorcycles. At the moment the new, bigger Twin Cam engine and six-speed transmission was announced in July 2006, orders began pouring into dealers. Annual sales of $6 billion were forecast. Another capability of Harley is a fast-growing overseas fan base that perceives the Harley-Davidson in the best possible sense, referring to being powerful and free. Over one-fifth of Harleys are sold outside the United States.

A major external threat facing Harley-Davidson was the long-time prediction that a demographic time bomb would blow up the company. The median age of a Harley buyer had leapt from 35 in 1987 to nearly 47 in 2006. The company has done little to shake its image with people in their twenties as Granddad's or Grandma's bike. "They haven't kept up with the younger riders," says a 44-year-old business analyst who owns two Harleys.

Establish Goals and Objectives

The second step in planning is to establish goals and identify objectives that contribute to the attainment of goals. (Goals are broader than objectives, whereas objectives function as smaller goals that support the bigger goals.) A major goal Harley management might establish is to continue to cultivate people over 30 who prefer the big loud bikes that allow for smooth rides on long trips. Another goal would be to promote the Harley as a retirement treat, especially for young retirees. Another goal would be to promote its lower-priced sports bikes in its Buell line.

Genevieve Schmitt, founding editor of *WomenRidersNow.com*, believes Harley should establish the goal of continuing to focus on what they do best. She says, "They've responded to the needs of smaller, less muscular riders by offering motorcycles with lower motors. They realize women are an up-and-coming segment and that they need to accommodate them. They don't market to a specific gender, but are gender-neutral. They market a lifestyle, with daughters and moms, dads and sons." Following this thought Harley might establish the goal of making their marketing more gender neutral.

Analyze the Environment to Forecast Aids and Barriers to Goals and Objectives

As an extension of defining the present situation, the manager or other planner attempts to predict which internal and external factors will foster or hinder attainment of the desired ends. A key strength of Harley being able to retain its prominence in the motorcycle business is that its brand is so well established. The loyal and talented Harley-Davidson workforce will be able to adapt to any shift toward smaller, sportier bikes.

A potential barrier in the environment to the continued success of Harley is that the Japanese bike makers quickly change to suit the shifting taste of customers. In contrast, Harley is over 100 years old and much more conservative. Company management is less than eager to mess with its iconic image. Kent Grayson, a marketing professor at Northwestern University says, "It's more than a brand. It's a culture." Another barrier to attaining goals is that European and Japanese motorcycle manufacturers far outsell the Harley Buell line of smaller bikes in the United States. For example, in 2006 the Japanese company Suzuki sold about 27,000 motorcycles with engines in the same class as the Buell line. Harley sold about 4,200 in this class.

Another external threat is that many individuals are concerned about motorcycle safety and the disturbance to the environment from the loud exhaust blast. The Hell's Angels image of motorcyclists is a potential barrier. Yet the barrier is offset somewhat by the fact that many would-be drivers are attracted to the rebellious image.

Develop Action Plans to Reach Goals and Objectives

Goals and objectives are only wishful thinking until action plans are drawn. An **action plan** consists of the specific steps necessary to achieve a goal or objective. The planners must figure out specifically how they will accomplish such ends as encouraging Harley users to keep motorcycling until later in life. Other action plans might include more advertising aimed at women, including the objective of featuring women celebrities in advertisements for Harley-Davidson. Additional action plans might include free seminars for seniors about the joy of motorcycle driving, and more extensive promotion of the Buell line.

Develop Budgets

Planning usually results in action plans that require money to implement. Among the expenses would be larger advertising and promotion budgets geared to seniors and women. Expenses for expanding the Buell line would be incentives for dealers to purchase them and increased production, so more Buells could be placed in dealer showrooms. Another budget item would include safe-driving campaigns to help soften the image of motorcycling being so dangerous.

Implement the Plans

If the plans developed in the previous five steps are to benefit the firm, they must be put to use. A frequent criticism of planners is that they develop elaborate plans and then abandon them in favor of conducting business as usual. One estimate is that 70 percent of the time when CEOs fail, the major cause of failure is poor execution, not poor planning. Poor execution in this study included not getting things done, being indecisive, and not delivering

action plan
The specific steps necessary to achieve a goal or an objective.

on commitments.[4] Furthermore, execution is considered to be a specific set of behaviors and techniques that companies need to master in order to maintain a competitive advantage.[5]

Part of the outstanding success of Toyota can be attributed to top-level management's penchant for implementing its many plans. CEO Fujio Cho believes that Toyota can never afford to take its foot off the gas (or relax in executing its plans). He believes that running Toyota is less like driving a car than "trying to pull a handcart up a steep hill—there's always tremendous danger that if we relax, even for a moment, we could lose momentum and be thrown to the bottom."[6]

The Harley managers and specialists seem poised to execute because their planning sessions heavily emphasize turning plans into action. Harley-Davidson management desperately wants the success of the Harley line of motorcycles to continue into the future.

Control the Plans

Planning does not end with implementation, because plans may not always proceed as conceived. The control process measures progress toward goal attainment and indicates corrective action if too much deviation is detected. The deviation from expected performance can be negative or positive. Progress against all of the goals and objectives mentioned above must be measured. One goal was to hold on to much of the existing customer base. Mark Barnett, an El Paso, Texas, Harley dealer believes that Harley is attaining this goal. He observes: "When they get into their 30s and 40s, people slow down and get tired of sports bikes. If you look at the sport bike demographics, the number on them over 40 is pretty low. As long as people don't quit riding motorcycles altogether, they're going to be our customer when they turn 40." Company management needs more time to know if the goal for getting more young riders to purchase sports cycles in the Buell line has been attained.

In Exhibit 4-1, note the phrase "Evaluation and Feedback" on the left. The phrase indicates that the control process allows for the fine-tuning of plans after their implementation. One common example of the need for fine-tuning is a budget that has been set too high or too low in the first attempt at implementing a plan. A manager controls by making the right adjustment.

Make Contingency Plans

contingency plan An alternative plan to be used if the original plan cannot be implemented or a crisis develops.

Many planners develop a set of backup plans to be used in case things do not proceed as hoped. A **contingency plan** is an alternative plan to be used if the original plan cannot be implemented or a crisis develops. (The familiar expression "Let's try plan B" gets at the essence of contingency planning.) One potential crisis for Harley management would be substantial climate changes in the form of much more rain, snow, and ice that would make

4 Ram Charan and Geoffrey Colvin, "Why CEOs Fail," *Fortune*, June 21, 1999, p. 70.

5 Larry Bossidy and Ram Charan with Charles Burck, *Execution: The Discipline of Getting Things Done* (New York: Crown Business, 2002).

6 Clay Chandler, "Full Speed Ahead," *Fortune*, February 7, 2005, p. 80.

motorcycle riding less feasible in many parts of the world. Another crisis would be the escalation of motorcycle insurance premiums to the point that the demand for on-the-road motorcycles would decline sharply.

Contingency plans are often developed from objectives in earlier steps in planning. The plans are triggered into action when the planner detects, however early in the planning process, deviations from objectives. Construction projects, such as building an airport hangar, are particularly prone to deviations from completion dates because so many different contractors and subcontractors are involved.

An *exit strategy* might be part of the contingency plan. If the demand for both the Harley big bikes and sports bikes declined to the point of major losses, the Harley facilities and dealerships might be sold to Suzuki. Harley management, of course, does not envision this crisis.

STRATEGIC PLANNING AND BUSINESS STRATEGIES

Learning Objective 2

Describe the nature of business strategy.

The framework for planning can be used to develop and implement strategic plans, as well as tactical and operational plans. The emphasis of strategic planning in the current era is to help the firm move into emerging markets, or invent the future of the firm. Strategic planning should result in managerial workers throughout the organization thinking strategically and wondering about how the firm adapts to its environment and how it will cope with its future. James R. Bailey remarks that one of the central challenges of modern organizations is for leaders at all levels of the firm to think strategically—including seeing the overall picture as they go about their work.[7]

A strategically minded worker at any level would think, "How does what I am doing right now support corporate strategy?" The call-center worker at Hewlett-Packard might say to himself, "Each time I help a customer solve a problem I am contributing to the strategy of having the highest-quality products in all the markets we serve."

Business strategy is a complex subject that can be viewed from many vantage points. Here we look at business strategy from three major perspectives: its nature, how it is developed, and a sampling of the various types of strategy in use.

The Nature of Business Strategy

strategy The organization's plan, or comprehensive program, for achieving its vision, mission, and goals in its environment.

What constitutes business strategy has been described in dozens of ways. A **strategy** is an integrated overall concept and plan of how the organization will achieve its goals and objectives.[8] For many managers, strategy simply refers to the direction in which the firm is pointed, such as a paycheck loan company deciding to set up shop in poor neighborhoods where many of the residents lack a bank account. An explanation of business

7 James R. Bailey, "The Mind of the Strategist," *Academy of Management Learning and Education*, December 2003, p. 385.
8 Donald C. Hambrick and James W. Fredericksson, "Are You Sure Your Have a Business Strategy?" *Academy of Management Executive*, November 2005, p. 51.

exhibit 4-2 The Nature of Strategy

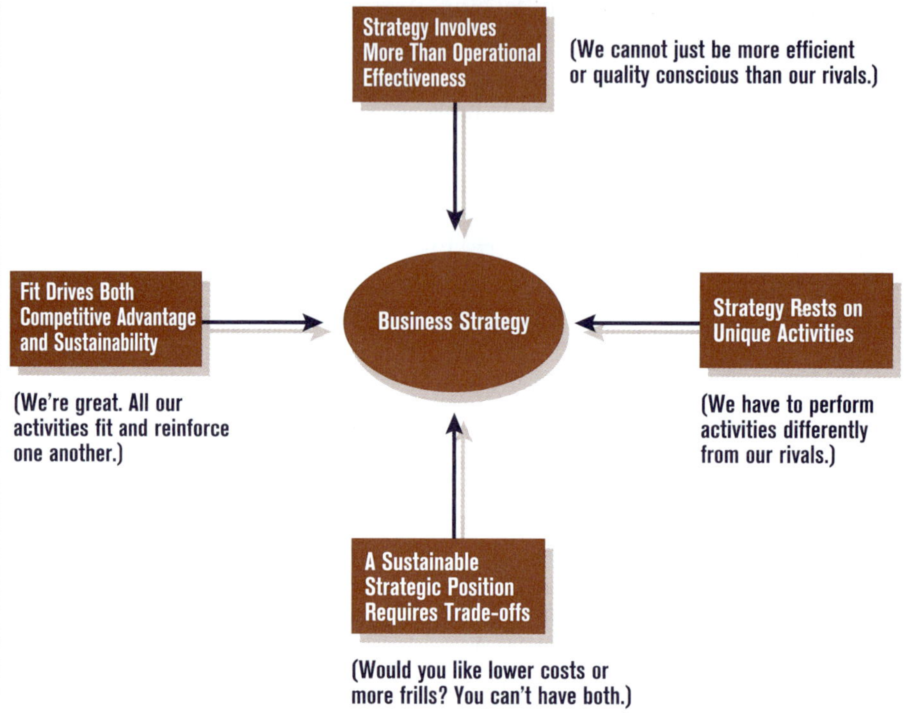

Source: Developed from Michael E. Porter, "What Is Strategy?" Harvard Business Review, November–December 1998, pp. 61–78.

strategy developed by Michael Porter, a leading authority, provides useful guidelines for managers who need to develop strategy. According to Porter, true business strategy has four components as outlined in Exhibit 4-2 and described next.[9]

Strategy Involves More Than Operational Effectiveness

A starting point in understanding the nature of business strategy is to understand that it involves more than operational effectiveness or being efficient. In recent years many firms in the private and public sector have become more efficient through such means as downsizing, performing work more efficiently, and outsourcing. Although the improvements in operations may often be dramatic, they rarely lead to sustainable improvements in profitability. As many top-level executives have said, "You can't cost-cut your way to growth." Strategy essentially involves performing activities differently, such as 1-800-MATTRESS, the company that pioneered selling mattresses over the phone. Being able to purchase a mattress over the phone is a convenience that adds value to the purchase of a mattress.

9 Michael E. Porter, "What Is Strategy?" *Harvard Business Review*, November–December 1996, pp. 61–78; John W. Bachmann, "Competitive Strategy: It's O.K. to be Different," *Academy of Management Executive*, May 2002, pp. 61–65.

Strategy Rests on Unique Activities

Competitive strategy means deliberately choosing a different set of activities to deliver a unique value. An often-cited example is Southwest Airlines. They offer short-haul, low-cost, direct service between midsized cities and secondary airports in large cities. Southwest's frequent departures and low fares attract price-conscious customers who would otherwise travel by car or bus. Southwest customers willingly forego the frill of in-flight meals to save money and have a wide choice of flight departures. All Southwest activities focus on delivering low-cost, convenient service on its routes. By doing away with added features such as meals and interline transfer of baggage, the airline can achieve gate turnarounds in about 15 minutes. Planes can then be airborne more of the time, allowing for more frequent flights. By using automated ticketing, passengers can bypass travel agents, saving Southwest money on commissions. Another unique activity is flying only 737 aircraft, which boosts the efficiency of maintenance.

Southwest has been so successful with its business model that several competitors have surfaced to implement the same strategy. Among these direct competitors are JetBlue and Ted (of United Airlines) in situations where these two carriers fly the same route as Southwest.

A Sustainable Strategic Position Requires Trade-Offs

After a firm finds a strategic position (or place in the market), it can best sustain it by making trade-offs with other positions. Trade-offs are necessary when activities are incompatible. A good example is shopping through the Internet. If you want the convenience of shopping anytime and from your home or office, you sacrifice interacting with a sales associate who can answer your questions. Another trade-off with e-commerce (and shopping by phone) is that defective or ill-fitting merchandise has to be repacked and shipped back to the manufacturer. Repacking and reshipping is more inconvenient for many people than, for example, driving back to the merchant with a computer that doesn't work.

Fit Drives Both Competitive Advantage and Sustainability

Strategy includes efficiently combining activities related to making a product or service. The chain of company activities fit and support each other to form an effective system. Bic Corporation is an example of the fit aspect of strategy. The company sells a narrow line of standard, low-priced ballpoint pens to the major customer markets (retail, commercial, promotional) through practically every available channel. Bic targets the common need for a low-price, acceptable pen throughout the markets it serves. The company gains the benefit of consistency across nearly all activities, meaning that they do not have to have different equipment or staff to conduct their business with different customer groups. Bic achieves fit by a product design that emphasizes ease of manufacturing, manufacturing plants designed for low-cost, large-scale purchasing to minimize material costs, and in-house parts production whenever cost effective.

As mentioned in passing at the outset of this section, business strategy also involves "thinking big," or taking an overall perspective even if it means glossing over some worrisome details.

THE DEVELOPMENT OF BUSINESS STRATEGY

Learning objective 3

Explain how business strategy is developed, including SWOT analysis.

Business strategy develops from planning. Strategic planning encompasses those activities that lead to the statement of goals and objectives and the choice of strategies to achieve them. The final outcomes of strategic planning are statements of vision, mission, strategy, and policy. A **vision** is an idealized picture of the future of the organization. The **mission** identifies the firm's purpose and where it fits into the world. Specifying a mission answers the question "What business are we really in?" A mission is more grounded in present-day realities than is a vision, but some companies use the terms interchangeably. A firm's mission may not be apparent to the casual observer. For example, Godiva Chocolates (the company that produces high-priced chocolate sold in separate displays in retail outlets) would appear to be in the candy business. In reality, their real mission places them in the luxury and pampering business. Exhibit 4-3 presents a few examples of company vision and mission statements. You will observe that companies vary considerably in what should be included in a mission or vision statement.

vision
An idealized picture of the future of an organization.

mission
The firm's purpose and where it fits into the world.

Planning alone does not create strategy. Corporate values also influence strategy because well-managed organizations tend to develop strategy to fit what the people in power think is important. If the company highly values innovation, it will not adopt a strategy of being successful by imitating (or benchmarking) other successful products. Piaget, for example, has remained successful for more than 200 years by staying with its own high-quality watches, and not imitating other trends in the watch industry.

Under ideal circumstances a firm arrives at strategy after completing strategic planning. In practice, many firms choose a strategy prior to strategic planning. Once the firm has the strategy, a plan is developed to implement it. A chief

exhibit 4-3 Sample Vision and Mission Statements

Microsoft: "Innovation is the core of providing opportunity."

Starfire Systems:

Vision: "Starfire Systems will pioneer the creation of new advanced materials through enabling technology based on a wide range of ceramic-forming polymers that meet the needs of customers."

Mission: "Starfire Systems invents, manufactures high-performance ceramic-forming polymers and provides the engineered material systems that will allow our customers to break through cost, performance and design barriers."

Bombardier: "Bombardier's mission is to be the leader in all the markets in which it operates. This objective will be achieved through excellence in design, manufacturing, and marketing in the fields of transportation equipment, aerospace, recreational products, financial services, and services related to its products and core competencies."

Roth Staffing Companies: "We are the preeminent staffing-services company, recognized as a creative industry leader, equally fulfilling the diverse needs of our customers, staffing associates, and coworkers."

Mrs. Fields Cookies: "I've always been in a feel good feeling business. My job was to sell joy, happiness, an experience, and my mission was to take my product to the extreme. You've got to strive to be the best in whatever you can." (As articulated by Debbi Fields, company founder)

executive might say, "Let's compete by becoming the most recognizable company in our field." The executive team would then develop specific plans to implement that strategy, rather than strategic planning leading to the conclusion that brand recognition would be an effective strategy. For many medium-sized and small organizations it is strategy first, followed by planning.

Three major approaches to developing strategy are gathering multiple inputs, analyzing the realities of the business situation, and doing a SWOT analysis. All three of these approaches are consistent with, and extensions of, the basic planning model presented in Exhibit 4-1.

Gathering Multiple Inputs to Formulate Strategy

Strategic managers and leaders are often thought of as mystics who work independently and conjure up great schemes for the future. In reality, many strategic leaders arrive at their ideas for the organization's future by consulting with a wide range of parties at interest. Strategy theorist Gary Hamel advises executives to make the strategy-creation process more democratic. He reasons that imagination is scarcer than resources. As a consequence, "We have to involve hundreds, if not thousands, of new voices in the strategy process if we want to increase the odds of seeing the future."[10]

An example of the democratization of strategic planning is how Walt Disney Co. CEO Robert Iger reduced in size the company's strategic planning unit when he came into power in 2005. The strategic planning unit's powers were then handed back to Disney business divisions. Previously the centralized planning unit shot down business strategies and deals that business unit company managers proposed—much to the displeasure of the managers. A corporate-planning group of ten replaced the 30-person strategic planning unit.[11]

An extreme approach to gathering multiple inputs for strategy is a new development termed *crowdcasting*. A consultancy, such as Idea Crossing, holds an online contest with 3,500 MBA students to solve strategic dilemmas. Companies pay Idea Crossing to obtain the input from the students. The payoff from crowdcasting is the opportunity to penetrate a closed-circuit corporate culture and profit from the fresh insights of a large group of smart and motivated outsiders. Contestants sign confidentiality agreements, and their strategic solutions become the property of the corporate sponsors. An example of a strategic problem tackled by the business students was to devise new services featuring high-speed wireless technologies for Sprint. Exhibit 4-4 outlines how crowdcasting involves so many business students in tackling business strategy problems. Many strategy experts might label the students' activities as problem solving rather than true strategy. Nevertheless, the consulting firm involved and the participating companies regard the activity as resolving strategic dilemmas.

Analyzing the Realities of the Business Situation

To develop effective business strategy, the strategist must make valid assumptions about the environment. When the assumptions are incorrect, the strategy might backfire. Let's get preposterous for a moment. Assume

---

10 John A. Byrne, "Three of the Busiest New Strategists," *Business Week*, August 26, 1996, p. 50.

11 Merissa Marr, "Disney Cuts Strategic-Planning Unit," *The Wall Street Journal*, March 28, 2005, p. A3.

exhibit 4-4 Seven Steps to the Next Big Idea through Crowdcasting

How the Innovation Challenge is Helping Companies to Develop New Strategies

1. *Team formation:* MBA students join teams that have three to five members each.
2. *Challenge sent:* Each team receives a carefully crafted strategic challenge.
3. *Conference call:* Team discusses their challenge with executives of participating companies.
4. *Brainstorming:* Teams have nine days to draft concept plans to solve the challenge.
5. *Ideas submitted:* A group of judges reviews the teams' concept plans outline.
6. *Final round:* Finalists present their plans at a two-day session at the University of Virginia.
7. *Winner named:* The team gets $20,000; the companies get rights to the team's ideas.

Source: Melanie Haiken, "Turning In to Crowdcasting," *Business 2.0,* November 2006, p. 68.

that Krispy Kreme regards e-commerce as the wave of the future, and therefore halts its plans to vend its donuts through stores of its own and in grocery stores and service stations. Instead, Krispy Kreme develops Web sites so people can purchase donuts and coffee online, and pay for quick delivery service. The wrong assumption is that potential Krispy Kreme customers throughout the world own computers, are online, and have credit cards, and will pay a premium to have donuts and coffee delivered to their home or office. The e-tailing strategy fails because assumptions about the potential customer base were flawed.

The general point here is that firms must constantly change in order to be aligned with their key environments.[12] Sometimes management can shape the nature of the business to match the external environment, such as Harley-Davidson crafting motorcycles that its aging customer base can continue to drive. (What about motorcycle tricycles such as the police vehicles with a side-car?) The assumption Harley would be making here is that motorcyclists want to continue driving motor cycles as late in life as possible.

Accurately analyzing the environment in terms of understanding customers, potential customers, production capability, and the relevant technology is a time-consuming and comprehensive activity. Yet for strategy to work well, the manager has to understand both the external environment and the capabilities of the firm, as already implied from the basic planning model. Exhibit 4-5 presents a series of questions the strategist is supposed to answer to accurately size up the environment. Finding valid answers to these questions will often require considerable interviewing, including interviewing groups of consumers, and information gathering.

SWOT analysis A method of considering the strengths, weaknesses, opportunities, and threats in a given situation.

Performing a SWOT Analysis

Quite often strategic planning takes the form of a **SWOT analysis**, a method of considering the strengths, weaknesses, opportunities, and threats in a given situation. The strengths and weaknesses take into account internal resources

12 Bob De Wit and Ron Meyer, *Strategy Synthesis: Resolving Strategy Paradoxes to Create Competitive Advantage* (London, UK: Thomson Learning, 2005).

exhibit 4-5 **A Strategic Inventory**

The purpose of the *strategic inventory* is to help a manager relate ideas about strategy to his or her own organization. By finding answers to these questions, the manager is likely to do a better job of sizing up the competition, the customers, and the technology necessary to compete effectively. The manager will often need the assistance of others in finding answers to these challenging questions.

Defining the Boundaries of the Competitive Environment

- What are the boundaries of our industry? What market do we serve? What products or services do we provide?
- Who are our customers? Who has chosen not to buy from us? What is the difference between these two groups?
- Who are our competitors? Which firms do not compete with us? What makes one firm a competitor and not the other?

Defining the Key Assumptions Made About the Environment, Customers, Competition, and the Capabilities of the Firm

- Who is our customer? What product or service features are important to that customer? How does the customer perceive us? What kind of relationship do we have with the customer?
- Who are our competitors? What are their strengths and weaknesses? How do they perceive us? What can we learn from our competitors?
- Who are our potential competitors? New entrants? What changes in the environment or their behavior would make them competitors?
- What is the industry's value chain (points along the way in which value is added)? Where is value added? What is the industry's cost structure? How does our firm compare? How about the cost structure of our competitors?
- What technologies are important in our industry? Product technologies? Delivery and service technologies? How does our firm compare? How about our competitors?
- What are the key factors of production? Who are the suppliers? Do we rely on just a few suppliers and sources? How critical are these relationships to our success? How solid are these relationships?
- What are the bases for competition in our industry? What are the key success factors? How do we measure up on these success factors? How do our competitors measure up?
- What trends and factors in the external environment are important in our industry? How are they likely to change? What is likely to be the time period for the changes?
- Are we able, in assessing our knowledge and assumptions, to clearly separate fact from assumption?
- Which of the preceding assumptions are the most important in terms of the impact on our business?

Examining the Process for Reviewing and Validating Our Key Assumptions and Premises

- Do we have a process already established? Have responsibilities been assigned? Are periodic reviews planned and scheduled?

Source: Adapted from Joseph C. Picken and Gregory G. Dess, "Right Strategy—Wrong Problem," *Organizational Dynamics*, Summer 1998, p. 47.

and capabilities, whereas opportunities and threats refer to factors external to the organization. SWOT is considered the most applicable to the early stages of strategic and marketing planning. Elements of a SWOT analysis are included in the general planning model, and in using the strategic inventory to size up the environment. Given SWOT's straightforward appeal, it has become a popular framework for strategic planning. The framework, or technique, can identify a niche the company has not already exploited.

Preparing for the Analysis Four steps are recommended to bring about a successful SWOT analysis.[13] First, it is important to be clear about what you

13 "Performing a SWOT Analysis," in *Business: The Ultimate Resource* (Cambridge, MA: Perseus Publishing, 2002), pp. 468–469.

are doing and why. The purpose might be to fine-tune a present strategy or to point the business in a new direction. Second, it is important to select appropriate contributors. Select people with appropriate experience, talent, and enthusiasm. Imaginative people are particularly useful for a SWOT analysis. Usually six to ten people are enough, but involving more people can be helpful to get more people involved in the changes that SWOT might trigger. Third, allocate research and information-gathering tasks. Several members of the team might concentrate on analyzing the firm, whereas others might concentrate on analyzing the outside environment. Step four is to create a workshop environment by encouraging open communication among participants. All present should feel free to criticize the status quo, even questioning what most people think is a company strength. A SWOT team member of a group at Starbucks might say, "Is having so many stores such a great strength? Could we be losing out to the coffee lovers who want a more unique, intimate experience?"

Conducting the Analysis

To illustrate the use of the model, we turn to Ulysse Nardin, a Swiss manufacturer of fine watches founded in 1846. The price range of Ulysse Nardin watches is between \$7,000 and \$25,000. Assume that top executives at Ulysse Nardin are thinking about finding another niche by manufacturing luxury pens in the \$200 to \$500 range. Some of their thinking in regard to a SWOT analysis might proceed as follows:

Strengths. *What are the good points about a particular alternative? Use your judgment and intuition; ask knowledgeable people.* Selling luxury pens appears to be a reasonable fit with the watch line because a luxury pen is often worn as jewelry. We are great at making small-size luxury items. People who just want a writing instrument could settle for a Bic or competitive brand. The profit margins on luxury pens are quite good, and they are not likely to be deeply discounted in department stores or discount stores. We can also maintain low inventories until we assess the true demand. As our sales representatives and distributors receive orders, we can manufacture the pens quickly. Our beautiful Web site, http://www.ulysse-nardin.com, could easily incorporate a line of luxury pens.

Weaknesses. *Consider the risks of pursuing a particular course of action, such as getting into a business you do not understand.* We are watchmakers, pure and simple. We would need to train our skilled craftspeople to make watches, or hire new workers. If only a handful of companies manufacture luxury pens, it could be because it is a tough market to crack. We are so well known for watches, that our clientele might not perceive us to be a crafter of fountain pens. (We will need to do some market research here.) Another risk is that we will cheapen the Ulysse Nardin name. The average price of a Ulysse Nardin product is now about \$11,000. With a brand of luxury pens, a person could take home a Ulysse Nardin brand product for about \$400, which could result in a scaling down of our image. Another problem is that we are not presently linked to all the distribution channels that sell luxury pens, such as office supply stores. We might have to rely on new distributors to get us into that channel.

Opportunities. *Think of the opportunities that welcome you if you choose a promising strategic alternative. Use your imagination and visualize the opportunities.* The opportunities could be quite good in terms of snob appeal. Maybe large numbers of consumers would welcome the opportunity to carry a Ulysse Nardin anything in their shirt pocket, handbag, or attaché case. Many of the people who become Ulysse Nardin luxury pen customers might want to take a step up to become a Ulysse Nardin watch owner.

Threats. *Every alternative has its downside, so think ahead to allow for contingency planning. Ask people who have tried in the past what you are attempting now. But don't be dissuaded by the naysayers, heel draggers, and pessimists. Just take action.* Several manufacturers of high-end products in jewelry, clothing, and automobiles have cheapened their image and lost market share when they spread their brand name too thin. Following this approach, we could wind up having Ulysse Nardin pens, wallets, and handbags. At that point the high prestige of the Ulysse Nardin brand would be at risk.

As a result of this SWOT analysis, Ulysse Nardin sticks to its knitting (or watch making) and continues to make world-class watches. Do you think they are making the right decision? Or do you think the brand equity (value of the brand name) warrants putting the Ulysse Nardin label on another product?

A caution about the SWOT analysis is that it is sometimes viewed as too superficial, and may rely on description instead of analysis and ignores prioritizing the alternatives it generates.

Levels of Strategy, Competitive Forces, and Types of Strategies

Learning Objective 4

Identify levels of business strategy, competitive forces, and types of business strategies.

The nature of strategy and how it is developed may appear complex. Yet strategy statements themselves, as expressed by managers and planners, are usually straightforward and expressed in a few words, such as "We will be cost leaders," or "We will be competitive by offering superior service." Keep in mind that businesspeople are likely to have a less precise and less scientific meaning of strategy than do strategy researchers. A variety of business strategies have already been mentioned in this chapter. Here we look at levels, competitive forces, and types of business strategies.

Levels of Business Strategies

A strategy chosen to reach an important goal depends considerably on the level of the organization. At the level of the overall firm, Amazon.com might decide that its strategy is to allow people throughout the world to purchase as many products online as they wish. Yet at the level of the distribution centers, the managers must develop a strategy for enabling world-wide distribution of products at a reasonable cost. Exhibit 4-6 provides a few details about strategy levels.

Two major concerns of *corporate-level strategy* are the total direction of the enterprise, and the selection of specific businesses. Usually the total

exhibit 4-6 Strategy Levels for Diversified and Single-Business Firms

Diversified Business Firms	*Single-Business Firms*
Corporate-Level Strategy What direction do we pursue for the total enterprise? Which businesses should be we enter?	**Corporate-Level Strategy** Which business should we be in? How do we compete within the market we have chosen?
Business-Level Strategy How do we compete within each of the businesses we have chosen?	**Functional-Level Strategy** How can each function best support each of our businesses? How do we get the various functions working together smoothly?
Functional-Level Strategy How can each function best support each of our businesses? How do we get the various functions working together smoothly?	

direction of the enterprise begins with the founding of the company such as the Boeing Co. being founded as an aerospace company. Later, a variety of businesses may emerge, such as the company forming a commercial division, a military division, and a service division. Executives in large, diversified firms invest considerable time in deciding which businesses to enter such as Yahoo! moving into various types of entertainment.

The *business-level strategy* focuses on the question of how to compete in each of our businesses. Several of these strategies will be mentioned in the next section.

Functional-level strategies are formulated to specify actions required to successfully implement strategies at the corporate and business level. An example is that a corporate-level strategy of Google is to be a leading innovator in any business it enters. The human resources function must then assist in attracting, selecting, and retaining imaginative workers. Fit among the various functions is another major consideration. For example, if the human resources department at Google recruits imaginative workers, these workers must be placed in functions such as marketing and finance that provide these people with stimulating work.

Under ideal circumstances, the activities of managers and other workers at the functional level support the business-level and corporate-level strategies. For example, if top-level management wants the firm to be world recognized for its quality products and services (such as IBM), business units would not engage in such businesses as selling refurbished personal computers. At the functional level, all IBM departments would hire talented people who can help deliver quality goods and services.

Five Competitive Forces

Before choosing the most appropriate strategy or strategies for the business, it is helpful to examine the relevant competitive forces. Michael E. Porter studied many business firms, leading him to conclude that business-level strategies are the result of five competitive forces in the company's environment.[14] The same five forces can also influence enterprise-level strategy. For example, strategists at PepsiCo might say, "Why bother going into the wine business? The market is already flooded." The competitive forces the organization has to take into account are as follows:

1. *The power of customers to affect pricing and reduce profit margins.* Informed customers become empowered customers. If customers can readily purchase your produce to service from a competitor, you need to keep costs low. A telecommunications company, for example, might shop worldwide for the least expensive fiber-optic cables.
2. *The power of suppliers to influence the company's pricing.* Manufacturing companies are dependent on suppliers for raw materials and components. With the growth of outsourcing, companies are sometimes dependent on suppliers for marketing, research and development, and even staffing. High-price suppliers could drive up costs, forcing a company to think of better ways of attracting customers other than low prices.
3. *The threat of similar or substitute products to limit market freedom and reduce prices and thus profits.* Alternatives to a company's products are a constant menace even for stable products and services. The Internet has accelerated the power of this competitive force, in such ways as people purchasing investments online, thus decreasing the perceived need for personal advice from a stockbroker. The in-person travel agency business has been severely reduced because of online travel agencies and direct purchases of airplane tickets and hotel rooms.
4. *The level of existing competition that impacts on investment in marketing and research and thus erodes profits.* As every shopper knows, the greater the competition the lower the price. A few years ago Wal-Mart priced over 300 generic drugs at $4 per prescription in 14 states. Within a couple of weeks many supermarkets and pharmacy chains followed suit, lowering profits for all.

---

14 Michael E. Porter, "Strategy and the Internet," *Harvard Business Review*, March 2001, pp. 63–78; Porter, "What Is Strategy?" *Business: The Ultimate Resource* (Cambridge, MA: Perseus Publishing, 2002), pp. 1038–1039.

5. *The threat of new market entrants to intensify competition and further impact on pricing and profitability.* Some businesses are more difficult to enter than others, often depending on the amount of investment and time required both in your own country and elsewhere. Relatively few new tire manufacturers emerge, but new online shopping sites emerge daily. Complexity and bigness tend to lower the competitive threat of new entrants. Yet the existence of even great enterprises like Ford Motor has been threatened by companies like Toyota and Kia.

Types of Business Strategies

Companies use a variety of strategies to survive and prosper, and these strategies have been classified in several ways. For convenience in integrating our discussion of strategy, we present eight types of strategy placed under the level in which they most nearly fit. Managers tend to think in terms of the strategy type rather than worrying about the type or which competitive force it best meets.

Corporate-Level Strategies Three examples of corporate-level strategies are strategic alliances, diversification, and sticking to core competencies.

1. *Strategic alliances.* A widely used business strategy is to form alliances, or share resources, with other companies to exploit a market opportunity. A major factor contributing to the growth of alliances is the enormous costs and time involved in developing and distributing products if a company starts from zero. According to the consultancy Booz-Allen & Hamilton, strategic alliances are sweeping through nearly every industry and are a driver of superior growth.[15] Apple and Nike formed an alliance, or partnership, with their first joint product being an iPod gizmo to put more rhythm into running: the Nike + iPod Sports Kit. The wireless kit enables Nike's Air Zoom Moire shoes to send fitness data to the runner's iPod Nano via a sensor tucked inside the running shoe and a small receiver that attaches to the Nano. As you run, the sensor records your distance, time, pace, and calories burned, displaying the data on the Nano.[16] Neither company could develop this breathtaking high-tech product working alone.
2. *Diversification of goods and services.* "Don't put all your eggs in one basket" is a standard business strategy. One of the many reasons that diversification is an effective strategy is that it serves as a hedge in case the market for one group of products or services softens. In recent years about three-fourths of GM's profitability has stemmed from lending money, not selling vehicles. The General Motors Acceptance Corporation, GM's lending division, earns most of the company's profits. Curiously, one-half of the profits from loaning money comes from home mortgages processed through Ditech.com, the online mortgage subsidiary.[17]

---

15 "Strategic Alliances," *Small Business Notes* (http://www.smallbusinessnotes.com), October 3, 2006.

16 Edward C. Gaig, "Apple, Nike Exercise iPods to Track Workouts," *USA Today* syndicated story, May 20, 2006.

17 David Welch, "For GM, Mortgages are the Motor," *Business Week*, August 4, 2003, p. 36; David Henry, "Corporate America's New Achilles' Heel," *Business Week*, March 28, 2005.

3. *Sticking to core competencies.* It may be valuable not only to not put all your eggs in one basket, but also to guard against spreading yourself too thin. Many firms of all sizes believe they will prosper if they confine their efforts to business activities they perform best—their core competencies. A current trend is for companies that have diversified to later sell off acquired assets in order to refocus on their core business. For instance, Xerox Corporation sold its European business that financed large purchases, which enabled Xerox to concentrate on selling document and digital products and services. (Xerox also needed the cash from the sale to pay off debt.) Divesting itself of divisions not related to its core business of telecommunications helped Xerox climb back to prosperity and vitality. A newer example is that Ford Motor Co. has sold to sell the Aston Martin line of cars (the vehicle preferred by James Bond) from its Premier Automotive Group. The major purpose was to free time and talent to concentrate on the problems affecting the company's core Ford, Lincoln, and Mercury brands.[18]

Business-Level Strategies Three examples of business-level strategies are product differentiation, focus and cost leadership.

1. *Product Differentiation.* A differentiation strategy attempts to find a niche or offer a product or service perceived by the customer as different from available alternatives. Most companies believe they have a differentiated product unless their strategy is to imitate another product or service, or produce *knock off* merchandise. Luxury brands often stem from a differentiation strategy. An example of a low-price luxury brand that has honed a differentiation strategy is Etón Corporation of Palo Alto, California. The etón® AM/FM/Shortwave radio retails for about $100, and offers the remarkable feature of receiving AM and FM stations from several hundred miles away. The radio is advertised in such elite places as *The Wall Street Journal.* The radios are also advertised under the Grundig brand, and the corporate Web site (http://www.etoncorp.com) has a differentiated, exciting appeal.

   An extension of the product differentiation strategy is to create a new market in which competition does not exist, referred to as a *blue ocean strategy.* A prime example is Cirque du Soleil that increased revenue 22-fold in a ten-year period by reinventing the circus with extravagant shows that combine several forms of entertainment at once. The 1984 Chrysler minivan that created a new class of automobile is another example of blue ocean strategy.[19]

2. *Focus.* In a focus strategy, the organization concentrates on a specific regional or buyer market. To gain market share, the company uses either a differentiation or a low-cost approach in a targeted market. Some companies have several products or services catering to a buyer market, such as vitamins for seniors, but it does not constitute a full focus strategy. Specialized medical products, such as leg and arm prostheses, are based on

---

18 John O'Dell, "For Sale: Ford's Aston Martin," *The Los Angeles Times* (http://www.latimes.com) September 1, 2006.
19 W. Chan Kim and Renée Mauborgne, "Blue Ocean Strategy," *Harvard Business Review*, October 2004, pp. 76–84.

a focus or niche strategy. Payday-loan stores are based on a focus strategy. Typically these stores, such as Advance America, focus on the working poor who live paycheck to paycheck. Yet in recent years, these payday-loan stores have developed a presence in some affluent neighborhoods. So the real focus of pay day-loan stores is people in financial need, and perhaps have already used up their credit or have poor credit. Check Into Cash opened a store in an Aurora, Colorado neighborhood with an annual median income of $95,347.[20]

3. *Cost leadership.* The cost leader provides a product or service at a low price in order to gain market share. Wal-Mart is a master at cost leadership because the company's massive buying power enables it to receive huge price concessions from suppliers. Save-A-Lot has become one of the United States's most successful grocery chains by serving a demographic that most supermarkets have long ignored—the poor. The Earth City, Mo. chain is covering the country with small, cheap stores catering to households earning less than $35,000 a year. Many Save-A-Lot stores are located in poor sections of the inner city, and offer prices lower than those of Wal-Mart.[21] Note that Save-A-Lot uses the focus and cost leadership strategy simultaneously, illustrating the point that business strategies overlap somewhat.

Southwest Airlines is another well-known company that emphasizes cost leadership. In addition to the low-cost maneuvers mentioned earlier in this chapter, the company uses one aircraft type to simplify training and maintenance. Also, you will not find such luxuries as a Southwest airport club. A cost leadership strategy can create ethical problems because of what suppliers must do to cut costs, such as having goods manufactured at sweatshops.

Functional-Level Strategy Two examples of functional-level strategy are finding and retaining the best people, and high speed.

1. *Find and retain the best people.* A foundation strategy for becoming and remaining a successful organization is to find and retain highly competent people. Such people will help the organization develop products and services that are in demand, and will find ways to reduce costs and behave ethically. Concentrating on hiring talent can be considered a functional-level strategy because people are usually hired into specific departments. Top management at Microsoft and Amazon.com attribute most of their success to hiring only intelligent, motivated job candidates. Fast Company magazine offers this advice to modern business executives.

> *Yes, you need an Internet strategy. Sure, you've got to stay on the good side of Wall Street. But when it comes to building great companies, the most urgent business charge is finding and keeping great people. In an economy driven by ideas and charged by the Web, brainpower is the real source of competitive advantage.*[22]

---

20 Andy Vuong, "Quick Cash Lenders Fill Rich Niche," *The Denver Post* (http://www.denverpost.com), September 25, 2005.
21 Janet Adamy, "To Find Growth, No-Frills Grocer Goes Where Other Chains Won't," August 30, 2005, *The Wall Street Journal* p. A1.
22 Bill Breen and Anna Mudio, "Peoplepalooza," *Fast Company*, January 2001, pp. 80–81.

2. *High speed.* Satisfy customer needs more quickly and you will make more money. High-speed managers focus on speed in all of their business activities, including speed in product development, sales response, and customer service. Knowing that "time is money," they choose to use time as a competitive resource. It is important to get products to market quickly because the competition might get there first. Part of Domino's Pizza's original success was based on getting pizzas delivered more quickly than competitors. The strategy had to be modified slightly when too many deliverers sacrificed auto safety to enhance delivery speed. Dell Computer relies on high speed as part of its strategy. A custom order placed at 9 a.m. Wednesday can *often* be on a delivery truck by 9 p.m. on Thursday. Not every customer has the same good fortune. Porter notes that speed is not good for its own sake. The effectiveness of speed depends on what the speed allows you to do that creates lower cost or differentiation. In Dell's case, the rapid delivery facilitates not keeping loads of products in inventory, and appeals to users who want equipment in a hurry.[23]

So now that you are a top executive, or an advisor to a top executive, which combination of strategies should you choose to triumph? Strategies must be selected carefully, and given a chance to work. When a strategy is agreed upon, it must be executed carefully. Jumping from strategy to strategy in the hopes of revitalizing a company has been cited as a major reason why companies fail. For example, a reason cited for the struggles of Gateway is that it attempted so many different business plans and strategies including direct sales, Gateway Country Stores, Internet access, the sale of branded electronic devices, and a merger with eMachines. Gateway still operates but became part of Acer Computer in 2007. Interim CEO Rick Snyder said, "We took a simple business and made it more complex than it needed to be."[24]

The accompanying Management in Action illustrates how one of the world's best-known companies has successfully developed and executed business strategy.

management in action

Pepsi Thinks Outside the Cola Wars

One November evening, Pepsi CEO Steve Reinemund laid out a smorgasbord of snacks for his board of directors to munch on. This was not gentlemanly hospitality; it was pure business. These snacks represented Pepsi's future: a line of products aimed at cashing in on consumers' continuing obsession with healthy food. If all goes well, the line will bring in billions for the company. According to one board member, the treats were "delightful." But more than just the future of Pepsi, this spread in many ways represents everything the company has done right for nearly a decade: finding new ways into people's stomachs—and wallets—and pulling off one of the great turnarounds in American business.

23 Cited in Nicholas Argyres and Anita M. McGahan, "Introduction: Michael Porter's," *Competitive Strategy, Academy of Management Executive*, May 2002, p. 47.

24 Robert Levine, "The Cow in Winter," *Fortune*, April 17, 2006, p. 55.

In December 2005, for the first time in this 108-year rivalry, Pepsi beat Coke in market capitalization. "Pepsi's been on fire," notes Robert van Brugge, beverage analyst with Sanford Bernstein. Part of Pepsi's progress in the food and beverage business is due to the rigor and competitiveness of CEO Reinemund. "Steve's an ex-Marine, and everything you would associate with that pertains," says Ken Harris, a consultant who has worked with Reinemund at PepsiCo.

"You'll leave a meeting knowing exactly what is expected of you and the time frame in which it should be done." Reinemund has put together one of the strongest management teams around, including president and CFO Indra Nooyi, and is a hands-on manager who's been known to personally make sales calls to help Pepsi win a contract. One Christmas Eve a few years back, while on vacation with his family, he found himself at a convenience store just as a Frito-Lay delivery arrived to replenish the shelves; he pushed aside his purchases and helped pack chips.

Nooyi worked so closely and so well with Reinemund that she was appointed chief executive officer in August 2006, when Reinemund decided to leave executive life and spend more time with his family. Nooyi said she felt fortunate to become CEO at a time when PepsiCo had such solid growth across all business units. Reinemund said, "I can't tell you how excited I am to pass the baton to Indra."

Pepsi's resurgence is not considered to be an accident. A decade ago Coke offered investors a compelling story: a recession-resistant product inexpensive enough that consumers would buy it in good times and bad, but valued enough that they would willingly pay an extra nickel or so above what no-name brands charged. What Coke investors didn't envision was that an emerging preference for other soft beverages—water, sports drinks—would fracture demand. By 2007, however, Coke was moving rapidly into non-carbonated beverages, as exemplified by two key purchases: Energy Brands which produces vitamin-enhanced water, and Fuze Beverage LLC, a producer of energy, tea, and vitamin-enhanced drinks.

Losing the cola wars, it turns out, was the best thing that ever happened to Pepsi. It prompted Pepsi's leaders to look outside the confines of their battle with Coke. "They were the first to recognize that the consumer was moving to noncarbonated products, and they innovated aggressively," observes Gary Hemphill of Beverage Marketing. PepsiCo embraced bottled water and sports drinks much earlier than its rival. Pepsi's Aquafina is the No. 1 water brand, with Coke's Dasani trailing; in sports drinks, Pepsi's Gatorade owns 80 percent of the market while Coke's Powerade has 15 percent.

Throughout the past five years the company has deftly moved with every shift in consumer tastes. "He's thinking about what the products should look like in the future," says Victor Dzau, a director of PepsiCo. For example, as COO in 2000, Reinemund had a hand in Pepsi's acquisition of Sobe, buying the company a critical foothold in an emerging category of New Age drinks—the business now pulls in an estimated $200 million a year. Through its partnership with Starbucks, PepsiCo now dominates the bottled-coffee market, with annual sales of over $300 million of Frappuccinos.

But Pepsi's strongest business lies outside drinks altogether. Over the past ten years, the Frito-Lay division has become a powerhouse, controlling 60 percent of the U.S. snack food market. So strong is Pepsi in this arena that many investors no longer judge it by how it stacks up against Coke. "Most people think of Pepsi and Coke as fighting it out," observes Eric Schoenstein, an analyst at Jensen Investment Management. "But we don't see it that way. Pepsi isn't really a beverage company anymore: It's a food company that also sells beverages." The company now boasts 16 brands that bring in more than $1 billion each year in revenue.

Questions

1. Why might this story about PepsiCo be considered an example of business strategy?
2. Which business strategy or strategies are illustrated in this story about PepsiCo?

Source: Katrina Brooker, "The Pepsi Machine," *Fortune*, February 6, 2006, pp. 68–72.; Vinnee Tong, "Woman Will Lead PepsiCo: Nooyi to be No. 2 Female CEO in Fortune 500," The Associated Press, August 15, 2006.

OPERATING PLANS, POLICIES, PROCEDURES, AND RULES

Learning Objective 5

Explain the use of operating plans, policies, procedures, and rules.

Strategic plans are formulated at the top of the organization. Four of the vehicles through which strategic plans are converted into action are operating plans, policies, procedures, and rules.

Operating Plans

Operating plans are the means through which strategic plans alter the destiny of the firm. Operating plans involve organizational efficiency (doing things right), whereas strategic plans involve effectiveness (doing the right things). Both strategic and operational plans involve such things as exploring alternatives and evaluating the effectiveness of the plan. In a well-planned organization, all managers take responsibility for making operating plans that mesh with the strategic plans of the business. Operational plans (a term used synonymously with operating plans) provide the details of how strategic plans will be accomplished. In many firms, suggestions to be incorporated into operating plans stem from employees at lower levels.

Operating plans focus more on the firm than on the external environment. To illustrate, the strategic plan of a local government might be to encourage the private sector to take over government functions. One operating unit within the local government might then formulate a plan for subcontracting refuse removal to private contractors and phasing out positions for civil-service sanitation workers.

Operating plans tend to be drawn for a shorter period than strategic plans. The plan for increasing the private sector's involvement in activities conducted by the local government might be a ten-year plan. In contrast, the phasing out of government sanitation workers might take two years.

Policies

Policies are general guidelines to follow in making decisions and taking action; as such, they are plans. Many policies are written; some are unwritten, or implied. Policies, designed to be consistent with strategic plans, must allow room for interpretation by the individual manager. An important managerial role is interpreting policies for employees. Here is an example of a policy and an analysis of how it might require interpretations.

> *Policy: When hiring employees from the outside, consider only those candidates who are technically competent or show promise of becoming technically competent and who show good personal character and motivation.*

A manager attempting to implement this policy with respect to a given job candidate would have to ask the following questions:

- What do we mean by "technical competence"?
- How do I measure technical competence?
- What do we mean by "show promise of becoming technically competent"?

operating plans
The means through which strategic plans alter the destiny of the firm.

policies
General guidelines to follow in making decisions and taking action.

procedures
A customary method for handling an activity. It guides action rather than thinking.

rule
A specific course of action or conduct that must be followed. It is the simplest type of plan.

- How do I rate the promise of technical competence?
- What do we mean by "good personal character and motivation"?
- How do I assess good personal character and motivation?

Policies are developed to support strategic plans in every area of the firm. Many firms have strict policies against employees accepting gifts and favors from vendors or potential vendors. For example, many schools endorse the Code of Ethics and Principles advocated by the National Association of Educational Buyers. One of the specific policies states that buyers should "decline personal gifts or gratuities which might in any way influence the purchase of materials."

Procedures

Procedures are considered plans because they establish a customary method of handling future activities. They guide action rather than thinking, in that they state the specific manner in which a certain activity must be accomplished. Procedures exist at every level in the organization, but they tend to be more complex and specific at lower levels. For instance, strict procedures may apply to the handling of checks by store associates. The procedures for check handling by managers may be much less strict.

Rules

A **rule** is a specific course of action or conduct that must be followed; it is the simplest type of plan. Ideally, each rule fits a strategic plan. In practice, however, many rules are not related to organizational strategy. When rules are violated, corrective action should be taken. Two examples of rules follow:

- Any employee engaged in an accident while in a company vehicle must report that accident immediately to his or her supervisor.
- No employee is authorized to use company photocopying machines for personal use, even if he or she reimburses the company for the cost of the copies.

MANAGEMENT BY OBJECTIVES: A SYSTEM OF PLANNING AND REVIEW

Learning objective 6
Present an overview of management by objectives.

Management by objectives (MBO) is a systematic application of goal setting and planning to help individuals and firms be more productive. The system began in the 1950s, and continues to contribute to organizational effectiveness. An MBO program typically involves people setting many objectives for themselves. However, management frequently imposes key organizational objectives upon people. An MBO program usually involves sequential steps, which are cited in the following list. (Note that these steps are related to those in the basic planning model shown in Exhibit 4-1.)

1. *Establishing organizational goals*. Top-level managers set organizational goals to begin the entire MBO process. Quite often these goals are strategic. A group of hospital administrators, for example, might decide upon the strategic goal of improving health care to poor people in the community. After these broad goals are established, managers determine what the organizational units must accomplish to meet these goals.
2. *Establishing unit objectives*. Unit heads then establish objectives for their units. A cascading of objectives takes place as the process moves down the line. Objectives set at lower levels of the firm must be designed to meet the general goals established by top management. Lower-level managers and operatives provide input because a general goal usually leaves considerable latitude for setting individual objectives to meet that goal. The head of inpatient admissions might decide that working more closely with the county welfare department must be accomplished if the health-care goal cited earlier in this list is to be met. Exhibit 4-7 suggests ways to set effective goals.
3. *Reviewing group members' proposals*. At this point, group members make proposals about how they will contribute to unit objectives. For example, the assistant to the manager of inpatient admissions might agree to set up a task force to work with the welfare department. Each team member is also given the opportunity to set objectives in addition to those that meet the strategic goals.
4. *Negotiating or agreeing*. Managers and team members confer together at this stage to either agree on the objectives set by the team members or negotiate further. In the hospital example, one department head might state that he or she wants to reserve ten beds on the ward for the exclusive use of indigent people. The supervisor might welcome the suggestion but point out that only five beds could be spared for such a purpose. They might settle for setting aside seven beds for the needy poor.

management by objectives (MBO) A systematic application of goal setting and planning to help individuals and firms be more productive.

exhibit 4-7 Guide to Establishing Goals and Objectives

Effective goals and objectives have certain characteristics in common. Effective goals and objectives

- **Are clear, concise, and unambiguous.** An example of such an objective is "Reduce damaged boxes of printer paper during April 27 to April 30 of this year."
- **Are accurate in terms of the true end state or condition sought.** An accurate objective might state, "The factory will be as neat and organized as the front office after the cleanup is completed."
- **Are achievable by competent workers.** Goals and objectives should not be so high or rigid that the majority of competent team members become frustrated and stressed by attempting to achieve them.
- **Include three difficulty levels: routine, challenging, and innovative.** Most objectives deal with routine aspects of a job, but they should also challenge workers to loftier goals.
- **Are achieved through team-member participation.** Subordinates should participate actively in setting objectives.
- **Relate to small chunks of accomplishment.** Many objectives should concern small, achievable activities, such as un-cluttering a work area. Accomplishing small objectives is the building block for achieving larger goals.
- **Specify what is going to be accomplished, who is going to accomplish it, when it is going to be accomplished, and how it is going to be accomplished.** Answering the what, who, when, and how questions reduces the chance for misinterpretation.

5. *Creating action plans to achieve objectives.* After the manager and team members agree upon objectives, action plans must be defined. Sometimes the action plan is self-evident. For example, if your objective as a call-center manager is to hire three new customer service representatives this year, you would begin by consulting with the human resources department.
6. *Reviewing performance.* Performance reviews are conducted at agreed-upon intervals. (A semiannual or annual review is typical.) Persons receive good performance reviews as to the extent they attain most of the major objectives. When objectives are not attain, the manager and group member mutually analyze what went wrong. Equally important, they discuss the corrective actions. New objectives are then set for the next review period. Because establishing new objectives is part of an MBO program, the process of management by objectives can continue for the life of an organization.

SUMMARY OF Key Points

1 Summarize a general framework for planning and apply it to enhance your planning skills.

A generalized planning model can be used for strategic planning, tactical planning, and operational planning. The model consists of seven related and sometimes overlapping elements: defining the present situation; establishing goals and objectives; analyzing the environment in terms of forecasting aids and barriers to goals and objectives; developing action plans; developing budgets; implementing the plan; and controlling the plan. Contingency plans should also be developed.

2 Describe the nature of business strategy.

A current explanation of business strategy emphasizes four characteristics. First, strategy involves more than operational effectiveness. Second, strategy rests on unique activities. Third, a sustainable strategic position requires trade-offs. Fourth, fit among organizational activities drives both competitive advantage and sustainability.

3 Explain how business strategy is developed, including a SWOT analysis.

Business strategy usually develops from planning, and is also influenced by values. Gathering multiple inputs, including the new technique of crowdcasting, is important in developing strategy. Strategists must also analyze the realities of the business situation to guard against false assumptions about customers, production capability, and the relevant technology. Strategy development often begins with a SWOT analysis, but first the group must prepare for the analysis. The SWOT analysis considers the strengths, weaknesses, opportunities, and threats in a given situation.

4 Identify levels of business strategy, competitive forces, and types of business strategies.

In a diversified business firm, strategy is formulated at the corporate level, the business level, and the functional level. Competitive forces facing the firm include customers affecting pricing, suppliers influencing pricing, substitute products, existing competition, and new market entrants. Types of strategies are s follows: Corporate-level strategies include diversification, strategic alliances, diversification of goods and services, and sticking to core competencies. Business-level strategies include product differentiation, focus, and cost leadership. Functional-level strategies include find and retain the best people, and high speed. The right strategy or combination of strategies must be chosen with care.

5 Explain the use of operating plans, policies, procedures, and rules.

Operating plans provide the details of how strategic plans will be accomplished or implemented. They deal with a shorter time span than do strategic plans. Policies are plans set in the form of general statements that guide thinking and action in decision making. Procedures establish a customary method of handling future activities. A rule sets a specific course of action or conduct and is the simplest type of plan.

6 Present an overview of management by objectives.

Management by objectives (MBO) is the most widely used formal system of goal setting, planning, and review. In general, it has six elements: establishing organizational goals, establishing unit objectives, obtaining proposals from group members about their objectives, negotiating or agreeing to proposals, developing action plans, and reviewing performance. After objectives are set, the manager must give feedback to team members on their progress toward reaching the objectives.

KEY TERMS AND PHRASES

Strategic planning, 114
Tactical planning, 114
Operational planning, 115
Action plan, 117
Contingency plan, 118
Strategy, 119
Vision, 122
Mission, 122
SWOT analysis, 124
Operating plans, 135
Policies, 135
Procedures, 136
Rule, 136
Management by objectives (MBO), 137

QUESTIONS

1. In what way does planning control the future?
2. How can you use the information in this chapter to help you achieve your career and personal goals?
3. Some business owners make a statement something to the effect, "We're too busy to bother with strategy. We have to take care of the present." What might be wrong with their reasoning?
4. How realistic is Microsoft's mission (or vision)? "To enable people and businesses throughout the world to realize their full potential."
5. Why are companies willing to spend up to $50,000 for business students to propose solutions to their strategic dilemmas? Shouldn't the company be relying on experienced business people?
6. Using the information presented in Exhibit 4-7 as a guide, prepare an effective goal for a call-center customer-service worker who is responsible for resolving call-in problems about digital cameras.
7. Give an example of how a rule could fit the corporate strategy of cost leadership.

SKILL-BUILDING EXERCISE 4-A: Conducting a SWOT Analysis

In this chapter you have read the basics of conducting a SWOT analysis. Now gather in small groups to conduct one. Develop a scenario for a SWOT analysis, such as the group starting a chain of coffee shops, pet-care service centers, or treatment centers for online addictions. Or, conduct a SWOT analysis for reorganizing a company from being mostly hierarchical to one that is mostly team based. Keep in mind one of the biggest challenges in doing a SWOT analysis—differentiate between internal strengths and weaknesses, and external opportunities and threats. Because most of your data are hypothetical, you will have to rely heavily on your imagination. Group leaders might share the results of the SWOT analysis with the rest of the class.

SKILL-BUILDING EXERCISE 4-B: Developing Business Strategy for Coca Cola

Imagine yourself as part of a strategy development team for the Coca Cola Co. You have gathered information indicating that the worldwide demand for carbonated soft drinks has been declining. More and more consumers are moving toward the purchase of specialty beverages such as energy drinks, including Red Bull, and flavored water. According to a *Beverage Digest* sales of non-soda drinks in the United States are rising about 14 percent per year, whereas the soda market is slipping about 2 percent. Coca Cola has diversified into a variety of bottle and canned drinks, as well as water (for example, Dasani). Yet top management is concerned about Coca Cola becoming a less dominant force in the beverage world. Work as part of small team to recommended a business strategy that will help invigorate the company. Your final strategy statement should be about 25 words long, yet powerful enough to add billions of dollars in annual profit to the Coca Cola Co.

INTERNET SKILL-BUILDING EXERCISE: Business Strategy Research

The purpose of this assignment is to find three examples of business strategy by searching the Internet. A good starting point is to obtain information about a company of interest to you by visiting its Web site. After copying down several strategic statements (or transferring them to a storage drive or your hard drive), compare them to the section of this chapter called "Types of Business Strategies." Attempt to match the company statement about its strategy to a type of strategy listed in the chapter. If you cannot find the information you need in the company Web sites, research companies you are curious about by inserting their name in a search engine.

Case Problem 4-A

Zales Jewelers Flops at the High End

Jewelry retailer Zale Corp. named interim chief executive officer Mary "Betsy" Burton to the post permanently and launched a search for a new chief financial officer. Zale's board tapped Burton, a director, as its interim CEO in late January after forcing the resignation of Mary Forté, CEO since 2002. Zale's board made the change following the failure of Forté's campaign to shift the advertising and merchandise at the retailer's flagship Zales Jewelers to appeal to a more upscale and fashion-conscious clientele.

Zale, Irving, Texas, has annual sales of over $2 billion. In the United States it operates under the Zales Jewelers, Zales Outlet, Gordon's Jewelers, Bailey Banks & Biddle and Piercing Pagoda brands. In Canada, its brands are Peoples Jewellers and Mapins Jewellers.

In Burton, Zale gets a CEO with extensive experience on the boards and retailers and in turning around struggling operations. She served as CEO of the hair-salon chain Supercuts Inc. from 1987 to 1991, of a printing concern from 1991 to 1992, and of Revlon Inc.'s 250-store Cosmetic Center Inc. chain from 1998 to 1999. She has served as CEO of two large private ventures: Toysrus.com in 1999 and Tower Records in 2003.

In January of 2005, after a disappointing Christmas season and amid worries about competition from discount retailers, Zale Corp., decided to shake things up: The self-proclaimed jeweler to Middle America was going to chase upscale customers. In a few months, Zale drew up a plan than involved replacing almost a third of the merchandise at its Zales Jewelers division. To dodge a battle with retailers such as Wal-Mart Stores Inc., Zales dropped inexpensive, low-quality diamond jewelry for fashionable 14-karat gold and silver pieces with higher margins. It started buying direct from overseas dealers, cutting out U.S. middlemen, and even dumped a decades-old marketing slogan: "The Diamond Store."

The move was a disaster. 'The Irving, Texas, retailer lost many of its traditional customers without winning the new ones it coveted. A second poor Christmas badly dented the company's annual profits. Within weeks, Forté was forced to resign.

In recent years, discounters such as Wal-Mart and J. C. Penney were grabbing an increasing amount of the jewelry business. At the same time, Internet retailers and TV shopping networks were selling more diamonds and other fine jewelry, encroaching on Zale's turf.

Early in 2005, Forté moved to cultivate a higher-income clientele. "We are in the process of really tearing things apart, now," Forté told Wall Street analysts. She proposed dumping many of the company's $99 diamonds as well as Zale's long-running TV campaign promoting those pieces. Forté also wanted to get rid of promotions on holidays such as Veteran's Day and Columbus Day, when Zales slashed its prices and saw sales soar, albeit at low margins. After sprucing up Zales Jewelers, Forté also began doing the same to Zale's existing upscale divisions. Bailey Banks & Biddle, she thought, could be like Tiffany & Co., say several former employees.

Zale couldn't do much to improve the quality of its diamonds—better gems would cost too much for some of its clientele. Instead, it stopped selling inexpensive diamond pieces, leaving only items that cost more than $200. In total, Zale changed 30 percent of its merchandise and replaced 15 percent of its suppliers.

Burton says, "The big mistake, and how we really broke Zales going into a key holiday season, was changing the product line-up, especially in diamonds. We literally had a broken category going into the all important quarter, the one where you make all your money."

Forté defends her strategy and argues that the company was beginning to work through its problems. "You don't have to go inexpensive to show great value," she says. Forté also claimed that Zales was able to offer better quality jewelry because it had finally started to buy products directly from overseas suppliers. "We were working to improve the business and these things take time," Forté says. "We were starting to hit our stride, but direct sourcing was still new and was just beginning to infiltrate the inventory."

Since taking the reins, Burton, 54 years old, has scrapped Forté's upscale strategy, recast Zales Jewelers' advertising campaign to focus on value rather than fashion and shifted the division's merchandise back to a heavy focus on diamond rings and jewelry. She also overhauled Zale's training and commission programs.

Zale put former chief financial officer Mark Lenz on administrative leave in May 2006 for allegedly failing to

Case Problem 4-A

inform Zale's auditors that roughly $8 million in payments to vendors recorded prior to the end of Zale's fiscal year on July 31, 2006 were actually received by the vendors in August. Zale has since April faced a Securities and Exchange Commission investigation focused on multiple topics, including vendor payments, warranty programs, leases, and executive severance and stock trading.

Discussion Questions

1. What do you think will be the effectiveness of Burton returning Zales Jewelers to its regular business strategy? In your answer, define or categorize that strategy.
2. What should Burton do about the ethical and legal problems facing Zales?
3. Do you think Mary Forté had a good strategy in attempting to move Zales upscale? As part of your answer think of your own experience at Zales, or anybody else who has shopped there.
4. If you were a board member at Zales would you be concerned about the job-hopping of Mary Burton?

Source: Ann Zimmerman and Kris Hudson, "Chasing Upscale Customers Tarnishes Mass-Market Jewelers," *The Wall Street Journal*, June 26, 2006, pp. A1, A12; Kris Hudson and Joann S. Lublin, "Zale Interim CEO, 'Betsy' Burton, Is Permanent Pick," *The Wall Street Journal*, July 24, 2006, p. A12.

Case Problem 4-B

What Should Dell Do Next?

Chris Conroy works at a publisher of scientific journals in Washington, D.C. He first logged onto Dell Inc.'s Web site to browse personal-computer offerings online. But because his laptop was dying quickly, the 31-year-old figured buying a PC on the Internet and getting it shipped home would take too long.

So Conroy went to a Circuit City Stores Inc., which doesn't stock any Dell computers. There, he checked out several laptops before snapping up a $1,200 Hewlett-Packard Co. model. "Most importantly, I could get my hands on it right then, without having to worry about it being shipped," he says.

Conroy's experience signals a fundamental problem facing Dell. For years, Dell—famous for selling products directly over the phone and Internet—was a dynamo thanks to bulk sales to corporations, mostly of desktop computers. Its direct-sales business model made the Round Rock, Texas, company a widely admired paragon of efficiency as it underpriced rivals such as H-P and Gateway, Inc.

But in the past few years, buying behavior in the PC world has changed. Much of the growth has come from consumer demand rather than the business market on which Dell focused. What's more, people looking for a new home computer are increasingly turning to laptops. There Dell is particularly weak (according to some observers): its models lack the pizzazz and features of its rivals. For laptops, especially, consumers prefer to hold and test models in a store, but Dell computers are not sold there. According to the NPD Group, 56 percent of laptops sold to consumers are now bought in stores, up from 50 percent two years ago.

Dell still considers consumers an important market. The company has poured money into corporate products such as printers, storage systems and computer servers. It nixed some overtures from retailers to sell its wares in stores. Yet the company has one retail store to display products (but not sell them), and operates more than 170 kiosks in malls around the country, where consumers can see and order a selection of Dell products.

At the same time, rivals such as H-P, Gateway, and Apple Computer Inc., have charged ahead in the consumer PC market. In particular, H-P cut costs to become competitive with Dell, began working more closely with retailers, and redoubled its marketing efforts. As Dell cut prices, H-P invested in consumer-friendly features on its notebooks. H-P computers, using a laser, can write a label on specially coated music CD with artist and title so users don't have to use a marker.

Early in 2006, Dell expanded more slowly than the overall U.S. PC market for the first time in more than a decade. Consumers make up about 30 percent of H-P's sales, in contrast to 15 percent of Dell sales.

Dell is now scrambling to contain the damage. It has overhauled its Web site and streamlined its pricing, and has introduced a new consumer advertising campaign with the tagline "Purely You." Chief Executive Kevin Rollins calls the consumer business volatile, and says it remains a secondary focus for the company. But privately, has admitted to some mistakes. At a meeting with 50 Dell employees in Round Rock to discuss a change in direction for the company, the CEO conceded that "historically we didn't pay enough attention to our customer experience. Some of our new competitors did."

Some on Wall Street are pushing for founder Michael Dell to take a more hands-on role in the company. Investors applauded Dell's recent acquisition of Miami's Allenware Corp., a maker of high-end videogame PCs. The company has said that deal, which boosted its offerings for consumers, was personally pushed by Mr. Dell.

In 2007, Rollins was released and replaced by Michael Dell. Later that year Dell began selling $700 desktop computers at 3,400 Wal-Mart Stores.

The desktop market began cooling a few years ago as many companies slowed the pace of upgrading their computers. Meanwhile, consumers gravitated to laptops as prices fell and new wireless technology made them more useful at home and on the go. While corporate demand focused on replacing the desktops employees already had, consumers were adding second, third and fourth computers at home as mod, dad, and the kids listened to digital music, shared digital photos and played games. The research firm IDC predicts that by 2010, consumers will likely be buying more laptops than do corporations.

The move to temporary workers at call centers backfired for Dell. Ro Parra, a senior vice president who was asked to look into the problem, discovered that the temporary call-center workers who wanted full-time jobs weren't being promoted. Turnover in the centers soared

Case Problem 4-B

to 300 percent a year from 30 percent in 2002. "We were very efficient, and we made those decisions that work with the short term, but they were really damaging to us over the long term," says Parra.

In late 2004, the profitability of Dell's consumer business began deteriorating. Dell told Wall Street its competitors were cutting prices to gain market share at the expense of profit, and said its focus was the high-end PC consumer. But Dell was also participating in a price war, dropping its prices as low as $299 for desktops.

Dell rolled out some new products to woo consumers. In October 2004, it released its first plasma-screen television sets, a digital music player and a new photo printer with a built-in display to preview photos. But many consumers were wary about buying some of these products sight unseen from a company not known as a consumer electronics maker.

In May 2006, the company pledged $100 million to improve the "customer experience," including hiring more than 2,000 new U.S. sales and support staff. It has since added another $50 million to the effort. Internal Dell data show that its efforts are reducing call volumes and call transfers for customers.

Discussion Questions

1. Identify several business strategies Dell has used so far.
2. Suggest a plan to Dell executives for continuing its past successes into the future.
3. Advise Dell management as to whether they should be so concerned about their recent downturn in sales.
4. What is your opinion of the quality of Dell desktops and laptops based upon what you have observed personally and what people in your network have said.

Source: Christopher Lawton, "Consumer Demand and Growth in Laptops Leave Dell Behind," *The Wall Street Journal*, August 30, 2006, pp. A1, A9.

chapter 5

Problem Solving and Decision Making

Twenty-two-year-old Stewart Beal sees a land of opportunity in the dilapidated buildings in downtown Detroit for his new interior demolition company, Beal Inc. Demolition and construction is in his blood—his company is affiliated with general contractor JC Beal Construction Inc. of Ann Arbor, Michigan, which was founded by his grandfather. That company got out of the interior demolition business in 2001. Beal sees the opportunity to fill this construction niche in Detroit where the trend of renovating old buildings is well underway and several more projects have been proposed.

Much of downtown Detroit is a historic district, and developers can obtain tax credits by meeting government guidelines for restoring historic buildings. "Detroit has the greatest collection of dilapidated old buildings in the country," he said. "That's a minus, but it's also an opportunity." That's one reason why he located the offices of his new company in downtown Detroit. According to a marketing study prepared for the Greater Downtown Partnership two years ago, vacant buildings in downtown Detroit have the potential for 2,000 lofts that should be built at the rate of 300 a year.

Interior demolition usually involves stripping down a building to the support structure, floor decking, and masonry. Beal Inc. has a construction crew of around 20 and can take jobs year round because the work is inside.

Objectives

After studying this chapter and doing the exercises, you should be able to:

1. Differentiate between nonprogrammed and programmed decisions.
2. Explain the steps involved in making a nonprogrammed decision.
3. Understand the major factors that influence decision making in organizations.
4. Appreciate the value and potential limitations of group decision making.
5. Understand the nature of creativity and how it contributes to managerial work.
6. Describe organizational programs for improving creativity and innovation.
7. Implement several suggestions for becoming a more creative problem solver.

Beal has bids out on ten projects and expects more opportunities coming up. He expects some work for JC Beal Construction and is bidding on projects in close-by cities. But he sees the greatest potential for his business in Detroit, especially if he is successful in obtaining the city's designation as a Detroit-based business.[1]

The story about Stewart Beal illustrates an important point about problem solving and decision making. Beal was imaginative enough to recognize that a problem existed—a bunch of old buildings in Detroit were ripe for internal demolition because a demand existed for renovated buildings that could be converted into lofts. The decision he chose to solve the problem was to locate his demolition company downtown so he could obtain more business. This chapter explores how managerial workers solve problems and make decisions individually, and in groups. A **problem** is a discrepancy between ideal and actual conditions. For example, a hospital might have too many beds unoccupied. The ideal would be to have an occupancy rate of 90 percent or greater. A **decision** is choosing among alternatives, such as affiliating with more doctors so as to receive more patient referrals.

problem
A discrepancy between ideal and actual conditions.

decision
A choice among alternatives.

Problem solving and decision making are required to carry out all management functions. For example, when managers control, they must make a series of decisions about how to solve the problem of getting performance back to standard. Decision making can also be seen as the heart of management. A distinguishing characteristic of a manager's job is the authority to make decisions.

NONPROGRAMMED VERSUS PROGRAMMED DECISIONS

Learning Objective 1

Distinguish between nonprogrammed and programmed decisions.

Managerial workers face a variety of decisions. A problem that has not taken the same form as in the past or is extremely complex or significant calls for a **nonprogrammed decision**. A complex problem contains many elements. Significant problems affect an important aspect of an organization such as the introduction of a new service. Virtually all strategic decisions are nonprogrammed. A well-planned and highly structured organization reduces the number of nonprogrammed decisions. It does so by formulating hundreds of policies to help managers know what to do when faced with a given problem. In contrast, many small firms do not offer much guidance about decision making.

nonprogrammed decision
A decision that is difficult because of its complexity and the fact that the person faces it infrequently.

Within the category of nonprogrammed decisions, there are wide variations in complexity.[2] A very complex nonprogrammed decision for a Harley-Davidson executive would be whether to outsource the manufacture of its heavy bikes to South Korea. Dozens of issues would be at stake, including the

1 Eric Pope, "Opportunity Knocks, Demolition Firm Bets," http://detnews.com, February 9, 2006.

2 Donald C. Hambrick, Sydney Finkelstein, and Ann C. Mooney, "Executive Job Demands: New Insights for Explaining Strategic Decisions and Leader Behaviors," *Academy of Management Review*, July 2005, pp. 472–491.

PLAY VIDEO

PROBLEM SOLVING AND DECISION MAKING

Go to academic.cengage.com/management/dubrin and view the video. When an organization is faced with unexpected change, what can managers do to help insure they make the correct choices?

reputation of Harley as a truly American icon, and weighing labor saving versus shipping costs. A less complex nonprogrammed decision would be whether to enlarge a given manufacturing plant in Milwaukee. A complex decision is more demanding than a less complex decision, just as studying some subjects may be more difficult than studying others.

Programmed decisions are repetitive, or routine, and made according to a specific procedure. Procedures specify how to handle these routine, uncomplicated decisions. Here is an example: A person who earns $26,000 per year applies to rent a two-bedroom apartment. The manager makes the decision to refuse the application on the basis of an established rule that families with annual incomes of $39,000 or less may not rent in the building.

Under ideal circumstances, top-level management concerns itself almost exclusively with nonroutine decisions, and lower-level management handles

management in action

Thirteen of the Greatest Management Decisions Ever Made

Many people consider good decision making to be the essence of management. So a business writer for *Management Review* asked experts for their nominations of the 75 greatest decisions ever made. All these decisions were successful and had a major impact. Here we list 11 of these decisions related directly to business rather than to government or religion. For example, we excluded Queen Isabella's decision to sponsor Christopher Columbus's voyage to the new world in 1492. Each decision's rank among 75 is listed in brackets. At the end of the list, we add two of 20 decisions that made history, according to *Fortune*.

1. **Walt Disney** listened to his wife and named his cartoon mouse Mickey instead of Mortimer. Entertainment was never the same after Mickey and Minnie debuted in "Steamboat Willie" in 1928 (1).
2. **Frank McNamara**, in 1950, found himself in a restaurant without money, prompting him to come up with the idea of the Diners Club Card. This first credit card changed the nature of buying and selling throughout the world (5).
3. **Thomas Watson Jr.**, of IBM, decided in 1962 to develop the System/360 computer, at a cost of $5 billion. Although IBM's market research suggested it would sell only two units worldwide, the result was the first mainframe computer (7).
4. **Robert Woodruff** was president of Coca-Cola during World War II when he committed to selling bottles of Coke to members of the armed services for a nickel a bottle, starting around 1941. The decision led to enormous customer loyalty, including the fact that returning soldiers influenced family members and friends to buy Coca-Cola (12).
5. **Jean Nidetch**, in 1961, was put on a diet in an obesity clinic in New York City. She invited six dieting friends to meet in her Queens apartment every week. The decision created Weight Watchers and the weight-loss industry (20).
6. **Bill Gates**, in 1981, decided to license MS/DOS to IBM, while IBM did not require control of the license for all non-IBM PCs. The decision laid the foundation for Microsoft's huge

success and a downturn in IBM's prestige and prominence (21).

7. A **Hewlett-Packard** engineer discovered in 1979 that heating metal in a specific way caused it to splatter. The management decision to exploit this discovery launched the ink-jet printer business, and laid the groundwork for more than $6 billion in revenue for HP (25).
8. **Sears, Roebuck and Co.**, in 1905, decided to open its Chicago mail-order plant. The Sears catalogue made goods available to an entirely new customer base, and also provided a model for mass production (40).
9. **Ray Kroc** liked the McDonald brothers' stand that sold hamburgers, french fries, and milk shakes so much that he decided to open his own franchised restaurant in 1955 and form McDonald's Corp. Kroc soon created a giant global company and a vast market for fast food (58).
10. **Procter & Gamble**, in 1931, introduced its brand management system, which showcased brands and provided a blueprint that management has followed ever since (62).
11. **Michael Dell** made the decision in 1986 to sell PCs direct and build them to order. Others in the industry are now trying to imitate Dell Computer's strategy (73).
12. **Citibank** chairman Walter Wriston gave top-level executive John Reed the go-ahead to invest $100 million into automatic teller machines (ATMs). During a major snow storm in New York City in 1978, customers started making extensive use of these new machines that gave you money.
13. **King Gillette**, at his boss's urging, developed a disposable razor blade, and in 1901 patented the first razor with a disposable blade. The U.S. Army gave 3.5 million Gillette Razors and 32 million blades to soldiers during World War I, capturing a generation of people—and created the beginnings of America's throwaway culture.

Source: Stuart Crainer, "The 75 Greatest Management Decisions Ever Made," *Management Review*, November 1998, pp. 16–24; Kate Bonamici and Ellen Florian Kratz, "20 that Made History," *Fortune*, June 27, 2005, pp. 62, 80.

all routine ones. In reality, executives do make many small, programmed decisions in addition to nonprogrammed ones. Some executives sign expense account vouchers and answer routine e-mail inquiries. Middle managers and first-level managers generally make both routine and nonroutine decisions, with first-level managers making a higher proportion of routine decisions. A well-managed organization encourages all managers to delegate as many nonprogrammed decisions as possible.

programmed decision
A decision that is repetitive, or routine, and made according to a specific procedure.

The Management in Action on pages 148-149 lists some of the most important decisions ever made by managers in business, all of which were nonprogrammed.

STEPS IN PROBLEM SOLVING AND DECISION MAKING

Learning Objective 2

Explain the steps involved in making a nonprogrammed decision.

Learning how to solve problems and make decisions properly is important because, according to a long-term study, being systematic about decision making helps avoid bad decisions. Paul C. Nutt studied 356 decisions in medium to large organizations in the United States and Canada. About one-quarter of the decisions were made in a public agency, one-quarter in nonprofit firms, and one-half in private companies. One-half of these decisions

exhibit 5-1 Steps in Problem Solving and Decision Making

Managers who are thorough in their decision making will often proceed through the steps shown here.

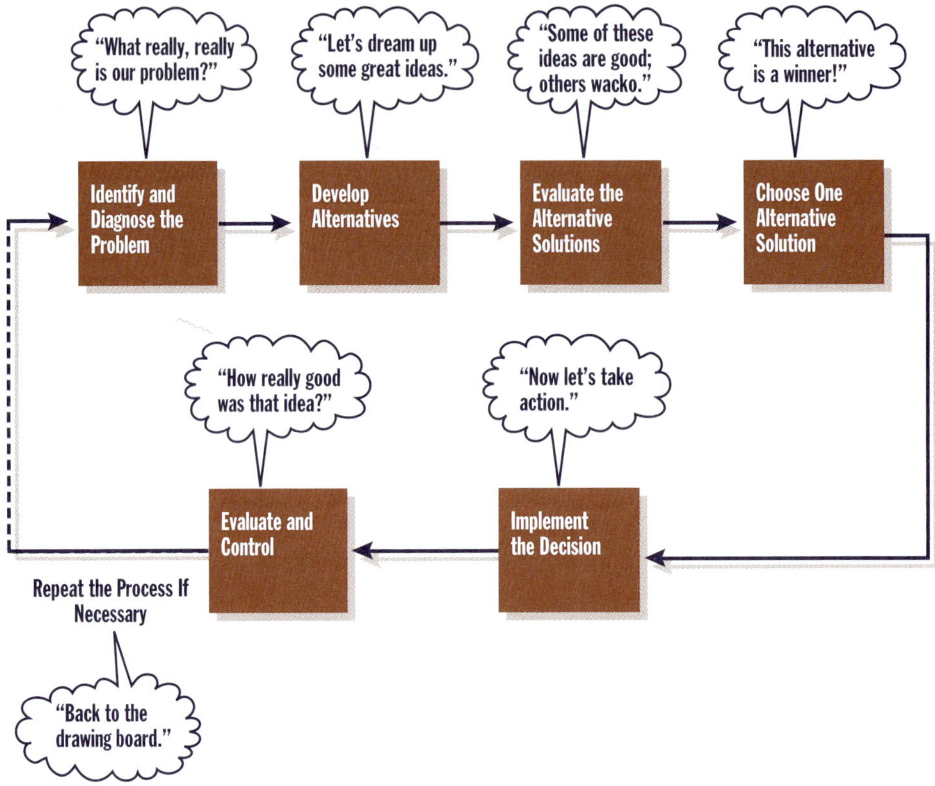

failed, such as a bank dropping Saturday service and losing customers as a result. Most instances of decision-making failure were attributed to poor tactics, including not exploring enough alternatives, and not obtaining enough input from group members.[3] Managers are more likely to find better solutions to complex problems—and therefore make better major decisions—when they follow an orderly process. Drawing a consistent distinction between problem solving and decision making is difficult because they are part of the same process. The basic purpose of making a decision is to solve a problem, but you must analyze the problem prior to making the decision.

As shown in Exhibit 5-1, and described next, problem solving and decision making can be divided into steps.

Identify and Diagnose the Problem

Problem solving and decision making begins with the awareness that a problem exists. In other words, the first step in problem solving and decision making is identifying a gap between desired and actual conditions. Being

3 Paul C. Nutt, "Surprising but True: Half the Decisions in Organizations Fail," *Academy of Management Executive*, November 1999, pp. 75–90.

attentive to the environment helps the manager identify problems, such as noticing that the department is receiving frequent criticism from outsiders and insiders. At times, a problem is imposed on a manager, such as when customer complaints increase. At other times, he or she has to search actively for a worthwhile problem or opportunity. For example, a sales manager actively pursued a problem by conducting an audit to find out why former customers stopped buying from the company.

A thorough diagnosis of the problem is important because the real problem may be different from the one that a first look suggests. The ability to think critically helps a person get at the real problem. To diagnose a problem properly, you must clarify its true nature. A frequent example is that a manager might attempt to reduce turnover by increasing wages. The manager assumes that the workers would stay with the company longer if their wages were higher. Yet the real problem is inflexible working hours that are triggering turnover.

Develop Alternative Solutions

The second step in decision making is to generate alternative solutions. In this intellectually freewheeling aspect of decision making, all kinds of possibilities are explored, even if they seem unrealistic. Often the difference between good and mediocre decision makers is that the former do not accept the first alternative they think of. Instead, they keep digging until they find the best solution. When Jeff Bezos, the founder of Amazon.com, was searching for a way to commercialize the Internet, he made a list of the top 20 mail-order products. He then looked for where he could create the most value for customers, and finally decided on the alternative of selling books.[4]

Often the problem solver will find a creative alternative solution to the problem. At other times, a standard solution will work adequately. For example, one small-business owner needing money to expand the business might choose the standard alternative of borrowing money from a bank or finance company. Another small-business owner might attempt the creative alternative of raising money by selling shares of the company to friends and family members. (If the company fails, however, the business owner will have created conflict with these people.)

Evaluate Alternative Solutions

The next step involves comparing the relative value of the alternatives. The problem solver examines the pros and cons of each one and considers the feasibility of each. Some alternatives may appear attractive, but implementing them would be impossible or counterproductive.

Comparing relative value often means performing a cost and savings analysis of each alternative. Alternatives that cost much more than they save are infeasible. The possible outcome of an alternative should be part of the analysis. If an unsatisfactory outcome is almost a certainty, the alternative should be rejected. For example, if a firm is faced with low profits, one

---

4 Joshua Quittner, "An Eye on the Future: Jeff Bezos Merely Wants Amazon.com to Be Earth's Biggest Seller of Everything," *Time*, December 27, 1999, p. 57.

alternative would be to cut pay by 20 percent. The outcome of this alternative would be to lower morale drastically and create high turnover, so a firm should not implement that alternative. High employee turnover is so expensive that it would override the cost savings.

One approach to examining the pros and cons of each alternative is to list them on a worksheet. This approach assumes that virtually all alternatives have both positive and negative consequences.

Choose One Alternative Solution

The process of weighing each alternative must stop at some point. You cannot solve a problem unless you choose one of the alternatives—that is, make a decision. Several factors influence the choice. A major factor is the goal the decision should achieve. The goals sought for in making the decision are also referred to as the *decision criteria*. The alternative chosen should be the one that appears to come closest to achieving it. If two alternatives appear almost equally good after considerable deliberation, it might be helpful to seek the opinion of one more person to decide which alternative is slightly better.

Despite a careful evaluation of alternatives, ambiguity remains in most decisions. The decisions faced by managers are often complex, and the factors involved in them are often unclear. Even when quantitative evidence strongly supports a particular alternative, the decision maker may be uncertain. Human resource decisions are often the most ambiguous because making precise predictions about human behavior is so difficult. Deciding which person to hire from a list of several strong candidates is always a challenge.

A problem some managers have in choosing an alternative is that they have a tendency to say yes to many alternatives proposed by staff members. The task for the manager is to choose to pursue what is most important and disregard the less critical alternatives. Being selective in this way helps the manager and the organization on those alternatives that hold the most promise.[5] For example, a turnaround manager (one who specializes in fixing a broken company) was brought into a failing fast-service food restaurant chain, and he was bombarded with suggestions for improving profitability in a hurry. Among them were immediately closing all underperforming restaurants, automating as much self-service as possible, updating the menu, improving customer service, and creating an advertising campaign featuring NFL and NBA stars. Instead of agreeing to all these ideas, the manager chose to upgrade the menu and the customer service in a hurry. As a result, the restaurant chain was salvaged.

Implement the Decision

Converting a decision into action is the next major step. Until a decision is implemented, it is not really a decision at all. A fruitful way of evaluating the merit of a decision is to observe its implementation. A decision is seldom a good one if people resist its implementation or if it is too cumbersome to

5 "Power Decision Making," *Executive Leadership*, Special Bonus Report, September 2006, p. 5.

implement. Suppose a firm tries to boost productivity by decreasing the time allotted for lunch or coffee breaks. If employees resist the decision by eating while working and then taking the allotted lunch break, productivity will decrease. Implementation problems indicate that the decision to boost productivity by decreasing break time would be a poor one.

Another perspective on implementation is that it represents execution, or putting plans into action. Implementation therefore involves focusing on the operations of a company or business unit. When Mark Hurd was appointed as the new CEO of Hewlett-Packard several years ago, he was praised for his decision to focus on execution rather than formulating new visions for the company. As part of execution, he focused on cost cutting and efficiency.[6] His predecessor Carly Fiorina was often accused of focusing too much on visions, and not enough on execution or business operations.

Evaluate and Control

The final step in the decision-making framework is to investigate how effectively the chosen alternative solved the problem. Controlling means ensuring that the results the decision obtained are the ones set forth during the problem-identification step. Evaluating and controlling your decisions will help you improve your decision-making skills. You can learn important lessons by comparing what actually happened with what you thought would happen. You can learn what you could have improved or done differently and use this information the next time you face a similar decision.

BOUNDED RATIONALITY AND INFLUENCES ON DECISION MAKING

Learning Objective 3

Understand bounded rationality and the major factors that influence decision making in organizations.

Decision making is usually not entirely rational, because so many factors influence the decision maker. Awareness of this fact stems from the research of psychologist and economist Herbert A. Simon. He proposed that bounds (or limits) to rationality are present in decision making. These bounds are the limitations of the human, particularly related to the processing and recall of information.[7] **Bounded rationality** means that people's finite (somewhat limited) mental abilities, combined with external influences over which they have little or no control, prevent them from making entirely rational decisions.

In more recent years, the irrational side of decision making became incorporated into a branch of behavioral economics called *neuroeconomics*. Behavioral economics emphasizes that people are not entirely rational decision makers, such as trying hard to avoid losing money in the stock market instead of on increasing profits. An individual might hang on to a losing stock or mutual fund too long, and a manager might hang on to a losing product for too long. At Princeton University, Daniel Kahneman, a psychologist,

6 Adam Lashinsky, "Take a Look at HP," *Fortune*, June 13, 2005, p. 117.
7 Herbert A. Simon, "Rational Choice and the Structure of the Environment," *Psychological Review*, 63 (1956), pp. 129–138.

bounded rationality The observation that people's limited mental abilities, combined with external influences over which they have little or no control, prevent them from making entirely rational decisions.

shared a Nobel Prize with Vernon Smith, an economist, for research about the irrational side of decision making.[8]

Neuroeconomics looks inside the brain with such tools as magnetic resonance imaging (MRI) to discover how parts of the brain control some aspects of decision making. The limbic system located deep inside the brain controls the intuitive and emotional parts of our psyches. In contrast, the analytic system controls the calculated, conscious, and future-oriented thinking. The limbic system will prompt us into being impatient, such as taking the first offer on a lot of unsold inventory. A fruitful avenue of neuroeconomic research helps explains how people make decisions that involve a time perspective. When people decide about the distant future, they tend to be rational. In contrast, when faced with a choice about whether to continue something now or delay gratification, they tend to be impulsive, as in the inventory example.[9]

Research and opinion on bounded rationality emphasizes that humans use problem-solving strategies which are reasonably rapid, reasonably accurate, and that fit the quantity and type of information available.[10] In short, people do the best with what they have while making decisions.

As a result of bounded rationality, most decision makers do not have the time or resources to wait for the best possible solution. Instead, they search for **satisficing decisions**, or those that suffice in providing a minimum standard of satisfaction. Such decisions are adequate, acceptable, or passable. Many decision makers stop their search for alternatives when they find a satisficing one. Successful managers recognize that it is difficult to obtain every possible fact before making a decision. In the words of Lawrence Weinbach, the former top executive at Unisys, and now a member of a capital management firm, "If we want to be leaders, we're going to have to make decision with maybe 75 percent of the facts. If you wait for 95 percent, you are going to be a follower."[11]

Accepting the first reasonable alternative may only postpone the need to implement a decision that truly solves the problem and meets the decision criteria. For example, slashing the price of a pickup truck to match the competition's price can be regarded as the result of a satisficing decision. A superior decision might call for the firm to demonstrate to end users that the difference in quality is worth the higher price.

satisficing decision A decision that meets the minimum standards of satisfaction.

heuristics A rule of thumb used in decision making.

Partly because of bounded rationality, decision makers often use simplified strategies, also known as **heuristics**. A heuristic becomes a rule of thumb in decision making, such as the policy to reject a job applicant who does not smile during the first three minutes of the job interview. A widely used investing heuristic is as follows: The percent of equity in your portfolio should equal 100 minus your age, with the remainder being invested in

8 "Daniel Kahneman wins Nobel Prize," *News from Princeton University* (http://www.princeton.edu), October 9, 2002.

9 "Neuroeconomics," *Harvard Magazine* (http://www.harvardmagazine.com), March–April 2006, pp. 54–55; Peter Coy, "Why Logic Often Takes a Backseat: The Study of Neuroeconomics May Topple the Notion of Rational Decision-Making," *Business Week*, March 28, 2005, pp. 94–95.

10 Gerd Gigerenzer and Reinhard Selten (eds.), *Bounded Rationality: The Adaptive Toolbox* (Cambridge, MA: MIT Press, 2001).

11 Quoted in Jeffrey E. Garten, *The Mind of the C.E.O.* (Cambridge, MA: Perseus Publishing, 2001).

fixed-income investments including cash. A 25-year-old would therefore have a portfolio consisting of 25 percent interest-bearing securities, such as bonds, and 75 percent in stocks. However, his or her 100-year-old grandparent should hold all fixed-income investments and no stocks! Heuristics help the decision maker cope with masses of information, but their oversimplification can lead to inaccurate or irrational decision making.

A host of influences on the decision-making process contribute to bounded rationality. We describe nine such influences, as outlined in Exhibit 5-2.

intuition
An experience-based way of knowing or reasoning in which weighing and balancing evidence are done unconsciously and automatically.

Intuition

Effective decision makers do not rely on analytical and methodological techniques alone. They also use their hunches and intuition. **Intuition** is an experience-based way of knowing or reasoning in which weighing and balancing evidence are done unconsciously and automatically. Intuition is also a way of arriving at a conclusion without using the step-by-step logical process. Intuition can be based mostly on experience or mostly on feeling. The fact that experience contributes to intuition means that decision makers can become more intuitive by solving many difficult problems because accumulated facts

exhibit 5-2 **Factors Influencing Decision Making**

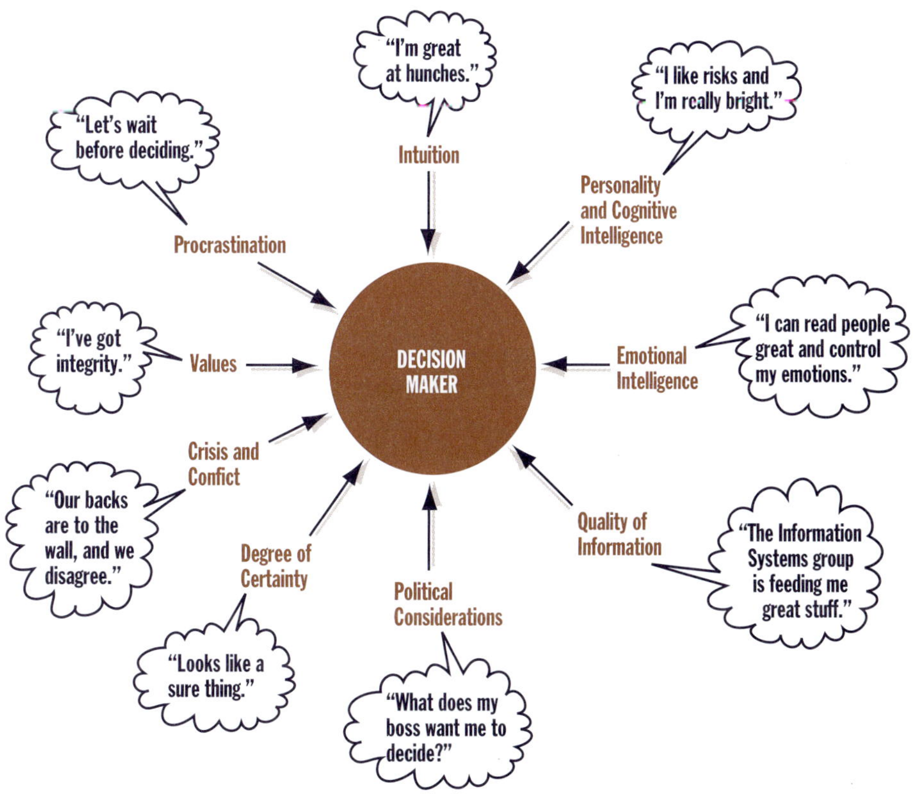

are an asset to intuition. It also means that decision makers will have better intuition if they perform the same work for a relatively long period of time.[12]

Although the use of intuition in managerial decision making is now widely recognized, researchers have also found limitations to intuition. When the stakes are high, such as a CEO contemplating acquiring a company in a different field, rational analysis is recommended. The analysis might include receiving input from many people and asking knowledgeable people loads of questions.[13] At the same time, intuition could help point the executive in the right direction, such as sizing up the overall merits of the company to be acquired. Major decisions usually begin with intuition. As Henry Ford said, "If I asked consumers what they wanted, they would have told me to build a faster horse and buggy." In short, you need to use your intuition to know when intuition or rational analysis is best!

Personality and Cognitive Intelligence

The personality and cognitive intelligence of the decision maker influence his or her ability to find effective solutions. A particularly relevant personality dimension is a person's propensity for taking risks. A cautious, conservative person typically opts for a low-risk solution. An extremely cautious person may avoid making major decisions for fear of being wrong. Organizational pressures can also influence a person's propensity for risk taking. In addition to being related to risk taking, cautiousness and conservatism influence **decisiveness**, the extent to which a person makes up his or her mind promptly and prudently. Good decision makers, by definition, are decisive. Take the quiz presented in Exhibit 5-3 to examine your degree of decisiveness.

Perfectionism exerts a notable impact on decision making. People who seek the perfect solution to a problem are usually indecisive because they hesitate to accept the fact that a particular alternative is good enough. Optimism versus pessimism is another relevant personality dimension. Optimists are more likely to find solutions than pessimists are. Pessimists are more likely to give up searching, because they perceive situations as being hopeless.

Cognitive (or traditional) intelligence carries a profound influence in decision-making effectiveness. Today psychologists recognize other types of intelligence also, such as being imaginative and adapting well to the environment, or having practical intelligence. In general, intelligent and well-educated people are more likely to identify problems and make sound decisions than are those who have less intelligence and education. A notable exception applies, however. Some intelligent, well-educated people have such a fondness for collecting facts and analyzing them that they suffer from "analysis paralysis." One plant manager put it this way: "I'll never hire a genius again. They dazzle you with facts, figures, and computer graphics. But when they get through with their analysis, they still haven't solved the problem."

decisiveness
The extent to which a person makes up his or her mind promptly and prudently.

12 Eugene Sadler-Smith and Erella Shefy, "The Intuitive Executive: Understanding and Applying 'Gut Feel' in Decision Making," *The Academy of Management Executive*, November 2004, pp. 76–91; Erik Dan and Michael G. Pratt, "Exploring Intuition and its Role in Managerial Decision Making," *Academy of Management Review*, January 2007, pp. 33–35.

13 C. Chet Miller and R. Duane Ireland, "Intuition in Strategic Decision Making: Friend or Foe in the Fast-Paced 21st Century?" *The Academy of Management Executive*, February 2005, pp. 19–30.

exhibit 5-3 How Decisive Are You?

Answer the following questions by placing a check in the appropriate space: N = never; R = rarely; Oc = occasionally; Of = often.

	N	R	Oc	Of
1. Do you let the opinions of others influence your decisions?	___	___	___	___
2. Do you procrastinate when it's time to make a decision?	___	___	___	___
3. Do you let others make your decisions for you?	___	___	___	___
4. Have you missed out on an opportunity because you couldn't make a decision?	___	___	___	___
5. After reaching a decision do you have second thoughts?	___	___	___	___
6. Did you hesitate while answering these questions?	___	___	___	___

Scoring and interpretation: Score one point for each "often" response, two points for each "occasionally," three points for each "rarely," and four points for each "never."

19–24	You are very decisive and probably have no problem assuming responsibility for the choices you make.
13–18	Decision making is difficult for you. You need to work at being more decisive.
12 or lower	You are going to have a big problem unless you learn to overcome your timidity. When a decision has to be made, face up to it and do it!

Source: Adapted from Roger Fritz, "A Systematic Approach to Problem Solving and Decision Making," *Supervisory Management*, March 1993, p. 4. Reprinted with permission of the American Management Association.

It is helpful for you to size up the environment in terms of how much analysis is required before making a decision. It is good to avoid being both impulsive (jumping too quickly to a decision) and indecisive because of overanalysis.

Emotional Intelligence

How effective you are in managing your feelings and reading other people can affect the quality of your decision making. For example, if you cannot control your anger you are likely to make decisions motivated by retaliation, hostility, and revenge. An example would be shouting and swearing at your team leader because of a work assignment you received. **Emotional intelligence** refers to qualities such as understanding one's own feelings, empathy for others, and the regulation of emotion to enhance living. This type of intelligence generally affects the ability to connect with people and understand their emotions. If you cannot read the emotions of others you are liable to make some bad decisions involving people, such as pushing your boss too hard to grant a request. Emotional intelligence contains four key factors, all of which can influence the quality of our decisions:[14]

emotional intelligence
The ability to connect with people and understand their emotions.

14 Daniel Goleman, Richard Boyatzis, and Annie McKee, "Primal Leadership: The Hidden Driver of Great Performance," *Harvard Business Review*, December 2001, pp. 42–51.

1. *Self-awareness.* The ability to understand your own emotions is the most essential of the four emotional intelligence competencies. Having high self-awareness allows people to know their strengths and limitations and have high self-esteem. (Effective managers seek feedback to see how well their actions are received by others. A manager with good self-awareness would recognize such factors as whether or he she was liked, or was exerting the right amount of pressure on people.)
2. *Self-management.* The ability to control one's emotions and act with honesty and integrity in a consistent and adaptable manner. The right degree of self-management helps prevent a person from throwing temper tantrums when activities do not go as planned. Effective workers do not let their occasional bad moods ruin their day. (A manager with high self-management would not suddenly decide to fire a group member because of one difference of opinion.)
3. *Social awareness.* This competency includes having empathy for others and having intuition about organizational problems. Socially aware workers go beyond sensing the emotions of others by showing that they care. (A team leader with social awareness, or empathy, would be able to assess whether a team member had enough enthusiasm for a project to assign him to that project.)
4. *Relationship management.* Includes the interpersonal skills of being able to communicate clearly and convincingly, disarming conflicts, and building strong personal bonds. Effective individuals use relationship management skills to spread their enthusiasm and solve disagreements, often with kindness and humor. (A manager with good relationship management skills would not burn bridges and would continue to enlarge his or her network of people to win support when support is needed.)

Quality and Accessibility of Information

Reaching an effective decision usually requires high-quality, valid information. The ability to supply managers with high-quality information forms the major justification for information systems. Part of having quality information is being able to base decisions upon solid data. The discussion in Chapter 1 abut evidence-based management emphasizes collecting information before making a decision, and we return to this topic in Chapter 6 about quantitative techniques for planning and decision making.

Accessibility may be even more important than quality in determining which information is used or not used. Sometimes it takes so much time and effort to search for quality information that the manager relies on lower-quality information that is close at hand. A frequent accessibility problem is to rely on information from the Internet because it is easy to access, without stopping to investigate the date of the information.

anchoring In the decision making process, placing too much value on the first information received and ignoring later information.

Closely related to quality and accessibility of information is the tendency to be influenced by the first information we receive when attempting to solve a problem or make a decision. **Anchoring** occurs during decision making when the mind gives too much weight to the first information it receives.

Initial impressions, estimates, or data hold back, or anchor, later thoughts and judgments.[15] The manager who uses the old information found on the Internet might be overly influenced by that information. Having been received first, the anchored information becomes the standard against which to judge other information. Anchoring can therefore lead to wasting useful information received after the first information.

Another decision-making trap is overconfidence. The risk here comes from associating confidence with accuracy. The problem then arises because accuracy reflects what we know, whereas confidence reflects what we think we know. You can test your opinions by searching for information that challenges your beliefs or facts as a way to help combat the overconfidence trap and thereby avoid the natural tendency to look only for supporting information.[16]

Political Considerations

Under ideal circumstances, managers make organizational decisions on the basis of the objective merits of competing alternatives. In reality, many decisions are based on political considerations, such as favoritism, alliances, or the desire of the decision maker to stay in favor with people who wield power.

Political factors sometimes influence which data are given serious consideration in evaluating alternatives. The decision maker may select data that support the position of an influential person whom he or she is trying to please. For instance, one financial analyst, asked to investigate the cost-effectiveness of the firm owning a corporate jet, gave considerable weight to the "facts" supplied by a manufacturer of corporate jets. This information allowed her to justify the expense of purchasing the plane—the decision the CEO favored.

The *status quo trap* ties decisions to political factors. Failure to challenge the status quo often stems from worry that being critical will invite criticism from key people. Breaking away from the status quo requires action, and when we take action, we take responsibility, thus opening ourselves up to criticism.[17] A barrier many sales representatives face in selling against a dominant product in the industry results from managers' fear of being criticized if the new product fails. As one systems administrator said, "You can never get fired for buying Cisco." (The implication is that if the manager bought Internet equipment from a smaller competitor, he would risk being reprimanded.)

A person with professional integrity arrives at what he or she thinks is the best decision and then makes a diligent attempt to convince management of the objective merits of that solution. The person with integrity is aware of not alienating people in power, yet supports what he or she thinks is the best decision.

---

15 John S. Hammond, Ralph L. Keeney, and Howard Raffia, "The Hidden Traps in Decision Making," *Harvard Business Review*, September–October 1998, p. 48.

16 "Are You 90% Sure You'll Hit That Target? Check Out Your Knowledge Calibration," Knowledge@Wharton, January 31–February 13, 2001.

17 Hammond, Keeney, and Raffia, "The Hidden Traps," pp. 48–49.

Degree of Certainty

The more certain a decision maker is of the outcome of a decision, the more calmly and confidently the person will make the decision. Degree of certainty is divided into three categories: certainty, risk, and uncertainty. A condition of certainty exists when the facts are well known and the outcome can be predicted accurately. A retail store manager might predict with certainty that more hours of operation will lead to more sales.

A condition of risk exists when a decision must be made based on incomplete, but accurate, factual information. Effective managers often accept a condition of risk. A calculated risk is where the potential return is well worth the cost that will be incurred if the effort fails. When Steve Jobs at Apple Computer (now Apple Inc.) spearheaded the development of the iPod for downloading and playing music, many insiders thought the company was taking a risk with dwindling funds. However, the iPod sold well beyond even Job's expectations, vindicating the risky decision. Part of the factual information here was that MP3 players were an established part of the culture, along with industry sales figures for the MP3.

Crisis and Conflict

In a crisis, many decision makers panic. They become less rational and more emotional than they would in a calm environment. Decision makers who are adversely affected by crisis perceive it to be a stressful event. As a consequence, they concentrate poorly, use poor judgment, and think impulsively. Under crisis, some managers do not bother dealing with differences of opinion because they are under so much pressure. A smaller number of managers perceive a crisis as an exciting challenge that energizes them toward their best level of problem solving and decision making.

A recommendation for becoming more adept at making decisions under crisis conditions is to anticipate crises. Visualize ahead of time how you will react to the situation. Visualization serves somewhat as a rehearsal for the real event. A hospital administrator might think to herself, "Here is what I would do if a patient dies during routine surgery, and the media grab hold of the story."

Conflict relates to crisis because both can be an emotional experience. When conflict is not overwhelming, and is directed at real issues, not personalities, it can be an asset to decision making. By virtue of opposing sides expressing different points of view, problems can be solved more thoroughly, which leads to better decisions.

Values of the Decision Maker

Ultimately, all decisions are based on values. A manager who places a high value on the personal welfare of employees tries to avoid alternatives that create hardship for workers and implements decisions in ways that lessen turmoil. Another value that significantly influences decision making is the pursuit of excellence. A manager who embraces the pursuit of excellence will search for the high-quality alternative solution.

Attempting to preserve the status quo mentioned above as a political factor is also a value. If you value the status quo too highly, you may fail to make a decision that could bring about major improvements. At one company, the vice president of human resources received numerous inquiries about when the firm would begin offering benefits for domestic partners (of the opposite or same sex). The vice president reasoned that since the vast majority of employees rated the benefit package highly, a change was not needed. A few employees took their complaints about "biased benefits" to the CEO. The vice president of human resources was then chastised by the CEO for not suggesting an initiative that would keep the company in the forefront of human resources management.

procrastinate
To delay in taking action without a valid reason.

decision-making style
A manager's typical pattern of making decisions.

Procrastination

Many people are poor decision makers because they **procrastinate**, or delay taking action without a valid reason. Procrastination results in indecisiveness and inaction and is a major cause of self-defeating behavior. Procrastination is a deeply ingrained behavior pattern, and may be based on such factors as being concerned about being judged as poorly. For example, if the oil company manager delays making a decision about drilling, he or she cannot be accused of having wasted resources on an oil source of limited value.

Although too much procrastination may interfere with effective decision making, rapid decision making is not always the most effective. When too much emphasis is placed on speed, financial data become less reliable, customer service might be compromised, and productivity suffers. Furthermore, critical information may not be shared, alternative solutions are dismissed too readily, and risks are ignored. Good decision makers recognize the balance between procrastination and impulsiveness. We will return to the problem of procrastination in Chapter 17.

Decision-Making Styles

The various factors that influence the quality of decision making also contribute to a manager's typical pattern of making decisions, or **decision-making style**. For example, a manager who relies heavily on intuition will tend to make decisions quickly without agonizing over data. And a manager with procrastination tendencies will ponder over as much information as possible and consult many people before reaching a decision. Kenneth R. Brousseau, the CEO of Decision Dynamics, and his colleagues have studied executive decision-making styles, using a database of 120,000 people.

According to the Decision Dynamic research, decision styles differ in two fundamental ways: how information is used, and how options are created. In terms of information, some managers want to pore over reams of information before making a decision. The opposite approach is to come to a decision as soon as enough information is available. (This approach is referred to as satisficing, as described earlier.) In terms of creating options, *single focus* decision makers are committed to taking one course of action. In contrast, their *multifocused* counterparts generate lists of possible options and may pursue multiple courses. Combining the dimensions of using information and creating options results in four styles, as follows:[18]

1. *Decisive (one option, less information).* Decisive decision makers value action, speed, efficiency, and consistency. After a plan is in place they stick with it and move on to the next decision. Time is precious to this type of decision maker, and he or she fits well into a setting like managing a brand for Procter & Gamble. For example, "Let's run a special promotion on Tide next month. Get the word out this afternoon."
2. *Flexible (many options, less information).* The flexible style also focuses on speed, yet adaptability is emphasized. Flexible decision makers gather just enough data to choose a line of attack, and quickly change course if needed. A marketing manager for Jeep with a flexible style might say, "Let's try a dealer incentive for the Jeep Compass. I've seen that work once with the Cherokee. If that doesn't work, let's quickly switch to zero percent financing."
3. *Hierarchic (one option, more information).* People using the hierarchic style analyze a great deal of information, and seek input from others. They expect a decision to be final and relatively permanent. An information technology manager might say, "We have studied the problem for several months, and have received inputs from hundreds of intelligent users. Our single source of new desktops and laptops will be Gateway Computer." (Gateway is now part of Acer.)
4. *Integrative (many options, more information).* Instead of looking for a single best solution, managers using the integrative style frame problems broadly. The integrative style uses input from many sources, and makes decisions involving multiple courses of action. Also, the decision may be modified in the future as circumstances change. An executive at Target might say, "For now, we are going to increase the proportion of full-time workers, based on the opinions of several hundred store managers. However, we will keep our eyes on the bottom line and employee morale to see how well this shift in the proportion of full-time staff works."

A key suggestion in relation to decision-making styles is to be aware that they exist. Next, reflect on your style, including receiving feedback from others. You might recognize, for example, that you tend to collect too much data before making a decision. You are much like the potential homebuyer who collects so much information before making a purchase offer that the property is sold to someone else.

---

18 Kenneth R. Brousseau, Michael J. Driver, Gary Hourihan, and Rikard Larsson, "The Seasoned Executive's Decision-Making Style," *Harvard Business Review*, February 2006, pp. 110–121.

GROUP PROBLEM SOLVING AND DECISION MAKING

Learning Objective 4

Appreciate the value and potential limitations of group decision making.

group decisions The process of several people contributing to a final decision.

We have described how individuals go about solving problems and making decisions. However, groups make most major decisions in organizations. **Group decisions** result when several people contribute to a final decision. Because so much emphasis has been placed on teams in organizations and participative decision making, an increasing number of decisions are made by groups rather than individuals. Group decision making is often used in complex and important situations such as developing a new product, or producing a list of the employees with the best potential for promotion. We will examine the advantages and disadvantages of group decision making, describe when it is useful, and present a general problem-solving method for groups, followed by a specific technique.

Advantages and Disadvantages of Group Decision Making

Group decision making offers several advantages over the same activity carried out individually. First, the quality of the decision might be higher because of the combined wisdom of group members. A second benefit is a by-product of the first. Group members evaluate each other's thinking, so major errors are likely to be avoided. The marketing vice president of a company that sells small appliances such as microwave ovens, toasters, and coffee pots decided the company should sell direct through e-commerce. Before asking others to begin implementing the decision, the executive brought up the matter for group discussion. A sales manager in the group pointed out that direct selling would enrage their dealers, thus doing damage to the vast majority of their sales. The marketing vice president then decided she would back off on direct marketing until a new product was developed that would not be sold through dealers.

Third, group decision making is helpful in gaining acceptance and commitment. People who participate in making a decision will often be more committed to the implementation than if they were not consulted. Fourth, groups can help people overcome blocks in their thinking, leading to more creative solutions to problems.

Group decision making also has some notable disadvantages. The group approach consumes considerable time and may result in compromises that do not really solve the problem. An intelligent individual might have the best solution to the problem, and relying on his or her judgment could save time.

The explosion of the space shuttle Columbia in 2003 presents a serious example of the disadvantages of group decision making. Sixteen months prior to the explosion of the spaceship, the General Accounting Office concluded that the downsizing of the NASA's workforce had left it ill equipped to manage its safety upgrade program for the shuttle. Furthermore, a Rand report released in 2002 said that, "Decaying infrastructure and shuttle component obsolescence are significant contributions to a future declining safety posture." Equally significant, NASA later released a batch of e-mails revealing that dozens of NASA workers at the Johnson Space Center were aware that engineers were concerned about a potentially catastrophic re-entry for Columbia. A NASA official later said it would have been impossible for him to be aware of all the conversations

groupthink
A psychological drive for consensus at any cost.

among NASA's 18,000 employees. Furthermore, the groups of NASA officials approved the launch of Columbia despite all the safety warnings.[19]

Flawed decisions of the type just described have generally been attributed to **groupthink**, a psychological drive for consensus at any cost. Groupthink makes group members lose their ability to evaluate bad ideas critically. Glen Whyte believes that many instances of groupthink are caused by decision makers who see themselves as choosing between inevitable losses. The group believes that a sure loss will occur unless action is taken. Caught up in the turmoil of trying to make the best of a bad situation, the group takes a bigger risk than any individual member would.[20] A group of executives might hold back on the recall of a potentially unsafe product because they fear the recall would bankrupt the company.

Even though groupthink is classified here as a negative influence on group decision making, one study showed that some aspects of groupthink may facilitate performance. The participants in the study—108 employees who made up 30 teams in five large business firms—answered a questionnaire about crisis events they had faced within the past year. The results surprised researchers: Three symptoms of groupthink combined together enhanced team performance. The three specific symptoms include belief in inherent group morality, illusion of unanimity, and illusion of invulnerability.[21] Apparently, having a strong faith in the group was associated with high group performance.

The negative aspects of groupthink can often be avoided if the team leader encourages group members to express doubts and criticisms of proposed solutions. It is helpful to show by example that you are willing to accept criticism. It is also important for someone to play the role of the devil's advocate. This person challenges the thinking of others by asking such questions as, "Why do you think so many employees, investors, and regulators are so stupid they will not find out that we virtually stole billions from the corporation with our wacky schemes?"

Because group decision making takes more time and people than individual decision making, it should not be used indiscriminately. Group decision making should be reserved for complex decisions of reasonable importance. Too many managers use the group method for solving such minor questions as "What should be on the menu at the company picnic?"

Aside from being used to enhance the quality of decisions, group decision making is often used to gain acceptance for a decision. If people contribute to a decision, they are more likely to be committed to its implementation.

A General Method of Group Problem Solving

When workers at any level gather to solve a problem, they typically hold a discussion rather than rely on a formal decision-making technique. These

19 The quote is from "Inquiry Puts Early Focus on Heat Tiles," *The New York Times*, February 2, 2003; Larry Wheeler, "NASA Chief Calls on Columbia," *The New York Times*, February 28, 2003.

20 Glen Whyte, "Decision Failures: Why They Occur and How to Prevent Them," *Academy of Management Executive*, August 1991, p. 25.

21 Jin Nam Choi and Myung Un Kim, "The Organizational Application of Groupthink and Its Limitations in Organizations," *Journal of Applied Psychology*, April 1999, pp. 297–306.

general meetings are likely to produce the best results when they follow the decision-making steps. Exhibit 5-4 recommends steps for conducting group decision making, which are quite similar to the decision-making steps presented in Exhibit 5-1.

nominal group technique (NGT) A group decision making technique that follows a highly structured format.

A Specific Method of Group Problem Solving: The Nominal Group Technique

A manager who must make a decision about an important issue sometimes needs to know what alternatives are available and how people would react to them. Another important consideration is for the group to reach consensus. An approach called the **nominal group technique** (**NGT**) has been developed to fit this situation. NGT is a group decision-making technique that follows a highly structured format. The term *nominal* means that, for much of the activity, the participants are a group in name only; they do not interact.

An appropriate candidate for NGT is the problem of deciding which plants of a multiplant firm should be closed because of declining demand for a product. This type of highly sensitive decision elicits many different opinions. Suppose Sherry McDivott, the division president, faces the plant-closing problem. A six-step decision process follows, using a basic version of the nominal-group technique, as summarized in Exhibit 5-5.[22]

exhibit 5-4 Steps for Effective Group Decision Making

1. **Identify the problem.** Describe specifically what the problem is and how it manifests itself.
2. **Clarify the problem.** If group members do not perceive the problem in the same way, they will offer divergent solutions. Make sure everyone shares the same definition of the problem.
3. **Analyze the cause.** To convert "what is" into "what we want," the group must understand the causes of the specific problem and find ways to overcome them.
4. **Search for alternative solutions.** Remember that multiple alternative solutions can be found to most problems.
5. **Select alternatives.** Identify the criteria that solutions must meet, and then discuss the pros and cons of the proposed alternatives. No solution should be laughed at or scorned.
6. **Plan for implementation.** Decide what actions are necessary to carry out the chosen solution.
7. **Clarify the contract.** The contract is a restatement of what group members have agreed to do, and it includes deadlines for accomplishment.
8. **Develop an action plan.** Specify who does what and when to carry out the contract.
9. **Provide evaluation and accountability.** After the plan is implemented, reconvene to discuss its progress and hold people accountable for results that have not been achieved.

Source: Adapted from Andrew E. Schwartz and Joy Levin, "Better Group Decision Making," *Supervisory Management*, June 1990, p. 4.

22 Andrew H. Van de Ven and Andrew L. Delbercq, "The Effectiveness of Nominal, Delphi, and Interacting Group Decision-Making Processes," *Academy of Management Journal*, December 1972, p. 606; Leigh Thompson, "Improving the Creativity of Organizational Work Groups," *Academy of Management Executive*, February 2003, p. 104; "Quality Tools: Nominal Group Technique," *American Society for Quality* (http://www.asq.org), 2004.

1. Group members (called the target group) are selected and assembled. McDivott includes her five top managers, each representing a key function of the business, and informs them in advance of the topic.
2. The group leader presents a specific question. McDivott tells the group, "Our corporate office says we have to consolidate our operations. Our output isn't high enough to justify keeping five plants open. Whatever we do, we must cut operating expenses by about 20 percent. Your assignment is to develop the rationale for choosing which plant to close. However, if the group can think of another way of cutting operating costs by 20 percent, I'll give it some consideration. I also need to know how you feel about the alternative you choose and how our employees might feel."
3. Individual members write down their ideas independently, without speaking to other members. Members are given a set period of time for developing their suggestions, usually about five to ten minutes. Using PowerPoint, the five managers write down their ideas about reducing operating costs by 20 percent.
4. Each participant, in turn, presents one idea to the group, projected on a large screen. The group shares the ideas in a round-robin manner. The group does not discuss the ideas. The administrative assistant summarizes each idea by writing it on a slide. Here are some of the group's ideas:

   Alternative A. Close the plant with the most obsolete equipment and facilities. We all know that the Harrisburg plant is running with equipment built about 100 years ago. Close the plant in 60 days. Give employees six months

exhibit 5-5 The Nominal Group Technique

Observe that when the group reaches Step 6, the job is completed except for implementation. An important purpose of the NGT is to find a high-quality solution to a problem that will result in an effective decision.

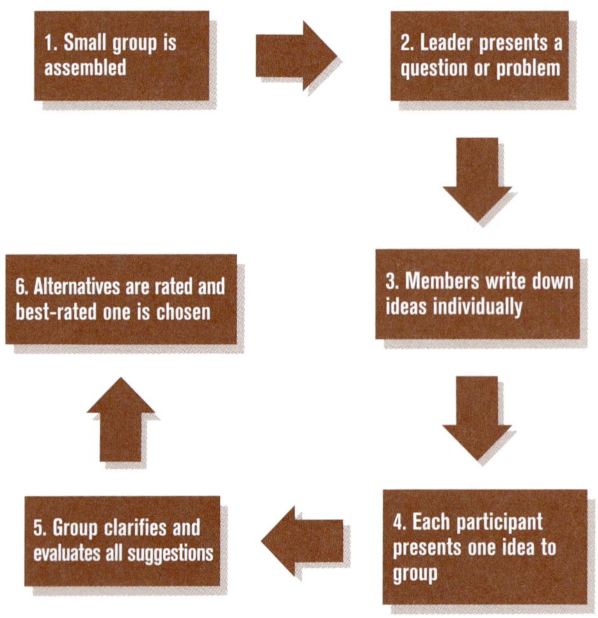

of severance pay and assist them to find new jobs. Transfer the most outstanding staff to our other plants.

Alternative B. Close the plant with the least flexible, most unproductive workforce. A lot of employees are likely to complain about this type of closing. But the rest of the workforce will get the message that we value productive employees.

Alternative C. Forget about closing a plant. Instead, take our least productive plant and transfer all its manufacturing to our other four plants. Then, work like fury to get subcontracting business for the emptied-out plant. I think our employees and stockholders will be pleased if we take such a brave stance.

Alternative D. We need a careful financial analysis of which plant is producing the lowest return on investment of capital, all factors considered. We simply close that plant. Employees will accept this decision because they all know that business is based on financial considerations.

Alternative E. Closing one plant would be too much of a hardship on one group of people. Let's share the hardship evenly. Cut everybody's pay by 25 percent, eliminate dividends to stockholders, do not replace anybody who quits or retires for the next year, and ask all our suppliers to give us a 10 percent discount. These measures would be the starting point. We could then appoint a committee to look for other savings. If everybody pulls together, morale will be saved.

5. After each group member has presented his or her idea, the group clarifies and evaluates the suggestions. At this point members are free to question the logic of the idea and express agreement and disagreement. The length of the discussion for each of the ideas varies substantially. For example, the discussion about cutting salaries 25 percent and eliminating dividends lasts only three minutes.
6. The meeting ends with a silent, independent rating of the alternatives. The final group decision is the pooled outcome of the individual votes. The target group is instructed to rate each alternative on a 1-to-10 scale, with 10 being the most favorable rating. The ratings that follow are the pooled ratings (the sum of the individual ratings) received for each alternative (50 represents the maximum score):

    Alternative A, close obsolete plant: 35
    Alternative B, close plant with unproductive workforce: 41
    Alternative C, make one plant a subcontractor: 19
    Alternative D, close plant with poorest return on investment: 26
    Alternative E, cut everybody's pay by 25 percent: 4

McDivott agrees with the group's preference for closing the plant with the least productive, most inflexible workforce. Ultimately, the board accepts Alternative B. The best employees in the factory chosen for closing are offered an opportunity to relocate to another company plant.

The NGT is effective because it follows the logic of the problem-solving and decision-making method and allows for group participation. As a result, the group usually attains consensus. The NGT also provides a discipline and rigor that are often missing in brainstorming.

Up to this point we have explored how decisions are made and characteristics that influence the decision-making situation, and have also studied group decision making. Next, we study in depth the aspect of decision making that moves organizations forward, and helps them stay competitive.

CREATIVITY AND INNOVATION IN MANAGERIAL WORK

Learning objective 5

Understand the nature of creativity and how it contributes to managerial work.

Creativity is an essential part of problem solving and decision making. To be creative is to see new relationships and produce imaginative solutions. **Creativity** can be defined simply as the process of developing novel ideas that can be put into action. By emphasizing the application of ideas, creativity is closely linked to innovation. To be innovative, a person must produce a new product, service, process, or procedure. Innovation can also be regarded as the commercialization or implementation of creative ideas. As explained by IBM, innovation continues to be the hottest topic in business today.[23]

Our discussion of managerial creativity focuses on the creative personality, the necessary conditions for creativity, the creative organization, creativity programs, and suggestions for becoming more creative.

The Creative Personality

creativity The process of developing novel ideas that can be put into action.

lateral thinking A thinking process that spreads out to find many alternative solutions to a problem.

vertical thinking An analytical, logical process that results in few answers.

Creative people tend to be more emotionally open and flexible than their less-creative counterparts. People who rarely exhibit creative behavior suffer from "hardening of the categories" and cannot overcome the traditional way of looking at things. In business jargon, creative people can *think outside the box*, or get beyond the usual constraints when solving problems.

Yet another way of characterizing creative thinkers is that they break the rules. As such, creative people are often mavericks.[24] They are unconventional and off-the-wall, such as Jack DeBoer, known as the father of the extended-stay hotel concept. His newest venture is the Value Place motel chain, mostly for business travelers paying their own expenses. Guests make their own bed, and go to the desk for sheets and towels. Says DeBoer, "As a generality, our competition is a 50-year old motel with exterior entrances and two cars with a least one flat tire in the parking lot."[25]

A key part of being creative is to think laterally. **Lateral thinking** spreads out to find many alternative solutions to a problem. **Vertical thinking**, in contrast, is an analytical, logical process that results in few answers. A problem

23 "It's a Long Journey from Inspiration to Reality," IBM advertisement in *The Wall Street Journal*, September 5, 2006, p. A12.

24 William C. Taylor and Polly LaBarre, *Mavericks at Work: Why the Most Original Minds in Business Win* (New York: William Morrow, 2006).

25 Quoted in Joe Sharkey, "Gun or Bed Spray Not Needed, but You Do Make Your Own Bed," *The New York Times* (http://www.nytimes.com), September 26, 2006.

requiring lateral thinking would be to specify a variety of ways in which a small-business owner could increase income. A vertical thinking problem would be to calculate how much more money the small-business owner needs each month to earn a 10 percent profit.

Lateral thinking is thus divergent, while vertical thinking is convergent. Creative people think divergently. They can expand the number of alternatives to a problem, thus moving away from a single solution. Yet the creative thinker also knows when it is time to think convergently. For example, the divergent thinker might generate 25 ways to reduce costs. Yet at some point he or she will have to converge toward choosing the best of several cost-cutting procedures.

Highly creative people are willing to support an unusual idea that the world is not ready to accept at the time. When Chester Carlson first toyed with the idea of a copying machine based on xerography, many questioned why anyone would want a photocopier when carbon paper was readily available. (As you may have guessed, the trade name Xerox stems from xerography.)

Conditions Necessary for Creativity

Certain individual and organizational conditions are necessary for, or at least enhance the production of, creative ideas. The most consistent of these conditions are described here and in the next section about the creative and innovative organization.

Expertise, Creative-Thinking Skills, and Internal Motivation

Creativity researcher Teresa M. Amabile summarized 22 years of research about the conditions necessary for creativity in organizations. Creativity takes place when three components join together: expertise, creative-thinking skills, and motivation.[26] Expertise refers to the necessary knowledge to put facts together. The more facts floating around in your head, the more likely you are to combine them in some useful way. A case in point is Deaf-Talk, a firm that offers a link between hospitals and American Sign Language interpreters. The founders, Dave Stauffer and Robert Fisher, were experts in teleconferencing equipment, and also knowledgeable about the needs of deaf patients, particularly when they face a medical emergency. With the Deaf-Talk service, a patient can be connected within minutes to a certified American Sign Language interpreter, who can translate via videoconferencing equipment. Deaf-Talk also offers the services of interpreters who speak dozens of languages.[27]

If you know how to keep digging for alternatives, and to avoid getting stuck in the status quo, your chances of being creative multiply. Persevering, or sticking with a problem to a conclusion, is essential for finding creative solutions. A few rest breaks to gain a fresh perspective may be helpful, but the creative person keeps coming back until a

---

26 Teresa M. Amabile, "How to Kill Creativity," *Harvard Business Review*, September–October 1998, pp. 78–79.

27 "Hospitals Hook Up for Deaf," The Associated Press, February 24, 2004.

solution emerges. You may recall the incident about Jeff Bezos exploring many different possibilities before the thought of the right product for Amazon.com.

The right type of motivation is the third essential ingredient for creative thought. A fascination with, or passion for, the task is more important than searching for external rewards. People will be the most creative when they are motivated primarily by the satisfaction and challenge of the work itself. The ultimate involvement in work is referred to as the **flow experience**, a condition of heightened focus, productivity, and happiness.[28] You are experiencing flow when you are "in the zone." Dineh Mohajer is the creative force behind Hard Candy (Urban Decay Cosmetics LLC). She became successful as a by-product of being passionate about making her own nail polish. Her intent was not to find a hobby that could lead to fame and fortune.

Environmental Need Plus Conflict and Tension

In addition to the internal conditions that foster creativity, two factors outside the person have a significant effect. An environmental need must stimulate the setting of a goal, which is another way of saying, "Necessity is the mother of invention." For example, after Hurricane Katrina ravaged the Gulf Coast of the United States, companies attempting reconstruction projects lacked housing for workers. Among the solutions was hiring cruise ships that stationed in the gulf as temporary hotels.

Enough conflict and tension to put people on edge also foster creativity. A practical way to create this conflict is for people to challenge each other's thinking, such as saying, "Offering construction workers tents as temporary housing won't attract enough of them to come down here. Let's try harder for a housing solution."

Encouragement from Others

Another external factor in creativity is encouragement, including a permissive atmosphere that welcomes new ideas. A manager who encourages imaginative and original thinking, and does not punish people for making honest mistakes, is likely to receive creative ideas from employees. A research study suggests that encouragement from family and friends, as well as from a supervisor, enhances creative thinking on the job. The participants in the study were both administrative and production employees in the Bulgarian knitwear industry. Support for creativity was measured by questions such as, "My family and friends outside this organization give me useful feedback about my ideas concerning the workplace." Supervisors rated employee creativity. The researchers concluded that (a) supervisors and coworkers, and (b) family and friends each made their own contribution to work creativity.[29]

Another aspect of encouragement that enhances creativity is to encourage risk taking. Employees are sometimes hesitant to make creative suggestions

flow experience The ultimate involvement in work or a condition of heightened focus, productivity, and happiness.

28 Ann Marsh, "The Art of Work," *Fast Company*, August 2005, pp. 76–79.

29 Nora Madjar, Greg R. Oldham, and Michael G. Pratt, "There's No Place Like Home? The Contributions of Work and Nonwork to Creativity Support to Employee's Creative Performance," *Academy of Management Journal*, August 2002, pp. 757–767.

for fear of being zapped if their new idea fails when implemented. In contrast, if risk taking is encouraged by informing employees that it is okay to fail, more people will take chances. For people to sustain creative effort, they need to feel that their work matters to the employer. The manager might say, "I love your idea for reducing shipping costs. Keep up the good work." In this way, the employee might be encouraged to take a risk.

The Creative and Innovative Organization

Another perspective on the conditions necessary for creativity is to recognize that certain managerial and organizational practices foster creativity. Five categories of activities summarize much of what is known about what managers can do to establish a creative atmosphere, as described next.[30] In extreme, the creative and innovative organization can be referred to as a culture of ideas, with Texas Instruments (TI) being an example. A group of senior people call themselves the Lunatic Fringe, and they are free to follow their curiosity wherever it goes.[31]

1. *Challenge.* Giving employees the right type and amount of challenge helps provide a creative atmosphere. Employees should be neither bored with the simplicity of the task, nor overwhelmed by its difficulty. A good creativity-inducer for a new sales representative might be for the manager to say, "How would you like to go through our ex-customer file, and attempt to bring back 5 percent of them? It would have a great impact on profits."
2. *Freedom.* To be creative, employees should have the freedom to choose how to accomplish a goal, but not which goal to accomplish. For example, creativity would be encouraged if a manager said to a group member, "I would like to improve our Internet service, and you figure out how." A creative result would be less likely if the manager said, "I would like you to improve our service, and you decide which service to improve and how to do it."
3. *Resources.* Managers need to allot time and money carefully to enhance creativity. Tight deadlines can get the creative juices flowing, but people still need enough time to let creative ideas swirl around in their heads. Employees also need large enough budgets to purchase the equipment and information necessary to get the job done. It is also important that the budget approval process for funding worthwhile ideas not be overly restrictive. Robert Iger, the CEO of Walt Disney Company, suggests that to manage creativity well, the approval process should not be unduly rigorous.[32]

---

30 Amabile, "How to Kill Creativity," pp. 81–84; Pamela Tierney, Steven M. Farmer, and George B. Graen, "An Examination of Leadership and Employee Creativity: The Relationship of Traits and Behaviors," *Personnel Psychology*, Autumn 1999, pp. 591–620; Dorothy Leonard and Walter Swap, *When Sparks Fly: Igniting Creativity in Groups* (Boston: Harvard Business School Press, 1999).

31 Peter Lewis, "Texas Instruments' Lunatic Fringe," *Fortune*, September 4, 2006, p. 122.

32 Merissa Marr, "Redirecting Disney," *The Wall Street Journal*, December 5, 2005, p. B1.

4. *Organizational support in terms of rewards.* Support in terms of encouragement was already mentioned as a condition necessary for creativity. Support can also take such forms as giving recognition and financial rewards for successful new ideas. 3M has long been recognized as an organization that supports creativity. One of the leading company-wide programs lets workers invest 15 percent of their time on their own projects. Such projects did not have to fit into the strategic business plan in the past. One of the most successful projects to come from the program is Post-it® notes, a top-selling product in the United States. However, in the last several years the new 3M CEO demands data about the marketing feasibility of a product before giving financial support. Other companies also offer employees time to pursue pet-project programs as a way of enhancing creativity and innovation. At Google, for example, engineers have "20 percent time" in which they are free to pursue projects they are passionate about.[33]
5. *Greater diversity in groups.* Managers can also cultivate creativity by establishing a group of people with diverse backgrounds. Intellectual diversity, in particular, fans the fire of creativity. A variety of perspectives leads to thinking outside the box and challenging existing paradigms. Tom Preston, the former head of MTV, then Viacom, says that one of the tips for managing a creative organization is to hire passionate, diverse employees.[34]

Exhibit 5-6 lists companies that have been successful in fostering creativity and innovation, making use of many of the practices mentioned in the last several pages.

exhibit 5-6 The World's Most Innovative Companies

The results of a poll of 1,070 senior executives in 63 countries by The Boston Consulting Group, shown below, are particularly useful because they include an explanation of why the companies selected are perceived to be innovative.

Rank	Company	Why
1	Apple	Hello, iPod World. Outstanding design and innovative software platforms create an unrivaled user experience.
2	Google	Allows one of the world's brightest corps of engineers time to experiment. Focuses on simplicity and the customer.
3	3M	Revamped its vaunted R&D labs in 2003 to centralize basic research.
4	Toyota	A master of manufacturing innovation, and now, hybrid technology. New cost-cutting strategy calls for reducing vehicle systems costs as a whole.
5	Microsoft	Primes Windows and Office sales with innovations. A new combo of Web and PC services, called Live, is off to a good start.

33 Ed Frauenheim, "On the Clock But Off on Their Own: Pet Project Programs Set to Gain Wider Acceptance," *Workforce Management*, April 24, 2006, p. 40.

34 Matthew Karnitschnig, "Mr. MTV Moves Up," *The Wall Street Journal*, January 9, 2006, p. B1.

6	General Electric	Transforming from an efficiency powerhouse to one that values bold ideas. Now rates managers on traits such as "imagination and courage."
7	Procter & Gamble	Its "connect and develop" model calls for 50 percent of new products to come from outside. Design and innovation executives are now part of the organization chart.
8	Nokia	Global handset leader. Diverse teams create future-oriented "world maps" to track macro trends. Designed low-cost phones for emerging markets.
9	Starbucks	Would you like a movie with your latte? The creator of the $3 coffee has started marketing films. Taps an army of baristas for customer insight.
10	IBM	Donated 500 of its more than 40,000 patents to help build new technology ecosystems. Co-invests in projects with clients and partners.
11	Virgin	Adds its hip lifestyle brand to everything from airlines to insurance. Enters new businesses at lightning speed.
12	Samsung	An intense design focus, speedy product cycles, and rigorous metrics make the South Korean company a creative force in electronics.
13	Sony	Fell eight spots this year; is trying to claw its way back with a focus on high-def products and a revamped management structure.
14	Dell	Revolutionized the PC supply chain and sales channels. But stuck in Apple's shadow, Dell fell eight spots this year.
15	IDEO	Designed the Palm V and Leap chair. Now helps some of the biggest companies learn design thinking and transform their cultures.
16	BMW	Brings teams together to collaborate inside an innovative research center.
17	Intel	Expanding beyond microprocessors and outside the PC. Poised to launch more products than at anytime in its history.
18	EBay	Built the world's largest online marketplace and a new way of doing business. Launching a fixed-price site to cater to busy consumers.
19	IKEA	A focus on affordable design and a different retail experience have turned the Swedish retailer's shoppers into cult fans.
20	Wal-Mart	Wields technology and pioneers processes to streamline its supply chain.
21	Amazon	Continuously focuses on improving the online experience. Ramping up R&D spending on search and Web services for outside merchants.
22	Target	Embraced design as a differentiator in the discount market. Creative marketing and temporary stores surprise devoted customers.
23	Honda	Known for excellent engineering, Honda is thinking outside the car, with its launch of solar cell production for homes and businesspersons.
24	Research in Motion	Breakthrough mobile devices changed the way business communicates. Dominates the wireless e-mail market.
25	Southwest Airlines	Created the low-cost airline model through operational innovation. Developed fare marketing software for consumers' desktops.

Questions

1. Is there any company not on this list that you would have voted to be included?
2. Is there any company on this list that you would not have voted to be included?
3. Does being on this list of 25 most innovative companies influence whether you would want to work for a particular company?

Source: Jena McGregor, "The World's Most Innovative Companies," *Business Week*, April 24, 2006, pp. 64–65.

Organizational Programs for Improving Creativity and Innovation

Learning objective 6

Describe organizational programs for improving creativity.

Another aspect of the creative organization is formal programs or mechanisms for creativity improvement. Four such mechanisms include creativity training, brainstorming, systematically gathering ideas, and appropriate physical surroundings.

Creativity Training

A standard approach to enhancing individual and organizational creativity is to offer creativity training to many workers throughout the organization. About 30 percent of medium-size and large firms provide some sort of creativity training. Much of creativity training encompasses the ideas already covered in this chapter, such as learning to overcome traditional thinking and engaging in some type of brainstorming. A variety of techniques are used to encourage more flexible thinking, such as engaging in child play, squirting each other with water guns, and scavenger hunts. An extreme technique is to deprive participants of food and rest for 24 hours so their defenses are weakened, and they are then mentally equipped to "think differently." Other creativity-training techniques are more cerebral, such as having participants solve puzzles and ask "what if" questions.

Brainstorming

The best-known method of improving creativity is **brainstorming**. This technique is a method of problem solving carried out by a group. Brainstorming is standard practice for solving real problems facing a company, and is also a creativity-training technique. Group members spontaneously generate numerous solutions to a problem, without being discouraged or controlled. Alex Osborn, the founder of modern brainstorming, believed that one of the main blocks to organizational creativity was the premature evaluation of ideas. The presence of a trained facilitator greatly enhances the productivity of brainstorming meetings.[35]

brainstorming A group method of solving problems, gathering information, and stimulating creative thinking. The basic technique is to generate numerous ideas through unrestrained and spontaneous participation by group members.

Brainstorming produces many ideas; it is not a technique for working out details during the first meeting. Some types of business problems are well suited to brainstorming, such as coming up with a name for a new sports car, identifying ways to attract new customers, and making cost-cutting suggestions. People typically use brainstorming when looking for tentative solutions to nontechnical problems, yet the technique is also used to improve computer programs and systems.

By brainstorming, people improve their ability to think creatively. To achieve the potential advantages of brainstorming, the session must be conducted properly. Exhibit 5-7 presents rules for conducting a brainstorming session, yet the technique continues to evolve. One new suggestion is to assign fieldwork to participants prior to the meeting. Staffers from the design firm Ideo, wanted to devise new high-tech gadgets for children. The team split into three groups: The first group did no preparation; the second group did some background reading; and the third group visited toy stores.

35 Thompson, "Improving the Creativity of Organizational Work Groups," p. 97; Michael Myser, "When Brainstorming Goes Bad," *Business 2.0*, October 2006, p. 76.

exhibit 5-7 Rules for Conducting a Brainstorming Session

RULE 1 Enroll five to eight participants. If you have too few people, you lose the flood of ideas; if you have too many, members feel that their ideas are not important, or too much chatter may result. Set a meeting limit of about 60 minutes because creativity tends to come in intense bursts, and these bursts are mentally draining.

RULE 2 Give everybody the opportunity to generate alternative solutions to the problem. Have them call out these alternatives spontaneously. Encouraging members to prepare for the meeting will often help participation. One useful modification of this procedure is for people to express their ideas one after another, to decrease possible confusion.

RULE 3 Do not allow criticism or value judgments during the brainstorming session. Make all suggestions welcome. Above all, members should not laugh derisively or make sarcastic comments about other people's ideas.

RULE 4 Encourage freewheeling. Welcome bizarre ideas. It is easier to tone down an idea than it is to think one up.

RULE 5 Strive for quantity rather than quality. The probability of discovering really good ideas increases in proportion to the number of ideas generated.

RULE 6 Encourage members to piggyback, or build, on the ideas of others.

RULE 7 The facilitator should record each idea or audio-record the session. Disallow participants from taking notes on a notebook computer or BlackBerry rather than actively participating. Written notes should not identify the author of an idea because participants may worry about saying something foolish.

RULE 8 After the brainstorming session, edit and refine the list of ideas and choose one or two for implementation.

Source: Parts of rules 1 and 8 are from "Finding Inspiration in a Group," *Business 2.0*, April 2005, p. 110.

The toy-store group produced the highest-quality ideas along with the highest quantity said Ideo general manager, Tom Kelley.[36] Another suggestion is to allow natural light into the brainstorming workspace. A sterile, windowless room may not be conducive to idea generation.[37]

Brainstorming can also be conducted through e-mail and other online collaboration tools, generally referred to as electronic brainstorming. The online collaboration tool might include video, audio, file sharing, and sketch pads.[38] In brainstorming by e-mail, group members simultaneously enter their suggestions into a computer. The ideas are distributed to the screens of other group members. Or ideas can be sent back at different times to a facilitator who passes the contributions along to other members. In either approach, although group members do not talk to each other, they are still able to build on each other's ideas and combine ideas.

Systematically Gathering Ideas

The major new thrust in developing an innovative organization is to systematically gather ideas from people inside and outside the firm. An

36 "Finding Inspiration in a Group," *Business 2.0*, April 2005, p. 110.

37 "Future Edisons of America: Turn Your Employees into Inventors," *WorkingSMART*, June 2001, p. 2.

38 Chris Penttila, "Fantastic Forum," *Entrepreneur*, September 2005, p. 92.

internal technique is to set quotas for employee suggestions. Being creative therefore becomes a concrete work goal. Google has taken the practice of idea quotas to the extreme. An intranet (internal Web site) regularly collects fresh ideas from employees, even those without Internet savvy. Every employee spends a fraction of the workday on research and development. One of the tangible outcomes of the intranet for creative ideas is a news-search feature.[39]

Procter & Gamble CEO A. G. Lafley has been searching for new product ideas externally as well as internally since 2000. The executive team identifies promising ideas throughout the world and applies its own capabilities to develop them. P&G collaborates with suppliers, competitors, scientists, entrepreneurs, and others to search for products it can market on its own or in collaboration with the idea source. In a two-year period the company launched more than 100 new products for which some aspect of the development came from outside the company. Two such product winners are the Crest SpinBrush and Mr. Clean Magic Eraser.[40]

The IBM Innovation Jam conducted in 2006 is another example of gathering ideas externally. IBM pulled together online the opinions of approximately 100,000 people with the hopes of finding innovations so powerful they will transform industries, alter human behavior, and lead to new businesses for the company. IBM invited clients, consultants, and employees' family members to tinker with its technologies in the pursuit of new ideas. Anybody who logs on can uses the ideas, and IBM stood ready to invest up to $100 million behind the most fruitful ideas.[41] The payoff in terms of a breathtaking innovation may be years into the future.

Appropriate Physical Surroundings

Creativity is facilitated when the physical environment allows for the flow of ideas, including a room with natural light as previously mentioned. Sun Microsystems provides a representative example of how physical space can be configured to enhance collaboration, including the exchange of ideas. Consultants observed that engineers tended to gather briefly in office doorways and kitchens, and then walk away. This observation spawned the idea that physical spaces should be designed that encourage informal conversations but discourage the workers dispersing. As a result "Forum" spaces extend from the kitchens as open areas designed to encourage informal, chance encounters. Conference rooms are available for spontaneous meetings. Wooden benches, tables, and chairs for reflection and quiet work are provided on company grounds. "Sun rooms" are designed to allow ideas to incubate, and also include white boards along with recreational equipment like Ping-Pong tables.[42]

---

39 Fara Warner, "How Google Searches Itself," *Fast Company*, July 2002, pp. 50, 52.

40 Larry Huston and Nabil Sakkab, "Connect and Develop: Inside Procter & Gamble's New Mode for Innovation," *Harvard Business Review*, March 2006, pp. 58–66.

41 Jessi Hempel, "Big Blue Brainstorm," August 7, 2006, p. 70.

42 Dorothy Leonard and Walter Swap, "Igniting Creativity," *Workforce*, October 1999, pp. 87–90.

The accompanying Management in Action provides details about providing a physical set up to enhance creativity. Despite the merits of physical spaces for idea sharing, many workers need private space to do their best creative thinking. After developing a creative idea, the person might want to refine the idea by interacting with others. Yet the time for independent thinking, away from the buzz of the office, is important. Microsoft makes sure that employees required to do creative work have access to private space, as well as the opportunity for group interaction.

As has been described, creativity and innovation are considered highly important in most organizations. Yet, a caution is in order. A company has to focus on the most important creative ideas, and not attempt every good idea. Too many products and services at the same time can lead to more

management in action

The Innovation Lab at Fisher-Price

Mattel Inc.'s preschool toy unit, Fisher-Price, has its center at company headquarters in East Aurora, N.Y., but it's clearly a separate part of the operation. Called the Cave, the center boasts bean-bag chairs, comfy couches, and adjustable lighting that make people feel as if they're far from the office. Teams of staffers from engineering, marketing, and design meet with child psychologists or other specialists to share ideas. After observing families at play in the field, they return to brainstorm—or "sketchstorm," as they call it. Then they build prototypes of toys from foam, cardboard, glue, and acrylic paint.

Mingling with people from various disciplines is emphasized at the operation. Staffers such as Tina Zinter-Chahin, senior vice-president for research and development, call the interaction spelunking, since it's based on the idea of taking a "deep dive" into product development. "People at first were skeptical," says Ziner-Chahin, noting that toy designers didn't care to spend so much time with marketers. "They said: 'Come on, I'm going to go away for five days and take a marketing person?' We found that while they aren't great with foam and glue guns, they're great at hashing out an idea and positioning the product."

Fisher-Price staffers can point to successes. After observing babies as they learned basic skills, the spelunkers realized that moms spent a lot of time teaching kids about such things in the house as doors, light switches, drawers, and kitchen utensils. While the company could boast about toys that make noise or flash lights, it was short on real-world, practical stuff. It solved the problem with Laugh and Learn Learning Home, a $65 model home made of plastic, where kids can crawl through a front door and explore the alphabet, numbers, music, speech, and different sounds. A smash hit in its 2004 debut, it's now a full line of toys. The outfit has high hopes for a couple of forthcoming products, such as Easy Clean high chair, the result of a spelunk about issues moms had feeding kids.

Questions

1. Why might bean-bag chairs, comfy couches, and adjustable lighting contribute to creativity?
2. From the standpoint of innovation, why does it help Fisher-Price to have toy designers work with marketers?

Source: The facts as reported in Joseph Weber, "'Mosh Pits' of Creativity: Innovation labs are Sparking Teamwork—and Breakthrough Products," *Business Week*, November 7, 2005, pp. 99–100.

complexity than the company can manage. The company needs to optimize revenues and profits by focusing on the most promising new offerings.[43] Yet if creativity and innovation are ignored, a company will not have promising new offerings (like the typewriter, electric coffee pot, personal computer, and cell phone) upon which to concentrate.

Self-Help Techniques for Improving Creativity

Learning objective 7

Implement several suggestions for becoming a more creative problem solver.

In addition to participating in organizational programs for creativity improvement, you can help yourself become more creative. Becoming a more creative problem solver and decision maker requires that you increase the flexibility of your thinking. Reading about creativity improvement or attending one or two brainstorming sessions is insufficient. You must also practice the methods described in the following sections. As with any serious effort at self-improvement, you must exercise the self-discipline to implement these suggestions regularly. Creative people must also be self-disciplined to carefully concentrate on going beyond the obvious in solving problems.

Six Specific Creativity-Building Suggestions

To develop habits of creative thinking, you must regularly practice the suggestions described in the list that follows.[44]

1. Keep track of your original ideas by maintaining an idea notebook or computer file. Few people have such uncluttered minds that they can recall all their past flashes of insight when they need them.
2. Stay current in your field, and be curious about your environment. Having current facts at hand gives you the raw material to link information creatively. (In practice, creativity usually takes the form of associating ideas that are unassociated, such as associating the idea of selling movie tickets with the idea of selling through vending machines.) The person who routinely questions how things work (or why they do not work) is most likely to have an idea for improvement.
3. Improve your sense of humor, including your ability to laugh at your own mistakes. Humor helps reduce stress and tensions, and you will be more creative when you are relaxed.
4. Adopt a risk-taking attitude when you try to find creative solutions. You will inevitably fail a few times. The best-known tale about creativity is that Thomas Edison got the lightbulb right after 99 false starts.
5. Identify the times when you are most creative and attempt to accomplish most of your creative work during that period. Most people are at their peak of creative productivity after ample rest, so try to work on your most vexing

43 Mark Gottfredson and Keith Aspinall, "Innovation Versus Complexity," *Harvard Business Review*, November 2005, pp. 62–71; Robin Hanson, "The Myth of Creativity," *Business Week*, July 3, 2006, p. 134.

44 Eugene Raudsepp, "Exercises for Creative Growth," *Success*, February 1981, pp. 46–47; Mike Vance and Diane Deacon, *Think Out of the Box* (Franklin Lakes, NJ: Career Press, 1995); Interview with John Cleese, "Test: Can You Laugh at His Advice?" *Fortune*, July 6, 1998, pp. 203–204.

problems at the start of the workday. Schedule routine decision making and paperwork for times when your energy level is lower than average.

6. When faced with a creativity block, step back from the problem and engage in a less mentally demanding task for a brief pause, or even a day. Sometimes by doing something quite different, your perspective will become clearer and a creative alternative will flash into your head when you return to your problem. Although creative problem solvers are persistent, they will sometimes put a problem away for awhile so they can come back stronger. The solution will eventually emerge. Patent whiz Steve Harrington says, "When you have a problem it doesn't leave you alone until you have a solution."[45]

Play the Roles of Explorer, Artist, Judge, and Lawyer

One method for improving creativity incorporates many of the suggestions discussed so far. It requires you to adopt four roles in your thinking. First, you must be an *explorer*. Speak to people in different fields to get ideas you can use. Second, be an *artist* by stretching your imagination. Strive to spend about 5 percent of your day asking "what if?" questions. For example, an executive in a swimsuit company might ask, "What if the surgeon general decides that since sunbathing causes skin cancer, we have to put warning labels on bathing suits?" Third, know when to be a *judge*. After developing some wild ideas, evaluate them. Fourth, achieve results with your creative thinking by playing the role of a *lawyer*. Negotiate and find ways to implement your ideas within your field or place of work. You may spend months or years getting your best ideas implemented.[46] One the biggest hurdles in bringing about innovation in an organization is to obtain funding for your brainchild.

---

45 David Tyler, "Patent Whiz Runs Out of Room On His Wall," Rochester, New York *Democrat and Chronicle*, September 13, 2006, p. 9D.

46 "Be a Creative Problem Solver," *Executive Strategies*, June 6, 1989, pp. 1–2.

SUMMARY OF Key Points

1 Differentiate between nonprogrammed and programmed decisions.

Unique and complex decisions are nonprogrammed decisions, whereas programmed decisions are repetitive or routine, and made according to a specific procedure.

2 Explain the steps involved in making a nonprogrammed decision.

The recommended steps for solving problems and making nonprogrammed decisions call for a problem solver to identify and diagnose the problem, develop alternative solutions, evaluate the alternatives, choose an alternative, implement the decision, evaluate and control, and repeat the process if necessary.

3 Understand the major factors that influence decision making in organizations.

Bounds (or limits) to rationality are present in decision making, leading many people to make decisions that suffice. Neuroeconomics helps explain the irrational side of decision making. People vary in their decision-making ability, and the situation can influence the quality of decisions. Factors that influence the quality of decisions are intuition, personality and cognitive intelligence, emotional intelligence, quality and accessibility of information, political considerations, degree of certainty, crisis and conflict, values of the decision maker, and procrastination. Decision-making style focuses on a combination of how information is used and how options are created, such as decisive—one option, less information.

4 Appreciate the value and potential limitations of group decision making.

Group decision making often results in high-quality solutions, because many people contribute. It also helps people feel more committed to the decision. However, the group approach consumes considerable time, may result in compromise solutions that do not really solve the problem, and may encourage groupthink. Groupthink occurs when consensus becomes so important that group members lose their ability to evaluate ideas. It is likely to occur when decision makers have to choose between inevitable losses. Yet, at times groupthink enhances performance.

General problem-solving groups are likely to produce the best results when the decision-making steps are followed closely. The nominal group technique (NGT) is recommended for a situation in which a manager needs to know what alternatives are available and how people will react to them, and wants consensus. Using the technique, a small group of people contribute written thoughts about the problem. Other members respond to their ideas later. Members rate each other's ideas numerically, and the final group decision is the value of the pooled individual votes.

5 Understand the nature of creativity and how it contributes to managerial work.

Creativity is the process of developing novel ideas that can be put into action. Creative people are generally more open and flexible than their less creative counterparts. They are also better able to think laterally, and will often hang on to an idea that the world is not ready to accept.

Creativity takes place when three components join together: expertise, creative-thinking skills, and internal motivation. Perseverance in digging for a solution is also important, and so is an environmental need that stimulates the setting of a goal. Conflict and tension can also prompt people toward creativity. Encouragement contributes to creativity. Certain managerial and organizational practices foster creativity and innovation. To establish a creative atmosphere, managers can (a) provide the right amount of job challenge, (b) give freedom on how to reach goals, (c) provide the right resources, (d) support creativity by such means as rewards, and (e) promote greater diversity in groups.

6 Describe organizational programs for improving creativity.

One organizational program for improving creativity is to conduct creativity training. Brainstorming is the best-known method of improving creativity. The method can also be conducted by e-mail and online collaboration tools. Systematically gathering ideas inside and outside the company often enhances creativity, as does appropriate physical surroundings.

7 Implement several suggestions for becoming a more creative problem solver.

Self-discipline improves creative thinking ability. Creativity-building techniques include staying current in your field and being curious about your environment, improving your sense of humor, and having a risk-taking attitude. A broad approach for improving creativity is to assume the roles of an explorer, artist, judge, and lawyer. Each role relates to a different aspect of creative thinking.

KEY TERMS AND PHRASES

Problem, 147
Decision, 147
Nonprogrammed decision, 147
Programmed decision, 149
Bounded rationality, 153
Satisficing decision, 154
Heuristics, 154
Intuition, 155
Decisiveness, 156
Emotional intelligence, 157
Anchoring, 158
Procrastinate, 161
Decision-making style, 161
Group decisions, 163
Groupthink, 164
Nominal group technique (NGT), 165
Creativity, 168
Lateral thinking, 168
Vertical thinking, 168
Flow experience, 170
Brainstorming, 174

QUESTIONS

1. Describe a problem the manager of a new restaurant might face, and point to the actual and ideal conditions in relation to this problem.
2. How might emotional factors in decision making influence the potential purchase of a business franchise, such as Dunkin' Donuts and Service Master among hundreds of others?
3. How might the use of Internet search engines help you make better decisions on the job?

4. Which one of the factors that influence decision making would likely give you the most trouble? What can you do to get this factor more in your favor?
5. Assume that the director of a social agency was exploring different alternatives for decreasing the number of homeless people in the area. Describe how a political factor might influence his or her decision making.
6. What is a potential disadvantage of giving employees prizes, such as a leather jacket for submitting 100 ideas in the idea quota program?
7. Describe the general approach a firm of five real-estate developers might take to use the nominal group technique for deciding which property to purchase next.

SKILL-BUILDING EXERCISE 5-A: The Forced-Association Technique

A widely used method for releasing creativity is to make forced associations between the properties of two objects to solve a problem. Apply the method by working in small groups. One group member selects a word at random from a dictionary, textbook, or newspaper. Next, the group lists all the properties and attributes of this word. Assume you randomly chose the word *rock*. Among its attributes are "durable," "low-priced," "abundant in supply," "decorative," and "expensive to ship."

You then force-fit these properties to the problem you are facing. Your team might be attempting to improve the quality of an office desk chair. Reviewing the properties of the rock might give you the idea to make the seat covering more durable because it is a quality hot point.

Think of a problem of your own, or perhaps the instructor will assign one. Another possibility is to use as your problem the question of how to expand the market for snow tires. The groups might work for about 15 minutes. To make the technique proceed smoothly, keep up the random search until you hit a noun or adjective. Prepositions usually do not work well in the forced-association technique. Group leaders share their findings with the rest of the class.

SKILL-BUILDING EXERCISE 5-B: Choose an Effective Domain Name

Using brainstorming, huddle in small groups. Your task is to develop original domain names for several products or services. An effective domain name is typically one that is easy to remember and will capture potential customers in an uncomplicated Web search. One reason this exercise is difficult is that "cybersquatters" grab unclaimed names they think business owners might want, and then sell these names later. For example, a cybersquatter (or domain name exploiter) might develop or buy the domain name www.dogfood.com, hoping that an e-tailer of dog food will want this name in the future. The owner of dogfood.com would charge a company like Pet Smart every time a surfer looking to purchase dog food over the Internet, entered dogfood.com and was then linked to Pet Smart.

After your team has brainstormed a few possible domain names, search the Internet to see if your domain name is already in use. Simply enter "www" plus the name you have chosen into your browser. Or visit the site of a company like http://www.DomainCollection.com/Inc. After you have developed your list of domain names not already in use, present your findings to the rest of the class.

- Hair salons
- Replacement parts for antique or classic autos
- A used-car chain
- Massage therapy salons
- Personal loans for people with poor (subprime) credit ratings
- Recycled steel for manufacturers
- You choose one of your own

INTERNET SKILL-BUILDING EXERCISE: Learning About Creativity Training

Use the Internet to learn more about what companies are doing to enhance employee creativity. Be specific when you make an entry in your search engine to avoid being deluged with a choice of Web sites far removed from your topic. A sample phrase to enter into your search engine would be "creativity training programs for business." When you have located one or two sites that give some details about a training program, compare the information you've found to the information in this chapter about creativity training. Note similarities and differences, and be prepared to discuss your findings in class.

Case Problem 5-A

The Sticky-Priced Condo

Jack Cauldron and Sarah Toomey, a married couple, live in Reston, Virginia. Upon getting married in 2002, they both gave up their rental apartments and jointly purchased a condominium apartment for $145,000. Jack and Sarah meticulously maintained their condo, including repainting each room, laying down new carpeting, and installing a closet organizing system in all three closets.

Several years later they decided they wanted to live in a condominium townhouse to give them more space and more privacy. Also, they wanted a private garage and the possibility of more room should they be fortunate enough to have a baby. Jack and Sarah signed a contract with Wendy McMaster, a real-estate agent referred to them by a neighbor. Wendy signed on to assist the couple both in the sale of their condominium and the purchase of their new home.

Within five days, Wendy found a condominium less than five miles away that fit their requirements: four bedrooms, three baths, two-car garage, finished basement, dining room, and sunroom. The asking price was $565,000 with perhaps a little room for price negotiation.

"Now, let's seriously discuss the pricing of your condo so we can sell it quickly, and move you into your dream home," said Wendy. "Unless your condo is on the market, you won't be able to make a contingency offer on the new place. As we mentioned earlier," said Sarah, "Jack and I agree that we should get at least $215,000 for our place."

Wendy replied, "Hold on Jack and Sarah, I think that you two are shooting for the moon. What makes you think your condo will haul in $215,000?"

Sarah said, "We have fixed up this place so much. It is so elegant. And just two months ago, a condo in this development much less nice than ours sold for $210,000. It would be an insult for us to sell for less than $215,000."

After reflecting for a few moments, Wendy said, "You are asking too much in the real-estate market as it stands today. I look at comparable condos that are selling for $190,000. Why don't you too think about the price over the weekend? I will get back to you. Keep in mind that the new condo you want will be ideal living. Also, it will be a great investment."

Wendy met again with Jack and Sarah on Monday night. She suggested to the couple that they set the selling price of their condo at $195,000 which would give them some wiggle room. Jack responded, "Absolutely not, Wendy. We have a gorgeous place that should have no problem fetching $215,000 in today's market."

Wendy said with a gasp and a smile, "It looks like you two are suffering from what we real-estate agents call *sticky prices*. These are people who won't cut their demands enough to make a deal possible."

Discussion Questions

1. What would you advise Jack and Sarah to do about pricing their condo for sale?
2. In what way are the sellers displaying neuroeconomics in making a decision about selling their condominium?
3. If you were Wendy McMaster, how would you attempt to convince Jack and Sarah to accept a lower price for their condo?

Source: Several of the facts in this case are from Kristin Downey, "For Sale, By the Owner's Ego," *The Washington Post*, November 4, 2006, pp. F1, F7, F8–F9.

Case Problem 5-B

Staple's Annual Creativity Contest

Henry Ford. Thomas Alva Edison. Adrian Chernoff? Maybe Chernoff isn't a household name like the first two inventors, but the 33-year-old Royal Oak, Michigan, man certainly shows potential. Chernoff's claim to fame—a handy little office product called Rubber Bandits—started gracing the shelves of every Staples store in North America a few years ago. The labeling bands, which retail at $2.99, also have their own Web site, and can be purchased online through Staples.

The General Motors Corp. employee was one of last year's finalists in Staples' Invention Quest. The contest is part of a broad effort by Staples to develop an exclusive product line to distinguish its private brand line from those of competitors. Inaugurated several years ago, the contest is aimed at budding inventors looking to create the next Post-it note or better. About 10,000 entries are received annually. Besides giving inventors the gratification of seeing their ideas hit the shelves in 1,600 office superstores, Staples promises to share the profits. Winners of the contest receive $25,000 and as high as an 8 percent royalty. One year's winner was a California man who created WordLock, a combination lock that allows users to select their combinations using letters rather than the traditional set of numbers.

Chernoff walked away with $5,000, a licensing agreement with the office-supply store and the official title of inventor. "The best part for me right now is seeing it actually make its way in the market place," Chernoff said. "The product is going into practice in the real world."

Maybe an extra-large rubber band with a wear-and-tear-resistance label won't solve the world's problems. But Rubber Bandits do make it easier to bundle and label piles of paperwork. And it definitely makes a nice workplace projectile, although Chernoff says that was not its original purpose.

Chernoff centered his career on creativity. Besides having a bachelor's degree and two master's degrees from the University of New Mexico, in business and engineering, his résumé includes jobs working on robots for the National Aeronautics and Space Administration and designing new rides for The Walt Disney Co.

Rubber Bandits popped into his mind on a shuttle bus ride between Denver and Boulder, Colorado, where he was visiting a brother. He started pondering office efficiency, and the problems people have of losing things in the shuffle.

Discussion Questions

1. Why should Rubber Bandits be classified as a creative idea?
2. What does this story illustrate about how creative ideas surface?
3. In what way might having studied both business and engineering helped Adrian Chernoff become an inventor?

Source: Karen Dyris, "Staples Hunting for Next Wave of Ideas, Inventors," *Detroit News* syndicated story, May 10, 2005; William M. Bulkeley, "Got a Better Letter Opener? Staples Solicits Inventive Ideas From the Public for Products It Can Sell Exclusively," *The Wall Street Journal*, July 13, 2006, pp. B1, B6.

chapter 6

Quantitative Techniques for Planning and Decision Making

Stores throughout the 7-Eleven empire have been turned into logistical marvels. In a matter of seconds, any store manager can tap into 7-Eleven's proprietary computer system and pull up real-time data on what products are selling best at that location or across the country. Instant weather reports, too, can dictate whether more umbrellas are needed for an impending storm of if a store should stock up on a muffin that sells particularly well when the temperature drops below 40 degrees F. Employees are trained to stay current on upcoming sporting events or school functions to prepare for a surge in beer runs or notebook purchases. The constant tweaking means that slow-moving items are cleared away, so managers can make way for some of the 50 or so new ones 7-Eleven introduces every week. That leads to fewer overstocks and understocks, which begets happier customers.

"There's no replenishment model in the world that can respond like the eyes and ears of a retailer," says CEO Jim Keyes. But even the most informed manager would flounder without the strong tech backbone. 7-Eleven stores are equipped with NEC handhelds designed exclusively for the chain. Using the handhelds, store operators place orders each morning for items that need replenishing the next day, and many of those requests are beamed to one of the 23 third-party distribution centers 7-Eleven has

Objectives

After studying this chapter and doing the exercises, you should be able to:

1 Explain how managers use data-based decision making.

2 Explain the use of forecasting techniques in planning.

3 Describe how to use Gantt charts, milestone charts, and PERT planning techniques.

4 Describe how to use break-even analysis and decision trees for problem solving and decision making.

5 Describe how to manage inventory by using the economic order quantity (EOQ), the just-in-time (JIT) system, and LIFO versus FIFO.

6 Describe how to identify problems using a Pareto diagram.

partnered with in the past decade. (The data also go to headquarters to be stored and analyzed.) At the centers, in warehouses akin to enormous refrigerators, local suppliers drop off their inventory for sorting.

The system is a godsend for entrepreneurially minded store managers like Andrey Vinogradsky. At 8:30 on a recent morning, Vinogradsky prowls the aisles of his San Francisco store with the NEC handheld, scanning best-sellers like the King's Hawaiian Sweet Roll. The device instantly calculates how many have moved since last week and suggests an order, but Vinogradsky decides to up the number to 17, knowing that tomorrow is Thursday, his busiest day. As he works his way through the store, he passes several items that are there only because of his own initiative. Six months ago, for example, when Vinogradsky arrived at the outlet, he immediately noticed a flood of tourists who came in asking for maps, postcards, and other items that the story didn't carry. Now it does, because Vinogradsky lined up a local vendor and began stocking them.

"All of these tools allow me to provide what my customers really want," Vinogradsky says. "Without them, my job would be twice as hard."

The technological overhaul has done more than empower store managers. It has helped 7-Eleven regain control over distribution and product decisions that for decades had been dictated but its major suppliers. Now 7-Eleven is getting suppliers to play by its rules, in part because the precise sales data it generates help the suppliers predict demand for their products nationwide. "They'd been doing it the old way for a hundred years," Keyes says. Anheuser, for one, resisted giving up control. But, Keyes says, it eventually saw the economic advantage in ceding stocking and distribution decisions to 7-Eleven. Today store managers can communicate directly with Anheuser's delivery staff (most often by handheld computer) to customize their mix of beverages. For the past four years, Keyes has seen a 6 to 10 percent annual increase in sales of Anheuser beer (including Budweiser) at 7-Eleven—a startling jump in an industry where 2 percent growth is considered healthy.[1]

The 7-Eleven push toward making better merchandising decisions based on quantitative facts illustrates how the modern manager often uses data-based decision making to improve profitability. To make planning and decision making more accurate, a variety of techniques based on the scientific method, mathematics, and statistics have been developed. This chapter will provide sufficient information for you to acquire basic skills in

---

1 Excerpted from Elizabeth Esfahani, "7-Eleven Gets Sophisticated," *Business 2.0*, January/February 2005, pp. 96, 98, 100.

several widely used techniques for planning and decision making. You can find more details about these techniques in courses and books about production and operations management and accounting. All these quantitative tools are useful, but they do not supplant human judgment and intuition. For example, a decision-making technique might tell a manager that it will take four months to complete a project. She might say, "Could be, but if I put my very best people on the project, we can beat that estimate."

As you read and work through the various techniques, recognize that software is available to carry them out. A sampling of appropriate software is presented in Exhibit 6-1. Before using a computer to run a technique, however, it is best to understand the technique and try it out manually or with a calculator. Such firsthand knowledge can prevent accepting computer-generated information that is way offtrack. Similarly, many people use spell checkers without a good grasp of word usage. The results can be misleading and humorous, such as "Each of our employees is assigned to a *manger*" or "The company picnic will proceed as scheduled *weather* or not we have good *whether*."

exhibit 6-1 Software for Quantitative Planning and Decision-Making Techniques

Managers and professionals generally rely on computers to make use of quantitative planning and decision-making techniques. Examples of applicable software are presented at the right, and should be referred to for on-the-job-application of these techniques.

Forecasting Techniques	Excel-Based ForecastX™ (John Galt Solutions Inc.); Forecast Pro (Business Forecast Systems Inc.); PROPHIX; spreadsheet programs can also be used to make forecasts based on trend data.
Gantt Charts and Milestone Charts	SmartDraw; E Project Management Software
PERT Diagrams	MinuteMan Plus (MinuteMan Systems); Envision Software; PERT Chart EXPERT (Critical Tools Inc.)
Break-Even Analysis	Orion Business Center; Business Plan Software
Decision Trees	TreeAge; SmartDraw
Economic Order Quantity	Software would be superfluous, use pocket calculator. However, the EOQs that you calculate can be entered into a spreadsheet and updated as needed.
Just-in-Time (JIT) Inventory Management	Blue Claw Database Design; Just-in-Time Software Solutions
Pareto Diagrams	Envision Software; SPC for Excel
All Techniques Combined	Enterprise software controls an entire company's operations, linking them together. The software automates finance, manufacturing, and human resources, incorporating stand-alone software such as that designed for PERT and break-even analysis. Enterprise software also helps make decisions based on market research. Specific types of enterprise software have several different names. (Four key suppliers are SAP; Oracle, Siebel; and NEC Enterprise Software Solutions.)

DATA-BASED DECISION MAKING

Learning Objective 1

Explain how managers use data-based decision making.

data-driven management
An attitude and approach to management rather than a specific technique that stems from data-based decision making.

The chapter opener about 7-Eleven stores making extensive use of quantitative data to make merchandising decisions illustrates how numbers and facts influence managerial decision making. **Data-driven management** refers to the idea that decisions are based on facts rather than impressions or guesses.[2] The idea is straightforward: before making a decision of consequence the managerial worker should gather facts that could influence the outcome of the decision. The quantitative techniques described in this chapter assist the process of data-driven management, yet simply gathering relevant facts can make data-driven management possible.

The discussion about using high-quality information in making decisions (Chapter 5) is part of data-driven management. Also, people who are scientifically oriented use data-driven management quite naturally. Executive dashboards, described in Chapter 14, give managers access to a wide variety of real-time information such as items sold, profit, and spending versus budget.

Many managers want to see the data before accepting a suggestion from a subordinate. Marissa Mayer, the vice president for search products and user experiences at Google Inc., is one such manager. One of her "9 notions of innovation" is "Don't politic, use data." She discourages the use of "I like" in meetings, pushing staffers instead to use "metrics."[3] How might this use of data work in practice?

During a meeting with Mayer, a staff member might make the comment, "I don't think we have much to worry about from A9.com, the Amazon search engine. Almost nobody has heard about it or is using it." Mayer might reply, "Get back to me when you can cite some hard data about how many people are using A9.com instead of Google when they conduct a search. At that point we can decide on the competitive threat posed by A9."

Data-driven management is more of an attitude and approach rather than a specific technique, and it is hardly new. You attempt to gather relevant facts before making a decision of consequence. Suppose a small-business owner wants to repaint the walls inside the office. The office manager suggests buying a premium brand of paint because such paint stays fresher looking longer and does not chip as readily. The data-driven manager would say, "Where is the evidence that if we have the painter use premium paint the walls will look better longer and resist chipping? Show me the evidence."

Although data-driven management is preferable in most situations, intuition and judgment still contribute to making major decisions. At times relevant data may not be available, so acting on hunches can be essential. A major new source of recruiting for truckers is early retiree couples who enjoy heavy travel.[4] Before actively recruiting older people as potential truckers to help with the acute trucker shortage, several trucking association executives guessed that this

2 http://www.pheatt.emporia.edu/courses/2002/, accessed November 17, 2006.

3 Michele Conlin, "Champions of Innovation," *Business Week*, June 2006, p. IN 20.

4 Stephanie Chen, "How Baby Boomers Turn Wanderlust Into Trucking Careers," *The Wall Street Journal*, August 24, 2006, pp. A1, A8.

demographic group might be attracted to trucking. Now trucking managers have some data to work with in terms of recruiting retiree couples as truckers.

The accompanying Management in Action presents more details of how a successful manager relies heavily on data before making major decisions.

management in action

Data-Driven Decision Making at Hewlett-Packard

When Mark Hurd was named chief executive of Hewlett-Packard Co. in March 2005, the board gave him a clear mission: fix the giant computer and printer make, which was suffering from slow growth and inconsistent results. Hurd took a big step forward attempting to fulfill that mandate when he embarked on a sweeping plan in July 2005 to cut costs and restructure the company. He planned to lay off 14,500 employees, or about 10 percent of the company's global workforce, modify its pension benefits, and revamp its sales force in an effort to make the company more efficient and better able to service customers. (All of these plans were implemented by 2007.)

But before Hurd could attempt to fix HP, he had to figure out HP. So, shortly after arriving at the Palo Alto, California, company, the 48-year-old former chief executive of NCR Corp. set about to collect information methodically. He spent time with senior executives, conducted extensive business reviews and even traveled with sales people to meet HP customers firsthand. He visited HP offices and factories from Boise to Beijing. At each site he spoke to employees and sought feedback. In all, he has collected more than 5,000 e-mails from HP staffers. With his findings, Hurd built two computer models—one financial and the other an operating model—designed to help plot the company's course.

"I have a pretty standard process," Hurd said. Getting out into the field "is some of the best market research I can get."

After reviewing the businesses at each site, Hurd typically held an employee "coffee talk" in the afternoon. For him, the aim is to trigger feedback from employees so that they can unearth facts not covered by managers. Many visits are dominated "by the biggest personalities," he says. "But it's some of the people who don't speak up who send the crispest two-page e-mails."

About 320 new e-mails arrive every day, the company says. Hurd has also encouraged staffers to call him directly: Hearing someone's voice helps him understand what they are emphasizing and their emotion, he says.

Then came the rigorous analysis. Back at his Palo Alto office, Hurd reviewed the findings from a site visit or business review with executives. Based on a series of spreadsheets, these models change daily as Hurd adds new facts and thoughts from his travels, such as the number of salespeople in an office versus the size of a sales territory, and ruminations on what kinds of capabilities need to be added or subtracted from a facility.

The goal of the models is to winnow down all the information being collected onto a single page that lays out a vision of HP's future and how to get there. "I want to get everything between us and the goal line on a piece of paper," says Hurd.

Questions

1. Why might employees and customers be a valuable source of input for Hurd in making decisions about the future of HP?
2. In what way is employee input shaping the future of HP?
3. What, if any, ethical issues might there be in collecting input from employees about fixing the company, then laying off 14,500 of them?

Source: Excerpted from Pui-Wing Tam, "Rewiring Hewlett-Packard," *The Wall Street Journal*, July 20, 2005, p. B1.

FORECASTING METHODS

Learning objective 2

Explain the use of forecasting techniques in planning.

All planning involves making forecasts, or predicting future events. Forecasting is important because if a manager fails to spot trends and react to them before the competition does, the competition can gain an invaluable edge. As noted in an executive newsletter: "The handwriting is on the wall. The way your business reacts to newly emerging trends is perhaps the best barometer of your future success."[5] The forecasts used in strategic planning are especially difficult to make because they involve long-range trends. Unknown factors might crop up between the time the forecast is made and the time about which predictions are made. This section will describe approaches to and types of forecasting.

Qualitative and Quantitative Approaches

Forecasts can be based on both qualitative and quantitative information. Most of the forecasting done for strategic planning relies on a combination of both. *Qualitative* methods of forecasting consist mainly of subjective hunches. For example, an experienced executive might predict that the high cost of housing will create a demand for small, less-expensive homes, even though this trend cannot be quantified. One qualitative method is a **judgmental forecast**, a prediction based on a collection of subjective opinions. It relies on analysis of subjective inputs from a variety of sources, including consumer surveys, sales representatives, managers, and panels of experts. For instance, a group of potential homebuyers might be asked how they would react to the possibility of purchasing a compact, less-expensive home.

PLAY VIDEO

QUANTITATIVE TECHNIQUES FOR PLANNING AND DECISION MAKING

"Go to academic.cengage.com/management/dubrin and view the video. Does Cold Stone Creamery represent a high performance approach to planning? Why or why not?"

Quantitative forecasting methods involve either the extension of historical data or the development of models to identify the cause of a particular outcome. A widely used historical approach is **time-series analysis**. This technique is simply an analysis of a sequence of observations that have taken place at regular intervals over a period of time (hourly, weekly, monthly, and so forth). The underlying assumption of this approach is that the future will be much like the past. Exhibit 6-2 shows a basic example of a time-series analysis chart. This information might be used to make forecasts about when people would be willing to take vacations. Such forecasts would be important for the resort and travel industry. A time-series forecast works best in a relatively stable situation. For example, an unusually strong or weak hurricane season makes it difficult to predict the demand for home improvement materials. Home Depot faced this problem in 2006 when a mild hurricane season contributed to lower numbers than forecast for sales to building contractors. If you use a spreadsheet program such as Excel to make forecasts, you will find that the input data are part of a time-series analysis. The future trends projected are based on historical data.

judgmental forecast
A qualitative forecasting method based on a collection of subjective opinions.

time-series analysis
An analysis of a sequence of observations that have taken place at regular intervals over a period of time (hourly, weekly, monthly, and so forth).

Many firms use quantitative and qualitative approaches to forecasting. Forecasting begins with a quantitative prediction, which provides basic data

5 Daniel Levinas, "How to Stop the Competition from Eating Your Lunch," *Executive Focus*, May 1998, pp. 55–58.

exhibit 6-2 **Time-Series Analysis Chart**

A time-series analysis uses the past to make predictions.

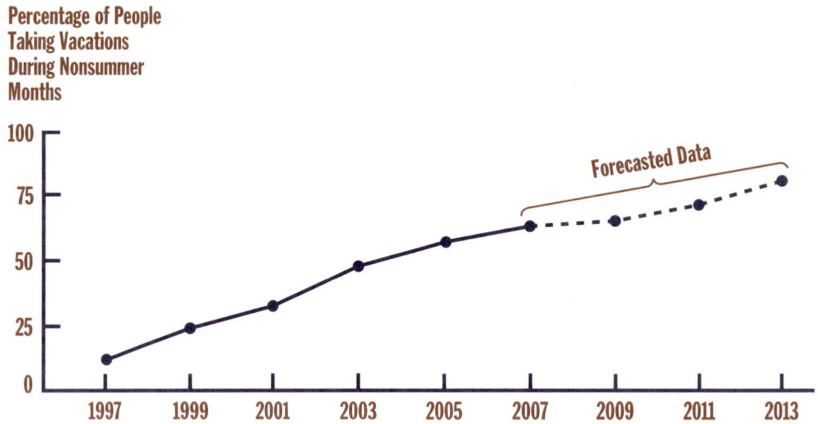

about a future trend. An example of a quantitative prediction is the forecast of a surge in demand for flat-screen television receivers, 50 inches or greater. Next, the qualitative forecast is added to the quantitative forecast, somewhat as a reality check. For example, a quantitative forecast might predict that if the current growth trend continues, every household in North America will contain three 50-inch TV sets by 2012.

The quantitative forecast is then adjusted according to the subjective data supplied by the qualitative forecast. In this case, it could be reasoned that the growth trend was extrapolated too aggressively. In many instances, a quantitative forecast will serve as a reality check on the qualitative forecasts because numerical data is more accurate than intuition.

Three errors or traps are particularly prevalent when making forecasts or estimates.[6] One is the *overconfidence trap*, whereby people overestimate the accuracy of their forecasts. A CEO might be so confident of the growth of her business that she moves the company into expensive new headquarters. Based on her confidence, she does not prepare contingency plans in case the estimated growth does not take place. A second problem is the *prudence trap*, in which people make cautious forecasts "just to be on the safe side." Being safe can mean taking extra measures just not to be caught short, such as a restaurant owner buying ten extra boxes of strawberries "just to be safe." If the strawberry desserts go unsold, the owner is stuck unless he can make strawberry pudding for tomorrow's menu.

A third problem is the *recallability trap* whereby our forecasts are influenced by extremely positive or negative incidents we recall. If a manager vividly recalls success stories from global expansion to Singapore, he might overestimate the chances of succeeding in that country.

6 John S. Hammond, Ralph L. Keeney, and Howard Raiffa, "The Hidden Traps in Decision Making," *Harvard Business Review*, September–October 1998, pp. 55–58.

Being aware of these traps can help you take a more disciplined approach to forecasting. For example, to reduce the effect of the overconfidence trap, start by considering the extremes—the possible highs and lows. Try to imagine a scenario in which your forecast could be way too high or way too low and make appropriate adjustments if necessary. For a reality check, discuss your forecasts with other knowledgeable people. To become a good forecaster, you need to make a large number of predictions and then look for feedback on the accuracy of these predictions.

Types of Forecasts

Three types of forecasts are used most widely: economic, sales, and technological. Each of these forecasts can be made by using both qualitative and quantitative methods. Forecasts that are updated regularly with fresh data are referred to as *rolling forecasts*. The presence or absence of hurricanes, as mentioned above, would be useful in updating a yearly sales forecast in the building-supply industry.

Economic Forecasting

No single factor is more important in managerial planning than predicting the level of future business activity. Strategic planners in large organizations rely often on economic forecasts made by specialists they hire. Planners in smaller firms are more likely to rely on government forecasts, or speaking to other business people. However, forecasts about the general economy do not necessarily correspond to business activity related to a particular product or service. Assume that you are a manager at an office-supply company, such as Office Max or Staples. The following forecast prepared by the World Future Society might prompt you to stock up on home-office systems:

> *More than 100 million people will telecommute to work by the year 2015. This increase will distribute worldwide wealth more rapidly, save energy, reduce global pollution, and transfer real estate values.*[7]

A major factor in the accuracy of forecasts is time span: Short-range predictions are more accurate than long-range predictions. Strategic planning is long-range planning, and many strategic plans have to be revised frequently to accommodate changes in business activity. For example, a sudden recession may abort plans for diversification into new products and services.

Sales Forecasting

The sales forecast is usually the primary planning document for a business. Even if the general economy is robust, an organization needs a promising sales forecast before it can be aggressive about capitalizing on new opportunities. Strategic planners themselves may not be involved in making sales forecasts, but to develop master plans they rely on forecasts from the marketing unit. For instance, the major tobacco companies have embarked on strategic plans to diversify into a number of nontobacco businesses, such as soft drinks and food products. An important factor in

---

7 *Special Report: Forecasts for the Next 25 Years*, p. 3 (Published by the World Future Society, 2004).

the decision to implement this strategic plan was a forecast of decreased demand for tobacco products in the domestic market. The cause for decreased demand was health concerns of the public, and numerous anti-smoking campaigns.

According to marketing consultant Terry Elliott, sales forecasts are likely to be more accurate if they are based on several types of data. A manager of a home-electronics store might include the following data sources in preparing a sales forecast for the present year: (1) average sales volume per square foot for similar stores in similar locations and size, (2) the number of households within five miles who intend to purchase home electronic devices, and (3) sales revenues for each type of item or service offered. A service might be in-home installation of electronic products. Elliott also recommends that the owner generate three figures: pessimistic, optimistic, and realistic. The pessimistic forecast might alert the owner to the importance of lining up credit or conserving cash.[8]

Technological Forecasting

A technological forecast predicts what types of technological changes will take place. Technological forecasts allow a firm to adapt to new technologies and thus stay competitive. For example, forecasts made in the late 1990s about the explosive growth of e-commerce have enabled many firms to ready themselves technologically for the future. At first a lot of the activity was unprofitable, yet the majority of industrial and consumer companies that prepared to buy and sell over the Internet soon found it to be profitable. By mid-2000 technological forecasts were made of the abundant availability of Wi-Fi at places of work, airports, hotels, and restaurants. This forecast encouraged the manufacturing and marketing of portable computers and personal digital assistants suited for the wireless environment. (*Wi-Fi* refers to Wireless Fidelity, a high-speed, high-capacity network built on radio signals.)

GANTT CHARTS AND MILESTONE CHARTS

Learning Objective 3

Describe how to use Gantt charts, milestone charts, and PERT planning techniques.

Two basic tools for monitoring the progress of scheduled projects are Gantt charts and milestone charts. Closely related to each other, they both help a manager keep track of whether activities are completed on time. Both techniques include the use of numbers, so they can be classified as quantitative.

Gantt Charts

During the era of scientific management, Henry Gantt developed a chart for displaying progress on a project. An early application was tracking the progress of building a ship.[9]

A **Gantt chart** graphically depicts the planned and actual progress of work over the period of time encompassed by a project. Gantt charts are

8 Terry Elliott, "Sales Forecasting by Multiple Methods Is Most Accurate," *About Small Business: Canada* (http://www.sbinfocanada.about.com), Accessed November 17, 2006.

9 "Gantt Chart," *NetMBA* (http://www.netmba.com/operations/project/gantt), accessed November 17, 2006, p. 1.

especially useful for scheduling one-time projects such as constructing buildings, making films, or building an airplane. Charts of this type are also called time-and-activity charts, because time and activity are the two key variables they consider. Time is plotted on the horizontal axis; activities listed on the vertical axis.

Gantt chart
A chart that depicts the planned and actual progress of work during the life of the project.

Despite its simplicity, the Gantt chart is a valuable and widely used control technique. It also provides the foundation of more sophisticated types of time-related charts, such as the PERT diagram described later.

Exhibit 6-3 shows a Gantt chart used to schedule the opening of a small office building. Gantt charts used for most other purposes would have a similar format. At the planning phase of the project, the manager lays out the schedule by using rectangular boxes. As each activity is completed, the appropriate box is shaded. At any given time, the manager can see which activities have been completed on time. For example, if the building owner has not hired a contractor for the grounds by August 31, the activity would be declared behind schedule.

The Gantt also depicts dependent activities, such as, in Exhibit 6-3, hiring contractors being dependent on first getting the building permit. The dependent activities must be completed in sequence. However, some of the activities are nondependent or "parallel." For example, some developers obtain leases before a building is completed.

The Gantt chart presented here is quite basic. On most Gantt charts, the bars are movable strips of plastic. Different colors indicate scheduled and actual progress. Mechanical boards with pegs to indicate scheduled dates and actual progress can also be used. Some managers and specialists now use

exhibit 6-3 **A Gantt Chart Used for Opening a Small Office Building**

A Gantt chart helps keep track of progress on a project.

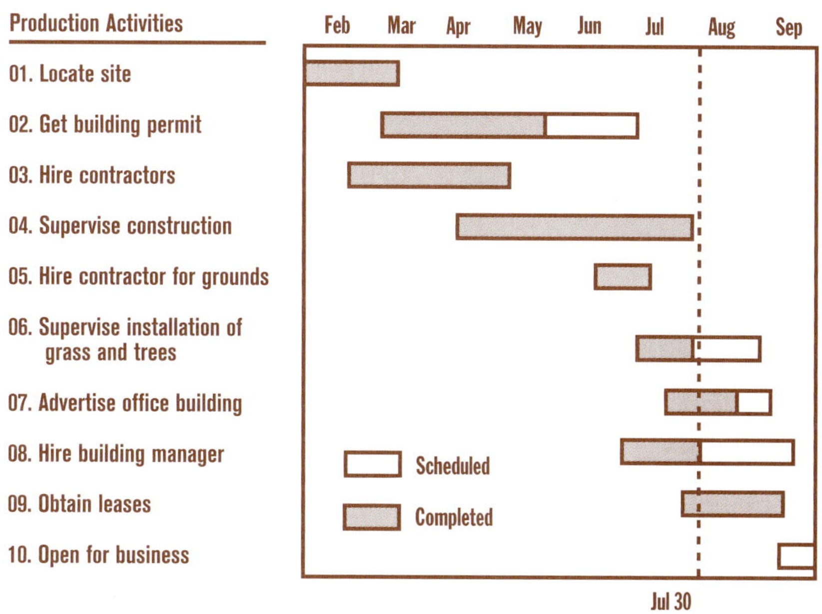

milestone chart An extension of the Gantt chart that provides a listing of the subactivities that must be completed to accomplish the major activities listed on the vertical axis.

computer graphics to prepare their own high-tech Gantt charts. You can also use a spreadsheet to readily construct a Gantt chart.

Because Gantt charts are used to monitor progress, they also act as control devices. When the chart shows that the building-permit activity has fallen behind schedule, the manager can investigate the problem and solve it. The Gantt chart gives a convenient overall view of the progress made against the schedule. However, its disadvantage is that it does not furnish enough details about the subactivities that need to be performed to accomplish each general item.

Milestone Charts

A **milestone chart** is an extension of the Gantt chart. It provides a listing of the subactivities that must be completed to accomplish the major activities listed on the vertical axis. The inclusion of milestones, which are the completion of individual phases of an activity, adds to the value of a Gantt chart as a scheduling and control technique. Each milestone serves as a checkpoint on progress. In Exhibit 6-4, the Gantt chart for constructing a small office building has been expanded into a milestone chart. The numbers in each

exhibit 6-4 A Milestone Chart Used for Opening a Small Office Building

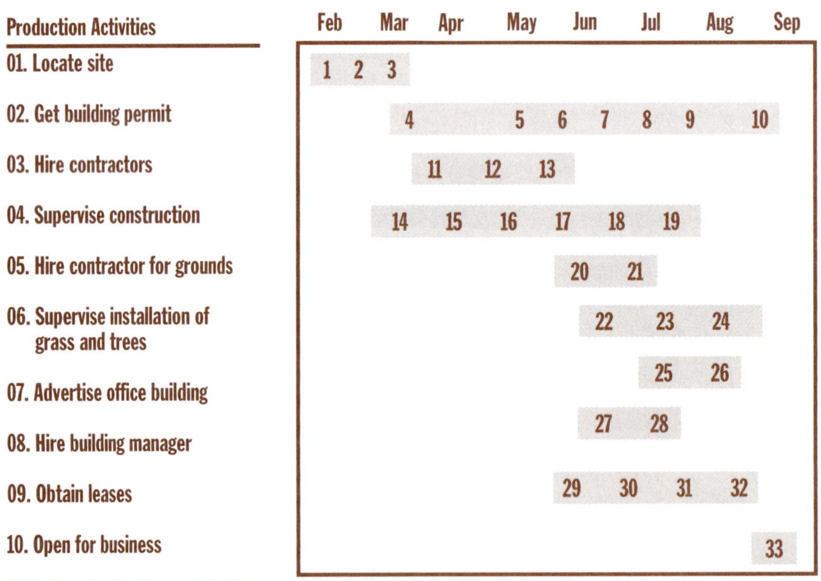

Milestones to Be Accomplished

- •
- •
- •

29. Speak to friends and acquaintances about space availability.
30. Put ad in local newspaper.
31. Conduct interviews with rental applicants and check credit history of best potential tenants.
32. Offer lease to most creditworthy candidates.
33. Have grand-opening celebration September 5.

rectangle represent milestones. A complete chart would list each of the 33 milestones. In Exhibit 6-4 only the milestones for obtaining leases (including screening tenants) and the opening date are listed.

PROGRAM EVALUATION AND REVIEW TECHNIQUE

Gantt and milestone charts are basic scheduling tools, exceeded in their basic versions only in simplicity by a to-do list. A more complicated method of scheduling activities and events uses a network model. The model depicts all the interrelated events that must take place for a project to be completed. The most widely used network-modeling tool is the **program evaluation and review technique** (**PERT**). It is used to track the planning activities required to complete a large-scale, nonrepetitive project. PERT was originally developed in 1958 by the United States Department of Defense to assist with the Polaris mobile submarine launch project. PERT has the potential to reduce the time and cost required to complete a project because activities can be sequenced efficiently.

A scheduling technique such as PERT is useful when certain tasks have to be completed before others if the total project is to be completed on time. In the small office building example, the site of the building must be specified before the owner can apply for a building permit. (The building commission will grant a permit only after approving a specific location.) The PERT diagram indicates such a necessary sequence of events.

PERT is used most often in engineering and construction projects. It has also been applied to such business problems as marketing campaigns, company relocations, and convention planning. Here we examine the basics of PERT, along with a few advanced considerations.

program evaluation and review technique (PERT)
A network model used to track the planning activities required to complete a large-scale, nonrepetitive project. It depicts all of the interrelated events that must take place.

Key PERT Concepts

Two concepts lie at the core of PERT: event and activity. An **event** is a point of decision or the accomplishment of an activity or task. Events are also called *milestones*. The events involved in the merger of two companies would include sending out announcements to shareholders, changing the company name, and letting customers know of the merger.

event
In the PERT method, a point of decision or the accomplishment of a task.

An **activity** is the time-consuming aspect of a project or simply a task that must be performed. Before an activity can begin, its preceding activities must be completed—such as installing dry wall before painting the wall. One activity in the merger example is working with a public relations firm to arrive at a suitable name for the new company. Activities that have to be accomplished in the building example include supervising contractors and interviewing potential tenants.

activity
In the PERT method, the physical and mental effort required to complete an event.

Steps Involved in Preparing a PERT Network

The events and activities included in a PERT network are laid out graphically, as shown in Exhibit 6-5. Preparing a PERT network consists of four steps:

exhibit 6-5 A PERT Network for Opening a Building

Each numeral in the diagram equals the expected time for an activity, such as 5 weeks to locate site (between circles A and B) and 13 weeks to supervise installation of grass and trees (between circles E and F). The critical path is the estimated time for all the activities shown above the thick arrows (13 + 30 + 6 + 13 + 8 + 14 + 8 + 1 = 93).

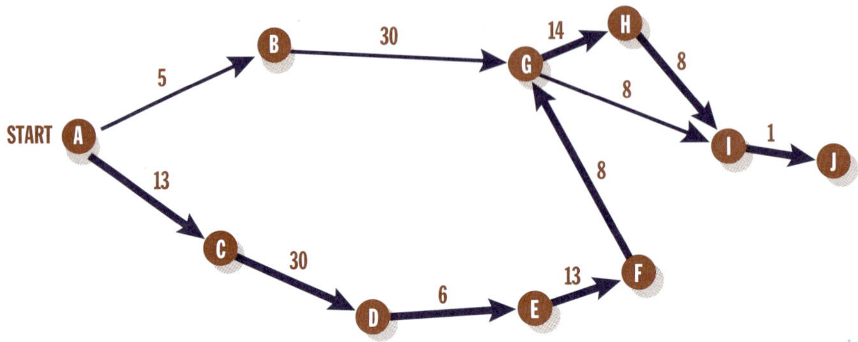

1. *Prepare a list of all the activities and events necessary to complete the project.* In the building example, the activities include locating the site, getting the building permit, and so forth. Many more activities and subactivities could be added to this example. The events are the completion of the activities such as (C) hiring the contractors.
2. *Design the actual PERT network, relating all the activities to each other in the proper sequence.* Anticipating all the activities in a major project requires considerable skill and judgment. In addition, activities must be sequenced—the planner must decide which activity must precede another. In the building example, the owner would want to hire a grounds contractor before hiring a building manager.
3. *Estimate the time required to complete each activity.* This step must be done carefully because the major output of the PERT method is a statement of the total time required by the project. Because the time estimate is critical, several people should be asked to make three different estimates: optimistic time, pessimistic time, and probable time.

   Optimistic time (O) is the shortest time an activity will take if everything goes well. In the construction industry, the optimistic time is rarely achieved because so many different trades are involved in completing a project.

   Pessimistic time (P) is the amount of time an activity will take if everything goes wrong (as it sometimes does with complicated projects such as installing a new subway system).

Most probable time (M) is the most realistic estimate of how much time an activity will take. The probable time for an activity can be an estimate of the time taken for similar activities on other projects. For instance, the time needed to build a cockpit for one aircraft might be based on the average time it took to build cockpits for comparable aircraft in the past.

After the planner has collected all the estimates, he or she uses a formula to calculate the **expected time**. The expected time is the time that will be used on the PERT diagram as the needed period for the completion of an activity. As the following formula shows, expected time is an "average" in which most probable time is given more weight than optimistic time and pessimistic time.

expected time
The time that will be used on the PERT diagram as the needed period for the completion of an activity.

$$\text{Expected time} = \frac{O + 4M + P}{6}$$

(The denominator is six because O counts for one, M for four, and P for one.)

Suppose the time estimates for choosing a site location for the building are as follows: optimistic time (O) is two weeks; most probable time (M) is five weeks; and pessimistic time (P) is eight weeks. Therefore,

$$\text{Expected time} = \frac{2 + (4 \times 5) + 8}{6} = \frac{30}{6} = 5 \text{ weeks}$$

As each event or milestone is completed, the project manager can insert the actual time required for its completion. The updates are helpful because if the completion time turns out to be the pessimistic one, more resources can be added to shorten the activity required to attain the next event.

4. *Calculate the **critical path**, the path through the PERT network that includes the most time-consuming sequence of events and activities.* The path with the longest elapsed time determines the length of the entire project. To calculate the critical path, you must first add the times needed to complete the activities in each sequence. The logic behind the critical path is this: A given project cannot be considered completed until its lengthiest component is completed. For example, if it takes six months to get the building construction permit, the office-building project cannot be completed in less than one year, even if all other events are completed earlier than scheduled. Sudden changes in the time required for an activity can change the critical path, such as unanticipated delays in obtaining enough plywood for the building project.

Exhibit 6-5 shows a critical path that requires a total elapsed time of 93 weeks. This total is calculated by adding the numerals that appear beside each thick line segment. Each numeral represents the number of weeks scheduled to complete the activities between each lettered label. Notice that activity completion must occur in the sequence of steps indicated by the direction of the arrows. In this case, if 93 weeks appeared to be an excessive length of time, the building owner would have to search for ways to shorten

critical path
The path through the PERT network that includes the most time-consuming sequence of events and activities.

the process. For example, the owner might be spending too much time supervising the construction.

When it comes to implementing the activities listed on the PERT diagram, control measures play a crucial role. The project manager must ensure that all critical events are completed on time. If activities in the critical path take too long to complete, the overall project will not be completed on time. If necessary, the manager must take corrective action to move the activity along. Such action might include hiring additional workers, dismissing substandard workers, or purchasing more productive equipment.

Advanced Considerations in PERT

Considering that PERT is used for projects as complicated as building a new type of airliner, the process can become quite complex. In practice, PERT networks often specify hundreds of events and activities. Each small event can have its own PERT diagram. Many computer programs are available to help perform the mechanics of computing paths. The PERT Chart EXPERT shown in Exhibit 6-6 is one such program. Here we look at two concepts that are used in complex applications of PERT.

exhibit 6-6 **The PERT Chart EXPERT Software**

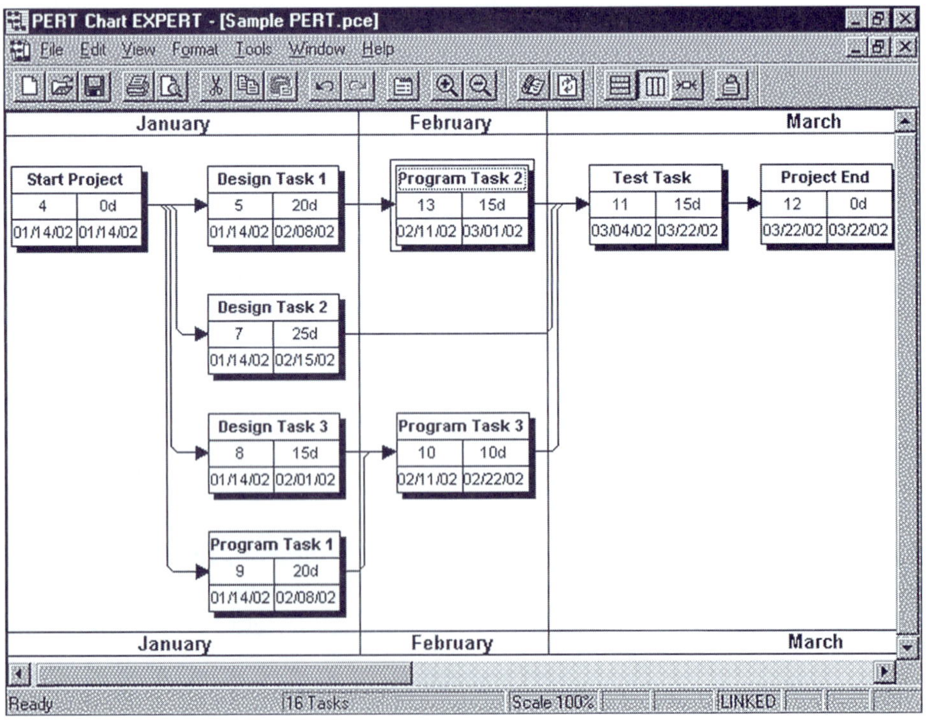

Source: Reprinted with permission from http://www.criticaltools.com.

Refined Calculation of Expected Times

The optimistic, pessimistic, and most probable times should be based on a frequency distribution of estimates. Instead of using one intuitive guess as to these durations, a specialist collects all available data about how long comparable activities took. For example: wiring a cockpit took seven weeks in ten different cases; six weeks in five cases; five weeks in three cases; and so forth. The optimistic and pessimistic times are then selected as the lower and upper ten percentiles of the distribution of times. In other words, it is optimistic to think that an event will be completed as rapidly as suggested by the briefest 10 percent of estimates. Also, it is pessimistic to think that the event will be completed in the longest 10 percent of estimated times. (Remember, the expected time is calculated based on a weighted average of the optimistic, most probable, and pessimistic times.)

It is often difficult to obtain data for comparable activities, so quantified guesswork will be required. To illustrate, a project manager might guess, "If we attempted to drill a hole for oil through that ice cap 100 times, I think it would take us 60 days 25 times, 90 days 35 times, 110 days 5 times, and 130 days 5 times." The guesses provided by this project manager might be combined with the guesses of another specialist, before calculating the pessimistic, optimistic, and most probable times.

Resource and Cost Estimates

In addition to estimating the time required for activities, advanced applications of PERT estimate the amount of resources required. Before a building contractor would establish a price for erecting a building, it would be prudent to estimate how much and what types of equipment would be needed. It would also be essential to estimate how many workers of different skills would be required. Considering that payroll runs about two-thirds of the cost for manufacturing, miscalculating costs can eliminate profits.

The resource and cost estimates can be calculated in the same manner as time estimates. Resource and cost estimates can then be attached to events, thereby suggesting at which point in the project they will most likely be incurred. For example, the building contractor might estimate that siding specialists will not be needed until 90 days into the project.

BREAK-EVEN ANALYSIS

Learning objective 4

Describe how to use break-even analysis and decision trees for problem solving and decision making.

"What do we have to do to break even?" is asked frequently in business. Managers often find the answer through **break-even analysis**, a method of determining the relationship between total costs and total revenues at various levels of production or sales activity. Managers use break-even analysis because—before adding new products, equipment, or human resources—they want to be sure that the changes will pay off. Break-even analysis tells managers the point at which it is profitable to go ahead with a new venture.

Exhibit 6-7 illustrates a typical break-even chart. It deals with a proposal to add a new product to an existing line. The point at which the Total Costs

break-even analysis A method of determining the relationship between total costs and total revenues at various levels of production or sales activity.

line and the Revenue line intersect is the break-even point. Sales shown to the right of the break-even point represent profit. Sales to the left of this point represent a loss.

Break-Even Formula

The break-even point (BE) is the situation in which total revenues equal fixed costs plus variable costs. It can be calculated with the following standard formula:

$$BE = \frac{FC}{P - VC}$$

where

P = selling price per unit

VC = variable cost per unit, the cost that varies with the amount produced

FC = fixed cost, the cost that remains constant no matter how many units are produced

The chart in Exhibit 6-7 is based on the plans of a small company to sell furniture over the Internet. For simplicity, we provide data only for the dining room sets. The average selling price (P) is \$1,000 per unit; the variable cost (VC) is \$500 per unit, including Internet commission fees for sales made through major Web sites. The fixed costs are \$300,000.

$$BE = \frac{\$300{,}000}{\$1{,}000 - \$500} = \frac{\$300{,}000}{\$500} = 600 \text{ unit}$$

exhibit 6-7 **Break-even Chart for Adding a New Product to an Existing Line**

A break-even chart indicates at what point a venture becomes profitable.

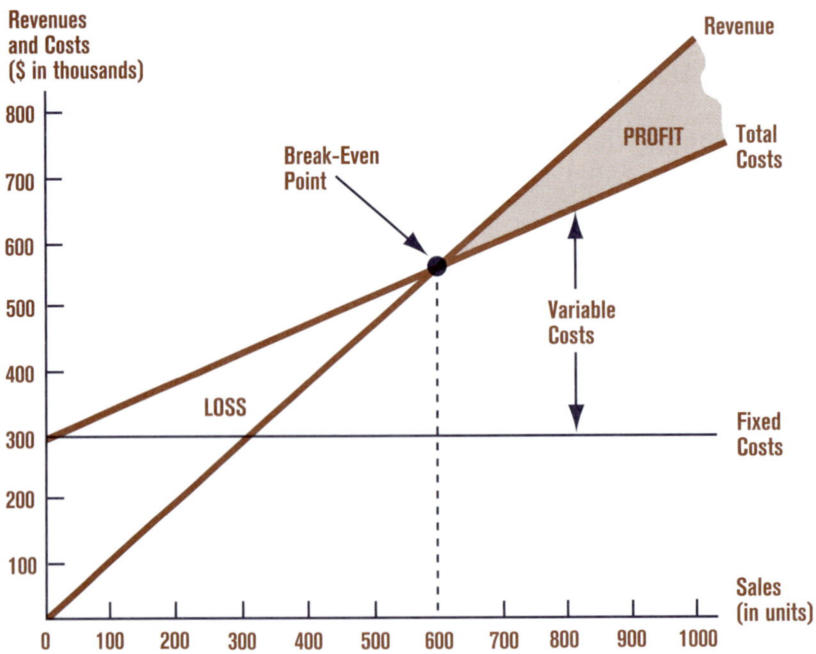

Under the conditions assumed and for the period of time in which these costs and revenue figures are valid, a sales volume of 600 dining room sets would be required for the furniture company to break even. Any volume above that level would produce a profit and anything below it would result in a loss. (We are referring to online sales only. Sales through their customary channels would have to be figured separately.) If the sales forecast for dining room sets sold through e-commerce is above 600 units, it would be a good decision to sell online. If the sales forecast is less than 600 units, the furniture company should not attempt e-commerce for now. However, if the husband-and-wife team is willing to absorb losses now to build for the long range, they might start e-commerce anyway. Break-even analysis would tell the owners how much money they are likely to lose. An encouraging note is that small operations like the furniture company in question have typically profited from e-tailing.

decision tree
A graphic illustration of the alternative solutions available to solve a problem.

Break-even analyses must be calculated frequently because fixed and variable costs may change quite suddenly. Imagine that you were the manager of a package-delivery service. One of your variable costs, gasoline, might fluctuate weekly. And a fixed cost like truck insurance might change each six months. Also, as an enterprise grows, new fixed costs may arise, such as needing to hire a human resources consulting firm to take care of payroll and benefits administration.

Advantages and Limitations of Break-Even Analysis

Break-even analysis helps managers keep their thinking focused on the volume of activity that will be necessary to justify a new expense. The technique is also useful because it applies to a number of operations problems. Break-even analysis can help a manager decide whether to drop an existing product from the line, to replace equipment, or to buy rather than make a part.

Break-even analysis has some drawbacks. First, it is only as valid as the estimates of costs and revenues that managers use to create it. Second, the relationship between variable costs and sales may be complicated. Exhibit 6-7 indicates that variable costs and sales increase together in a direct relationship. In reality, unit costs may decrease with increased volume. It is also possible that costs may increase with volume: Suppose that increased production leads to higher turnover because employees prefer not to work overtime.

Break-even analysis relates to decisions about whether to proceed or not to proceed. The next section will examine a more complicated decision-making technique that relates to the desirability of several alternative solutions.

DECISION TREES

Another useful planning tool is called a **decision tree**, a graphic illustration of the alternative solutions available to solve a problem. Analyzing the outcomes of a few alternative actions before making a decision is useful because it helps predict if you have made a decision that produces the most favorable,

expected value The average return on a particular decision being made a large number of times.

or least painful, consequences.[10] Decision trees are designed to estimate the outcome of a series of decisions. As the sequences of the major decision are drawn, the resulting diagram resembles a tree with branches.

To illustrate the essentials of using a decision tree for making financial decisions, return to the building owner who used the Gantt and milestone charts. One major decision facing the owner is whether to open an office building only or open an office building with an attached conference facility (rented to the public as needed). According to data from a local real-estate association, the probability of having a good first year is 0.6 and the probability of a poor one is 0.4.

Discussion with an accountant indicates that the payout, or net cash flow, from a good year with the building only would be \$100,000. The payout from a poor first year with the same alternative would be a loss of \$10,000. Both these figures are conditional because they depend on business conditions and tenants paying their rent. The owner and accountant predict that a good first year with the alternative of a building and public conference facility would be \$150,000. A poor first year would result in a loss of \$30,000.

Using this information, the manager computes the expected values and adds them for the two alternatives. An **expected value** is the average value incurred if a particular decision is made a large number of times. Sometimes the alternative would earn more, and sometimes less, with the expected value being the alternative's average return.

Expected value: Office building only	=0.6×\$100,000=	\$60,000
	0.4×−\$10,000=	−\$4,000
		\$56,000
Expected value: Office building and conference facility	=0.6×\$150,000=	\$90,000
	0.4×−\$30,000=	−\$12,000
		\$78,000

As Exhibit 6-8 graphically portrays, the decision tree suggests that the building and conference room will probably turn a first-year profit of \$78,000. The building-only alternative is likely to show a profit of \$56,000. Over one year, operating a building and public conference center would be \$22,000 more profitable.

The advantage of a decision tree is that it can be used to help make sequences of decisions. After having one year of experience in running a building and conference center, the owner may think of expanding. One logical possibility for expansion would be to open a public warehouse for the use of small business firms and individuals. The building owner would now have more accurate information about the conditional values for an office building and conference room—the choice the owner made when opening his new enterprise. With one year of success with the office building and conference center, the probability of having a second good season might

10 Carole Matthews, "Decision Making with Decision Trees," Inc.com, April 2003, p. 1.

exhibit 6-8 First-Year Decision Tree for Building Owner

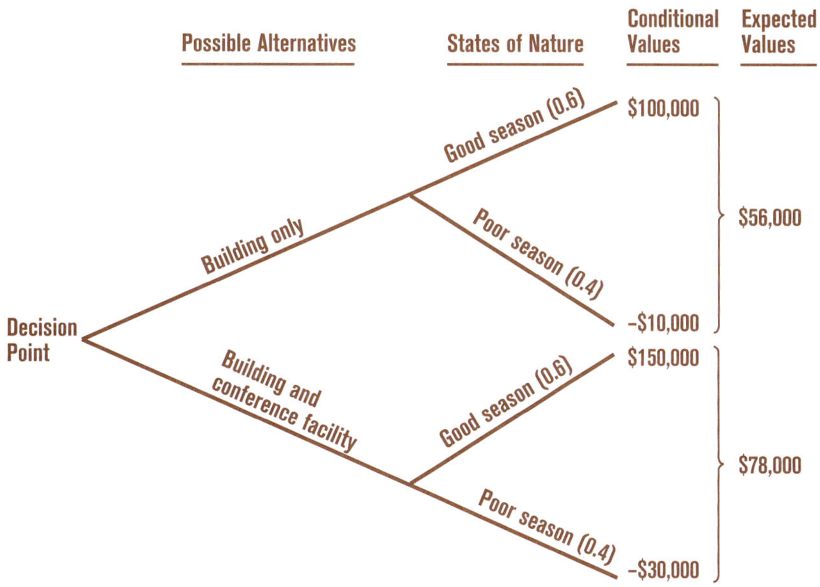

be raised to 0.8. With each successive year, the owner would have increasingly accurate information about the conditional values.

Following is an explanation of how the expected values are calculated for the new branch of the decision tree in question, shown in Exhibit 6-9.

exhibit 6-9 Second-Year Decision Tree for Building Owner

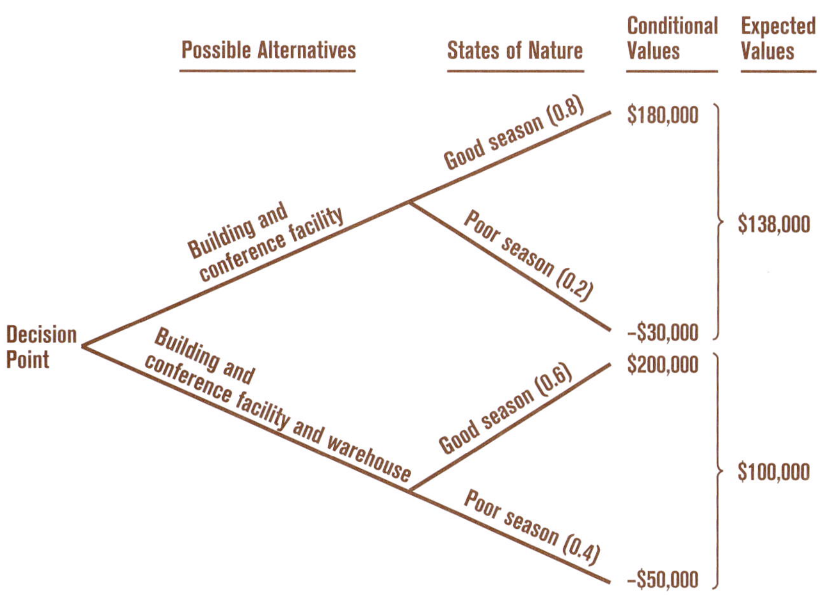

INVENTORY CONTROL TECHNIQUES

Learning Objective 5

Describe how to manage inventory by using the economic order quantity (EOQ), the just-in-time (JIT) system, and LIFO versus FIFO.

Managers of manufacturing and sales organizations face the problem of how much inventory to keep on hand. If a firm maintains a large inventory, goods can be made quickly, customers can make immediate purchases, or orders can be shipped rapidly. However, stocking goods is expensive. The goods themselves are costly, and the money tied up in inventory cannot be invested elsewhere. Dell Computers and Wal-Mart are examples of companies that owe some of their competitive advantage to their efficient management of inventory. Dell minimizes the need for large inventory by building a computer only after an order is received. Of course, Dell still keeps lots of computer components on hand, but they do not have warehouses filled with yet-to-be sold computers. Wal-Mart collaborates with its suppliers to keep shelves stocked with the right amount and quantity of merchandise to minimize inventory accumulation.

This section will describe three decision-making techniques used to manage inventory and control production: the economic order quantity (EOQ), the just-in-time (JIT) system, and brief mention of LIFO versus FIFO.

Economic Order Quantity

The **economic order quantity (EOQ)** is the inventory level that minimizes both administrative costs and carrying costs. The EOQ represents the reorder quantity of the least cost. Carrying costs include the cost of loans, the interest foregone because money is tied up in inventory, and the cost of handling the inventory. EOQ is expressed mathematically as

$$EOQ = \sqrt{\frac{2DO}{C}}$$

where

D=annual demand in units for the product

O=fixed cost of placing and receiving an order

C=annual carrying cost per unit (taxes, insurance, storage cost, interest, and other expenses)

The economic order quantity is found to be the most useful when a company has repetitive purchasing and demand for an item, such as truck tires or hospital supplies. Assume that the annual demand for coffee tables is 100 units and that it costs $1,000 to order each unit. Furthermore, suppose the carrying cost per unit is $200. The equation to calculate the most economic number of coffee tables to keep in inventory is

$$\begin{aligned} EOQ &= \sqrt{\frac{2 \times 100 \times \$1{,}000}{\$200}} \\ &= \sqrt{\frac{\$200{,}000}{\$200}} \\ &= \sqrt{1{,}000} \\ &= 32 \text{ coffee tables (rounded figure)} \end{aligned}$$

economic order quantity (EOQ) The inventory level that minimizes both administrative costs and carrying costs.

Therefore, the owners of the online furniture store conclude that the most economical number of coffee tables to keep in inventory during the selling season is 32. (The assumption is that the company has a large storage area.) If the figures entered into the EOQ formula are accurate, EOQ calculations can vastly improve inventory management.

just-in-time (JIT) system
A system to minimize inventory and move it into the plant exactly when needed.

Just-in-Time System

An important thrust in manufacturing is to keep just enough parts and components on hand to fill current orders. The **just-in-time (JIT) system** is an inventory control method designed to minimize inventory and move it into the plant exactly when needed. Note also that JIT is part of a manufacturing system that focuses on making manufacturing more efficient by eliminating waste wherever possible. The key principle of the system is to eliminate excess inventory by producing or purchasing parts, subassemblies, and final products only when—and in the exact amounts—needed. JIT helps a manufacturing division stay *lean* by minimizing waste. A lean manufacturing organization adopts a culture of continuously looking for ways to be more efficient. A specific example would be redesigning a work area from a linear operation to a U-shaped station to improve efficiency.[11]

The JIT is quantitative in the sense that it relies heavily on numbers, such as specifying the number of parts and components accumulated as inventory. Also, under JIT the company would track data such as the number of hours or days of accumulated inventory.

Imagine the small furniture company having raw wood delivered to its door within an hour or so after an order is received over the Internet. JIT is generally used in a repetitive, single-product, manufacturing environment. However, the system is now also used to improve operations in sales and service organizations.

Reducing waste is the core JIT philosophy. Three such wastes are overproduction, waiting, and stock. *Overproduction waste* can be reduced by producing only what is needed when an order is received. *Waiting waste* can be reduced by synchronizing the work flow, such as technicians preparing a computer-monitor housing when the internal mechanisms are coming down the line. *Stock waste* can be reduced by keeping inventory at a minimum.

Procedures and Techniques

Just-in-time inventory control is part of a system of manufacturing control. Therefore, it involves many different techniques and procedures. Seven of the major techniques and procedures are described in the list that follows.[12] Knowing them provides insight into the system of manufacturing used by many successful Japanese companies, and companies located in other countries as well.

1. *Kanbans.* The JIT system of inventory control relies on *kanbans,* or cards, to communicate production requirements from the final point of assembly to the

11 Neal Haldene, "Novi Center Teaches Lean Way of Working," *Detroit News* (http://www.detnews.com), September 21, 2006.

12 Ramon L. Aldag and Timothy M. Stearns, *Management,* 2nd ed. (Cincinnati: South-Western College Publishing, 1991), pp. 645–646.

manufacturing operations that precede it. When an order is received for a product, a kanban is issued that directs employees to finish the product. The finishing department selects components and assembles the product. The kanban is then passed back to earlier stations. This kanban tells workers to resupply the components. New stock is ordered when stock reaches the reorder level. Kanban communication continues all the way back to the material suppliers. In many JIT systems, suppliers locate their companies so they can be close to major customers. Proximity allows suppliers to make shipments promptly. At each stage, parts and other materials are delivered just in time for use.

2. *Demand-driven pull system.* The JIT technique requires producing exactly what is needed to match the demand created by customer orders. Demand drives final assembly schedules, and assembly drives subassembly timetables. The result is a pull system—that is, customer demand pulls along activities to meet that demand.
3. *Short production lead times.* A JIT system minimizes the time between the arrival of raw material or components in the plant and the shipment of a finished product to a customer.
4. *High inventory turnover (with the goal of zero inventory and stockless production).* The levels of finished goods, work in process, and raw materials are purposely reduced. Raw material in a warehouse is regarded as waste, and so is idle work in process. (A person who applied JIT to the household would regard backup supplies of ketchup or motor oil as shameful!)
5. *Designated areas for receiving materials.* Certain areas on the shop floor or in the receiving and shipping department are designated for receiving specific items from suppliers. At a Toyota plant in Japan, the receiving area is about half the size of a football field. The designated spaces for specific items are marked with yellow paint.
6. *Designated containers.* Specifying where to store items allows for easy access to parts, and it eliminates counting. For example, at Toyota the bed of a truck has metal frame mounts for exactly eight engines. A truckload of engines means eight engines—no more, no less. No one has to count them.
7. *Neatness.* A JIT plant that follows Japanese tradition is immaculate. All unnecessary materials, tools, rags, and files are discarded. The factory floor is as neat and clean as the showroom.

Advantages and Disadvantages of the JIT Inventory System

Manufacturing companies have realized several benefits from adopting JIT. The expenses associated with maintaining a large inventory can be dramatically reduced, providing suppliers do not raise their prices for making deliveries as needed. JIT controls can lead to organizational commitment to quality in design, materials, parts, employee–management and supplier–user relations, and finished goods. With minimum levels of inventory on hand, finished products are more visible and defects are more readily detected. Quality problems can therefore be attacked before they escalate to an insurmountable degree. Low levels of inventory also shorten cycle times.

Despite the advantages JIT management can offer large manufacturers, it has some potential disadvantages. Above all, a JIT system must be placed in a supportive or compatible environment. JIT is applicable only to highly repetitive manufacturing operations such as car or residential furnace manufacturing. Also, product demand must be predictable with a minimum of surges in demand. Reliable suppliers are also needed.

Small companies with short runs of a variety of products often may suffer financial losses from JIT practices. One problem they have is that suppliers are often unwilling to promptly ship small batches to meet the weekly needs of a small customer.

The savings from JIT management can be deceptive. Suppliers might simply build up inventories in their own plants and add that cost to their prices. JIT inventory practices also leave a company vulnerable to work stoppages, such as a strike. With a large inventory of finished products or parts, the company can continue to meet customer demand while the work stoppage is being settled.

The accompanying Management in Action will help you develop a feel for what it is like to work under a JIT management system and philosophy.

management in action

Supervisor at a Toyota Supplier

I worked for Arvin Sango Inc. The company supplies Toyota with instrument panels and body parts. Instead of using the "push" philosophy of producing as many parts as we could, we had a daily production. The trucks from Toyota arrived "just in time" to pick up the parts we produced. Typically no more than four hours elapsed between the time the parts were made and when they were picked up. If the production line broke down, there was a possibility that we would miss our truck. We had to pay Toyota if our inability to keep them supplied resulted in them halting production.

When we had produced the number of parts that was set, we were done working for the day. We might help workers on another line, but we were not allowed to produce any more of our parts. JIT is the opposite of the warehousing philosophy, where you fill up your warehouse with inventory and wait for someone to order it. JIT saves warehouse space and helps assure quality between the customer and the producer. Typically the producer and customer are both on a JIT schedule. Some times we would have a slight flaw in our parts and Toyota noticed it right away and notified us of the quality deficiency. We were then able to correct the deficiency before we produced a warehouse full of flawed parts.

Questions

1. In what way did using just-in-time inventory management help the supplier, Arvin Sango?
2. In what way did using just-in-time inventory management help the customer, Toyota?

Source: "What are Examples of a Company Using Just in Time (JIT) Management Philosophy?" *Yahoo! Answers*, accessed November 17, 2006.

Last In, First Out (LIFO) Selling an item first that was received last in inventory.

First In, First Out (FIFO) Selling an item first that has been in inventory the longest.

LIFO versus FIFO

Another method of inventory control is more of a method of accounting than a method of managing physical inventory, yet it does relate to stocking inventory. Imagine that you were running a tire warehouse, and had hundreds of tires of many sizes in stock. When an automotive service center ordered four tires, would you ship the center the oldest tires in your warehouse? Or would you ship the center, the tires you most recently acquired? Which tires you ship could have important implications.

Last in, First Out (LIFO) means that when there is more than one item in stock, you sell the last one received first. In the example at hand, you sell the latest four tires you received from the manufacturer, of the size ordered. The rationale here is that the newest is probably the most expensive. **First in, First Out (FIFO)** means that when there is more than one item in stock, you sell the one you have had in inventory the longest.

In choosing between LIFO and FIFO, you have both physical and financial considerations. Getting rid of older inventory first can be a good idea because the longer it sits around, the higher the probability of the item getting damaged, including the packing looking old and being torn. In some situations, the company has borrowed money to purchase inventory, so you want to move the inventory you have been paying for the longest. This is particularly true for business firms such as automobile and boat dealers.

One of several financial, and tax, considerations is that if you value your inventory at the cost of the time you purchased it, your profits will look better when you sell at today's prices. In returning to the tire example, suppose you sell your four tires to the service center for $400. If you ship four tires for which you paid $50 each three years ago, your gross profit would be $200 (four tires times $50). You have to pay income tax on $200. However, if you ship four tires for which you paid $75 each last month, your profit is now $100. You have earned less profit, but you will pay less tax. (Please consult your accounting professor or tax accountant for the latest rulings! For example, it might be possible to value the older tires at today's prices, thus reducing your reported revenue.)

PARETO DIAGRAMS FOR PROBLEM IDENTIFICATION

Learning Objective 6

Describe how to identify problems using a Pareto diagram.

Pareto diagram A bar graph that ranks types of output variations by frequency of occurrence.

Managers and professionals frequently must identify the major causes of their problem, such as "What features of our product are receiving the most complaints from consumers?" or "Our agency is offering more services to the public than we can afford. Which services might we drop without hurting too many people?" One problem-identification technique uses a **Pareto diagram**, a bar graph (or histogram) that ranks types of output variations by frequency of occurrence. Managers and other workers often use Pareto diagrams to identify the most important problems or causes of problems that affect output quality. Identification of the "vital few" allows management or product improvement teams to focus on the major cause of a production or service problem. Based on quantitative data, effort is then directed where it will do the most good.

An example of Pareto analysis is an investigation of the delay associated with processing credit card applications. The data are grouped in the following categories:[13]

- No signature
- Residential address not valid
- Non-legible handwriting
- Already a customer
- Other

As Exhibit 6-10 shows, the cause of a problem is plotted on the x-axis (horizontal). The cumulative effects both in frequency and percent are plotted on the y-axis (vertical). In a Pareto diagram, the bars are arranged in descending order of height (or frequency of occurrence) from left to right across the x-axis. As a consequence, the most important causes are at the left of the chart. Priorities are then established for taking action on the few causes that account for most of the effect. According to the Pareto principle, generally 20 percent or fewer of the causes contribute to 80 percent or more of the effects. It is widely recognized, for example, that about 20 percent of the customers of an industrial company account for 80 percent of sales. And also, about 20 percent of customers account for about 80 percent of complaints.

A while back a crisis-management team of Ford managers and professionals did a Pareto analysis of problems with Bridgestone/Firestone tires used on the Ford Explorer. The Ford team analyzed the data based on tire

exhibit 6-10 Sample Pareto Chart Depiction

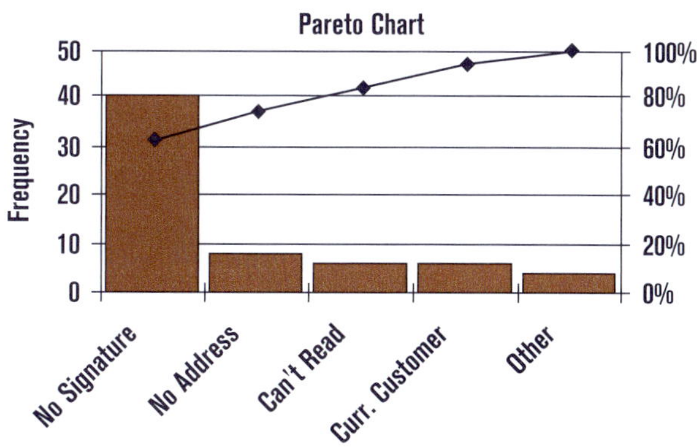

Source: Kerri Simon, "Pareto Chart," *Six Sigma* (http://www.isixsigma.com), accessed November 18, 2006.

13 Kerri Simon, "Pareto Chart," *Six Sigma* (http://www.isixsigma.com), accessed November 18, 2006.

sizes that had more than 30 reported warranty claims. The key results of their analysis, reported as follows, strongly support the Pareto principle:

> *Of 2,498 complaints involving eight separate size categories, 2,030, or 81 percent, involved the 15-inch P235/75R15 models, which included the Firestone ATX and Wilderness tires. Of the 1,699 reported complaints of tread separations on 13 different size tires, 1,424, or 84 percent, were for the P234/75R15 series of tires used on Ford's Explorer and Bronco SUVs and its F-150 and Ranger pickup trucks.*[14]

As you probably observed, one model created 81 percent of the problems, and another series 84 percent. Although, the 80/20 (Pareto) principle is a general guide, it is a close approximation of reality in many situations.

The Pareto Diagram fits data-driven management and decision making. In the example in Exhibit 6-10, the manager can say, "About 80 percent of our credit card applications are being rejected because the signature is missing. I think we can coach our customers to do a better job signing their applications."

14 Bill Vlasic, "Tire Recall Rife with Blame, Tragedy," *The Detroit News*, March 9, 2000.

SUMMARY OF
Key Points

1 Explain how managers use data-based decision making.

Using data-driven management, decisions are based on facts rather than impressions or guesses. Many managers want to see the data before accepting a suggestion from a subordinate. Data-driven management is more of an attitude and approach rather than a specific technique. Although data-driven management is preferable in most situations, intuition and judgment still contribute to making major decisions.

2 Explain the use of forecasting techniques in planning.

All planning includes making forecasts, both qualitative and quantitative. A judgmental forecast makes predictions on subjective opinions. Time-series analysis is a widely used method of making quantitative forecasts. Three widely used forecasts are economic, sales, and technological.

3 Describe how to use Gantt charts, milestone charts, and PERT planning techniques.

Gantt and milestone charts are simple methods of monitoring schedules that are particularly useful for one-time projects. Gantt charts graphically depict the planned and actual progress of work over the period of time encompassed by a project. A milestone chart lists the subactivities that must be completed to accomplish the major activities.

Managers use PERT networks to track complicated projects when sequences of events must be planned carefully. In a PERT network, an event is a point of decision or accomplishment. An activity is the task that must be performed to complete an event. To complete a PERT diagram, a manager must sequence all the events and estimate the time required for each activity. The expected time for each activity takes into account optimistic, pessimistic, and probable estimates of time. The critical path is the most time-consuming sequence of activities and events that must be followed to implement the project. The duration of the project is determined by the critical path. Frequency distributions are sometimes used to calculate expected times, and PERT can also be used to estimate resources and costs that will be needed.

4 Describe how to use break-even analysis and decision trees for problem solving and decision making.

Managers use break-even analysis to estimate the point at which it is profitable to go ahead with a new venture. It is a method of determining the relationship between total costs and total revenues at various levels of sales activity or operation. Break-even analysis determines the ratio of total fixed costs to the difference between the selling price and the variable cost for each unit. The results of break-even analysis are often depicted on a graph. Break-even analysis has to be done frequently as fixed and variable costs change.

A decision tree provides a quantitative estimate of the best alternative. It is a tool for estimating the outcome of a series of decisions. When the sequences of the major decisions are drawn, they resemble a tree with branches.

5 Describe how to manage inventory by using the economic order quantity (EOQ), the just-in-time (JIT) system, and LIFO versus FIFO.

The economic order quantity (EOQ) is a decision-support technique widely used to manage inventory. The EOQ is the inventory level that minimizes both ordering and carrying costs. The EOQ technique helps managers in a manufacturing or sales organization decide how much inventory to keep on hand.

Just-in-time (JIT) inventory management minimizes stock on hand. Instead, stock is moved into the plant exactly when needed. Although not specifically a decision-making technique, JIT helps shape decisions about inventory. The key principle underlying JIT systems is the elimination of excess inventory by producing or purchasing items only when and in the exact amounts they are needed. JIT is part of lean manufacturing.

Just-in-time processes involve (1) kanbans, or cards for communicating production requirements to the previous operation, (2) a customer demand–driven system, (3) short production lead times, (4) high inventory turnover, (5) designated areas for receiving materials, (6) designated containers, and (7) neatness throughout the factory.

JIT inventory management is best suited for repetitive manufacturing processes. One drawback of JIT is that it places heavy pressures on suppliers to build up their inventories to satisfy sudden demands of their customers who use the system.

LIFO versus FIFO helps manage inventory, but is mostly an accounting technique. With LIFO, you sell the last one received, first. With FIFO, you sell the item first that you have had in inventory the longest.

6 Describe how to identify problems using a Pareto diagram.

Problems or causes of problems can often be identified by a problem-identification technique called the Pareto diagram. The Pareto principle stems from the diagram, and suggests that about 20 percent or fewer of the causes contribute to 80 percent or more of the effects.

KEY TERMS AND PHRASES

QUESTIONS

1. Visualize yourself as the manager of an athletic club. Give three examples of data you might be able to use in making decisions about how to improve the profitability of the club.
2. What is the difference between a milestone chart and a to-do list?
3. Describe two possible job applications for a PERT network.
4. What similarities do you see between the purposes of break-even analysis and a decision tree?
5. How might the Pareto principle apply to the profits an automobile company earns on the sales of its vehicles?
6. At least one-half of new restaurants fail within the first couple of years, even when these restaurants appear to be busy much of the time. Describe how two of the techniques described in this chapter might help a person prevent opening a restaurant that is doomed to fail.
7. An important part of management is dealing with people. Where is the human touch in any of the techniques described in this chapter?

SKILL-BUILDING EXERCISE 6-A: Developing a PERT Network

Use the following information about a safety improvement project to construct a PERT diagram. Be sure to indicate the critical path with a dark arrow. Work individually or in small groups.

Event	Description	Time Required (units)	Preceding Event
A	Complete safety audit	6	none
B	Benchmark	15	A
C	Collect internal information	6	A
D	Identify safety problems	3	B, C
E	Identify improvement practices	7	D
F	Elicit employee participation	20	A
G	Implement safety program	6	E, F
H	Measure results	8	G

Source: Adapted and reprinted with permission from Raymond L. Hilgert and Edwin C. Leonard Jr., *Supervision: Concepts and Practices of Management*, 6th ed. (Cincinnati: South-Western College Publishing, 1995), p. 191.

SKILL-BUILDING EXERCISE 6-B: Break-Even Analysis

On recent vacation trips to Juarez, Mexico, you noticed retail stores and street vendors selling inexpensive digital cameras. (The photo stores also sold brand-name digital cameras at close to U.S. prices.) The prices for the inexpensive cameras ranged from \$25 to \$40 U.S. A flash of inspiration hit you. Why not sell Mexican-assembled digital cameras back home to Americans, using a van as your store? Every three months you would drive the 350 miles to Mexico and load up on these novelty digital cameras. You are thinking of negotiating to receive large-quantity discounts.

You would park your van on busy streets and nearby parks, wherever you could obtain a permit. Typically you would display the cameras outside the van, but on a rainy day people could step inside. Your intention is to operate your traveling camera sale about 12 hours per week. If you could make enough money from your business, you could attend classes full-time during the day. You intend to sell the cameras at an average of \$65 a unit.

Based on preliminary analysis, you have discovered that your primary fixed costs per month would be: \$550 for payments on a van, $175 for gas and maintenance, $75 for insurance, and $60 for a street vendor's permit. You will also be driving down to Mexico every three months at $600 per trip, resulting in a $200 per month travel cost. Your variable costs would be an average of $30 per camera and 45¢ for placing each camera in an attractive box.

1. How many cameras will you have to sell each month before you start to make a profit?
2. If the average cost of your cameras rises to $35, how many cameras will you have to sell each month if you hold your price to $65 per unit?

INTERNET SKILL-BUILDING EXERCISE: The Reality of the Pareto Principle

The Pareto principle stating that 80 percent of effects are created by 20 percent of causes has become entrenched in management thinking. We regularly hear such glib statements as "20 percent of our customers account for 80 percent of our sales." The text furnished other examples of the Pareto principle. Conduct research on the Internet to find at least five examples of the 80/20 rule. At the same time, see if you can find any evidence that refutes the reliability of this principle or rule. In other words, can you find an example of a situation in which 20 percent of the causes did not produce 80 percent of the effects?

Case Problem 6-A

Just-In-Time Worries at the University of Utah Hospital

Like many big hospitals, the University of Utah Hospital carries a 30-day supply of drugs, in part because it would be too costly or wasteful to stockpile more. Some of its hepatitis vaccine supply has been diverted to the hurricane-ravaged Gulf, leaving it vulnerable should an outbreak occur closer to home. About 77 other drugs are in short supply because of manufacturing and other glitches, such as a drug maker shutting down a factory.

"The supply chain is horribly thin," says Erin Fox, a drug-information specialist at the Salt Lake City Hospital. In the event of a pandemic flu outbreak, that chain is almost certain to break. Thousands of drug-company workers in the United States and elsewhere could be sickened, prompting factories to close. Truck routes could be blocked and borders may be closed, particularly perilous at a time when 80 percent of raw materials for U.S. drugs come from abroad. The likely result: shortages of important medicines—such as insulin, blood products, or the anesthetics used in surgery—quite apart from any shortages of medicine to treat the flu itself.

A problem facing Utah Hospital, as well as other hospitals, is that production of drugs takes place offshore because that's cheaper. The federal government doesn't intervene as a guaranteed buyer of flu drugs, as it does with weapons. Investors and tax rules conspire to eliminate redundancy and reserves. Antitrust rules prevent private companies from collaborating to speed development of new drugs.

A report issued by the Trust for America's Health, a public-health advocacy group in Washington, concluded that 40 percent of the states lack enough backup medical supplies to cope with a pandemic flu or other major disease outbreak.

"Most if not all of the medical products or protective-device companies in this country are operating almost at full capacity," says Michael Osterholm, director of the Center for Infectious Disease Research and Policy at the University of Minnesota. "That's the reality of today's economy: just-in-time delivery with no surge capacity."

One significant concern is what Michael Leavitt, the secretary of health and human services, described in an interview as the "Albertson's syndrome," referring to the grocery-store chain. At the first sign of panic, all supplies disappear from shelves, something that routinely happens when there is the threat of even a modest storm.

Discussion Questions

1. How suitable is the just-in-time inventory management system for the University of Utah Hospital (as well as for other large hospitals)?
2. What recommendations would you make to the hospital in question to have drugs available to deal with a pandemic or other emergency?

Source: Bernard Wysocki Jr. and Sara Lueck, "Just-in-Time Inventories Make U.S. Vulnerable in a Pandemic," *The Wall Street Journal*, January 12, 2006, pp. A1, A7.

Case Problem 6-B

Imbalances at Family Services

Gisela Sanchez is the director at Downtown Family Services, a social agency that provides various forms of assistance to low-income and no-income citizens in the northeast section of the city. Family Services receives funding from the city, state, and federal governments along with charitable contributions. Among the services the agency provides are family counseling, abortion counseling, home care for the infirm, and emergency shelters for battered or homeless people.

Seventeen professionals work at Family Services, including nurses and counselors, 19 paraprofessionals who assist the professionals, and a support staff of six people. Although the premises at Family Services are far from luxurious, the offices are adequately equipped with furniture, restrooms, break rooms, and office technology. The biggest problem facing the agency is an overworked staff, accompanied by complaints of burnout.

After the Christmas season, Sanchez was particularly worried about the haggard look of many staff members. As a preliminary step in dealing with the problem, Sanchez called a staff meeting at 4:30, two Fridays after the New Year. Sanchez served snacks and beverages. Sanchez began the meeting with these words: "I know you've been overworked, underpaid, and feel unappreciated, but I love you all. I think it's time to take some managerial action about our problems."

Gil Toomey, the director of social work, responded: "Oh, Gisela, are you going to merge us with another agency, and lay off duplicate positions?"

"Not at all Gil," responded Sanchez. "I want to know where we are spending the most of our time, what's dragging us down, and how we can improve the situation. We've known for a long time we're spreading ourselves too thin."

"I sure feel spread too thin," said Marcie Beaudoin, the director of home-health care. "My staff is also spread dangerously thin."

Sanchez then explained that she would like to analyze where the human resources are being used in the agency. She explained, "After we know what we are really doing with our time, we can develop a plan to ease the workload. The most we can hope for in the budget is to hire one new professional, and one paraprofessional. My suspicion is that a small number of our clients are draining us. Because of these needy people, we are not devoting enough attention to some other worthy clients."

Discussion Questions

1. Recommend a technique that Family Services can use to evaluate how much of their time is being spent on a relatively few number of clients.
2. After making this analysis and perhaps furnishing some illustrative data, explain what can be done about the situation.
3. How might forecasting techniques help Family Services do a better job of managing their workload?

chapter 7

Job Design and Work Schedules

Objectives

After studying this chapter and doing the exercises, you should be able to:

1 Explain the four major dimensions of job design plus job specialization and job descriptions.

2 Describe job enrichment, including the job characteristics model.

3 Describe job involvement, enlargement, and rotation.

4 Explain how workers use job crafting to modify their jobs.

5 Illustrate how ergonomic factors can be part of job design.

6 Summarize the various modified work schedules.

7 Explain how job design can contribute to a high-performance work system.

A year ago, it took 20 to 30 craftsmen to put together each Louis Vuitton "Reade" tote bag. Over the course of about eight days, separate workers would sew together leather panels, glue in linings, and attach handles. Later on, inspired by car maker Toyota Corp. and egged on by management consultants from McKinsey & Co., the venerable French luxury-goods house discovered efficiency. Today, clusters of 6 to 12 workers, each of them performing several tasks, can assemble the $680 shiny, LV-logo bags in a single day.

The factory floor changes are part of a sweeping effort by Louis Vuitton to serve customers better by keeping its boutiques fully stocked with popular merchandise—to operate, in other words, more like a successful modern retailer. It supply-chain overhaul includes changes to its distribution system and to the way salespeople serve customers in its tony stores.

For years, high-end fashion houses like Louis Vuitton—best known for its expensive brown-and-gold logo bags—paid far more attention to product design, craftsmanship, and image than to the mechanics of keeping the stores stocked. When new designs caught on, they often sold out and the companies were often ill prepared to speed up production and distribution.

Chic but less-expensive fashion labels such as Zara and H&M have thrived by spotting trends quickly and filling shelves with new products every fortnight. Their success has forced higher-end rivals to rethink how they do business. Part of the overhaul by Louis Vuitton to stay competitive was to make its manufacturing process more flexible, borrowing techniques pioneered by car makers and consumer-electronic companies.

Tampering with Vuitton's production poses a risk to the brand's image. Customers pay hundreds of dollars for its logo canvas bags, for example, partly because they have bought into the notion that skilled craftsmen make them the old-fashioned way. Although the company has been modernizing gradually for some time, the high-quality reputation is still vital to the company's success.

The new factory format is called Pégase (Pegasus in English), after the mythological winged horse and a Vuitton rolling suitcase. Under the new system, it take less time to assemble bags, in part because they no longer sit around on carts waiting to be moved from one workstation to another. That enables the company to ship fresh collections to its boutiques every six weeks—more than twice as frequently as in the past. "It's about finding the best ratio between quality and speed," says Patrick-Louis Vuitton, a fifth-generation member of the company's founding family, who is in charge of special orders.[1]

The Louis Vuitton story illustrates how modifying job design is a major part of helping a company stay competitive. By adding tasks to the production workers' jobs, they became more productive to the point that the tote bag could be produced in one day. (Yet the company does not want to lose the benefits of workers having expertise.) Modifying job design can also contribute to the success of a workplace in many manufacturing and service settings. Employers use a variety of job designs and work schedules to increase productivity and job satisfaction. Modifying job design and giving workers more control over schedules are the two major topics of this chapter.

To accomplish large tasks, such as building ships or operating a hotel, you must divide work among individuals and groups. Subdividing the overall tasks of an enterprise can be achieved in two primary ways. One way is to design specific jobs for individuals and groups to accomplish. The shipbuilding company must design jobs for welders, metal workers, engineers, purchasing agents, and contract administrators. In addition, many workers may be assigned to teams that assume

---

1 Adapted from Christina Passariello, "Louis Vuitton Tries Modern Methods on Factory Lines," *The Wall Street Journal*, October 9, 2006, pp. A1, A15.

considerable responsibility for productivity and quality. The other primary way of subdividing work assigns tasks to different units within the organization—units such as departments and divisions.

This chapter will explain basic concepts relating to job design, such as making jobs more challenging and giving employees more control over their working hours and place of work. We also look at how workers often shape their own jobs, the importance of ergonomics, and job designs for high-performance work systems. The next chapter will describe how work is divided throughout an organization.

FOUR MAJOR DIMENSIONS OF JOB DESIGN PLUS JOB SPECIALIZATION AND JOB DESCRIPTION

Learning Objective 1

Explain the four major dimensions of job design plus job specialization and job descriptions.

A useful starting point in understanding job design is to examine the major dimensions or components of jobs. **Job design** is the process of laying out job responsibilities and duties and describing how they are to be performed. The different ways in which work can be designed has been studied for a long time. Frederick P. Morgeson and Stephen E. Humphrey have recently integrated this information and added a study of their own with 540 job holders, to arrive at a new understanding of job dimensions and the nature of work.[2] Each of the four dimensions has several components. Almost any job, from a door person to a CEO, can be described according to how much of each dimension and sub-dimension is contained in the job. Understanding these dimensions leads to an understanding of the nature of work because the dimensions refer to what an incumbent actually does on the job.

The dimensions and sub-dimensions are described next, and outlined in Exhibit 7-1. In this section we also explain job specialization and job descriptions because they are a logical follow up to knowing job dimensions. The various approaches to job design described in this chapter contain similar dimensions because this new framework includes many previous findings about job design.

PLAY VIDEO

JOB DESIGN AND WORK SCHEDULES

Go to academic.cengage.com/management/dubrin. Why does Zingerman seek to hire emotionally intelligent people?

Task Characteristics

Task characteristics focus on how the work itself is accomplished and the range and nature of the tasks associated with a particular job. A task characteristic for a manager at a steel mill might be using a spreadsheet to make a time-series analysis of the demand for recycled steel by manufacturers of washing machines.

job design
The process of laying out job responsibilities and duties and describing how they are to be performed.

2 The entire discussion in this section is based on Frederick P. Morgeson and Stephen E. Humphrey, "The Work Design Questionnaire (WDQ): Developing and Validating a Comprehensive Measure for Assessing the Job Design and the Nature of Work," *Journal of Applied Psychology*, November 2006, pp. 1321–1329. However, the Morgeson and Humphrey article is based partly on much of the research on job enrichment and the job characteristics model presented later in this chapter.

exhibit 7-1 The Four Job Dimensions and their Sub-Dimensions

Task Characteristics

Work-scheduling autonomy
Decision-making autonomy
Work-methods autonomy
Task variety
Task significance
Task identity
Feedback from the job

Knowledge Characteristics

Job complexity
Information processing
Problem solving
Skill variety
Specialization

Social Characteristics

Social support
Initiated interdependence
Received interdependence
Interaction outside organization
Feedback from others

Contextual Characteristics

Ergonomics
Physical demands
Work conditions
Equipment use

Source: Abridged from Frederick P. Morgeson and Stephen E. Humphrey, "The Work Design Questionnaire (WDQ): Developing and Validating a Comprehensive Measure for Assessing the Job Design and the Nature of Work," *Journal of Applied Psychology*, November 2006, p. 1327.

Autonomy in general refers to how much freedom and independence the incumbent has to carry out his or her work assignment. The freedom aspect includes (a) work scheduling, (b) decision making, and (c) work methods. The steel manager with high autonomy might decide when to do the forecast, make decisions based on the forecast, and choose the method for making the forecast (maybe not using a spreadsheet).

Task variety refers to the degree to which the job requires the worker to use a wide range of tasks, such as the steel-company manager making forecasts, selecting employees, and motivating workers. *Task significance* indicates the extent to which a job influences the lives or work of others, whether inside or outside the organization. Because the steel our manager helps produce is contained in the vehicles and home appliances of many people, the manager's job has high task significance.

Task identity reflects the extent to which a job involves a whole piece of work that can readily be identified. An audiologist who administered hearing tests to customers in a shopping mall would have high task identity. The business analyst who performs some financial analysis that only contributes to a larger report would have low task identity.

Feedback from job refers to the extent to which the job provides direct and clear information about the task performance. The focus is on feedback directly from the job itself, as opposed to feedback from others. An installer of satellite TV would have considerable feedback because before leaving the customer's home, he or she would know if the rig were working. One of the potential frustrations in a manager's job is that the manager does not know right away if he or she has done any good, such as in attempting to motivate workers.

Knowledge Characteristics

An obvious job dimension is the amount of knowledge, skill, and ability demands placed on the job holder because of the activities built into the job. The security person at the door of a bar has to know the difference between a valid and a fake I.D. card, and the chief financial officer has to understand the various meanings ways in which *profits* might be stated.

Job complexity refers to the degree to which the job tasks are complex and difficult to perform. Work that involves complex tasks requires many high-level skills and is mentally demanding and challenging. Even some basic jobs, such as production technician, have become more complex because of the math and computer skills required to carry out these jobs today. Most managerial positions involve high complexity, including the many skills described in Chapter 1 and throughout this book.

Information processing refers to the degree to which a job requires attending to and processing data and information. (Information is the result of making data useful, such as making sense of a survey about customer satisfaction.) Some jobs require higher levels of monitoring and processing information than others. As managers dash about consulting their BlackBerry, a high level of information processing is required. A student's life is filled with processing information and so is the life of a professional-level worker in any field.

Problem solving refers to the degree to which a job requires unique ideas or solutions, and also involves diagnosing and solving nonroutine problems, and preventing or fixing errors. Creativity is often required to effectively handle problem solving. Without problem-solving skills, a worker could be replaced by software or a handbook. Managers and professional-level workers are essentially problem solvers, yet some managerial jobs require heavier problem solving than others—for example, the CEO of Ford Motor Co. trying to solve the problem of how to make the automotive division profitable.

Skill variety refers to the extent to which a job requires the incumbent to use a variety of skills to perform the work. Skill variety and task variety are not the same thing because the use of multiple skills is different from the performance of multiple tasks. Your task might be to assemble a PowerPoint presentation, and you would need a variety of skills to perform this one task. Among the skills would be keyboarding, operating software, data analysis, and being artistic.

Specialization refers to the extent to which a job involves performing specialized tasks or possessing specialized knowledge and skills. A depth of knowledge and skill is required to be an effective specialist, such as a municipal-bond analyst or brain surgeon. A manager's job is typically that of a generalist rather than a specialist, yet the manager was most likely a specialist on the way to becoming a manager. A basic example would be a purchasing specialist later becoming a purchasing manager. Later we add a few more comments about job specialization because of its importance in defining jobs and careers.

Social Characteristics

Social characteristics relate to the interpersonal aspects of a job or the extent to which the job requires interaction with others. *Social support* refers to the degree to which a job involves the opportunity for advice and assistance from others in the workplace. Social support often contributes to the job holder's well-being, such as being able to turn to coworkers for technical assistance.

Interdependence reflects the degree to which the job depends on others—and others depend on the job—to accomplish the task. Visualize a team putting together a proposal for a large government contract to build an airplane. The various team members have to provide each other input such as manufacturing time and cost figures, such as the quality of a particular component being somewhat dependent on how much money is available for its manufacture.

Interaction outside the organization refers to how much the job requires the employee to interact and communicate with people outside the organization. Customer-contact workers obviously have to interact with outsiders, and so do C-level managers such as the CFO speaking with Wall Street financial analysts. *Feedback from others* refers to the extent to which other workers in the organization provide information about performance. Supervisors and coworkers are typical sources of feedback, yet feedback can also be received from those outside the immediate work area. For example, a senior manager might encounter a specialist in the hallway and say, "Jackie, I heard you're doing a great job for us. Keep up the good work."

Contextual Characteristics

Contextual characteristics refer to the setting or environment of the job, such as working in extreme temperatures. *Ergonomics* indicates the degree to which a job allows correct posture or movement. A chicken cutter in a poultry factory might suffer from tendonitis as a result of the repetitive movements, whereas most managerial jobs do not contain ergonomics problems.

Physical demands refer to the level of physical activity or effort required by the job, particularly with respect to the physical strength, endurance, effort, and activity aspects of the job. The job of a furniture mover obviously has high physical demands, yet many managerial positions have heavier physical demands than outsiders imagine. Among these demands can be heavy travel requiring endurance, lugging a heavy laptop computer and accessories, standing for long hours at a trade show, plus working long hours.

Work conditions relate directly to the environment in which the work is performed, including the presence of health hazards, noise, temperature, and cleanliness of the workplace. A project manager on a building site would face more environmental challenges than would his or her counterpart working in a climate-controlled office. *Equipment use* is a sub-dimension of contextual characteristics that reflects the variety and complexity of the technology and equipment incorporated into the job. Although managers would not ordinarily be considered equipment operators, they often make use of computers, printers, personal digital assistants, telephones, pocket calculators, and coffee pots.

Job Dimension Differences between Professional and Nonprofessional Jobs

As we described the above dimensions, we have made several references to occupational differences on the standing of the dimensions. Morgeson and Humphrey collected data on differences on the dimensions between the occupational categories of professionals (such as managers, accountants, and engineers) versus nonprofessional (such as food preparation specialist and personal-service provider). Nonprofessional jobs required more physical demands. Professionals scored significantly higher on the work characteristics as follows:

- Job complexity
- Information processing
- Problem solving
- Skill variety
- Work-scheduling autonomy
- Decision-making autonomy
- Work-methods autonomy
- Work conditions (more favorable).

Another analysis compared the job demands of occupations that were human-life focused (such as a supervisor) versus those that were nonhuman-life focused (such as lab technician). The human-life—focused jobs scored higher on the dimension of significance, or impact on others.

A career suggestion here is that if you think the dimensions in the bulleted-list along with the dimension of significance are important, you would be more satisfied occupying a professional rather than a nonprofessional job.

Job Specialization and Job Design

A major consideration in job design is how specialized the job holder must be (as shown in the specialization sub-dimension of *knowledge characteristics*). **Job specialization** is the degree to which a jobholder performs only a limited number of tasks. Specialists handle a narrow range of tasks especially well. High occupational-level specialists include the investment consultant who specializes in municipal bonds and the surgeon who concentrates on liver transplants. Specialists at the first occupational level are often referred to as entry-level workers, production specialists, support workers, or operatives.

A generalized job requires the handling of many different tasks. An extreme example of a top-level generalist is the owner of a small business who performs such varied tasks as making the product, selling it, negotiating with banks for loans, and hiring new employees. An extreme example of a generalist at the first (or entry) occupational level is the maintenance worker who packs boxes, sweeps, shovels snow in winter, mows the lawn, and cleans the lavatories.

job specialization
The degree to which a job holder performs only a limited number of tasks.

Advantages and Disadvantages of Job Specialization

Job specialization allows for the development of expertise at all occupational levels. When employees perform the same task repeatedly, they become highly knowledgeable. Many employees derive status and self-esteem from being experts at some task. Specialized jobs at lower occupational levels require less training time and less learning ability, which can prove to be a key advantage when the available labor force lacks special skills. For example, McDonald's could never have grown so large if each restaurant needed expert chefs. Instead, newcomers to the workforce can quickly learn such specialized skills as preparing hamburgers and french fries. These newcomers can be paid entry-level wages—an advantage from a management perspective only!

Job specialization also has disadvantages. Coordinating the work force can be difficult when several employees do small parts of one job. Somebody must take responsibility for pulling together the small pieces of the total task. Some employees prefer narrowly specialized jobs but the majority prefers broad tasks that give them a feeling of control over what they are doing. Although many technical and professional workers join the workforce as specialists, they often become bored by performing a narrow range of tasks.

Automation and Job Specialization

Automation has been used to replace some aspects of human endeavor in the office and the factory ever since the Industrial Revolution. Automation typically involves a machine that performs a specialized task previously performed by people. Automation is widely used in factories, offices, and stores. A major purpose of automation is to increase productivity by reducing the labor content required to deliver a product or service. A representative example is robotic equipment that can polish parts. Kason Industries in Atlanta, Georgia, found that the robotic polisher costing $500,000 paid for itself in two years.[3]

Two automation devices in the store are optical scanners and the automatic recording of remaining inventory when a customer checks out. The computerization of the workplace represents automation in hundreds of ways, such as personal computers decreasing the need for clerical support in organizations. Today, only high-level managers have personal secretaries. Others rely on their computers to perform many chores. E-mail has automated the delivery of many types of messages once sent by postal mail or messenger service, including sending photos and graphics around the world.

Automation enhances job satisfaction when annoying or dangerous tasks are removed, and automation does not result in job elimination. When automation helps a business organization become more productive, the net result is often the creation of more jobs. A curious case in point is the self-service kiosks at many McDonald's restaurants. Sales have increased so much where kiosks have been installed that the owners found it necessary to add two more employees at each store.[4]

---

3 Michael E. Kanell, "Productivity Lull Raises Concerns," *The Atlanta Journal Constitution* (http://www.ajc.com), November 24, 2006.

4 Charles Fishman, "The Toll of a New Machine," *Fast Company*, May 2004, p. 95.

exhibit 7-2 Job Description for Branch Manager, Insurance

Manages the branch office, including such functions as underwriting, claims processing, loss prevention, marketing, and auditing, and resolves related technical questions and issues. Hires new insurance agents, develops new business, and updates the regional manager regarding the profit-and-loss operating results of the branch office, insurance trends, matters having impact on the branch-office function, and competitor methods. The manager makes extensive use of information technology to carry out all of these activities, including spreadsheet analyses and giving direction to establishing customer databases.

Job Description and Job Design

Before choosing a job design, managers and human resource professionals develop a job description. The **job description** is a written statement of the key features of a job, along with the activities required to perform it effectively. Sometimes a description must be modified to fit basic principles of job design. For example, the job description of a customer-service representative might call for an excessive amount of listening to complaints, thus creating too much stress. Exhibit 7-2 presents a job description of a middle-level manager.

job description
A written statement of the key features of a job along with the activities required to perform it effectively.

The various job dimensions described above are found in the job design, even if these dimensions are not made explicit in the design. For example, in the job description for the branch manager the knowledge characteristics are heavy. The manager also has social characteristics demands, including hiring new insurance agents and developing new business.

JOB ENRICHMENT AND THE JOB CHARACTERISTICS MODEL

Learning Objective 2
Describe job enrichment including the job characteristics model.

Job enrichment is an approach to including more challenge and responsibility in jobs to make them more appealing to most employees. At its best, job enrichment gives workers a sense of ownership, responsibility, and accountability for their work. Because job enrichment leads to a more exciting job, it often increases employee job satisfaction and motivation. People usually work harder at tasks they find enjoyable and rewarding, just as they put effort into a favorite hobby. The general approach to enriching a job is to build into it more planning and decision making, controlling, and responsibility. Most managers have enriched jobs; most data entry specialists do not.

job enrichment
An approach to including more challenge and responsibility in jobs to make them more appealing to employees.

Characteristics of an Enriched Job

The design of an enriched job includes as many of the characteristics in the following list as possible, based on the pioneering work of Frederick Herzberg as well as updated research.[5] (Exhibit 7-3 summarizes the characteristics and

5 Frederick Herzberg, "The Wise Old Turk," *Harvard Business Review*, September–October 1974, pp. 70–80; Nico W. Van Yperen and Mariët Hagedoorn, "Do High Job Demands Increase Intrinsic Motivation or Fatigue or Both? The Role of Job Control and Job Social Support," *Academy of Management Journal*, June 2003, pp. 339–348.

exhibit 7-3 Characteristics and Consequences of an Enriched Job

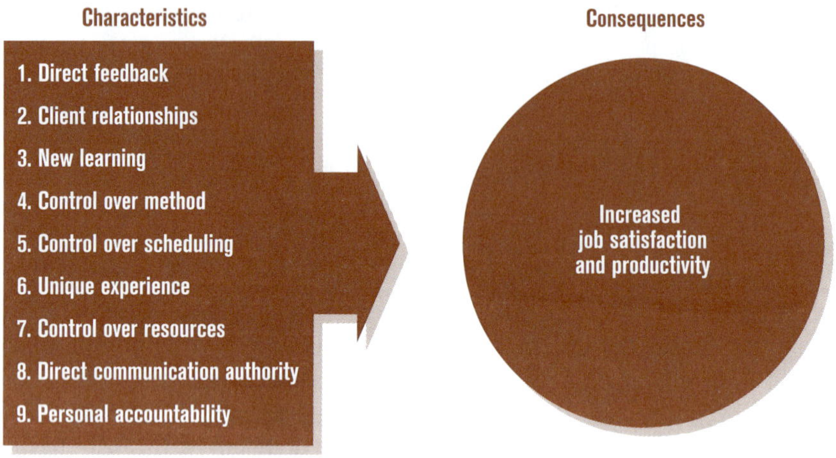

consequences of enriched jobs.) The person holding the job must perceive these characteristics as part of the job. You will notice that characteristics 1, 4, and 5 are also found as sub-dimensions of the four major dimensions that were described earlier in this chapter. Research indicates that supervisors and group members frequently have different perceptions of job characteristics. For example, supervisors are more likely to think that a job has a big impact on the organization.[6] A worker who is responsible for placing used soft-drink cans in a recycling bin might not think his job is significant. Yet the supervisor might perceive the individual to be contributing to the social-responsibility goal of creating a cleaner, less-congested environment.

1. *Direct feedback.* Employees should receive immediate evaluation of their work. This feedback can be built into the job (such as the feedback that closing a sale gives a sales representative) or provided by the supervisor.
2. *Client relationships.* A job is automatically enriched when an employee has a client or customer to serve, whether that client is inside or outside the firm. Serving a client is more satisfying to most people than performing work solely for a manager.
3. *New learning.* An enriched job allows its holder to acquire new knowledge. The learning can stem from job experiences themselves or from training programs associated with the job.
4. *Control over method.* When a worker has some control over which method to choose to accomplish a task, his or her task motivation generally increases. An office manager, for example, might be told to decrease energy costs by 10 percent in the building. She would have control over method if

6 Marc C. Marchese and Robert P. Delprino, "Do Supervisors and Subordinates See Eye-to-Eye on Job Enrichment?" *Journal of Business and Psychology*, Winter 1998, pp. 179–192.

empowered to decide *how* to decrease costs, such as adjusting the thermostat or finding a lower-cost energy supplier.

5. *Control over scheduling.* The ability to schedule one's own work contributes to job enrichment. Scheduling includes the authority to decide when to tackle which assignment and having some say in setting working hours.
6. *Unique experience.* An enriched job exhibits some unique qualities or features. A public-relations assistant, for example, has the opportunity to interact with visiting celebrities.
7. *Control over resources.* Another contribution to enrichment comes from some control over resources, such as money, material, or people.
8. *Direct communication authority.* An enriched job provides workers the opportunity to communicate directly with other people who use their output. A software specialist with an enriched job, for example, handles complaints about the software he or she developed. The advantages of this dimension of an enriched job are similar to those derived from maintaining client relationships.
9. *Personal accountability.* In an enriched job, workers take responsibility for their results. They accept credit for a job done well and blame for a job done poorly.

A highly enriched job with all nine of the preceding characteristics gives the jobholder an opportunity to satisfy high-level psychological needs, such as self-fulfillment. Sometimes the jobs of managers are too enriched, with too much responsibility and too many risks. A job with some of these characteristics would be moderately enriched. An impoverished job has none. Information technology workers are another occupational group that may suffer from over-enriched jobs. Working with computers and software at an advanced level may represent healthy job enrichment for many workers—working directly with information technology gives a person direct feedback, new learning, and personal accountability. However, many other computer workers feel stressed by the complexity of information technology, the amount of continuous learning involved, and frequent hardware and software breakdowns beyond the control of the worker.

The Job Characteristics Model of Job Enrichment

Expanding the concept of job enrichment creates the **job characteristics model,** a method of job enrichment that focuses on the task and interpersonal dimensions of a job.[7] As Exhibit 7-4 shows, five measurable characteristics of jobs improve employee motivation, satisfaction, and performance. All five characteristics have been incorporated into the four major dimensions of job design, and were defined previously.

job characteristics model
A method of job enrichment that focuses on the task and interpersonal dimensions of a job.

As Exhibit 7-4 reports, these core job characteristics relate to critical psychological states or key mental attitudes. Skill variety, task identity, and task significance lead to a feeling that the work is meaningful. The task dimension of autonomy leads quite logically to a feeling of responsibility for

7 John Richard Hackman and Greg R. Oldham, *Work Redesign* (Reading, MA: Addison-Wesley, 1980), p. 77.

exhibit 7-4 **The Job Characteristics Model of Job Enrichment**

Job enrichment can be made more precise and scientific by following the model presented here.

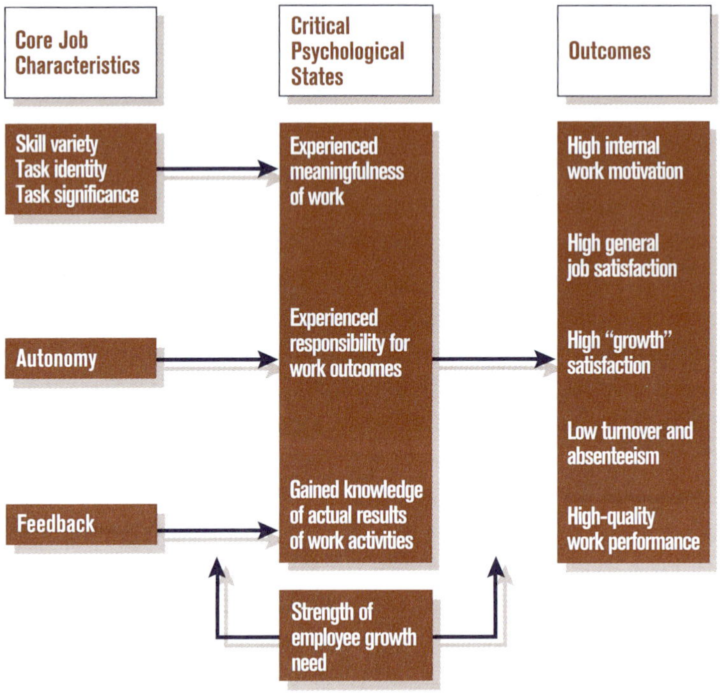

work outcomes. And the feedback dimension leads to knowledge of results. According to the model, a redesigned job must lead to these three psychological states for workers to achieve the outcomes of internal motivation, job satisfaction, low turnover and absenteeism, and high-quality performance.

Guidelines for Implementing a Job Enrichment Program

The notation in Exhibit 7-4, strength of employee growth need, provides guidelines for managers. The link between the job characteristics and outcomes strengthens as workers want to grow and develop. Before implementing a program of job enrichment, a manager must first ask whether the workers need or want more responsibility, variety, and growth. Some employees already have jobs that are enriched enough. Many employees do not want an enriched job because they prefer to avoid the challenge and stress of responsibility. Brainstorming is useful in pinpointing changes that will enrich jobs for those who want enrichment.[8] The brainstorming group would be composed of job incumbents, supervisors, and perhaps an industrial engineer. The workers' participation in planning changes can be useful. Workers may suggest, for example, how to increase client contact or how they could self-schedule some tasks.

8 J. Barton Cunningham and Ted Eberle, "A Guide to Job Enrichment and Redesign," *Personnel*, February 1990, p. 59.

JOB INVOLVEMENT, ENLARGEMENT, AND ROTATION

Learning Objective 3

Describe job involvement, enlargement, and rotation.

Job enrichment, including the job characteristics model, requires a comprehensive program. Managers can also improve the motivational aspects of job design through less complicated procedures: job involvement, job enlargement, and job rotation. All three processes are built into the more comprehensive job enrichment.

Job involvement is the degree to which individuals identify psychologically with their work. It also refers to the importance of work to a person's total self-image. If an insurance claims examiner regards his job as a major part of his identity, he experiences high job involvement. For example, at a social gathering the claims examiner would inform people shortly after meeting them, "I'm a claims examiner with Nationwide." The employee-involvement groups in quality management are based on job involvement. By making decisions about quality improvement, the team members ideally identify psychologically with their work. Exhibit 7-5 gives you an opportunity to think about job involvement as it applies to you.

Job enlargement refers to increasing the number and variety of tasks within a job. The technique was developed to help workers combat boredom. Because the tasks are approximately at the same level of responsibility, job enlargement is also referred to as horizontal job loading. In contrast, *job enrichment* is referred to as vertical job loading, because the jobholder takes on higher-level job responsibility. The claims examiner would experience job enlargement if he were given additional responsibilities such as examining claims for boats and motorcycles as well as automobiles.

As responsibilities expand in job enlargement, jobholders usually find themselves juggling multiple priorities. Two, three, four, or even more demands might be facing the worker. In one approach to handling multiple priorities, a jobholder ranks them in order of importance and then tackles the most important one first. With this approach, the lowest-priority tasks may be neglected. With a more recommended approach, the jobholder finishes the top-priority task, and then moves immediately to all other tasks. Top-priority items can be tackled again after the lesser tasks are completed. Yet if the manager or team leader insists that a specific task must be done immediately, it is good office politics to work on that task. Some catch-up time at night or on weekends might then be invested in work to avoid falling behind on other projects.

Job rotation is a temporary switching of job assignments. In this way employees develop new skills and learn about how other aspects of the unit or organization work. However, the potential advantages of job rotation are lost if a person is rotated from one dull job to another. A motivational form of job rotation would be for the claims examiner to investigate auto and small-truck claims one month, and large trucks the next. Job rotation helps prevent workers from feeling bored or in a rut. In addition to learning new skills, job rotation gives workers an opportunity to learn more about how the organization operates. A marketing specialist who was rotated into a finance position for six months commented, "Now I really understand firsthand how every penny counts when the company is attempting to obtain a good return on investment."

job involvement
The degree to which individuals identify psychologically with their work.

job enlargement
Increasing the number and variety of tasks within a job.

job rotation
A temporary switching of job assignments.

exhibit 7-5 How Involved Are You?

Indicate the strength of your agreement with the following statements by circling the number that appears below the appropriate heading: DS = disagree strongly; D = disagree; N = neutral; A = agree; AS=agree strongly. Respond in relation to a present job, the job you hope to have, or schoolwork.

	DS	D	N	A	AS
1. The major satisfaction in my life comes from my work.	1	2	3	4	5
2. Work is just a means to an end.	5	4	3	2	1
3. The most important things that happen to me involve my work.	1	2	3	4	5
4. I often concentrate so hard on my work that I'm unaware of what is going on around me.	1	2	3	4	5
5. If I inherited enough money, I would spend the rest of my life on vacation.	5	4	3	2	1
6. I'm a perfectionist about my work.	1	2	3	4	5
7. I am very much involved personally in my work.	1	2	3	4	5
8. Most things in life are more important than work.	5	4	3	2	1
9. Working full time is boring.	5	4	3	2	1
10. My work is intensely exciting.	1	2	3	4	5

Score ________________

Scoring and interpretation: Total the numbers circled, and then use the following guide to interpretation.

45–50 Your attitudes suggest intense job involvement. Such attitudes should contribute highly to productivity, quality, and satisfaction.

28–44 Your attitudes suggest a moderate degree of job involvement. To sustain a high level of productivity and quality, you would need to work toward becoming more involved in your work.

10–27 Your attitudes suggest a low degree of job involvement. It would be difficult to sustain a successful, professional career with such low involvement.

Source: Adapted from Myron Gable and Frank Dangello, "Job Involvement, Machiavellianism, and Job Performance," *Journal of Business and Psychology*, Winter 1994, p. 163.

Job enlargement and job rotation offer similar advantages and disadvantages to the individual and the organization. Through job enlargement and job rotation, workers develop a broader set of skills, making them more valuable and flexible. Pushed to extremes, however, job enlargement and rotation lead to feelings of being overworked.

JOB CRAFTING AND JOB DESIGN

In the traditional view of a job, a competent worker carefully follows a job description, and good performance means that the person accomplishes what is specified in the job description. A contemporary view sees a job description as only a guideline: the competent worker exceeds the constraints of a job description. He or she takes on constructive activities not mentioned in the job description.

Learning Objective 4

Explain how workers use job crafting to modify their jobs.

The flexible work roles carried out by many workers contribute to the move away from tightly following job descriptions that are too rigid. An emerging trend finds companies hiring people "to work" rather than to fill a specific job slot. As the pharmaceutical industry has become increasingly competitive and unpredictable, Pfizer has shifted its hiring strategy to find workers who are versatile. The giant drug maker now hires and develops employees who can shift from one position to another. In the past the company hired mostly on the basis of job descriptions. Now Pfizer evaluates what competencies (such as problem solving and communications skills) the candidate demonstrates.[9]

Workers sometimes deviate from their job descriptions by modifying their job to fit their personal preferences and capabilities. According to the research of Amy Wrzesniewski and Jane E. Dutton, employees craft their jobs by changing the tasks they perform and their contacts with others to make their jobs more meaningful.[10] To add variety to her job, for example, a team leader might make nutritional recommendations to team members. The team leader alters her task of coaching about strictly work-related issues to also coaching about personal health. In this way, she broadens her role in terms of her impact on the lives of work associates.

job crafting The physical and mental changes individuals make in the task or relationship aspects of their job.

ergonomic principles The practice of matching machines to worker requirements.

Job crafting refers to the physical and mental changes individuals make in the task or relationship aspects of their job. Three common types of job crafting include (1) the number and types of job tasks, (2) the interactions with others on the job, and (3) one's view of the job. The most frequent purpose of crafting is to make the job more meaningful or enriched. A cook, for example, might add flair to a meal, which was not required, just to inject a little personal creativity. Exhibit 7-6 illustrates these three forms of job crafting, including how crafting affects the meaning of work. After studying the exhibit think through whether you have ever engaged in job crafting.

ERGONOMICS AND JOB DESIGN

Learning Objective 5

Illustrate how ergonomic factors can be part of job design.

A key principle of job design is that the job should be laid out to decrease the chances that it will physically harm the incumbent. According to the U.S. Occupational and Health Agency (OSHA), **ergonomics** is the science of fitting the worker to the job. Ergonomics seeks to minimize the physical demands on workers and optimize system performance, and therefore has considerable relevance to job design. Three principles of ergonomics are recommended when designing jobs:

9 Jessica Marquez, "A Talent Strategy Overhaul at Pfizer," *Workforce Management*, February 12, 2007, pp. 1, 3.

10 Amy Wrzesniewski and Jane E. Dutton, "Crafting a Job: Revisioning Employees as Active Crafters of Their Work," *The Academy of Management Review*, April 2001, pp. 179–201.

exhibit 7-6 Forms of Job Crafting

Form	Example	Effect on Meaning of Work
Changing number, scope, and type of job tasks	Design engineers engage in changing the quality or amount of interactions with people, thereby moving a project to completion.	Work is completed in a more timely fashion; engineers change the meaning of their jobs to be guardians or movers of projects.
Changing quality and/or amount of interaction with others encountered in the job	Hospital cleaners actively caring for patients and families, integrating themselves into the work flow of their floor units.	Cleaners change the meaning of their jobs to be helpers of the sick; they see the work of the floor unit as an integrated whole of which they are a vital part.
Changing the view of the job	Nurses take responsibility for all information and "insignificant" tasks that may help them to care more appropriately for a patient.	Nurses change the way they see the work to be more about patient advocacy, as well as high-quality technical care.

Source: Adapted from Amy Wrzesniewski and Jane E. Dutton, "Crafting a Job: Revisioning Employees as Active Crafters of Their Work," Academy of Management Review, April 2001, p. 185.

- Workers should be able to adopt several different postures that are safe and comfortable.
- When workers exert muscular force, they should be encouraged to use the largest muscle groups (such as using the legs and body to help lift a box rather than only the arms).
- Whenever possible, workers should be able to perform regular work activities with their joints, in the middle range of movement.[11]

It is important for managers to help prevent ergonomic problems for ethical and humanitarian reasons. In addition, injuries and illnesses stemming from ergonomic problems drive up health costs, including insurance premiums.

Musculoskeletal Disorders Including Carpal Tunnel Syndrome

A frequent problem in factories, mills, supermarkets, and offices is work-related musculoskeletal disorders (MSDs) or problems involving muscle and bones. Musculoskeletal disorders represent more than 100 injures that take place when there is a mismatch between the physical requirements of the job and the physical capacity of the human body. Overuse is a common problem. A supermarket cashier might stay in good shape working a few hours a day, but lifting several hundred bags of groceries in eight hours may create

11 "Ergonomics," http://www.referencesforbusiness.com/management/Em-Exp/Ergnomics.html, accessed November 26, 2006, p. 1.

a severe back injury. OSHA recommends that designing check-out counters to reduce ergonomic risk factors, such as twisting or extended reaching, can improve cashier effectiveness and productivity.

Solutions to some potential ergonomic problems can be quite simple. For example, working the back of a deep display case to face or stock merchandise can be awkward and uncomfortable, especially when heavy items are involved. One solution to this problem OSHA recommends is display cases that are stocked from the back. The product, such as cartons of milk, slides down an inclined shelf so that it is always in front of the customer. The employee stocking the shelf experiences less physical strain.[12]

Musculoskeletal disorders also include **cumulative trauma disorders**—injuries caused by repetitive motions over prolonged periods of time. These disorders now account for almost half of occupational injuries and illnesses in the United States. Any occupation involving excessive repetitive motions, including bricklayer and meat cutter or fishery worker, can lead to cumulative trauma disorder. Vibrating tools, such as jackhammers, also cause such disorder. The use of computers and other high-tech equipment such as price scanners contributes to the surge in the number of cumulative trauma disorders. Extensive keyboarding places severe strain on hand and wrist muscles, often leading to **carpal tunnel syndrome**. This syndrome occurs when frequent bending of the wrist causes swelling in a tunnel of bones and ligaments in the wrist. The nerve that gives feeling to the hand is pinched, resulting in tingling and numbness in the fingers. Overuse of the computer mouse is a major contributor to wrist and tendon injury.

The symptoms of carpal tunnel syndrome are severe. Many workers suffering from the syndrome are unable to differentiate hot and cold by touch and lose finger strength. They often appear clumsy because they have difficulty with everyday tasks such as tying their shoes or picking up small objects. Treatment of carpal tunnel syndrome may involve surgery to release pressure on the median nerve. Another approach is anti-inflammatory drugs to reduce tendon swelling.

To help prevent and decrease the incidence of cumulative trauma disorders, many companies select equipment designed for that purpose. Exhibit 7-7 depicts a workstation based on ergonomic principles developed to engineer a good fit between person and machine. In addition, the following steps should be taken to prevent cumulative trauma disorders:[13]

- Analyze each job with an eye toward possible hazards on that job, including equipment that is difficult to operate.
- Install equipment that minimizes awkward hand and body movements. Try ergonomically designed keyboards to see whether they make a difference.

cumulative trauma disorders
Injuries caused by repetitive motions over prolonged periods of time.

carpal tunnel syndrome
The most frequent cumulative trauma disorder which occurs when frequent wrist bending results in swelling, leading to a pinched nerve.

12 "Ergonomics for the Prevention of Musculoskeletal Disorders-Guidelines for Retail Grocers," http://www.osha.gov/ergonomics/guidelines/retailgrocery/retailgrocery.html, accessed November 26, 2006, p. 4.

13 Albert R. Karr, "An Ergo-Unfriendly Home Office Can Hurt You," *The Wall Street Journal*, September 30, 2003, p. D6; "Preventing Carpal Tunnel Syndrome," *HRfocus*, August 1995, p. 4; Neil Gross and Paul C. Judge, "Let's Talk," *Business Week*, February 23, 1998, pp. 61–72.

exhibit 7-7 An Ergonomically Designed Workstation

- Screen is below eye level.
- Elbows are on same level with the home key row, keeping wrists and lower arms parallel to the floor.
- Back and thighs are supported.
- Upper legs are parallel to the floor.
- Feet are placed flat on the floor.
- Task lamp supplements adequate room lighting.

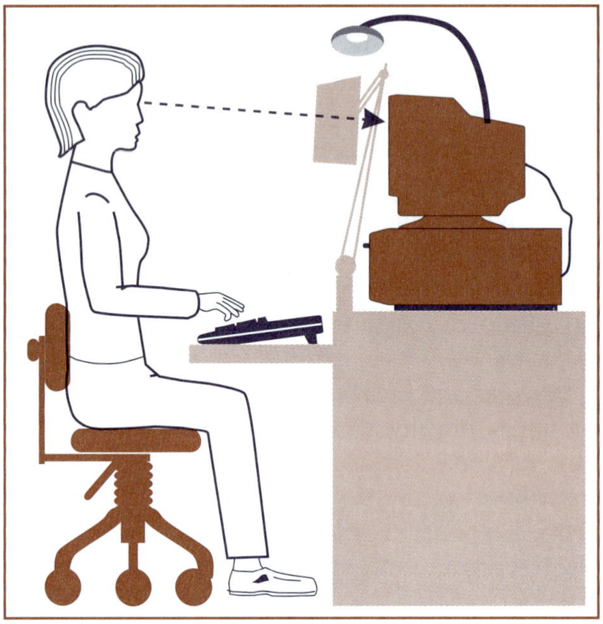

- Encourage workers to take frequent breaks, and rotate jobs so that repetitive hand and body movements are reduced.
- Encourage workers to maintain good posture when seated at the keyboard. Poor posture can lead to carpal tunnel syndrome from extending the wrists too far, as well as to neck ache and backache.
- Make less use of the mouse by using more key commands. Overuse of the mouse can cause repetitive motion injury. Find ways to use the left hand more, such as for tapping function keys.

Workers must also recognize that if they spend many nonworking hours using a keyboard, they increase the probability of developing carpal tunnel syndrome. Other factors that predispose workers to carpal tunnel syndrome are obesity, particularly when the obese person is diabetic, and shortages of vitamins B_6 and C.[14]

Noise Problems

Repetitive motion disorders and other musculoskeletal disorders, including tendonitis, sciatica, and lower-back pain, are well-publicized ergonomic problems. Another recurring problem relates to uncomfortable noise levels. Although industrial noise problems are usually associated with manufacturing

14 William Atkinson, "The Carpal Tunnel Conundrum," *Workforce*, September 2002, p. 17.

and mills, the constant buzz in offices can also create discomfort and physical problems. Also, many workers complain about the ringing of personal cell phones during the work day.

An experiment was conducted in which 40 female clerical workers were assigned to a control (low-noise) group or to a high-noise group. The noise was a three-hour exposure to low-intensity noise designed to simulate open-office noise levels. Workers exposed to the noise experienced negative consequences, not experienced by the control (comparison) group. One effect was an increase in epinephrine, a hormone that enters the urine in response to stress. The group exposed to noise also performed more poorly on a puzzle given to participants. Also, the group exposed to noise made less use of work-furniture features designed to provide opportunities for postural adjustment during work.[15] In this way one ergonomics problem (noise) could lead to increased ergonomic problems (repetitive motion disorder and back problems).

MODIFIED WORK SCHEDULES AND JOB DESIGN

Learning Objective 6

Summarize the various modified work schedules.

A key characteristic of job enrichment gives workers authority in scheduling their own work. Closely related is the widespread practice of giving workers some choice in deviating from the traditional five-day, 40-hour workweek. A **modified work schedule** is any formal departure from the traditional hours of work, excluding shift work and staggered work hours. Yet shift work presents enough unique managerial challenges that it will be described here. Modified work schedules include flexible working hours, a compressed workweek, job sharing, telecommuting, and part-time and temporary work.

Modified work schedules serve several important organizational purposes in addition to being part of job design. They potentially increase job satisfaction and motivation and attract workers who prefer to avoid a traditional schedule. Modified work schedules are also popular with the physically disabled because the rigors of commuting may decrease. Many single parents need flexible hours to cope with childcare. Flexible working hours are popular with many employees. Working at home continues to gain popularity with a subset of the workforce.

Flexible Working Hours

For about 35 million American employees, the standard eight-hour day with fixed starting and stopping times is a thing of the past. Instead, these employees exert some control over their work schedules through a system or informal arrangement of flexible working hours. The vast majority of workers with flexible working hours adjust their working hours through informal agreements with their managers, rather than as part of a formal program.[16]

modified work schedule
Any formal departure from the traditional hours of work, excluding shift work and staggered work hours.

15 Gary W. Evans and Dana Johnson, "Stress and Open-Office Noise," *Journal of Applied Psychology*, October 2000, pp. 779–783.

16 Sarah Fister Gale, "Formalized Flextime: The Perk That Brings Productivity," *Workforce*, February 2001, p. 39. Data are extrapolated to 2006.

Employees with flexible working hours work certain core hours, such as 10:00 a.m. to 3:30 p.m. However, they are able to choose which hours they work from 7:00 a.m. to 10:00 a.m. and from 3:30 p.m. to 6:30 p.m. Exhibit 7-8 presents a basic model of flexible working hours. Time-recording devices frequently monitor employees' required hours for the week.

Flexible working hours are far more likely to be an option for employees on the nonexempt payroll. Such workers receive additional pay for work beyond 40 hours per week and premium pay for Saturdays and Sundays. Managers, professional-level workers, and salespeople generally have some flexibility in choosing their work hours. In addition, managers and professionals in corporations work an average of 55 hours per week, making concerns about fitting in a 40-hour-per-week flextime schedule irrelevant.

Many employers believe that flexible working hours enhance productivity for reasons such as decreasing employee absenteeism and stress. Also, flexible working hours tend to increase efficiency during core times, and decrease the need for overtime because more gets accomplished during the core.[17]

Many employees hesitate to use flexible working hours (as well as other work/life programs) for fear of being perceived as not strongly committed to the organization. In a survey of 505 working employees, 59 percent indicated they were reluctant to ask their employer about flexible working options. The most common reason given was fear of the perception that they were not serious about their careers. The employees surveyed had interviewed with Flexible Resources Inc., a placement firm specializing in flexible workplace arrangements.[18]

exhibit 7-8 **A Typical Flexible-Working-Hours Schedule**

Flexible working hours have a fixed core time in the middle.

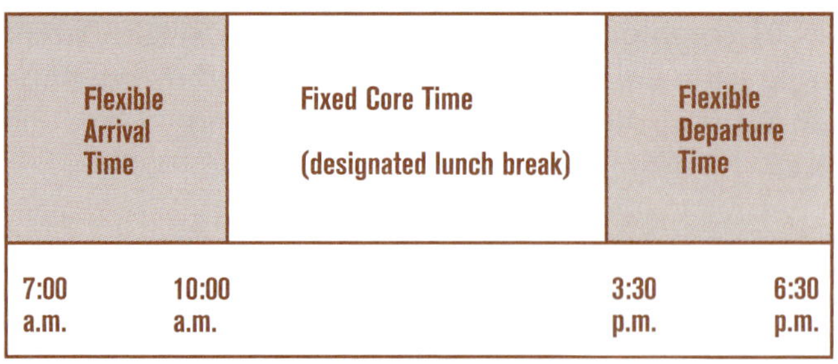

Sample schedules: **Early Schedule, 7:00—3:30**
Standard Schedule, 9:00—5:30
Late Schedule, 10:00—6:30

17 "Introducing Flexible Working Hours Into Your Organization," in *Business: The Ultimate Resource* (Cambridge, MA: Perseus Publishing, 2002), p. 358.

18 *BNA Daily Labor Report* article cited in "Workers May Want Flexibility, but Don't Always Ask for It," *Leading for Results*, sample issue 2006. Published by Ragan's Management Resources.

A major problem for the career-oriented employee who chooses flextime is that meetings might be held at times beyond the employee's scheduled quitting time. Suppose you have agreed to work from 7 a.m. until 4 p.m. on Thursday. The team leader schedules an important meeting at 4:30 for Thursday. You now face a conflict between taking care of personal obligations and appearing to be a dedicated worker.

Flextime often comes about after an employee requests the opportunity to participate in a program. Finding answers to the following questions can help the manager evaluate a flextime request:[19] (The same questions also apply generally to other types of modified work schedules.)

1. *Does the nature of the job allow for a flexible schedule*? Employees who must turn around work quickly or respond to crises might not be good candidates for flexible working hours. Negative indicators for flextime also include other employees being inconvenienced by the altered schedule, and a job that requires frequent interaction with others.
2. *Will this individual work well independently*? Some employees thrive on working solo, such as being in the office at 6 a.m. or 7 p.m. Others lose momentum when working alone. Does the employee have a high level of initiative and self-motivation?
3. *Are you comfortable managing a flex-worker*? A manager who feels the need to frequently monitor the work of employees will become anxious when the employees are working by themselves during noncore hours.
4. *Can you arrange tasks so the employee will have enough to do when you or other workers are not present*? Some employees can find ways to make a contribution on their own, while others must be fed work in small doses.

Flexible working hours can also be attained outside of a formal program by the manager granting flexibility as needed. Smith-Winchester, a Michigan company that provides advertising and other business communication services, has a year-round policy that permits workers to leave early as needed, as long as they make up the time. The company also grants workers five personal days a year.[20]

Compressed Workweek

A **compressed workweek** is a full-time work schedule that allows 40 hours of work in less than five days. The usual arrangement is 4–40 (working four 10-hour days). Many employees enjoy the 4–40 schedule because it enables them to have three consecutive days off from work. Employees often invest this time in leisure activities or part-time jobs. A 4–40 schedule usually allows most employees to take off Saturdays and Sundays. Important exceptions include police workers, hospital employees, and computer operators.

compressed workweek
A full-time work schedule that allows 40 hours of work in less than five days.

19 "A Time for Change? Maybe Not—Flextime Isn't for Everyone," *WorkingSMART*, September 1996, pp. 1–2.
20 Joyce M. Rosenberg, "Bosses Can Help Relieve Holiday Pressure," Associated Press, November 27, 2006.

Two lesser used versions of the compressed workweek are the three-day workweek, and the 5/4–9 compressed plan. The basic work requirement for the three-day workweek is 13 hours and 20 minutes per day. Under 5/4–9, an employee works eight 9-hour days and one 8-hour day for a total of 80 hours every two weeks. As you can imagine, the three-day workweek is much desired by camping and skiing enthusiasts but is not effective for career advancement.

Compressed workweeks are well liked by employees whose lifestyle fits such a schedule. Morale sometimes increases because employees have more days off per month. (Yet, some employees do not want so much time away from work each month.) However, the 4–40 week has many built-in problems. Many workers are fatigued during the last two hours and suffer from losses in concentration. From a personal standpoint, working for ten consecutive hours can be inconvenient.

Telecommuting and the Distributed Workforce

An estimated 12 percent of the U.S. workforce conducts most of its work away from the company office, with this figure forecast to rise to 40 percent by 2012.[21] **Telecommuting** is an arrangement in which employees use computers to perform their regular work responsibilities at home, in a satellite office, or remote worksite. Telework also takes place at coffee shops, Wi-Fi (or Internet) cafés, boats, and RVs (recreational vehicles). Another possibility is working from a community center alongside other teleworkers. In total such workers are often referred to as part of the *distributed workforce* because they are distributed away from the traditional workplace.

Employees who telecommute usually use computers tied to the company's main office. Or they can simply use e-mail to communicate with people in the traditional office. People who work at home are referred to as *teleworkers*. The vast majority of people who work at home make use of computers and related equipment. Yet a person might do piecework at home, such as making garments or furniture, without using a computer—and is therefore not classified as a telecommuter.

In addition to using computers to communicate with their employer's office, telecommuters attend meetings on company premises and stay in contact by telephone and teleconferences. Some telecommuting programs are huge. At IBM, 40 percent of the workforce has no office or dedicated workspace at the office. The Mobility Initiative at IBM, for example, has resulted in 12,500 sales representatives giving up their dedicated workspaces. The sales representative's residence, along with an automobile trunk, becomes his or her office. At AT&T, 39 percent of managers work from home at least once a week, and another 24 percent do so occasionally, as needed. Many small businesses operate with informal telecommuting programs.[22]

telecommuting
An arrangement with one's employer to use a computer to perform work at home or in a satellite office.

The accompanying Management in Action describes a telecommuting experience at a well-known retailer.

---

21 Michelle Conlin, "The Easiest Commute of All," *Business Week*, December 12, 2005, p. 79.

22 "Creating a Network-Centric Future: Summary of 2003 AT&T Employee Telework Research," *AT&T Telework White Paper*, February 3, 2004, p. 1; Conlin, "The Easiest Commute of All," p. 78.

management in action

Steve Hance, Best Buy Employee Relations Manager Works from Wherever He Wants

Back when he worked in a conventional corporate office for a previous employer, Best Buy employee relations manager Steven Hance admits he sometimes got through long, unproductive meetings by fantasizing about fishing or hunting. But since he began working for the Richfield, Minnesota, national electronics retailing chain in March 2005, the outdoorsman no longer has to daydream.

Instead, when Hance participates in a morning teleconference with his coworkers or in-house clients, he is sometimes calling in via cell phone from his fishing boat on a lake or from the woods where he's spent the hours since dawn stalking wild turkeys. "No one at Best Buy really knows where I am," he explains. "Nor do they really care."

Gone are the days when Hance needed to spend morning until night seated in a cubicle surrounded by papers and charts he'd carefully arranged to ensure that coworkers and bosses who peeked in would see he was hard at work. At Best Buy, he's free to set his own schedule, to work wherever he wants—whether it's a desk at headquarters or a table in a coffee shop—and whatever days and hours he chooses.

"It used to be that I had to schedule my life around my work," he says. "Now I schedule my work around my life."

Welcome to Best Buy's Results-Only Work Environment, or ROWE, a radical experiment whose aim is to reshape the corporate workplace, achieve an unparalleled degree of work/life balance and redefine the very nature of the work itself. In ROWE, most of the rules, restrictions, and expectations with which corporate workers traditionally labor—such as keeping regular hours, and showing up at the office each morning—are discarded.

Instead, employees are allowed to decide how, when, and where they get the job done. Whether they choose to work in the office or somewhere else, such as a spare bedroom, salaried employees are required to put in only as much time as it actually takes to do their work. (Hourly employees in the program have to work a set of number of hours to comply with federal labor regulations, but they still get to choose when they do it.)

"In the standard corporate work environment, you have to put in face time because that's how you show your commitment to the organization and your level of dedication," Hance says. "When you come into the office, you've got to make sure you're always seen by the right people. That becomes the goal, rather then actually getting things done. With ROWE, all those little rules that we've grown used to living by are out the door. Instead, the work itself is the only thing that matters."

Questions

1. How can a retailer like Best Buy offer telecommuting to employees? What about serving customers face to face?
2. Can an employee relations manager really be *working* while he is chasing down wild turkeys in the woods?
3. What impact might the ROWE experiment have on the recruitment and retention of workers?

Source: Patrick J. Kiger, "Throwing Out the Rules of Work," *Workforce Management*, September 25, 2006, pp. 1, 16.

Advantages of Telecommuting

Telecommuting can work well with self-reliant and self-starting employees who have relevant work experience. Work-at-home employees usually volunteer for such an arrangement. As a result, they are likely to find telecommuting satisfying.

Employees derive many benefits from working at home, including easier management of personal life; lowered costs for commuting, work clothing, and lunch; much less time spent commuting; and fewer distractions such as office noise. Telecommuting offers the following advantages to the employer:[23]

1. *Increased productivity.* Surveys consistently show that telecommuting programs increase productivity, usually by at least 25 percent. AT&T managers consistently report that they gain about one extra productive hour per day when working at home. The gain comes from saving time by not physically commuting, the ability to concentrate better by not being distracted, and better time management. Work design consultant Jim Ware notes that distributed workers are more productive because they spend less time commuting, in hallways gabbing, or unproductive meetings.[24]
2. *Low overhead.* Because the employees provide some of their own office space, the company can operate with much less office space. A vice president of marketing research operations noted that, because of its work-at-home program, the company was able to greatly expand its client load without acquiring additional space. At Sun Microsystems Inc., nearly one-half of employees are part of the distributed workforce, saving the company $300 million annually in real-estate costs. (Sun would probably have to sell $3 billion in equipment to earn the same amount of profit.)
3. *Access to a wider range of employee talent.* Companies with regular work-at-home programs are usually deluged with résumés from eager job applicants. The talent bank includes parents (mostly mothers) with young children, employees who find commuting unpleasant, and others who live far way from their firms. The Department of Labor regards telework as an option for disabled workers who traditionally have few opportunities in the workplace. The disabled workers may have talents that otherwise might be overlooked.

Disadvantages of Telecommuting

Work-at-home programs must be used selectively because they pose disadvantages for both employee and employer. The careers of telecommuters may suffer because they are not visible to management. Many telecommuters complain of the isolation from coworkers.

Also, telecommuters can be exploited if they feel compelled to work on company problems late into the night and on weekends. The many potential distractions at home make it difficult for some telecommuters to concentrate on work. Finally, telecommuters are sometimes part-time employees who receive limited benefits and are paid only for what they produce. As one telecommuter, a data entry specialist, said, "If I let up for an afternoon, I earn hardly anything." Working at home can reinforce negative tendencies:

---

23 Mahlon Apgar IV, "The Alternative Workplace: Changing Where and How People Work," *Harvard Business Review*, May–June 1998, p. 121; "What Is the Future of Telework?" *HRfocus*, March 2001, pp. 5–6; "Creating a Network-Centric Future," p. 2; Conlin, "The Easiest Commute of All," p. 79.

24 Cited in "Workplace 1.5: Managing Teleworkers—at Home, at Work, at Starbucks," *Fast Company*, November 2005, p. 105.

It will facilitate a workaholic to work harder and longer, and it will give a procrastinator ample opportunity to delay work.[25]

Telecommuting programs can be disadvantageous to the employer because building loyalty and teamwork is difficult when so many workers are away from the office. In 2006, a group of Hewlett-Packard employees who manage the company's internal software and computers were no longer allowed to telecommute. The HP chief information officer made the change as part of a plan to increase face-to-face interaction and team effectiveness in the information technology unit.[26]

Telecommuters who are not performing measured work are difficult to supervise—working at home gives an employee much more latitude in attending to personal matters during work time. With so many teleworkers conducting work at coffee shops, many of them may drift away from being focused on company goals during the working day.

A major concern is that the organization may miss out on some of the creativity that stems from the exchange of ideas in the traditional office. Another problem is that telecommuting can impact a worker's identity toward being self-employed, and away from being part of the organization.[27] A worker who spends very little time on company premises is less likely to express a sentiment such as "I am a Yahoo! woman."

To maximize the advantages and minimize the disadvantages of telecommuting, managers should follow a few key suggestions presented in Exhibit 7-9. If you are in the process of building your career and want to develop valuable contacts on the job, minimize telecommuting. Establishing face-to-face relationships remains highly important for career advancement.

Sharing Office Space and Hoteling

Another major aspect of the alternative workplace is for workers to share offices or cubicles, or have use of a shared office (similar to a hotel) only when on premises. *Shared office space* means simply that more than one employee is assigned to the same office or cubicle because their work schedules allow for such an arrangement. Among the factors allowing for sharing office space are complementary travel schedules, working different shifts, and working from home on different schedules. AT&T discovered that for some groups of employees, as many as six people could use the same desk and equipment formerly assigned to one. The company now has 14,000 employees in shared-desk arrangements. The savings on real-estate costs can be enormous from sharing office space.

In *hoteling*, the company provides workspaces equipped and supported with typical office services. The worker who travels frequently might even be assigned a locker for personal storage. A computer system routes phone calls and e-mail as necessary. However, the office space, similar to a hotel (or rented temporary office space) is reserved by the hour, day, or week instead

---

25 Jenny C. McCune, "Telecommuting Revisited," *Management Review*, February 1998, p. 13.

26 Ed Frauenheim, "Telecommuting Cutbacks at HP Represent Shift," *Workforce, Management*, June 26, 2006, p. 4.

27 Sherry M. B. Thatcher and Xiumei Zhu, "Changing Identities in a Changing Workplace: Identification, Identity, Enactment, Self-Verification, and Telecommuting," *Academy of Management Review*, October 2006, p. 1079.

exhibit 7-9 How to Manage Teleworkers

1. *Develop a formal telecommuting policy*. The expectations of teleworkers should be made explicit in writing. The type of electronic equipment required to telecommute should be specified, including both hardware and software. Employees must know how much the company will pay for or subsidize home-office equipment. The policy should cover many of the points in this list. Having a formal policy is an effective way of knowing if workers are abusing the system.
2. *Choose the right type of work for working at home*. If a job requires frequent monitoring, such as reviewing progress on a complex report, it is not well suited for telecommuting. Jobs requiring the use of complicated, large-scale equipment, such as medical laboratory work or manufacturing, cannot be done off premises. Work that requires clients or customers to visit the employee is best done on company premises. In general, positions with measurable work output are best suited for working at home.
3. *Teleworkers should be chosen with care*. Working at home is best suited for self-disciplined, well-motivated, and deadline-conscious workers. Make sure the telecommuter has a suitable home environment for telecommuting. The designated work area should be as separate from the household as possible and relatively free from distractions, including interaction with family members, friends, and domestic animals.
4. *Agree early on the number of days or months for telecommuting*. The optimum number of days depends somewhat on the position and the worker. For corporate telecommuters, about two days per week of working at home is typical.
5. *Clearly define productivity goals and deadlines*. The more measurable the work output, such as lines of computer code or insurance claims forms processed, the better suited it is for telecommuting. Collect weekly data that relate to the results being achieved, such as orders filled or cases settled.
6. *Keep in contact through a variety of means, including e-mail and instant messaging, telephone, phone meetings, and conference calls*. Agree on working hours during which the teleworker can be reached. Remember, the manager is not disturbing the worker at home by telephoning that person during regularly scheduled working hours. Also, agree on how frequently the worker will be checking e-mail.
7. *Use telecommuting as a reward for good performance in the traditional office*. Poor performers should not be offered the opportunity to telecommute. Employees who volunteer to become telecommuters should only be accepted if they can demonstrate average or above-average performance records.
8. *Make periodic visits to the workers at home, but give them appropriate lead time*. During the visit, look to see if equipment is being used in a way that is ergonomically sound. Field visits, as long as they are not perceived as spying, communicate the fact that teleworkers are an important part of the team.

Source: "Don't Give Up On Telecommuters," *Manager's Edge*, July 2006, p. 8; "Managing Telecommuters: Taking the Mystery Out of Tracking Work from Afar," *Executive Strategies*, March 1998, p. 6; "What Is the Future of Telework?" p. 6; Stephen L. Schilling, "The Basics of a Successful Telework Network," *HRfocus*, June 1999, p. 10.

of being permanently assigned. Employees can sometimes book workstations closer to their home than their assigned office, or when they are traveling for business. The U.S. Patent and Trademark Office conducts a shared office space, or hoteling program that allows patent examiners to telecommute four days a week and used shared office space on the fifth day. In addition to attempting to improve morale and reduce automobile traffic, the Patent and Trademark Office seeks to avoid overcrowded office space through hoteling combined with telecommuting.[28]

From the perspective of top management, requiring workers to share office space or have no permanent office space provides an excellent method of cost control. In a traditional office, up to one-half of desks, offices, and work stations are unused at a given time on a typical workday. From the perspective of many employees, not having a permanent office or cubicle can be an indignity and an inconvenience. As many workers lament, "I have no home." Years ago ambitious workers aspired toward having a corner office. Now they aspire toward having any office.

28 Deborah Keary, Dyane Holt, and Ruhal Dooley, "Appraising Performance, 'Hoteling,' Volunteering," *HR Magazine*, May 2003, p. 42.

Job Sharing

Another way to accommodate workers is to give them half a job. **Job sharing** is a work arrangement in which two people who work part-time share one job. Salary and benefits are prorated for the half-time workers. The sharers divide up the job according to their needs. Each may work selected days of the workweek. Or, one person might work mornings and the other work afternoons. The job sharers might be two friends, a husband and wife, or two employees who did not know each other before sharing a job. For complex jobs, the sharers may spend work time discussing it.[29]

Job sharing appeals mostly to workers whose family commitments do not allow them to work full time. The person wanting to job share often feels that because of personal responsibilities, he or she can no longer work full time. Job sharing allows for a sense of balance in one's life, yet being able to hold on to a career.[30] A typical job-sharing situation involves two friends who want a responsible position but can only work part-time. Job sharing offers the employer an advantage in that two people working half-time usually produce more than one person working full time, which is particularly noticeable in creative work. Also, if one employee is sick, the other is still available to handle the job for half the time.

Part-Time and Temporary Work

Part-time work is a modified work schedule offered by about two-thirds of employers. The category of part-time workers includes employees who work reduced weekly, annual, or seasonal hours and those who have project-based occasional work. For example, a marketing brand manager might work full days on Mondays, Wednesdays, and Fridays. Many people, such as students and semi-retired people, choose part-time work because it fits their lifestyle. Also, many people work part-time because they cannot find full-time employment.

Temporary employment is at an all-time high, with some employers even hiring part-time managers, engineers, lawyers, and other high-level workers. A survey of 488 human resources specialists indicated that 33 percent have a formal policy permitting part-time work for professionals.[31] Collectively, part-time and temporary employees constitute one-fourth to one-third of the workforce. Given that they are hired according to, or contingent upon, an employer's need, they are referred to as **contingent workers**. Some contingent workers receive modest benefits. Other contingent workers function as independent contractors who are paid for services rendered but do not receive benefits. A familiar example would be a plumber hired by a business owner to make a repair. The plumber sets the wage, and receives no benefits.

Many employees enjoy part-time work, which allows them to willingly trade off the low pay for personal convenience. Employers, particularly in the retailing and restaurant industries, are eager to hire contingent workers

job sharing
A work arrangement in which two people who work part-time share one job.

contingent workers
Part-time or temporary employees who are not members of the employer's permanent workforce.

29 Tom Ramstack, "Patent Workers Being 'Hoteling'," *The Washington Times* (http://www.washingtontime.com), April 6, 2006.
30 Dawn Rosenberg McKay, "Job Sharing: An Interview, Part I," http://www.careerplanning.about.com, accessed November 27, 2006.
31 Survey cited in Erin White, "The Jungle: Focus on Recruitment, Pay, and Getting Ahead," *The Wall Street Journal*, October 24, 2006.

to avoid the expense of hiring full-time workers. Paying limited or no benefits to part-time workers can save employers as much as 35 percent of the cost of full-time compensation. Also, contingent workers can be readily laid off if business conditions warrant. Some seasonally oriented businesses, such as gift-catalogue sales firms, hire mostly part-time workers.

Shift Work

To accommodate the needs of employers rather than employees, many workers are assigned to shift work. The purpose of shift work is to provide coverage during nonstandard hours. The most common shift schedules are days (7 a.m. to 3 p.m.), evenings (3 p.m. to 11 p.m.), and nights (11 p.m. to 7 a.m.). Manufacturing uses shift work to meet high demand for products without having to expand facilities. It is more economical to run a factory 16 or 24 hours per day than to run two or three factories eight hours per day. Service industries make even more extensive use of shift work to meet the demands of customers around the clock, such as in a hotel. Shift work is necessary in public service operations such as police work, fire fighting, and healthcare.

Catering to clients in faraway time zones may require some modification of a typical shift, such as a stockbroker in Seattle, Washington, being on call to converse with clients in Tokyo, Japan. According to the Sleep Channel, nearly 20 percent of employees in industrialized countries are assigned to shift work that requires them to drastically change their sleep habits weekly or even daily. Changes in the work shift affects circadian rhythm, which similar to jet lag, desynchronizes the body's sleep-wake schedule.[32]

Shift work involves more than a deviation from a traditional work schedule. It creates a lifestyle that affects productivity, health, family, and social life. Approximately 20 percent of shift workers report falling asleep during work, leading to more accidents and lower productivity. Three times the average incidence of drug and alcohol abuse fosters an increased risk of errors and accidents. Many industrial catastrophes, such as shipwrecks, oil spills, and chemical leaks have taken place during the night ("graveyard") shift. People who work in nontraditional hours that interfere with their biological clock are also at risk for automobile crashes.[33]

Shift workers also experience difficulty in integrating their schedules with the social needs of friends and families. With proper training, employees can adjust better to shift work. A shift-work consultant, for example, recommends: "Create healthy sleep environments by keeping rooms cool and eliminating daylight with dark shades and curtains or even Styrofoam cutouts or black plastic taped to the window frame."[34]

---

32 "Shift Work Sleep Disorder," http://www.sleepdisorderchannel.com/shiftwork, accessed November 27, 2006.

33 "Who's at Risk? Shift Workers and People with Long Work Hours," http://www.drowsydriving.org, accessed May 30, 2004; "Shift Work Sleep Disorder."

34 Cited in Ellen Hale, "Lack of Sleep Is Now Grounds for Filing Suit—Or Being Sued," *Gannett News Service*, August 15, 1993.

JOB DESIGN AND HIGH-PERFORMANCE WORK SYSTEMS

As implied throughout this chapter, a major purpose of job design is to enhance job performance and productivity. As such, job design contributes to work systems that perform exceptionally well. High-performing work systems have been proposed in terms of both manufacturing settings, and the total work environment. We look at both approaches briefly because essentially every topic in the formal study of management is geared toward producing a high-performing work system. Why study management to produce a low-performing work system?

Learning Objective 7

Explain how job design can contribute to a high-performance work system.

high-performance work system
A way of organizing work so that front-line workers participate in decisions that have an impact on their jobs and the wider organization.

High-Performance Work Systems in a Manufacturing Environment

High-performing work systems based on the contribution of individual workers overlap with several of components of job enrichment and the job characteristics model. A **high-performance work system** is a way of organizing work so that front-line workers participate in decisions that have an impact on their jobs and the wider organization.

The United Auto Workers, as well as other labor unions, favor high-performance work systems as a way of saving jobs by boosting the productivity of U.S. manufacturing plants. However, for a plant to boost productivity, four workplace practices must be incorporated into the operation of the plant. First, the workers must have a reasonable degree of autonomy in their jobs, such as making decisions about job tasks and work methods. A second practice is for workers to have access to coworkers, managers, and supporting professionals such as manufacturing engineers and product designers. Third, the teams on the production floor must be self-managing to a large extent. Fourth, is the presence of problem-solving and quality-improvement teams that are removed from assembly line responsibilities. Most of these ideas will be touched upon again in the study of effective work groups in Chapter 13.

Another consideration is that these four practices must be supported by the company's overall approach to human resource management. Among these supportive human resources practices are extensive screening of new employees to establish a high-quality workforce; increased training for production workers; a commitment to employment security; and financial incentives linked to group performance.

The researchers studying high-performance work systems concluded that high-performance practices were associated with higher productivity and lower costs in three different manufacturing industries: steel, apparel, and medical equipment. Other improvements from using these practices also took place. For example, in the apparel industry, high-performance practices helped companies respond more rapidly to unanticipated changes in consumer demand. In turn, sales and profits increased independent of any change in productivity. Worker satisfaction often increased under high-performance work systems, yet the results were more mixed in comparison to boosts in productivity.[35]

High-Performance Jobs through Adjusting Worker Resources

Another twist on high-performance work systems and job design is to adjust resources available to all workers. According to Harvard Business School professor Robert Simons, for a company to attain its potential, each employee's supply of organizational resources should equal his or her demand, or need, for these resources. The same supply–demand balance must apply to every function, every business unit, and the entire organization. To carry out his or her job, each employee must find answers to four questions:

1. What resources do I control for accomplishing my tasks?
2. What measures will be used to evaluate my performance?
3. Who do I need to interact with and influence to achieve my goals?
4. How much support can I expect when I ask others for assistance?

Each question refers to the four basic *spans* of a job. Question 1 refers to the control span; Question 2, accountability; Question 3, influence; and Question 4, support. Each span can be adjusted so that it is narrow or wide, or somewhere in between the extremes. If the manager adjusts to the right settings, the job can be designed so a talented individual can execute the company's strategy with success. If the resources are adjusted incorrectly, the worker will be less effective.

The heart of this proposed system is an executive manipulating resources as if they were a high-to-low sliding volume control. According to this system of achieving high performance, the supply of resources for each job and each unit must be equivalent to demand. This means that the span of control plus span of support must equal the span of accountability plus span of influence. An example of this type of fine-tuning, would be in making adjustment in spans for a marketing and sales manager at a software company. The manager might be given a narrow *span of control* and a relatively wide *span of accountability*. The discrepancy would be geared toward forcing the manager to be entrepreneurial. If you lack many resources, yet you are still accountable for many different outcomes such as market share and customer satisfaction, you have to take an entrepreneurial, innovative approach.[36]

The approach to job design just presented usually requires a top-level manager to implement. The several other approaches to job design described in this chapter are much more realistic for most managers.

---

35 "High Performance Work Systems: What's the Payoff?" http://www.uaw.org/publications/jobs_pay, accessed November 22, 2006; Eileen Appelbaum, Thomas Bailey, Peter Berg, and Arne Kallbgberg, *Manufacturing Advantage* (Ithaca, NY: Cornell University Press, 2000).

36 Robert Simons, "Designing High-Performance Jobs," *Harvard Business Review*, July–August 2005, pp. 54–72.

SUMMARY OF
Key Points

1 Explain the four major dimensions of job design plus job specialization and job descriptions.

The four major dimensions of job design are task characteristics, knowledge characteristics, social characteristics, and contextual characteristics. Each dimension has sub-dimensions. Professional and nonprofessional jobs differ on sub-dimensions, such as professional jobs having more job complexity, information processing, and problem solving. Also, human-life–focused jobs score higher on the dimensions of significance.

Job specialization is the degree to which a jobholder performs only a limited number of tasks. Specialists are found at different occupational levels. Job specialization enhances workforce expertise at all levels and can reduce training time at the operative level. Specialization, however, can lead to problems. Coordinating the work of specialists can be difficult, and some employees may become bored. Automation contributes to job specialization. A major purpose of automation is to increase productivity by reducing the labor content required to deliver a product or service.

2 Describe job enrichment, including the job characteristics model.

Job enrichment is a method of making jobs involve more challenges and responsibility so they will be more appealing to most employees. The person holding the job must perceive these enriched characteristics of a job. An enriched job provides direct feedback, client relationships, new learning, control over methods, scheduling by the employee, unique experience, control over resources, direct communication authority, and personal accountability.

Expanding on the idea of job enrichment creates the job characteristics model, which focuses on the task and interpersonal dimensions of a job. Five characteristics of jobs improve employee motivation, satisfaction, and performance: skill variety, task identity, task significance, autonomy, and feedback. These characteristics relate to critical psychological states, which in turn lead to outcomes such as internal motivation, satisfaction, low absenteeism, and high quality.

Implementing job enrichment begins by finding out which employees want an enriched job. The groups of employees most likely to want and enjoy enriched jobs are those with a strong need for personal growth.

3 Describe job involvement, enlargement, and rotation.

Job involvement reflects psychological involvement with one's work and how much work is part of the self-image. Job enlargement increases the number and variety of job tasks. Job rotation switches assignments and can contribute heavily to career development.

4 Explain how workers use job crafting to modify their jobs.

The rigidity of some job descriptions does not fit the flexible work roles carried out by many workers. Following an emerging trend, many companies hire people "to work" rather than to fill a specific job slot. Another way of deviating from job descriptions is for workers to modify their job to fit their personal preferences and capabilities. Employees often craft their jobs by changing the tasks they perform and their contacts with others to make their jobs more meaningful.

5 Illustrate how ergonomic factors can be part of job design.

A key principle of job design is that the job should be laid out to decrease the chances that it will physically harm the incumbent. Ergonomics seeks to minimize the physical demands on workers and optimize system performance. Musculoskeletal (muscle and bones) injuries include cumulative trauma disorders—injuries caused by repetitive motions over prolonged periods of time, and that occur in many different types of work. Workstations can be designed to minimize these problems by such measures as supporting the back and thighs, and placing the feet flat on the floor. Uncomfortable noise levels present another ergonomic problem to be addressed.

6 Summarize the various modified work schedules.

Work scheduling is another part of job design. A modified work schedule departs from the traditional hours of work. Modified work-scheduling options include flexible working hours, a compressed workweek, the alternative workplace and telecommuting, job sharing, and part-time and temporary work. Shift work involves more than a deviation from a traditional work schedule because it creates a lifestyle that affects productivity, health, family, and social life.

7 Explain how job design can contribute to a high-performance work system.

A high-performing work system organizes work so that front-line workers participate in decisions that have an impact on their jobs and the wider organization. Such a work system includes job autonomy, access to support form work associates, self-managing work teams, along with problem-solving and quality-improvement teams. The company human resource management approach should support the high-performing work system.

A proposed approach to high-performing work systems is to adjust resources available to workers. For a company to attain its potential, each employee's supply of resources should equal demand for these resources. Also, employees should know their span of controlling resources, how performance will be measured, who they need to influence to accomplish their goals, and the amount of support available. The span of control plus the span of support must equal the span of accountability plus the span of influence.

KEY TERMS AND PHRASES

Job design, 221
Job specialization, 225
Job description, 227
Job enrichment, 227
Job characteristics model, 229
Job involvement, 231
Job enlargement, 231
Job rotation, 231
Job crafting, 233
Ergonomics, 233
Cumulative trauma disorders, 235
Carpal tunnel syndrome, 235
Modified work schedule, 237
Compressed workweek, 239
Telecommuting, 240
Job sharing, 245
Contingent workers, 245
High-performance work system, 247

QUESTIONS

1. In about 35 words, write the job description for (a) a restaurant manager, (b) the top executive at Target, and (c) the head coach of one of your favorite athletic teams.
2. Why is job rotation often more exciting to workers than job enlargement?
3. What are the benefits of frequent job rotation for a person who would like to become a high-level manager?
4. How might a customer-service representative who works at the call center for a consumer electronics company craft his or her job?
5. How well suited would a work schedule of three 13 1/3-hour days per week be for an employee whose job demanded considerable creativity?
6. Would you be satisfied as a telecommuter? Why or why not?
7. How would a manager know if the jobs he or she supervised fit well into a high-performance work system?

SKILL-BUILDING EXERCISE 7-A: The Ideal Home-Based Office

Gather into teams of about five people to design an ideal office at home for a professional worker. Take about 20 minutes to develop suggestions for the following aspects of a home office: (1) hardware and software, (2) equipment other than computers, (3) furniture, (4) ergonomics design, (5) office layout, and (6) location within home. Consider both productivity and job satisfaction when designing your office. After the designs are completed, the team leaders might present the design to the rest of the class.

SKILL-BUILDING EXERCISE 7-B: The Job-Improvement Interview

Interview two people performing essentially the same job, such as two accountants, two truck drivers, or two clerical support workers. Dig for information about what these workers like and dislike about their job, and what improvements they would like to see in their jobs. Based on your interview findings, and the information in this chapter, prepare a 150-word report on how to improve the job in question. Make recommendations about improving both job satisfaction and productivity.

INTERNET SKILL-BUILDING EXERCISE: Worst Jobs Trophy

The assignment here is to gain insight into how intensely some people dislike their jobs, and to speculate what managers can do to improve such jobs. Stuart Macfarlane, a Glasgow, Scotland, information technology consultant, launched the website http://www.worstjobs.com to give people an opportunity to complain publicly about their jobs. He invites brief entries for his "Worst Jobs Trophy." So far, about 1,000 people per day worldwide are submitting descriptions of their unsatisfying jobs. Select one of these jobs (sometimes a work assignment too gross to describe here), and recommend what could be done to make the job more satisfying. Also, speculate about whether some of these submitters are just chronic gripers.

According to Janiece Pompa, president of the Utah Psychological Association, the therapeutic value of a complaint site such as this should not be dismissed. "I love sites like this. If we read about someone in worse condition than we are, we seem to feel better. It's a human thing, the way we are built."[37]

37 Quoted in "Is Your Job on this List of Bad Jobs?" *Salt Lake Tribune* syndicated story, November 24, 2006.

Case Problem 7-A

The Sub Shop Blues

Serge Staglione runs a profitable chain of five rapid-service restaurants that sell submarine sandwiches along with nonalcoholic beverages, and related snacks such as potato chips and pretzels. Customers either take out the sandwiches or eat them on the restaurant premises. "Serge's Subs" also caters sub sandwiches to local businesses for luncheon parties, and for sports gathering in homes.

Asked to identify his biggest management challenge, Serge replied,

"Keeping good employees. Most of our workers are part-timers. Some are students, some are older people. Most of them want part-time employment. Making a submarine sandwich may look easy, but there is skill involved. For example, you have to remember what the customer asked for. A beginner might ask the same question a few times about what the customer wants on the sub.

"It takes a few weeks for a sub maker to get sharp, and to move quickly enough take care of a surge in orders, like Friday lunch.

"The problem is that too many of the good sub makers leave after a couple of months. So my store managers have to keep finding and training new employees."

Asked what he and his managers have attempted so far to increase retention, Serge replied,

"We have tried increasing pay 15 cents per hour. We have also been more generous about the employees being allowed to make their own subs to eat on premises or take home.

"So far these two initiatives haven't had much of an effect on reducing turnover."

Asked what reason workers give for leaving, Serge answered. "Sometimes a worker will say that he or she needs more money. Sometimes that answer is that school has become too demanding to work. Sometimes a senior person will say that he or she finds the work too physically demanding, especially standing up all the time.

"But the biggest complaint I get is that the work is boring. Instead of thinking of preparing a sub as a work of art, a lot of the guys and gals say that the work is boring. Once you've prepared a hundred sandwiches, it's all the same."

"So far, I haven't figured out how to make job of our basic worker more interesting."

Discussion Questions

1. How does this case relate to job design?
2. What recommendations might you offer Serge Staglione for making the position of subshop preparer more satisfying?
3. What else can Staglione do to find out what is lacking in the job of sub shop preparer?

Case Problem 7-B

Homeless at New Wave Machinery

Amy Wentworth, the human resources director at New Wave Machinery, feels triumphant today. After working with other members of top management on the project for several months, the company has initiated a program of hoteling for all employees who spend at least 50 percent of their time in the field working with customers. The field staff consists primarily of sales representatives and service technicians who service and repair the complicated machinery New Wave sells to manufacturers, banks, retail stores, and large restaurants. The line of machinery includes packing and labeling machines, large-scale shredders, and postage machines.

The switch to hoteling means that all employees who spend 50 percent of the time or more in the field will no longer be assigned permanent space in a cubicle or office. A typical arrangement up until now was for two service technicians or sales representatives to share a cubicle. However, three more senior sales reps would share one small office. Under the new policy, each field worker will be assigned a small file cabinet with wheels, or drawer, to store his or her work records and personal possessions such as a photo or coffee mug. When the field representative is coming to town, he or she must book space in a conference room or cubicle to work in the office. It is the representative's responsibility to roll the file cabinet, or carry the contents of the draw, to the conference room or cubicle.

Wentworth estimates that the company will be able to save about $450,000 per year by consolidating office workers into one building, and selling the second building that was required with so many people occupying cubicles and offices. "Besides," said Wentworth, "by having less attractive office space, our sales reps and service reps will spend more time out in the field with our customers—where they belong. This should result in increased revenue for New Wave."

Upon learning of the new policy, most of the customer and service representatives were a little skeptical, but did not express open opposition to the new work arrangement. Group discussions about the changes were held, and management mentioned that saving money on office space is preferable to thinking about downsizing to save money.

Four months into the policy, Wentworth and the directors of sales and service met to discuss how the new policy was going. They agreed among themselves that so far, no major opposition to the policy was discovered. Yet to gain more insight into how well hoteling was being accepted, the three managers decided to invite e-mail comments from the sales and service reps about how their work lives were affected. Among the e-mails received were the following:

Sales representative with nine years of experience: Enough of this Dilbert style management. I racked up $1 million in sales for the company last year. So when I come to the office I'm treated less well than a temporary worker. I have to roll my cabinet down the hall to my assigned cubicle for the afternoon. The last time I was here, somebody had moved by file cabinet, and it took two hours to find the missing cabinet. I still love the company, but hoteling is the pits. I won't stay at New Wave forever if I don't get back some decent place to work when I'm in town.

Sales representative with one year of experience: I like hoteling. It's kind of cool. My job is with my customers, so I don't have too much need to spend time in the office. Besides, I have a desk in my apartment that I use for an office so I don't have too much need for a physical office at headquarters.

Service technician with three years of experience: My biggest problem is that I feel like a homeless person. When I'm out in the field I obviously do not have a permanent work area. When I get back to the office, I have loads of computer work and paper work to do. It wastes so much time getting set up when I come to headquarters. Hoteling doesn't make me feel like a valued member of New Wave. When I'm at headquarters, I feel like I'm a service rep visiting New Wave Machinery. I keep most of my records on my laptop, but still I need more than a small file cabinet for my paperwork.

Service technician with one year of experience. Service techs are in big demand in today's world. Why should be we put up with an indignity like storing my stuff in a drawer? Also, it feels like I'm treated so impersonally. I think I should be able to keep a family photo in one place without having to take it out of a cabinet for a

Case Problem 7-B

day. If you want to save the company some big bucks, how about taking a slice out of some of those salaries in the executive suite?

Discussion Questions

(To help analyze this case, you might refer to the information about gaining support for change in Chapter 8.)

1. What might management at New Wave Machinery do to make hoteling a bigger success?
2. How should management respond to the service technician's suggestion that they take a pay cut to save the company money?
3. What should management do to find out if the decision to move to hoteling is successful?

Source: The company name has been changed to protect confidentiality.

chapter 8

Organization Structure, Culture, and Change

Objectives

After studying this chapter and doing the exercises, you should be able to:

1 Describe the bureaucratic organization structure and discuss its advantages and disadvantages.

2 Explain the major ways in which organizations are divided into departments.

3 Describe three modifications of the bureaucratic structure.

4 Identify key factors that influence the selection of organization structure.

5 Specify how delegation, empowerment, and decentralization spread authority in an organization.

6 Identify major aspects of organizational culture.

7 Describe key aspects of managing change, including gaining support for change, and the DICE framework for successful change management.

Kent Thiry, chief executive of DaVita of El Segundo, California, the No. 2 dialysis-treatment operator in the country, starts worrying he is out of touch when all he hears is good news. At a recent annual staff gathering, thousands of employees said yes when he asked if integrating recently acquired Gambro Healthcare was "a fun process." His response? "Either you're all on drugs or better than me because integrations are a god-awful nightmare."

He also told employees how much he depended on their frank feedback to avoid "messing up" the Gambro integration. He said he was paying attention to complaints from former Gambro managers who were being asked to adjust to dozens of new systems and employee practices. Among the issues was an order to assign one employee at each center to greet patients or sit with them in the waiting room. "Gambro people told us to grow a brain" about greeters, he said, and that prompted him to rescind the directive.

DaVita was a mess when Thiry took the helm nearly six years ago, in default on its bank loans and barely able to make payroll. Turnover was a steep 45 percent a year, and it included employees with the most knowledge about which problems were most acute and which needed to be fixed first.

Thiry's encouragement of frank feedback has helped the company cut employee turnover by 50 percent and grow revenues to

organization structure The arrangement of people and tasks to accomplish organizational goals.

bureaucracy A rational, systematic, and precise form of organization in which rules, regulations, and techniques of control are specifically defined.

more than $5 billion and achieve the industry's best clinical outcomes. At the outset, he sold off assets and overhauled payment systems. Rather than issuing orders, he made front-line employees an integral part of turnaround decision making, seeking their views on equipment maintenance, inventory management, and cutting costs by reusing supplies.

Most important, says Thiry, is for executives who seek frank feedback to be candid about their own shortcomings. In the performance review he recently received from his 13 senior executives, he received a bad grade for giving too much negative feedback. He said, "They say I'm not harder on them than I am on myself but my negativity isn't constructive."[1]

A key point the DaVita anecdote illustrates is that adjusting an organization's culture can help the company succeed. At DaVita, the culture was fine-tuned toward more truth telling and honest feedback. Organization culture is one of the several major themes in this chapter. In Chapter 7, we described how the tasks of an organization are divided into jobs for individuals and groups. Companies also subdivide work through an **organization structure**—the arrangement of people and tasks to accomplish organizational goals. The structure specifies who reports to whom and who does what, and is also a method for implementing a strategy, or for accomplishing the purpose of the organization. For example, top management at Subway wants to sell millions and millions of sandwiches and beverages, so it places thousands of stores and counters in convenient locations, even at some service stations.

In addition to structure and culture, this chapter explains how to manage change. All three topics are fundamental aspects of understanding how organizations function.

BUREAUCRACY AS AN ORGANIZATION STRUCTURE

Learning Objective 1

Describe the bureaucratic organization structure and discuss its advantages and disadvantages.

A **bureaucracy** is a rational, systematic, and precise form of organization in which rules, regulations, and techniques of control are specifically defined. Think of bureaucracy as the traditional form of organization, with other structures as variations of, or supplements to, bureaucracy. Do not confuse the word *bureaucracy* with bigness. Although most big organizations are bureaucratic, small firms can also follow the bureaucratic model. An example might be a small, carefully organized bank.

Principles of Organization in a Bureaucracy

The entire classical school of management contributes to our understanding of bureaucracy. Yet the essence of bureaucracy can be identified by its major characteristics and principles as listed next:

1 Excerpted from Carol Hymowitz, "Executives Who Build Truth-Telling Cultures Learn Fast What Works," *The Wall Street Journal*, June 12, 2006, p. B1.

1. *Hierarchy of authority*. The dominant characteristic of a bureaucracy is that each lower organizational unit is controlled and supervised by a higher one. The person granted the most formal authority (the right to act) occupies the top place of the hierarchy. Exhibit 8-1 presents a bureaucracy as pyramid-shaped. The number of employees increases substantially as one moves down each successive level. Most of the formal authority concentrates at the top and decreases with each lower level.

> PLAY VIDEO
>
> **ORGANIZATION STRUCTURE, CULTURE, AND CHANGE**
>
> "Go to academic.cengage.com/management/dubrin and view the video. What do you think Boyne's organizational structure formally became after Everett Kircher's death in 2002?"

2. *Unity of command*. A classic management principle, **unity of command**, states that each subordinate receives assigned duties from one superior only and is accountable to that superior. In the modern organization many people serve on projects and teams in addition to reporting to their regular boss, thus violating the unity of command.

> **unity of command**
> The classical management principle stating that each subordinate receives assigned duties from one superior only and is accountable to that superior.

3. *Task specialization*. In a bureaucracy, division of labor is based on task specialization. To achieve task specialization, organizations designate separate divisions or departments, such as new product development, customer service, and information technology. Workers assigned to these organizational units employ specialized knowledge and skills that contribute to the overall effectiveness of the firm.
4. *Responsibilities and job descriptions*. Bureaucracies are characterized by rules that define the responsibilities of employees. In a highly bureaucratic organization, each employee follows a precise job description, and therefore knows his or her job expectations. Also, the responsibility and authority of

exhibit 8-1 The Bureaucratic Form of Organization

In a bureaucracy, power is concentrated at the top, yet many more employees occupy lower levels in the organization. Note that team leaders are typically found at the first level or middle level of management.

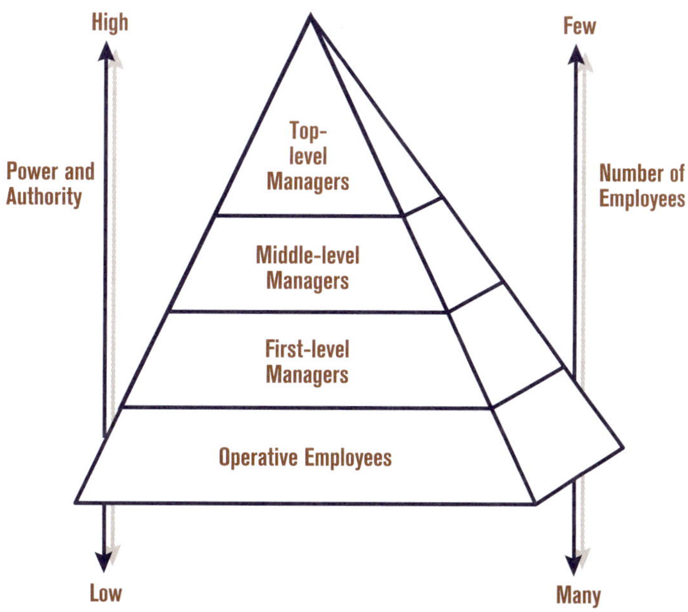

each manager is defined clearly in writing. Responsibility defined in writing lets managers know what is expected of them and what limits are set to their authority.

5. *Line and staff functions.* A bureaucracy identifies the various organizational units as being line or staff. Line functions involve the primary purpose of an organization or its primary outputs. In a bank, line managers supervise work related to borrowing and lending money. Staff functions assist the line functions. Staff managers take responsibility for important functions such as human resources and purchasing. Although staff functions do not deal with the primary purposes of the firm, they play an essential role in achieving the organization's mission.

Advantages and Disadvantages of Bureaucracy

Bureaucracy made modern civilization possible. Without large, complex organizations to coordinate the efforts of thousands of people, we would not have airplanes, automobiles, skyscrapers, universities, vaccines, or space satellites. Many large bureaucratic organizations successfully continue to grow at an impressive pace, such as Wal-Mart and General Electric. A major reason that hierarchies continue to thrive is that they fill the basic need for order and security. People want order, predictability, and structures they can understand, such as getting in touch with the tech center when a desktop computer breaks down. Hierarchies help us satisfy other psychological needs through such mechanisms as career ladders, and giving us identity by belonging to a stable organization.[2] Also, organizations such as banks, pharmaceutical firms, and hospitals have to follow tight regulations for the good of the public.

In an attempt to make their companies less bureaucratic, many executives eliminate policies, rules, and regulations. However, these procedures often embody an invaluable source of effective organizational practices. Paul S. Adler says, "Having tossed out the manuals, many organizations discover that their employees are frustrated because now they have to improvise without even a common melody line let alone a complete score."[3]

Despite the contributions of bureaucracy, several key disadvantages exist. A bureaucracy can be rigid in handling people and problems. Its well-intended rules and regulations sometimes create inconvenience and inefficiency. For example, requiring several layers of approval to make a decision causes the process to take a long time. Another substantial problem in a pronounced bureaucracy is that many workers pass responsibility to another department for dealing with a problem. A typical comment is, "You will have to be in touch with (another department) to solve that problem." Other frequent problems in a bureaucracy are frustration from sources such as red

2 Harold J. Leavitt, "Why Hierarchies Thrive," *Harvard Business Review*, March 2003, p. 99; Leavitt, *Top Down: Why Hierarchies Are Here to Stay and How to Manage Them More Effectively* (Boston: HBS Press, 2004).

3 Paul S. Adler, "Building Better Bureaucracies," *Academy of Management Executive*, November 1999, pp. 26–37.

tape, slow decision making based on the layers of approval required, and the occurrence of frequent meetings.

An example of the rigidity and heavy-handedness possible in a bureaucracy took place at General Motors Corp. In December 2005, GM ran ads across the United States showing Cadillacs being driven through snow. The decision was made by executives in Detroit, where snow often falls during winter. The ads also ran in Miami, a bustling car market where GM has struggled for 15 years. According to one analysis, one reason GM is having a difficult time persuading Americans to buy its cars is the company's cumbersome and unresponsive bureaucracy[4]. (In defense of GM, the company has also had big successes in marketing the Cadillac, including the appeal of the Escalade to affluent young people.)

To examine your own orientation to the bureaucratic form of organization, take the self-quiz presented in Exhibit 8-2.

exhibit 8-2 Understanding Your Bureaucratic Orientation

Answer each question "mostly agree" (MA) or "mostly disagree" (MD). Assume the mind-set of attempting to learn something about you rather than impressing a prospective employer.

	MA	MD
1. I value stability in my job.	_______	_______
2. I like a predictable organization.	_______	_______
3. I enjoy working without the benefit of a carefully specified job description.	_______	_______
4. I would enjoy working for an organization in which promotions were generally determined by seniority.	_______	_______
5. Rules, policies, and procedures generally frustrate me.	_______	_______
6. I would enjoy working for a company that employed 95,000 people worldwide.	_______	_______
7. Being self-employed would involve more risk than I'm willing to take.	_______	_______
8. Before accepting a position, I would like to see an exact job description.	_______	_______
9. I would prefer a job as a freelance landscape artist to one as a supervisor for the Department of Motor Vehicles.	_______	_______
10. Seniority should be as important as performance in determining pay increases and promotion.	_______	_______
11. It would give me a feeling of pride to work for the largest and most successful company in its field.	_______	_______
12. Given a choice, I would prefer to make $100,000 per year as a vice-president in a small company than $120,000 per year as a middle manager in a large company.	_______	_______

(Continued)

4 Lee Hawkins Jr., "Behind GM's Slide: Bosses Misjudged New Urban Tastes," *The Wall Street Journal*, March 8, 2006, p. A1.

exhibit 8-2 Understanding Your Bureaucratic Orientation *(Continued)*

13. I would feel uncomfortable if I were required to wear an employee badge with a number on it. _______ _______
14. Parking spaces in a company lot should be assigned according to job level. _______ _______
15. I would generally prefer working as a specialist to performing many different tasks. _______ _______
16. Before accepting a job, I would want to make sure that the company had a good program of employee benefits. _______ _______
17. A company will not be successful unless it establishes a clear set of rules and regulations. _______ _______
18. I would prefer to work in a department with a manager in charge than to work on a team where managerial responsibility is shared. _______ _______
19. You should respect people according to their rank. _______ _______
20. Rules are meant to be broken. _______ _______

Score: _______

Scoring and interpretation: Give yourself one point for each question you answered in the bureaucratic direction, then total your score.

1. Mostly agree	8. Mostly agree	15. Mostly disagree
2. Mostly agree	9. Mostly disagree	16. Mostly agree
3. Mostly disagree	10. Mostly agree	17. Mostly agree
4. Mostly agree	11. Mostly agree	18. Mostly agree
5. Mostly disagree	12. Mostly disagree	19. Mostly agree
6. Mostly agree	13. Mostly disagree	20. Mostly disagree
7. Mostly agree	14. Mostly agree	

15–20 You would enjoy working in a bureaucracy.
8–14 You would experience a mixture of satisfactions and dissatisfactions if working in a bureaucracy.
0–7 You would most likely be frustrated by working in a bureaucracy, especially a large one.

Source: Adapted and updated from Andrew J. DuBrin, *Human Relations: A Job Oriented Approach*, 5th ed. (Upper Saddle River, NJ: Prentice Hall, 1991), pp. 434–435.

DEPARTMENTALIZATION

Learning objective 2

Explain the major ways in which organizations are divided into departments.

Bureaucratic and other forms of organization subdivide the work into departments, or other units, to prevent total confusion. Can you imagine an organization of 300,000 people, or even 300, in which all employees worked in one large department? The process of subdividing work into departments is called **departmentalization**.

This chapter uses charts to illustrate four frequently used forms of departmentalization: functional, geographic, product–service, and customer. In practice, most organization charts show a combination of the various types, and therefore have *hybrid organization structures*. The most appropriate form of departmentalization is the one that provides the best chance of achieving the organization's objectives. The organization's environment is an important factor in this decision. Assume that a company needs to use substantially different approaches to manufacturing, marketing, and distributing a product. It would organize the firm according to the product, such as pharmaceuticals and beauty products.

departmentalization
The process of subdividing work into departments.

Functional Departmentalization

Functional departmentalization defines departments by the function each one performs, such as accounting or purchasing. Dividing work according to activity is the traditional way of organizing the efforts of people. In a functional organization, each department carries out a specialized activity, such as information processing, purchasing, sales, accounting, or maintenance. Exhibit 8-3 illustrates an organization arranged on purely functional lines. The major subdivisions further divide along their own functional lines as shown in Exhibit 8-4. The exhibit shows the functional organization within the materials management department.

functional departmentalization
An arrangement that defines departments by the function each one performs, such as accounting or purchasing.

The list of advantages and disadvantages of the functional organization, the traditional form of organization, reads the same as for bureaucracy. Functional departmentalization works particularly well when large batches of work have to be processed on a recurring basis and when the expertise of specialists is required. As with any form of departmentalization, a major problem is that the people within a unit may not communicate sufficiently with workers in other units.

geographic departmentalization
An arrangement of departments according to the geographic area or territory served.

Geographic Departmentalization

Geographic departmentalization is an arrangement of departments according to the geographic area or territory served. In this organization structure, people performing all the activities for a firm in a given geographic area report to one manager, often with a title like "Regional Vice-President." Marketing divisions often use territorial departmentalization; the sales force may be divided into the northeastern, southeastern, midwestern, northwestern, and southwestern regions.

Geographic departmentalization that divides an organization into geographic regions generally works well for international business. Yet in a

exhibit 8-3 Functional Departmentalization Within the Davenport Machine Company

Observe that each box below the level of CEO indicates an executive in charge of a specific function or activity, such as sales and marketing.

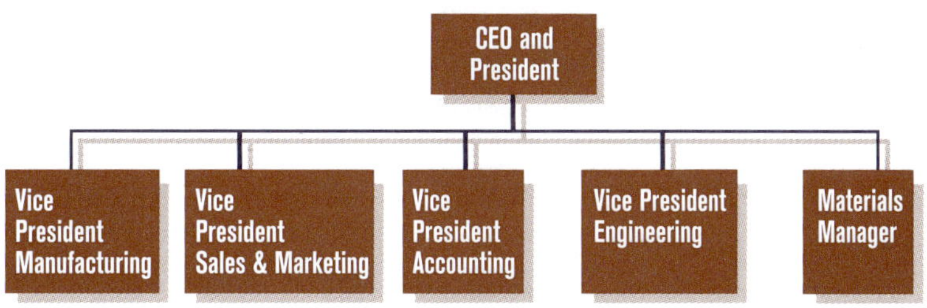

exhibit 8-4 **Functional Departmentalization Within a Department of the Davenport Machine Company**

Observe that the materials management department, as with other departments, has its own functional structure.

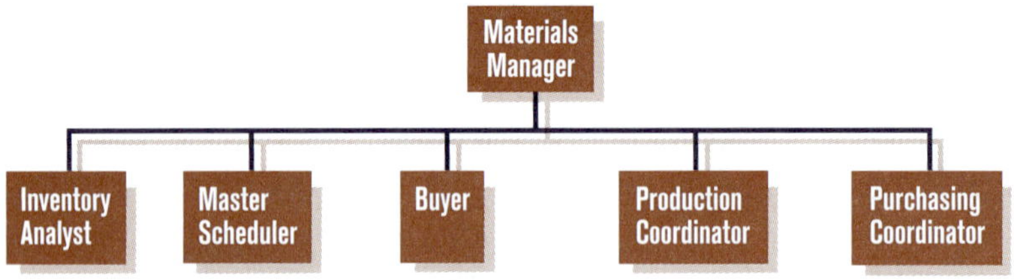

new global business trend, organizations develop a central structure that serves operations in various geographic locations. A case in point is Ford Motor Company. To economize, Ford merged its manufacturing, sales, and product development operations in North America, Europe, Latin America, and Asia.

A key advantage of geographic departmentalization is that it allows for decision making at a local level, where the personnel are most familiar with the problems and the local culture, including tastes in fashion, product styling, and food. Geographic departmentalization also presents some potential disadvantages. The arrangement can be quite expensive because of duplication of costs and effort. For instance, each region may build service departments (such as for purchasing) that duplicate activities carried out at headquarters. A bigger problem arises if top-level management experiences difficulty controlling the performance of field units.

Product–Service Departmentalization

Product–service departmentalization is the arrangement of departments according to the products or services they provide. When specific products or services are so important that the units that create and support them almost become independent companies, product–service departmentalization makes sense. The departments of this size are usually labeled as divisions. With very successful products, the organizational unit making the product becomes a division, such as the wireless product division of Verizon.

Exhibit 8-5 presents a version of product–service departmentalization. Notice that the four finance divisions offer products or services with unique demands of their own. For example, the sale of insurance and investment products is a different business than lending money to business firms. Notice also that the same customer might purchase services from one or more divisions, such as a small business purchasing life insurance from one unit, and borrowing money to finance a new machine from another. As a consequence, the structure is not customer departmentalization.

product-service departmentalization The arrangement of departments according to the products or services they provide.

Organizing by product line offers numerous benefits because employees focus on a product or service, which allows each division or department the

exhibit 8-5 Product–Service Departmentalization at GE Capital

Notice that the four divisions of GE Capital could be considered separate business firms.

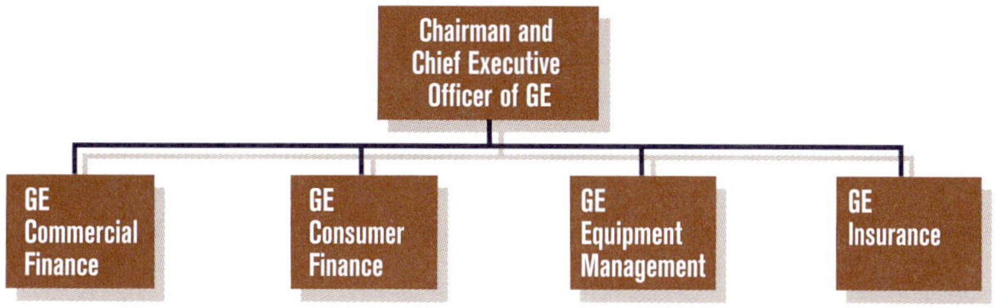

maximum opportunity to grow and prosper. An important marketing and sales advantage is that sales representatives are assigned to one product or service group in which they become experts, rather than being sales generalists. Several years ago Hewlett-Packard shifted back to product-specific reps so they would no longer be sending generalist account reps up against the "razor-focused sales people from the likes of Dell, printer specialist Lexmark International Inc., and storage giant EMC Corp."[5]

In a smooth-running organization with open communication, the various product or service units cooperate with each other for mutual benefit. A case in point is the healthcare giant Johnson & Johnson. A division that develops an improved method of delivering drugs (such as a skin patch) would typically share that development with another division. Human care could therefore improve pet care and vice versa! Similar to geographic departmentalization, grouping by product or service fosters high morale, and allows decisions to be made at the local level. Departmentalization by product poses the same potential problems as geographic departmentalization. It can be expensive because of duplication of effort, and top-level management may find it difficult to control the separate units.

MODIFICATIONS OF THE BUREAUCRATIC ORGANIZATION

Learning Objective 3

Describe three modifications of the bureaucratic structure: the matrix structure; flat structures, downsizing, and outsourcing; and the horizontal structure.

To overcome some of the problems of the bureaucratic (including the functional) structure, several other organization structures have been developed. Virtually all large organizations combine bureaucratic and less bureaucratic forms. This section describes three popular modifications of bureaucracy: the matrix organization; flat structures, downsizing, and outsourcing; and the horizontal structure.

The Matrix Organization

Departmentalization tends to be poorly suited to performing special tasks that differ substantially from the normal activities of a firm. **Project organization,**

5 Peter Burrows, "The Un-Carly Unveils His Game Plan," *Business Week*, June 27, 2005, p. 36.

project organization A temporary group of specialists working under one manager to accomplish a fixed objective.

matrix organization A project structure superimposed on a functional structure.

in which a temporary group of specialists works under one manager to accomplish a fixed objective, offers one widely used solution to this problem. Used most extensively in the military, aerospace, construction, motion picture, and computer industries, project management is so widespread that software has been developed to help managers plot out details and make all tasks visible. The project manager has long been a central figure in getting major tasks accomplished, such as seeing a new product to completion. A more recent role emphasized for the project manager is as a linking pin between an organization providing service and the client.[6] An example would be a project manager at the General Electric division that services airplane engines spending time on the premises of United Airlines to help with the service project.

The best-known application of project management is the **matrix organization**, a project structure superimposed on a functional structure. Matrix organizations evolved to capitalize on the advantages of project and functional structures, while minimizing their disadvantages. The project groups act as mini-companies within the firm in which they operate. However, the group usually disbands after completing its mission. In some instances, the project proves so successful that it becomes a new and separate division of the company.

Exhibit 8-6 shows a popular version of the matrix structure. Notice that functional managers exert some functional authority over specialists assigned to the projects. For example, the quality manager occasionally meets with the quality specialists assigned to the projects to discuss their professional activities. The project managers hold line authority over the people assigned to their projects.

The project managers borrow resources from the functional departments, a feature that distinguishes the matrix from other organizational structures. Also, each person working on the project reports to two superiors: the project manager and the functional manager. For example, observe the quality analyst in the lower right corner of Exhibit 8-6. The analyst reports to the manager of quality three boxes above him or her and to the project manager for the digital camera/camcorder project located five boxes to the left.

Users of the matrix structure include banks, insurance companies, aerospace companies, and educational institutions. Colleges often use matrix structures for setting up special interest programs. Among them are African American studies, industrial training, and an executive MBA program. A director who uses resources from traditional departments heads each of these programs.

Flat Structures, Downsizing, and Outsourcing

Three closely related approaches to simplifying an organization structure include creating flat structures, downsizing, and outsourcing. Reducing the number of layers typically makes an organization less bureaucratic.

---

6 Shelia Simsarian Webber and Maria T. Torti, "Project Managers Doubling as Client Account Executives," *Academy of Management Executive*, February 2004, p. 70.

exhibit 8-6 **Matrix Organization Structure in an Electronics Company**

Personnel assigned to a project all report to two managers: a project head and a functional manager.

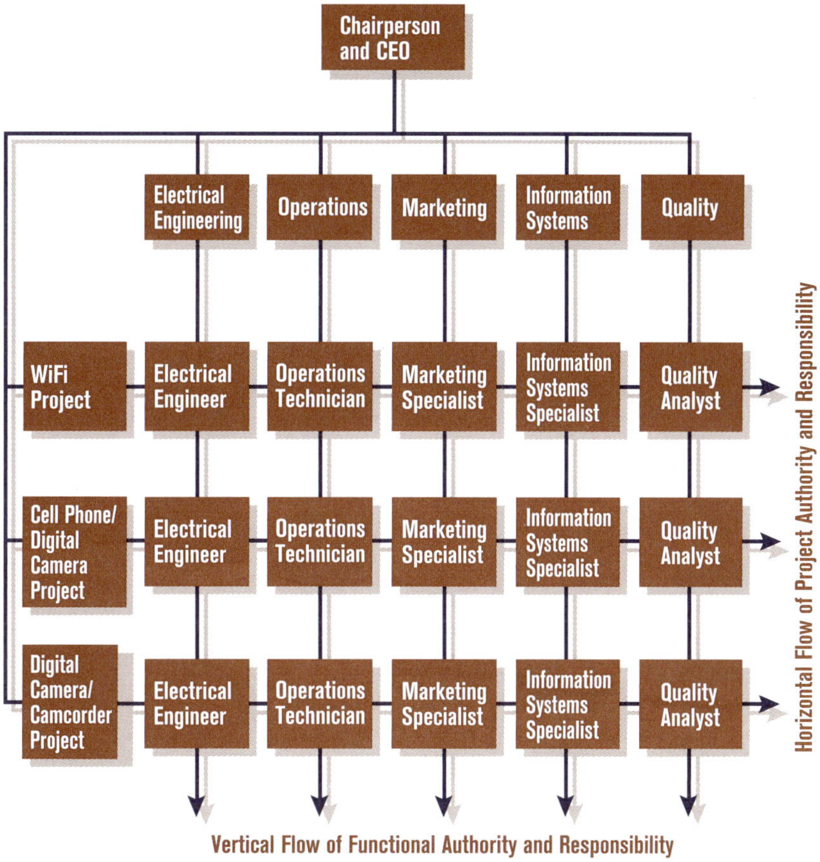

Flat Structures

Organizations with a bureaucratic structure tend to accumulate many layers of managers, and often too many employees in general. For example, before Hewlett Packard was overhauled in 2005, there were 11 layers of management between the CEO and the customer. At times, staff groups outnumber the line groups. Top management may then decide to create a **flat organization structure**, a form of organization with relatively few layers. A flat organization structure acts less bureaucratically for two reasons. First, fewer available managers review the decisions of other workers. Second, a shorter chain of command means that managers and workers at lower levels can make decisions more independently.

An important consequence of creating flat structures leaves the remaining managers with a larger **span of control**—the number of workers reporting directly to a manager. A large span of control works best with competent and efficient managers and group members. When group members do relatively similar work, the manager can supervise more people.

flat organization structure
A form of organization with relatively few layers of management, making it less bureaucratic.

span of control
The number of workers reporting directly to a manager.

Small enterprises often use flat structures. Bill Gilmer runs his 16-person commercial printing company with as few managers as possible. "We're an extremely flat organization," says the owner of Wordsprint Inc., in Wytheville, Virginia. Gilmer has made big investments in technology to make sure each of his press operators and other key employees has all the information he or she needs to make decisions without a supervisor.[7]

Management writer Mark Henricks observes that an organization can be too flat. The key is to make sure your organization doesn't have too many managers—nor too few. When you have too little hierarchy, decisions don't get made or are made wrongly by employees who lack experience, accountability, or motivation to do the work of the missing managers.[8]

Downsizing

In Chapter 3 we analyzed downsizing as it related to social responsibility. Downsizing can also be viewed as a way of simplifying an organization to make it less bureaucratic. Under ideal circumstances, downsizing also leads to better profits and higher stock prices. The motivation behind most downsizings of both assets (such as company divisions or buildings) and workers comes from the drive to reduce costs and increase profits. Yet, downsizing can be expensive. Among the costs associated with downsizing that need to be considered are severance pay, supplements to early retirement plans, disability claims, and lowered productivity resulting from possible decline in staff morale.[9]

For downsizing to help the company in the long run, *it should be part of a business strategy to improve the company, not just a stopgap measure to save money*. Examples would be using downsizing to eliminate duplication of jobs after a merger, or to exit a business that does not fit a new strategy. *Eliminating low-volume and no-value activities* provides an early step in effective restructuring. This *activity-based reduction* systematically compares the costs of a firm's activities to their value to the customer. In searching for low-value activity, workers monitor the output of others. *Keeping the future work requirements in mind* also contributes to effective restructuring. Letting go of people who will be an important part of the firm's future rarely provides an effective answer to overstaffing. *Sensible criteria should be used to decide which workers to let go*. In general, the poorest performers should be released first. Offering early retirement and asking for voluntary resignations also leads to less disruption. Laid-off workers should be *offered assistance in finding new employment or reorienting their career*.

A comprehensive principle of downsizing or resizing a company is to *involve employees in the resizing process*. Top-level management may have to decide which employees will be terminated, yet workers can be involved in making suggestions about how the work should be reassigned. At a successful resizing in a publishing company, middle-level managers helped design the

---

7 Quoted in Mark Henricks, "Falling Flat?" *Entrepreneur*, January 2005, pp. 69–70.

8 Hendricks, "Falling Flat?" p. 70.

9 Assa Birati and Aharon Tziner, "Cost-Benefit Analysis of Organizational Interventions: The Case of Downsizing," *Journal of Business and Psychology*, Winter 2000, p. 285.

resized organization. They also identified opportunities such as eliminating unnecessary work and redeploying workers to support more profitable divisions of the publisher.[10]

Outsourcing

Outsourcing is part of globalization but is also part of the organization structure by having other companies perform part of your work. By outsourcing, a company can reduce its need for employees and physical assets and their associated costs. Outsourcing to low-wage regions also saves money if the work is performed properly. Productivity can increase because work is performed more economically. A major justification for outsourcing is that a company is likely to profit when it focuses its effort on activities it performs best, while noncore activities such as human resources and information systems are performed by outside experts. Yet, as outsourcing has evolved, considerable core work, including research and development, and marketing, is being outsourced. Companies such as Dell, Motorola, and Philips purchase complete designs for some digital devices from Asian developers. Later the designs are modified to the well-known company's specifications and labeled as the company's own brand.[11]

The outsourcing movement continues to grow through many small and medium-sized firms that perform stable work for larger organizations. At the same time smaller enterprises themselves outsource considerable work such as paperwork processing, and labeling, mailing, and shipping.

United Parcel Service (UPS) exemplifies how far outsourcing has advanced. The world's largest delivery company provides a wide variety of services for other companies through its subsidiary, UPS Supply Chain Solutions. The services other companies outsource to UPS include emergency electronic repairs, fixing laptops, installing giant X-ray machines, operating customer-service hotlines, packaging consumer electronics, and issuing corporate credit cards. The type of work Supply Chain provides lends itself to domestic outsourcing because much of the work is needed urgently. UPS stores every conceivable part in its giant warehouse in Louisville, Kentucky, so it can perform repairs quickly. (For this type of operation, the just-in-time inventory system would be counterproductive because speed of repair is a success factor.) The highly regarded brand name, UPS, has facilitated the growth of the outsourcing business.[12] Outsourcing partners like UPS work so closely with their customers that they become virtually part of their client's business.

A rapidly growing development in outsourcing is **homeshoring**, or moving customer service into workers' homes as a form of telecommuting. Instead of customer service work being performed at domestic and foreign call centers, it is performed by teleworkers. At JetBlue Airways, all 1,400 reservation agents work from home as company employees. The majority of the new homeshoring jobs are for independent contractors given assignments

homeshoring
Moving customer service into workers' homes as a form of telecommuting.

---

10 Mitchell Lee Marks and Kenneth P. De Meuse, "Resizing the Organization: Maximizing the Gain While Minimizing the Pain of Layoffs, Divestitures, and Closings," *Organizational Dynamics*, No. 1, 2005, p. 28.

11 Peter Engardio and Bruce Einhorn, "Outsourcing," *Business Week*, March 21, 2005, p. 86.

12 Chuck Salter, "Surprise Package," *Fast Company*, February 2004, pp. 62–66.

by outsourcing companies. The agents pay for their own health care insurance, telephone, and computer equipment. Home-based agents are typically stay-at-home moms, with a higher level of education than call center workers. Two key advantages of homeshoring are that the workers know the culture of the country and are a flexible, just-in-time workforce, with shifts lasting as little as 15 minutes.[13]

Homeshoring has all the advantages and disadvantages of telecommuting, yet the domestic call agent has to be extra careful about background noises such as a television set, phone calls, children playing, and dogs barking. If you supervise homeshore workers, it is important to stay in touch and offer encouragement and recognition.

Outsourcing is a form of organization structure that management must carefully evaluate. Outsourcing may save money and acquire expertise not available in-house, yet there is much to be said for building a company with a loyal workforce that has company pride. Great companies built in the past and the present, such as Colgate Palmolive and Google, did not achieve their greatness through outsourcing every conceivable business process.

The Horizontal Structure (Organization by Team and Process)

In the traditional organization, people in various organization units are assigned specialized tasks such as assembly, purchasing, marketing, and shipping. In another approach to organization structure, a group of people concerns itself with a process, such as filling an order or developing a new product. Instead of focusing on a specialized task, all team members focus on achieving the purpose of all the activity, such as getting a product in the hands of a customer.

A **horizontal structure** is the arrangement of work by multidisciplinary teams that are responsible for accomplishing a process. Exhibit 8-7 illustrates a horizontal structure, as do the projects shown in Exhibit 8-6. The employees take collective responsibility for customers, and they work together to accomplish the task. Instead of one department handing off work to another department, the team members work together on the task of meeting customer requirements. A horizontal structure can therefore also be considered a team structure, and teams will be reintroduced in Chapter 13.

horizontal structure
The arrangement of work by teams that are responsible for accomplishing a process.

reengineering
The radical redesign of work to achieve substantial improvements in performance.

As with other modifications of the bureaucratic structure, the horizontal structure coexists with vertical structures. The process teams offer a balanced focus so that employees direct their effort and attention toward adding value for the customer.[14] The UPS groups that provide packaging services for clients use a horizontal structure because a project manager is responsible for making sure that client needs are met. The team members focus on a single purpose such as "We have to get these Nikon cameras packed and ready for shipment."

Switching from a vertical (task) emphasis to a horizontal (process) emphasis can be done through **reengineering**, the radical redesign of work to

---

13 Michele Conlin, "Call Centers in the Rec Room," *Business Week*, January 23, 2006, pp. 76–77.

14 Frank Ostroff, *The Horizontal Organization: What the Organization of the Future Actually Looks Like and How It Delivers Value to Customers* (New York: Oxford University Press, 1999); Ann Majchrzak and Qianwei Wang, "Breaking the Functional Mind-Set in Process Organizations," *Harvard Business Review*, January 1998, p. 21.

exhibit 8-7 **A Horizontal Organization Structure**

In a horizontal organization, even though specialists are assigned to the team, they are expected to understand one another's tasks, and perform some of those tasks as needed.

achieve substantial improvements in performance. Reengineering searches for the most efficient way to perform a large task. At the same time, reengineering is process innovation because it searches for new ways to perform the same process, such as revamping the way merchandise is ordered and shipped to a department store. Reengineering emphasizes uncovering wasted steps, such as people handing off documents to one another to obtain their approval. E-commerce considerably reengineers the work of sales representatives. If goods are exchanged over the Internet, the need for industrial sales representatives shrinks.

As a result of reengineering, work is organized horizontally rather than vertically. The people in charge of the process function as team leaders who guide the team toward completion of a core process such as new product development or filling a complicated order. Key performance objectives for the team would include "reduce cycle time," "reduce costs," and "reduce throughput time." Team members usually have to develop a process mentality instead of the task mentality of focusing on their specialty.

The push toward the horizontal structures and a process mentality should not be embraced without qualification, however. Having a task mentality remains important because expertise is still crucial in many endeavors. A building construction team, for example, still relies on highly proficient specialists such as mechanical and electrical engineers. Wouldn't you prefer to ride in an elevator that was designed by a highly proficient specialist?

Informal Structures and Communication Networks

The formal structures described in this chapter are an essential part of planning how work is performed. Nevertheless, an organization chart does not tell the whole story of how work gets accomplished. The **informal organization structure** is a set of unofficial relationships that emerge to take care of events and transactions not covered by the formal structure. The informal structure supplements the formal structure by adding a degree of flexibility and speed. A widespread application of the informal structure is the presence of "tech fixers" who supplement the technical

informal organization structure
A set of unofficial relationships that emerge to take care of events and transactions not covered by the formal structure.

support center. For example, marketing assistant Jason might be skilled at resolving software problems created by computer viruses. As a consequence, many people call on Jason for some quick assistance even though the formal organization indicates that they should use the tech center for help with virus problems.

Informal structures are also referred to as informal networks because of the focus on how people use personal contacts to obtain information in a hurry and get work done.[15] The informal networks reveal how well connected people are, as well as how work really gets done. An application of mapping the informal network would be in spotting talent. Some of the most respected workers might not be found on the organization chart but could be indicated by a network map because of the number of times these individuals are consulted by other workers. The highly respected workers might be tapped for key projects.[16]

Also as part of informal networks, all organization structures described so far in this chapter are influenced by information technology. Workers from various units throughout an organization can solve problems together through information networks without being concerned with "who reports to whom," as indicated by organization charts. Furthermore, entry-level workers can leapfrog layers of management and communicate directly with senior executives through e-mail. However, now, as in the past, entry-level workers almost never telephone a member of upper management.

Enough different organization structures have been described to create some confusion and blurring. Exhibit 8-8 indicates the unique aspect of each structure. We have added the conglomerate structure, referring to a collection of independent companies under one corporate roof. Although a term that is fading from frequent use, conglomerates still exist, with Tyco International being one of the best known.

Key Factors that Influence the Selection of an Organization Structure

Learning objective 4

Identify key factors that influence the selection of organization structure.

With so many organization structures, how do managers choose the best one? The answer lies in contingency management—the most effective structure depends on certain factors. Among these factors are strategy, technology, size, financial condition, and environmental stability.

1. *Strategy and goals.* As described in the history of management presented in Chapter 1, structure is supposed to follow strategy. Assume that the strategy of a business machine company is to be the friend of small businesses and individuals who want to operate business equipment in their homes. The company would choose a geographically dispersed marketing organization that gives them maximum access to small customers, such as OfficeMax and Radio Shack.
2. *Technology.* High-technology firms such as aerospace companies make extensive use of flexible structures, such as project and matrix structures.

15 Rob Cross and Laurence Prusak, "The People Who Make Organizations Go—or Stop," *Harvard Business Review*, June 2002, p. 104.
16 Jena McGregor, "The Office Chart That Really Counts: Mapping Informal Relationships at a Company is Revealing and Useful," *Business Week*, February 27, 2006, pp. 48–49.

exhibit 8-8 Unique Feature of Various Organization Structures

Type of Structure or Modification	Unique Feature or Emphasis
Bureaucracy	Hierarchical, with clear rules and regulations
Functional	Departments are defined by the function, or activity, they perform
Geographic	Departments are defined by their geographic location
Product-Service	Departments or divisions are defined by the major product or service they offer
Matrix	A project, or program, structure is superimposed on a functional structure
Flat and Downsized	One or more layers is removed from the structure, and the staff is reduced
Outsourcing and Homesourcing	Work activities are deployed outside the organization, including having it performed at peoples' homes
Horizontal or team	Work is performed by multidisciplinary teams, and communication among workers is enhanced
Informal	People work cooperatively to fill in the gaps not taken care of by the formal organization
Hybrid	A structure that combines several of the above structures, such as a traditional bureaucracy also having several product or service divisions
Conglomerate	A large company that is really a collection of loosely related independent companies, with a minimum of direction and control from headquarters

Relatively low-technology firms such as lumber mills and refuse-collection firms rely more on bureaucratic structures. Organizations based on digital technology like Cisco Systems and Amazon.com typically use horizontal and network structures for two key reasons.[17] The primary reason is that the technology allows for linking workers, customers, and suppliers together. A more subtle reason is that information technology–oriented workers are naturally inclined toward horizontal, free-flowing communication.

3. *Size.* As an organization grows and matures, it inevitably needs centralized controls and some degree of bureaucracy, or formalization. Yet when the firm becomes very large, it is necessary to develop smaller, more flexible units, such as projects and task forces. These units help the firm remain adaptive, and are found in every large organization. Large size and bureaucracy, however, are not synonymous. Some small firms, such as a local bank, might be bureaucratic because they are tightly regulated by banking laws.
4. *Financial condition of the firm.* Size influences structure, and the financial condition of the firm influences both size and structure. Many large business organizations have moved toward a flatter structure to trim costs. Trimming down the number of corporate positions influences structure because with fewer headquarters executives left to supervise divisions, decision-making authority becomes more decentralized. A representative example is the

17 Richard L. Daft, *Management*, 7th ed. (Mason, Ohio: Thomson/South-Western, 2005), p. 380.

10 percent workforce reduction by Intel during 2006 and 2007. The reduction included the elimination of 1,000 management jobs because company executives thought that the ranks of managers had grown faster than its overall headcount, resulting in slowed decision making at Intel.[18]

5. *Environmental stability.* When a business firm faces an uncertain and unstable environment, such as the market for high-fashion clothing or domestic electronics, it needs a highly flexible structure. Task forces and projects are often called into action to deal with a rapidly changing marketplace. Conversely, a more bureaucratic structure is better suited to dealing with more certain (stable) environments. An example is the market for leading candy bars, which has proved to be both recession-proof and resistant to competitors. The manufacturing and marketing of candy bars is more stable than the distribution because the latter has to respond to rapid changes in technology such as just-in-time shipping.

DELEGATION, EMPOWERMENT, AND DECENTRALIZATION

Learning Objective 5

Specify how delegation, empowerment, and decentralization spread authority in an organization.

Collective effort would not be possible, and organizations could not grow and prosper, if a handful of managers did all the work themselves. In recognition of this fact, managers divide up their work. Subdividing work through the process of departmentalization has already been described. The section that follows will discuss subdivision of work using the chain of command through delegation and empowerment, and decentralization.

Delegation of Responsibility and Empowerment

Delegation refers to assigning formal authority and responsibility for accomplishing a specific task to another person. If managers do not delegate any of their work, they are acting as individual contributors—not true managers. Delegation relates closely to **empowerment**, the process by which managers share power with group members, thereby enhancing employees' feelings of personal effectiveness. Delegation is a specific way of empowering employees, thereby increasing motivation.

delegation Assigning formal authority and responsibility for accomplishing a specific task to another person.

empowerment The process by which managers share power with group members, thereby enhancing employees' feelings of personal effectiveness.

A major goal of delegation is the transfer of responsibility as a means of increasing one's own productivity. At the same time, delegation allows team members to develop by learning how to handle more responsibility and to become more productive. Even though a manager may hold a group member responsible for a task, final accountability belongs to the manager. (To be accountable is to accept credit or blame for results.) If the group member fails miserably, the manager must accept the final blame; the manager chose the person who failed.

Delegation and empowerment lie at the heart of effective management. For example, a study was conducted with management teams in 102 hotel properties in the United States. A major finding was that empowering leadership increased the sharing of job knowledge among employees, and

18 Don Clark, "Intel to Slash 10% of Work Force in Restructuring," *The Wall Street Journal*, September 6, 2006, p. A3.

effective teamwork. In turn, the improved knowledge sharing and teamwork were related to good performance.[19]

Following the five suggestions presented next improves the manager's chance of increasing productivity by delegating to and empowering individuals and teams.[20] (Note that teams as well as individuals can be the unit of delegation and power sharing, such as asking a team to find a way of filling orders more rapidly.)

1. *Assign duties to the right people.* The chances for effective delegation and empowerment improve when capable, responsible, well-motivated group members receive the delegated tasks. The manager must be aware of the strengths and weaknesses of staff members to delegate effectively. However, if the purpose of delegation is to develop a group member, the present capabilities of the person receiving the delegated tasks are less important. The manager is willing to accept some mistakes as the cost of development.
2. *Delegate the whole task and step back from the details.* In the spirit of job enrichment, a manager should delegate an entire task to one subordinate rather than dividing it among several. So doing gives the group member complete responsibility and enhances motivation, and gives the manager more control over results. After the whole task is delegated, step back from the details. If a manager cannot let go of details, he or she will never be effective at delegation or empowerment.
3. *Give as much instruction as needed.* Some group members will require highly detailed instructions, while others can operate effectively with general instructions. Many delegation and empowerment failures occur because instruction was insufficient. *Dumping* is the negative term given to the process of dropping a task on a group member without instructions. Under ideal circumstances, delegating should be an opportunity for coaching employees and sharing skills with them.
4. *Retain some important tasks for yourself.* Managers need to retain some high-output or sensitive tasks for themselves. In general, the manager should handle any task that involves the survival of the unit or employee discipline. However, which tasks the manager should retain always depend on the circumstances. Strategic planning is ordinarily not delegated except to obtain input from group members.
5. *Obtain feedback on the delegated task.* A responsible manager does not delegate a complex assignment to a subordinate, then wait until the assignment is complete before discussing it again. Managers must establish checkpoints and milestones to obtain feedback on progress.

---

19 Abhishek Srivastava, Kathryn M. Bartol, and Edwin A. Locke, "Empowering Leadership in Management Teams: Effects on Knowledge Sharing, Efficacy, and Performance," *Academy of Management Journal*, December 2006, pp. 1239–1251.

20 Sharon Gazda, "The Art of Delegating," *HR Magazine*, January 2002, pp. 75–77; "Boost Delegation with this Master List," *Manager's Edge*, June 2002, p. 7; "The Power of Powersharing," *HR/OD*, July–August 1998, p. 2.

decentralization The extent to which authority is passed down to lower levels in an organization.

centralization The extent to which authority is retained at the top of the organization.

Decentralization

Decentralization is the extent to which authority is passed down to lower levels in an organization. It comes about as a consequence of managers delegating work to lower levels. However, the term also refers to decentralization by geography. Geographic decentralization often results in passing down authority because managers in the decentralized units are granted decision-making authority. Unless so noted, this text uses the term *decentralization* in reference to authority. **Centralization** is the extent to which authority is retained at the top of the organization. Decentralization and centralization lie on two ends of a continuum. No firm operates as completely centralized or decentralized.

How much control top management wants to retain determines how much to decentralize an organization. Organizations favor decentralization when a large number of decisions must be made at lower organizational levels, often based on responding to customer needs. Johnson & Johnson, the medical and personal care products giant, favors decentralization in part because the company consists of a collection of different businesses, many with vastly different customer requirements. Division management is much more aware of these needs than are people at company headquarters. In general, a centralized firm exercises more control over organization units than a decentralized firm.

Many firms centralize and decentralize operations simultaneously. Certain aspects of their operations are centralized, whereas others are decentralized. Quick-service franchise restaurants such as Subway, Long John Silver's, and Wendy's illustrate this trend. Central headquarters exercises tight control over such matters as menu selection, food quality, and advertising. Individual franchise operators, however, make human resource decisions, such as hiring.

An advanced technique of juggling the forces of centralization and decentralization simultaneously is for decentralized units to remain somewhat autonomous, yet cooperate with each other for the common good. For example, the basic structure of Johnson & Johnson is a decentralized firm with 204 nearly autonomous units organized into three divisions: drugs, medical and diagnostic devices, and consumer products (such as Band-Aids and Johnson's Baby Powder). The current emphasis at J&J is for the autonomous divisions to cooperate with each other to achieve better products—such as sutures from one division being coated with drugs from another, to help prevent infections.[21]

ORGANIZATIONAL CULTURE

Learning Objective 6

Identify major aspects of organizational culture, including its determinants, how it is learned, managed, and sustained.

Organization structure has sometimes been referred to as the "hard side" of how a firm operates; yet understanding the "soft side" of an organization is also essential. **Organizational culture (or corporate culture)** is the system of shared values and beliefs that actively influence the behavior of organization members. The term *shared* implies that many people are guided by the same values and that they interpret them in the same way. Values develop over

21 Amy Barrett, "Staying on Top," *Business Week*, May 5, 2003, p. 62.

time and reflect a firm's history and traditions. Organizational culture is important to understand because it is a major factor in the success of any company. In the words of Douglas R. Conant, the dynamic CEO of Campbell Soup Co., "If you want to be a sustainably good company, you have to have a sustainably good culture."[22]

organizational culture (or corporate culture)
The system of shared values and beliefs that actively influence the behavior of organization members.

This section describes significant aspects of organizational culture: how it is learned, and its determinants, dimensions, consequences, and management and maintenance.

Determinants of Organizational Culture

Many forces shape a firm's culture. Often its origin lies in the values, administrative practices, and personality of the founder or founders. Also, the leader's vision can have a heavy impact on culture, such as John Chambers' dream of Cisco Systems becoming one of the world's greatest companies in history. A much-publicized example of the impact of a leader on culture is Herb Kelleher, the founder of Southwest Airlines, who is considered pivotal in shaping one of the most distinctive organizational cultures. Up until Kelleher's retirement several years ago, Southwest was considered very dependent on his personality and character. After his retirement for health reasons, his personality could still be felt. At the core of Southwest are the values of humor and altruism. Flight attendants and pilots use jokes and games to put customers at ease (a practice now copied by JetBlue Airlines). An example of altruism is that Southwest employees have established a catastrophe fund to help workers who need more assistance than usual employee benefits cover.[23]

Organizational culture responds to and mirrors the conscious and unconscious choices, behavioral patterns, and prejudices of top-level managers. As the founders leave or become less active, other top-level managers help define the culture. One of the ways in which Robert Nardelli, the former CEO and chair of Home Depot, changed the company culture was to make the company more disciplined and military-like through implementing business processes from his former employer GE, and hiring hundreds of former junior military officers.

The culture in which a society operates also helps determine the culture of the firm. Sooner or later, society's norms, beliefs, and values find their way into the firm. Societal values are communicated through such means as the media, conversations, and education. The emphasis on sexual and racial equality in U.S. society has become incorporated into the value culture of many employers. The emphasis on collegiality translates into harmony and cooperation in the workplace at many Scandinavian companies, including Nokia. Another perspective on national culture is that the introduction of values from another society into a retail business can be a competitive advantage. For example, the Japanese values of high quality and reliability,

22 Quoted in Harold Brubaker, "Souper Saver," *Philadelphia Inquirer* (http://www.philly.com), July 25, 2006, p. 1.

23 Katrina Brooker, "Can Anyone Replace Herb?" *Fortune*, April 17, 2000, pp. 186–192; Tom Belden, "Will Fun Be Enough?" http://www.philly.com, January 24, 2006.

subculture
A pocket in which the organizational culture differs from the dominant culture, as well as other pockets of the subculture.

and spotless factories have helped fuel the success of the Toyota car brand in the United States.

The industry to which a firm belongs helps shape its culture. For example, a public utility will have a culture different from a food manufacturer of comparable size. Heavy competition and low profit margins may force the food manufacturer to operate at a faster pace than the utility, which usually competes with only several other utilities.

Dimensions of Organizational Culture

The dimensions of organizational culture help explain the subtle forces that influence employee actions. In addition to the dominant culture of a firm, the subculture also influences behavior. A **subculture** is a pocket in which the organizational culture differs from the dominant culture, as well as other pockets of subculture. A frequently observed difference in subcultures can be found between the marketing and production groups, even in such matters as dress and behavior. The marketing people are likely to be more style conscious and people-oriented. Six dimensions significantly influence organizational culture.[24]

1. *Values.* Values provide the foundation of any organizational culture. The organization's philosophy expressed through values guides behavior on a day-to-day basis. Representative values of a firm might include ethical behavior, concern for employee welfare, a belief that the customer is always right, a commitment to quality, and the importance of equality and independence. A pervasive value is the importance of formality, with a heavily bureaucratic culture believing strongly in formality, including following procedures and protocol.
2. *Relative diversity.* The existence of an organizational culture assumes some degree of homogeneity. Nevertheless, organizations differ in terms of how much deviation can be tolerated. Many firms are highly homogeneous; executives talk in a similar manner and even look alike. Furthermore, those executives promote people from similar educational backgrounds and fields of specialty into key jobs. The diversity of a culture also reflects itself in the dress code. Some organizations insist on uniformity of dress, such as wearing a jacket and tie (for men) when interacting with customers or clients. Strongly encouraging all workers to conform to dress-down Fridays discourages diversity.
3. *Resource allocations and rewards.* The allocation of money and other resources exerts a critical influence on culture. The investment of resources sends a message to people about what is valued in the firm. If a customer-service department is fully staffed and nicely furnished, employees and customers can assume that the company values customer service.
4. *Degree of change.* The culture in a fast-paced, dynamic organization differs from that of a slow paced, stable one. A highly competitive environment

24 J. Steven Ott, *The Organizational Culture Perspective* (Chicago: Dorsey Press, 1989), pp. 20–48; Personal communication from Lynn H. Suksdorf, Salt Lake City Community College, October 1998.

might encourage a fast-paced climate. Top-level managers, by the energy or lethargy of their stance, send signals about how much they welcome innovation. The degree of change also influences whether a culture can take root and how strong that culture can be.

5. *A sense of ownership.* The movement toward employee stock ownership in companies creates an ownership culture and inspires workers to think and act like owners. An ownership culture increases loyalty, improves work effort, and aligns worker interests with those of the company. An ownership culture can be reflected in such everyday actions as conserving electricity, making gradual improvements, and not tolerating sloppiness by coworkers. An ownership culture can backfire, however, if employee wealth stays flat or decreases as a result of stock ownership.
6. *Strength of the culture.* The strength of the culture, or how much influence it exerts, emerges partially as a by-product of the other dimensions. A strong culture guides employees in everyday actions. It determines, for example, whether an employee will inconvenience himself or herself to satisfy a customer. Without a strong culture, employees are more likely to follow their own whims—they may decide to please customers only when convenient. Unfortunately, strong cultures may develop a cult-like atmosphere in which employees become more attached to the firm than to outside life. The corporation takes over as the major source of satisfying emotional needs.[25] A research study with 123 organizations found that the climate (or culture) tended to be strongest when it was unambiguous, such as clearly bureaucratic or clearly flexible.[26]

These dimensions represent a formal and systematic way of understanding organizational culture. In practice, people use more glib expressions in describing culture, as illustrated in Exhibit 8-9.

How Workers Learn the Culture

Employees learn the organizational culture primarily through **socialization**, the process of coming to understand the values, norms, and customs essential for adapting to the organization. Socialization is therefore a method of indoctrinating employees into the organization in such a way that they perpetuate the culture. The socialization process takes place mostly by learning through imitation and observation.

Another important way in which workers learn the culture is through the teachings of leaders, as implied in the cultural dimension of resource allocations and rewards. Organizational members learn the culture to some extent by observing what leaders pay attention to, measure, and control. Suppose a coworker of yours is praised publicly for doing community service. You are likely to conclude that an important part of the culture is to help people outside the company. Senior executives will sometimes

socialization
The process of coming to understand the values, norms, and customs essential for adapting to the organization.

25 Dave Arnott, *Corporate Cults: The Insidious Lure of the All-Consuming Organization* (New York: AMACOM, 1999).

26 Marcus W. Dickson, Christian J. Resick, and Paul J. Hanges, "When Organizational Climate Is Unambiguous, It Is Also Strong," *Journal of Applied Psychology*, March 2006, pp. 351–364.

exhibit 8-9 A Sampling of Organizational Cultures of Well-Known Companies

IKEA Very informal culture with roots in Swedish culture. Emphasis on informality, cost consciousness, and a humble, down-to-earth approach. Workers are allowed considerable responsibility.

Nike Go-it-alone, insular culture characterized by a desire for growth within, rather than taking on the hassles of integrating a merger with another company. Very difficult for outside executives to be accepted by the inner circle.

United Airlines Ailing culture, long plagued by tension between management and unions. Employees are hired for functional skills rather than relational skills. Performance is measured in a functionally specific, divisive way rather than allowing cross-functional responsibility for performance. Company bankruptcy tended to increase the negative aspects of the culture.

Apple inc. Attitude of smugness and superiority, with a tendency to perceive other technology companies as mere imitators of the real thing (Apple), with these attitudes being strengthened with the success of the iPod. Intense fondness for innovation and freethinking, combined with a strong dislike for bureaucracy.

Toyota Highly disciplined approach to work with fanatic attitudes toward cleanliness, even on the manufacturing floor. Heavy orientation toward cost control and superb engineering. More concerned about efficiency than style or flash, and slow to introduce significant changes in methods or design.

Source: Katarina Kling and Ingela Goteman, "IKEA CEO Anders Dahlvig on International Growth and IKEA's Unique Corporate Culture and Brand Identity," *Academy of Management Executive*, February 2003, pp. 31–37; January 24, 2006. Patrick J. Kiger, "Unite or Die," *Workforce*, February 2003, pp. 26–29; Carleen Hawn, "If He's So Smart..." *Fast Company*, January 2004, pp. 68–74; Alex Taylor III, "The Americanization of Toyota," *Fortune*, December 8, 2003, pp. 165–170.

publicly express expectations that help shape the culture of the firm, such as demanding data-driven decision making.

Consequences and Implications of Organizational Culture

The attention to organizational culture stems from its pervasive impact on organizational effectiveness. Exhibit 8-10 outlines several key consequences of organizational culture. The right organizational culture *contributes to gaining competitive advantage and therefore achieving financial success.* The consistently strong performance of Google can be partially attributed to its culture that values intelligence, imagination, and hard work.

The right organizational culture can enhance *productivity, quality, and morale.* A culture that emphasizes productivity and quality encourages workers to be more productive and quality conscious. A culture that values the dignity of human beings fosters high morale and job satisfaction. A corporate culture that *encourages creative behavior contributes to innovation,* as described in Chapter 5 about problem solving and decision making. Amazon chief executive Jeff Bezos notes that a culture of experimentation is crucial in a fast-changing world. He says that "Invention always leads you down paths that people think are weird."[27]

27 Robert D. Hof, "How to Hit a Moving Target," *Business Week*, August 21/28, 2006, p. 81.

exhibit 8-10 Consequences and Implications of Organizational Culture

Although organizational culture is a soft concept, it has many hard consequences.

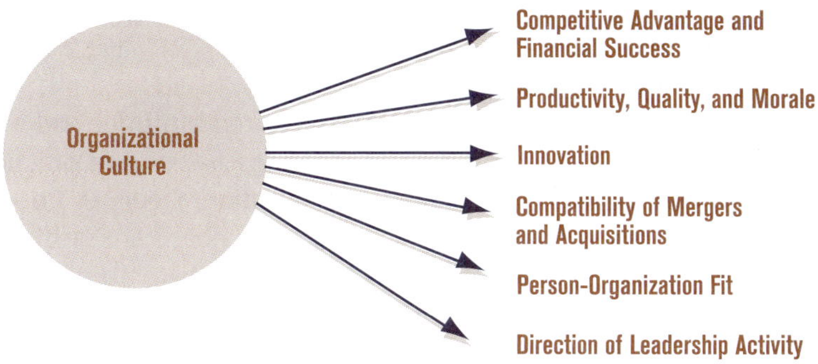

A reliable predictor of success in merging two or more firms is *compatibility of their respective cultures*. When the cultures clash, such as a hierarchical firm merging with an egalitarian one, the result can be negative synergy. When US Airways merged with American West several years ago, the company created the position of "vice president of culture integration" to help meld the two air carriers. US Airways had a highly formal culture, and American had an easygoing, informal culture. Larry LeSueur, the new vice president, said, "I want to mold the two companies into one culture but still keep the best of both cultures." The techniques included town hall meetings with managers and workers.[28]

Individuals can contribute to their own success by *finding a good person—organization fit*, an organization that fits his or her personality. The person who finds a good fit is more likely to experience job satisfaction, commitment to the organization, and a lesser interest in quitting.[29] Similarly, an organization will be more successful when the personalities of most members fit its culture. One study measured organizations on such dimensions as stability, experimenting, risk taking, and rule orientation. Researchers then compared the preferences of professional employees regarding culture to the culture of their firms and found good person—organization fit resulted in more commitment and higher job satisfaction.[30]

Organizational culture powerfully influences the *direction of leadership activity*. Top-level managers spend much of their time working with the forces that shape the attitudes and values of employees at all levels. Leaders in key roles establish what type of culture is needed for the firm and then shape the existing culture to match that ideal, which is why outsiders are sometimes brought in to head a company.

---

28 Eve Tahmincioglu, "Double Vision," *Workforce Management*, January 16, 2006, pp. 1, 22.

29 Amy L. Kristof-Brown, Ryan D. Zimmerman, and Erin C. Johnson, "Consequences of Individuals' Fit at Work: A Meta-Analysis of Person-Job, Person-Organization, Person-Group, and Person-Supervisor Fit," *Personnel Psychology*, Summer 2005, p. 310.

30 Charles A. O'Reilly III, Jennifer A. Chairman, and David F. Caldwell, "People and Organizational Culture: A Profile Comparison Approach to Assessing Person-Organization Fit," *Academy of Management Journal*, September 1991, pp. 487–516.

Managing and Sustaining the Culture

After a new CEO is appointed, the person typically makes a public statement to the effect, "My number-one job is to change the culture." A manager might do the following to bring about change as well assuring that a healthy corporate culture is maintained.

- Serve as a role model for the desired attitudes and behaviors. Leaders must behave in ways consistent with the values and practices they wish to see imitated throughout the organization. Deere & Co. went through a major cultural change in which customer needs are satisfied through mass customization. For a strongly traditional company to undergo such change, considerable new training is necessary. Top managers at Deere both set up teams for training and participate in the training sessions themselves.[31]
- Impose a new approach through executive edict. The accompanying Management in Action illustrates a forceful approach by the top executive to revamp the culture of one of the world's most admired companies.
- Establish a reward system that reinforces the culture, such as giving huge suggestion awards to promote an innovative culture. At Boeing Co., CEO W. James McNerney Jr. wants to create a common culture and work toward a shared goal. So to discourage negative internal competition and the hoarding of information, part of executive compensation is based on how well they share information with other units across the company.[32]
- Select candidates for positions at all levels whose values mesh with the values of the desired culture. Many firms hire only those candidates whose work and school suggest that they might be good team players—a cultural value.
- Sponsor new training and development programs that support the desired cultural values. Among many examples, top management might sponsor diversity training to support the importance of cultural diversity, or training in quality to support the value of quality. Edward W. Lambert, the chairman of Sears Holding Company (a merger of Sears and Kmart), wanted to create a culture based on selling, including improving team work and customer service. One of his techniques to achieve this goal was a training session for 500 managers in which he showed clips from *Miracle on Ice,* about the U.S. hockey team that won the gold medal in the 1980 Winter Olympics.[33]
- Conduct conference calls in a large company to discuss progress toward building the new culture. One of the biggest cultural change initiatives of all time took place at Home Depot when Nardelli wanted to the make the company more disciplined like a big-company and less free wheeling. Monday-morning conference calls were established with the top 15 executives, during which the business results and promises made the previous week are discussed to emphasize accountability. Also, information was shared bout operations, customers, markets, and competitive conditions.[34]

---

31 Anita Lienert, "Plowing Ahead in Uncertain Times," *Management Review*, November 1998, p. 19.

32 Stanley Holmes, "Cleaning Up Boeing," *Business Week*, March 13, 2006, p. 64.

33 Michael Barbaro, "Sears Chairman Works to Emphasize Selling," *The New York Times* (http://www.nytimes.com), April 13, 2006.

34 Ram Charan, "Home Depot's Blueprint for Culture Change," *Harvard Business Review*, April 2006, p. 65.

management in action

Overhauling the GE Culture

Despite his air of easy-going confidence, Jeffrey R. Immelt admits to two fears: that General Electric will become boring, and that his top people might act like cowards. That's right: cowards. He worries that GE's famous obsession with bottom-line results—and the tendency to get rid of those who don't meet them—will make some execs shy away from taking risks that could revolutionize the company.

Immelt, 49, is clearly pushing for a cultural revolution. For the past three and half years, the GE chairman and CEO has been on a mission to transform the hard-driving, process-oriented company into one steeped in creativity and wired for growth. He wants to move GE's average organic growth rate—the increase in revenue that comes from existing operations, rather than from deals and currency fluctuations—to be at least 8 percent from about 5 percent over the past decade. Under his former boss, the renowned Jack Welch, the skills GE prized above all others were cost-cutting, efficiency, and deal-making. What mattered was the continual improvement of operations. Immelt hasn't turned his back on the old ways. But in his GE, the new imperatives are risk-taking, sophisticated marketing, and above all, innovation.

Immelt has plans for making the ingrained GE culture sizzle with bold thinking and creative energy. To start, he has banished some long-cherished traditions and beliefs. Immelt has welcomed outsiders into the highest ranks. He is pushing hard for a more global workforce that reflects the communities in which GE operates. Immelt is also encouraging his homegrown managers to become experts in their industries rather than just experts in managing. He's diversifying the top ranks and urging his lieutenants to stay put and make a difference where they are.

In true GE fashion, Immelt has engineered a quantifiable and scalable process for coming up with money-making "eureka!" moments. The members of the Commercial Council hold phone meetings every month and meet each quarter to discuss growth strategies, think up new ways to reach customers, and evaluate ideas from the senior ranks that aim to take GE out on a limb. Business leaders must submit at least three "Imagination Breakthrough" proposals per year that ultimately go before the council for review and discussion. The projects have to take GE into a new line of business, geographic area, or customer base. And each one has to give GE incremental growth of at least $100 million.

The GE chief is tying executives' compensation to the managers' ability to come up with ideas, show improved customer service, generate cash growth, and boost sales instead of simply meeting bottom-line targets. Twenty percent of bonuses will come from meeting pre-established measures of how well a business is improving its ability to meet customer needs. Risking failure is a badge of honor at GE these days.

The pressure to produce at the company could not be more intense. Many of the company's 307,000 workers weren't exactly hired to be part of a diverse, creative, fleet-footed army of visionaries who are acutely sensitive to customers' needs. "These guys just aren't dreamer types," says one consultant who has worked with the company. "It almost seems painful to them, like a waste of time. Even insiders who are openly euphoric about the changes under Chairman Jeff admit to feeling some fear in the depth of their guts."

A summary of how Immelt is trying to shift the GE mindset is as follows:

- *Pay*. Link bonuses to new ideas, customer satisfaction, and sales growth, with less emphasis on bottom-line results.
- *Risk*. Spend billions to fund "Imagination Breakthrough" projects that extend the boundaries of GE.
- *Experts*. Rotate experts less often, and bring in more outsiders to create industry experts instead of professional managers. (Management skills are still vital, but they should be combined with industry expertise.)

(Continued)

management in action (Continued)

Overhauling the GE Culture

Questions

1. Why doesn't a preoccupation with bottom-line results fit the new GE culture that Immelt is attempting to develop?
2. In what way is Immelt using idea quotas?
3. How well would the new GE culture fit for your talents and personality?

Source: Adapted from Diane Brady, "The Immelt Revolution: He's Turning GE's Culture Upside Down, Demanding Far More Risk and Innovation," *Business Week,* March 28, 2005, pp. 64–66, 71–73.

A suggestion in relation to organizational culture is to find employment where you fit the culture, or quickly adapt your values and behavior to create a fit. For example, if the culture emphasizes data-driven decision making and a highly disciplined approach to management, act in this manner to survive and prosper.

MANAGING CHANGE

Learning Objective 7

Describe key aspects of managing change, including gaining support for change, and the DICE framework for successful change management.

To meet their objectives, managers must manage change effectively almost daily. Change in the workplace relates to any factor with an impact on people, including changes in technology, organization structure, competition, human resources, and budgets. The following description of managing change contains six components: (1) change at the individual versus organizational level, (2) a model of the change process, (3) resistance to change, (4) gaining support for change, (5) bringing about planned change through Six Sigma, and (6) the DICE framework for successful change management. Knowledge of these components helps in managing change that affects oneself and others.

Creating Change at the Individual Versus Organizational Level

Many useful changes in organizations take place at the individual and small group level, rather than at the organizational level. Quite often individual contributors, middle-level managers, and team leaders identify a small need for change and make it happen. For example, a supermarket manager observed that several meat department workers did not understand fractions. He therefore suggested that each supermarket should have a designated "fraction trainer" who would assist meat workers who could not work with fractions.

One study researched the effective change brought about by individuals in a variety of organizations. Each of the more than 100 participants was identified as a "mover and shaker," someone who brought about constructive change. Constructive change included, for example, modifying a software product so as to open new markets. A common characteristic of these people who brought about change was a greater focus on results rather than on trying not to offend anyone. At the same time, they concentrated more on exerting individual initiative than on blending into the group.[35]

Change at the organizational level receives much more attention than the small, incremental changes brought about by individuals. One of these major changes has already been described: changing the organizational culture. Later we describe how Six Sigma changes an organization. Change at the organizational level can be regarded as change in the fundamental way in which the company operates, such as moving from a government-regulated utility to a competitive organization.

The Unfreezing-Changing-Refreezing Model of Change

Psychologist Kurt Lewin developed a three-step analysis of the change process widely used by managers to help bring about constructive change.[36] Many other approaches to initiating change stem from this simple model illustrated in Exhibit 8-11. *Unfreezing* involves reducing or eliminating resistance to change. As long as employees oppose a change, it will not be implemented effectively. To accept change, employees must first deal with and resolve their feelings about letting go of the old. Only after people have dealt effectively with endings can they readily make transitions.

Changing, or moving on to a new level, usually involves considerable two-way communication, including group discussion. According to Lewin, "Rather than a one-way flow of commands or recommendations, the person implementing the change should make suggestions. The changee should be encouraged to contribute and participate." Refreezing includes pointing out the success of the change and looking for ways to reward people involved in implementing the change.

Resistance to Change

Before a company's managers can gain support for change, they must understand why people resist change. People resist changes for reasons they think are important, the most common being the fear of an unfavorable outcome, such as less money or personal inconvenience. People also resist change for such varied reasons as not wanting to break well-established habits. Change

exhibit 8-11 The Change Process

To bring about change, you have to break old habits, create new ones, and solidify the new habits.

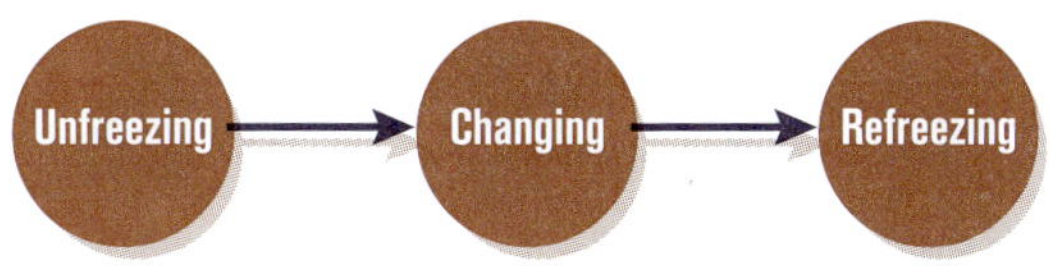

35 Alan H. Frohman, "Igniting Organizational Change from Below: The Power of Individual Initiative," *Organizational Dynamics*, Winter 1997, pp. 39–53.

36 Kurt Lewin, *Field Theory and Social Science* (New York: Harper & Brothers, 1951).

may also be unwelcome because it upsets the balance of an activity, such as the old system of in-person meetings versus video conferencing.

Personality factors also contribute to resistance to change. For example, a rigid person might be more naturally disposed to maintaining the status quo. Workers who feel they lack the skills to deal effectively with the change, such as working in a team rather than individually, will sometimes resist change. Even when people do not view a change as potentially damaging, they may sometimes cling to a system they dislike rather than change. According to folk wisdom, "People would rather deal with the devil they know than the devil they do not know." Workers may also resist change based on weaknesses in the proposed changes that may have been overlooked or disregarded by management. For example, managers might not be aware of how upset many customers would be when a voice recognition system replaces live customer-service agents. Because workers have more contact with customers, they might predict the customer dissatisfaction.

Gaining Support for Change

Gaining support for change, and therefore overcoming resistance, is an important managerial responsibility. A study investigated how organizational change in 32 different public and private organizations affected individual's commitment to the change and their broader commitment to the organization. One of the conclusions reached was that long-term benefits of change occur only when employees actively work to support the change and are aligned with the organization's goals and values.[37] Here we look at six techniques for gaining support for change.

1. *Allow for discussion and negotiation.* Support for change can be increased by discussing and negotiating the more sensitive aspects of the change. It is important to acknowledge the potential hardships associated with the change, such as longer working hours or higher output to earn the same compensation. The two-way communication incorporated into the discussion helps reduce some employee concerns. Discussion often leads to negotiation, which further involves employees in the change process.
2. *Allow for participation.* To overcome resistance to change, allow people to participate in the changes that will affect them. In applying this concept, a manager can allow employees to set their own rules to increase compliance. A powerful participation technique is to encourage people who already favor the change to help in planning and implementation. These active supporters of the change will be even more strongly motivated to enlist the support of others. Participation is also useful because it gives the manager additional input into developing a careful plan for the change, including implementation.
3. *Point out the financial benefits.* Given that so many employees express concern about the financial effects of work changes, it is helpful to discuss these effects openly. If employees will earn more money as a result of the change,

37 Donald B. Fedor, Steven Caldwell, and David M. Herold, "The Effect of Organizational Changes on Employee Commitment: A Multilevel Investigation," *Personnel Psychology*, Spring 2006, p. 26.

this fact can be used as a selling point. For example, a company owner told his employees, "I know you are inconvenienced and upset because we have cut way back on clerical support. But some of the savings will be invested in bigger bonuses for you." Much of the grumbling subsided.

4. *Avoid change overload.* Too much change too soon leads to negative stress. Too many sweeping changes in a brief period of time, or simultaneous changes, also causes confusion, and it leads to foot dragging about the workplace innovation. When change is perceived as excessive, employees often focus too much on the change and not enough on primary tasks such as the product, service, or customers. Explaining how the large-scale changes fit the company strategy can sometimes lessen the sting of change.[38]
5. *Allow for first-hand observation of successful change.* Support for change can sometimes be overcome by giving workers an opportunity to see first-hand an example of a model of the change in question.[39] Suppose, for example, top management decides that the company should shift to a virtually paperless company without secretarial assistance. Many managers and staff professionals would be quite skeptical. If feasible, it would be helpful for a small team of company skeptics to visit a company that has become a paperless office. Seeing is believing, and it also helps overcome resistance to change.
6. *Get the best people behind the program.* A powerful tactic for bringing about change is to enlist the cooperation of people whom others in the organization respect, and who are flexible. When Eastman Kodak Company chief executive Antonio M. Perez wanted to move the company more quickly into digital and away from film products he assembled a group of "rebels" (talented people who were skeptical by nature). He asked them to make suggestions on how the company could be improved, including coming up with new digital services and commercializing existing technology. Once these people thought they were part of the change, they spread the word throughout the organization that Perez was a good leader. Based on the credibility of the rebels, their opinions influenced many others.[40]

The above techniques for overcoming resistance to change are more likely to be successful when the manager has a good working relationship with staff members, including being trusted. For example, allowing for discussion and participation is less likely to be perceived as manipulation when the manager is trusted.

Six Sigma and Planned Change

The shift to a more quality-conscious firm can be classified as a total systems approach to organization change. Having high-quality goods and services is considered a necessary minimum to compete effectively. Most customers today require high-quality standards from vendors. One such standard is

---

38 Inger Stensaker et al., "Excessive Change: Coping Mechanisms and Consequences," *Organizational Dynamics*, No. 3, 2002, pp. 308, 310.

39 Jeffrey Pfeffer, *The Human Equation: Building Profits by Putting People First* (Boston, MA: Harvard Business School Press, 1998), pp. 126–128.

40 Steve Hamm and William C. Symonds, "Mistakes Made on the Road to Innovation," *Business Week*, November 2006, p. IN 30.

Six Sigma
A data-driven method for achieving near-perfect quality with an emphasis on preventing problems.

Six Sigma, or 3.4 errors in 1 million opportunities. (The figure is derived from the area under the normal curve from −6 to +6 standard deviations from the mean.) A number of organizations formalized this quality standard as part of company-wide programs for attaining high quality. With capital first letters, **Six Sigma** refers to a philosophy of driving out waste and improving quality and the cost and time performance of a company. Three examples of companies with Six Sigma programs in some or all their divisions are GE, the Vanguard Group (investment management), Dow Chemical, and Xerox.

Six Sigma is regarded as a data-driven method for achieving near-perfect quality, with an emphasis on preventing problems. The focus is on identifying, quantifying, and eliminating errors in business processes. Six Sigma emphasizes statistical analysis and measurement in design, manufacturing, and the entire area of customer-oriented activities. Decision making becomes heavily based on numbers. Six Sigma also contains a strong behavioral aspect, with a focus on motivating people to work together to achieve higher levels of productivity. The system creates specialized positions in the company instead of placing additional responsibility on already overburdened managers and specialists. Employees chosen to be "black belts" or Six Sigma specialists work full time as a Six Sigma project leader. Six Sigma teams carry out most of an organization's quality improvement efforts. Nevertheless, everybody in the company is supposed to be involved to some extent in the change effort.[41] As with all programs of organizational improvement, top management commitment is vital.

An example of the application of Six Sigma to fix a quality problem took place in a manufacturing unit of Xerox. Software for translating technical manuals into foreign languages could not deal with some of the engineering jargon. Identifying and eradicating the problematic phrases led to more rapid translations, fewer errors, and savings of up to $1 million.[42]

Six Sigma, as with other quality programs, can help an organization achieve reliable products and services. However, the program must fit into the company culture. Companies more attuned to Six Sigma are those where the culture emphasizes discipline and measurement, such as Xerox and Pitney-Bowes. However, Six Sigma is less likely to be accepted in a more free-wheeling and less disciplined culture such as a large advertising agency. A concern bout pushing too far with Six Sigma is that it sometimes takes away from the innovation and customer relationships partially because of its heavy emphasis on measurement and paperwork (or electronic work).[43]

The DICE Framework for Successful Change Management

New approaches to managing change in organizations continue to evolve. One such approach is proposed by consultants Harold S. Sirkin, Perry Keenan, and Alan Jackson, who studied change initiatives at 225 companies.[44] They

41 Sara Fister Gale, "Building Frameworks for Six Sigma Success," *Workforce*, May 2003, pp. 64–69.

42 Faith Arner and Adam Aston, "How Xerox Got Up to Speed," *Business Week*, May 3, 2004, p. 104.

43 Brian Hindo and Brian Grow, "Six Sigma: So Yesterday?" *Business Week*, June 2007 **IN**, p. 11.

44 Harold L. Sirkin, Perry Keenan, and Alan Jackson, "The Hard Side of Change Management," *Harvard Business Review*, October 2005, pp. 108–118.

found a consistent correlation between success in these programs and four objective factors, referred to collectively as the DICE framework.

D. Project *duration* refers to how long the project takes to complete or the time between project reviews. A project might be an improved approach to product development. A successful project should not drag on too long. If the project is of long duration, frequent reviews are more likely to contribute to successful change than are infrequent reviews.

I. *Integrity of performance* refers to the capability of project teams, with talented teams being more able to facilitate successful change—a finding which will not surprise an experienced manager.

C. *Commitment of senior executives and staff* emphasizes that top-level management as well as others involved must want the change to take place. A good example here is Six Sigma. Unless top management really wants and values quality improvement, not much improvement in quality and work processes is likely to be sustained. At the same time, workers throughout the organization must be committed to making the process improvements indicated by Six Sigma.

E. *Effort* refers to the additional effort required of employees directly affected by the change. A successful change initiative requires that employees dig in and push for the changes to work, such as a new self-service benefits system using kiosks or going online. Bringing about change requires effort beyond what is required for the usual work.

The consultants developed a formula to calculate the DICE score, with Commitment being divided into top-management commitment (C_1) and local-level commitment (C_2). The formula is: DICE Score $= D + (2 \times I) = (2 \times C_1) = C_2 + E$.

In the 1(high)-to-4(low) scoring, the formula yields overall scores that range from 7 to 28. The lower the score, the better—with scores between 7 and 14 indicating the best chance of a new project succeeding. Although the authors of this approach refer to DICE as the *hard* side of change management, it really deals with the *soft* side of bringing about change—getting talented and committed people to invest in a change project, and giving them feedback as they go along.

SUMMARY OF Key Points

1 Describe the bureaucratic form of organization and discuss its advantages and disadvantages.

The most widely used form of organization is the bureaucracy, a multilevel organization in which authority flows downward and rules and regulations are carefully specified. Bureaucracies can be highly efficient organizations that are well suited to handling repetitive, recurring tasks. Also, a bureaucracy fits the human need for order and security, among other needs. However, they may be rigid in terms of handling people and problems, and decision-making delays are frequent in bureaucracies.

2 Explain the major ways in which organizations are divided into departments.

The usual way of subdividing effort in organizations, particularly in bureaucracies, is to create departments. Three common types of departmentalization are functional, geographic, and product–service.

3 Describe three modifications of the bureaucratic structure.

The matrix organization consists of a project structure superimposed on a functional structure. Personnel assigned to the projects within the matrix report to a project manager, yet they report to a functional manager also. Flat organizations have fewer layers than traditional hierarchies, and are often the result of downsizing. They are created for such purposes as reducing human resource costs and speeding up decision making. Downsizing can also be looked upon as a way of simplifying an organization to make it less bureaucratic. Unless downsizing is done carefully, it can backfire in terms of increasing efficiency. By outsourcing, a company can reduce its need for employees and physical assets, and associated payroll costs. Outsourcing is part of globalization but is also part of the organization structure by having other companies perform part of your work. Homeshoring, or having customer-service work performed in workers' homes, is growing rapidly.

Another approach to organization structure is to organize horizontally, or for a group of people to concern themselves with a process, such as filling an order or development of a new product. Team members focus on their purpose rather than their specialty, and take collective responsibility for customers. Switching from a task to a process emphasis can often be done through reengineering.

In addition to the formal structures, organizations also have informal structures that consist of personal relationships and networks to accomplish work. Information technology facilitates communication in all types of organization structures.

4 Identify key factors that influence the selection of organization structure.

The most effective structure depends on four key factors. The organization's strategy and goals are the most influential factor. High technology favors a flexible structure, whereas low technology favors bureaucracy. Large size often moves a company toward bureaucracy. Finances influence structure because flatter structures lower costs. An unstable environment favors a flexible structure.

5 Specify how delegation, empowerment, and decentralization spread authority in an organization.

Delegation is assigning formal authority and responsibility for accomplishing a task to another person. Delegation fosters empowerment. The manager remains accountable for the result of subordinates' efforts. Effective delegation includes assigning duties to the right people and obtaining feedback on the delegated task. Decentralization stems from delegation. It is the extent to which authority is passed down to lower levels in an organization. Decentralization sometimes refers to geographic dispersion. Although units may be decentralized and autonomous, in some organizations these units cooperate with each other for the common good.

6 Identify major aspects of organizational culture.

The organizational culture is shaped by such forces as the values and personality of the founder, the attitudes of top-level managers, society, and the industry. Six key dimensions of organizational culture are values, relative diversity, resource allocation and rewards, degree of change, a sense of ownership, and the strength of culture. Employees learn the culture primarily through socialization. Culture has important consequences and implications for factors such as competitive advantage, productivity, quality, and morale. Top management is responsible for shaping, managing, and controlling culture. Although culture is slow to change, the manager can take positive steps to being about change. The manager can act as a role model, impose a new approach through edict, reward behaviors that fit the desired cultural values, select the right people, and conduct training programs and conference calls to bring about the desired culture.

7 Describe key aspects of managing change, including gaining support for change, and the DICE framework for successful change management.

Change can take place at the individual and small group levels as well as at the organizational level. A model of change suggests that the process has three stages: unfreezing attitudes, followed by attitude change, then refreezing to point out the success of the change. People resist change for reasons they think are important, the most common being the fear of an unfavorable outcome.

Six techniques for gaining support for change are as follows: allow for discussion and negotiation; allow for participation; point out the financial benefits; avoid change overload; allow for first-hand observation of successful change; and get the best people behind the program. Six Sigma is an important organizational change strategy. It is a data-driven method for achieving near-perfect quality, and is administered by Six Sigma teams with the cooperation of most managers and executives.

According to the DICE framework for successful change management, four factors are essential: short project duration or frequent progress reviews; integrity of performance; commitment by top management and staff workers; and effort by all involved.

KEY TERMS AND PHRASES

Organization structure, 256
Bureaucracy, 256
Unity of command, 257
Departmentalization, 261
Functional departmentalization, 261
Geographic departmentalization, 261
Product–service departmentalization, 262
Project organization, 264
Matrix organization, 264
Flat organization structure, 265
Span of control, 265
Homeshoring, 267
Horizontal structure, 268
Reengineering, 268
Informal organization structure, 269
Delegation, 272
Empowerment, 272
Decentralization, 274
Centralization, 274
Organizational culture (or corporate culture), 275
Subculture, 276
Socialization, 277
Six Sigma, 286

QUESTIONS

1. Over the years, large business organizations have steadily reduced the number of layers in the organization structure. What purposes has this profound change in structure served?
2. Small and medium-sized companies are often eager to hire people with about five years of experience working in a large, successful bureaucratic firm like IBM or General Foods. What might be the reason behind the demand for these workers with experience in a bureaucracy?
3. What is the basis for departmentalization in the last hospital you visited, read about, or saw on television? Explain the basis for your answer.
4. Describe the culture of a highly visible organization such as Wal-Mart or Starbucks. Perhaps make first-hand observations should you be visiting either one of these establishments. Use the dimensions of organizational culture to help you build your description.
5. What can first- and middle-level managers, as well as team leaders, do about shaping the culture of a firm?
6. Many career counselors believe that you are more likely to succeed in an organization in which you fit the culture. How could you determine before joining an organization whether you fit its culture?
7. How can a manager tell whether an employee is resisting change?

SKILL-BUILDING EXERCISE 8-A: Comparing Organization Structures

Work individually or in groups to find the organization structure at a local company or any type of organization. It may be possible to accomplish the tasks by e-mail and telephone. Whatever structure you find, provide some kind of explanation for why the particular structure is useful for the organization. For example, a hospital would have a departmental structure such as "emergency room" and "ob-gyn." The reason would be that the departments serve clienteles with radically different needs. Compare your organization structures in class, and see how many different types of structures were found.

SKILL-BUILDING EXERCISE 8-B: The Art of Delegation

Delegation is one of the most important managerial skills, yet delegation does not come easily to most people. For example, two major problems in delegating are (a) turning over an assignment to someone else and neglecting to check progress, or (b) turning over an assignment to someone else yet telling the person exactly how to perform the task, and (c) checking up on the person too frequently. The chapter section about delegation, empowerment, and decentralization presented suggestions for effective delegation that should be consulted to perform the exercise at hand. Your task is to delegate a work or personal-life task to somebody within the next ten days. Then reflect on what happened in terms of such factors as,

- How much difficulty did you have in getting the person to accept the delegation?
- How much checking up on the person did you need?
- Did the task get accomplished?
- What did you learn about delegation?

INTERNET SKILL-BUILDING EXERCISE: Analyzing an Organizational Culture

Every organization has a culture even if the organization has not developed a description of its culture. Search the Internet for several articles about one of your favorite companies, as well as the company Web site. Find at least three statements that describe its culture, such as "this is a highly disciplined organization where every worker keeps focused on the goal," or "this place is a bunch of cowboys and cowgirls running wild." Arrive at a tentative conclusion about the company's culture, based on your findings.

Case Problem 8-A

Reshaping Microsoft

A few years ago a team of business columnists wrote the following commentary:

"Bill Gates is ending his day-to-day involvement with Microsoft and focusing on charity. Because the move offers a time to reflect, here is something Gates should ponder. His reputation as a software developer is assured. But wouldn't breaking up his creation be the best way to secure his legacy?

"Sprawling companies are difficult to manage. Microsoft's businesses stretch from its ubiquitous Windows software to videogame consoles to an Internet portal. Moreover, the company seems to have lost its touch. It has fallen behind Google in Web searching, and its latest operating system is severely delayed. Microsoft may be just too big for Chief Executive Steve Ballmer, or indeed anyone, to handle. Gate's plan to step back may only intensify managerial problems.

"The company has three distinct businesses. Its operating systems are growing slowly, but produce tons of cash. Its suite of Office software products is in a similar position. Meanwhile, Microsoft's other efforts are potentially fast growers, yet mostly burn cash. Separating the company into three business units, or more, would make them easier for mere mortals to manage.

"Moreover, divvying up the company would help to secure Gate's reputation as a great philanthropist. He already plans to give away nearly the entirety of his fortune. Breaking up Microsoft would mean that he has more to give away. Value investors think Microsoft allocates the capital generated by its cash cows poorly. Growth investors think some of the company's efforts, like cell phone-software production, are smothered in such a large organization. Both sets are unhappy, so Microsoft trades at a measly 16 times estimated earnings. A breakup could raise this multiple.

"Of course, the company is still earning billions of dollars and has significantly improved operating results. But Gates was violently against governmental efforts to break up his company in 2001. He may be less defensive if he comes to the decision himself, especially once he removes himself from the daily grind and potentially gains some objectivity.

"And there's one last appealing point: No one would expect Gates to be involved in every offshoot company to the same degree. He can concentrate his interests on the parts of the business he likes best. And who knows, it may even bring out some youthful fire."

Discussion Questions

1. What do you see as the advantages and disadvantages of breaking up Microsoft?
2. Draw an organization chart to reflect the new proposed Microsoft. Draw only the major organizational units and one organizational layer below. Compare your structure to those developed by other individual class member or teams of class members.

Source: Robert Cyran, Rob Cox, and David Vise, "Gates Should Weigh Microsoft Breakup: Divisions Would Aid Value," *The Wall Street Journal*, June 17, 2006, p. B14. Article based on information form *breakingviews.com*.

Case Problem 8-B

Sparking Change at Coke

The faces at Coca-Cola haven't changed much through the decades. The board is a tight-knit group of people whose average age is 67. Seven have served Coke for 20 years or more. The annual meeting in 2006 marked a turning point. The crowd the board faced was altogether different from the complacent gatherings of years past. The audience of roughly 400 people was an odd assemblage of simmering college students, angry water-rights activists, angrier labor-rights activities, dismayed employees, watchful plainclothes security, and white-haired shareholders bewildered by the stock's 52 percent plunge from its high.

CEO Neville Isdell told the crowd, "Next month the Coca-Cola Co. will celebrate its 120th anniversary—120 years since someone paid a nickel for Doc Pemberton's inspiration-in-a-glass at Jacobs Pharmacy. Today consumers invite us into their lives more than a billion times a day for enjoyment, fun, and refreshment. We understand, however, that what has sustained us these first 12 decades will not be sufficient for the future."

When Isdell came out of retirement in 2004 to take over at Coke, he inherited a company that had utterly lost faith in itself, governed by a board that could not leave it alone. A social worker by training, he knew that a transition would take two years. During that time he repaired morale. He and his management team set out to understand how Coke's world had changed—analyzing what beverages people drink and why and when they drink them—and to devise a new roadmap called the Manifesto for Growth. Coke would not diversify away from beverages, they decided. Rather, Coke would deliver on its promise to be a nonalcoholic beverage company with an expanding portfolio to meet consumer needs.

At this annual meeting Isdell declared the transition over. The new Coca-Cola, he promised, will innovate—as it did in the first quarter, launching new products with strange-sounding names like Tab Energy (diet energy drink) and Full Throttle Fury (a citrus-flavored energy concoction). The company has also created glow-in-the-dark aluminum bottles of Coca-Cola to sell at night clubs. "You'll see better marketing and stronger connections with consumers," he told the audience. Coke, he said, would be bold. "You'll see some failures," Isdell said. "As we take more risks, this is something we must accept as part of the regeneration process."

For many years Coke had stayed defiantly rooted in the past, holding on to the belief that its business model was as good as gold: Make cola concentrate for pennies, then sell it for dollars through a global bottling system to a mass market that still pretty much drank what it saw on TV. When bottled water came along, one director called it a "low-margin road to nowhere." The company was late to the game in sports drinks, energy drinks, and coffee, regarding them as low-volume distractions. Coke's board nixed the acquisition of Gatorade, which was then bought by rival Pepsi. Coca-Cola depends on soft drinks for 80 percent of its total sales volume.

In an interview after the annual meeting, Isdell said, "I don't believe we've done more in the past than dabble outside carbonated soft drinks. We have not been able to think creatively enough about sodas themselves. We've often chased volume to the detriment of the business." Now his team is looking at sodas as "potential carriers of health and wellness," searching for new, natural sweeteners, and trying to convince Coke and its bottlers that they can distribute 1,000 brands and packages when they think they can handle only 200. Isdell says part of this job has been to lead the board into this regeneration of the Coca-Cola company.

A key player in Coke's planned transformation is Mary Minnick, the company's head of marketing, strategy, and innovation. "There was a culture of politeness and consensus and talking around an issue, rather than taking it head-on," she says. If Coke employees are upset by the change, too bad: "That's one thing I won't work on."

To Minnick, growth means more than simply boosting sales of Coca-Cola Classic. An innovation involves more than repackaging existing beverages in slightly different flavors. Minnick is exploring new products as far a field as beauty and health care. If she accomplishes even half of what's on the drawing board, she'll usher in the greatest flowering of creativity in the company's history.

Coke is still the most valuable brand in history, according to consultancy Interbrand, which measures how much a company's brand drives its sales and profits. Yet the value of the Coke brand has declined 20 percent since 1999, to $67 billion, according to Interbrand. The

Case Problem 8-B

challenge of reversing this trend, of making Coke more exciting, innovative, and relevant, falls largely on Minnick's shoulders. The marketing dynamo has helped bring a new sense of urgency to everything, from how the company advertises to how it develops new drinks.

Minnick's top priority has been jump-staring Coke's product development. Under her leadership, Coke has launched more than 1,000 new drinks or new variations of existing brands in a 12-month period, including a new male-oriented diet drink called Coca-Cola Zero, as well as a brisk-selling coffee-flavored cola called Coca-Cola Blak. But Minnick knows that, in the long run, new flavors and brand extension won't be enough to make Coke a growth company again. So with the solid backing of Isdell, to whom she reports, Minnick is pushing to transform Coke from a soda-centric organization that was long content to offer "me-too" products in emerging categories to one on the cutting edge of consumer trends.

At a meeting of Coke's top 200 global marketers in Istanbul, Minnick implored her troops to stop thinking in terms of existing drink categories and to start thinking broadly about why people consume beverages in the first place. The goal: to come to market with products which satisfy those needs before the competition does. An example might be a drink that is fortified with vitamins or nutrients that provide women with the same benefits as a facial scrub or cold cream.

In the future, Minnick says, the winners will be the beverage companies that develop breakthrough products that, more often than not, cross over traditional beverage categories—just as Red Bull did when it single-handedly created the energy drink segment. "Like Henry Ford said, 'If I'd asked the consumer[s] what they wanted, they'd have said a faster horse,'" she told her staff in Istanbul.

Another one of Minnick's initiatives has been to instill a culture of accountability in the marketing department and with the company's ad agencies. "Historically, we had a culture where putting the hard issue on the table made some people uncomfortable," she says.

In April 2007, Minnick took a position at a British private equity firm, Lion Capital, as a partner. A contributing factor to her decision to leave was being passed over for the position of chief operating officer.

Discussion Questions

1. Why does this story belong in a chapter that deals with organization change? Shouldn't the Coke story be placed in a chapter exclusively about marketing?
2. In what ways does the Coca-Cola Co. transformation require changes in the attitudes of employees and in the organizational culture?
3. What advice can you offer Isdell Minnick, and her successor to make the Coca-Cola Co. even more successful?

Source: Betsy Morris, "Coke Gets a Jolt," *Fortune*, May 15, 2006, pp. 77–78; Dean Foust, "Meet Mary Minnick. She's Blunt. She's Impatient. And She's Putting the Fizz Back in Tired Coke," *Business Week*, August 7, 2006; Mary Jane Credeur, "Coca-Cola Seeks More Fizz with Non-Soda Lines," *Los Angeles Times* (http://www.latimes.com), August 21, 2006; Renuka Rayasam, "The Pause that Refreshes," *US News and World Report* (www.usnews.com), May 20, 2007.

chapter 9

Staffing and Human Resource Management

Objectives

After studying this chapter and doing the exercises, you should be able to:

1. Explain how human resource management is part of business strategy.
2. Describe the components of organizational staffing.
3. Present an overview of recruitment and selection.
4. Present an overview of employee orientation, training, and development.
5. Explain the basics of a performance evaluation system.
6. Summarize the basics of employee compensation.
7. Understand the role of labor unions in human resource management.

After Kelly Emo joined BEA Systems Inc. she occasionally left during work hours to run personal errands. Soon the San Jose, California, software company began changing her routine. A car detailer started coming to the office. Emo now has her family's Explorer and Jetta scrubbed in the parking lot. BEA soon brought in massage therapists, so she started treating herself to an occasional 20-minute massage. More recently, a roving farmer's market also began visiting, so Emo did some of her grocery shopping outside the corporate cafeteria.

Emo says she seldom has to leave BEA's campus to run errands any more. "I can definitely spend more quality time at work," says the 40-year-old marketing manager, who estimates she squeezes in an extra 45 minutes a day on the job because of the new on-site services.

Jeanne Wu, BEA's senior vice president of human resources, says the on-site services offer benefits for both the company and employees. The convenience of the on-site services makes for happier employees who have more reason to remain on campus.

Mike Lee, who manages a group of engineers at Yahoo!, says he has a budget allocated to employee perks that include gift certificates for on-site services. He recently handed out $60-certificates to his 15-person team for hour-long on-site massages. "It's true that I can keep the team working here longer hours," by using these services, Lee says.

Lee, 29, gets his own car washed every three weeks and his hair cut once a month, all at work. "I'm basically buying time to be more productive at work," he says. Yahoo! also offers valet parking so employees don't waste time finding parking spots.[1]

The on-site personal services offered by BEA and Yahoo! illustrate an imaginative way in which human resource management (HRM) initiatives can be used to enhance employee productivity and retention. This chapter deals with key aspects of human resource management, including how it fits into business strategy, and staffing, including the subactivities of recruitment and selection, training, development, evaluation, and compensation. All managers engage in human resource management to some extent because they engage in activities including recruiting, selecting, training, and evaluating employees. The human resource department assists in these activities and also provides leadership.

HUMAN RESOURCE MANAGEMENT AND BUSINESS STRATEGY

Learning Objective 1

Explain how human resource management is part of business strategy.

The modern role for human resource professionals is that of a partner in helping the organization implement its business strategy. In the words of many HR professionals, "We finally have a seat at the executive table." The implication is that human resource management is an integral part of business strategy. (Human resource management is often referred to as *strategic human resource* management.) Without effective human resource management the company cannot accomplish high-level goals such as competing globally, grabbing market share, and being innovative. For example, unless talented and imaginative employees are recruited (even through outsourcing) innovation cannot be sustained. A major purpose of HRM is to maximize human capital so workers achieve the goals of the organization.

In many organizations, however, human resource managers and professionals are still seen as occupying a minor operational role, carrying out activities such as processing payroll, filing government forms about equal employment opportunity, and recruiting and selecting entry-level workers. Also, in small enterprises, the HR function might be part of the office manager's or owner's responsibility.

Dennis Donovan, the former executive vice-president of human resources in Home Depot, exemplifies how the human resources function contributes

1 Pui Wing Tam and Mylene Mangalindan, "Parking-Lot Perks: Haircuts, Car Washes for Busy Tech Workers," *The Wall Street Journal*, November 9, 2005, pp. A1, A10.

to accomplishing business strategy. He established recruiting partnerships with groups such as AARP and the Department of Veterans Affairs to ensure that Home Depot has ongoing access to talent. One result of the recruiting was merchandising deals with AARP that focused on in-store clinics, and grandparent/grandchild workshops. Another of Donovan's strategic accomplishment was to help form a new organization structure for centralizing merchandising. He formed cross-functional teams to help develop the new organization structure.[2]

PLAY VIDEO

STAFFING AND HUMAN RESOURCE MANAGEMENT

Go to academic.cengage.com/management/dubrin and view the video. In what way does AllState's human resource management philosophy adhere to the new social contract between organization and employee?

A specific way in which HRM contributes to business strategy is by helping to build high-performance work practices. Several of these approaches were mentioned in Chapter 7 about designing jobs for high performance and establishing flexible working hours. Aspects of high-performance work practices described in the present chapter include selection, incentive compensation, and training. The self-managing teams described in Chapter 13 also contribute to high performance. A recent integration of 92 studies found that organizations can increase their performance by 20 percent by implementing high-performance work practices, with the relationship more evident in manufacturing than service settings. The results demonstrate that human resource methods contribute substantially to an organization's performance goals.[3]

A concise way of understanding the strategic role of human resource management is to recognize that human resource activities create value only when they create a sustainable competitive advantage.[4] Assume that a training program developed by human resources helped employees be more responsive to customer needs, and that as a result customer retention increased and so did profits. We can then conclude that human resources helped create a sustainable competitive advantage.

THE STAFFING MODEL AND STRATEGIC HUMAN RESOURCE PLANNING

Learning Objective 2

Describe the components of organizational staffing.

In the model in Exhibit 9-1 the staffing process flows in a logical sequence. Although not every organization follows the same steps in the same sequence, staffing ordinarily proceeds in the way this section will discuss. The arrows pointing to "Retention" in the model suggest that a major strategy of staffing is to retain valuable employees, and that any aspect of staffing can contribute to retention. For example, selecting the right person for the job increases the probability that he or she will enjoy the job and stay with the firm.

2 Jessica Marquez, "Measuring Up," *Workforce Management*, September 11, 2006, pp. 16–17.

3 James Combs, Yongmei Liu, Angela Hall, and David Ketchen, "How Much Do High-Performance Work Practices Matter? A Meta-Analysis of Their Effects on Organizational Performance," *Personnel Psychology*, Autumn 2006, pp. 501–528.

4 Dave Ulrich and Wayne Brockbank, "Focusing on Customers," *HR Magazine*, June 2005, p. 63.

exhibit 9-1 **The Organization Staffing Model**

Under ideal circumstances, organization staffing would proceed through the stages as shown, and would improve employee retention. Terminating employees might also be considered part of staffing.

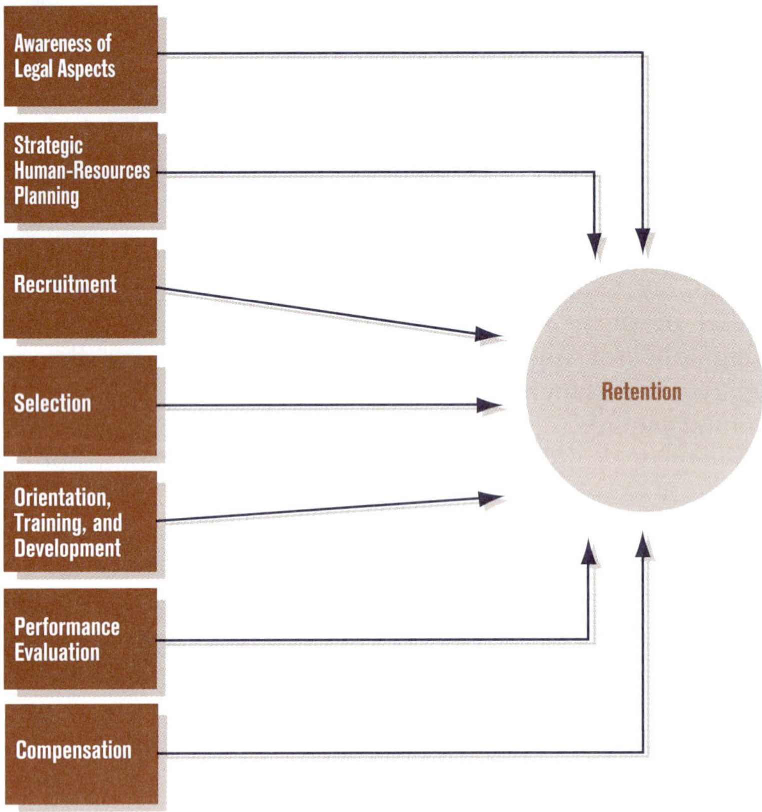

Turnover (or employees not being retained) occurs mainly due to individual, environmental and workplace factors, and these three main factors often work in combination.[5] An example of an *individual factor* might be that a person is not smart enough to cope with all the new learning in a job so he or she quits. However, if the job had been modified, the person might have stayed. *Environmental factors* would include the economy. Employees are more likely to explore job possibilities outside the firm during good economic conditions and low unemployment. Yet workers who believe they are working for an outstanding company are less likely to poke around for a new job even during boom times.

Workplace factors include job enrichment and giving emotional support to workers, both of which are likely to reduce turnover. However, an employee who wanted to live in another climate might quit even an enriched job. Managers have more control over workplace than individual or environmental factors in reducing turnover.

A Monster.com study found that approximately 70 percent of HR managers thought that employee retention is a primary business concern, and

5 Joseph Rosse and Robert Levin, *Talent Flow: A Strategic Approach to Keeping Good Employees, Helping Then Grow, and Letting Them Go* (San Francisco: Jossey-Bass, 2001).

40 percent reported that turnover is increasing. The study also concluded that long-term demographic changes including the retiring baby boomer population might aggravate the problem. Among the retention strategies suggested by the Monster.com study, as well as one conducted by CareerJournal.com are enhancing compensation including benefits, providing opportunities for professional growth and development, creating opportunities for work–life balance, and improving communication with employees.[6] All these topics are discussed in this chapter and other places in the text.

A recent theory of turnover called **job embeddedness** is based on research in a variety of work settings. The theory suggests that a combination of many factors influences whether employees stay with a firm. Among these influences are factors about the job itself, such as bonds with coworkers, the fit between one's skills and job demands, and organization-sponsored community service that the employee perceives as valuable. Off-the-job factors influencing retention include personal, family, and community commitments. For example, a person is less likely to relocate for job purposes when he or she has good contacts on the job and the family is committed to staying in the community.[7]

job embeddedness
A theory of turnover suggesting that a combination of many factors influences whether employees stay with a firm.

affirmative action
An employment practice that complies with antidiscrimination law and correcting past discriminatory practices.

Legal Aspects of Staffing

Federal, state, provincial, and local laws influence every aspect of organizational staffing. Managers and human resource specialists must keep the major provisions of these laws in mind whenever they make decisions about any phase of employment. Exhibit 9-2 summarizes major pieces of U.S. federal legislation that influence various aspects of staffing—not just employee selection. Canada has comparable legislation in both the federal and provincial levels. Managers need to be aware that such legislation exists, and also be familiar with the general provisions of each law or executive order. When a possible legal issue arises, the manager should review the relevant legislation in depth and confer with a company specialist in employment law.

A key aspect of implementing the spirit and letter of employment discrimination law in the United States has been affirmative action programs. To comply with the Civil Rights Act of 1964, employers with federal contracts or subcontracts must develop such programs to end discrimination. **Affirmative action** consists of complying with antidiscrimination law and correcting past discriminatory practices. Under an affirmative action program, employers actively recruit, employ, train, and promote minorities and women who may have been discriminated against by the employer in the past, which resulted in their underrepresentation in certain positions. Part of an affirmative action plan might include a career development program for Native American workers to help them qualify for management positions.

---

6 Study cited in Susan Meisinger, "Workforce Retention: A Growing Concern," *HR Magazine*, April 2006, p. 12.

7 Brooks C. Holtom, Terence R. Mitchell, and Thomas W. Lee, "Increasing Human and Social Capital by Applying Job Embeddedness Theory," No. 4, 2006, p. 319.

exhibit 9-2 Federal Laws Prohibiting Job Discrimination

- Title VII of the Civil Rights Act of 1964 (Title VII) prohibits employment discrimination based on race, color, religion, sex, or national origin.
- The Equal Pay Act of 1963 (EPA) protects men and women who perform substantially equal work in the same establishment from sex-based wage discrimination.
- The Age Discrimination in Employment Act of 1967 (ADEA) protects individuals who are 40 years of age or older.
- Title I and Title V of the Americans with Disabilities Act of 1990 (ADA) prohibits employment discrimination against qualified individuals with disabilities in the private sector, and in state and local governments.
- Sections 501 and 505 of the Rehabilitation Act of 1973 prohibits discrimination against qualified individuals with disabilities who work in the federal government.
- The Civil Rights Act of 1991, which, among other things, provides monetary damages in cases of intentional employment discrimination.

The U.S. Equal Employment Opportunity Commission (EEOC) enforces all of these laws. EEOC also provides oversight and coordination of all federal equal employment opportunity regulations, practices, and policies.

Source: http://www.eeoc.gov/abouteeo/overview_laws.html.

A national debate continues over whether any person in a competitive situation deserves a preference because of race, ethnicity, or sex. The opposing point of view to affirmative action programs is that race, ethnicity, or sex should not be a factor in making employment or business decisions. For example, a job candidate should not be given an edge over other applicants because she is a Hispanic female. What is your opinion on this issue?

An effective way of understanding how these laws might affect the individual is to specify the discriminatory practices prohibited by these laws. Under Title VII, the ADA, and the ADEA, it is illegal to discriminate in any aspect of employment, including hiring and firing; compensation, assignment, or classification of employees; transfer, promotion, layoff, or recall; job advertisements; recruitment; testing; use of company facilities; training and apprenticeship programs; fringe benefits; pay, retirement plans, and disability leave; or other terms and conditions of employment. Discriminatory practices under these laws also include the following:

1. Harassment on the basis of race, color, religion, sex, national origin, disability, or age;
2. Retaliation against an individual for filing a charge of discrimination, participating in an investigation, or opposing discriminatory practices;
3. Employment decisions based on stereotypes or assumptions about the abilities, traits, or performance of individuals of a certain sex, race, age, religion, or ethnic group, or individuals with disabilities; and
4. Denying employment opportunities to a person because of marriage to, or association with, an individual of a particular race, religion, national origin, or an individual with a disability. Title VII also prohibits discrimination because of participation in schools or places of worship associated with a particular racial, ethnic, or religious group.

Although all of the above forms of discrimination may appear clear-cut, a good deal of interpretation is required to decide if a given employee is the subject of discrimination. For example, assume that a woman files a charge of sex discrimination. Later on she is bypassed for promotion. She claims she is now the victim of discrimination, yet the company claims that she did not have the appropriate interpersonal skills to be promoted to a supervisory position.

Among the remedies awarded to individuals judged to be discriminated against are back pay, promotion, reinstatement, and the employer paying attorney's fees and court costs. Compensatory and punitive damages are also possible.

strategic human-resource planning
The process of anticipating and providing for the movement of people into, within, and out of an organization to support the firm's business strategy.

Strategic Human Resource Planning

Staffing begins with a prediction about how many and what types of people will be needed to conduct the work of the firm. Such activity is referred to as **strategic human resource planning.** It is the process of anticipating and providing for the movement of people into, within, and out of an organization to support the firm's business strategy. Management attempts, through planning, to have the right number and right kinds of people at the right time.

Business strategy addresses the financial priorities of the organization with respect to identifying what business the firm should be in, product direction, profit targets, and so forth. Human resource planning addresses the question "What skills are needed for the success of this business?" Planning helps identify the gaps between current employee competencies and behavior and the competencies and behavior needed in the organization's future. Strategic human resource planning consists of four basic steps:[8]

1. *Planning for future needs.* A human resource planner estimates how many people, and with what abilities, the firm will need to operate in the foreseeable future.
2. *Planning for future turnover.* A planner predicts how many current employees are likely to remain with the organization. The difference between this number and the number of employees needed leads to the next step.
3. *Planning for recruitment, selection, and layoffs.* The organization must engage in recruitment, employee selection, or layoffs to attain the required number of employees. A major choice between the commitment strategy in which the firm seeks to develop its own human capital and the secondary strategy of acquiring human capital in the market must be made. Most firms find a balance between training and promoting current employees, and hiring needed talent from the outside.
4. *Planning for training and development.* An organization always needs experienced and competent workers. This step involves planning and providing for training and development programs that ensure the continued supply of people with the right skills.

8 James A. F. Stoner and R. Edwards Freeman, *Management*, 4th ed. (Upper Saddle River, NJ: Prentice Hall, 1989), p. 331; Peter Bamberger and Ilan Meshoulam, *Human Resource Strategy: Formulation, Implementation, and Impact* (Thousand Oaks, CA: Sage, 2000).

management in action

Pinpointing Talent within IBM

Nestled within its forested corporate campus in Armonk, N.Y., an easy stroll from the CEO's office, is IBM's stone-and-glass leadership training center. Big Blue is one of those companies—along with General Electric Co. and Procter & Gamble Co.—that are often cited as the gold standard for talent management. But if the Armonk school is a window on IBM's human-resources history, its future is a technology-powered staff-deployment tool the company is calling its Workforce Management Initiative. Think of the system as a sort of in-house version of Monster.com, the online job site. Built on a database of 33,000 résumés, it lets managers search for employees with the precise skills they'll need for particular projects.

The initiative, which applies what the company learned about logistics over its decades as a computer hardware manufacturer to its human assets, has already become more efficient, saving IBM $500 million. It has also improved productivity. At one time, for example, a healthcare client needed a consultant with a clinical background. The system almost instantly targeted Lynn Yarbrough, a former registered nurse—a search that would have taken more than a week in the old days.

But the initiative's greatest impact may be its ability to help managers analyze what skills staffers possess and how those talents match up to the business outlook. The goal is to train people ahead of anticipated changes. In a recent year, IBM spent $400 million of its $750 million employee-education budget on instructing people in the skills it thinks will be hot in the future.

Questions

1. Identify two skills you would enter into the Workforce Management Initiative if you were an IBM employee.
2. Do you think the Workforce Management Initiative should include both hard (technical or discipline related) and soft (interpersonal) skills? Explain your reasoning.

Source: Nanette Byrnes, "Pinpointing Inside Up-and-Comers at IBM," *Business Week,* October 10, 2005, p. 72.

Strategic business plans usually involve shifting around or training people. Human resource planning can therefore be an important element in the success of strategies. Human resource planning can also be a strategic objective in itself. For example, one strategic objective of PepsiCo is the development of talented people. Human resource planning contributes to attaining this objective by suggesting on- and off-the-job experiences to develop talent.

The accompanying Management in Action illustrates how one of the world's best-known companies searches for talent within the organization to meet its forecast for its business outlook. The talent search can also be perceived as a recruiting tool.

RECRUITMENT

Learning Objective 3

Present an overview of recruitment and selection.

Recruitment is the process of attracting job candidates with the right characteristics and skills to fit job openings. The preferred recruiting method is to begin with a large number of possible job candidates and then give serious consideration to a much smaller number. However, if few candidates are available, the recruiter must be less selective or not fill the position.

Purposes of Recruitment

recruitment
The process of attracting job candidates with the right characteristics and skills to fill job openings.

A major purpose of recruiting and selection is to find qualified employees who fit well into the culture of the organization. Most job failures are attributed to workers being a "poor fit" rather than because of poor technical skills or experience. The poor fit often implies poor relationships with coworkers. A positive person—organization fit is usually based on a mesh between the person's values and those of the organization. For example, a person who values technology and diversity among people—and is qualified—would be a good candidate to work for Xerox. A synthesis of many studies indicates that person—organization fit is positively related to job satisfaction, commitment to the firm, and intention to quit.[9] An important implication is that a good person—organization fit helps increase retention.

Another important purpose of recruiting is to sell the organization to high-quality prospective candidates. Recruiters must select candidates who can function in one job today and be retrained and promoted later, as company needs dictate. Flexible candidates of this type are in demand; therefore, a recruiter may need to sell the advantages of his or her company to entice them to work there. However, an important principle of successful recruiting is to present an honest picture of the firm about such factors as growth opportunities, the amount of travel, and the type of culture.[10]

Job Descriptions and Job Specifications

A starting point in recruiting is to understand the nature of the job to be filled and the qualifications sought. Toward this end, the recruiter should be supplied with job descriptions and job specifications. The job description explains in detail what the jobholder is supposed to do. It is therefore a vital document in human resource planning and performance evaluation. An exception is that in some high-level positions, such as CEO, the person creates part of his or her own job description. Refer back to Exhibit 7-2 for a sample job description. A **job specification** (or person specification) stems directly from the job description. It is a statement of the personal characteristics needed to perform the job. A job specification usually includes the education, experience, knowledge, and skills required to perform the job successfully.

Many firms see job descriptions and job specifications decreasing in relevance, as explained in the study of job design in Chapter 7. Organizations often expect workers to occupy flexible roles rather than specific positions, to meet the need for rapid change. An example of flexibility might be a worker whose role is to learn new job-related software, whereas a job description might mention specific software that must be mastered.

job specification
A statement of the personal characteristics needed to perform the job.

9 Amy L. Kristof-Brown, Ryan D. Zimmerman, and Eric C. Johnson, "Consequences of Individuals' Fit at Work: A Meta-Analysis of Person-Job, Person-Organization, Person-Group, and Person-Supervisor Fit," *Personnel Psychology*, Summer 2005, p. 310.
10 Carolyn Brandon, "Truth in Recruitment Branding," *HR Magazine*, November 2005, pp. 89–96.

exhibit 9-3 Sources of External Hires

Despite extensive Internet activity, the largest source of external hires continues to be employee referrals. (Figures refer to percentage of referrals from the source. Because of rounding errors, both tables add to 100.1 percent.)

Employee referrals 27.1	Walk-ins 4.2
Internet 24.7	Temp-to-hire 3.2
College 8.0	Internet Sources
Direct sourcing 7.4	Company Web site 49.2
Other 5.5	Monster 15.2
Career fairs 5.2	Career Builder 9.0
Third-party agencies 5.2	HotJobs 4.2
Don't know 5.0	All niche sites 22.5
Print 4.6	

Source: Based on data from the Society for Human Resource Management, reported in John Zappe, "Be Aggressive or Be Gone," *Workforce Management*, February 27, 2006, p. 29.

Recruiting Sources

The term *recruitment* covers a wide variety of methods for attracting employees to the firm, even through such methods as a manager handing out business cards to people she meets while skiing. Recruiting sources are classified into four major categories, as described below. Exhibit 9-3 presents a more detailed breakdown of recruiting sources used by a variety of companies.

1. *Present employees.* As a standard recruiting method, companies post job openings so the current employees may apply. Managers also recommend current employees for transfer or promotion. A human resources information system can identify current employees with the right skills and competencies which minimizes the need to reject unqualified internal applicants. Temporary workers are another source of potential full-time workers, providing the company has a temp-to-hire agreement with the employment agency. T-Mobile used this approach successfully to hire cell engineers and technicians.[11]
2. *Referrals by present and former employees.* For established firms, present employees can be the primary recruiters. Satisfied employees may be willing to nominate relatives, friends, acquaintances, and neighbors for job openings. The effectiveness of current employees in the recruiting process comes from their ability to explain the culture of the firm to prospects, such as pointing out that the company expects its employees to work hard and long.[12] An effective approach is to dedicate a company Web site (Intranet)

11 John Zappe, "Temp-to-Hire is Becoming a Full-Time Practice at Many Firms," *Workforce Management*, June 2005, p. 82.
12 Kerri Koss Morehart, "How to Create an Employee Referral Program That Really Works," *HRfocus*, January 2001, pp. 3–4.

for employee referrals. Former employees can be effective recruiting sources, providing they left the company on good terms. An angry former employee might be prompted to refer poorly qualified candidates. Employee referral programs sometimes offer financial incentives to employees when a referred person joins the firm.

3. *External sources other than online approaches.* Potential employees outside an organization can be reached in many ways. The best known of these methods is a recruiting advertisement, including print, radio, and sometimes television. Other external sources include (a) placement offices, (b) private and public employment agencies, (c) labor union hiring halls, (d) walk-ins (people who show up at the firm without invitation), and (d) write-ins (people who write unsolicited job-seeking letters). Labor union officials believe that they simplify the hiring process for employers because only qualified workers are admitted to the union.
4. *Online recruiting including company Web sites.* The Internet is a standard source of recruiting job candidates. It offers hundreds of Web sites free to job candidates, and sometimes to employers. Online recruiting includes listing open positions on company Web sites and on job boards, and surfing sites for possible candidates. A key part of the service is the job board for posting openings, to which candidates submit their credentials. Many companies focus their online recruiting on the career section of the company Web site. Also, many job seekers go directly to company Web sites instead of using job boards.

A new variation of online recruiting is for companies to create pages on social-networking Web sites such as Facebook and MySpace to attract possible candidates. The page will often contain information and discussion boards aimed at students. The social Web site offers the advantage of allowing for continuing dialogue with potential job candidates.[13]

Finding employees or finding a job is best done through a variety of methods mentioned here. A noteworthy example is the approach taken by Wynn Las Vegas, when searching for 9,000 poker dealers, housekeepers, and cocktail servers for a new Las Vegas hotel and casino. A full-page ad in the local newspaper drew 100,000 applications. The ad was followed up by a Web site, http://www.wynnjobs.com, that allows for applying for positions and tracking their progress online. Managers can access the site any time to measure recruiting results, such as how many people applied for the poker dealer positions.[14]

A logical career interpretation to make of the data presented in Exhibit 9-3 is that being referred by another employee or using the Internet are the two most productive sources of finding a job for yourself.

---

13 Erin White, "Employers Are Putting New Face on Web Recruiting," *The Wall Street Journal*, January 8, 2007, p. B3.

14 Jennifer C. Berkshire, "For Massive Hiring Effort, Vegas Resort Wagers on High-Tech, Tried-and-True," *Workforce Management*, March 2005, pp. 65–66.

Global Recruiting

Global recruiting presents unique challenges. Multinational businesses must have the capability to connect with other parts of the globe to locate talent. Company recruiters must meet job specifications calling for multiculturalism (being able to conduct business in other cultures) on top of more traditional skills. To fill international positions, the recruiter may have to develop overseas recruiting sources. The recruiter may also require the assistance of a bilingual interviewer to help assess the candidate's ability to conduct business in more than one language.

Global recruiting for managers can be difficult because candidates must be found who can blend the work practices of two cultures. A Dell representative noted in relation to finding a manager for a facility in China that veteran executives in China often have a Confucian mind-set that views hands-on management as suited to lower-level workers. In contrast, Dell needs leaders familiar with the Chinese business culture, but also willing to use a hands-on approach to daily operations.[15]

SELECTION

Selecting qualified candidates is the lifeblood of the firm. Selecting the right candidate for a job is part of a process that includes recruitment, as shown in Exhibit 9-4. A hiring decision is based on information gathered in two or more of these steps. For instance, a person might receive a job offer if he or she was impressive in the interview, scored well on the tests, and had good references. Another important feature of this selection model allows for an applicant to be

exhibit 9-4 A Model for Selection

The selection process generally proceeds in the steps as indicated here, yet many exceptions can occur in terms of which steps are included and in what order. For example, some employers do not use psychological testing, and others have candidates complete the application form first.

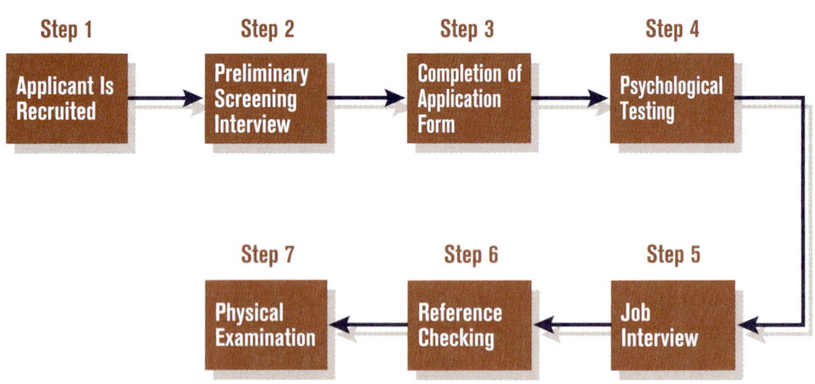

15 Ed Frauenheim, "Dell Reboots Recruitment for International Approach," *Workforce Management*, April 10, 2006, p. 24.

rejected at any point. An applicant who is abusive to the employment specialist might not be asked to fill out an application form.

Preliminary Screening Interview

Selection begins as soon as candidates come to the attention of the recruiter, often by cover letter and job résumé. If candidates come close to fitting the job specifications, a brief screening interview follows, frequently by telephone. The purpose of the screening interview is to determine whether the candidate should be given further consideration. One area of disqualification would be for the candidate to demonstrate such poor oral communication skills over the phone that the person is excluded from consideration for a job requiring considerable customer contact. "Knockout" questions are sometimes used for quickly disqualifying candidates. Assume a person applying for a supervisory position in a nursing home is asked, "How well do you get along with senior citizens?" A candidate who responds, "Very poorly" is immediately disqualified.

An important suggestion here is to be at your best for the telephone interview, including total concentration on the tasks at hand. Rehearse your presentation in advance.

Psychological Testing

Hundreds of different tests are used in employment testing, and such testing is standard practice in about one-half of firms. All tests are psychological tests in the sense that measuring human ability is an important part of psychology.

Types of Psychological Tests

The four principle types of psychological tests used in employment screening are achievement, aptitude, personality, and honesty and integrity.

1. *Achievement tests* sample and measure an applicant's knowledge and skills. They require applicants to demonstrate their competency on job tasks or related subjects. A test requiring the applicant to deal with customer situations is an achievement test. The most widely used achievement tests relate to computer skills: typing/data entry, word-processing software, and spreadsheet analysis.
2. *Aptitude tests* measure the potential for performing satisfactorily on the job, given sufficient training. Mental ability tests, the best-known variety of aptitude tests, measure the ability to solve problems and learn new material. Mental ability tests measure such specific aptitudes as verbal reasoning, numerical reasoning, and spatial relations (the ability to visualize in three dimensions). Many National Football League teams still use the Wonderlic Personnel Test, a brief test of mental ability, to help screen draftees. The highest scores on the mental ability tests are attained by quarterbacks and offensive linemen.[16] Tests of *emotional intelligence* are gaining in popularity whereby the candidate is measured on the ability to deal with people's feelings and emotions. However, emotional intelligence can also be classified as an aspect of personality.

16 Allen Barra, "Do These NFL Scores Count for Anything?" *The Wall Street Journal*, April 25, 2006, p. D6.

3. *Personality tests* measure personal traits and characteristics that could be related to job performance. The use of personality tests still sparks controversy, but research during the past decade shows positive connection between certain personality tests and subsequent job performance. Critics express concern that these tests invade privacy and are too imprecise to be useful. Nevertheless, personality factors can profoundly influence job performance. Personality tests are increasingly used to screen applicants for entry-level jobs at call centers, retail stores, and other customer-contact positions.[17] Exhibit 9-5 lists the major personality factors related to job performance.

   Personality tests were included in three studies that followed participants from early childhood to retirement. Conscientiousness, one of the major personality factors, was found to be a good predictor of career success as measured by compensation and promotions, as well as personal satisfaction. Also, having tendencies toward emotional instability was negatively related to compensation and promotions.[18]

4. *Honesty and integrity tests* are designed to measure a person's honesty or integrity as it relates to job behavior. (Honesty relates most specifically to lying, whereas integrity refers to sticking with your principles.) These tests are frequently used in workplaces such as retail stores, banks, and warehouses, where employees have access to cash or merchandise. Other types of work in which employees may potentially damage computers or access secret documents also require a prediction of employee honesty. A major factor measured by integrity

exhibit 9-5 The Big Five Personality Factors

Many psychologists believe that the basic structure of human personality is represented by what they call the Big Five factors. These factors influence job performance. Conscientiousness, for example, is related to the tendency to produce quality work. Furthermore, these factors can be measured by psychological tests.

I. **Neuroticism.** This factor relates to whether a person is anxious, depressed, angry, embarrassed, emotional, or worried. A person of low neuroticism—or high emotional stability—is calm and confident, and usually in control.

II. **Extraversion.** Extraversion (which is the same as extroversion) relates to whether a person is social, gregarious, assertive, talkative, or active. A shy person scores high on introversion.

III. **Openness to experience.** This factor relates to whether a person is imaginative, cultured, curious, original, broad-minded, intelligent, or artistically sensitive.

IV. **Agreeableness.** This factor relates to whether a person is courteous, flexible, trusting, good-natured, cooperative, forgiving, soft hearted, or tolerant.

V. **Conscientiousness.** This factor relates to whether a person is careful, thorough, responsible, organized, or prepared. Conscientiousness also relates to whether a person is hard-working, achievement-oriented, and persevering.

---

17 Erin White, "Personality Tests Aim to Stop 'Fakers'," *The Wall Street Journal*, November 6, 2006, p. B3.

18 Timothy A. Judge et al., "The Big Five Personality Traits, General Mental Ability, and Career Success Across the Life Span," *Personnel Psychology*, Autumn 1999, pp. 621–652.

tests is social conscientiousness. People who score high on this personality factor show a much greater likelihood of following organizational rules. Despite controversy over their use, honesty and integrity tests are widely used. Years of experience with integrity and honesty tests indicate that these tests can help identify job candidates with a propensity to steal and engage in other counterproductive behavior (such as computer hacking).[19]

Validity and Equal Employment Opportunity

The EEOC insists that psychological tests (integrity tests included) be scientifically accurate, job-related, and not discriminatory against any group. These rules also apply to other selection instruments, including application forms and interviews. A specific provision requires a validity study when a selection procedure shows an adverse impact on any race, sex, or ethnic group. A *validity study* is a statistical and scientific method of seeing if a selection device does predict job performance. Do high scorers perform well on the job? Do low scorers tend to be poor performers? An adverse impact as defined by the EEOC occurs when the selection ratio (acceptance rate) for protected groups is less than four-fifths of the selection ratio for the unprotected group. For example, if 80 out of 100 while males are accepted through a company-wide selection procedure then, 64 out of 100 Hispanic males should be accepted ($4/5 \times 80 = 64$).

The most consistent finding about the effectiveness of psychological tests in predicting job performance stems from a long series of studies concerning general intelligence and conscientiousness. In general, employees who have good problem-solving ability and are conscientious are likely to perform well in most jobs.[20] (These findings assume that the employee also has the necessary education and job skills. Yet for basic jobs, the ability to learn and dependability are more important than experience and already existing skills.) General problem-solving ability is measured by mental ability tests, and conscientiousness by a Big Five personality test. A straightforward explanation of these findings is that a bright person will learn quickly, and a conscientious person will try hard to get the job done.

The Job Interview and Job Simulations

The job interview is more comprehensive than the screening interview, covering topics such as education, work experience, special skills and abilities, hobbies, and interests. Interviewers frequently use the candidate's résumé as a source of topics. For example, "I notice you have worked for four employers in three years. Why is that?" Testing results may also provide clues for additional questioning. If a candidate scored low on a scale measuring conscientiousness, the interviewer might ask about the candidate's punctuality and error rate.

---

19 Leonard D. Goodstein and Richard I. Lanyon, "Applications of Personality Assessment to the Workplace: A Review," *Journal of Business and Psychology*, Spring 1999, p. 317; James E. Wanek, Paul R. Sackett, and Deniz S. Ones, "Towards and Understanding of Integrity Test Similarities and Differences: An Item-Level Analysis of Seven Tests," *Personnel Psychology*, Winter 2003, pp. 873–894.

20 Orlando Behling, "Employee Selection: Will Intelligence and Conscientiousness Do the Job?" *Academy of Management Executive*, February 1998, pp. 77–86; Goodstein and Lanyon, "Applications of Personality Assessment," p. 295.

realistic job preview A complete disclosure of the potential negative features of a job to a job candidate.

behavioral interviewing A style of interviewing in which the interviewer asks questions whose answers reveal behaviors that would be either strengths or weaknesses in a given position.

Employment interviews are more valid when the interviewer is trained and experienced. Evidence also suggests that when the interviewer carefully follows a format, predictions about job performance tend to be more accurate.[21] Validity may also increase when several candidates are interviewed for each position, because comparisons can be made among the applicants.

Job interviews serve a dual purpose. The interviewer tries to decide whether the interviewee is appropriate for the organization. At the same time, the interviewee tries to decide whether the job and organization fit him or her. An important approach to helping both the organization and the individual to make the right decision is to offer a **realistic job preview,** a complete disclosure of the potential negative features of a job to a job candidate.[22] For example, an applicant for a call-center position might be told, "At times customers will scream and swear at you because a computer file has crashed. Around holiday time many frustrated customers go ballistic." Telling job applicants about potential problems leads to fewer negative surprises and less turnover.

Exhibit 9-6 presents guidelines for conducting a job interview. Several of the suggestions reflect a screening approach referred to as **behavioral interviewing** because the answers to many of the questions reveal actual job behaviors relevant to a given position. The airline marketing manager might be instructed, "Give me an example of what you have done in the past to compete with a lower-price competitor." If the candidate lacks much job experience, a behavioral question can be asked about a characteristic important to the job, such as resiliency.[23] The candidate might be asked, "Tell me about how you acted the last time you were rejected for something you really wanted?"

An extension of behavioral interviewing is to give the job applicant a job simulation (work task to perform) to help determine job qualifications. An applicant for a tax preparer position might be asked to complete a tax form based on raw data supplied by the interviewer. An applicant for a managerial position might be observed handling a bunch of urgent e-mail messages including customer complaints. A public relations firm in Los Angeles asks candidates for account rep positions to study a client and then write a pitch.[24]

Job simulations are mostly relevant for experienced candidates, whereas as many people are hired for positions they have never performed. An advantage of job simulations is that they tend to be perceived as fair by job applicants because the simulations appear to be relevant, as suggested by a study with 754 applicants for U.S. government positions.[25]

21 Richard A. Posthuma, Frederick Pl. Morgeson, and Michael A. Campion, "Beyond Employment Interview Validity: A Comprehensive Narrative Review of Recent Research and Trends Over Time," *Personnel Psychology*, Spring 2002, p. 42.

22 Robert D. Bretz Jr. and Timothy A. Judge, "Realistic Job Previews: A Test of the Adverse Self-Selection Hypothesis," *Journal of Applied Psychology*, April 1998, pp. 330–337.

23 Andrea C. Poe, "Graduate Work: Behavioral Interviewing Can Tell You If an Applicant Just Out of College Has Traits Needed for the Job," *HR Magazine*, October 2003, pp. 95–100.

24 "Reduce the Cost & Grief of Bad Hires," *Executive Leadership*, November 2006, p. 5.

25 Deidra J. Schleicher, Vija Venkataramani, Frederick P. Morgeson, and Michael A. Campion, "So You Didn't Get the Job ... Now What Do You Think? Examining Opportunity-To-Perform Fairness Perceptions," *Personnel Psychology*, Autumn 2006, pp. 559–590.

exhibit 9-6 **Guidelines for Conducting an Effective Selection Interview**

1. **Prepare in advance.** Prior to the interview, carefully review the applicant's job application form and résumé. Keep in mind several questions worthy of exploration, such as "I notice you have done no previous selling. Why do you want a sales job now?" Job candidates who submit a video résumé will often provide some additional areas for questioning, such as asking about the quality of the candidate's oral communication skills and ability to smile at customers.
2. **Find a quiet place free from interruptions.** Effective interviewing requires careful concentration. Also, the candidate deserves the courtesy of an uninterrupted interview. Do not access e-mail, look at the computer screen, use a BlackBerry, or engage in telephone conversations during the interview.
3. **Take notes during the interview.** Take notes on the content of what is said during the interview. Also, record your observations about the person's statements and behavior. For example, "Candidate gets very nervous when we talk about previous work history."
4. **Use a brief warm-up period.** A standard way of relaxing a job candidate is to spend about five minutes talking about neutral topics, such as the weather. This brief period can be extended by asking about basic facts, such as the person's address and education.
5. **Ask open-ended questions.** To encourage the employee to talk, ask questions that call for more than a one- or two-word answer. Sometimes a request for information—a statement like "Tell me about your days at business school"—works like an open-ended question.
6. **Follow an interview format.** Effective interviewers carefully follow a predetermined interview format. They ask additional questions that are based on responses to the structured questions.
7. **Encourage the job candidate.** The easiest way to keep an interviewee talking is to give that person encouragement. Standard encouragements include "That's very good," "How interesting," "I like your answer," and "Excellent."
8. **Dig for additional details.** When the interviewee brings up a topic worthy of exploration, dig for additional facts. Assume the interviewee says, "I used to work as a private chauffeur, but then I lost my driver's license." Noticing a red flag, the interviewer might respond, "Why did you lose your license?"
9. **Spend most of the interview time listening.** An experienced job interviewer spends little time talking. It is the interviewee who should be doing the talking.
10. **Provide the candidate ample information about the organization.** Answer any relevant questions.

The accompanying Management in Action illustrates how complex and subtle job interviews can be, and how anything you do during the selection process might be observed and interpreted.

management in action

The Job Audition at Southwest Airlines

You don't just get interviewed when you apply for at job at Southwest Airlines. You get auditioned—and it starts the moment you call for an application. Given that ultra-friendly service is critical to the carrier's success, it is little wonder that HR managers don't wait until the interview to start screening. When a candidate calls for an application, managers jot down anything memorable about the conversation, be it good or bad. The same is true when the company flies recruits out for interviews. They receive special tickets, which alert gate agents, flight attendants, and others to pay special attention: Are they friendly to others or griping about service and slurping cocktails at 8 a.m.? If the candidate behavior employees observe seems promising—or not—they're likely to pass it on to HR.

Even when recruits aren't on the spot, they're on the spot. During group interviews for

(Continued)

management in action (Continued)

The Job Audition at Southwest Airlines

screening flight attendants, applicants take turns giving three-minute speeches about themselves in front of as many as 50 others. The catch? Managers are watching the audience as closely as the speaker. Candidates who pay attention pass the test; those who seem bored or distracted get bounced. "We want to know how they interact with people when they think they are not being evaluated," says Southwest recruiter Michael Burkhardt. The screening method not only keeps turnover low (about 5.5 percent annually) but keeps customers happy. Every year since 1987, the carrier has received the lowest number of passenger complaints in the industry.

Questions

1. How ethical is it for Southwest managers and HR specialists to make observations about the behavior of job candidates even when the candidates do not know that they are being evaluated?
2. How good a predictor of how people will perform on the job is spontaneous behavior, such as seeming bored or distracted when watching other job candidates make presentations?

Source: Michael V. Copeland, "Secret 08: Turn the Interview Into an All-Encompassing Tryout," *Business 2.0*, April 2006, p. 85.

To personalize the job interview process, go through the checklist presented in Exhibit 9-7 just to assure that you are on the top of your game for your next interview.

Reference Checking and Background Investigation

A **reference check** is an inquiry to a second party about a job candidate's suitability for employment. The two main topics explored in reference checks are past job performance and the ability to get along with coworkers. However, asking about any evidence of violent behavior has become more frequent. Former and prospective employers have a qualified privilege to discuss an employee's past performance. As long as the information is given to a person with a legitimate interest in receiving it, discussion of an employee's past misconduct or poor performance is permissible under law. Also, many state laws hold employers blameless if the information they share with a reference checker is truthful and without malice.[26] In spite of such rulings, many past employers are hesitant to provide complete references because job applicants have legal access to written references unless they specifically waive this right in writing (Privacy Act of 1974).

reference check An inquiry to a second party about a job candidate's suitability for employment.

Background investigations are closely related to reference checks, except that they focus on information from sources other than former employers. A survey by the Society for Human Resource Management indicates that 96 percent of employers use background checks. The growth of databases accessible through the Internet has facilitated reference checking.[27] Areas investigated include driving record, possible criminal charges or convictions, creditworthiness, disputes

26 Joe Mullich, "Cracking the ex-Files," *Workforce Management*, September 2003, pp. 51–54.
27 Jennifer Schramm, "Background Checking," *HR Magazine*, January 2005, p. 128.

exhibit 9-7 The Job Interviewee Checklist

Most readers are already familiar with most of the behaviors and attitudes associated with having a successful job interview. Nevertheless, going through the checklist of behaviors presented below in the form of questions can serve as a quick reminder of how to be at your best during a job interview.

1. Have I visited the organization's Web site to learn more about the company, and done an Internet search to read a few articles about the company?
2. Have I investigated which style of clothing (such as business formal versus business casual) would be preferred by HR and the interviewing manager?
3. Do I plan to look relaxed and fresh during the interview by resting, exercising, and showering as close to interview time as feasible?
4. Have I rehearsed a discussion of my strengths and areas for needed development?
5. Have I rehearsed a scenario of how I solved a difficult job problem or took care of an emergency?
6. Can I describe my job and educational history without hesitation?
7. Am I prepared to put away my cell phone (and keep it turned off) or personal digital assistant during the entire interview?
8. Will I be able to resist the temptation of frequently glancing at the interviewer's computer monitor?
9. Do I have a few intelligent questions in mind to ask the interviewer?
10. Am I prepared to listen to the interviewer as well as ask questions?
11. Will I ask questions about the nature of the work and challenges instead of asking about factors such as vacation time and personal leave time?
12. Will I be able to refrain from making negative statements about people I worked with in the past?
13. Will I be able to give examples of how I have been a team player?
14. Will I be able to give examples of having taken on some leadership responsibility (even for a project)?
15. Am I prepared to look relaxed and smile frequently?
16. Am I prepared to make a few comments about current events if the topic is relevant to the interview?
17. Am I prepared to explain how I would like to make a contribution?
18. Will I be able to refrain from talking about how this job will give me the experience I need to achieve my career goals?
19. Will I make only statements of facts about me that can be verified?
20. If the job interests me, will I have enough courage to indicate that I would accept an offer?
21. After the interview is completed will I remember to thank the interviewer for his or her time?

Interpretation: I can hear you saying "Duh" in response to a few of the above checklist items. Yet, you would be surprised how many candidates—even for top-level executive positions—blow job interviews by violating these suggestions. The more yes answers you gave, and assuming you are qualified for the position, the better your chances are for receiving a job offer.

with the IRS, and coworkers' and neighbors' comments about a candidate's reputation. Many employers believe that a good credit record reflects dependability, and the opposite as well. A concern for both employers and job candidates is that many credit reports are inaccurate.

Fingerprint checking to screen out applicants with a criminal record is gaining in use, mostly because of legal requirements for a variety of professional and nonprofessional positions. About 9 million fingerprint impressions are sent to the Federal Bureau of Investigation annually for a criminal-background check. As you can imagine, many privacy advocates and forensic experts are concerned about using fingerprints as part of background checking.[28]

---

28 Gary Fields, "Ten-Digit Truth Check," *The Wall Street Journal*, June 7, 2005, p. B1.

One justification for background investigations is that so many job candidates present untrue information in résumés and job interviews. An estimated 40 percent to 70 percent of job applicants enhance their work histories in their résumés and during the interview.[29] The many financial scandals in the executive suite in recent years have prompted more thorough background investigations of candidates for top-level management positions. Executives also have been found to misrepresent facts on their résumé, such as claiming a college degree never earned.

Physical Examination and Drug Testing

The physical examination remains a key part of preemployment screening. The exam gives some indication as to the person's physical ability to handle the requirements of particular jobs. For example, a person with a history of four heart attacks would be a poor candidate for a high-stress managerial position. The physical exam also provides a basis for later comparisons. This step lessens the potential for an employee to claim that the job caused a particular injury or disease. For example, after one year on the job, an employee might claim that the job created a fusion of two vertebrae. If the preemployment physical showed evidence of two fused vertebrae before the employee was hired, the employer would have little to fear from the claim.

The importance of the physical examination continues to increase since the passage of the Americans with Disabilities Act. As long as the candidate can perform the essential aspects of the job, including the employer making reasonable accommodations, he or she cannot be disqualified. However, if the person's disability prevents him or her from performing key aspects of the job, the person could be disqualified physically. For example, a person with vision in only one eye might lack the depth perception required to be a helicopter pilot.

About 60 percent of large companies test all job applicants for use of illegal drugs, showing a gradual decline as an employment practice. (Executives as well as entry-level workers can be drug abusers.) Abuse of prescription drugs is also a widespread problem. Testing for substance abuse includes blood analysis, urinalysis, analysis of hair samples, observations of eyes, and examination of skin for punctures.

Some people raise the concern that inaccurate drug testing may unfairly deny employment to worthy candidates. A strong argument in favor of drug testing, however, is that employees who are drug abusers may create such problems as lowered productivity, lost time from work, and misappropriation of funds. Accident and absenteeism rates for drug (as well as alcohol) abusers are substantial, and they also experience more health problems.

Cross-Cultural Selection

As with cross-cultural recruitment, most of the selection guidelines and techniques already mentioned can be applied cross-culturally. Many selection devices, such as widely used psychological tests, are published in languages

29 Joey George and Kent Marett, "The Truth About Lies," *HR Magazine*, May 2004, p. 87.

besides English, especially Spanish. Managers and employment interviewers gathering information about job candidates from other countries should familiarize themselves with key facts about the other culture. For example, in some countries a baccalaureate (or "bac") is equivalent to an American high school diploma, not a bachelor's degree.

A key aspect of cross-cultural selection is choosing workers who will fit well as *expatriates*, those individuals sent to work in affiliates in other countries. One predictor of success is the desire for an out-of-the-country assignment. Key personality traits of relevance for overseas assignments are flexibility, openness to experience, sense of humor, and interest in others. Matching the person's style to the culture is another key success factor. A human resources professional says, "You could have a top sales person in the United States who is aggressive and a high achiever, but who will fail in Japan for the very reason he's a success in the United States."[30]

After being recruited, job candidates pass through all the selection screens, such as the physical exam, before being hired. After making the hiring decision and applicant acceptance, human resource specialists and new employees complete all the necessary forms, such as those relating to taxes and benefits. Next is orientation.

ORIENTATION, TRAINING, AND DEVELOPMENT

Learning Objective 4

Present an overview of employee orientation, training, and development.

Most firms no longer operate under a "sink or swim" philosophy when it comes to employee learning. Instead, employees are oriented to the firm, and later trained and developed.

Employee Orientation

A new employee usually begins his or her new job by attending an orientation program. An **employee orientation program** more formally acquaints new employees with the company and imparts information about the corporate culture. Part of the orientation may deal with small but important matters, such as telling the employee how to get a parking sticker. Large firms offer elaborate orientation programs conducted by human resource specialists. The program may include tours of the buildings, talks by department heads, video presentations, printed information, and visits to the company Web site.

Employee orientation also conveys to new employees the specific nature of their job and expectations in terms of performance. In some firms, a buddy system is part of the orientation. A buddy, a peer from the new employee's department, shows the new employee around and fills in information gaps. A growing orientation practice is to assign a new employee a mentor who will help him or her better understand the organization, and also serve as a resource person for resolving problems. Your mentor is supposed to check in with you regularly to discuss progress, even by instant messaging.

employee orientation program
A formal activity designed to acquaint new employees with the organization.

30 The quote and information in the same paragraph are from Andrea C. Poe, "Selection Savvy," *HR Magazine*, April 2002, p. 78.

training
Any procedure intended to foster and enhance learning among employees, particularly directed at acquiring job skills.

e-learning
A Web-based form of computer-based training.

Another aspect of orientation is informal socialization. In this process, coworkers introduce new employees to aspects of the organizational culture. Coworkers might convey, for example, how well motivated a new employee should be or the competence level of key people in the organization. The disadvantage of informal orientation is that it may furnish the new employee with misinformation.

Training and Development

Training and development deal with systematic approaches to improve employee skills and performance. **Training** is any procedure intended to foster and enhance learning among employees and particularly directed at acquiring job skills. Rapid changes in technology and the globalization of business have spurred the growth of training programs. Training programs exist to teach hundreds of different skills such as equipment repair, performance evaluation, software utilization, and budget preparation. Training can develop both hard skills (technical, scientific, and numerical) and soft skills (interpersonal skills and attitudes). Employee training and development are both based on the belief that developing talent internally is a good investment.

A substantial amount of skills training in industry is delivered through computers, including the Internet. **E-learning** is a Web-based form of computer-based training. Many learning programs are computer-based without being delivered over the Internet. For example, a CD might be used for product training. An e-learning course is usually carefully structured, with specific lesson plans for the student. E-learning helps deal with the challenge of training workers who are geographically dispersed. (Of course, books and training manuals could also deal with this problem.) Another feature of e-learning is that it is often interactive. The computer provides a stimulus or prompt, to which the trainee responds. The computer then analyzes the response and provides feedback to the student. A question in a customer service course might ask trainees to evaluate the following response to a customer complaint: "If you don't like my answer, go speak to my boss." A message would then appear suggesting that the trainee take more ownership of the problem.

Related to e-learning is delivering training content by MP3 players, enabling workers to receive training at any spare moment, or just-in-time, such as when trying to understand how to use a new machine or fix a customer problem. The system works by transforming training content into podcasts, so the employee can train anywhere, even on an airplane or while bike riding. Steve Arneson, senior vice president of learning and development at Capital One (financial services) emphasizes that the audio learning is part of the company's focus on blended learning—classroom, multimedia, and written materials.[31]

Nike provides an example of the potential benefits of e-learning. The company wanted to offer product training to its sales associates as well as other retailers that sell its products. Centralized classroom training was not

31 Elizabeth Agnvall, "Just-in-Time Training," *HR Magazine*, May 2006, pp. 66–71.

feasible because store associates are so dispersed and turnover is so high. Training in short increments is also important because the trainees are on duty at the stores. Working with training consultants, Nike developed a program called Sports Knowledge Underground. It resembles a subway map with different stations representing different training themes, such as Apparel Union Station. Each segment runs between three and seven minutes and gives associates the basic knowledge they need about specific products. Stores that have implemented the e-learning program have experienced a 4 to 5 percent sales increase.[32]

Despite the substantial contribution and growth of e-learning, many students learn better when they can interact with people such as fellow students and instructors. Nonverbal cues, so important for many types of learning, are minimal at best when interacting with software.

Many companies are now taking a balanced approach of classroom training combined with e-learning. Computer-based learning is effective in helping workers learn conceptual information and hard skills such as product information and principles of customer service. Yet developing interpersonal skills requires face-to-face practice. For example, Home Depot relies heavily on computer-based training for training cashiers how to make change and process credit cards. In contrast, personal mentoring is used more often to coach store associates about product knowledge and dealing with customers.[33] Also, as with telecommuting, many workers lack enough self-discipline and self-motivation to follow through with e-learning.

Development is a form of personal improvement that usually consists of enhancing knowledge and skills of a complex and unstructured nature. For example, a development program might help managers become better leaders or develop multicultural skills.

Managers play an important role in most types of training and development, particularly with respect to on-the-job training and development. We return to the top of the manager as a teacher in discussions about mentoring in Chapter 10 and coaching in Chapter 16.

Most of this text and its accompanying course could be considered an experience in management training and development. The next paragraphs describe two vital aspects of training and development for employees and managers: needs assessment and the selection of an appropriate training program.

development
A form of personal improvement that usually consists of enhancing knowledge and skills of a complex and unstructured nature.

Needs Assessment and Selecting an Appropriate Training Program

Before embarking on a training program, an organization needs to determine what type of training is needed. When training programs fail, including traditional training as well as e-learning, it is often because there is no connection between learning and defined business needs.[34] Such an assessment generally

32 Jessica Marquez, "Faced with High Turnover, Retailers Boot Up e-Learning Programs for Quick Training," *Workforce Management*, August 2005, pp. 74–75.

33 Joe Mullich, "A Second Act for E-Learning," *Workforce Management*, February 2004, p. 51; George Anders, "Companies Find Online Training Has Its Limits," *The Wall Street Journal*, March 26, 2007, p. B3.

34 Sister Fister Gale, "Making E-Learning More Than Pixie Dust," *Workforce*, March 2003, p. 58.

benefits from including a job analysis and asking the managers themselves, their managers, and group members about the managers' need for training. Training and development needs can also be identified for the entire organization, or portions of it. For example, a few years ago IBM trained all of its 10,000 managers and executives in its new on-demand business model (responding immediately to customer needs) and its implementation.[35]

Despite the importance of matching training and development programs to specific individual and organizational needs, universal training needs also require attention. The training would include elements such as communication, motivation, decision making, coaching, and time management.

After needs are assessed, a program must often be tailored to fit company requirements. The person assigning employees to training and development programs must be familiar with their needs for training and development, know the content of various programs, and enroll employees in programs that will meet their needs. Exhibit 9-8 presents a sample listing of training and development programs.

In addition to training and development programs, substantial learning takes place outside of the classroom or away from the computer. Many employees learn job skills and information by asking each other questions, sharing ideas, and observing each other. Such learning is spontaneous,

exhibit 9-8 **A Sample Listing of Training Programs versus Development Programs**

Training programs listed in the left column are often included in a program of management development. The programs on the right, however, are rarely considered to be specific skill-based training programs.

Training Programs	Management Development
World-class customer service	Effective team leadership
Applying ergonomics to the office	Gourmet cooking for teamwork
Introduction to human resources law	Strategic leadership
Salary administration	Maintaining a healthy workforce
Preventing and controlling sexual harassment	Strategic diversity
Telemarketing skills	Developing cultural sensitivity
Understanding financial statements	Open book management
Getting started in e-commerce	Principle-centered leadership
Fundamentals of e-learning	Retaining valued employees
Six Sigma basics	Becoming a charismatic leader
Dealing with difficult employees	Strategic human resources planning
Accident prevention	Developing a winning corporate ISO 9000 certification culture

35 Jessica Marquez, "IBM Cuts Costs and Reduces Layoffs as it Prepares Workers for an 'On Demand' World," *Workforce Management*, May 2005, p. 85.

immediate, and task specific. Much **informal learning** takes place in meetings, on breaks, and in customer interactions. Also the digitalization of information facilitates informal learning because workers can exchange information so readily.[36] Some companies have now installed high round tables and white boards around the company so workers can informally exchange ideas in addition to small talk.

informal learning Any learning in which the learning process is not determined or designed by the organization.

PERFORMANCE EVALUATION (OR APPRAISAL)

Learning Objective 5

Explain the basics of a performance evaluation system.

Up to this point in the staffing model, employees have been recruited, selected, oriented, and trained. The next step is to evaluate performance. A **performance evaluation (or appraisal)** is a formal system for measuring, evaluating, and reviewing performance. The results of the evaluation can be recorded on paper or online. The term *performance* appears self-explanatory, yet an analysis of dozens of studies indicates that performance has three major components:[37]

- *Task performance* is the accomplishment of duties and responsibilities associated with a given job (like maintaining inventory at a profitable level).
- *Citizenship performance* is behavior that contributes to the goals of the organization by contributing to its social and psychological environment (like voluntarily help a coworker with a technical problem).
- *Counterproductive performance* is voluntary behavior that harms the well-being of the organization (like consistently insulting customers).

When managers evaluate performance, they are thinking of these components even if they are not explicitly aware of the components. For example, when a manager rates marketing assistant Maria "outstanding," the manager is most likely reacting to the fact that Maria (a) accomplished her marketing tasks, (b) was a cooperative company citizen, and (c) did not engage in counterproductive behavior such as disrupting meetings or regularly arrive late to work.

performance evaluation A formal system for measuring, evaluating, and reviewing performance.

An offshoot of evaluating employees against a performance standard is to use **forced rankings** in which employees are measured against each other. Using this system, employees are ranked into three, four, or five "baskets," usually with a different number of employees in each basket. The baskets represent the best workers, the worst workers, and intermediate categories. One ranking approach is forcing employees into the categories of "Top 20 percent, Vital 70 percent, and Bottom 10 percent." Assignment to categories is supposed to be based on performance, but can also be made on the basis of favoritism. However, in some companies including GE, the rankings are considered to be guidelines over time and every grading period does not have to include workers being forced into the bottom 10 percent. Forced rankings

forced rankings An offshoot of evaluating employees against a performance standard in which employees are measured against one another.

36 Nancy Day, "Informal Learning Gets Results," *Workforce*, June 1998, p. 31; Allison Rossett and Kendra Sheldon, *Beyond the Podium: Delivering Training and Performance to a Digital World* (San Francisco: Jossey-Bass/Pfeiffer, 2001).

37 Maria Rotundo and Paul R. Sackett, "The Relative Importance of Task, Citizenship, and Counterproductive Performance to Global Ratings of Job Performance: A Policy-Capturing Approach," *Journal of Applied Psychology*, February 2002, pp. 66–80.

360-degree feedback
A performance appraisal in which a person is evaluated by a sampling of all the people with whom he or she interacts.

are also referred to as "rank and yank" because the employees ranked in the bottom basket are dismissed—often during a downsizing. Yet sometimes the bottom 10 percent is coached and trained toward higher performance.[38]

Forced rankings are highly controversial. A major criticism is that a manager might be responsible for a group of outstanding performers, yet be forced to declare a few as "bottom performers." Teamwork and cooperation are likely to suffer under such a zero-sum game. Another concern about forced rankings is that workers may believe they have been victims of discrimination. Ford Motor Company and Capital One settled class-action suits in which former employees (or their lawyers) contended that a disproportionate numbers of employees of a particular sex, age group, or race had been laid off.[39] In another recent suit, the general counsel for GE's transportation division complained that she was the victim of anti-woman discrimination. She claims she was moved down from the top 20 percent to the middle 70 percent despite strong performance so she could be demoted. GE management says that the decision to demote the lawyer was based on merit.[40]

The current emphasis on team structures changes performance appraisals in two major ways. One, groups as well as individuals are now subject to regular evaluation. Another change comes in the widespread use of multirating systems whereby several workers evaluate an individual. The most frequently used multirater system is **360-degree feedback**, in which a person is evaluated by most of the people with whom he or she interacts. An evaluation form for a manager might incorporate input from the manager's manager, all group members, other managers at his or her level, and even a sampling of customers when feasible. The manager's manager would then synthesize all the information and discuss it with him or her. Dimensions for rating a manager might include "gives direction," "listens to group members," "coaches effectively," and "helps the group achieve key results."

The rationale for using 360-degree feedback for performance evaluation is based on its ability to present a complete picture of performance. This technique is used as much for management and leadership development as for performance appraisal.

Purposes of Performance Evaluation

Performance evaluations serve a number of administrative purposes and can also help the manager carry out the leadership function. A major purpose is to decide whether an employee should receive merit increases and the relative size of the increases. The evaluation process also identifies employees with potential for promotion. High-performing teams can be identified as well. Employee reviews are widely used to provide documentation for discharging, demoting, and downsizing employees who are not meeting performance standards. The results of performance evaluation should be tied closely to organizational

38 Steve Bates, "Forced Rankings," *HR Magazine*, June 2003, pp. 63–68; Jack and Suzy Welch, "The Case for 20-70-10," *Business Week*, October 2, 2006, p. 108.

39 Kelley Holland, "Performance Reviews: Many Need Improvement," *The New York Times* (http://www.nytimes.com), September 10, 2006.

40 Jessica Marquez, "Is GE's Ranking System Broken?" *Workforce Management*, June 25, 2007, pp. 1, 3.

rewards: workers who receive the highest evaluations should receive the most rewards including higher compensation and more promotions.[41]

Performance appraisals help managers carry out the leadership function in several ways. Suggesting areas for needed improvement can increase productivity. Also, the manager can help employees identify their needs for self-improvement and self-development. Appraisal results can be used to motivate employees by providing feedback on performance. Finally, a performance appraisal gives employees a chance to express their ambitions, hopes, and concerns, thereby enhancing career development.

traits
Stable aspects of people, closely related to personality.

behavior
In performance evaluation, what people actually do on the job.

results
In performance evaluation, what people accomplish, or the objectives they attain.

Design of the Performance Evaluation System

Organizations currently use a number of different formats and methods of performance evaluation designed to measure traits, behavior, or results. **Traits** are stable aspects of people, which are closely related to personality. Job-related traits include enthusiasm, dependability, and honesty. **Behavior**, or activity, is what people do on the job. Job-related behavior includes working hard, keeping the work area clean, maintaining a good appearance, and showing concern for customer service. **Results** are what people accomplish, or the objectives they attain. Following is an example of a performance factor on an employee evaluation form that focuses on results:

	5	4	3	2	1
	☐	☐	☐	☐	☐
Quality of work is the accuracy, and thoroughness of work.	Consistently unsatisfactory	Occasionally unsatisfactory	Consistently satisfactory	Sometimes superior	Consistently superior

Many performance evaluation systems take into account results, as well as traits and behaviors. For example, a worker might have achieved work goals (results), and also be described as having initiative (a behavior linked to a trait). Another important consideration is that the performance evaluation system should encourage some risk-taking behavior even if it could mean not reaching agreed-upon goals. Without prudent risk taking, innovation would be stifled.[42]

Employees are the most satisfied with performance evaluation when they participate in the process. Participation can take a number of forms such as jointly setting goals with the manager, submitting a self-appraisal as part of the evaluation, and having the opportunity to fully discuss the results.[43]

Many workers dislike having their performance evaluated, and many managers dislike evaluating workers, particularly when negative feedback is involved. Some researchers therefore propose eliminating performance appraisals. Such a move would be tantamount to abolishing grades in school.

---

41 Edward E. Lawler III, "Reward Practices and Performance Management System Effectiveness," *Organizational Dynamics*, No. 4, 2003, pp. 396–404.

42 Jena McGregor, "The Struggle to Measure Performance," *Business Week*, January 9, 2006, p. 28.

43 Brian D. Cawley, Lisa M. Keeping, and Paul E. Levy, "Participation in the Performance Appraisal Process and Employee Reactions: A Meta-Analytic Review of Field Investigations," *Journal of Applied Psychology*, August 1998, pp. 615–633.

One alternative to performance appraisals is for managers to have face-to-face conversations with workers about their performance on a regular basis, at a minimum three or four times annually. Managers make written note of any problems that workers experience, which creates the necessary documentation to support any necessary discipline or termination.[44] In reality, regular conversations that accommodate documentation of poor performance simply translate into an informal system of performance appraisal, not its replacement.

COMPENSATION

Learning Objective 6

Summarize the basics of employee compensation.

Compensation, the combination of pay and benefits, is closely related to staffing. A major reason compensation requires so much managerial attention is that it constitutes about two-thirds of the cost of running most enterprises. Compensation, including pay and benefits, plays a major role in attracting and retaining valued employees in general, and particularly during a labor shortage. Even when a firm is downsizing, key employees will be recruited and retained by juggling benefits. Companies often attempt to attract desirable employees with incentives like a $5,000 signing bonus or a company-paid vehicle. On the other hand, some key employees receive bonuses for staying with a firm during periods when many employees are switching firms. Here we look at several types of pay and employee benefits. Chapter 11 will describe how compensation is used as a motivational device.

Types of Pay

Wages and salary are the most common forms of pay. Wages are payments to employees for their services, computed on an hourly basis or on the basis of the amount of work produced. Salary is an annual amount of money paid to a worker and does not depend directly on output or hours worked. Nevertheless, future salary is dependent to some extent on how well the worker produced in the previous year. Many workers are eligible for bonuses or incentives to supplement their salary. To determine how much a given job should receive in wages or pay, many companies perform a **job evaluation**, the process of rank-ordering jobs based on job content, to demonstrate the worth of one job in comparison to another. Among the factors contributing to the content of a job are education, skill, mental demands, and physical demands. Each factor receives a weight, and the weights are added to determine how many points a job is worth. The greater the total points, the higher the pay.[45]

job evaluation The process of rank-ordering jobs based on job content, to demonstrate the worth of one job in comparison to another.

The major thrust in compensation for workers at all levels is **variable pay**, in which the amount of money a worker receives is partially dependent on his or her performance. A worker might receive a bonus for having surpassed a performance standard, or a salary increase for the same reason. Performance-based compensation is increasing rapidly as employers struggle to remain competitive in price, yet attract and retain capable workers. The assumption is that a talented worker will accept lower guaranteed pay,

variable pay When the amount of money a worker receives is partially dependent on his or her performance.

44 Dayton Fandray, "The New Thinking in Performance Appraisals," *Workforce*, May 2001, p. 40; Jena McGregor, "The Struggle to Measure Performance," *Business Week*, January 9, 2006, p. 28.

45 Deborah Keary, Saundra Jackson, and Vicki Neal, "Job Evaluations, Health Coverage, Discipline," *HR Magazine*, January 2004, p. 39.

if higher incentive pay is possible.[46] Variable pay is considered motivational because the worker has to produce more to earn more.

Another approach to variable pay, **stack-ranking**, requires managers to rank each employee within each unit, and distribute raises and bonuses accordingly. Yahoo! uses stack ranking to help retain top performers. According to the method, each member of a group of 25 people would be ranked 1 through 25, with person number 1 receiving the biggest share of the raise and bonus money allotted to the group. If the person ranked 25 was meeting job standards, he or she could still receive a raise or bonus. Yet, during performance evaluation the Yahoo! workers are not told their specific ranking.[47]

stack-ranking
A ranking system that requires managers to rank each employee within each unit, and distribute raises and bonuses accordingly.

Employee Benefits

An **employee benefit** is any noncash payment given to workers as part of compensation for their employment. Employee benefits cost employers about 35 percent of salaries. Therefore an employee earning $40,000 per year in salary probably receives a combined salary and benefit package of $54,000. Under ideal circumstances, employee benefits should be linked to business strategy, meaning that these benefits should reward employees for achieving key business goals. Some companies only offer tuition assistance for courses that directly improve job performance. Honda of America would thus reimburse an engineer for studying fuel cell technology, but would not reimburse an engineer for a course in acupuncture.

employee benefit
Any noncash payment given to workers as part of compensation for their employment.

A substantial number of firms offer a **flexible benefit package** that allows employees to select a group of benefits tailored to their preferences. Flexible compensation plans generally provide employees with one category of fixed benefits—minimum standards such as medical and disability insurance. The second category is flexible, with a menu of benefits from which each employee is allowed to select, up to a certain total cost. An employee who prefers less vacation time, for instance, might choose more life insurance.

flexible benefit package
A compensation plan that allows employees to select a group of benefits tailored to their preferences.

Exhibit 9-9 presents a representative list of employee benefits, organized by type and frequency. Organizations vary considerably in the benefits and services they offer employees. No one firm is likely to have the same portfolio of benefits, particularly for nonstandard benefits such as back massage services, or on-company-premises dry-cleaning.

Benefits, especially healthcare insurance and pensions, have been looked upon carefully by management in recent years as a detriment to competing successfully against foreign competitors who do not bear such a heavy cost. In many countries, for example, health care is paid for directly or administered by the federal government. Many business firms in recent years have either decreased benefits to present employees or required them to pay a larger share, particularly with respect to healthcare. Furthermore, many companies have even eliminated healthcare and pension benefits, claiming they can no longer afford the benefits.

Employee benefits can be quite costly. GM pays about $1,600 per vehicle in healthcare costs, more than the price of steel that goes into the vehicle. In contrast,

46 Jessica Marquez, "Premium on Productivity," *Workforce Management*, November 7, 2005, p. 22.
47 McGregor, "The Struggle to Measure Performance," p. 28.

exhibit 9-9 A Variety of Employee Benefits

Employers find that the right package of benefits for an individual worker will increase the chances he or she will stay with the firm for a relatively long time.

Frequent HealthCare Benefits

Mental and dental insurance
Life insurance
Drug prescription program
Mental health insurance
Employee assistance program
Weight-loss program

Frequent Financial Benefits

ATM
Direct deposit
Credit union
Educational assistance
Defined-contribution retirement plan
Automobile allowance/expenses
Incentive bonus plan
Employee stock ownership

Frequent Family-Friendly Benefits

Dependent care flexible spending account
Flexible working hours
Compressed workweeks
Telecommuting
Job sharing
Bring child to work in emergency
Child-care referral service

Frequent Personal Services

Professional development opportunities (seminars, conferences, courses, etc.)
Professional memberships
Casual dress every day
Casual dress one day per week
Organization-sponsored sports teams
Food services/subsidized cafeteria
Club memberships

Infrequent Benefits of All Types

Oil change/auto care
Massage therapy at work area
Lactation rooms for mothers of infants
Car-pooling subsidy
Company-supported childcare center
Company-supported eldercare center
Subsidize cost of elder care
Onsite laundry
Drop off packages for shipping service
Naptime during the workday
Animal pet health insurance
Animal pet allowed on company premises

Source: Stephanie Armour, "Voluntary Benefits Retain Their Luster," *USA Today* syndicated story, December 29, 2003; "What Benefits Are Companies Offering Now?" *HRfocus*, June 2000, p. 6; Jennifer Saranow, "Anybody Want to Take a Nap?" *The Wall Street Journal*, January 24, 2005, p. R5.

healthcare costs for Toyota are about $350 per vehicle. A frequent method of reducing the cost of healthcare insurance is shifting workers to a *consumer driven health plan* in which the worker assumes a much larger deductible before receiving reimbursement from the insurance company. For example, the worker might pay the first $1,000 in healthcare fees before reimbursement. Eleven percent of large employers now make high-deductible plan their only healthcare benefit. "Consumer driven" refers to the idea that the worker as a consumer is likely to be sensitive to price and pay for healthcare only when really needed. However, unhealthy employees tend to quickly burn through their deductibles and are no longer sensitive to price, so the employer's cost savings may not be substantial.[48]

48 Jeremy Smerd, "Aetna Official Says CDHP Alone Won't Cut Costs," *Workforce Management*, August 14, 2006, p. 6; Smerd, "Bedside Manner in Switching to a Consumer Plan," *Workforce Management*, May 22, 2006, p. 33.

Some companies have eliminated company pension plans by declaring bankruptcy, and then forcing the federal government to pay partial benefits through the Pension Benefit Guaranty Corp. (PGBC). The PBGC in 2005 assumed responsibility for the pensions of 36,000 United Airline grounds workers and retirees. The current maximum guarantee by the PBGC for a worker who retires at age 65 is $45,000 annually.

General Motors Corp. illustrates how companies have reduced benefits to help stay competitive. In 2006 the company reduced pensions for salaried (and also, nonunion) employees and shifted to a defined contribution plan. Instead of guaranteeing a defined benefit, such as $3,500 per month for life, GM shifted to a defined contribution, such as 4 percent of annual salary or wages to the employee's pension fund.[49] Defined contribution plans, often referred to as 401(k), make the employee partially responsible for contributing to the fund and making investment choices.

Another way of reducing pension costs is through *cash-balance plans*. In a traditional pension, benefits are calculated by multiplying years of service by average salary, or basing the monthly payout on the last three years of service. Employers who convert to cash-balance plans basically freeze the traditional pension's growth. The value of the pension that a worker has already earned is converted to a cash-out amount. The account grows with annual company contributions based on a percentage of an employee's pay.[50]

THE ROLE OF LABOR UNIONS IN HUMAN RESOURCE MANAGEMENT

Learning Objective 7

Understand the role of labor unions in human resource management.

When a public or private organization is unionized, the labor union influences almost all human resource programs and practices. The reason is that a major purpose of a labor union is to attain fair treatment for workers in such areas as compensation, including health and retirement benefits, safe working conditions, working hours, job security, and work-life programs.

According to the United States Bureau of Labor Statistics, about 12.5 percent of wage and salary workers are union members. The union membership rate has declined from a high of 20.1 percent in 1983, partially because of the manufacturing decline in North America. The unionization rate for government workers is 36.5 percent, whereas the rate for private industry workers is 7.8 percent. The most heavily unionized public sector workers are teachers, police officers, and firefighters. Among private industries, transportation and utilities have the highest union membership rate at 24.0 percent. Thirteen percent of manufacturing workers are organized.[51]

Because the manufacturing sector has been the hardest hit by foreign competition, union leaders are often unable to push for improved compensation including wages, and health retirement benefits. Company executives

49 Jui Chakravorty, "GM Cuts Pension Benefits for Salaried Workers," http://www.boston.com, March 7, 2006.

50 Ellen E. Shultz, "Workers of All Ages Lose Benefits in Switch to Cash-Balance Plans," *The Wall Street Journal*, November 5–6, 2005, p. A4.

51 This section follows closely "Union Members Summary," *Bureau of Labor Statistics News*, January 20, 2006.

can use the threat of sending work offshore when union demands are too high. Another antiunion tactic, as in the case of automotive parts supplier Delphi Corporation, is to declare bankruptcy, and have a judge nullify the union–management contract. Delphi then hired temporary workers at a lower wage rate to replace the union workers.

Management can also counter the thrust of unionization outside of the manufacturing sector, as evidenced by an event that took place in Quebec, Canada. Wal-Mart had resisted unionization at its 3,600 stores in the United States. The Wal-Mart in Jonquière, Québec, achieved unionization after an intense campaign—the first unionized Wal-Mart in North America. Shortly thereafter the company closed the store that had been in existence for three years. Wal-Mart officials said the store was losing money, and the demands of the union aggravated the loss.[52]

In contrast to the several negative scenarios just cited, many instances exist of healthy partnerships between management and labor unions in which both sides gain advantage. The American Rights to Work Group notes that the companies on its list of partners excel in one or more of the following human resource management practices:

- Collaborating as equal partners with workers and their unions to craft innovative strategies on compensation, performance, and productivity to meet business goals and address challenges
- Providing sustainable wages or progressive increases and worker-friendly benefits
- Creating new jobs and implementing employee-retention strategies
- Protecting workers' safety and health
- Fostering diversity and inclusion in the workforce
- Offering training and professional development opportunities

Two examples of companies partnering so well with unions, as described by the Rights to Work Group, are as follows:

1. *Costco Wholesale Corporation (International Brotherhood of Teamsters).* By providing wages and benefits above industry standards, this retail membership warehouse chain demonstrates that treating employees well is good for business.
2. *Harley-Davidson Motor Company (International Association of Machinists, United Steel Workers)* This leading motorcycle manufacturer partners with its employees' unions at every level, which boosts productivity and quality, and keeps job in America.[53]

Perhaps not every business firm is in a position to have such progressive labor relations, yet the message is clear that working well with all stakeholders is associated with business success.

52 Doug Struck, "Wal-Mart Leaves Bitter Chill: Quebec Store Closes after Vote to Unionize," *Washington Post Foreign Service*, April 14, 2005, p. E01.

53 Quoted from "The Labor Day List: Partnerships that Work," *American Rights to Work*, September 2005, pp. 1–2.

SUMMARY OF
Key Points

1 Explain how human resource management is part of business strategy.

Human resource management is an integral part of business strategy. Without effective human resource management the company cannot accomplish high-level goals such as competing globally, grabbing market share, and being innovative.

2 Describe the components of organizational staffing.

The staffing model consists of seven phases: awareness of the legal aspects of staffing; strategic human resources planning; recruitment; selection; orientation, training, and development; performance appraisal; and compensation. All phases can influence employee retention.

3 Present an overview of recruitment and selection.

Recruitment is the process of attracting job candidates with the right characteristics and skills to fit job openings and the organizational culture. Job descriptions and job specifications are necessary for recruiting. External and internal sources are used in recruiting, including expanded use of online recruiting.

Selecting candidates who will perform well is the lifeblood of the firm. Selecting the right candidate from among those recruited may involve a preliminary screening interview, psychological and personnel testing, a job interview, reference checking, and a physical examination. The four types of psychological and personnel tests used most frequently in employee selection are achievement, aptitude, personality, and honesty and integrity. Tests should be scientifically accurate and nondiscriminatory against any group.

Interviews are more valid when the interviewer is trained and experienced. Job interviews help both the interviewer and the interviewee acquire important information. Behavioral interviewing helps make the interview job-related. Job simulations are essentially a job tryout. Reference checks and background investigations are useful in making sound selection decisions, as does the physical examination.

4 Present an overview of employee orientation, training, and development.

An employee orientation program helps acquaint the newly hired employee with the firm. Training includes any procedure intended to foster and enhance employee skills. Development is a form of personal improvement that generally enhances knowledge and skills of a complex and unstructured nature. A needs assessment should be conducted prior to selecting training and development programs.

5 Explain the basics of a performance evaluation system.

A performance evaluation (or appraisal) is a standard method of measuring, evaluating, and reviewing performance of individuals as well as teams. The 360-degree appraisal involves feedback from many people. The forced-ranking method compares employees to each other. Performance evaluations serve important administrative purposes, such as helping managers make decisions about pay increases and promotions and carry out the leadership function. Appraisal systems measure traits, behavior, and results, with some systems taking into account more than one factor.

6 Summarize the basics of employee compensation.

Workers are typically paid salaries, bonuses, and sometimes payment for job skills. The purpose of job evaluations is to determine how much a job is worth. Variable pay is used to motivate employees and reduce company expenses. Employee benefits are a major part of compensation. Flexible benefit packages allow employees to select a group of benefits tailored to their preferences. Compensation is a major factor in recruiting and retaining employees, yet expensive benefits such as health insurance and pensions have been reduced in recent years to help companies face global competition.

7 Understand the role of labor unions in human resource management.

The labor union influences almost all human resource programs and practices. A major purpose of a labor union is to attain fair treatment for workers in such areas as compensation including health and retirement benefits, safe working conditions, flexible working hours, job security, and work-life programs. Companies can counterinfluence unions through offshoring, declaring bankruptcy to nullify union contracts, and closing down facilities that unionize. Many instances exist of healthy partnerships between management and labor unions, as described by the American Rights to Work Group.

KEY TERMS AND PHRASES

Job embeddedness, 299
Affirmative action, 299
Strategic human-resource planning, 301
Recruitment, 303
Job specification, 303
Realistic job preview, 310
Behavioral interviewing, 310
Reference check, 312
Employee orientation program, 315
Training, 316
E-learning, 316
Development, 317
Informal learning, 319
Performance evaluation (or appraisal), 319
Forced rankings, 319
360-degree feedback, 320
Traits, 321
Behavior, 321
Results, 321
Job evaluation, 322
Variable pay, 322
Stack-ranking, 323
Employee benefit, 323
Flexible benefit package, 323

QUESTIONS

1. What is your opinion about paying human resource managers as much as managers in other functions such as marketing, operations, and finance?
2. If you were applying for a professional position in your chosen field, what would be your reaction to being fingerprinted as part of the screening process?
3. Why should a manager who does not work in the human resources department be familiar with the various aspects of staffing?
4. Noted psychologist David McLelland once said, "They say you can teach a squirrel to fly. But it's easier to hire the eagle." Assuming the statement is true, what implications does the statement have for staffing and human resource management?
5. What have you learned about staffing that you might apply to your own job search?

6. What would be the advantages and disadvantages to the organization and individuals if a company abolished performance evaluations?

7. What is your opinion of the ethics of American business firms reducing healthcare benefits and pensions of retirees to help compete against foreign manufacturers?

SKILL-BUILDING EXERCISE 9-A: Presenting Yourself in 30 Seconds

A well-accepted belief about recruiters, hiring managers, and employment interviewers is that they form a quick impression of a candidate, often within the first ten seconds. With this fact in mind, develop a 30-second opening presentation about yourself with the goal of creating a favorable impression on people making judgments about your job qualifications. Facts to pack into your 30-second statement might include your name, type of work sought, education, experience, and key accomplishments. However, be creative. Many job seekers have found the 30-second self-promotion speech invaluable when meeting with recruiters or attending job fairs. Give your 30-second presentation to a few fellow students to obtain their feedback, and return the favor to them.

SKILL-BUILDING EXERCISE 9-B: The Selection Interview

Assume the role of the manager or employment interviewer of the call center for Apple Inc. The call center provides support to customers who already own Apple computers and consumer electronic devices including the iPod. After thinking through the job demands of a call center representative, conduct a 15-minute interview of a classmate who pretends to apply for the call center rep position. Before conducting the interview, review the guidelines in Exhibit 9-6. Other students on your team might observe the interview and then provide constructive feedback.

INTERNET SKILL-BUILDING EXERCISE: Recruiting on the Net

Place yourself in the role of a manager who is recruiting qualified job applicants to fill one or more of the following positions: (a) sales representative of machine tools, (b) customer service supervisor who speaks English and Spanish, (c) and Web site developer. Use the Internet to conduct your search for a pool of candidates. A good starting point might be the job boards (Web sites for job hunters). Remember, in this exercise you are looking for job candidates, not a position for yourself. Try to determine whether you can locate any job applicants without paying an employer fee.

Case Problem 9-A

Can Boomer Road Warriors Really Solve Our Problems?

Marilyn Gomez, the HR Director at an interstate trucking company, told the CEO, Bert Jackson, that she may have hit upon a solution to the severe truck driver shortage facing their company, and the entire industry. "So far, the industry has made some progress in looking for new sources of drivers, but not enough. The nationwide program of recruiting Hispanics has gone along okay, but we and the rest of the industry needs another major recruiting source. The boomer retirees with wanderlust might take a big bite out of our driver shortage."

Gomez then pulled out for discussion an article in *The Wall Street Journal* that contained some novel ideas for recruiting long-haul truckers. Excerpts of the article that stimulated Gomez's thinking follow:

At a truck stop diner along Interstate 5 near Tigard, Oregon, Daniel and Becky Ford were fueling up on pancakes and black coffee for the 2,500-mile run to Dallas they were about to make in a Freightliner tractor-trailer stuffed with auto parts. It was the tenth week on the open road for Mr. Ford, 57 years old, and his 51-year-old wife, who chucked their old life in rural Pennsylvania in May for a cramped truck cab that keeps them moving 22 hours a day.

Their new career is taking them to places they always dreamed of visiting but couldn't afford. "When the money is tight and you have other worries, you can't be too adventurous," says Mrs. Ford, a former hair stylist. "Becky and I serve as our own boss," says Mr. Ford, a former carpenter. The Fords can stop wherever they want along their company-assignment routes, as long as their loads are delivered on time. They already have visited 44 states, stashing postcards on the dashboard from stops along the way.

Faced with a worsening shortage of long-haul truck drivers, freight carriers are turning to the RV generation, aggressively recruiting older couples like the Fords to climb behind the wheel. Schneider National Inc., the Green Bay, Wisconsin, company that hired the Fords and put them through driving school, fishes for applicants through the AARP, the advocacy group for people 50 and older, and has a Web page for "mature workers." This fall, the American Trucking Association plans a billboard and television blitz to lure older drivers.

"We just thought that if Ma and Pa can drive the Winnebago, maybe they can drive the 18-wheeler," says Tim Lynch, a senior vice president in the trade group. Since 2000, the number of service and truck drivers 55 or older has surged 19 percent, to about 616,000, according to the Federal Bureau of Labor Statistics. The percentage drop is quadruple that of truck drivers overall. At Schneider, about 3,000 of the carrier's 15,000 drivers and independent contractors are older people.

The hiring binge has dramatically increased the number of husband-and-wife driving teams, and truck makers are trying to make their big rigs feel more like rolling homes away from home. Paccar Inc.'s Kenworth Truck Co. unit introduced a new model in March with leather beds and heated seats. Volvo Trucks North American has begun production of trucks with a full-size bed in the cam, comfortable for couples.

Women drivers at Prime Inc. can get their hair and nails done at a salon that opened two years ago in a 40,000-square-foot facility that the Springfield, Missouri, refrigerated-truck carrier runs in its hometown for drivers and other employees. "Even if they are away from home, we want to give them the same amenities everyone else would have," says Don Lacy, the company's safety director.

Older drivers don't face any extra requirements because of their age. Most carriers send recruits to commercial driving school. Drivers must pass a physical exam required by the federal government, but there is no mandatory requirement age as there is for commercial pilots, who under Federal Aviation Administration rules must retire at 60. On the road, among all drivers, those 55 to 69 have the lowest fatality rates for adults, according to a National Highway Traffic Safety Administration report.

Truck companies with baby boomer drivers insist their safety record is at least as good as that of younger drivers. Older derivers are especially cautious, says Steve Vogel, president of Vogel Safety & Risk Inc., a safety consulting firm. Riding shotgun with a spouse can also make drivers less likely to speed, tailgate, or go berserk at road-hogging cars.

At larger carriers, older husband-and-wife teams often get health insurance, a 401(k) plan, and two or three days off every two weeks. Annual starting pay is roughly $66,000 to $90,000 per couple, enough to entice many

Case Problem 9-A

middle-aged spouses approaching a financially precarious retirement.

Jackson, the CEO, said to Gomez, the HR Director, "Come to think of it. I am aware of some truckers that have hired older couples as a driving team. I think we should explore the possibilities further. Yet, can hiring boomers be all gold? For one, I would be a little concerned about hiring a couple to do the job of one trucker."

Discussion Questions

1. What advice would you offer the trucking company about recruiting retired baby boomer couples as drivers?
2. Would the trucker in question really be hiring two people to do the job of one trucker?
3. What other out-of-the-ordinary recruiting source for truckers could you offer this company, as well as other truckers?
4. What advice can you offer the trucking company in question to avoid practicing job discrimination against young applicants for their trucking jobs?

Source: Stephanie Chen, "How Baby Boomers Turn Wanderlust Into Trucking Careers," The Wall Street Journal, August 24, 2006, pp. A1, A8.

Case Problem 9-B

The Scrutinized Job Candidates

Dora Vell, managing partner of Vell & Associates, high tech recruiters in Waltham, Massachusetts, explains that a job candidate's demeanor comes under scrutiny the moment he or she arrives at a search (executive placement) firm. "We are building a picture of you, piece by piece."

The receptionist notices whether you read your *National Enquirer* rather than the employer's annual report. She may also keep tabs on your hygiene habits. Ms. Fell once worked for a small Boston search firm where the receptionist alerted partners if candidates using the guest bathroom failed to wash their hands. (She could hear the faucet.)

Escorted to a partner's office doorway, you march right in—even though he's engrossed in a confidential call. Bad idea. Wait outside until he finishes. You chat briefly, repeatedly peeking at your BlackBerry. Another dumb move. Twice in the past six months, aspiring vice presidents have pulled out these e-mail devices during interviews with Dean Bare, a managing partner of recruiters Stanton Chase International in Atlanta. "It's time to turn that off," he sternly told them.

"I wouldn't want to recommend anyone that insensitive and lacking in social graces," Bare adds. "To appear more considerate, inform the recruiter upfront that work crises require frequent e-mail checks."

He next suggests taking your car to a restaurant for lunch because yours is parked nearby. There is a hidden motive: "Assume you're being judged by how you drive," cautions Jane Howze, a managing director at the Alexander Group, a Houston search firm, who says driving habits are a good measure of character.

A job seeker keen to become a partner at a management consultancy hit a vehicle during one such trip with Bare. The collision crumbled the prospect's car hood. "It was clearly his fault," the recruiter recalls. But the man blamed the other driver. His poor road etiquette bothered Bare so much that Stanton Chase didn't recommend him. He should have admitted his culpability.

A well-qualified manager sought a post with an annual salary of about $450,000. He arrived early for his 1 p.m. appointment with the head of human resources. He asked to use the conference room to make an important call. It lasted until 1:15. He didn't apologize to the HR executive about the delay. Following their abbreviated session, she was ready to take him to his 2 p.m. session with the finance chief.

That didn't happen on time either. "I have a 2 p.m. conference call I have to get on," the potential recruit announced, ducking back into the conference room. The call took 40 minutes. After finishing his second delayed interview, he refused to meet again with the human resources chief because he needed to catch a flight.

The prospect's boorish behavior struck company and search-firm officials as a fatal red flag. "We said, 'This person has a real strong etiquette and judgment problem,'" recollects David W. Gallagher, a managing director for Boyden Global Executive Search in Atlanta. He suspects many ill-mannered job seekers suffer from a similar, excessive sense of self-importance. "If you're going to interview for a job, interview 100 percent." Gallagher advises. "Put everything else out of your mind."

Discussion Questions

1. How fair is it for the recruiters described here to reject candidates because they display poor manners, such as receiving e-mail messages during the job interviews or while talking to the human resource representative?
2. Of what significance is it if the candidate who is waiting reads the *National Enquirer* instead of the company annual report?
3. How valid is the management recruiter's belief that the way a person drives is related to job performance in aspects of a job that does not involve driving?
4. What lessons do these recruiters have for graduates seeking entry-level technical and professional jobs?

Source: Excerpted from Joann S. Lublin, "Interview Etiquette Begins the Minute You Walk in the Door," *The Wall Street Journal*, August 1, 2006, p. B1, Permission cleared through the Copyright Clearance Center.

chapter 10

Leadership

Objectives

After studying this chapter and doing the exercises, you should be able to:

1. Differentiate between leadership and management.
2. Describe how leaders are able to influence and empower team members.
3. Identify important leadership characteristics and behaviors.
4. Describe participative leadership, authoritarian leadership, the Leadership Grid, situational, and entrepreneurial leadership.
5. Describe transformational and charismatic leadership.
6. Explain the leadership role of mentoring and coaching.
7. Identify the skills that contribute to leadership.

Connie Lindsey can testify to getting by with a little help from her friends—those who are highly placed and influential in the corporate world. She learned that lesson soon after joining The Northern Trust Co. in 1993, when a mentor suggested she make the transition from marketing to managing a sales consulting team even though she had no sales experience.

"He made it very clear that we are a sales culture, and one of the most important ways to learn the business and to advance is to take this opportunity in sales," remembers Lindsey. "He said, 'you are a strong leader, Connie. You understand the products and services from the client's point of view. Now I need you to translate that understanding and passion from the clients into a successful strategy for the sales team.'"

Today the 47-year-old Milwaukee is a senior vice president and deputy business unit head in charge of the Chicago-based bank's financial management, strategic planning, business continuity, and disaster recovery, with nearly 3,000 partners worldwide.[1]

The story about the successful bank executive's career illustrates one of the many important functions an effective leader carries out, mentoring and coaching subordinates. **Leadership** is the ability to inspire confidence and support among the

1 Maureen Jenkins, "Why You Need a Mentor," *Black Enterprise*, March 2005, p. 81.

leadership The ability to inspire confidence and support among the people who are needed to achieve organizational goals.

people who are needed to achieve organizational goals.[2] This chapter focuses on leadership in business firms, which is important at every organizational level. For example, an office manager who is an effective leader helps keep the company running smoothly by motivating and encouraging the office workers to perform at their best. Successful professionals, regardless of their job titles, generally possess leadership capabilities. In order to cope with frequent change and to solve problems, people exercise initiative and leadership in taking new approaches to their job. Furthermore, in the modern organization, people slip in and out of leadership roles such as a temporary assignment as a task force leader.

In this chapter we describe the characteristics and behaviors of leaders in organizations, as well as useful leadership theories, and key leadership skills.

THE LINK BETWEEN LEADERSHIP AND MANAGEMENT

Learning Objective 1
Differentiate between leadership and management.

Today's managers must know how to lead as well as manage in order to have an effective organization. (You will recall that leadership—along with planning, organizing, and controlling—is one of the basic functions of management.) Three representative distinctions between leadership and management follow:[3]

- Management is more formal and scientific than leadership. It relies on universal skills, such as planning, budgeting, and controlling. Management is a set of explicit tools and techniques, based on reasoning and testing, that can be used in a variety of situations.
- Leadership, by contrast, involves having a vision of what the organization can become. Leadership requires eliciting cooperation and teamwork from a large network of people and keeping the key people in that network motivated, using every manner of persuasion.
- Management involves getting things done through other people. Leadership places more emphasis on helping others do the things they know need to be done to achieve the common vision.

Leaders must have many of the skills mentioned throughout this book, such as being able to formulate strategy. C-level executives are supposed to exercise strategic leadership that sets the course for the organization.

Effective leadership and management are both required in the modern workplace because to be an effective leader, one must also be an effective

2 W. Chan Kim and Renee A. Maubourgne, "Parables of Leadership," *Harvard Business Review*, July–August 1992, p. 123.
3 John P. Kotter, *A Force for Change: How Leadership Differs from Management* (New York: Free Press, 1990); David Fagiano, "Managers versus Leaders," *Management Review*, November 1997, p. 5.

manager.[4] Managers must be leaders, but leaders must also be good managers. Workers need to be inspired and persuaded, but they also need assistance in developing a smoothly functioning workplace. One such effective manager and leader is Kevin Johnson, the president of the Windows platform and services division at Microsoft. He has been described as a hard-headed operator with the shrewdness of Bill Gates and the personal skills of Oprah Winfrey. "I love business, I love technology, I love customers, and I love people," he says.[5]

PLAY VIDEO

LEADERSHIP

"Go to academic.cengage.com/management/dubrin and view the video. As a leader in the first years of McDonald's, what kind of power did Ray Kroc have? What are the benefits of a corporate leadership strategy?"

Exhibit 10-1 presents an overview of the link between leadership and management. It also highlights several of the major topics presented in this chapter. The figure illustrates that to bring about improved productivity and morale, managers do two things. First, they use power, authority, influence, and personal traits and characteristics. Second, they apply leadership behaviors and practices.

THE LEADERSHIP USE OF POWER AND AUTHORITY

Learning Objective 2

Describe how leaders are able to influence and empower team members.

Leaders influence people to do things through the use of power and authority. **Power** is the ability or potential to influence decisions and control resources. Powerful people have the potential to exercise influence, and they exercise it frequently. For example, a powerful executive might influence an executive from another company to do business with his or her company. **Authority** is the formal right to get people to do things or the formal right to control resources. Factors within a person, such as talent or charm, help

exhibit 10-1 The Links Between Management and Leadership

Management and leadership are both applied to improve productivity and morale.

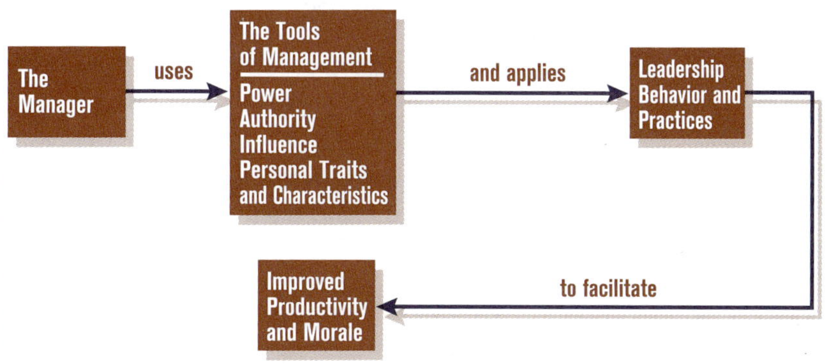

Source: Adapted from John R. Schermerhorn, Jr., *Management for Productivity,* 4th ed. (New York: Wiley, 1993).

4 Gary Yukl and Richard Lepsinger, "Why Integrating the Leading and Managing Roles is Essential for Organizational Effectiveness," *Organizational Dynamics*, No. 4, 2005, pp. 361–373.

5 "Star Power," *Fortune*, February 6, 2006, p. 58.

power The ability or potential to influence decisions and control resources.

authority The formal right to get people to do things or the formal right to control resources.

them achieve power. Only the organization, however, can grant authority. To understand how leaders use power and authority, we examine the various types of power, influence tactics, and how leaders share power with team members. Understanding these different approaches to exerting influence can help a manager become a more effective leader.

Types of Power

Leaders use various types of power to influence others. However, the power exercised by group members, or subordinates, acts as a constraint on how much power leaders can exercise. The list that follows describes the types of power exercised by leaders and sometimes by group members.[6]

1. *Legitimate power* is the authentic right of a leader to make certain types of requests. These requests are based on internalized social and cultural values in an organization. It is the easiest type of influence for most subordinates to accept. For example, virtually all employees accept the manager's authority to conduct a performance evaluation.
2. *Reward power* is a leader's control over rewards of value to the group members. Exercising this power includes giving salary increases and recommending employees for promotion. Being wealthy leads to having considerable reward power, and being an extremely wealthy leader has become almost synonymous with power.
3. *Coercive power* is a leader's control over punishments. Organizational punishments include assignment to undesirable working hours, demotion, and firing. Effective leaders generally avoid heavy reliance on coercive power because it creates resentment and sometimes retaliation.
4. *Expert power* derives from a leader's job-related knowledge as perceived by group members. This type of power stems from having specialized skills, knowledge, or talent. Expert power can be exercised even when a person does not occupy a formal leadership position. An advertising copywriter with a proven record of writing winning ad slogans has expert power, and so does a marketing manager who knows how to create demand for a product.
5. *Referent power* refers to the ability to control based on loyalty to the leader and the group members' desire to please that person. Having referent power contributes to being perceived as charismatic, but expert power also enhances charisma.[7] Part of the loyalty to the leader is based on identification with the leader's personal characteristics. Referent power and charisma are both based on the subjective perception of the leader's traits and characteristics.

---

6 John R. P. French Jr. and Bertram Raven, "The Bases of Social Power," in Dorwin Cartwright and Alvin Zander (eds.), *Group Dynamics: Research and Theory* (New York: Harper & Row, 1960), pp. 607–623.

7 Jeffrey D. Kudisch et al., "Expert Power, Referent Power, and Charisma: Toward the Resolution of a Theoretical Debate," *Journal of Business and Psychology*, Winter 1995, p. 189.

6. *Subordinate power* is any type of power that employees can exert upward in an organization, based on justice and legal considerations. This type of power restricts the extent to which power can be used to control them. For example, certain categories of workers cannot be asked to work overtime without compensation, and a worker does not have to put up with being sexually harassed by the boss.

Despite some constraints on leadership power, a small number of executives abuse power, such as using company funds for private use including using the corporate jet for vacations, and paying for personal services such as home renovation with company funds. Another abuse of power is to order company employees to work on the executives' home-improvement projects or car care.

Influence Tactics

In addition to various types of power, leaders use many other influence tactics to get things done. Influence tactics are especially important because in the modern organization you often have to influence people over whom you lack formal authority. At IBM one of the key behaviors on which executives are graded is the ability to influence without direct authority or collaborative influence. Various groups team up informally to accomplish work without the benefit of a command-and-control hierarchy.[8] Eight frequently used influence tactics follow.

1. *Leading by example* means that the leader influences group members by serving as a positive model of desirable behavior. A manager who leads by example shows consistency between actions and words. For example, suppose a firm has a strict policy on punctuality. The manager explains the policy and is always punctual. The manager's words and actions provide a consistent model. A popular connotation of leading by example is for the manager to demonstrate a strong work ethic by working long and hard, and expecting others to do the same.
2. *Leading by values* means the leader influences people by articulating and demonstrating values that guide the behaviors of others. Using values to influence others is similar to the organizational culture guiding behavior. The ideal values for a leader to pursue would be mutual respect, trust, honesty, fairness, kindness, and doing good.[9] According to Medtronic executive Bill George, an important part of leading by values is to be authentic by staying true to your values, such as being more concerned about employee welfare than trying to appease outside financial analysts.[10]
3. *Assertiveness* refers to being forthright in your demands. It involves expressing what you want done and how you feel about it. Assertiveness also refers to making orders clear. A supervisor might say, for example, "This break room is a mess. It nauseates me, and I want it cleaned up by tomorrow morning at 8:30."

---

8 Linda Tischler, "IBM's Management Makeover," *Fast Company*, November 2004, pp. 112–113.

9 Manuel London, *Principled Leadership and Business Diplomacy: Value-Based Strategies for Management Development* (Westport, CT: Quorum Books, 1999).

10 Bill George, *Authentic Leadership: Rediscovering the Secrets to Creating Lasting Value* (San Francisco: Jossey-Bass, 2003).

4. *Rationality* means appealing to reason and logic. Strong leaders use this tactic frequently. Pointing out the facts of a situation to group members in order to get them to do something is an example of rationality. For example, a middle-level manager might tell a supervisor, "If our department goes over budget this year, we are likely to be cut further next year." Knowing this information, the supervisor will probably become more cost conscious. Appealing to reason and logic works best when the leader is perceived as knowledgeable.
5. *Ingratiation* refers to getting somebody else to like you, often through the use of political skill. A typical ingratiating tactic would be to act in a friendly manner just before making a demand. Effective managers treat people well consistently to get cooperation when it is needed. A representative example is Timothy D. Cook, the second-in-command executive at Apple Inc. Part of his ability to influence others is based on his being so well liked. Cook is said to have "the courtly demeanor of a Southern Gentleman."[11]
6. *Exchange* is a method of influencing others by offering to reciprocate if they meet your demands. Leaders with limited expert, referent, and legitimate power are likely to use exchange and make bargains with subordinates. A manager might say to a group member, "If you can help me out this time, I'll go out of my way to return the favor." Using exchange is like using reward power. The emphasis in exchange, however, is that the manager goes out of his or her way to strike a bargain that pleases the team members.
7. *Coalition formation* is a way of gaining both power and influence. A **coalition** is a specific arrangement of parties working together to combine their power, thus exerting influence on another individual or group. Coalitions in business are a numbers game—the more people you can get on your side, the better. For example, a manager might band with several other managers to gain support for a major initiative such as merging with another company.
8. *Joking and kidding* are widely used to influence others on the job. Good-natured ribbing is especially effective when a straightforward statement might be interpreted as harsh criticism. In an effort to get an employee to stop Internet surfing so much during the work day, the supervisor said, "I know that you have over 7,000 friends on MySpace, but please just stay in touch with only your business contacts during the day."

coalition
A specific arrangement of parties working together to combine their power, thus exerting influence on another individual or group.

So which influence tactic should a leader choose? Leaders are unlikely to use all the influence tactics in a given situation. Instead, they tend to choose an influence tactic that fits the demands of the circumstances. For example, leading by values works best when a manager is highly placed in the organization and the influencing does not have to be done in a hurry. Rationality might work best in a fast-paced team setting such as a meeting to discuss a product introduction.

---

11 Nick Wingfield, "Apple's No. 2 Has Low Profile, High Impact," *The Wall Street Journal*, October 16, 2006, p. B9.

Employee Empowerment and the Exercise of Power

Self-leadership
The process of influencing oneself.

Chapter 8 emphasized empowerment as a way of distributing authority in the organization. Empowerment is similarly a way for leaders to share power, and empowerment is also referred to as distributed leadership. When leaders share power, employees experience a greater sense of personal effectiveness and job ownership. Sharing power with group members enables them to feel better about themselves and become better motivated. The extra motivation stems from a feeling of being in charge. An important use of empowerment is to enhance customer service. As employees acquire more authority to take care of customer problems, these problems can be handled promptly, or sometimes right on the spot.

A key component of empowerment is the leader's acceptance of the employee as a partner in decision making. Because the team member's experience and information are regarded as equal to those of the leader, he or she shares control. Both the leader and team member must agree on what is to be accomplished. The partnering approach to empowerment builds trust between the employee and the leader.[12]

Self-Leadership and Empowerment

For empowerment to work well, people have to exercise **self-leadership**, the process of influencing oneself.[13] Self-leadership is possible because most people have the capacity to lead themselves particularly when faced with difficult yet important tasks. At the same time people are intrinsically (internally) motivated to perform well when they engage in challenging tasks, as in job enrichment. A manager could give the group an opportunity to practice self-leadership with an assignment such as this: "We need to find a way to boost productivity 10 percent in our division starting next month. I am going to Ireland on a business trip for ten days. You can stay in touch with me by e-mail if you like, but the assignment is yours. When I return, I will accept your three best suggestions for boosting productivity."

According to Charles C. Manz, Henry Sims, and Christopher P. Neck, managers can help group members to practice effective self-leadership through three core steps.[14] First, the leader must set an example of self-leadership through such means as setting his or her own goals, making work enjoyable, and accepting rather than avoiding challenges. Second, the leader should give encouragement and instruction in self-leadership skills. Asking appropriate questions can be helpful, such as "What goals have you established?" "What aspects of your work give you the biggest kick" and "What obstacles have you overcome lately?" Third, the leader should reward accomplishment in self-leadership, such as giving feedback on progress and praising initiative. The manager above upon returning from Ireland might

12 Frank J. Navran, "Empowering Employees to Excel," *Supervisory Management*, August 1992, p. 5.

13 Charles C. Manz and Christopher P. Neck, *Mastering Self-Leadership: Empowering Yourself for Personal Excellence*, 3rd ed. (Upper Saddle River, NJ: Pearson Prentice Hall, 2004), p. 5; Neck and Manz, *Mastering Self-Leadership*, 4th ed., 2007.

14 Manz and Neck, *Mastering Self-Leadership*, pp. 138–139; Charles Manz and Henry P. Sims Jr., "Self-Management as a Substitute for Leadership: A Social Learning Theory Perspective," *Academy of Management Review*, No. 5, 1980, pp. 361–367.

say (if true), "These two productivity boosting suggestions you made look like winners. I really appreciate the way you followed through on this project."

Cross-cultural Factors and Empowerment

Empowerment as a leadership technique works better in some cultures than in others. To the extent that cultural values support the manager sharing power with group members, the more likely empowerment will lead to higher productivity and morale. A team of researchers investigated how well the management practice of empowerment fit different cultures. Data were collected from employees from a U.S.-based multinational corporation with operations in the United States, Mexico, Poland, and India. The results associated with empowerment varied with the country and culture. Workers in the United States, Mexico, and Poland had favorable views of their supervisors when they used a high degree of empowerment. Indian employees, however, rated their supervisor low when empowerment was high. (Indians value unequal power between superiors and subordinates, and therefore expect the supervisor to retain most of the power.)[15]

CHARACTERISTICS, TRAITS, AND BEHAVIORS OF EFFECTIVE LEADERS

Learning Objective 3

Identify important leadership characteristics and behaviors.

Understanding leadership requires an understanding of leaders as individuals. This section will highlight findings about the personal characteristics and behaviors of effective managerial leaders. An assessment of the characteristics and behaviors of leaders translates into the idea that these same positive attributes of a leader will facilitate his or her effectiveness in comparable settings, such as customer service departments in different companies.

A key point to recognize in your development as a leader is that leadership encompasses a wide variety of personal qualities and behaviors that could be relevant in a given situation. David Corderman, chief of the Leadership Development Institute at the FBI, notes: "Effective leadership entails such a wide variety of behaviors and skills across an extensive array of circumstances that no one person could possibly be born with all of the qualities necessary to serve in that capacity for all situations. Effective leadership therefore involves in most cases a substantial degree of acquired learning."[16]

Characteristics and Traits of Effective Leaders

Possessing certain characteristics and traits does not in itself guarantee success. Yet effective leaders differ from others in certain respects. Studying leadership traits is also important because a person who is perceived to

15 Christopher Robert et al., "Empowerment and Continuous Improvement in the United States, Mexico, Poland, and India: Predicting Fit on the Dimensions of Power Distance and Individualism," *Journal of Applied Psychology*, October 2000, pp. 643–658.

16 Quoted in "What Is Leadership? The FBI Takes It On," *Executive Leadership*, October 2006, p. 4, Adapted from *The FBI Law Enforcement Bulletin*.

embody certain traits is more likely to be accepted as a leader. For example, people see managers whom they believe to be good problem solvers as able to help overcome obstacles and create a better workplace. Hundreds of human qualities can enhance leadership effectiveness in some situations. Recent scholarly writing emphasizes that leadership effectiveness arises from the combined influence of several characteristics.[17] For example, to develop strategy the leader should need high intelligence and self-confidence, yet would also need effective interpersonal skills to implement the strategy. Here we present a sampling of factors relevant to many work settings[18]

management in action

The Enthusiastic Aylwin B. Lewis of Sears Holding Corp.

As Aylin B. Lewis addresses a group of Kmart managers at a dinner meeting, the years spent at the Baptist church where his father served as a deacon show through. "Our worst stores are dungeons!" bellows the new chief executive at Sears Holding Corp. "Well, who wants to work in a dungeon? Who wants to shop in a dungeon? Who wants to walk into an environment that is so dull and lifeless that it is sucking the air out of your body?" At the end of his 25-minute unscripted speech, the managers—whom he has been implicitly criticizing—hoot loudly and give him a standing ovation.

Lewis is the right-hand man in billionaire Edward S. "Eddie" Lampert's unprecedented—many say impossible—bid to get the 330,000 employees of the two ailing retail icons to think as if they are working for a $55 billion-in-annual-sales start-up.

In many ways, Lewis is Lampert's indispensable alter ego. The 43-year-old Lampert spends most of his time at his Greenwich, Connecticut, investment partnership, ESL Investments, often patched in via video conference. Lewis, 51, is the leader whose physical presence is felt most at Sears' Chicago area headquarters and its 3,500 U.S. stores. Lampert can seem aloof; Lewis is an engaging orator.

The duo share two sides of what most companies would consider one job. At Sears, it is Chairman Lampert who sets strategy. It is CEO Lewis who must remake the retailer's cultures in order to firmly implement Lampert's vision. "I am in the forest, and he is on the 50th floor," says Lewis. "It's hard to see him in the mud." Adds Lampert: "He has demonstrated to me, more than I thought before, what it takes to get people aligned around ideas."

Rowena, one of two younger siblings, says her brother developed a knack for public speaking in Sunday school, where students had to tell Bible stories. After gaining dual degrees in English and business management from the University of Houston, he pursued a Masters in English, intent on becoming a professor. But a job as an assistant manager of a Jack in the Box restaurant changed that. He found that leading his restaurant staff, "satisfied my need to teach."

For the next 26 years, Lewis stuck with restaurants, climbing the management ranks at Jack in the Box, then YUM! Brands Inc., a former PepsiCo Inc. division. A recruiter and a person close to PepsiCo says executives were divided on Lewis's potential to handle the broader strategic role of CEO at YUM!. But as operations head for

(Continued)

17 Stephen J. Zaccaro, "Trait-Based Perspectives on Leadership," *American Psychologist*, January 2007, p. 12.

18 Orlando Behling, "Employee Selection: Will Intelligence and Conscientiousness Do the Job?" *Academy of Management Executive*, February 1998, pp. 77–86; Shelly A. Kirkpatrick and Edwin A. Locke, "Leadership: Do Traits Matter?" *Academy of Management Executive*, May 1991, pp. 48–60.

management in action (Continued)

The Enthusiastic Aylwin B. Lewis of Sears Holding Corp.

the company's KFC and then Pizza Hut restaurants, he left no doubt about his ability to manage nitty-gritty details. He helped lead turnarounds in both chains, ultimately rising to president of YUM!. "He was the best operating guy we had," says YUM! founding chairman Andrall Pearson.

One reason for his success was his deep understanding of the business. Former colleagues say he spent at least three days a week visiting restaurants. They also praise his leadership skills. Although Lewis set tough objectives, he developed loyal subordinates by working closely with them to meet targets. This is why, at YUM!, he changed titles such as "district manager" to "district coach" to reinforce management's development role. He was quick at identifying talent so businesses would continue to perform once he moved on—what Lewis calls making "footprints in concrete."

As one of the most visible African American executives in the United States, Lewis has held high-profile director posts at Halliburton Co. and Disney Co. Robert A. Iger, the CEO of Disney, says Lewis is a strong communicator who cuts to the heart of issues.

Lewis and his human resources team have started to put the framework for a new culture in place. They're re-jiggering work flows to allow some store employees to spend less time in back rooms and more time on the floor interacting with customers. Since the merger, Lewis has required all 3,800 Sears headquarter employees to spend a day a week working in a store (many never had). He practices what he preaches, spending Thursday through Saturday visiting stores. He stays at each one for three hours, probing managers to see whether they know, say, the profit margins for the electronics department and asking what they need to run a store better. He and Lampert want employees throughout the business to be more financially literate. The highest compliment an employee can get is to be called "commercial"—meaning someone who has a sense of how to make money.

Lewis has identified 500 potential leaders in the company and is bringing them in 40 at a time for a daylong course, "Sowing the Seeds of Our Culture," that he runs. Lewis tells the participants, "Make no mistake, we have to change," so either they "drink the Kool-Aid" or they should leave. It remains to be seen whether Kmart and Sears will ever get religion.

Questions

1. In what ways does Lewis appear to be a hands-on leader?17
2. How might have Lewis's studies of English and telling Bible stories been effective supplements to his business education for purpose of becoming a corporate leader?
3. What is implied by the statement that opinion was divided about Lewis's ability to handle the broader strategic role even though he was outstanding at managing nitty-gritty details?

Source: Robert Berner, "At Sears, a Great Communicator," *Business Week*, October 31, 2005, pp. 50, 52.

1. *Drive and passion.* Leaders are noted for the effort they invest in their work and the passion they have for work and work associates. Carol Bartz, the former CEO of Autodesk, observes, "If you're not excited, how can you get others excited? People will know. It's like how kids and dogs can sense when people don't like them."[19] The accompanying Management in Action presents more details about how passion contributes to leadership effectiveness.

19 "Top Leaders Tell their Secrets," *Fortune*, December 12, 2005, p. 128.

2. *Power motive.* Successful leaders exhibit **power motivation**, a strong desire to control others and resources or get them to do things on your behalf. A leader with a strong power need enjoys exercising power and using influence tactics. A manager who uses power constructively would more likely be promoted rapidly in an ethical corporation. Bill Gates of Microsoft exemplifies a power-obsessed leader who aggressively pursued a market domination strategy. He now uses his power through his foundation to help combat malnutrition and AIDS throughout the world.

power motivation
A strong desire to control others and resources or get them to do things on your behalf.

3. *Self-confidence combined with humility.* Self-confidence contributes to effective leadership in several ways. Above all, self-confident leaders project an image that encourages subordinates to have faith in them. Self-confidence also helps leaders make some of the tough business decisions they face regularly. When a dose of humility is combined with self-confidence, the leader is likely to be even more influential. Tim Cook of Apple, mentioned above, leads the organization confidently, but is self-effacing enough to show humility. A key aspect of humility as a leader is being able to put other people in the limelight, thereby enhancing their self-esteem.[20]
4. *Trustworthiness and honesty.* Trust is regarded as one of the major leadership attributes. Continuing waves of downsizings, financial scandals, and gigantic compensation to executives have eroded employee trust and commitment in many organizations. Effective leaders know they must build strong employee trust to obtain high productivity and commitment. A major strategy for being perceived as trustworthy is to make your behavior consistent with your intentions. Such behavior is also referred to as the leader being authentic. Practice what you preach and set the example. Allowing group members to participate in decisions is another trust builder.[21] A good example of a trusted leader is Linus Torvalds, the head of the open-source software company Linux. He runs his company not by being autocratic, but by making people trust him through such means as listening carefully to each point of view and making good decisions.[22]

   Closely related to honesty and integrity is being open with employees about the financial operations and other sensitive information about the company. In an **open-book company** every employee is trained, empowered, and motivated to understand and pursue the company's business goals. In this way employees become business partners. A company in Texas that repairs airplane parts reduced the bill for shop supplies by 91 percent through open-book management. One saving was to substitute heavy-duty tape that cost $25 a roll with tape that cost $2.50 per roll.[23]

open-book company
A firm in which every employee is trained, empowered, and motivated to understand and pursue the company's business goals.

---

20 Martha Finney, *In the Face of Uncertainty: 25 Top Leaders Speak Out on Challenge, Change, and the Future of American Business* (New York: AMACOM, 2002).

21 Kurt T. Dirks and Donald L. Ferrin, "Trust in Leadership: Meta-Analytic Findings and Implications for Research and Practice," *Journal of Applied Psychology*, August 2002, p. 622; Rob Goffee and Gareth Jones, "Managing Authenticity: The Paradox of Great Leadership," *Harvard Business Review*, December 2005, pp. 86–94.

22 Steve Hamm, "Linux Inc.," *Business Week*, January 31, 2005, p. 65.

23 John Case, "HR Learns How to Open the Books," *HR Magazine*, May 1998, p. 72; Stan Luxenberg, "Open Those Books: Boost Your Biz by Sharing Info," *Business Week Small Biz*, Summer 2006, p. 32.

To help you link the abstract concept of trust to day-by-day behavior, take the self-quiz in Exhibit 10-2. You might use the same quiz in relation to any manager you have worked for.

5. *Good intellectual ability, knowledge, and technical competence.* Effective leaders are good problem solvers and knowledgeable about the business or technology for which they are responsible. They are likely to combine

exhibit 10-2 Behaviors and Attitudes of a Trustworthy Leader

The following behaviors and attitudes characterize leaders who are generally trusted by their group members and other constituents. After you read each characteristic, indicate whether this behavior or attitude is one you have developed already, or does not fit you at present.

	Fits Me	Does Not Fit Me
1. Tells people he or she is going to do something, and then always follows through and gets it done	☐	☐
2. Is described by others as being reliable	☐	☐
3. Keeps secrets and confidences well	☐	☐
4. Tells the truth consistently	☐	☐
5. Minimizes telling people what they want to hear	☐	☐
6. Is described by others as "walking the talk"	☐	☐
7. Delivers consistent messages to others in terms of matching words and deeds	☐	☐
8. Does what he or she expects others to do	☐	☐
9. Minimizes hypocrisy by not engaging in activities he or she tells others are wrong	☐	☐
10. Readily accepts feedback on behavior from others	☐	☐
11. Maintains eye contact with people when talking to them	☐	☐
12. Appears relaxed and confident when explaining his or her side of a story	☐	☐
13. Individualizes compliments to others rather than saying something like "You look great" to a large number of people	☐	☐
14. Does not expect lavish perks for himself or herself while expecting others to go on an austerity diet	☐	☐
15. Does not tell others a crisis is pending (when it isn't) just to gain their cooperation	☐	☐
16. Collaborates with others to make creative decisions	☐	☐
17. Communicates information to people at all organizational levels	☐	☐
18. Readily shares financial information with others	☐	☐
19. Listens to people and then acts on many of their suggestions	☐	☐
20. Generally engages in predictable behavior	☐	☐

Scoring: These statements are mostly for self-reflection, so no specific scoring key exists. However, the more statements that fit you, the more trustworthy you are—assuming you are answering truthfully. The usefulness of this self-quiz increases if somebody who knows you well answers it for you to supplement your self-perceptions.

academic intelligence with practical intelligence (the ability to solve everyday problems based on experience). An analysis of 151 studies found a positive relationship between intelligence and the job performance of leaders. The relationship is likely to be higher when the leader plays an active role in decision making, and he or she is not overly stressed.[24]

Technical competence, or knowledge of the business, often translates into close attention to details about products and services. A representative example of how knowledge of the business fits into leadership was the appointment of Muhtar Kent to the No. 2 executive at Coca-Cola Co. in 2006. In addition to having good leadership qualities, Kent had developed strategies for sales turnarounds in Australia and parts of Western Europe in his role as director of international operations.[25]

6. *Sense of humor.* An effective sense of humor is an important part of a leader's job. In the workplace, humor relieves tension and boredom, defuses hostility, and helps build relationships with group members. The manager who makes the occasional witty comment is likely to be perceived as approachable and friendly.
7. *Emotional intelligence.* Effective leaders demonstrate good emotional intelligence, the ability to manage themselves and their relationships effectively. Emotional intelligence broadly encompasses many traits and behaviors related to leadership effectiveness, including self-confidence, empathy, passion for the task, and visionary leadership. Being sensitive to the needs of others (and not insulting or verbally abusing them) is another part of emotional intelligence. Another important aspect of emotional intelligence is to create good feelings in those they lead. The good moods and positive emotions help group members perform at their best because they become excited about the task, and might even be more creative. One way in which the leader brings about good moods is to encourage the positive expression of feelings in others, and avoid being cranky, hostile, and miserable most of the time himself or herself.[26]

Behaviors and Skills of Effective Leaders

Traits alone are not sufficient to lead effectively. A leader must also behave in certain ways and possess key skills. The actions or behaviors described in the following list are linked to leadership effectiveness. Recognize, however, that behaviors are related to skills. For example, in giving emotional support to team members, a leader uses interpersonal skills. A valuable part of understanding leadership behaviors for your career is that they are activities that can be learned because they can be translated into doable tasks.[27]

24 Timothy A. Judge, Amy E. Colbert, and Remus Ilies, "Intelligence and Leadership: A Quantitative Review and Test of Theoretical Propositions," *Journal of Applied Psychology*, June 2004, pp. 542–552.

25 Duane D. Stanford, "Coke's New President is Polished, Worldly," *The Atlanta Journal-Constitution*, December 8, 2006.

26 Daniel Goleman, "Leadership That Gets Results," *Harvard Business Review*, March–April 2000, p. 80; Goleman, Richard Boyatzis, and Annie McKee, *Primal Leadership: Realizing the Power of Emotional Intelligence* (Boston: Harvard Business School Press, 2002).

27 Sharon Daloz Parks, *Leadership Can Be Taught: A Bold Approach for a Complex World* (Boston: Harvard Business School Press, 2005).

1. *Is adaptable to the situation.* Adaptability reflects the contingency viewpoint: A tactic is chosen based on the unique circumstances at hand. Research with trauma resuscitation teams (as in an emergency room) at a medical center documents this tried and true observation about leadership behavior. Empowering leadership was found to be more effective when severity of the trauma was low (e.g., broken leg) and team experience was high. In contrast, directive leadership was more effective when trauma severity was high (e.g., gunshot wound to head) or when the team was inexperienced.[28] Another important aspect of adaptability is for a leader to be able to function effectively in different situations, such as leading in a manufacturing or office setting or even with a different cultural group. A former Coke director said of Muhtar Kent (mentioned above), "He can meet with the janitor in a bottling plant and minutes later go meet with a prime minister and be equally effective."[29] The ability to size up people and situations and adapt tactics accordingly is a vital leadership behavior.
2. *Establishes a direction for and demands high standards of performance from group members.* A major contribution of the leader at any level is to point the group in the right direction, or work with them to figure out what the group should be doing. The direction becomes a clear vision of the future. After setting a direction, effective leaders consistently hold group members to high standards of performance, which raises productivity. (However, the leader might also set high standards for directions already in place.) Setting high expectations for subordinates becomes a self-fulfilling prophecy. People tend to live up to the expectations set for them by their superiors. Setting high expectations might take the form of encouraging team members to establish difficult objectives.

   Carlos Ghosn, CEO of both Nissan and Renault, exemplifies a leader who establishes a direction while setting high standards at the same time. (Renault owns 44 percent of Nissan.) Several years ago he pointed Renault in the direction of becoming a more profitable company without engaging in downsizing. His plan called for a doubling of profit margins to 6 percent, and expanding world-wide vehicle production by nearly one-third to 800,000 per year by 2009. "It's not a target," snapped Ghosn. "Either management performs or it's out—and that applies to me as well."[30]
3. *Is visible and maintains a social presence.* An effective way of making an impact as a leader is to be visible to group members, thereby maintaining the perception of being present. There is a strong temptation for leaders to stay in their own work area performing analytical work or dealing with e-mail. Being visible allows for spontaneous communication with group members, and a relaxed atmosphere in which to hear about problems. Being visible also creates the opportunity for coaching group members. Jeff Immelt, the chairman and CEO of General Electric, believes that being

28 Seokhwa Yun, Samer Faraj, and Henry P. Sims Jr., "Contingent Leadership Effectiveness of Trauma Resuscitation Teams," *Journal of Applied Psychology*, November 2005, pp. 1288–1296.

29 Duane D. Stanford, "Coke's New President is Polished, Worldly," *The Atlanta Journal-Constitution*, December 8, 2006.

30 Monica Langley, "For Carlos Ghosn, Fast Lane Gets bumpy," *The Wall Street Journal*, October 28–29, 2006, pp. A1, A8.

visible is essential for carrying out his leadership role. He spends more than one-half his time on the road visiting customers, employees, and shareholders.[31]

4. *Provides emotional support to group members.* Supportive behavior toward subordinates usually increases leadership effectiveness. A supportive leader frequently gives encouragement and praise, such as, "Jack, if it were not for your super effort over the weekend we could have never opened the store today." The emotional support generally improves morale and sometimes improves productivity. Being emotionally supportive comes naturally to the leader who has empathy for people and who is a warm person.
5. *Gives frequent feedback and accepts feedback.* Giving group members frequent feedback on their performance is another vital leadership behavior. The manager rarely can influence the behavior of group members without appropriate performance feedback. Feedback helps in two ways. First, it informs employees of how well they are doing, so they can take corrective action if needed. Second, positive feedback encourages subordinates to keep up the good work. The effective leader also listens to feedback from group members, and acts on positive suggestions. Lydia Whitefield, a vice president of marketing at Avaya, learned from her group members that she was perceived as being angry quite often. What employees perceived as anger, Whitefield perceived as passion. She learned to be more contained when discussing assignments with group members and to minimize acting vehemently.[32]
6. *Recovers quickly from setbacks, including crises.* Effective managerial leaders are resilient: They bounce back quickly from setbacks such as budget cuts, demotions, and being fired. Leadership resiliency serves as a positive model for employees at all levels when the organization confronts difficult times. During such times effective leaders sprinkle their speech with clichés such as "Tough times don't last, but tough people do," or "When times get tough, the tough get going." Delivered with sincerity, such messages are inspirational to many employees.

   Leading group members through a crisis is part of resiliency. Crisis leadership is a subject within itself. Trust that the leader or leaders can deal with the crisis is critical, and can often be attained by communicating openly, honestly, and often about the crisis.[33] In dealing with a crisis, it is helpful for the leader to project confident body language, such as appearing relaxed while delivering the crisis plan.

   Another key part of managing a crisis well is for the leader to present a plan for dealing with the crisis, and at the same time to be calm and reassuring. When Meg Whitman, the CEO of eBay, was at a company meeting in Germany, the managers present were concerned about a weakness in

---

31 Carol Hymowitz, "GE Chief is Charting His Own Strategy, Focusing on Technology," *The Wall Street Journal*, September 23, 2003, p. B1.

32 Carol Hymowitz, "Managers See Feedback from Their Staffers As the Most Valuable," *The Wall Street Journal*, November 11, 2003, p. B1.

33 Erika Hayes James and Lynn Perry Wooten, "How to Display Competence in Times of Crisis," *Organizational Dynamics*, No. 2, 2005, p, 146.

their business. She suggested that additional marketing spending would help boost activity, and that no one should panic because there are many solutions at their disposal.[34]

7. *Plays the role of servant leader.* Some effective leaders believe that their primary mission is to serve the needs of their constituents. They measure their effectiveness in terms of their ability to help others. Servant leaders are more concerned about the needs of their constituents so they usually show qualities such as patience, honesty, good listening skills, and appreciation of others. Instead of seeking individual recognition, servant leaders see themselves as working for the group members. The servant leader uses his or her talents to help group members. For example, if the leader happens to be a good planner, he engages in planning because it will help the group attain its goals.[35] Many academic administrators see themselves as servant leaders; they take care of administrative work so instructors can devote more time to teaching and scholarship. To be an effective servant leader, a person needs the many leadership traits and behaviors described in this chapter.

LEADERSHIP STYLES

Learning Objective 4

Describe participative leadership, authoritarian leadership, the Leadership Grid, situational, and entrepreneurial leadership.

Another important part of the leadership function is **leadership style.** It is the typical pattern of behavior that a leader uses to influence his or her employees to achieve organizational goals. Several different approaches to describing leadership styles have developed over the years. Most of these involve how much authority and control the leader turns over to the group. The historically important Theory X and Theory Y presented in Chapter 1 can be interpreted as two contrasting leadership styles. First, this section will describe two basic leadership styles, the participative and the autocratic. We then describe the Leadership Grid, the situational model of leadership, and the entrepreneurial leadership style. A skill-building exercise at the end of the chapter gives you a chance to measure certain aspects of your leadership style.

Participative Leadership Style

leadership style
The typical pattern of behavior that a leader uses to influence his or her employees to achieve organizational goals.

A **participative leader** is one who shares decision making with group members. The modern organization generally favors the leader sharing decision making with group members. One key reason is that in this complex world, the leader does not have all the answers. Research suggests that team leaders and team members can share leadership. In many teams, the leadership rotates to the person with the key knowledge, skills, and abilities for the task facing the team at the time.[36] For example, if the team were facing a

34 Adam Lashinsky, "Meg and the Machine," *Fortune*, September 1, 2003, p. 70.

35 Robert K. Greenleaf, *The Power of Servant Leadership* (San Francisco: Berrett-Koehler Publishers Inc., 1998); James C. Hunter, *The World's Most Powerful Leadership Principle* (New York: Crown Business, 2004).

36 Craig L. Pearse, "The Future of Leadership: Combining Vertical and Shared Leadership to Transform Knowledge Work," *Academy of Management Executive*, February 2004, pp. 47–57.

customer dissatisfaction issue, the team member with the most experience in resolving customer problems might be assigned leadership responsibility for resolving the problem. Team leaders use the participative style so frequently that participative leadership is also referred to as the *team leadership style.*

participative leader
A leader who shares decision making with group leaders.

Three closely related subtypes of participative leaders include consultative, consensus, and democratic. *Consultative leaders* confer with subordinates before making a decision. However, they retain the final authority to make decisions. *Consensus leaders* encourage group discussion about an issue and then make a decision that reflects the general opinion (consensus) of group members. All workers who will be involved in the consequences of a decision have an opportunity to provide input. A decision is not considered final until all parties involved agree with the decision. *Democratic leaders* confer final authority on the group. They function as collectors of opinion and take a vote before making a decision.

Although a pure democratic style of leadership may seem unsuited to business, it has been a cornerstone philosophy at the highly successful Brazilian equipment supplier, Semco. Of the employees' 3,000 votes on a variety of work issues, CEO Ricardo Semler gets only one. Employees even played a major role in setting their own compensation.[37]

Participative leaders can be found in all types of organizations, and at all levels. When the celebrated business consulting firm McKinsey & Co. wanted to reinvigorate the firm, they chose Ian Davis, a company veteran known for his consensus building, as the new managing director. His analytical skills and unassuming personality were considered appropriate for a person who has to share (or distribute) leadership to some extent with 900 partners. Davis says, "A managing director is a servant leader: elected, not appointed."[38] Participative leadership takes many forms. The group decision-making techniques described in Chapter 5 are participative because group input is relied on heavily.

Participative leadership works well with people who want to share decision making, and whose cultural values accept group members sharing leadership. Yet, using consensus and democratic leadership is time consuming and results in much time spent in physical and electronic meetings. Executive Chairman Bill Ford Jr. in analyzing the problems at Ford Motor Company said, "Maybe one of the drawbacks of our culture is that we've been too democratic, and that may have slowed us down."[39]

Autocratic Leadership Style

Autocratic leaders retain most of the authority for themselves. They make decisions in a confident manner and assume that group members will comply.

autocratic leader
A task-oriented leader who retains most of the authority for himself or herself and is not generally concerned with group members' attitudes toward decisions.

37 "Ricardo Semler's Huge Leap of Faith," *Executive Leadership*, April 2006, Adapted from Lawrence M. Fisher, "Ricardo Semler Won't Take Control," *strategy+business*.

38 Kemba J. Dunham, "McKinsey Taps Low-Key Leader For Tough Times," *The Wall Street Journal*, March 7, 2002, pp. B1, B4; "Our Managing Director," http://www.mckinsey.com, accessed December 22, 2006.

39 Bryce G. Hoffman, "Mulally Already Shaking up Ford," *The Detroit News* (http://www.detnews.com), September 22, 2006.

An autocratic leader is not usually concerned with the group members' attitudes toward the decision. Typical autocratic leaders tell people what to do, assert themselves, and serve as models for group members. During a crisis, autocratic leadership is often welcome because group members want someone to point them in the right direction in a hurry. Also, the situation may be so dire the leader does not have sufficient time to attain consensus on a recovery plan.

Donald Trump is a power-oriented business leader and celebrity with a brusque and autocratic leadership style. He contributes heavily to decisions such as which type of marble to choose for a hotel lobby. Trump is well liked by construction workers, as well as many staff members. "The Donald" may be autocratic, but he is not vicious. In Trump's words, "One of the most important lessons my parents taught me was to treat people with respect, even if I'm angry with them."[40]

Leadership Grid Leadership Styles

Several approaches to understanding leadership styles focus on two major dimensions of leadership: tasks and relationships. Research extending over 50 years has shown that the dimensions of tasks and relationships contribute to both performance and satisfaction. Task behavior is more related to performance, and relationship behaviors are more closely related to satisfaction.[41] The best known approach to basing style on tasks and relationships is the **Leadership Grid.®** It is based on different integrations of the leader's concern for production (results) and people (relationships). The Grid (a.k.a., The Managerial Grid) is part of a comprehensive program of management and leadership training that addresses the fundamental values and attitudes that influence behavior. The Grid has evolved over the years, and its most recent version is presented in Exhibit 10-3.

Concern for results is rated on the Grid's horizontal axis. Concern for production includes results, bottom line, performance, profits, and mission. Concern for people is rated on the vertical axis, and it includes concern for group members and coworkers. Both concerns are leadership attitudes or ways of thinking about leadership. Each of these concerns (or dimensions) exists in varying degrees along a continuum from 1 to 9. A manager's standing on one concern is not supposed to influence his or her standing on the other. As shown in Exhibit 10-3, the Grid encompasses seven leadership styles.

Leadership Grid® A visual representation of different combinations of a leader's degree of concern for task-related issues.

The developers of the grid argue strongly for the value of sound management (9, 9). According to their research, the sound management approach pays off. It results in improved performance, low absenteeism and turnover, and high morale. Team management relies on trust and respect, which help bring about good results.[42]

---

40 Quoted in Robert Kiyosaki, "Why the Rich Get Richer," *Yahoo! Finance* (http://www.finance.yahoo.com), November 29, 2006.

41 Timothy A. Judge, Ronald F. Piccolo, and Remus Ilies, "The Forgotten Ones? The Validity of Consideration and Initiating Structure in Leadership Research," *Journal of Applied Psychology*, February 2004, pp. 36–51.

42 Robert R. Blake and Anne Adams McCanse, *Leadership Dilemmas—Grid Solutions* (Houston: Gulf Publishing, 1991).

exhibit 10-3 The Leadership Grid™

The Managerial Grid graphic below is a very simple framework that elegantly defines seven basic styles that characterize workplace behavior and the resulting relationships. The seven managerial Grid styles are based on how two fundamental concerns (concern for people and concern for results) are manifested at varying levels whenever people interact.

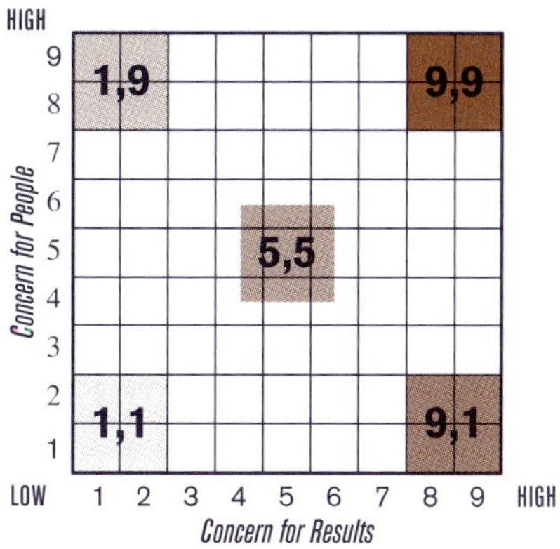

The Seven Managerial Grid Styles:

9,1 Controlling (Direct & Dominate)

I expect results and take control by clearly stating a course of action. I enforce rules that sustain high results and do not permit deviation.

1,9 Accommodating (Yield & Comply)

I support results that establish and reinforce harmony. I generate enthusiasm by focusing on positive and pleasing aspects of work.

5,5 Status Quo (Balance & Compromise)

I endorse results that are popular but caution against taking unnecessary risk. I test my opinions with others involved to assure ongoing acceptability.

1,1 Indifferent (Evade & Elude)

I distance myself from taking active responsibility for results to avoid getting entangled in problems. If forced, I take a passive or supportive position.

PAT Paternalistic (prescribe & Guide)

I provide leadership by defining initiatives for myself and others. I offer praise and appreciation for support, and discourage challenges to my thinking.

OPP Opportunistic (Exploit & Manipulate)

I persuade others to support results that offer me private benefit. If they also benefit, that's even better in gaining support. I rely on whatever approach is needed to secure an advantage.

9,9 Sound (Contribute & Commit)

I initiate team action in a way that invites involvement and commitment. I explore all facts and alternative views to reach a shared understanding of the best solution.

Source:

situational leadership model An explanation of leadership that matches leadership style to the readiness of group members.

Situational Leadership®II (SLII)

In another major perspective on leadership, effective leaders adapt their leadership style to the requirements of the situation, such as whether the group is facing a crisis, and swift, decisive action is called for by the leader.[43] Many other variables are also important such as the organizational culture and the characteristics of group members. **Situational leadership II (SLII)** of Kenneth H. Blanchard and his colleagues explains how to match the leadership style to capabilities of group members on a given task.[44] For example, you might need less guidance from the supervisor when you are skilled in a task than when you are performing a new task.

Situational Leadership II is designed to increase the frequency and quality of conversations about performance and professional development between managers and group members so that competence is developed, commitment takes place, and turnover among talented workers is reduced. Leaders are taught to use the leadership style that matches or responds to the needs of the situation.

Situational Leadership II stems from the original situational model that has been widely studied in leadership and used in training programs. The major premise of SLII is that the basis for effective leadership is managing the relationship between a leader and a subordinate on a given task. The major concepts of the SLII model are presented in Exhibit 10-4. According to SLII, effective leaders adapt their behavior to the level of *commitment* and

exhibit 10-4 Situational Leadership II (SLII)

For best results on a given task, the leader is required to match style to the developmental level of the group member. Each quadrant indicates the desired match between leader style and subordinate development level.

Style 3 **Supporting**: Low on directing and high on supporting behaviors **Developmental level 3** **Capable but cautious performer**: Growing competence and variable commitment	**Style 2** **Coaching**: High on directing and high on supporting behaviors **Developmental level 2** **Disillusioned learner**: Some competence but low commitment
Style 4 **Delegating**: Low on directing and low in supporting behaviors **Developmental level 4** **Self-reliant achiever**: Highest level of commitment and competence	**Style 1** **Directing**: High on directing and low on supporting behaviors **Developmental level 1** **Enthusiastic Beginner**: Low competence but high commitment

↕ **Supporting (relationship behaviors)**

← **Directing (task-related behaviors)** →

43 Victor H. Vroom and Arthur G. Jago, "The Role of the Situation in Leadership," *The American Psychologist*, January 2007, pp. 17–24.

44 Kenneth H. Blanchard, David Zigarmi, and Robert Nelson, "Situational Leadership after 25 Years: A Retrospective," *Journal of Leadership Studies 1*, 1993, pp. 22–26: "Building Materials Leader Builds Better Leaders," http://www.kenblanchard.com.

competence of a particular subordinate to complete a given task. For example, team member Russ might be committed to renting some empty office space by year-end, and also highly skilled at such activity. Or he might feel that the task is drudgery, and not have much skill in selling office space. The combination of the subordinate's commitment and competence determines his or her *developmental level*, as follows:

- **D1**—Enthusiastic Beginner. The learner has low competence but high commitment.
- **D2**—Disillusioned Learner. The individual has gained some competence but has been disappointed after having experienced several setbacks. Commitment at this stage is low.
- **D3**—Capable but Cautious Performer. The learner has growing competence, yet commitment is variable.
- **D4**—Self-reliant Achiever. The learner has high competence and commitment.

Situational Leadership II explains that effective leadership depends on two independent behaviors: *supporting* and *directing*. Supporting refers to relationship behaviors such as the leader listening, giving recognition, communicating, and encouraging. Directing refers to task-related behaviors such as the leader giving careful directions and controlling. As shown in Exhibit 10-4, the four basic styles are as follows:

- **S1**—Directing. High directive behavior/low supportive behavior.
- **S2**—Coaching. High directive behavior/high supportive behavior.
- **S3**—Supporting. Low directive behavior/high supportive behavior.
- **S4**—Delegating. Low directive behavior/low supportive behavior.

A key point of SLII is that no one style is best: an effective leader uses all four styles depending on the subordinate's developmental level on a given task. The most appropriate leadership style among S1 to S4 corresponds to the subordinate developmental levels of D1 to D4 respectively. Specifically, enthusiastic beginners (D1) require a directing (S1) leader; disillusioned learners (D2) need a coaching (S2) leader; capable but cautious workers (D3) need a supporting-style (S3) leader; and self-reliant achievers (D4) need a delegating (S4) style of leader.

Situational leadership represents a consensus of thinking about leadership behavior in relation to group members: competent people require less specific direction than do less competent people. The model is also useful because it builds on other explanations of leadership that emphasize the role of task and relationship behaviors. As a result, it has proved to be useful as the basis for leadership training. The situational model also corroborates common sense and is therefore intuitively appealing. You can benefit from this model by attempting to diagnose the commitment and competence of group members before choosing the right leadership style.

A challenge in applying SLII is that the leader has to stay tuned into which task a group member is performing at a given time, and then implement the correct style. Given that assignments change rapidly, and group members are often working on more than one task in a day, the leader would have to keep shifting styles. SLII presents categories and guidelines so precisely that it gives the impression of infallibility. In reality, leadership situations are less clear-cut than the four quadrants suggest. Also, the prescriptions for leadership will work only some of the time. For example, many supervisors use a coaching style (S2) with a disillusioned learner (D2) and still achieve poor results.

For an example of how the situational model might work in practice, consider the approach used by Lois Melbourne, the CEO of TimeVision Inc. of Irving, Texas, in selecting a new salesperson. When the company needed to add to its 20-person sales staff, Melbourne assigned the task to two of her salespeople. They created the job specification, posted it online, reviewed résumés, conducted interviews, and made the final recommendation. A Time-Vision manager did not get involved until salary negotiations, and Melbourne did not see the sales rep until her first day on the job. Melbourne used the delegating leadership style because she believed that her salespeople were competent and motivated enough to handle this personnel assignment by themselves.[45]

The Entrepreneurial Leadership Style

Interest in entrepreneurial leadership continues to grow as start-up companies and other small enterprises become an important source of new employment. Many new small businesses arise to meet the demand of larger firms that outsource work. Managers who initiate one or more innovative business enterprises show some similarity in leadership style. Entrepreneurs often possess the following personal characteristics and behaviors:

1. *A strong achievement need.* Entrepreneurs have stronger achievement needs than most managers. Building a business is an excellent vehicle for accomplishment. The high achiever shows three consistent behaviors and attitudes. He or she (a) takes personal responsibility to solve problems, (b) attempts to achieve moderate goals at moderate risks, and (c) prefers situations that provide frequent feedback on results (readily found in starting a new enterprise).[46] As part of their achievement need, entrepreneurs are often in a hurry to get projects accomplished and move on to the next project.
2. *High enthusiasm, creativity, and visionary perspective.* Related to the achievement need, entrepreneurs are typically enthusiastic, creative, and visionary. Their enthusiasm in turn makes them persuasive. As a result, entrepreneurs are often perceived as charismatic by their employees and customers. The enthusiasm of entrepreneurs propels them into a hurrying mode much of the time. Creativity is needed to find new business ideas. Successful entrepreneurs carefully observe the world around them, in constant

45 Mark Henricks, "Give It Away," *Entrepreneur*, May 2000, p. 117.
46 David C. McClelland, *The Achieving Society* (New York: Van Nostrand Reinhold, 1961).

search for their next big marketable idea, leading to a vision. They see opportunities others fail to observe. One example is Andy Taylor, who founded Enterprise Rent-a-Car. The opportunity he saw was to build a car rental agency that specialized in renting cars to airline travelers and people whose car was being repaired. Enterprise is now a major player in the car rental business.

3. *Uncomfortable with hierarchy and bureaucracy.* Entrepreneurs, by temperament, are not ideally suited to working within the mainstream of a bureaucracy. Many successful entrepreneurs are people who were frustrated by the constraints of a bureaucratic system. Once the typical entrepreneur launches a successful business, he or she often hires a professional manager to take over the internal workings of the firm. The entrepreneur is then free to concentrate on making sales, raising capital, and pursuing other external contacts. One of the reasons entrepreneurs have difficulty with bureaucracy is that they focus their energies on products, services, and customers. Some entrepreneurs are gracious to customers and moneylenders but brusque with company insiders.

transformational leader
A leader who helps organizations and people make positive changes in the way they do things.

Leadership styles relate directly to the leadership behavior of adaptability to the situation. A study of the leadership styles of 3,871 executives revealed that leaders who achieve the best results do not stick with one leadership style. The effective executive selects the best style to fit a given situation, much like a golf player selecting the most appropriate club for a particular shot. The study looked at styles similar to the styles and influence tactics already mentioned in this chapter, including authoritarian and democratic. An example of a leader fitting his style to the situation was "Tom," the vice president of marketing for a pizza chain. The chain was floundering, and the company held regular meetings to attempt to repair the damage. So Tom made a decisive move.

During a meeting he made an impassioned plea for his colleagues to think about pizza from the customer's perspective, and to strive for convenience. With his enthusiasm and clear vision, Tom filled a leadership vacuum at the company. Convenience became part of the mission statement, and it motivated pizza store operators to make buying pizza easier for customers. One such convenience was operating kiosks on busy street corners. Tom's shift to an authoritarian style saved the company.[47]

TRANSFORMATIONAL AND CHARISMATIC LEADERSHIP

Learning Objective 5
Describe transformational and charismatic leadership.

The study of leadership often emphasizes the **transformational leader**—one who helps organizations and people make positive changes in the way they do things. Transformational leadership combines charisma, inspirational leadership, and intellectual stimulation. It plays an especially critical role in the revitalization of existing business organizations. The transformational leader develops new visions for the organization and mobilizes employees to

47 Daniel Goleman, "Leadership That Gets Results," *Harvard Business Review*, March–April 2000, pp. 78, 83.

accept and work toward attaining these visions. An example of a transformational leader is William Bratton, the Los Angeles Chief of Police and former police commissioner of New York City. In two years Bratton turned New York into one of the safest large cities in the United States and had made substantial progress in combating crime in Los Angeles. He had previously turned around four other law enforcement agencies.[48] This section will describe how transformations take place, the role of charisma, how to become charismatic, and the downside of charismatic leadership.

How Transformations Take Place

The transformational leader attempts to overhaul the organizational culture or subculture, and to make a difference in people's lives. To bring about the overhaul, transformations take place in one or more of three ways.[49] First, the transformational leader raises people's awareness of the importance and value of certain rewards and how to achieve them. He or she points out the pride workers would experience if the firm became number one in its field. Second, the transformational leader gets people to look beyond their self-interests for the sake of the work group and the firm. Such a leader might say, "I know you would like more healthcare benefits. But, if we don't cut expenses, we'll all be out of a job." Third, the transformational leader helps people go beyond a focus on minor satisfactions to a quest for self-fulfillment. He or she might explain, "I know that a long lunch break is nice. But, just think, if we get this project done on time, we'll be the envy of the company."

One of many studies indicating that transformational leadership makes a difference in performance was conducted by Robert T. Keller with 118 research and development project teams from five firms. Subordinate perceptions of transformational leadership (including charisma) were measured by a standard measure of such leadership. The results demonstrated that transformational leadership was positively related to technical quality of the projects produced and performing on schedule one year later. Even more impressive, perceptions of transformational leadership were related to the five-year profitability of the products developed by the project teams as well as product speed to market.[50]

charisma The ability to lead or influence others based on personal charm, magnetism, inspiration, and emotion.

Charismatic Leadership

A leader's personality can be a big part of his or her effectiveness. **Charisma** is the ability to lead or influence others based on personal charm, magnetism, inspiration, and emotion. Jack and Suzy Welch explain that charisma is vital in today's competitive worlds because workers needed to be energized more

48 W. Chan Kaim and Renée Mauborgne, "Tipping Point Leadership," *Harvard Business Review*, April 2003, pp. 60–69; "Chief William J. Bratton's Welcome Message," http://www.lapdblo.typepad.com, May 11, 2006.

49 John J. Hater and Bernard M. Bass, "Superiors' Evaluations and Subordinates' Perceptions of Transformational and Transactional Leadership," *Journal of Applied Psychology*, November 1988, p. 69; Nick Turner et al., "Transformational Leadership and Moral Reasoning," *Journal of Applied Psychology*, April 2002, pp. 304–311.

50 Robert T. Keller, "Transformational Leadership, Initiating Structure, and Substitutes for Leadership: A Longitudinal Study of Research and Development Project Team Performance," *Journal of Applied Psychology*, January 2006, pp. 202–210.

than ever.[51] To label a leader as charismatic does not mean that everybody shares that opinion. Even the most popular and inspiring leaders are perceived negatively by some members of their organization or their constituents. Quite often these negative perceptions are communicated on blogs. The list that follows presents leaders' qualities that relate specifically to charisma.[52]

1. *Vision.* Charismatic leaders offer an exciting image of where the organization is headed and how to get there. A vision is more than a forecast, because it describes an ideal version of the future for an organization or organizational unit.
2. *Masterful communication style.* To inspire people, charismatic and transformational leaders use colorful language and exciting metaphors and analogies. A former CEO of Coca-Cola told people, "We give people around the world a moment of pleasure in their daily lives." Another key aspect of the communication style of transformational leaders is that they tell captivating stories that relate to the goals of the firm. For example, some leaders use the fairy tale "The Three Little Pigs" to illustrate how business firms must make products and services stronger to withstand competitive force.
3. *Inspires trust.* People believe so strongly in the integrity of charismatic leaders that they will risk their careers to pursue the leader's vision. Also, when a charismatic leader leaves an organization, several subordinates often follow the leader to his or her next firm.
4. *Energy and action orientation.* Similar to entrepreneurs, most charismatic leaders are energetic and serve as a model for getting things done on time.
5. *Inspiring leadership.* Partly as a result of the four preceding characteristics, transformational and charismatic leaders emotionally arouse people to the point that they want to achieve higher goals than they thought of previously. In short, the charismatic leader stands as an inspiration to many others.

Charisma may indeed be related to personality factors, but often a leader is perceived as charismatic because he or she attained outstanding performance. For example, a study found that CEOs tended to be perceived as charismatic following good organizational performance. Yet CEOs being perceived as charismatic was not related to future good business results.[53] So, it is possible that good organizational performance leads to charisma rather than the opposite.

---

51 Jack and Suzy Welch, "It's Not about Empty Suits," *Business Week*, October 16, 2006, p. 132.

52 Alan J. Dubinsky, Francis J. Yammarino, and Marvin A. Jolson, "An Examination of Linkages Between Personal Characteristics and Dimensions of Transformational Leadership," *Journal of Business and Psychology*, Spring 1995, p. 315; Timothy A. Judge and Joyce E. Bono, "Five-Factor Model of Personality and Transformational Leadership," *Journal of Applied Psychology*, October 2000, pp. 751–765.

53 Bradely R. Agle, Nandu J. Nagarajan, Jeffrey A. Sonnenfeld, and Dhinu Srinivasan, "Does CEO Charisma Matter? An Empirical Analysis of the Relationships among Organizational Performance, Environmental Uncertainty, and top Management Perceptions of CEO Charisma," *Academy of Management Journal*, February 2006, pp. 161–174.

Developing Charisma

Managers can improve their image as charismatic by engaging in favorable interactions with group members through a variety of techniques.[54] A starting point is to *use visioning*. Develop a dream about the future of your unit and discuss it with others. *Make frequent use of metaphors.* Develop metaphors to inspire the people around you. A commonly used one after the group has experienced a substantial setback is to say, "Like the phoenix, we will rise from the ashes of defeat." *It is important to inspire trust and confidence.* Get people to believe in your competence by making your accomplishments known in a polite, tactful way.

Be highly energetic and goal oriented so your energy and resourcefulness become contagious. To increase your energy supply, exercise frequently, eat well, and get ample rest. It is important to express your emotions frequently. Freely express warmth, joy, happiness, and enthusiasm. *Smile frequently*, even if you are not in a happy mood. A warm smile indicates a confident, caring person, which contributes to perceptions of charisma. *Make everybody you meet feel important.* For example, at a company meeting shake the hand of every person you meet. Another way of making people feel important is giving them assignments in which they have a high chance of succeeding, and then give positive feedback.

A relatively easy characteristic to develop is to *multiply the effectiveness of your handshake.* Shake firmly without creating pain, and make enough eye contact to notice the color of the other person's eyes. When you take that much trouble, you project care and concern. Finally, *stand up straight and use nonverbal signs of self-confidence.* Practice good posture and minimize fidgeting and speaking in a monotone.

David Brandon, now the CEO of Domino's Pizza, provides a good illustration of a transformational and charismatic leader. During his first eight years at Domino's he has unleashed the company's once patriarchal culture and created an energized and fast-growing company. Brandon is highly people focused and uses such techniques as creating new labels for business functions. Human resources became "People First," and marketing became "Build the Brand."[55] Brandon frequently praises people, offers financial incentives for reaching goals, and tells stories with messages about company values. Brandon is seen as a future political star.

The Downside of Charismatic Leadership

Charismatic business leaders are seen as corporate heroes when they can turn around a failing business or launch a new enterprise. Nevertheless, this type of leadership has a dark side. Some charismatic leaders manipulate and take advantage of people, such as by getting them to invest retirement savings in risky company stock. Some charismatic leaders are unethical and

---

54 Andrew J. DuBrin, *Personal Magnetism: Discover Your Own Charisma and Learn How to Charm, Inspire, and Influence Others* (New York: AMACOM, 1997), pp. 93–111; Monica Larner, "The Man Who Saved Ferrari," *Business Week*, March 8, 1999, pp. 74–75.

55 Dorothy Bourdet, "Domino Effect," *Detroit News Online*, December 9, 2006.

lead their organizations toward illegal and immoral ends. People are willing to follow the charismatic leader down a quasi-legal path because of his or her charisma. Gary Winnick, the former CEO and chairman of Global Crossing, was perceived as charming and persuasive. He encouraged people to invest in his company, or hold on to their stock, while he sold more than $735 million in stock just before the company's downfall.

Another concern about some charismatic business leaders is that they begin to perceive of themselves as superstars who accomplish most of the company leadership by themselves. Some of these charismatic executives become so caught up in receiving publicity and mingling with politicians and investors, they neglect the operations of the business. Because of this, more low-key executive leaders—especially those who focus on internal operations—are more in style than previously. On such example is Mark Hurd, the chairman and CEO of Hewlett-Packard, who is considered to be a whiz at making a company more efficient yet is moderately charismatic.

mentor
A more experienced person who develops a protégé's abilities through tutoring, coaching, guidance, and emotional support.

THE LEADER AS A MENTOR AND COACH

Learning Objective 6

Explain the leadership role of mentoring and coaching.

Another vital part of leadership is directly assisting less experienced workers to improve their job performance and advance their careers. A **mentor** is a more experienced person who develops a protégé's abilities through tutoring, coaching, guidance, and emotional support. The mentor helps the person being mentored grow by challenging him or her to deal with difficult situations (such as joining a task force) or deal with a difficult work problem. The idea of mentoring traces back to ancient Greece when a warrior entrusted his son to the tutor Mentor. Although never out of style, mentoring is more important than ever as workers face complex and rapidly changing job demands. Coaching deals with helping others improve performance, and will be described more fully in Chapter 16. Quite often the mentor is also a coach, but a manager who coaches another person may not be a mentor. The manager mentioned in the chapter opener functioned as both a mentor and coach.

The mentor, a trusted counselor and guide, is typically a person's manager or team leader. Mentors are typically within the field of expertise of the protégé, but can also come from another specialty. For example, a manufacturing manager might mentor an accountant. A leader can be a mentor to several people at the same time, and successful individuals often have several mentors during their career.

Helping the protégé solve problems is an important part of mentoring. Mentors help their protégés solve problems by themselves and make their own discoveries. A comment frequently made to mentors is, "I'm glad you made me think through the problem. You put me on the right track." A mentor can also give specific assistance in technical problem solving. If the mentor knows more about the new technology than the protégé, he or she can shorten the person's learning time. Many developments in information technology are likely to be taught by a coworker serving as a mentor, because a manager often has less current technology knowledge than a group member.

shadowing
Directly observing the work activities of the mentor by following the manager around for a stated period of time, such as one day per month.

Mentoring has traditionally been an informal relationship based on compatibility between two personalities. As with other trusted friends, good chemistry should exist between the mentor and the protégé. Many mentoring programs assign a mentor to selected new employees. Formal mentors often supplement the work of managers by assisting a newcomer to acquire job skills and understand the organization culture.

A recently popular approach to mentoring is **shadowing**, or directly observing the work activities of the mentor by following the manager around for a stated period of time, such as one day per month. The protégé might be invited to strategy meetings, visits with key customers, discussions with union leaders, and the like. The protégé makes observations about how the mentor handles situations, and a debriefing session might be held to discuss how and why certain tactics were used.

To capitalize on the potential advantages of mentoring, develop or build on good relationships with superiors and request feedback on performance at least once a year. Find and identify an informal mentor who is willing to be an advocate for your upward mobility within the organization, help you learn the informal rules of the workplace, and help you make valuable contacts. Your mentor will help you identify the informal rules of the company that are helpful in navigating through the organization. (An example would be "Never turn down a request from upper management.")

A mentor usually becomes a better manager because of mentoring. Keith R. Wyche, the president, U.S. Operations of Pitney Bowe's Management Services, observes that mentoring enhances the leadership capacity of the mentor. "The first law of leadership," he says, "is a true leader helps create future leaders. It also helps the mentor move from being just successful to being significant. Individual success is admirable, but taking time to help others achieve success is much more satisfying and significant."[56]

LEADERSHIP SKILLS

Learning Objective 7
Identify the skills that contribute to leadership.

As already explained, leadership involves personal qualities, behaviors, and skills. A skill refers to a present capability, such as being able to resolve conflict or create a vision statement. Many of these leadership skills have been mentioned or implied throughout the book. A prime example would be the five general skills for managers described in Chapter 1: technical, interpersonal, conceptual, diagnostic, and political. For example, to exercise strategic leadership, a manager would need to have strong conceptual skills. To inspire people, a leader would need interpersonal skills, and to negotiate well, he or she would need good political skills. To be an effective face-to-face leader, the manager would need coaching skills, as described in Chapter 16.

The leadership roles presented in Chapter 1 directly associated with leadership skills are as follows: negotiator, coach, team builder, technical

56 Quoted in Laura Egodigwe, "His Brother's Keeper: A Mentor Learns the True Meaning of Leadership of Leadership," *Black Enterprise*, December 2006, p. 69.

problem solver, and entrepreneur. The following checklist provides some additional skills that can contribute to leadership effectiveness, depending on the people and the task.

- Sizing up situations in order to apply the best leadership approach
- Exerting influence through various approaches such as rational persuasion, inspirational appeal, and being assertive
- Motivating team members through such specific techniques as goal setting and positive reinforcement
- Motivating people from diverse cultures and nations
- Resolving conflict with superiors and group members
- Solving problems creatively in ways that point group members in new directions
- Developing a mission statement that inspires others to perform well

As implied by this discussion, leadership involves dozens of different skills. An effective manager's toolkit combines various skills according to the leader's needs and the situation. Holding a leadership position offers a wonderful opportunity for personal growth through skill development.

SUMMARY OF Key Points

1 Differentiate between leadership and management.

Management is a set of explicit tools and techniques based on reasoning and testing that can be used in a variety of situations. Leadership is concerned with vision, change, motivation, persuasion, creativity, and influence.

2 Describe how leaders are able to influence and empower team members.

Power is the ability to get other people to do things or the ability to control resources. Authority is the formal right to wield power. Six types of power include legitimate, reward, coercive, expert, referent (stemming from charisma), and subordinate. Through subordinate power, team members limit the authority of leaders. To get others to act, leaders also use tactics such as leading by example, leading by values, assertiveness, rationality, ingratiation, exchange, coalition formation, and joking and kidding.

Empowerment is the process of sharing power with team members to enhance their feelings of personal effectiveness. Empowerment increases employee motivation, because the employee is accepted as a partner in decision making. For empowerment to work well, people have to exercise self-leadership, and cross-cultural factors in the acceptance of empowerment must be considered.

3 Identify important leadership characteristics and behaviors.

Certain personal characteristics are associated with successful managerial leadership in many situations, including the following: drive and passion; power motive; self-confidence combined with humility; trustworthiness and honesty; good intellectual ability, knowledge, and technical competence; sense of humor; and emotional intelligence.

Effective leaders need to demonstrate adaptability, establish a direction and set high standards of performance, and provide emotional support to group members. They should give and accept feedback, exhibit a strong customer orientation, recover quickly from setbacks and crises, and perhaps be a servant leader.

4 Describe participative leadership, authoritarian leadership, Leadership Grid, situational, and entrepreneurial styles of leadership.

Leadership style is the typical pattern of behavior that a leader uses to influence employees to achieve organizational goals. Participative leaders share decision making with the group. One subtype of participative leader is the consultative leader, who involves subordinates in decision making but retains final authority. A consensus leader also involves subordinates in decision making and bases the final decision on group consensus. A democratic leader confers final authority on the group. Autocratic leaders attempt to retain most of the authority.

The Leadership Grid classifies leaders according to how much concern they have for both results and people. Sound management, with its high emphasis on results and people, is considered the ideal.

The Situational Leadership II model explains how to match the leadership style to the capabilities of group members on a given task. The basic premise of SLII is that the basis for effective leadership is managing the relationship between a leader and a subordinate on a given task. Effective leaders adapt to the level of commitment and competence of a subordinate. The leader adjusts the amount of supporting and directing which results in the four leadership styles shown in Exhibit 10-4.

Entrepreneurial leaders often have a strong achievement need, high enthusiasm and creativity, and a visionary perspective. They are uncomfortable with hierarchy and bureaucracy, often because they focus their energies on products, services, and customers.

5 Describe transformational and charismatic leadership.

The transformational leader helps organizations and people make positive changes. He or she combines charisma, inspirational leadership, and intellectual stimulation. Transformations take place through such means as pointing to relevant rewards, getting people to look beyond self-interest, and encouraging people to work toward self-fulfillment. Charismatic leaders provide vision and masterful communication. They can inspire trust and help people feel capable, and they are action-oriented. Performing well may lead to being perceived as charismatic. Some charismatic leaders are unethical and use their power to accomplish illegal and immoral ends. Managers can improve their image as charismatic by engaging in favorable interactions with group members through a variety of techniques including visioning, and having an effective handshake.

6 Explain the leadership role of mentoring and coaching.

Mentoring is more important than ever as workers face complex and rapidly changing job demands. Coaching is part of mentoring. Mentors help protégés solve problems by themselves and make their own discoveries. Mentoring can be an informal or formal relationship. Shadowing is a useful part of mentoring.

7 Identify the skills that contribute to leadership.

To be an effective leader, a manager must possess a wide variety of skills, many of which are described throughout this chapter and this book. Among these diverse skills are exerting influence, motivating others, and solving problems creatively.

KEY TERMS AND PHRASES

Leadership, 334
Power, 336
Authority, 336
Coalition, 338
Self-leadership, 339
Power motivation, 343
Open-book company, 343
Leadership style, 348
Participative leader, 348
Autocratic leader, 349
Leadership Grid, 350
Situational leadership II (SLII), 352
Transformational leader, 355
Charisma, 356
Mentor, 359
Shadowing, 360

QUESTIONS

1. In what way does a first-level supervisor play an important leadership role in the organization?
2. Describe how a businessperson could be an effective leader yet an ineffective manager. Also describe how a businessperson could be an effective manager yet an ineffective leader.
3. Which of the influence tactics described in this chapter do you think is the least ethical? Explain your reasoning.

4. Identify and describe the behavior of a public figure who appears to have low emotional intelligence. Do you think the person can be helped?
5. The entrepreneurial spirit has become increasingly welcome in corporations of all sizes. What do you think you could do to develop your entrepreneurial spirit?
6. Suppose you believed that you would be more effective as a leader or potential leader if you were more charismatic. What would be a realistic action plan for you to begin this month to become more charismatic?
7. New hires for technical and professional positions at many companies are assigned a mentor, in addition to having a manager. In what way might this practice be less effective than finding a mentor by oneself?

SKILL-BUILDING EXERCISE 10-A: My Leadership Journal

A potentially important aid in your development as a leader is to maintain a journal or diary of your experiences. Make a journal entry within 24 hours after you carried out a significant leadership action, or failed to do so when the opportunity arose. You therefore will have entries dealing with leadership opportunities both capitalized upon and missed. An example, "A few of my neighbors were complaining about all the vandalism in the neighborhood. Cars were getting dented and scratched, and lamplights were being smashed. A few bricks were thrown into home windows. I volunteer to organize a neighborhood patrol. The patrol actually helped cut back on the vandalism." Or, in contrast: "A few of my neighbors. . . . windows. I thought to myself that someone else should take care of the problem. My time is too valuable."

Also include in your journal such entries as feedback you receive on your leadership ability, leadership traits you appear to be developing, and key leadership ideas you read about. Review your journal monthly, and make note of any progress you think you have made in developing your leadership skills. Also consider preparing a graph of your leadership skill development. The vertical axis can represent skill level on a 1-to-100 scale, and the horizontal axis might be divided into time internals, such as calendar quarters.

SKILL-BUILDING EXERCISE 10-B: What Style of Leader Are You?

Directions: Answer the following questions, keeping in mind what you have done, or think you would do in the scenarios and attitudes described.

	Mostly True	Mostly False
1. I am more likely to take care of a high-impact assignment myself than turn it over to a group member.	___	___
2. I would prefer the analytical aspects of a manager's job rather than working directly with group members.	___	___
3. An important part of my approach to managing a group is to keep the members informed almost daily of any information that could affect their work.	___	___
4. It is a good idea to give two people in the group the same problem, and then choose what appears to be the best solution.	___	___
5. It makes good sense for the leader or manager to stay somewhat aloof from the group, in order to make a tough decision when necessary.	___	___
6. I look for opportunities to obtain group input before making a decision, even on straightforward issues.	___	___
7. I would reverse a decision if several of the group members presented evidence that I was wrong.	___	___
8. Differences of opinion in the work group are healthy.	___	___

9. I think that activities to build team spirit, like the team fixing up a poor family's house on a Saturday, are an excellent investment of time.	___	___
10. If my group were hiring a new member, I would like the person to be interviewed by the entire group.	___	___
11. An effective team leader today uses e-mail for about 98 percent of communication with team members.	___	___
12. Some of the best ideas are likely to come from the group members rather than from the manager.	___	___
13. If our group were going to have a banquet, I would seek input from each member on what type of food should be served.	___	___
14. I have never seen a statue of a committee in a museum or park, so why bother making decisions by committee if you want to be recognized?	___	___
15. I dislike it intensely when a group member challenges my position on an issue.	___	___
16. I typically explain to group members how (what method they should use) to accomplish an assigned task.	___	___
17. If I were out of the office for a week, most of the important work in the department would get accomplished anyway.	___	___
18. Delegation of important tasks is something that would be (or is) very difficult for me.	___	___
19. When a group member comes to me with a problem, I tend to jump right in with a proposed solution.	___	___
20. When a group member comes to me with a problem, I typically ask that person something like, "What alternative solutions have you thought of so far?"	___	___

Scoring and Interpretation: The answers in the participative/team-style leader direction are as follows:

Mostly True: 3, 6, 7, 8, 9, 10, 12, 13, 17, 20

Mostly False: 1, 2, 4, 5, 11, 14, 15, 16, 18, 19

Skill development: The quiz you just completed is also an opportunity for skill development. Review the 20 questions and look for implied suggestions for engaging in participative leadership. For example, question 20 suggests that you encourage group members to work through their own solutions to problems. If your goal is to become an authoritarian leader, the questions can also serve as useful guidelines. For example, question 19 suggests that an authoritarian leader looks first to solve problems for group members.

INTERNET SKILL-BUILDING EXERCISE: Charisma Tips from the Net

A section in this chapter offered suggestions for becoming more charismatic. Search the Internet for additional suggestions and compare them to the suggestions in the text. Be alert to contradictions, and offer a possible explanation for them. You might want to classify the suggestions into two categories: those dealing with the inner person, and those dealing with more superficial aspects of behavior. A suggestion of more depth would be to become a visionary, and a suggestion of less depth would be to wear eye-catching clothing.

Use a search phrase such as "How to become more charismatic." An all-encompassing phrase such as "developing leadership effectiveness" is unlikely to direct you to the information you need. You might consult a search engine and look for information about developing charisma.

Case Problem 10-A

Tough as Nails at Home Depot

Don R. Ray spent three years with the 82nd Airborne Division, one of the U.S. Army's elite divisions. Much of his activity involved terrorist hunting. Nowadays, Ray commands a different kind of operation. He has replaced crack-of-dawn physical training and green Army fatigues with sunrise store openings and an orange Home Depot apron. A store manager in Clarksville, Tenn., Ray runs a 110,000-square-foot box with 35,000 products and a 100-member staff, 30 of them former military. "In the military, we win battles and conquer the enemy," says Ray. At Home Depot, "we do that with customers."

Military analogies are commonplace at Home Depot Inc. Five years after his arrival, Chief Executive Robert L. Nardelli is putting his stamp on what was long a decentralized, entrepreneurial business. Nardelli loves to hire soldiers. The military, to a large extent, has become the management model for his entire enterprise. Of the 1,142 people hired into Home Depot's store leadership program, a two-year regimen for future store managers, 528 are junior military officers. More than 100 of them now run Home Depots. Recruits such as Ray "understand the mission," says Nardelli. "It's one thing to have faced a tough customer. It's another to face the enemy shooting at you. So they probably will be pretty calm under fire."

Nardelli is a detail-obsessed, diamond-cut precise manager, who believes in the military style of organization. Overall, some 13 percent of Home Depot's 345,000 employees have military experience, versus. 4 percent at Wal-Mart stores Inc. Importing ideas, people, and platitudes from the military is a key part of Nardelli's sweeping move to reshape Home Depot, the world's third-largest retailer, into a more centralized organization. It's a critical element of his strategy to rein in an unwieldy 2,048-store chain and prepare for the next leg of growth.

Nardelli is trying to build a disciplined corps, one predisposed to following orders, operating in high-pressure environments, and executing with high standards. A financial analyst points out, "Bob believes in a command-and-control organization." These days every major decision and goal at Home Depot flows down from Nardelli's office. "There's no question; Bob's the general," says Joe DeAngelo, 44, executive vice president of Home Depot Supply (HDS), a wholesale unit selling to contractors and repair specialists.

Profits and sales have increased substantially during Nardelli's reign, yet some managers and workers oppose his approach to rebuilding Home Depot. Some describe a demoralized staff, and a "culture of fear." Some workers object to Nardelli's annual compensation of approximately $30 million. Before Nardelli's arrival, managers ran Home Depot's stores on "tribal knowledge," based on years of experienced about what sold and what didn't. Now they click nervously through BlackBerry's at the end of each week, hoping they "made plan," a combination of sales and profit targets. Underperforming executives are routinely culled from the ranks. Says one former executive: "Every single week you shuddered when you looked at e-mail because another officer was gone."

As a manager, Nardelli is relentless, demanding, and determined to prove wrong every critic of Home Depot. He treats Saturdays and Sundays as ordinary working days and often expects those around him to do the same.

Nardelli's cultural transformation has prompted some new lingo among Home Depot employees, including the following phrases:

- *The Aprons.* Like, "troops," a term used by some senior executives to refer to Home Depot store workers (who wear aprons).
- *Home Despot.* For the most disenchanted workers, the moniker imposed on the mighty home-improvement chain.
- *Bob's Army.* Slang for the "store leadership program," wherein almost 50 percent of the 1,142 managers hired are ex-military personnel.
- *Bobaganda.* The always-on Home Depot television channel, a.k.a., HD-TV, shown in rooms where employees take their breaks.

To improve customer service, employees carry in their apron pocket a 25-page booklet dubbed *How to Be Orange Every Day*. The booklet contains aphorisms such as "we create an atmosphere of high-energy fun," and "every person, penny and product counts."

Case Problem 10-A

The 2006 University of Michigan American Customer Satisfaction Index shows Home Depot slipped to dead last among U.S. retailers. Home Depot scored 11 points below Lowe's and 3 points below Kmart. Home Depot management disputes these findings, pointing out that with so many customer transactions it is inevitable that about 1 percent will be unsatisfactory. For a company that processes 1.3 billion transactions a year, even 99 percent satisfaction would leave 1.3 million unhappy customers. Home Depot is now providing incentives for workers who provide exceptional customer service.

Some Home Depot former managers blame Nardelli's hardball approach for corroding the service ethic at the home-improvement chain. The also describe a culture so paralyzed with fear that they didn't worry about whether they would be terminated, but when.

In January 2007, the Home Depot board decided it had enough with the company's slowing sales, lagging stock price, and Nardelli's abrasive leadership style. Nardelli's refusal to amend his giant compensation package, however, was a major factor in his dismissal. Investors also were becoming increasingly angry with Nardelli's compensation including the $38 million he pulled down in 2006. He left with an exit package of $210 million, including $20 million in cash severance. Shortly after Nardelli's departure became known, many employees at some Home Depot stores celebrated, and exchanged high-fives.

Nardelli was immediately replaced by Frank Blake, a former GE executive who prefers to build consensus rather than dictate orders. Shortly after taking office, he vowed to change back the culture of Home Depot to its former years, although he too is short on retail experience.

In August 2007, Cerberus Capital Management hired Nardelli as Chairman of Chrysler with the hope that his expertise in operations could help squeeze profits out of the ailing auto giant. Critics wondered if Nardelli could work well with unions and dealers.

Discussion Questions

1. What, if any, improvements in leadership style might Nardelli have made?
2. What is your opinion of the fairness of giving so many Home Depot management positions to former military personnel?
3. What impact do you think Nardelli's leadership style might have had on customer service at Home Depot stores?
4. To what extent should expertise in retailing be a requirement for the CEO position at Home Depot?

Source: Brian Grow, "Renovating Home Depot," *Business Week*, March 6, 2006, pp. 50–58; Brian Hindo, "Satisfaction Not Guaranteed," *Business Week*, June 19, 2006, p. 34; Grow, "Out at Home Depot," *Business Week*, January 15, 2007, pp. 56–62; *Breakingviews.com*, "Can nardelli Help Chrysler?" *The Wall Street Journal*, August 7, 2007, p. C12.

Case Problem 10-B

VW Gets a Turnaround Artist

Eighteen months after joining Volkswagen AG, Wolfgang Bernhard is making big waves at Europe's biggest car maker with his American-style notions of cost cutting. Bernhard, who sits on the company's board of management and is responsible for its VW brand, has been playing the bad cop in the company's restructuring. The 45-year-old executive has publicly bemoaned the poor quality of VW cars, disclosed productivity problems at its factories, and pronounced Volkswagen "a company in crisis."

The German-born, American-trained former McKinsey & Co. consultant has overturned some long-standing practices. At his urging, Volkswagen for the first time opened its European factories to American quality experts and has resolved internal disagreements over how to build new models by forcing hundreds of employees into the same room to debate.

Now he is spearheading Volkswagen's drive to slash labor costs in Germany, and is threatening to shift production abroad if he doesn't get his way. Germany is noted for its consensual approach to labor–management relations. At one point Bernhard announced that Volkswagen could move production of its best-selling model, the Golf, out of the company's hometown of Wolfsburg—a provocative threat for a community so dependent on the car that it once temporarily renamed itself "Golfsburg" to promote it. Bernhard belongs to a new generation of German executives who have worked in the United States and are demanding painful sacrifices from their work forces. He is moving to cut jobs and scale back investments in underperforming units.

His hard-charging style has rankled Volkswagen's old guard and has sometimes left him looking out of synch with fellow VW executives. Bernhard sizes up the company's challenges in the bluntest possible terms: Volkswagen has "nothing coming that is basically positive," in the next year, he says. "If the company can't profitably export cars," he says, "part of Europe is going to die." He also has criticized one of Germany's most hallowed traditions: its so-called co-determination law, which requires major companies to give employees equal representation on their boards of directors.

Bernhard offers no apologies to those who don't like his approach. "I am quick and focused, and I like to cut the formalities," he says. One of his initiatives is to extend the workweek at Volkswagen's German factories to 35 hours from 28, without a pay increase. The German labor movement has long touted Volkswagen as a model for how companies should treat workers. During Volkswagen's last downturn in the early 1990s, the company shortened its workweek by roughly 20 percent rather than shed tens of thousands of jobs.

Volkswagen is trying to reverse a slide in profits, which have fallen 60 percent since 2001. In North America, it has lost roughly $2.5 billion over the past three years. Bernhard says the company's mounting problems abroad means the company has to make changes at home. The auto maker warns that as many as 20,000 jobs, most of them in Germany, could be cut over the next three years.

Bernhard's current challenge resembles the one he faced at his former employer, DaimlerChrysler: expand the company's model line-up while drastically slashing costs. Volkswagen offers only one SUV and no minivans or pickups in the United States, even though those vehicles account for roughly half of U.S. auto sales.

A group of consultants discovered that Volkswagen takes twice as long to build a car as its most efficient competitors. Bernhard says the company must close that gap to ensure its survival. "He's trying to motivate his organization and wake people up," says Ronald Harbour, the consulting group's president. "He says some of this is painful, but he thinks that if he's open and honest, he'll have more credibility."

A few years ago, he ordered more than 200 VW employees to report to an auditorium a few miles from headquarters. He broke them into teams and instructed them to figure out how to cut the planned SUV's cost by $2,500 per vehicle. He told them not to return to their workplaces until they were done.

Each evening at about 6, he returned to the auditorium to watch as the teams, often working until midnight, presented cost-cutting recommendations. "One person would say, 'I want to reduce the number of welding points,'" in the car, recalls Rudolf Krebs, a senior VW engineer. "Then someone at another table would stand up and say, 'No, we can't do that because it reduces safety.' Krebs says, "Bernhard would look to his

Case Problem 10-B

senior managers and say: 'Is it a good idea? Yes or no?' Then all of a sudden, you had a decision."

Bernhard began to scrutinize other areas of spending at VW. For years, Volkswagen has sent employees—including those from its finance, legal, and human resources—to Scandinavia, Africa, and other regions to test drive new models in a variety of conditions. The idea was to create a corporate culture in which any employee's prospects for advancement would depend on knowing its products. Bernhard concluded that the number of invitations was excessive. He slashed the budgets for such events, restricting participation mainly to employees directly involved in developing and building cars.

Bernhard's most public struggle has been extracting concessions from Volkswagen's union. During the summer of 2005, he asked the union for ideas for reducing the cost of the compact SUV by roughly $1,000 per vehicle. The union balked.

Union leaders complain that Bernhard's public criticisms of Volkswagen are hurting morale. At a company meeting, one of Volkswagen's top union leaders chastised Bernhard in front of workers for divulging VW's low standing in the Harbour survey.

Bernhard says he has taken steps to boost Volkswagen's quality levels, such as tying managers' bonuses to demonstrated improvements. Despite the attention his cost cutting has attracted, he says his success will depend more on whether he can deliver on a promise to introduce five to ten new vehicles by 2010, and to price each of them competitively.

Discussion Questions

1. In what ways is Bernhard a transformational leader, or at least trying to be a transformational leader?
2. How would you describe Bernhard's leadership style?
3. What suggestions might you offer Bernhard to be more successful as the chief executive of Volkswagen?

Source: Stephen Power, "Top Volkswagen Executive Tries U.S.—Style Turnaround Tactics," *The Wall Street Journal*, July 18, 2006, pp. A1, A11.

chapter 11

Motivation

At the $4.7-billion Whole Foods Market, when store department "teams" finish a four-week period under their payroll budget, the company doesn't keep the surplus (money not used for payroll). Rather, it gets handed back to the employees whose efficiency created the savings. Here's how it works: Managers constantly track their payroll spending against their budget. Every four week they divide any surplus by the hours logged and add the "gainshare" to workers' hourly wages. If the surplus is $2,000, on 1,200 hours, each employee gets an extra $1.67 per hour.

The company claims the incentive not only pushes workers to step it up a notch, but also aids in recruiting. Newcomers need a two-thirds vote from colleagues to be brought on permanently. As company spokeswoman Amy Schaffer notes, "It's a chance for team members to say, 'This person is not catching on, he or she is not productive,' because they're going to share their gainsharing with him or her."[1]

Management at Whole Food recognizes that profit margins in the grocery business are quite thin, so every bit of added efficiency helps. Furthermore, management recognizes that an effective motivational technique can be to allow employees to share in the savings they create by economizing on the number of workers required to get the job done.

1 "Secret 23: Pass Cost Savings on to those Who Achieved Them," *Business 2.0*, April 2006, p. 96.

Objectives

After studying this chapter and doing the exercises, you should be able to:

1 Explain the relationship between motivation and performance.

2 Present an overview of major theories of need satisfaction in explaining motivation.

3 Explain how goal setting is used to motivate people.

4 Describe the application of behavior modification to worker motivation.

5 Explain the conditions under which a person will be motivated according to expectancy theory.

6 Describe the role of financial incentives, profit sharing and gainsharing, in worker motivation.

Gainsharing is one of the motivational techniques described in this chapter. For many managers, the purpose of motivation is to get people to work hard toward achieving company objectives. Understanding motivation is also important because low motivation contributes to low-quality work, superficial effort, indifference toward customers, and high absenteeism and tardiness.

motivation
The expenditure of effort to accomplish results.

The term *motivation* refers to two different but related ideas. From the standpoint of the individual, motivation is an internal state that leads to the pursuit of objectives. Personal motivation affects the initiation, direction, intensity, and persistence of effort. (A motivated worker gets going, focuses effort in the right direction, works with intensity, and sustains the effort.) From the standpoint of the manager, motivation is the process of getting people to pursue objectives. Both concepts have an important meaning in common. **Motivation** is the expenditure of effort to accomplish results. The effort results from a force that stems from within the person. However, the manager or team leader, or the group, can be helpful in igniting the force.

This chapter will present several theories or explanations of motivation in the workplace. In addition, it will provide descriptions of specific approaches to motivating employees. Exhibit 11-1 presents an overview of various motivation theories and techniques. All the ideas presented in this chapter can be applied to motivating oneself as well as others. For instance, when you read about the expectancy theory of

exhibit 11-1 Overview of Motivation Theories and Techniques

In this chapter we present both theories and explanations of motivation, along with techniques based on them.

I. Theories and explanations of motivation
   1. Motivation through need satisfaction
      a. Maslow's need hierarchy
      b. Satisfaction of needs such as achievement, power, affiliation, pride, recognition, and risk taking and thrill seeking
      c. Herzberg's two-factor theory
   2. Goal theory
   3. Behavior modification
   4. Expectancy theory

II. Specific motivational techniques stemming from theories
   1. Recognition programs
   2. Positive reinforcement programs
   3. Motivation through financial incentives
      a. Linking pay to performance including bonuses
      b. Bonuses, profit sharing and gainsharing
      c. Employee stock ownership programs and stock option plans

motivation, ask yourself: "What rewards do I value strongly enough for me to work extra hard?"

THE RELATIONSHIP BETWEEN MOTIVATION, PERFORMANCE, AND COMMITMENT

Learning Objective 1

Explain the relationship between motivation and performance.

Many people believe the statements "You can accomplish anything you want" and "Think positively and you will achieve all your goals." In truth, motivation is but one important contributor to productivity and performance. Abilities, skills, and the right equipment are also indispensable. An office assistant might be strongly motivated to become a brand manager for Cheerios at General Mills, but she must first acquire knowledge about marketing and project management, develop her leadership skills, and make the right connections—among other factors.

Exhibit 11-2 shows the relationship between motivation and performance. It can also be expressed by the equation $P = M \times A$, where P refers to performance, M to motivation, and A to ability. Note that skill and technology contribute to ability. For instance, if you are skilled at using information technology, and you have the right hardware and software, you can accomplish the task of producing a company blog. Commitment in the diagram is essentially an extension of motivation. The committed employee works joyfully toward achieving organizational objectives. A study of about 30 prosperous business firms suggested that these organizations are able to sustain high performance levels because they achieve the emotional commitment of their workforces. Employees are treated well and rewarded, and as a result they become loyal dedicated workers who help give the firm a competitive advantage.[2]

PLAY VIDEO

MOTIVATION

"Go to academic.cengage.com/management/dubrin and view the video. What motivates Washburn Guitar employees? What is the connection between quality guitars and workforce motivation?"

Gaining employee commitment is especially important in the current era because several studies have found that most American workers are not fully engaged in their work.[3] They do what is expected of them but do not contribute extra mental and physical effort to be outstanding. Many of these workers want to be good organizational citizens, yet many of them feel they have a poor relationship with the supervisor or believe that the organization does not care about them. According to a Gallup study, about 70 percent of employees are "disengaged," meaning that they are no longer committed to the company. Furthermore, the longer employees stay, the more disengaged they become.[4] The gravity of the problem is highlighted by the observation that the turnaround of a company like

$P = M \times A$ An expression of the relationship between motivation and performance, where P refers to performance, M to motivation, and A to ability.

2 John Katzenbach, *Peak Performance: Aligning the Hearts and Minds of Your Employees* (Boston: Harvard Business School Press, 2000).

3 Quoted in Steve Bates, "Getting Engaged," *HR Magazine*, February 2004, p. 46.

4 Ibid.

exhibit 11-2 Motivation and Ability as Factors in Performance

Motivation does contribute substantially to performance, but not as directly as many people think.

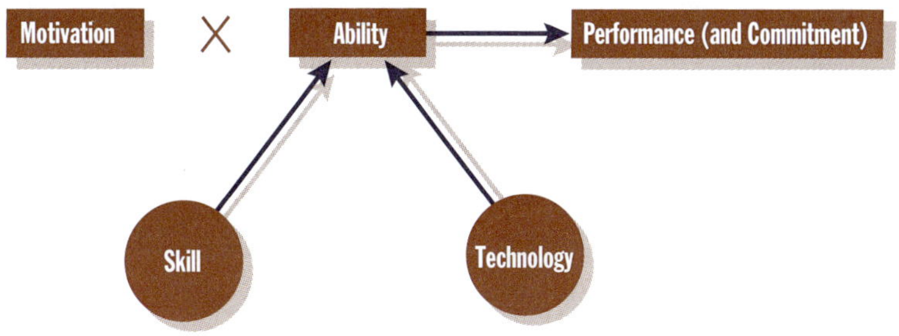

Ford Motor is dependent on fully engaging and motivating the workforce in the effort.[5]

Decreased job security caused by downsizing and outsourcing and offshoring, along with reduced benefits, are probable contributors to less than full engagement by employees. The techniques described in this chapter, as well as other places in this text, are designed to help employees commit to the organization. High-performance work design as described in Chapter 7 leads to commitment. High motivation for a given task is different from emotional commitment that translates into intense motivation for a long period of time. The process works as follows:

Day-by-day motivation and good treatment of workers → Long-term motivation of workers → Emotional commitment to the firm → Competitive advantage → Elevated profits and stock price

Group norms also contribute to both motivation and performance. If group norms and organizational culture encourage high motivation and performance, the individual worker will feel compelled to work hard. To do otherwise isolates the worker from the group and the culture. Group norms and an organizational culture favoring low motivation will often lower individual output.

A manager contributes to performance by motivating group members, improving their ability, and helping to create a positive work culture. Before studying specific explanations of motivation, do the accompanying self-assessment quiz (Exhibit 11-3). Taking the quiz will give you a preliminary idea of your current level of knowledge about motivation.

5 John Hollon, "Workers at the Wheel," *Workforce Management*, January 30, 2006, p. 50.

exhibit 11-3 Self-Assessment Exercise: My Approach to Motivating Others

Describe how often you act or think in the way indicated by the following statements when attempting to motivate another person. Use the following scale: very infrequently (VI); infrequently (I); sometimes (S); frequently (F); very frequently (VF).

	VI	I	S	F	VF
1. I ask the other person what he or she is hoping to achieve in the situation.	1	2	3	4	5
2. I attempt to figure out whether the person has the ability to do what I need done.	1	2	3	4	5
3. When another person is heel-dragging, it usually means he or she is lazy.	5	4	3	2	1
4. I tell the person I'm trying to motivate exactly what I want.	1	2	3	4	5
5. I like to give the other person a reward up front so he or she will be motivated.	5	4	3	2	1
6. I give lots of feedback when another person is performing a task for me.	1	2	3	4	5
7. I like to belittle another person enough so that he or she will be intimidated into doing what I need done.	5	4	3	2	1
8. I make sure that the other person feels treated fairly.	1	2	3	4	5
9. I figure that if I smile nicely enough I can get the other person to work as hard as I need.	5	4	3	2	1
10. I attempt to get what I need done by instilling fear in the other person.	5	4	3	2	1
11. I specify exactly what needs to be accomplished.	1	2	3	4	5
12. I generously praise people who help me get my work accomplished.	1	2	3	4	5
13. A job well done is its own reward. I therefore keep praise to a minimum.	5	4	3	2	1
14. I make sure to let people know how well they have done in meeting my expectations on a task.	1	2	3	4	5
15. To be fair, I attempt to reward people about the same no matter how well they have performed.	5	4	3	2	1
16. When somebody doing work for me performs well, I recognize his or her accomplishments promptly.	1	2	3	4	5
17. Before giving somebody a reward, I attempt to find out what would appeal to that person.	1	2	3	4	5
18. I make it a policy not to thank somebody for doing a job he or she is paid to do.	5	4	3	2	1
19. If people do not know how to perform a task, their motivation will suffer.	1	2	3	4	5
20. If properly designed, many jobs can be self-rewarding.	1	2	3	4	5

Total Score ____________________

Scoring and interpretation: Add the numbers circled to obtain your total score.

90–100 You have advanced knowledge and skill with respect to motivating others in a work environment. Continue to build on the solid base you have established.

50–89 You have average knowledge and skill with respect to motivating others. With additional study and experience, you will probably develop advanced motivational skills.

20–49 To effectively motivate others in a work environment, you will need to greatly expand your knowledge of motivation theory and techniques.

Source: The idea for this quiz and a couple of statements stem from David A. Whetton and Kim S. Cameron, *Developing Management Skills*, 3rd ed. (New York: HarperCollins, 1995), pp. 358–359.

MOTIVATION THROUGH NEED SATISFACTION

The simplest explanation of motivation is one of the most powerful: People are willing to expend effort toward achieving a goal because it satisfies one of their important needs. A **need** is a deficit within an individual, such as a craving for water or affection. Self-interest is thus a driving force. The principle is referred to as "What's in it for me?" or WIIFM (pronounced wiff'em). Reflect on your own experiences. Before working hard to accomplish a task, you probably want to know how you will benefit. If your manager asks you to work extra hours to take care of an emergency, you will most likely oblige. Yet underneath you might be thinking, "If I work these extra hours, my boss will think highly of me. As a result, I will probably receive a good performance evaluation and maybe a better-than-average salary increase."

Learning Objective 2

Present an overview of major theories of need satisfaction in explaining motivation.

need
A deficit within an individual, such as a craving for water or affection.

Our behaviors are ruled partly by our need intensity, such as having an intense desire for recognition might propel a person to win an employee-of-the month award.[6] Similarly, people are motivated to fulfill needs that are not currently satisfied. The need-satisfaction approach requires two key steps in motivating workers. First, you must know what people want—what needs they are trying to satisfy. To learn what the needs are, you can ask directly or observe the person. You can obtain knowledge indirectly by getting to know employees better. To gain insight into employee needs, find out something about the employee's personal life, education, work history, outside interests, and career goals.

Second, you must give each person a chance to satisfy needs on the job. To illustrate, one way to motivate a person with a strong need for autonomy is to allow that person to work independently.

This section examines needs and motivation from three related perspectives. First, we describe the best-known theory of motivation, Maslow's need hierarchy. Then we discuss several specific needs related to job motivation and move on to another cornerstone idea, Herzberg's two-factor theory.

Maslow's need hierarchy
The motivation theory that arranges human needs into a pyramid-shaped model with basic physiological needs at the bottom and self-actualizing needs at the top.

Maslow's Need Hierarchy

Based on his work as a clinical psychologist, Abraham M. Maslow developed a comprehensive view of individual motivation.[7] **Maslow's need hierarchy** arranges human needs into a pyramid-shaped model with basic physiological needs at the bottom and self-actualization needs at the top. (See Exhibit 11-4.) Lower-order needs, called **deficiency needs**, must be satisfied to ensure a person's existence, security, and requirements for human contact. Higher-order needs, or **growth needs**, are concerned with personal development and reaching one's potential. Before higher-level needs are activated, the lower-order needs must be satisfied. The five levels of needs are described next.

deficiency needs
Lower-order needs that must be satisfied to ensure a person's existence, security, and requirements for human contact.

growth needs
Higher-order needs that are concerned with personal development and reaching one's potential.

6 Piers Steel and Cornelius J. König, "Integrating Theories of Motivation," *Academy of Management Review*, October 2006, pp. 895–897.

7 Abraham M. Maslow, "A Theory of Human Motivation," *Psychological Review*, July 1943, pp. 370–396; Abraham M. Maslow, *Motivation and Personality* (New York: Harper & Row, 1954), Chapter 5.

exhibit 11-4 Maslow's Need Hierarchy

As you move up the hierarchy, the needs become more difficult to achieve. Some physiological needs could be satisfied with pizza and a soft drink, whereas it might take becoming rich and famous to satisfy the self-actualization need.

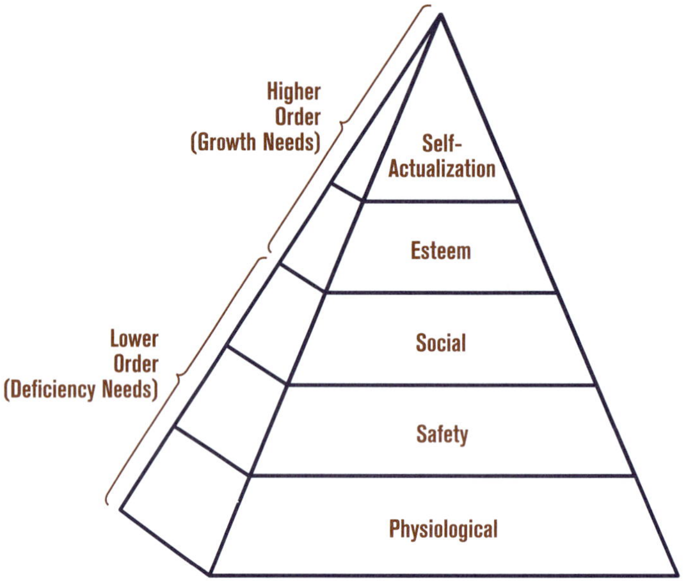

1. *Physiological needs* refer to basic bodily requirements such as nutrition, water, shelter, moderate temperatures, rest, and sleep. Most office jobs allow us to satisfy physiological needs. Naps to reduce stress and boost productivity help workers satisfy an important physiological need. Fire fighting is an occupation with potential to frustrate some physiological needs. Smoke inhalation can block the satisfaction of physiological needs.
2. *Safety needs* include the desire to be safe from both physical and emotional injury. Many workers who hold dangerous jobs would be motivated by the prospects of obtaining safety. For example, computer operators who are suffering from cumulative trauma disorder would prefer a job that requires less intense pressure on their wrists. Any highly stressful job can frustrate the need for emotional safety.
3. *Social needs* are the needs for love, belonging, and affiliation with people. Managers can contribute to the satisfaction of these needs by promoting teamwork and allowing people to discuss work problems with each other. Many employees see their jobs as a major source for satisfying social needs.
4. *Esteem needs* reflect people's desire to be seen by themselves and others as a person of worth. Occupations with high status are a primary source for the satisfaction of esteem needs. Managers can help employees satisfy their esteem needs by praising the quality of their work.
5. *Self-actualization needs* relate to the desire to reach one's potential. They include needs for self-fulfillment and personal development. True self-actualization is an ideal to strive for, rather than something that automatically stems from occupying a challenging position. Self-actualized people are those who are becoming all they are capable of becoming. Managers can help group members move

toward self-actualization by giving them challenging assignments and the chance for advancement and new learning.

Maslow's need hierarchy is a convenient way of classifying needs and has spurred thousands of managers to take the subject of human motivation more seriously. Its primary value lies in recognition of the importance of satisfying needs in order to motivate employees. Furthermore, Maslow shows why people are difficult to satisfy. As one need is satisfied, people want to satisfy other needs or different forms of the same need. The need hierarchy has helped three generations of students understand that it is normal to be constantly searching for new satisfactions.

The need hierarchy is relevant in the current era because so many workers have to worry about satisfying lower-level needs. Despite the general prosperity, job security and having limited or no healthcare benefits are still concerns for many workers. Even if finding new employment is relatively easy, many workers feel their security is jeopardized when they have to worry about conducting a job search to pay for necessities.

Specific Needs People Attempt to Satisfy

Maslow's need hierarchy refers to classes of needs, and represents but one way of understanding human needs. The work setting offers the opportunity to satisfy dozens of psychological needs. This section will describe six of the most important of these needs, including programs specially designed to satisfy the recognition need.

Achievement, Power, and Affiliation

According to David McClelland and his associates, much job behavior can be explained by the strength of people's needs for achievement, power, and affiliation.[8] The power need (or motive) has already been described in relation to leadership. The **achievement need** refers to finding joy in accomplishment for its own sake. High achievers find satisfaction in completing challenging tasks, attaining high standards, and developing better ways of doing things. The **affiliation need** is a desire to have close relationships with others and to be a loyal employee or friend. Affiliation is a social need, while achievement and power are self-actualizing needs.

achievement need
The need that refers to finding joy in accomplishment for its own sake.

affiliation need
A desire to have close relationships with others and to be a loyal employee or friend.

A person with a strong need for affiliation finds compatible working relationships more important than high-level accomplishment and the exercise of power. Successful executives, therefore, usually have stronger needs for achievement and power than for affiliation. Workers with strong affiliation needs, however, typically enjoy contributing to a team effort. Befriending others and working cooperatively with them satisfies the need for affiliation.

Recognition

The workplace provides a natural opportunity to satisfy the **recognition need**, the desire to be acknowledged for one's contributions and efforts and

recognition need
The desire to be acknowledged for one's contributions and efforts and to feel important.

8 Michael J. Stahl, "Achievement, Power, and Managerial Motivation: Selecting Managerial Talent with Job Choice Exercise," *Personnel Psychology*, Winter 1983; David C. McClelland, *Power: The Inner Experience* (New York: Irvington, 1975).

to feel important. A manager can thus motivate many employees by making them feel important. Employee needs for recognition can be satisfied both through informal recognition and by formal recognition programs. Praising workers for good performance is a type of informal recognition. An effective form of praise describes the worker's performance rather than merely making an evaluation. Describing good performance might take this form: "You turned an angry customer into an ally who has referred new business to us." A straightforward evaluation would be "You did a great job with that angry customer." Even more effective would be to combine the two statements. Exhibit 11-5 provides a list of statements of praise that might be used with team members.

Although praise costs no money and only requires a few moments of time, many workers feel they do not receive enough praise. Managers therefore have a good opportunity to increase motivation by the simple act of praising good deeds. Other informal approaches to recognizing good performance include taking an employee to lunch, a handshake from the manager or team leader, and putting flowers on an employee's desk. E-mail is another handy tool for giving praise and recognition.

Formal *recognition and reward* programs are more popular than ever as companies attempt to retain the right employees, and keep workers productive who worry about losing their jobs or having no private work area. These recognition programs usually include the term reward because good performers are recognized with rewards. Among the rewards are dinner certificates, watches and jewelry, candles, plaques, and on-the-spot cash awards (around $25 to $50) for good performance. Employee recognition programs are so widespread, that several companies including Maritz Inc. specialize in

exhibit 11-5 **21 Ways to Say "Well Done"**

Sometimes, offering praise is harder than it should be. In a busy office, it's easy to forget to compliment and voice your appreciation. But praise can really make a team member's day. Here are some reminders of how easy it really is to say, "Thanks, well done."

1. I'm proud you're on my team.
2. Congratulations on a terrific job.
3. You're so helpful. Thank you.
4. You really made a difference by. . ."
5. Thanks so much for your considerate effort.
6. I really admire your perseverance.
7. You've made my day because of. . .
8. You're a champion.
9. Wow, what an incredible accomplishment.
10. Great effort. You make us all look good.
11. I have great confidence in you.
12. You've grasped the concept well.
13. Your customer service skills are sensational.
14. Your sales results are outstanding.
15. You're a valuable part of the team.
16. Your efforts are really making a difference.
17. You are hitting high productivity.
18. Our customers are crazy about you.
19. You have helped us attain our goals.
20. Your work ethic motivates the team.

developing reward incentive and recognition programs for other companies. Maritz has annual revenues of around $1.3 billion.[9]

FedEx had a recognition program called Bravo Zulu. Managers are authorized to make awards on the spot by giving employees a set of flags symbolizing a job well done. FedEx managers present personalized Bravo Zulu letters to employees in front of their work groups. It appears that the recognition award works equally well as previous financial awards.[10]

More sophisticated recognition programs recognize behavior that supports organizational values so the awards are a reminder of what is important to the company. TEOCO, an information technology company near Washington DC links rewards to the company name and values. Managers give on-the-spot "TEO-Star" awards when they observe workers displaying one of the company's core values: alignment with interests of employees, clients, and community; integrity, honesty, and respect; courageous action; and striving for progress through ownership.[11] An IT technician might receive such an award for salvaging a client's data during a blackout.

Teams, as well as individuals, should receive recognition to enhance motivation. Motivation consultant Bob Nelson recommends that to build a high-performing team, the manager should acknowledge the success of all team members. As with individual recognition, a personal touch works best. Examples include a manager thanking group members for their involvement, suggestions, and initiatives. Holding a group luncheon for outstanding team performance is also a potential motivator.[12] *Potential* is emphasized because team recognition does not take into account individual differences in preferences for rewards. For example, some employees object to group luncheons because it diverts time they might want to use for personal purposes.

As with most motivation and retention programs, recognition and rewards have to be carefully planned, otherwise they may backfire and lose money for the company. One example is giving out turkeys or gift baskets at holiday time that many employees perceive to be insulting and patronizing. An advanced procedure is to ask employees what types of recognition they prefer.

The Need to Be Proud

Wanting to feel proud motivates many workers even if *pride* is not exactly a psychological need. Striving to experience the emotion of pride most likely stems from the desire to satisfy the needs for self-esteem and self-fulfillment. Being proud of what you accomplish is more of an internal (intrinsic) motivator than an external (extrinsic) motivator such as receiving a gift. Giving workers an opportunity to experience pride can therefore be a strong internal motivator.

---

9 Sheree R. Curry, "Family Turmoil Aside, the Incentives Business Has Proved Rewarding for Maritz," *Workforce Management*, July 2005, p. 74.

10 Bob Nelson, "Motivation Matters," in *Corporate Meetings & Incentives* (Primedia Magazines & Media Inc., 2003), http://www.meetingsnet.com.

11 "Branded Recognition," *Manager's Edge*, December 2006, p. 4.

12 Bob Nelson, "Does One Reward Fit All?" *Workforce*, February 1997, pp. 67–70.

Imagine that you are the assistant service manager at a company that customizes corporate jets to meet the requirements of individual clients. Your manager asks you to prepare a PowerPoint presentation of trends in equipment problems. You make your presentation to top management, the group applauds, executives shake your hand, and later you receive several congratulatory e-mail messages. One of the many emotions you experience is likely to be pride in having performed well. You are motivated to keep up the good work.

Workers can also experience pride in relation to external motivators. For example, a worker might receive a crystal vase for having saved the company thousands of dollars in shipping costs. The vase might be more valuable to the worker as a symbol of accomplishment than as a household decoration. The feeling of pride stems from having accomplished a worthwhile activity (saving the company money) rather than from being awarded a vase.

According to consultant Jon R. Katzenbach, managers can take steps to motivate through pride. A key tactic is for the manager to set his or her compass on pride, not money. It is more important for workers to be proud of what they are doing day by day, than for them to be proud of reaching a major goal. The manager should celebrate "steps" (or attaining small goals) as much as the "landings" (the major goal). The most effective pride builders are masters at identifying and recognizing the small achievements that will instill pride in their people.[13]

Risk Taking and Thrill Seeking

The willingness to take risks and pursue thrills is a need that has grown in importance in the high-technology era. Many people work for employers, start businesses, and purchase stock with uncertain futures. Both the search for giant payoffs and daily thrills motivate these individuals, and they are attracted to high-stress careers such as computer security specialists or investment banking.[14] A strong craving for thrills may have some positive consequences for the organization, including willingness to perform such dangerous feats as setting explosives, capping an oil well, controlling a radiation leak, and introducing a product in a highly competitive environment. However, extreme risk takers and thrill seekers can create problems such as being involved in a disproportionate number of vehicular accidents and making imprudent investments.

A manager can appeal to the need for risk taking and thrill seeking, and therefore enhance the motivation of a person so inclined by rewarding good behavior with adventuresome assignments such as the following:

- Dealing with an irate, hostile customer
- Working on a product development team under time constraints
- Repairing equipment under heavy time pressures and customer demands
- Attending dangerous team-building activities such as cliff hanging and race-car driving

---

13 Cited in John A. Byrne, "How to Lead Now," *Fast Company*, August 2003, p. 66.
14 Christopher Munsey, "Frisky, but Risky," *Monitor on Psychology*, July/August 2006, p. 40.

If you are too strong a thrill seeker, you have to be on guard for your own safety and that of others while on the job. Or, seek thrills off the job, such as in mountain climbing and betting on changes in foreign currencies.

two-factor theory of work motivation
The theory contending that there are two different sets of job factors. One set can satisfy and motivate people, and the other set can only prevent dissatisfaction.

Herzberg's Two-Factor Theory

The study of the need hierarchy led to the **two-factor theory of work motivation**, which focuses on the idea of two different sets of job factors. One set of factors can satisfy and motivate people. The other can only prevent dissatisfaction. The late industrial psychologist Frederick Herzberg and his associates interviewed hundreds of professionals about their work.[15] They discovered that some factors of a job give people a chance to satisfy higher-level needs. Such elements are satisfiers or motivators. A *satisfier* is a job factor that, if present, leads to job satisfaction. Similarly, a *motivator* is a job factor that, if present, leads to motivation. When a motivator is not present, the effect on motivation is neutral rather than negative.

Satisfiers and motivators generally refer to the content (the heart or guts) of a job. These factors are achievement, recognition, challenging work, responsibility, and the opportunity for advancement. All the factors are self-rewarding. The important implication for managers is that most people can be motivated by providing an opportunity to do interesting work or to be promoted. The two-factor theory thus underlies the philosophy of job design through job enrichment and the job characteristics model, as described in Chapter 7.

Herzberg also discovered that some job elements are more relevant to lower-level needs than upper-level needs. Referred to as dissatisfiers, or hygiene factors, these elements are noticed primarily by their absence. A *dissatisfier* is a job element that, when present, prevents dissatisfaction; it does not, however, create satisfaction. People will not be satisfied with their jobs just because hygiene factors are present. For example, not having a handy place to park your car would create dissatisfaction. But having a place to park would not make you happier about your job.

Dissatisfiers relate mostly to the context of a job (the job setting or external elements). These include relationships with coworkers, company policy and administration, job security, and money. All these factors deal with external rewards. Money, however, does work as a satisfier for many people. A key point of the two-factor theory is that the opposite of satisfaction is no satisfaction—not dissatisfaction. Similarly, the opposite of dissatisfaction is no dissatisfaction—not satisfaction.

The two-factor theory has prompted managers to ask, "What really motivates our employees?" Nevertheless, Herzberg's assumption—that all workers seek more responsibility and challenge on the job—may be incorrect. It is more likely that people in higher-level occupations strive for more responsibility and challenge. But even in a given occupational group, such as managers or production workers, not everybody has the same motivational pattern. Many workers are motivated by a secure job when they have heavy financial obligations.

15 Frederick Herzberg, *Work and the Nature of Man* (Cleveland: World, 1966).

The two-factor theory becomes more current when we look at job factors that are considered important today for attracting, motivating, and retaining professional workers of the millennial generation (born in 1980 or later). In terms of suggestions to managers, these motivator and hygiene factors are as follows:

- *Let them have a life.* Millennials are wary of their parents' 80-hour work-weeks, so liberal vacations are a must.
- *No time clocks, please.* Recent grads are willing to work long hours if they set the schedule. Lockheed Martin allows employees to work nine-hour days and take alternate Fridays off.
- *Give them responsibility.* An opportunity to work on fulfilling projects and develop ones of their own is important to millennials. PepsiCo allows young employees with potential to manage a small team within six months of joining.
- *Feedback and more feedback.* Career-planning advice and frequent performance appraisals are helpful in retaining new hires.
- *Giving back matters.* Today's young workers expect to have the opportunity to engage in community service. Wells Fargo encourages its employees to teach financial literacy classes in the community.[16]

Cross-Cultural Differences in Needs and Suitable Recognition Awards

A person's culture can influence which needs are strongest for him or her, and therefore which approach to motivating that person is the most effective. A manager can study different cultures in general to get some ideas but it is also important to make some observations within the work group. According to popular stereotype, a worker raised in Japan would more likely be motivated by recognition in private than by public recognition. In contrast, an American-raised worker would be more likely to experience need satisfaction when given public recognition such as during a staff meeting.

On a more superficial level than psychological needs, cultural differences exist about suitability of recognition gifts. Globoforce CEO Eric Mosley notes that companies should be sensitive to differences in desirability of gift certificates. The United States has a department-store culture, so awarding American workers gift certificates to big retail chains and restaurants is desirable. Italians may prefer gift certificates to a small fashion boutique, and Germans, a sports store. In most parts of Asia gift certificates are not prevalent, and employees would prefer a tangible gift as a reward.[17]

Cross-cultural differences in standards of living also influence the effectiveness of recognition awards. In the United States an outstanding performer might be rewarded with a luxury item like a Mont Blanc pen or watch worth about $1,000 retail. Yet in India or China where standards of

---

16 Lindsey Gerdes, "The Best Places to Launch a Career," *Business Week*, September 18, 2006, p. 70.
17 Sheree R. Curry, "A Reward in the U.S. May Not Be a Reward Overseas," http://www.workforce.com, July 2005.

living are still rising and where bicycles remain an important mode of transportation, $1,000 might be better invested to buy a motor bike for a top employee. Incentives consultant Eugene Less says, "You might not give a mo-ped away in the U.S., but giving one in China or India is a huge thing."[18]

Despite cultural and geographic differences, the manager must still investigate. In general, a mo-ped is a better gift than an expensive fountain pen for a high-performing Chinese worker. Nevertheless, beauty products giant Mary Kay has found that pink cell phones, pink Buicks, and pink Cadillacs are cherished gifts for outstanding sales representatives in China.[19]

MOTIVATION THROUGH GOAL SETTING

Learning Objective 3

Explain how goal setting is used to motivate people.

Goal setting plays an important role in most formal motivational programs and managerial methods of motivating employees. The premise underlying goal theory is that behavior is regulated by values and goals. A *value* is a strongly held personal standard or conviction. It is a belief about something important to the individual, such as dignity of work or honesty. Our values create within us a desire to behave consistently with them. If an executive values honesty, the executive will establish a goal of trying to hire only honest employees. He or she would therefore make extensive use of reference checks and honesty testing. A **goal** is an overall condition one is trying to achieve, or a conscious intention to act. Exhibit 11-6 summarizes some of the more consistent findings and the following list describes them.[20]

1. *Specific goals lead to higher performance than do generalized goals.* Telling someone to "do your best" is a generalized goal. A specific goal would be "Decrease the turnaround time on customer inquiries to an average of two working days."
2. *Performance generally increases in direct proportion to goal difficulty.* The harder one's goal, the more one accomplishes. An important exception occurs, however, when goals are too difficult. Difficulty in reaching the goal leads to frustration, which in turn leads to lowered performance. On the other hand, lofty goals can be inspirational. A new development in goal theory recognizes the importance of **superordinate goals**, an overarching goal that captures the imagination of people.[21] The superordinate goal is similar to a vision because it relates to an ideal, and is often inspirational. The construction manager of a sewer-pipe company might explain to all workers that "We are working together to improve sanitation and help rid the world of deadly diseases stemming from poor sewage systems."

goal
An overall condition one is trying to achieve, or a conscious intention to act.

superordinate goals
An overarching goal that captures the imagination.

18 Irwin Speizer, "Incentives Catch On Overseas, but Value of Awards Can Too Easily Get Lost in Translation," *Workforce Management*, November 21, 2005, p. 46.

19 Martin Booe, "Sales Force at Mary Kay China Embraces the American Way," *Workforce Management*, April 2005, pp. 24–25.

20 Edwin A. Locke and Gary P. Latham, *A Theory of Goal Setting and Task Performance* (Upper Saddle River, NJ: Prentice Hall, 1990); Gary P. Latham, "Goal Setting: A Five-Step Approach to Behavior Change," *Organizational Dynamics*, Vol. 32, No. 3, 2003, pp. 309–317.

21 Latham, "Goal Setting: A Five-Step Approach," p. 309.

exhibit 11-6 **The Basics of Goal Theory**

Goals that meet the illustrated conditions have a positive impact on motivation, as revealed by a wide variety of research studies.

3. *For goals to improve performance, the employee must accept them.* If you reject a goal, you will not incorporate it into your planning. For this reason, it is often helpful to discuss goals with employees, rather than just imposing the goals on them. Participating in setting goals has no major effect on the level of job performance, except when it improves goal acceptance. Yet participation is valuable because it can lead to higher satisfaction with the goal-setting process.

   A study of pizza deliverers compared the contribution of assigned versus participative goal setting. All the deliverers were college students, whose average age was 21. At one store the employees participated in setting goals about making complete stops at intersections. At the other store, the pizza-delivery specialists were assigned a goal. Both groups significantly increased their number of complete stops at intersections, as measured by trained observers hiding behind nearby windows. A surprising finding was that the participative groups also increased the use of turn signals and safety belts.[22] Perhaps participating in goal setting made the deliverers feel more responsible.
4. *Goals are more effective when they are used to evaluate performance.* When workers know that their performance will be evaluated in terms of how well they attained their goals, the impact of goals increases. Management by objectives is built around this important idea.
5. *Goals should be linked to feedback and rewards.* Workers should receive feedback on their progress toward goals and be rewarded for reaching them. Rewarding people for reaching goals is perhaps the best-accepted principle of management. Feedback is also important because it is a motivational principle within itself. The process of receiving positive feedback encourages us to repeat the behavior; receiving negative feedback encourages us to discontinue

---

22 Timothy D. Ludwig and E. Scott Geller, "Assigned Versus Participative Goal Setting and Response Generalization: Managing Injury Control Among Professional Pizza Deliverers," *Journal of Applied Psychology*, April 1997, pp. 253–261.

the behavior. A practical way of building more feedback into goal setting is to set achievable short-term goals. In this way, goal accomplishment gets measured more frequently, giving the goal setter regular feedback. Short-term goals also increase motivation because many people do not have the patience and self-discipline to work long and hard without seeing results.

6. *Group goal setting is as important as individual goal setting.* Having employees work as teams with a specific team goal, rather than as individuals with only individual goals, increases productivity. Furthermore, the combination of the compatible group and individual goals is more effective than either individual or group goals.

Pygmalion effect
The idea that people live up to the expectations set for them.

behavior modification
A way of changing behavior by rewarding the right responses and punishing or ignoring the wrong responses.

Closely related to goal theory is the **Pygmalion effect**—the idea that people live up to the expectations set for them. If the manager establishes high goals and projects confidence that these goals will be achieved, the workers will rise to the occasion. The confidence might be projected though such means as a firm handshake or an accepting smile. Holding high expectations for employees can help overcome some of the motivational problems of a low work ethic. Many employees with a low work ethic will change their attitude and behaviors if management expects these employees to perform well.[23]

A potential problem with relying on goals to motivate workers is that they might use unethical means to attain goals. Examples include booking sales for a quarter in which the money is yet to be received, and using low-quality components in order to attain a cost goal for a part. To meet profit goals, some CEOs will cut back on research and development, fire capable workers, and sell off valuable company assets. A risk specialist wrote about financial goal setting, "In over 30 years as a banker, I have seen the toll that the relentless pressure to turn in ever better quarterly and annual numbers has on business and personal ethics."[24] Another problem with goals is that the continual pursuit of goals that stretch your capability can be stressful, as workers keep extending their workweek to "make their numbers."

To overcome this potential problem with goals, it is important for the worker pursuing the goal and the goal setter to agree on the method of attaining the goal. Unethical and dysfunctional methods might be declared out of bounds.

BEHAVIOR MODIFICATION

Learning Objective 4
Describe the application of behavior modification to worker motivation.

The most systematic method of motivating people is **behavior modification.** It is a way of changing behavior by rewarding the right responses and punishing or ignoring the wrong responses. A *reward* is something of value received as a consequence of having attained a goal. This section will describe several key concepts and strategies of behavior modification (also referred to as OB Mod).

23 Dov Eden, *Pygmalion in Management: Productivity as a Self-fulfilling Prophecy* (Lexington, MA: Lexington Books, 1990).

24 Quoted in Carol Hymowitz, "Readers Share Tales Of Jobs Where Strategy Became Meeting Target," *The Wall Street Journal*, March 22, 2005, p. B1.

law of effect The underlying principle of behavior modification stating that behavior leading to positive consequences tends to be repeated and that behavior leading to negative consequences tends not to be repeated.

Key Concepts of Behavior Modification

The **law of effect** is the foundation principle of behavior modification. According to this principle, behavior that leads to positive consequences tends to be repeated. Similarly, behavior that leads to negative consequences tends not to be repeated. Perceptive managers rely on the law of effect virtually every day. Assume that a supervisor of a paint shop wants her employees to comply with safety regulations by putting on a face mask every time they use a spray gun. When she sees an employee using a mask properly, she might comment, "Good to see that you're wearing the safety mask today." If the supervisor noticed that an employee was not wearing a mask, she might say, "Please put down the spray gun, and go get your mask. If this happens again, I will be forced to suspend you for one day."

Positive reinforcement and punishment are by far the two most frequently used behavior modification techniques in the workplace. (In Chapter 16, the topic of punishment will be reintroduced in the form of employee discipline.) *Positive reinforcement* increases the probability that behavior will be repeated by rewarding people for making the right response. The phrase "increases the probability" is noteworthy. No behavior modification strategy guarantees that people will always make the right response in the future. However, it increases the chance that they will repeat the desired behavior. The term *reinforcement* means that the behavior (or response) is strengthened or entrenched. For example, your response of touching F7 in Word to reach the spelling and grammar function has been reinforced so many times that the response is now probably automatic.

Positive reinforcement is the most effective behavior modification strategy. Most people respond better to being rewarded for the right response than to being punished for the wrong response, such as receiving a bonus for good customer service versus being fined for poor customer service.

Punishment is the presentation of an undesirable consequence for a specific behavior. Yelling at an employee for making a mistake is a direct form of punishment. Another form of punishment is taking away a privilege, such as working on an interesting project, because of some undesirable behavior. In order to be effective, punishment not only tells people what not to do, it teaches them the right behavior. A serious disadvantage of punishment is that it may cause adverse consequences for managers and the organization. Employees who are punished often become defensive, angry, and eager to seek revenge. Many incidents of workplace violence, such as killing a former supervisor, occur after a mentally unstable employee has been fired—even when the dismissal is justified.

Successful Application of Positive Reinforcement

Behavior modification may take the form of an overall company program, such as a highly structured behavior modification program, or a rewards and recognition program. Managers use positive reinforcement more frequently, on an informal, daily basis. The following list presents suggestions for making effective use of positive reinforcement, whether as part of a company program or more informally.

1. *State clearly what behavior will lead to a reward, and supply ample feedback.* The nature of good performance, or the goals, must be agreed to by both manager and group member. Clarification could take this form: "What I need are inventory reports without missing data. When you achieve this, you'll be credited with good performance." As workers attain the performance goals, they should receive frequent feedback. Telling people they have done something correctly, or notifying them by e-mail, are efficient forms of feedback.
2. *Use appropriate rewards.* An appropriate reward proves effective when it is valued by the person being motivated. Examine the list of rewards in Exhibit 11-7. Note that some have more appeal to you than do others. The best way to motivate people is to offer them their preferred rewards for good performance. Managers should ask employees what they are interested in attaining.
3. *Make rewards contingent on good performance.* Contingent reinforcement means that getting the reward depends on giving a certain performance. Unless a reward is linked to the desired behavior or performance it will have little effect on whether the behavior or performance is repeated. For example, saying "You're doing great" in response to anything an employee does will not lead to good performance. Yet if the manager reserves the "doing great" response for truly outstanding performance, he or she may reinforce the good performance.
4. *Administer rewards intermittently.* Positive reinforcement can be administered under different types of schedules. The most effective and sensible type is an intermittent schedule, in which rewards are administered often, but not always, when the appropriate behavior occurs. A reward loses its effect if given every time the employee makes the right response. Thus intermittent rewards sustain desired behavior for a longer time by helping to prevent the behavior from fading away when it is not rewarded. In addition to being more effective, intermittent rewards are generally more practical than continuous rewards. Few managers have enough time to dispense rewards every time team members attain performance goals.
5. *Administer rewards promptly.* The proper timing of rewards may be difficult because the manager is not present at the time of good performance. In this case, an e-mail message or telephone call of appreciation within several days of the good performance is appropriate.
6. *Change rewards periodically.* Rewards grow stale quickly; they must be changed periodically. A repetitive reward can even become an annoyance. How many times can one be motivated by the phrase "nice job"? Suppose the reward for making a sales quota is an iPod. How many iPods can one person use (assuming the award is not re-gifted)?
7. *Make the rewards visible.* When other workers notice the reward, its impact multiplies because the other people observe what kind of behavior is rewarded. Assume that you were informed about a coworker's exciting assignment, given because of high performance. You might strive to accomplish the same level of performance.

exhibit 11-7 Rewards Suitable for Use in Positive Reinforcement

A large number of potential rewards can be used to motivate individuals and teams, and many of them are low-cost or no-cost. An important condition for a reward is the perception of its value by the individual being motivated. The viewpoint of the reward giver alone about the value of a reward is not sufficient.

Monetary
Salary increases or bonuses
Instant cash awards
Company stock
Bonus or profit sharing
Stock options
Paid personal holiday (such as birthday)
Extra paid-vacation days
Movie, concert, or athletic event tickets
Free or discount airline tickets
Discounts on company products or services
Gift selection from online catalog
Race-car driving camp

Job and Career Related
Challenging work assignment
Empowerment of employee
Change of job status from temporary to permanent
Promise of job security
Assignment to high-prestige team or project
Favorable performance appraisal
Freedom to choose own work activity
Promotion
Flexible working hours
Creating own schedule for peak work loads
Do more of preferred task
Role as boss's stand-in when he or she is away
Job rotation
Seminars and continuous education
Opportunity to set own goals

Food and Dining
Business luncheon paid by company
Company picnics
Department parties or banquet
Lunch catered into office

Recognition and Pride Related
Compliments
Encouragement
Access to confidential information
Pat on back or handshake
Public expression of appreciation
Meeting of appreciation with executive
Open note of thanks distributed by e-mail
Flattering letter from customer distributed by e-mail
Employee-of-the-month award
Wall plaque indicating accomplishment
Visit to manager's office just to receive praise
Team uniforms, hats, or T-shirts
Designated parking space for outstanding performance

Status Symbols
Bigger office or cubicle
Office or cubicle with window
Freedom to personalize work area
Private office

Time Off
Three-day weekend
Company time bank with deposits made for unusual success
Time off gift certificates
Personal leave days for events chosen by employee

Source: Melinda Ligos, "Those Year-End Bonuses Aren't Always Green," *The New York Times* (http://nytimes.com) December 28, 2003; "Do Incentive Rewards Work?" *HRfocus*, October 2000, pp. 1, 14–15; "Retain Top Workers with Time Off," *Manager's Edge*, October 2006; Cindy Krischer Goodman, "Managers Use Perks for Young Workers," McClatchy Newspapers, September 24, 2006.

8. *Reward groups and teams as well as individuals.* To improve organizational productivity, groups as well as individuals should receive rewards for good performance. A combination of group and individual rewards encourages teamwork yet does not discourage outstanding individual performance. As Jack and Suzy Welch recommend, "When an individual or team does

something notable, make a big deal of it. Announce it publicly, talk about it at every opportunity. Hand out awards."[25]

Behavior Modification Effectiveness

Behavior modification has a long history of improving productivity on the job, including the control of absenteeism.[26] Discount-store chain Dollar General turned to the behavior modification company Aubrey Daniels International to tackle absenteeism when it reached 16 percent at the company's distribution center. Dollar General introduced a point system, put workers into teams, and drew a racetrack on the wall with each team represented by a race car. Following OB Mod principles, team members could earn points by arriving on time. However, if they arrived late, they could still earn points for their teams in other ways such as returning from breaks on time. Each day, the race cars advanced by the number of points earned.

expectancy theory of motivation The belief that people will expend effort if they expect the effort to lead to performance and the performance to lead to a reward.

Jeff Sims, the Dollar General senior vice president, says, "And we talked to all of our supervisors and got rid of the punishing behavior of yelling at them if they were late. We started thanking them for coming to work and then saying, 'We really need your help to get those points tomorrow morning.'" After a certain number of laps were completed, the team with the most points was authorized to choose the food served at the distribution center. Within two weeks of the program's introduction, attendance had moved up to 95 percent (from 84 percent).[27]

Whether or not you think the Dollar General motivational approach is hokey, there is a message. With even modest rewards, positive reinforcement can help a company attain key goals.

EXPECTANCY THEORY OF MOTIVATION

Learning Objective 5

Explain the conditions under which a person will be motivated according to expectancy theory.

According to the **expectancy theory of motivation**, people will put forth the greatest effort if they expect the effort to lead to performance that in turn leads to a reward. The various versions of expectancy theory suggest that a process similar to rational gambling determines choices among courses of action. Employees are motivated by what they expect will be the consequences of their efforts. At the same time, they must be confident they can perform the task.[28]

A Basic Model of Expectancy Theory

Expectancy theory integrates important ideas found in other generally accepted motivation theories, including those presented in this chapter. Exhibit 11-8 presents a basic version of expectancy theory. According to

25 Jack and Suzy Welch, "Keeping Your People Pumped," *Business Week*, March 27, 2006, p. 122.

26 Alexander D. Stajkovic and Fred Luthans, "Differential Effects of Incentive Motivators on Work Performance," *Academy of Management Journal*, June 2001, pp. 580–590.

27 Todd Henneman, "Daniels' Scientific Method," *Workforce Management*, October 10, 2005, p. 46.

28 Steel and König, "Integrating Theories of Motivation," p. 893.

exhibit 11-8 Basic Version of Expectancy Theory of Motivation

An individual will be motivated when:

A. The individual believes effort (E) will lead to favorable performance (P)—that is, when $E \rightarrow P$ (also referred to as expectancy).

B. The individual believes performance will lead to favorable outcome (O)—that is, when $P \rightarrow O$ (also referred to as instrumentality).

C. Outcome or reward satisfies an important need (in other words, valence is strong).

D. Need satisfaction is intense enough to make effort seem worthwhile.

the version of expectancy theory developed by Victor H. Vroom, four conditions must exist for motivated behavior to occur.[29]

Condition A refers to *expectancy*, which means that people will expend effort because they believe it will lead to performance. In this $E \rightarrow P$ expectancy, subjective probabilities range between 0.0 and 1.0. Rational people ask themselves, "If I work hard, will I really get the job done?" If they evaluate the probability as being high, they probably will invest the effort to achieve the goal. People have higher $E \rightarrow P$ expectancies when they have the appropriate skills, training, and self-confidence.

Condition B is based on the fact that people are more willing to expend effort if they think that good performance will lead to a reward, referred to as $P \rightarrow O$ instrumentality. It too ranges between 0.0 and 1.0. (*Instrumentality* refers to the idea that the behavior is instrumental in achieving an important end.) The rational person says, "I'm much more willing to perform well if I'm assured that I'll receive the reward I deserve." A cautious employee might even ask other employees if they received their promised rewards for exceptional performance. To strengthen a subordinate's $P \rightarrow O$ instrumentality, the manager should give reassurance that the reward will be forthcoming.

Condition C refers to *valence*, the value a person attaches to certain outcomes. The greater the valence, the greater the effort. Valences can be either positive or negative. If a student believes that receiving an A is important, he or she will work hard. Also, if a student believes that avoiding a C or a lower grade is important, he or she will work hard. Valences range from −1 to +1 in most versions of expectancy theory. A positive valence indicates a preference for a particular reward. A clearer picture of individual differences in human motivation spreads valences out over a range of −100 to +100.

Most work situations present the possibility of several outcomes, with a different valence attached to each. Assume that a purchasing manager is pondering whether becoming a certified purchasing manager (CPM) would be worth the effort. The list that follows cites possible outcomes or rewards from achieving certification, along with their valences (on a scale of −100 to +100).

29 Victor H. Vroom, *Work and Motivation* (New York: Wiley, 1964).

- Status from being a CPM, 75
- Promotion to purchasing manager, 95
- Plaque to hang on office wall, 25
- Bigger salary increase next year, 90
- Letters of congratulations from friends and relatives, 50
- Expressions of envy from one or two coworkers, –25

Valences are useful in explaining why some people will put forth the effort to do things with low expectancies. For example, most people know the chance of winning a lottery, inventing something as successful as the Internet, or writing a best-selling novel is only one in a million. Nevertheless, a number of people vigorously pursue these goals. They do so because they attach an extraordinary positive valence to these outcomes (perhaps 100!).

Condition D indicates that the need satisfaction stemming from each outcome must be intense enough to make the effort worthwhile. Would you walk two miles on a hot day for one glass of ice water? The water would undoubtedly satisfy your thirst need, but the magnitude of the satisfaction would probably not be worth the effort. Similarly, a production technician turned down a promotion to the position of inspector because the raise offered was only 50 cents per hour. The worker told his supervisor, "I need more money. But I'm not willing to take on that much added responsibility for $30 a week."

Implications for Management

Expectancy theory has several important implications for the effective management of people. The theory helps pinpoint what a manager must do to motivate group members and diagnose motivational problems.[30]

1. *Individual differences among employees must be taken into account.* Different people attach different valences to different rewards, so a manager should try to match rewards with individual preferences. Behavior modification also makes use of this principle.
2. *Rewards should be closely tied to those actions the organization sees as worthwhile.* For example, if the organization values customer service, people should be rewarded for providing good customer service. Home Depot has a program called Orange Juiced that offers store employees bonuses as much as $2,000 for exceptional customer service.[31]
3. *Employees should be given the appropriate training and encouragement.* An investment in training will strengthen their subjective hunches that effort will lead to good performance.
4. *Employees should be presented with credible evidence that good performance does lead to anticipated rewards.* Similarly, a manager should reassure employees that good work will be both noticed and rewarded. As part

---

30 Walter B. Newsom, "Motivate Now!" *Personnel Journal*, February 1999, pp. 51–52.
31 Bruce Upbin, "Hammered," *Forbes*, January 8, 2007, p. 37.

of this implication, managers must listen carefully to understand the perceived link employees have between hard work and rewards. If instrumentality is unjustifiably low, the manager must reassure the employee that hard work will be rewarded.

5. *The meaning and implications of outcomes should be explained.* It can be motivational for employees to know the values of certain outcomes. If an employee knows that a high rating on a performance evaluation increases the chances of receiving favorable assignments and promotions, plus a bigger salary increase, he or she will strive harder to perform well.

MOTIVATION THROUGH FINANCIAL INCENTIVES

Learning Objective 6

Describe the role of financial incentives, including profit sharing and gainsharing, in worker motivation.

A natural way to motivate workers at any level is to offer them financial incentives for good performance. Linking pay to performance improves the motivation value of money. Using financial incentives to motivate people fits behavior modification principles. Financial incentives, however, predate behavior modification. The paragraphs that follow discuss linking pay to performance, profit sharing and gainsharing, and employee stock ownership and stock options, and problems associated with financial incentives. Exhibit 11-9 outlines this information.

A useful principle for using financial incentives to motivate workers at all levels is to investigate which incentives are most appealing to groups as well as individuals. Many workers are motivated to work hard for salary increases, yet some others would work harder for the opportunity to obtain a bonus or stock options. Another group of workers might value increased health benefits more than a salary increase.[32]

Linking Pay to Performance Including Bonuses

Financial incentives are more effective when they are linked to (or contingent upon) good performance. Linking pay to performance motivates people to work harder. Production workers and sales workers have long

exhibit 11-9 **Linking Pay to Performance Including Bonuses**

Multiple approaches to motivate workers by using financial incentives are possible.

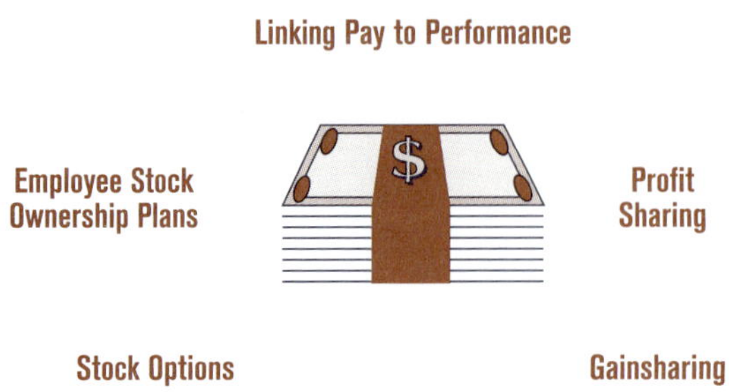

32 Pamela Babcock, "Find What Workers Want," *HR Magazine*, April 2005, p. 51.

received contingent financial incentives. Many production workers receive, after meeting a quota, bonuses per unit of production. Most industrial sales representatives receive salary plus commissions. Managers increasingly use bonuses to retain and motivate employees, according to a survey of over 1,000 companies by Hewett Associates Inc. Bonuses help control fixed costs, and also tend to keep employees focused on business objectives.[33]

Exhibit 11-10 presents a typical approach to linking employee pay to performance, a plan that is often referred to as *merit pay*. Note carefully the information about assigning lump sum payments, rather than percentages, to each performance category. This approach helps more junior workers receive large merit increases. A cost-of-living adjustment is not considered merit pay because it is not related to performance. Merit pay for both individual contributors and managers is based on actual results.

An increasing effort of managers and compensation specialists to link pay to performance supports many business strategies—workers receive financial incentives for performing in ways consistent with the business strategy. The Home Depot bonuses for good customer service mentioned above came about because the company was not rated as highly on customer service as management wanted, so improved customer service was incorporated into strategy.

A radical approach to pay-for-performance is to distribute almost all the variable pay to outstanding performers, and give no bonus pay to less-than-

exhibit 11-10 Guidelines for Performance-Based Merit Increases at a Hospital

Merit pay is additional income earned for meeting performance standards.

Performance Level of Staff Members	Merit Increase (Percentage of Pay)
Demonstrate exceptional performance and make outstanding contributions during the year	4.75–5.50
Give consistently productive performance that meets all standards and exceeds some	3.75–4.74
Give consistently productive performance that meets expectations	2.00–3.74
Demonstrate performance that is not wholly satisfactory, even though some expectations may be met or even exceeded	1.00–1.99
Generally fail to meet key expectations and standards; substantial improvement is necessary and essential	0.00

Note: To help equalize wages more, some organizations assign an absolute amount of salary increase to each performance category. For example, all workers in the top category would receive a $2,500 increase; those in the second category $1,500; those in the third category, $1,000; and those in the fourth category, zero dollars. Assigning absolute dollar amounts to each category prevents junior workers receiving relatively small increases because their base pay is so much lower. Under the new system a more junior top-performing worker making $30,000 per year would receive a new salary of $32,500 ($30,000 + $2,500). Under the old percentage system, his or her maximum new salary might be $31,650 ($30,000 + 0.055 × $30,000).

33 Study cited in Erin White, "Employers Increasingly Favor Bonuses to Raises," *The Wall Street Journal*, August 28, 2006, p. B3.

profit-sharing plan A method of giving workers supplemental income based on the profitability of the entire firm or a selected unit.

gainsharing A formal program allowing employees to participate financially in the productivity gains they have achieved.

outstanding performers. A compensation consultant defends restricting bonus pay to top performers in these words: "The biggest risk is mediocrity if a company fails to reward its top employees adequately. Your stars are going to look elsewhere, and your average and below-average employees will say 'I'm going to stick around.' "[34] Many potential morale problems exist with this approach, including charges that a handful of favorites profit from the hard work of other employees.

Profit Sharing and Gainsharing

The pay plans mentioned so far link rewards to individual effort. Numerous organizations attempt to increase motivation and productivity through a company-wide plan linking incentive pay to increases in performance. Here we describe profit sharing in general, and a specific form of sharing profits called gainsharing.

Profit Sharing

Profit-sharing plans give workers supplemental income based on the profitability of the entire firm or a selected unit. The motivational principle is an employee belief in working harder to contribute to profitability because they will eventually share some of the profits. The larger the company, the more difficult it is for the individual employee to visualize how his or her work efforts translate into corporate profits. Ideally, all employees need to be committed to working for a common good. Employee contributions to profits may take a variety of forms such as product quantity, product quality, reducing costs, or improving work methods.

A major challenge in administering profit-sharing plans as well as any of the other financial incentives described here is making precise judgments about who should receive how much, and whether the variable pay contributes to organizational performance.

Gainsharing

Another approach to profit sharing focuses on productivity increases more directly attributable to worker ideas and effort. **Gainsharing** is a formal program that allows employees to participate financially in the productivity gains they have achieved. It is accomplished through establishing a payout formula and getting employees involved. Productivity gains are typically manufacturing related, but can also be in service, such as customer service. Rewards are distributed after performance improves. As in other forms of profit sharing, the participants can be the entire organization or a unit within the firm. Gainsharing is based on factors in the work environment that employees can control directly. Furthermore, rewards are shared with all members of the gainsharing unit, regardless of individual contribution toward productivity improvement.[35]

---

34 Steve Bates, "Top Pay for Best Performance," *HR Magazine*, January 2003, p. 37.

35 Luis R. Gomez-Meija, Theresa M. Welbourn, and Robert M. Wiseman, "The Role of Risk Sharing and Risk Taking Under Gainsharing," *Academy of Management Review*, July 2000, p. 493; http://www.gainsharing.com.

The formulas used in gainsharing vary widely, but share common elements. Managers begin by comparing what employees are paid to what they sell or produce. Assume that labor costs make up 50 percent of production costs. Any reductions below 50 percent are placed in a bonus pool. Part of the money in the bonus pool is shared among workers. The company's share of the productivity savings in the pool can be distributed to shareholders as increased profits. The savings may allow managers to lower prices, a move that could make the company more competitive.

The second element of gainsharing is employee involvement. Managers establish a mechanism that actively solicits, reviews, and implements employee suggestions about productivity improvement. A committee of managers and employees reviews the ideas and then implements the most promising suggestions. The third key element is employee cooperation. To achieve the bonuses for productivity improvement, group members must work harmoniously with each other. Departments must also cooperate with each other, because some suggestions involve the work of more than one organizational unit.[36]

Gainsharing can lead to a dramatic increase in productive capacity, in record time. Most companies will achieve a productivity gain of 10 to 30 percent within 30 to 90 days after implementing gainsharing. Also, unnecessary overtime is reduced. Because pay is based more on performance than on number of hours worked, employees find ways to get their work accomplished with a minimum of overtime.[37]

Employee Stock Ownership and Stock Option Plans

An increasingly popular way of motivating workers with financial incentives is to make them part owners of the business through stock purchases. Two variations of the same idea of giving workers equity in the business are stock ownership and stock option plans. Stock ownership can be motivational because employees participate in the financial success of the firm as measured by its stock price. If employees work hard, the company may become more successful and the value of the stock increases. Executives are supposed to be strongly motivated by stock ownership because if the stock increases in price, the executives earn so many company shares. If the stock increases substantially in value, the executive can sell the stock and earn millions of dollars.

Under an *employee stock ownership plan* (ESOP), employees at all levels in the organization are given stock. The employer either contributes shares of its stock or the money to purchase the stock on the open market. Stock shares are usually deposited in employee retirement accounts. Upon retirement, employees can choose to receive company stock instead of cash. ESOPs are also significant because they offer tax incentives to the employer. For example, a portion of the earnings paid to the retirement fund are tax deductible.

---

36 Susan C. Hanlon, David C. Meyer, and Robert K. Taylor, "Consequences of Gainsharing: A Field Experiment Revisited," *Group and Organization Management*, Vol. 19, No. 1 (1994), pp. 87–111.

37 http://www.gainsharing.com, accessed December 15, 2006.

Employee stock ownership plans are popular because they are easy to understand, and contribute to an ownership culture. The only notable downside is that employees might rely too heavily on company stock in their investment portfolio, thereby forgoing the advantages of having a diversified investment portfolio. If the company stock plunges dramatically, the value of the employee's investments shrink to almost nothing.

Employee stock options are more complicated than straightforward stock ownership. Stock options give employees the right to purchase company stock at a specified price at some point in the future. If the stock rises in value, you can purchase it at a discount. If the stock sinks below your designated purchase price, your option is worthless. Thousands of workers in the information technology field, particularly in Silicon Valley, have become millionaires and multimillionaires with their stock options—particularly those who cashed in their options at the right time.

However, stock options can also be worthless. When it comes time for employees to cash their options, the stock price can be much less than option (striking) price. Furthermore, many workers who chose relatively small base pay and big options are especially disappointed should the stock market plunge. Stock options become sources of discouragement and anger rather than motivation. To help remedy the situation, many technology companies enable employees to trade in *underwater* options for new options that are more likely to be profitable. (An *underwater option* is one whose strike price is more than the stock's current value, or the water level!) The new lower-price options are more likely to be exercised.[38]

Stock options have also encouraged practices of questionable ethics. A high-ranking official backdates the option price to a time when it was much lower than the time at which the holder of the options wants to sell the stock. A few instances have been found in which backdates have been forged to make the grants seem legitimate. The person is assigned a "favorable date." The ethical issue is that the option holder is almost guaranteed a big profit even if the stock did not increase in value from the time the original option was issued. In 2006, several dozen executives and directors in Silicon Valley were fired or suspended or have resigned in relation to option probes. In the most high-profile probe, the *Financial Times* found that Steve Jobs of Apple Corp. received a grant of 7.5 million stock options without approval from that board in 2001, and that reports of board approval were falsified. By 2006, the value of these falsified options was $442 million.[39] (Is Jobs an evil charismatic?)

Another serious potential source of dissatisfaction with stock options is the tax owed on the gains at the time the employee exercises the option. If you hold the stock and the price plunges, you pay taxes on paper profits. Exhibit 11-11 shows you the arithmetic behind a stock option.

---

38 Gregory Zuckerman, "Tech Companies Find Options Hard to Kick," *The Wall Street Journal*, August 11, 2003, p. C1.

39 Reported in Ian King and Connie Gugielmo, "Report: Job Got Options without OK," Bloomberg News, December 29, 2006, p. 9D.

Problems Associated with Financial Incentives

Although financial incentives are widely used as motivators, they can create problems. A major problem is that workers may not agree with managers about the value of their contributions. Financial incentives can also pit individuals and groups against each other. The result may be unhealthy competition rather than cooperation and teamwork.

Many critics of financial incentives are concerned that American business executives siphon off too much money from corporations that could go to shareholders, employees, and to customers in the form of lower prices. Top-level managers may deserve large financial rewards for good performance, but how much is too much? A glaring example is that Goldman Sachs (a major investment bank) chief executive Lloyd Blankfein received a performance bonus of $53.4 million in 2006. One study demonstrated that during a two-year period, top-executive compensation amounted to 9.8 percent of the companies' net income.[40] A 2005 survey of executive pay at 350 major U.S. corporations revealed that the median total compensation—including salary, bonuses, and a variety of stock payouts—for chief executives was $6,049,504.[41]

People who justify such high executive compensation say the large payments are necessary to attract and retain top talent, and to keep the executives motivated. And besides, executive pay is a small percentage of total revenues. You have probably heard the same argument for paying some professional athletes $12 million per year. Another argument in favor of giant compensation for executives is that managerial skills are highly valued in society, and top business managers and leaders are worth at least as much as entertainment stars.

The most researched argument against financial rewards is that it focuses the attention of workers too much on the reward such as money or stocks. In the process, the workers lose out on intrinsic rewards such as joy in accomplishment. Instead of being passionate about the work they are doing, people become overly concerned with the size of their reward. One argument is that external rewards do not create a lasting commitment. Instead, they create temporary compliance, such as working hard in the short run to earn a bonus. A frequent problem with merit pay systems is that a person who does not receive a merit increase for one pay period then feels that he or she has been punished.

In reality, workers at all levels want a combination of internal (intrinsic) rewards and financial rewards along with other external rewards such as praise. Workers also want a work environment that enables them to manage their life well off the job, such as ample vacation and some flexibility in working hours. Workers also search for meaning and satisfaction as well as financial rewards.[42] The ideal combination is to offer exciting (intrinsically motivating) work to people, and simultaneously pay them enough money so they are not preoccupied with matters such as salary and bonuses.

---

40 Study reported in Jesse Eisinger, "Lavish Pay Puts a Bite on Profits," *The Wall Street Journal*, January 11, 2006, p. C1.

41 "The Boss's Pay: The WSJ/Mercer 2005 CEO Compensation Survey," *The Wall Street Journal*, April 16, 2006, p. R7.

42 Gardiner Morse, "Why We Misread Motives," *Harvard Business Review*, January 2003, p. 18.

A useful perspective for managers is that for financial rewards to be effective motivators, they must be combined with meaningful responsibility, respect for the worker, constructive relationships on the job, and recognition. All these factors combined make for an effective motivation strategy.[43]

The accompanying Management in Action illustrates how a company famous for its worker output motivates using financial incentives as well as other motivators.

management in action

Worker Motivation at Nucor

It was about 2 p.m. on March 9, 2006 when three Nucor Corp. electricians got the call from their colleagues at the Hickman, Arkansas, plant. It was bad news; Hickman's electrical grid had failed. For a mini-mill steelmaker like Nucor, which melts scrap steel from autos, dishwashers, mobile homes, and the like in an electric arc furnace to make new steel, there's little that could be worse. The trio immediately dropped what they were doing and headed out to the plant. Malcolm McDonald, an electrician from the Decatur, Alabama, mill was in Indiana visiting another facility. He drove down, arriving at 9 o'clock that night. Less Hart and Bryson Trumble, from Nucor's facility in Hartford County, NC, boarded a plane that landed in Memphis at 11 p.m. Then they drove two hours to the troubled plant.

No supervisor had asked them to make the trip, and no one had to. They went on their own. Camping out in the electrical substation with the Hickman staff, the team worked 20-hour shifts to get the plant up and running again in three days instead of the anticipated full week. There wasn't any direct financial incentive for them to blow their weekends, no extra money in their next paycheck, but for the company their contribution was huge. Hickman went on to post a first-quarter record for tons of steel shipped.

At Nucor, the heroic act of the three electricians is not considered particularly remarkable. "It could easily have been a Hickman operator going to help the Crawfordville [Indiana] mill," says Executive Vice-President John J. Ferriola, who overseas the Hickman plant and seven others. "It happens daily."

In an industry as Rust Belt as they come, Nucor has nurtured one of the most dynamic and engaged workforces around. The 11,300 non-union employees at the Charlotte, NC, company don't see themselves as worker bees waiting for instructions from above. Nucor's flattened hierarchy and emphasis on pushing power to the front line led its employees to adopt the mind-set of owner-operators. Nucor's 387 percent return to shareholders during a five-year stretch handily beats almost all other companies in the Standard & Poor's 500-stock index.

Nucor gained renown in the late 1980s for its radical pay practices, which base the vast majority of most workers' income on their performance. An upstart nipping at the heels of the integrated steel giants, Nucor had a close-knit culture that was the natural outgrowth of its underdog identity. Legendary leader F. Kenneth Iverson's radical insight was that employees, even hourly clock-punchers, will make an extraordinary effort if you

43 R. Brayton Bowen, "Today's Workforce Requires New Age Currency," *HR Magazine*, March 2004, p. 101.

reward them richly, treat them with respect, and give them real power.

Nucor's unusual pay system is the single most daring element of the company's model and the hardest for outsiders and acquired companies to embrace. An experienced steelworker at another company can easily earn $16 to $20 an hour. At Nucor the guarantee is closer to $10. A bonus tied to the production of defect-free steel by an employee's entire shift can triple the average steelworker's take-home pay. The average Nucor steelworker took home nearly $79,000 in 2005. Add to that a $2,000 one-time bonus to mark the company's record earnings and almost $18,000, on average, in profit sharing.

Not only is good work rewarded, but bad work is penalized. Bonuses are calculated on every order and paid out every week. At the Berkeley Mill in Huger, SC, if workers make a bad batch of steel and catch it before it has moved on, they lose the bonus they otherwise would have made on that shipment. But if it gets to the customer, they lose three times that. The take-home pay of managers depends heavily on results as well. Department managers typically get a base pay that is 75 to 90 percent of market average. But in a great year that same manager might get a bonus of 75 percent or even 90 percent, based on the return on assets of the whole plant.

"In average-to-bad years, we can earn less than our peers in other companies. That's supposed to teach us that we don't want to be average or bad. We want to be good," says James M. Coblin, Nucor's vice-president for human resources.

Questions

1. Identify the motivational techniques Nucor management uses.
2. In what way does Nucor management use punishment as a motivational technique?
3. How can Nucor still be so profitable even though steelworkers can earn as much as $100,000 in salary and bonuses in a given year?

Source: Nanette Byrnes, "The Art of Motivation," *Business Week*, May 1, 2006, pp. 57–62.

SUMMARY OF Key Points

1 Explain the relationship between motivation and performance.

From the standpoint of the individual, motivation is an internal state that leads to the pursuit of objectives. From the standpoint of the manager, motivation is an activity that gets subordinates to pursue objectives. The purpose of motivating employees is to get them to achieve results and commitment. A problem today is that so many workers are not engaged in their work. Motivation is but one important contributor to productivity and performance. Other important contributors are abilities, skills, technology, and group norms.

2 Present an overview of major theories of need satisfaction in explaining motivation.

Workers can be motivated through need satisfaction, particularly because most people want to know "What's in it for me?" First, needs must be identified. Second, the person must be given an opportunity to satisfy those needs.

Maslow's need hierarchy states that people strive to become self-actualized. However, before higher-level needs are activated, certain lower-level needs must be satisfied. When a person's needs are satisfied at one level, he or she looks toward satisfaction at a higher level. Specific needs playing an important role in work motivation include achievement, power, affiliation, recognition, pride, risk taking and thrill seeking.

The two-factor theory of work motivation includes two different sets of job motivation factors: One set gives people a chance to satisfy higher-level needs. These are satisfiers and motivators. When present, they increase satisfaction and motivation. When satisfiers and motivators are absent, the impact is neutral. Satisfiers and motivators generally relate to the content of a job. They include achievement, recognition, and opportunity for advancement. Dissatisfiers are job elements that appeal more to lower-level needs. When they are present, they prevent dissatisfaction, but they do not create satisfaction or motivation. Dissatisfiers relate mostly to the context of a job. They include company policy and administration, job security, and money. Current satisfiers for young workers include flexible work schedules and engaging in community service.

3 Explain how goal setting is used to motivate people.

Goal setting is an important part of most motivational programs, and it is a managerial method of motivating group members. It is based on these ideas: (a) specific goals are better than generalized goals; (b) the more difficult the goal, the better the performance, yet superordinate goals are important; (c) only goals that are accepted improve performance; (d) goals are more effective when used to evaluate performance; (e) goals should be linked to feedback and rewards; and (f) group goal setting is important. The Pygmalion effect contributes to goal setting.

4 Describe the application of behavior modification to worker motivation.

Behavior modification is the most systematic method of motivating people. It changes behavior by rewarding the right responses and punishing or ignoring the wrong ones. Behavior modification is based on the law of effect: Behavior that leads to positive consequences tends to be repeated, and behavior that leads to negative consequences tends not to be repeated.

Positive reinforcement and punishment are the most used behavior modification strategies. Positive reinforcement rewards people for making the right response. Punishment is the presentation of an undesirable consequence for a specific behavior, and is often counterproductive. If used appropriately, however, punishment can be motivational.

Suggestions for the informal use of positive reinforcement in a work setting include (a) state clearly what behavior leads to a reward, and supply feedback, (b) use appropriate rewards, (c) make rewards contingent on good performance, (d) administer intermittent rewards, (e) administer rewards promptly, (f) change rewards periodically, (g) make rewards visible, and (h) reward the team as well as the individual.

5 Explain the conditions under which a person will be motivated according to expectancy theory.

Expectancy theory contends that people will expend effort if they expect the effort to lead to performance and the performance to lead to a reward. According to the expectancy model presented here, a person will be motivated if the person believes effort will lead to performance, the performance will lead to a reward, the reward satisfies an important need, and the need satisfaction is intense enough to make the effort seem worthwhile.

6 Describe the role of financial incentives, including profit sharing and gainsharing, in worker motivation.

A natural way to motivate workers at any level is to offer financial incentives for good performance. Linking pay to performance improves the motivational value of financial incentives. A radical approach to pay-for-performance is to distribute almost all the variable pay to outstanding performers.

Profit-sharing plans give out money related to company or large-unit performance. Gainsharing is a formal program that allows employees to participate financially in productivity gains they have achieved. Bonuses are distributed to employees based on how much they decrease the labor cost involved in producing or selling goods. Employee involvement in increasing productivity is an important part of gainsharing.

Employee stock ownership plans set aside a block of company stock for employee purchase, often redeemable at retirement. Stock option plans give employees the right to purchase company stock at a specified price at some future time. Both plans attempt to motivate workers by making them part owners of the business. Stock option plans have been subject to the abuse of backdating the strike price.

Financial motivators can create problems, such as executives siphoning off too much money from shareholders and employees, and even customers. Financial incentives also encourage workers to focus on the reward instead of the work. For best results, financial incentives should be combined with internal motivators such as meaningful responsibility and recognition.

KEY TERMS AND PHRASES

Motivation, 371
$P = M \times A$, 372
Need, 375
Maslow's need hierarchy, 375
Deficiency needs, 375
Growth needs, 375
Achievement need, 377
Affiliation need, 377
Recognition need, 377
Two-factor theory of work motivation, 381
Goal, 383
Superordinate goals, 383
Pygmalion effect, 385
Behavior modification, 385
Law of effect, 386
Expectancy theory of motivation, 389
Profit-sharing plan, 394
Gainsharing, 394

QUESTIONS

1. Visualize yourself as a Whole Foods store manager. What might be the unintended negative consequences of allowing employees to split the money saved from minimizing the number of workers on a team?
2. How could you use expectancy theory to increase your own motivation level?
3. What similarities do you see between motivating professional athletes and workers in business?
4. What information does this chapter have to offer the manager who is already working with a well-motivated team?
5. Some managers object to systematic approaches to motivating employees by expressing the thought "Why should we have to go out of our way to motivate workers to do what they are paid to do?" What is your reaction to this objection?
6. How would a company know if recognition awards, such as an expensive watch containing the company logo, actually contributed to employee motivation or retention?
7. What is your opinion of the ethics of paying a business executive $45 million in one year, salary and bonus included?

SKILL-BUILDING EXERCISE 11-A: Recognizing the Good Work of Others

The evidence about the effectiveness of recognition and other forms of positive reinforcement is impressive. However, we want you to study the results of recognition first hand. Think of someone who performs a service for you whom you might have an opportunity to see more than once or twice. Examples here include cashiers at a supermarket, servers at a restaurant, or bank tellers. When you receive good service from that person, give him or her appropriate recognition (or a super tip if tipping is expected). When you encounter that person again, see if he or she behaves differently, or performs at an even higher level. If no change occurs, analyze the reason for the lack of change. For example, is there a possibility that you did not deliver the recognition effectively?

SKILL-BUILDING EXERCISE 11.B: Identifying the Most Powerful Motivators

The class divides itself into small groups. Working alone, group members first attach a valence to all the rewards in Exhibit 11-7. Use the expectancy theory scale of −100 to +100. Next, do an analysis of the top ten motivators identified by the group, perhaps by calculating the average valence attached to the rewards that at first glance were assigned high valences by most group members. After each group has identified its top ten motivators, the group leaders can post the results for the other class members to see. After comparing results, answer these questions:

1. What appear to be the top three motivators for the entire class?
2. Do the class members tend to favor internal or external rewards?
3. Did career experience or gender influence the results within the groups?
4. Of what value to managers would this exercise be in estimating valences?

INTERNET SKILL-BUILDING EXERCISE: Analyzing a Motivational Program

Hundreds of programs for motivating employees are described on the Internet. We direct you, however, to http://www.nelson-motivation.com. After watching the video, answer these questions:

1. Which theory of motivation appears to underlie the work of Bob Nelson?
2. Nelson describes the position of "turkey administrator" created by a specific company. What does this new position tell us about the importance of valence in motivation?
3. Based on the brief video clip, how effective do you think Nelson is in motivating his audience?

Case Problem 11-A

Motivating the Staff at HROutsource

Kelly Winters is a program manager at HROutsource, a company that supplies human resource services to small and medium-size organizations, including businesses, hospitals, and a variety of nonprofit firms. The human resources services include administering payroll and employee benefits, bonus plans, and training. Winters is the program manager for training services, a small but growing part of client work for HROutsource.

The three members of Winters' staff are Christina Conway, Peter Wang, and Maria Sanchez, all of whom hold the job title of human resources consultant. All three consultants are performing adequately, yet Winters has been thinking lately about enhancing their performance. Winters' immediate manager, the vice president of client programs, agrees that her staff has room for improvement in terms of effort and commitment. Winters' preliminary action plan for enhancing the motivation of her staff is to interview them to search for specific motivators.

In Winters' words, "As an HR professional, I'm not naïve enough to think that a one-size-fits-all approach to motivation is going to work. I'm not going to offer each member of my team a gift certificate to their favorite online shopping service as a reward for outstanding performance. Gifts are nice, but I want to try something a little more sophisticated."

Excerpts from the interviews are as follows:

WINTERS: "Chris, what do you really want from working at HROutsource? What would it take to get you to the next level of effort?"

CONWAY: "Thanks for asking me, Kelly. I haven't given the issue much thought yet. But off the top of my head, I would say I want your job, and then keep moving. I see a great future in human resource programs being outsourced, and I want to be part of that future. I'm 26 right now, and I can see myself as a CEO of a human resources outsourcing firm by the time I hit 35. So if I could see some clear signs of career advancement, I would put a little more pressure on the accelerator."

WINTERS: "Peter, what do you want to get out of working for HROutsource? How could we get you to be even more strongly motivated?"

WANG: "I like what I see at the company, yet I'm falling into a little bit of a routine. I keep doing safety training and diversity training for clients. It's getting a little repetitious. I have to appear excited and enthused even if I've given the identical training program seven times in one month. I want to branch out, and maybe help install a bonus system for a client or two. I want to get into other aspects of HR.

"I don't want to feel like I'm finished growing as an HR professional. I'm only 31."

WINTERS: "Good morning Maria. How are you doing today? I wanted to learn a little bit more about what makes you happy and motivated. What do you hope to get out of working for HROutsource? What type of work would get you even more fired up?"

SANCHEZ: "I thought I was pretty fired up. I think I could be more committed to the company if the company was more committed to me. I feel I am only as good as my last client assignment. Supposed the company runs out of client assignments for me. Does that mean I'm out the door?

"Stable employment is pretty important for me. I have a child, and my husband is a full-time student in a field with little prospect for high-paying work. I would like to wake up every morning and feel that my job at HROutsource will be there."

Discussion Questions

1. What needs are Conway, Wang, and Sanchez attempting to satisfy?
2. Make a suggestion to Winters and her manager for motivating Conway, Wang, and Sanchez.
3. Should Winters have asked each staff member exactly the same question in order to understand more clearly their potential motivators?

Case Problem 11-B

We Need More Engagement Around Here

Peggy Bates is the CEO of a regional HMO (health maintenance organization) with 25 local offices serving business and nonprofit organizations. The competition for business has become more intense in recent years as organizations continue to look for ways to reduce costs for medical and dental insurance. A particular concern is that a given company might shift to another HMO if that healthcare provider can offer lower costs.

Bates expressed her concern at a meeting with the management staff in these words: "I think our HMO could provide better service and lower costs if our employees put in more effort. A lot of the employees I have seen are so laid back, and almost indifferent. They don't seem to have a sense of urgency.

"I don't think that by simply downsizing the company we will reduce costs. Having fewer workers to accomplish our important work would just make things worse. We would get less work accomplished, and the quality would suffer."

After listening to Bates, Jerry Falcone, the vice president of marketing, commented: "Peggy you might be right about some of our employees not being totally engaged in our efforts. Yet, I cannot understand why. Taking care of people's health is one of the most important responsibilities in the world. I mean, we are often increasing life span as well as saving lives."

Melissa Mitchell, director of human resources, said: "Jerry from your point of view, you are correct. Healthcare is a noble undertaking. Yet when a person is seated at a keyboard and terminal for eight hours processing claims, he or she might not feel like an angel of mercy.

"We can speculate all we want about how well our employees are engaged and motivated, and what we should do about the situation. I propose that we get some data to work with so we can learn more about the nature of the problem we are working with. I propose we hire a human resources consulting firm to conduct a survey about employee engagement. It could prove to be a good investment."

Bates said with a smile, "Here I am concerned about our costs being too high, and Melissa makes a suggestion for spending money."

Mitchell retorted, "Peggy, I am talking about *investing* not spending money. If we could boost our employee level of motivation 10 percent, we would get a tremendous return on investment."

Bates, Mitchell, and the rest of the executive team agreed on hiring a firm to conduct the survey. Four months later, the survey was completed, and the results presented to management. The consultant, Ken Ho, focused on the data presented in the accompanying Exhibit as the key findings of the survey. He said, "Folks, here is the meat of the study. Let's discuss what calls for action are revealed by the data."

CASE EXHIBIT: Data from Employee Attitude Survey

Question	Percent Yes	Percent No
1. Do you know what is expected of you at work?	72	28
2. Do you have the opportunity to do what you do best every day?	55	45
3. Do you put your full effort into the job most days?	44	56
4. Do you think your immediate boss is doing a good job?	85	15
5. Do you expect to be working for this company for at least another three years?	34	66
6. Do you ever take work home with you (assuming you have the type of work that can be done off company premises)?	41	59
7. In the past year, have you had opportunities at work to learn and grow?	38	62
8. How satisfied are you with your compensation (salary and benefits combined)?	69	31

Case Problem 11-B

Discussion Questions

1. How bad is employee motivation and engagement as revealed by the Exhibit?
2. What actions can management take to increase motivation?
3. Should management focus on intrinsic, or extrinsic, motivators in attempting to enhance the motivation and engagement level of these HMO workers?

chapter 12

Communication

Objectives

After studying this chapter and doing the exercises, you should be able to:

1 Describe the steps in the communication process.

2 Recognize the major types of nonverbal communication in the workplace.

3 Explain and illustrate the difference between formal and informal communication channels.

4 Identify major communication barriers in organizations.

5 Develop tactics for overcoming communication barriers.

6 Describe how to conduct more effective meetings.

7 Describe how organizational (or office) politics affect interpersonal communication.

Thomas Swidarski was a senior vice president at Diebold, the Canton, Ohio, maker of automated teller machines. Hardly anything was going smoothly. New ATMs had fancy features but also costly bugs. A supply-chain quagmire in overseas plants slowed the flow of products. Earnings plummeted. Every C-level executive left: The chief financial officer jumped ship and the COO and CEO both were ousted.

That's when directors named Swidarski, 47 years old, president and CEO. Before accepting the top job, he reminded Diebold's lead director that he didn't have any manufacturing experience. What the ten-year veteran did have was experience overseeing marketing, global business development, and acquisitions. And he hasn't lacked the ability to identify problems quickly and mobilize employees to work toward solutions.

Swidarski began his first day as CEO by asking himself what he'd want from a new top boss. His answer: candid communication. He sent an e-mail to Diebold's 14,500 employees inviting comments and outlining his priorities, including building customer loyalty by speeding the flow of products through the supply chain and "providing quality products and outstanding service." He told them that leading Diebold "does not rest with one person—it rests with each and every one of us."

He received more than 1,000 responses. Some employees simply said "thanks for writing," but others wrote about a problem they wanted to solve. "People cared and were passionate, which is what you always want and need" to make changes, says Swidarski.

Straightforward and unpretentious, Swidarski drops by employees' desks to ask about their work or invite them to lunch. He reminds executives to "make sure associates know the work they do is important, whatever their title," says Debbie Metzger, who oversees Diebold's global customer-satisfaction program.[1]

The story about the newly appointed CEO illustrates the key role communication with employees plays in a manager accomplishing his or her mission of running a successful business.

Communication has been described as the glue that holds the organization together. According to one study, companies with highly effective internal communication posted shareholder returns over a five-year period that were 57 percent higher than those of companies that communicated less well with employees.[2] Also, many sales are gained when the sales staff has the skills to develop rapport with customers, to listen, to inform, and to problem solve—either in person, by telephone, or by e-mail.[3] Looking at the negative side, poor communication is the number one problem in virtually all organizations and the cause of most problems.

Communication is an integral part of all managerial functions. Unless managers communicate with others, they cannot plan, organize, control, or lead. Effective communication is a leader's most potent tool for inspiring workers to take responsibility for creating a better future (implementing the vision).[4] Person-to-person communication is as much a part of managerial, professional, technical, and sales work as running is a part of basketball and soccer. Furthermore, the ability to communicate effectively relates closely to career advancement. Employees who are poor communicators are often bypassed for promotion, particularly if the job includes people contact. Well-known investor and executive Warren Buffet told a group of business students that good communication skills are the most important skills needed to succeed.[5]

The information in this chapter is designed to improve communication among people in the workplace. Two approaches are used to achieve this end. First, the chapter describes key aspects of organizational communication, including communication channels and barriers. Second, the chapter presents many suggestions about how managers and others can overcome communication barriers and conduct effective meetings. We also study a subtle aspect of communications called organizational politics.

---

1 Carol Hymowitz, "Diebold's New Chief Shows How to Lead After a Sudden Rise," *The Wall Street Journal*, May 8, 2006, p. B1.
2 Study reported in Eric Krell, "The Unintended Word," *HR Magazine*, August 2006, pp. 51–52.
3 David Saxby, "Sales Unfold Naturally When You Train Employees to Be Skilled Communicators with Customers," http://www.measure-x.com/tips/salesunfold.html, accessed June 25, 2004.
4 John Hamm, "The Five Messages Leaders Must Manage," *Harvard Business Review*, May 2006, p. 114.
5 Josh Funk, "Buffet Devotes Time to College Students," Associated Press, April 14, 2006.

THE COMMUNICATION PROCESS

Learning Objective 1

Describe the steps in the communication process.

Anytime people send information back and forth to each other they are communicating. **Communication** is the process of exchanging information by the use of words, letters, symbols, or nonverbal behavior. Sending messages to other people, and having the messages interpreted as intended, generally proves to be complex and difficult. The difficulty arises because communication depends on perception. People may perceive words, symbols, actions, and even colors differently, depending on their background and interests.

A typical communication snafu took place at a product-improvement meeting. The supervisor said to a technician, "Product desirability is in the eye of the beholder." The technician responded, "Oh, how interesting." Later the technician told the rest of the team, "It's no use striving for product improvement. The boss thinks product desirability is too subjective to achieve." The supervisor's message—that the consumer is the final judge of product desirability—got lost in the process; communication failed.

PLAY VIDEO

COMMUNICATION

"Go to academic.cengage.com/management/dubrin and view the video. Explain why the communication skills and techniques used within a business unit are not always effective in communicating across business units or up and down the corporate ladder."

Steps in the Communication Process

Exhibit 12-1 illustrates the complexity of the communication process. This diagram simplifies the baffling process of sending and receiving messages. The model of two-way communication involves four major steps, each subject to interference, or noise. The four steps are encoding, transmission, decoding, and feedback.

Encoding the Message

Encoding is the process of organizing ideas into a series of symbols, such as words and gestures, designed to communicate with the receiver. Word choice strongly influences communication effectiveness. The better a person's grasp of language, the easier it is for him or her to encode. Appropriate choices of words or any other symbol increase the chance that communication will flow

communication The process of exchanging information by the use of words, letters, symbols, or nonverbal behavior.

exhibit 12-1 The Communication Process

Exchanging message as intended is complex because noise, or interference, so often gets in the way.

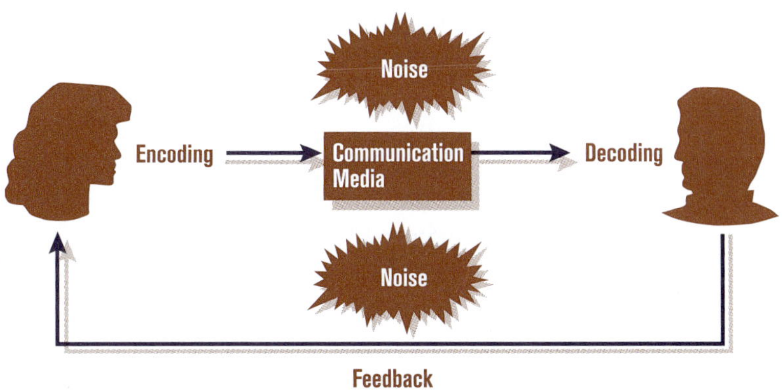

smoothly. The supervisor mentioned at the beginning of this section chose to use the somewhat vague phrase: "Product desirability is in the eye of the beholder." A more effective message might be "Product desirability is measured by customer acceptance."

Communication Media

The message is sent via a communication medium, such as voice, e-mail, instant message, Web log, or telephone. Selecting a medium that fits the message contributes to its effectiveness. In general, more emotional, sensitive, and negative topics are better communicated face-to-face, such as offering a worker a promotion or disciplining him or her. It would be appropriate to use the spoken word to inform a coworker that his shirt was torn. It would be inappropriate to send the same message through e-mail or voice mail because the message might appear too harsh and ridiculing. Many messages in organizations are communicated nonverbally, through the use of gestures and facial expressions. For example, a smile from a superior in a meeting effectively communicates the message "I agree with your comment."

Decoding the Message

In **decoding**, the receiver interprets the message and translates it into meaningful information. Barriers to communication often surface at the decoding step. People may interpret messages according to their psychological needs and motives. The technician mentioned earlier may have been looking for an out—a reason not to be so concerned about achieving high standards. So he interpreted the message in a way that minimized the need to strive for product desirability.

After understanding comes action—the receiver does something about the message. If the receiver acts in the manner the sender wants, the communication process is successful. From the manager's perspective, the success of a message is measured in terms of the action taken by a group member. Understanding alone is not sufficient. Many people understand messages but take no constructive action.

encoding
The process of organizing ideas into a series of symbols designed to communicate with the receiver.

decoding
The communication stage in which the receiver interprets the message and translates it into meaningful information.

feedback
The communication stage in which the receiver responds to the sender's message.

Feedback

The receiver's response to the sender's message is referred to as **feedback**. Without feedback, it is difficult to know whether a message has been received and understood. Also, many people are offended when they are forced to listen to a message but not given the opportunity for feedback. Seven months before Robert Nardelli was fired as CEO of Home Depot he held an annual meeting in which he knew he would be criticized for his gigantic compensation and the company's low stock price. So Nardelli convinced other board members to stay away from the meeting, and limited shareholder questions to one minute. His attempt to limit dialogue reinforced his public image as a callous and entrenched corporate leader,[6] and also as an autocratic leader who does not want to listen to criticism.

---

6 Joann S. Lublin, Ann Zimmerman, and Chad Terhune, "Behind Nardelli's Abrupt Exit: Executive's Fatal Flaw: Failing to Understand New Demands on CEOs," *The Wall Street Journal*, January 4, 2007, p. A12.

The feedback step also includes the reactions of the receiver. If the receiver takes actions as intended by the sender, the message has been received satisfactorily. Action represents a form of feedback, because it results in a message sent to the original sender from the receiver. Suppose a small-business owner receives this message from a supplier: "Please send us $450 within 10 days to cover your overdue account. If we do not receive payment within 10 days, your account will be turned over to a collection agent." The owner understands the message but decides not to comply because the parts for which the $450 is owed were defective. The owner's noncompliance is not due to a lack of understanding.

noise
In communication, unwanted interference that can distort or block a message.

The feedback from the receiver to the sender is likely to be better accepted when it contains an analysis, rather than merely an opinion.[7] An opinion would be, "Your idea about sending payroll notices exclusively online is bad." An analysis on the same subject would be, "Many of our employees do not have computers, so it would be difficult for them to access the information that previously came in the mail to their homes."

Many missteps can occur between encoding and decoding a message. **Noise**, or unwanted interference, can distort or block the message. Later in the chapter the discussion of communication barriers will examine the problem of noise and how it prevents the smooth flow of ideas between sender and receiver.

NONVERBAL COMMUNICATION IN ORGANIZATIONS

Learning Objective 2
Recognize the major types of nonverbal communication in the workplace.

The most obvious modes of communication are speaking, writing, and sign language. A substantial amount of interpersonal communication also occurs through **nonverbal communication**, the transmission of messages by means other than words. Nonverbal communication usually supplements rather than substitutes for writing, speaking, and sign language. The general purpose of nonverbal communication is to express the feeling behind a message, such as nodding one's head vigorously to indicate an emphatic "yes." Six frequently used aspects of nonverbal communication are presented next.

1. *Hand and body gestures.* Your hand and body movements convey specific information to others. Frequent gesturing shows a positive attitude toward another person. In contrast, dislike or disinterest usually produces few gestures. An important exception here occurs when some people wave their hands while in an argument, sometimes to the point of making threatening gestures. The type of gesture displayed also communicates a specific message. For example, moving your hand toward your body in a waving motion communicates the message "Come here, I like you" or "Tell me more." Palms spread outward indicate perplexity.

nonverbal communication
The transmission of messages by means other than words.

7 Seth Godin, "How to Give Feedback," *Fast Company*, March 2004, p. 103.

Gesturing should not be ignored because it is a natural part of speech and thinking. Scientific evidence suggests that gesturing literally takes a load off your mind while engaged in heavy cognitive activity, such as explaining financial ratio. The gesturing off-loads some of the mental effort, enabling you to accomplish more.[8]

2. *Facial expressions and movement.* The particular look on a person's face and movements of the person's head provide reliable cues as to approval, disapproval, or disbelief. A smile from the receiver often indicates support for what you are saying.
3. *Posture.* Another widely used clue to a person's attitude is his or her posture. Leaning toward another person suggests a favorable attitude toward the message a person is trying to communicate. Tilting your head and leaning in indicates your concern and attentiveness. Leaning backward communicates the opposite. Standing up straight generally conveys self-confidence, while slouching can be interpreted as a sign of low self-confidence.
4. *Body placement.* The placement of one's body in relation to someone else is widely used to transmit messages. Facing a person in a casual, relaxed style indicates acceptance. Moving close to another person also generally indicates acceptance. Yet moving too close may be perceived as a violation of personal space, and the message sender will be rejected. Speechwriter and speaking coach Nick Morgan says that to effectively relate to an audience, you need a kinesthetic connection (effective movement of the body). This would include the other forms of nonverbal communication as well as moving around effectively. For example, vary the distance between yourself and your audience, and do not turn away from the audience to cue your next slide.[9]
5. *Voice quality.* Aspects of the voice such as pitch, volume, tone, and speech rate may communicate confidence, nervousness, and enthusiasm. People often judge intelligence by how a person sounds. The most annoying voice quality is a whining, complaining, or nagging tone.[10] Another aspect of voice quality is a person's accent. A study conducted in Texas found that job candidates with strong regional accents were less likely to be offered a high-prestige job or one with high public contact. The recommendation offered is to soften but not necessarily completely change a regional accent because a complete change could make a person feel unnatural.[11] Many professionals hire speech pathologists to serve as coaches for improving their voice, and thereby improve their chances for advancing in their career. The emphasis is not on speech therapy but on voice beautification to come across as more intelligent and persuasive.[12]

---

8 Nick Morgan, "The Kinesthetic Speaker: Putting Action Into Words," *Harvard Business Review*, April 2001, p. 115.

9 Research reported in Sharon Begley, "Gesturing as You Talk Can Help You Take a Load Off Your Mind," *The Wall Street Journal*, November 14, 2003, p. B1.

10 Jeffrey Jacobi, *The Vocal Advantage* (Upper Saddle River, NJ: Prentice-Hall, 1996).

11 Carla D'Nan Bass, "Strong Accent Can Hurt Chances for Employment," *Knight Ridder*, October 1, 2000.

12 Jennifer Saranow, "A Personal Trainer for Your Voice," *The Wall Street Journal*, February 3, 2004, pp. D1, D4.

6. *Clothing, dress, and appearance.* The image a person conveys communicates such messages as "I feel powerful" and "I think this meeting is important." For example, wearing one's best business attire to a performance evaluation interview would communicate that the person thinks the meeting is important. Another important meaning of dress is that it communicates how willing the employee is to comply with organizational standards. By deviating too radically from standard, such as wearing a suit on "Dress Down" day, the person communicates indifference.

   Aside from helping people communicate effectively, nonverbal communication has other applications. One example is to assist in screening airline passengers who might be a security threat. Unusual body language such as trembling, lack of eye contact with security officials, and a swollen carotid artery (in the neck) could suggest a passenger with evil intent. Wearing a big coat on a summer day would be an example of unusual and suspicious behavior. Odd gestures and split-second expressions could indicate an attempt to conceal emotions. Passengers displaying any of the preceding behaviors would then be interviewed for further screening. Screening possible security threats by nonverbal communication rather than by cultural stereotypes is much more acceptable to defenders of civil liberties.[13]

   Keep in mind that many nonverbal signals are ambiguous. For example, a smile usually indicates agreement and warmth, but at times it can indicate nervousness. Even if nonverbal signals are not highly reliable, they are used to judge your behavior, particularly in meetings.

ORGANIZATIONAL CHANNELS AND DIRECTIONS OF COMMUNICATION

Messages in organizations travel over many different channels, or paths. Communication channels can be formal or informal, and can be categorized as downward, upward, horizontal, or diagonal. The widespread use of e-mail, including instant messaging, and intranets has greatly facilitated sending messages in all directions.

Learning Objective 3

Explain and illustrate the difference between form and informal communication channels.

Formal Communication Channels

Formal communication channels are the official pathways for sending information inside and outside an organization. The organization chart formally indicates the channels messages are supposed to follow. By carefully following the organization chart, a maintenance technician would know how to transmit a message to the chief operating officer. In many large organizations, the worker may have to go through as many as eight management or organizational levels. Modern organizations, however, make it easier for lower-ranking workers to communicate with high-level managers.

formal communication channels
The official pathways for sending information inside and outside an organization.

13 Daniel Michaels, "Queues Caused by Airport Searches Spur Calls for Passenger Profiling," *The Wall Street Journal*, August 17, 2006, p. A5.

The Saturday Morning Meeting at Wal-Mart is a large-scale example of a formal communication channel. The meeting is held at 7 a.m. 52 weeks a year at company headquarters in Bentonville, Arkansas, and is attended by about 600 workers, invited from different regions. The meetings are designed to discuss business plans, boost morale, and reinforce the Wal-Mart culture, and are considered the soul of the company. Wal-Mart also has many other meetings, including five company-wide mega-meetings each year attended by more than 10,000 participants each.[14]

In addition to being pathways for communication, formal channels are also means of sending messages. These means include publications such as intranets, e-mail, videoconferences, and physical meetings. The company *Web log* or *blog* is a formal communication channel rapidly growing in use. A point of potential confusion here is that the blog, a formal channel, is written in a casual, informal way. Blogs were first used by businesses to communicate with customers in a personal, direct manner. The blog communicates professional information, but with a soft, human touch. For example, a product manager for single-use cameras might say, "Just the other day, I heard from an off-the-road bike rider, Lily. She carries a few single-use cameras with her to every rally. Lily says she would rather smash one of our cameras than her $600 digital rig."

Some senior executives publish blogs, such as Robert Lutz, the vice chairman of General Motors, having a Web log about car talk (http://www.FastLane.bmblogs.com), The company Web log can also be used to communicate with employees in a relaxed, casual tone. Employees as well as customers can interact with the Web log by providing comments that can be a source of valuable feedback to management, and communicated directly to other visitors to the site.

If an employee publishes a blog with company information, and the blog is not authorized by the company, this does not constitute a formal communication channel. Many employees have been fired for making nasty statements about the company on their blogs. Revealing trade secrets on your blog can also get you fired.

The use of information technology to enhance formal communication continues to evolve, with RSS (really simple syndication) being one example. It is the technology that enables Web sites and blogs to send out automatic updates about new content that workers might need to know, including price changes and inventory shortages. The updates can be sent via e-mail, mobile phones, or through the browser.[15]

One important communication channel can be classified as both formal and informal. With *management by walking around,* managers intermingle freely with workers on the shop floor, in the office, with customers, and at company social events. By spending time in personal contact with employees, the manager enhances open communication. Because management by walking around is systematic, it could be considered formal. However, a manager who circulates throughout the company violates the chain of command. She

---

14 Brent Schlender, "Wal-Mart's $22 Billion Meeting," *Fortune,* April 18, 2005, p. 93.
15 Alison Overholt, "Learning to Love RSS," *Fast Company,* October 2005, p. 43.

exhibit 12-2 How to Succeed in Management by Walking Around

Here's a checklist of walk-around tips a manager can start using today, as provided by communications consultant Linda Duyle:

- *Get out of the office.* Dedicate some time each week to get out and talk with your workforce.
- *Leave behind your cell phone and BlackBerry.* Minimize distractions that can tug on your attention. You want to demonstrate courtesy and respect during your time on the floor.
- *Start slowly.* Don't feel the need to dive right into your discussion even in you have prepared an agenda. Effective listening requires you to focus on the person with whom you are speaking. Clear your mind of distractions.
- *Make eye contact.* Look directly at the people with whom you are speaking.
- *Make it two-way communication.* When you're asked a question that you can't answer, tell the employee that you don't have the answer but will get back to him or her.
- *Be honest.* If times are tough, don't sugarcoat reality. For example, if the company lost a big contract, bring it up in your casual conversation.
- *Process information.* You may want to bring a small notepad with you to write down questions or comments that you'd like to remember or that require follow-up. You will learn some great new things about your people and operations.
- *Show appreciation.* Thank the person for his or her time and comments.
- *Never quit.* People may not be comfortable during the early months of the walk-around process. But as they see you more frequently and your willingness to be visible, comfort in the process will improve.

Source: Adapted and abridged from Linda Dulye, "Get Our of Your Office," *HR Magazine*, July 2006, pp. 100–101.

or he, therefore, invites more informal communication. Visualize yourself as a manager doing a walk-around. Exhibit 12-2 offers you a few suggestions.

Informal Communication Channels

Organizations could not function by formal communication channels alone. Another system of communication, called an **informal communication channel**, is also needed. The informal organization structure is created from informal communication networks. Informal communication channels form the unofficial network that supplements the formal channels. Most of these informal channels arise out of necessity. For example, people sometimes depart from the official communication channels to consult with a person with specialized knowledge, such as a marketing manager consulting with a worker from another department who is up to date on hip-hop culture. Anytime two or more employees consult each other outside formal communication channels, an informal communication channel has been used. Here we look at three aspects of informal communication channels: networks created by leaders, chance encounters, and the grapevine including rumors.

informal communication channel
An unofficial network that supplements the formal channels in an organization.

Networks Created by Leaders

Leaders make extensive use of informal networks to accomplish goals. Successful leaders have a knack for knowing whom to tap to get things done. For example, Melissa in finance might be highly creative when cost-cutting ideas are needed, and Tim in human resources might be outstanding at negotiating with union leaders.

Based on a study of 30 emerging leaders, Herminia Ibarra and Mark Hunter identified three distinct forms of networking.[16] *Operational networking* is aimed at doing one's assigned task more effectively. It involves cultivating stronger relationships with coworkers whose membership in the network is clear. Some of these relationships may be part of the formal structure, such as getting cost data from a member of the finance department. *Personal networking* engages cooperative people from outside the organization in a person's effort to develop personally and advance. This type of networking might involve being mentored on how to deal with a challenge such as dealing with the problem of sexual harassment by a senior manager. *Strategic networking* focuses networking on attaining business goals directly. At this level, the manager creates a network that will help identify and capitalize on new opportunities for the company, such as breaking into the Indian market.

Chance Encounters

Unscheduled informal contact between managers and employees can be an efficient and effective informal communication channel.[17] Spontaneous communication events may occur in the cafeteria, near the water fountain, in the halls, and on the elevator. For example, during an elevator ride, a manager might spot a purchasing agent and ask, "Whatever happened to the just-in-time inventory purchasing proposal?" In two minutes the manager might obtain the information that would typically be solicited in a meeting or e-mail exchange. Also, the chance meeting might trigger the manager's thinking of the topic. A chance encounter differs from management by walking around in that the latter is a planned event; the former occurs unintentionally.

The Grapevine and Rumor Control

The **grapevine** is the informal means by which information is transmitted in organizations. As such, it is the major informal communication channel. The term *grapevine* refers to tangled pathways that can distort information. Rumors and gossip are the two major components of the grapevine. Conditions of anxiety and uncertainty breed rumors. Rumors are typically about something people wish to happen (such as double bonuses this year) or something people dread (such as jobs being outsourced).

Gossip is fueled by the need for affiliation, and helps people bond because by sharing information we develop a sense of trust and intimacy.[18] Gossip is usually spread by word of mouth, but electronic transmission is also a vehicle. Positive gossip (Did you hear that our accounts payable supervisor at age 57 is getting married for the first time?) travels over the grapevine. The negative type (Did you hear that our chief ethics officer was convicted of DWI?) travels even faster. The grapevine often creates a bigger impact on employees than do messages sent over formal channels. Messages received through formal communication channels often carry the perception of stale news. Information usually travels along the grapevine with considerable speed.

grapevine
The informal means by which information is transmitted in organizations.

16 Herminia Ibarr and Mark Hunter, "How Leaders Create and Use Networks," *Harvard Business Review*, January 2007, pp. 40–47.
17 John P. Kotter, *The General Manager* (New York: The Free Press, 1991).
18 Zak Stambor, "Bonding Over Others' Business," *Monitor on Psychology*, April 2006, pp. 58–59.

Approximately three-fourths of messages transmitted along the grapevine are true. Because so many grapevine messages are essentially correct, employees believe most of them. Nevertheless, messages frequently become distorted and misunderstood. By the time a rumor reaches the majority of employees, it is likely to contain false elements. An example would be the case of a company CEO who gave a personal donation to a gay-rights group. The funds were to be used to promote local legislation in favor of equal employment opportunities for gay people. The last version of the story that traveled over the grapevine took this form: "The CEO has finally come out of the closet. He's hiring three gay managers and is giving some year-end bonus money to the Gay Alliance."

False rumors can be disruptive to morale and productivity, and can create employee stress. Some employees take actions that hurt the company and themselves in response to a rumor. Employees might leave a firm in response to rumors about an impending layoff. The valuable workers often leave first because they have skills and contacts in demand at other firms. Severe negative rumors dealing with products or services, especially about product defects or poisonings, must be neutralized to prevent permanent damage to an organization. A couple of years ago rumors spread quickly that part of a human finger was found in a bowl of chili eaten at a fast-food restaurant. (It would not be fair to mention the restaurant.) The company had to work hard to explain the truth—a woman planted the finger so she could sue the company. She had pulled such a stunt in the past with another restaurant chain.

Rumors about the financial health of a company are another concern for managers. Several years ago the rumor was circulating that because of heavy losses, GM had plans to file for bankruptcy. Mark LaNeve, the vice president of GM's North American marketing, spearheaded a positive campaign to tell the truth about GM's progress. LaNeve was particularly concerned because a survey showed that 75 percent of Americans would not purchase a vehicle from a bankrupt company.[19]

Rumors can be combated by enhancing formal communication. Employees naturally seek more information during times of intense rumors. Move quickly on reaching a decision rather than waiting for so many departments to sign off on the decision, such as waiting for buy-in on the shift from a traditional company pension to a 401(k) plan where employees make a larger contribution.[20] Explain why you cannot comment or give full information. For example, during the preliminary stages of a merger, management is legally obligated to make no comment.

Confirm the rumor. For example, "Yes, it is true. We are going to outsource the manufacture of all paper clips and staples." Encourage employees to discuss rumors they hear with you. Be readily accessible, including management by walking around. Make it clear that you are willing to clear up rumors, and that you will investigate whatever facts you do not have at hand.[21]

---

19 Gina Chon, "Are Rumors Hurting Sales?" *The Wall Street Journal*, January 16, 2006, p. B1.

20 Francine Russo, "Meet the Nicheperts," *Time*, October 9, 2006, p. A29.

21 "Make the Rumor Mill Work for You," *Executive Leadership*, May 2003, p. 7.

Communication Directions

communication network A pattern or flow of messages that traces the communication from start to finish.

Messages in organizations travel in four directions: downward, upward, horizontally, and diagonally. Over time, an organization develops communication networks corresponding to these directions. A **communication network** is a pattern or flow of messages that traces the communication from start to finish.

In *downward communication*, messages flow from one level to a lower level. For example, a supervisor gives orders to a team member, or top-level managers send an announcement to employees. *Upward communication* transmits messages from lower to higher levels in an organization. Although it may not be as frequent as downward communication, it is equally important. Upward communication tells management how well messages have been received. The upward communication path also provides an essential network for keeping management informed about problems. Management by walking around and simply speaking to employees facilitate upward communication. Many companies develop their own programs and policies to facilitate bottom-up communication. Four such approaches follow:

1. *Open-door policy.* An open-door policy allows any employee to bring a gripe to top management's attention—without first checking with his or her immediate manager. The open-door policy can be considered a grievance procedure that helps employees resolve problems. However, the policy also enhances upward communication because it informs top management about problems employees are experiencing.
2. *Town hall meetings.* Top-level executives often meet with employees in a town hall format to gather employee concerns and opinions. For example, General Electric conducts three-day town meetings across the company, attended by a cross-section of about 50 company personnel—senior and junior managers, and salaried and hourly workers. Facilitators encourage the audience to express their concerns freely. Participants evaluate various aspects of their business, such as reports and meetings. They discuss whether each one makes sense and attempt to resolve problems. By using upward communication, GE attempts to achieve more speed and simplicity in its operations.
3. *Complaint program and hotlines.* Many organizations institute formal complaint programs. Complaints sent up through channels include those about supervisors, working conditions, personality conflicts, sexual harassment, and inefficient work methods.
4. *Web logs.* Blogs are useful vehicles for upward communication, while at the same time being a vehicle for downward communication. The employee has the opportunity to interact with the message sent by management, such as "We plan to base more of your compensation on variable pay next year." The employee might reply, "Sounds good to me so long as I have the opportunity to earn more money."

Through *horizontal communication*, managers as well as other workers send messages to others at the same organizational level. Horizontal communication frequently takes the form of coworkers from the same department talking to or sending e-mail messages to each other. Coworkers who fail to share information with and respond to each other are likely to fall behind schedules and miss deadlines. Horizontal communication provides the basis for cooperation. People need to communicate with each other to work effectively in joint efforts. For example, they advise each other of work problems and ask each other for help when needed. Moreover, extensive lateral communication enhances creativity. Exchanging and "batting around" ideas with peers sharpens imagination. The accompanying Management in Action illustrates a mechanism for facilitating horizontal communication and exchanging ideas among employees.

Diagonal communication is the transmission of messages to higher or lower organizational levels in different departments. A typical diagonal communication event occurs when the head of the marketing department needs some pricing information. She sends an e-mail to a supervisor in the finance department to get his input. The supervisor, in turn, sends an e-mail to a specialist in the data processing department to get the necessary piece of information. The marketing person has thus started a chain of communication that goes down and across the organization.

Organizational Learning as Part of Communication in Organizations

An important output of both formal and informal communication channels is to transmit information to other workers so as to advance knowledge and learning throughout the organization.

An effective organization engages in continuous learning by proactively adapting to the external environment. In the process, the organization profits from its experiences. Instead of repeating the same old mistakes, the

management in action

Google Encourages Office Graffiti

For a company that has nearly doubled its workforce each year since 2002 (current headcount 5,800), Google doesn't much act like the big company it has become. One of the ways it has preserved its tech-start-up ethos is decidedly low-tech: dozens of whiteboards placed in common areas and corridors through its Mountain View, California, campus. Some are businesslike, used by product teams to swap ideas. But the two longest ones, about 30 feet long, are devoted to the equivalent of corporate graffiti. One is packed with cartoons and jokes that workers have scrawled under the slogan, "Google's Plan for World Domination." "It's collaborative art," says David Krane, Google's director of communications and one it its earliest whiteboard posters. "We're in a growth period, and when new hires see the boards, they get a quick, comprehensive snapshot of our personality."

Questions

1. What constructive purposes might the whiteboards at Google have?
2. How might the whiteboards contribute to creativity and innovation at Google?

Source: Paul Kaihla, "Secret 14: Let Office Workers Speak their Minds," *Business 2.*, April 2006, p. 90.

learning organization An organization that is skilled at creating, acquiring, and transferring knowledge.

knowledge management The ways and means by which a company leverages its knowledge resources to generate business value.

organization learns. A **learning organization** is skilled at creating, acquiring, and transferring knowledge. It also modifies its behavior to reflect new knowledge and new insights.[22] All of these activities are facilitated by effective communication.

Learning organizations find ways to manage knowledge more productively and encourage organizational members to share information by communicating relevant topics to each other. IBM defines **knowledge management** as the ways and means by which a company leverages its knowledge resources to generate business value. More simply, knowledge management involves "getting the right knowledge to the right people at the right time."[23]

Most organizations employ many people with useful knowledge, such as how to solve a particular problem. Because this information may be stored solely in the person's brain, other workers who need the information do not know who possesses it. Systematizing such knowledge develops a sort of corporate yellow pages.

In addition to the specialized work of the *chief knowledge officer* in a learning organization, managers also manage knowledge. They should actively contribute to knowledge management. Firms that fail to codify and share knowledge lose the knowledge of workers who leave. Shared knowledge, such as knowing who the real decision makers are within a particular customer's business, can be retained. In a learning organization, considerable learning takes place in teams as members share expertise. A major block to knowledge sharing is that many workers jealously guard their best ideas, believing that their creative ideas are their ticket to success. So the chief knowledge officer and the manager have to work hard to overcome people's natural resistance to sharing their best ideas.

BARRIERS TO COMMUNICATION

Learning Objective 4

Identify major communication barriers in organizations.

Barriers to communication influence the receipt of messages, as shown in Exhibit 12-3. The input is the message sent by the sender. Barriers to communication, or noise, affect throughput, the processing of input. Noise poses a potential threat to effective communication because it can interfere with the accuracy of a message. The output in this model is the message as received.

Interference occurs most frequently when a message is complex, arouses emotion, or clashes with a receiver's mind-set. An emotionally arousing message deals with such topics as money or personal inconvenience, such as change in working hours. A message that clashes with a receiver's usual way of viewing things requires the person to change his or her typical pattern of receiving messages. To illustrate this problem, try this experiment. The next time you order food at a restaurant, order

22 David A. Garvin, "Building a Learning Organization," *Harvard Business Review*, July–August 1993, p. 80.

23 "Are Your Up to Speed on Knowledge Management?" *HRfocus*, August 200, pp. 5–6.

exhibit 12-3 Barriers to Communication

Many factors make it difficult to get a message across as intended. A sampling of these barriers to communication (or noise) is listed here.

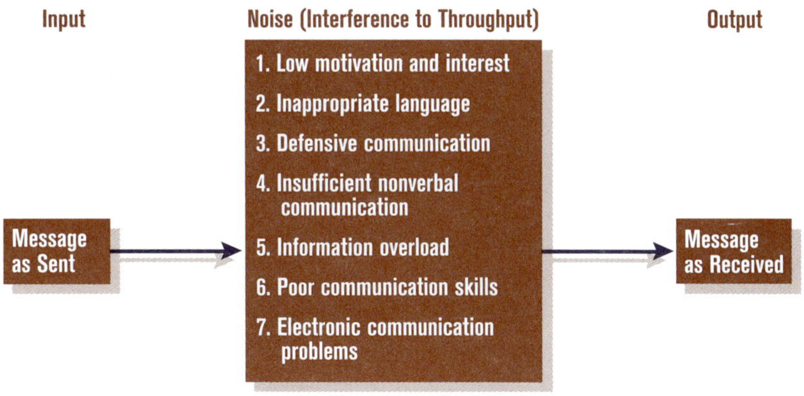

the dessert first and the entrée second. The server will probably not hear your dessert order.

Low Motivation and Interest

Many messages never get through because the intended receiver is not motivated to hear the message or is not interested. The challenge to the sender is to frame the message in such a way that it appeals to the needs and interests of the receiver. This principle can be applied to conducting a job campaign. When sending a message, the job seeker should emphasize the needs of the prospective employer. An example would be: "If I were hired, what problem would you like me to tackle first?" Many job seekers send low-interest messages of this type: "Would this job give me good experience?" Sending a message at the right time contributes to motivation and interest. Messages should be sent at a time when they are most likely to meet with a good reception, such as asking for new equipment when the company is doing quite well.

Inappropriate Language

The language used to frame a message must be suited to the intended receivers. Language can be inappropriate for a host of reasons. Two factors of language that are of particular significance in a work setting—semantics and difficulty level—may affect appropriateness.

Semantics is the study of meaning in language forms. The message sender should give careful thought to what certain terms will mean to receivers. Take, for example, the term *productive.* To prevent communication barriers, you may have to clarify this term. Assume a manager says to the group members, "Our department must become more productive." Most employees will correctly interpret the term to mean "more efficient," but some employees will interpret it as "work harder and longer at the same rate of pay." Consequently, these latter employees may resist the message.

defensive communication The tendency to receive messages in a way that protects self-esteem.

information overload A condition in which an individual receives so much information that he or she becomes overwhelmed.

The difficulty level of language affects receiver comprehension. Communicators are typically urged to speak and write at a low difficulty level. At times, however, a low difficulty level is inappropriate. For instance, when a manager communicates with technically sophisticated employees, using a low difficulty level can create barriers. The employees may perceive the manager as patronizing and may tune him or her out. The use of jargon, or insider language, is closely related to difficulty level. When dealing with outsiders, jargon may be inappropriate; with insiders (people who share a common technical language), it may be appropriate.

Defensive Communication

An important general communication barrier is **defensive communication**—the tendency to receive messages in a way that protects self-esteem. Defensive communication also allows people to send messages to make themselves look good. People communicate defensively through the process of *denial*, the suppression of information one finds uncomfortable. It serves as a major barrier to communication because many messages sent in organizations are potentially uncomfortable. Top management might decide, for example, to require employees to enroll in a physical fitness program so the company might be able to reduce healthcare costs. Many physically unfit employees might dismiss the requirement as simply a joke.

Insufficient Nonverbal Communication

Effective communicators rely on both verbal and nonverbal communication. If verbal communication is not supplemented by nonverbal communication, messages may not be convincing, as the following situation illustrates. For example, if the manager expresses approval for an idea with a blank expression on his or her face the approval message might not get through. As one worker said, "My manager is a zombie so I never know what she is really thinking."

Information Overload

Information overload occurs when an individual receives so much information that he or she becomes overwhelmed. As a result, the person does a poor job of processing information and receiving new messages. Many managers suffer from information overload because of extensive e-mail including instant messages, in addition to the phone messages, the intranet, Web logs, and trade magazines. Many managers receive about 150 e-mail messages daily. The problem of being overloaded by e-mail is intensified by the sending of e-mail signatures, those inspirational messages and brief statements of personal philosophy at the bottom of e-mail messages. Included here are quotes from famous people and axioms, including "Too often we underestimate the power of a smile."[24] The thoughts contained in e-mail signatures might be entertaining and constructive, yet they contribute to information

24 Jared Sandberg, "A Friend Is Someone Who Senses How to Sign Off an Email," *The Wall Street Journal*, June 27, 2006, p. B1.

overload on the job. Perhaps it is better to include these sayings on personal, not business e-mail.

Many workers are learning how to manage e-mail better, such as dealing with e-mail during certain blocks of time, yet information overload is still a widespread problem.

Poor Communication Skills

A message may fail to register because the sender lacks effective communication skills. The sender might garble a written or spoken message so severely that the receiver cannot understand it, or the sender may deliver the message so poorly that the receiver does not take it seriously. The plain language movement instructs workers in government, the sciences, business, and the legal profession to write more clearly.[25] Documents prepared by human resource departments and lawyers are difficult to understand because the terminology has to be precise to meet legal requirements. Yet, for most purposes the average reader should be able to understand the intent of the written message. Unclear voice-mail messages, including presenting difficult-to-follow return numbers or e-mail addresses, are a widespread problem. Another form of poor communication skills stems from not focusing on the receiver while sending a message. When speaking on the phone it is helpful to focus on the other person rather than reading e-mails or doing other work at the same time.[26]

Communication barriers can also result from deficiencies within the receiver. A common barrier is a receiver who is a poor listener. Have you ever encountered a person who repeats "okay" several times but then does nothing in response to your request?

Electronic Communication Problems

Information technology plays a major role in workplace communication, yet it creates several problems. The problems associated with e-mail are representative of these barriers, particularly the problem of impersonality. Many people conduct business with each other exclusively by e-mail and instant messaging, thus missing out on the nuances of human interaction. Some managers and staff professionals discourage face-to-face meetings with workers who ask for help, and instead demand communication by e-mail.

Face-to-face communication offers the advantage of a smile and an expression of sympathy through a nod of the head. When somebody asks or answers a question in person, it is easier to probe for more information than if the interaction took place through e-mail. Many people supplement their e-mail messages with emoticons to add warmth and humor. Yet many times, an electronic message can seem much harsher than a spoken message.

E-mail, in general, is better suited to communicating routine rather than complex or sensitive messages. When dealing with sensitive information it is better to deliver the message face to face or at least in a telephone conversation.

---

25 Mary Ann Lammers, "Plain English," *Business Education Forum*, February 2005, p. 6.

26 Anita Bruzzese, "Bad Phone Etiquette Mars the Face of Many Businesses," Gannett News Service, April 3, 2006.

In this way both parties can have questions answered and minimize misunderstandings.[27] RadioShack Corp. received considerable criticism from company insiders and outsiders when management sent layoff notices by e-mail to 400 headquarters workers: "The workforce reduction notification is currently in progress. Unfortunately your position is one that has been eliminated."[28]

Videoconferencing is another example of an advanced electronic device that has built-in communication problems despite its many productivity advantages. Exchanging information back and forth through camcorders is perceived as too impersonal by some businesspeople. Videoconferencing saw a big boost after the terrorist attacks of September 11, 2000, but cooled down shortly thereafter. Tim Smith, a spokesperson for American Airlines said of videoconferencing, "It's out there, but it hasn't replaced us yet."[29]

Computer graphic presentations, such as PowerPoint, present problems of their own. In most organizations, PowerPoint presentations are expected. Some major suggestions for communicating effectively with slide presentations are first to maintain eye contact with your audience, and to avoid looking too much at your slides thereby giving the impression that you are reading the slides to your audience. Another suggestion is to present enough slides to keep the audience interested and focused, but do not overwhelm them with slides containing considerable detail.

OVERCOMING BARRIERS TO COMMUNICATION

Learning Objective 5

Develop tactics for overcoming communication barriers.

Most barriers to communication are surmountable. First, however, you must be aware that these potential barriers exist. Then as part of a strategy to overcome the barriers, you develop a tactic to deal with each one. For example, when you have an important message to deliver, make sure you answer the following question from the standpoint of the receiver: "What's in it for me?" This section will describe eight strategies and tactics for overcoming communication barriers. Exhibit 12-4 lists the strategies.

Understand the Receiver

A common communication error is to think about communication as tool for getting others to agree with you. It is more effective to strive for understanding rather than agreement.[30]

Understanding the receiver provides a strategy that can assist in overcoming every communication barrier. For example, part of understanding the receiver comes from an awareness that he or she may be overloaded with information or be poorly motivated. Achieving understanding takes empathy, the ability to see things as another person does. Empathy leads to improved communication, because people more willingly engage in dialog when they

27 "New Etiquette for Evolving Technologies: Using E-Mail and Voice Mail Effectively," *Business Education Forum*, October 1998, p. 8; Edward M. Hallowell, "The Human Moment at Work," *Harvard Business Review*, January–February 1999, pp. 58–66.

28 "RadioShack Uses E-mail to Fire 400 Employees as Part of Planned Job Cuts," Associated Press, August 30, 2006.

29 Martin Zimmerman, "Video Meetings Didn't Take Off Despite Fear of Flying," *Los Angeles Times*, http://latimes.com, September 11, 2006.

30 Timothy G. Habbershon, "Can't We All Just Get Along?" *Business Week Small Biz*, Summer 2005, p. 16.

exhibit 12-4 Overcoming Communication Barriers

The chances of getting around the noise in the communication process increase when the sender uses specific strategies and tactics.

1. Understand the receiver
2. Communicate assertively and directly
3. Use two-way communication and ask for clarification
4. Elict verbal and nonverbal feedback
5. Enhance listening skills
6. Unite with a common vocabulary
7. Be sensitive to cultural differences
8. Engage in metacommunication

→ Effective Communication

feel understood. Also, communication improves because empathy builds rapport with the other person. Rapport, in turn, substantially improves communication. You may notice that conversation flows smoothly when you achieve rapport with a work associate or friend.

Communicate Assertively and Directly

Many people create their own communication barriers by expressing their ideas in a passive or indirect mode. If instead they explain their ideas explicitly and directly—and with feeling—the message is more likely to be received. Being assertive also contributes to effective communication because assertiveness enhances persuasiveness. When both sides are persuasive, they are more likely to find a shared solution.[31] Notice the difference between a passive (indirect) phrasing of a request versus an assertive (direct) approach:

> *Passive*
>
> Team member: *By any chance would there be some money left over in the budget? If there would happen to be, I would like to know.*
>
> Manager: *I'll have to investigate. Try me again soon.*
>
> *Assertive*
>
> Team member: *We have an urgent need for a high-speed color copier in our department. Running to the document center to use their copier is draining our productivity. I am therefore submitting a requisition for a high-speed color copier.*
>
> Manager: *Your request makes sense. I'll see what's left in the budget right now.*

Another use of assertiveness in overcoming communication barriers in the workplace is **informative confrontation,** a technique of inquiring about

informative confrontation
A technique of inquiring about discrepancies, conflicts, and mixed messages.

31 Jay A. Conger, "The Necessary Art of Persuasion," *Harvard Business Review*, May–June 1998, p. 86.

discrepancies, conflicts, and mixed messages.[32] Confronting people about the discrepancies in their message provides more accurate information. As a manager, here is how you might handle a discrepancy between verbal and nonverbal messages:

You're talking with a team member you suspect is experiencing problems. The person says, "Everything is going great" (verbal message). At the same time the team member is fidgeting and clenching his fist (nonverbal message). Your informative confrontation might be: "You say things are great, yet you're fidgeting and clenching your fist."

As another way of being assertive, you repeat your message and use multiple channels. By being persistent, your message is more likely to be received. An important message should be repeated when it is first delivered and repeated again one or two days later. Repetition of the message becomes even more effective when more than one communication channel is used. Effective communicators follow up spoken agreements with written documentation. The use of multiple channels helps accommodate the fact that some people respond better to one communication mode than another. For example, a supervisor asked an employee why she did not follow through with the supervisor's request that she wear safety shoes. The employee replied, "I didn't think you were serious. You didn't send me an e-mail."

Another way of being assertive is to be direct, rather than indirect and evasive, when delivering bad news. A manager might say, "Today is a good day for a change," when he has to deliver some bad news about demoting a few staff members, or the loss of a major customer. Indirect communication of this type is often referred to as *spin*, which is intended to look at the bright side of a bad situation.

Use Two-Way Communication and Ask for Clarification

A dialog helps reduce misunderstanding by communicating feelings as well as facts. At times a brief amount of small talk, such as commenting on a popular movie or sporting event can set the stage for comfortable two-way communication. Both receiver and sender can ask questions of each other in two-way communication. Here is an example:

> Manager: *I want you here early tomorrow. We have a big meeting planned with our regional manager.*
>
> Employee: *I'll certainly be here early. But are you implying that I'm usually late?*
>
> Manager: *Not at all. I know you come to work on time. It's just that we need you here tomorrow about 30 minutes earlier than usual.*
>
> Employee: *I'm glad I asked. I'm proud of my punctuality.*

A manager who takes the initiative to communicate face to face with employees encourages two-way communication. Two-way interaction also

---

32 William Cormier and Sherilyn Cormier, *Interviewing Strategies for Helpers* (Monterey, CA: Brooks/Cole, 1990).

overcomes communication barriers because it helps build connections among people. Interaction is also useful in obtaining clarification on what the other person means by a phrase such as "you need to provide better customer service." One of the reasons that instant messaging is gaining hold in business is that it allows for more immediate two-way communication and clarification than does e-mail. Also, the telephone is making a comeback as a communications device because it allows for more authentic two-way communication than does e-mail.[33] Some small enterprises have even moved to a "no e-mail Friday" to encourage more personal and two-way communication among employees.

Elicit Verbal and Nonverbal Feedback

To be sure that the message has been understood, ask for verbal feedback. A recommended managerial practice is to conclude a meeting with a question such as, "To what have we agreed this morning?" The receiver of a message should also take the responsibility to offer feedback to the sender. The expression "This is what I heard you say" is an effective feedback device. Feedback can also be used to facilitate communication in a group meeting. After the meeting, provide everyone in attendance with written follow-up to make sure they all left with the same understanding.

It is also important to observe and send nonverbal feedback. Nonverbal indicators of comprehension or acceptance can be more important than verbal indicators. For example, the manner in which somebody says "Sure, sure" can indicate if that person is truly in agreement. If the "Sure, sure" is a brush-off, the message may need more selling. The expression on the receiver's face can also be due to acceptance or rejection.

Enhance Listening Skills

Many communication problems stem from the intended receiver not listening carefully. Managers need to be good listeners because so much of their work involves eliciting information from others in order to solve problems. Based on his 65 years of consulting and writing, Peter Drucker said that a rule for managers is to listen first, speak last.[34] Reducing communication barriers takes active listening. **Active listening** means listening for full meaning, without making premature judgments or interpretations. Five suggestions should be followed.[35]

1. *The receiver listens for total meaning of the sender's message.* By carefully analyzing what is said, what is not said, and nonverbal signals, you will uncover a fuller meaning in the message.
2. *The receiver reflects the message back to the sender.* Show the sender that you understand by providing summary reflections such as "You tell me you are behind schedule because our customers keep modifying their orders."

active listening
Listening for full meaning, without making premature judgments or interpretations.

33 Jared Sandberg, "Employees Forsake Dreaded Email For the Beloved Phone," *The Wall Street Journal*, September 26, 2006, p. B1.
34 Peter F. Drucker, "What Makes an Effective Executive," *Harvard Business Review*, June 2004, p. 63.
35 Andrew E. Schwartz, "The Importance of Listening: It Can't Be Stressed Enough," *Supervisory Management*, July 1991, p. 7; "Train Yourself in the Art of Listening," *Positive Leadership*, p. 10, sample issue, 2001.

3. *The sender and receiver both understand the message and engage in a concluding discussion.* In the preceding situation, the manager and the employee would converse about the challenges of making on-time deliveries despite changes in customer requirements.
4. *The receiver asks questions instead of making statements.* For example, do not say, "Maurice, don't forget that the Zytex report needs to be completed on Friday morning." Rather, ask, "Maurice, How is the Zytex report coming along? Any problems with making the deadline?" By asking questions you will start the type of dialog that facilitates active listening.
5. *The receiver does not blurt out questions as soon as the employee is finished speaking.* Being too quick to ask questions gives the impression that you were formulating your reply rather than listening. Before you ask a question, paraphrase the speaker's words. An example is, "So what you're saying is..." Then, ask your question. Paraphrasing followed by asking a question will often decrease miscommunication.

Note that active listening incorporates the two previous suggestions about two-way communication, and eliciting verbal and nonverbal feedback.

Unite with a Common Vocabulary

People from the various units within an organization may speak in terms so different that communication barriers are erected. For example, the information technology group and the marketing group may use some words and phrases not used by the other. Steve Patterson recommends that managers first identify the core work of a business, and then describe it in a shared business vocabulary.[36] All key terms should be clearly defined, and people should agree on the meaning. Assume that a company aims to provide "high-quality long-distance telephone service." Workers should agree on the meaning of high quality in reference to long distance. The various departments might retain some jargon and their unique perspectives but a common language would unite them. Exhibit 12-5 lists some current business jargon that could contribute to a common vocabulary but must be used cautiously to avoid misunderstanding.

Be Sensitive to Cultural Differences

Effective communication in a global environment requires sensitivity to cultural differences. Awareness of these potential barriers alerts you to the importance of modifying your communication approach. The list that follows presents several specific ideas to help overcome cross-cultural communication barriers.

- *Show respect for all workers.* An effective strategy for overcoming cross-cultural communication barriers is to simply respect all others in the workplace. A key component of respect is to perceive other cultures as different from but not inferior to your own. Respecting other people's customs can translate into specific attitudes, such as respecting one coworker for wearing a yarmulke on Friday, or another for wearing native African dress to celebrate Kwanzaa.

36 Steve Patterson, "Returning to Babel," *Management Review*, June 1994, pp. 44–48.

exhibit 12-5 A Sampler of Current Business Buzzwords

A new crop of business buzzwords usually sprouts every three or five years. Some can be useful in swiftly communicating, and spreading, new business concepts. Others are less useful, even devious. "Too often people use buzzwords to muddy or cover up what they are actually saying," says Warren Bennis, management professor at the University of Southern California in Los Angeles. A few of the recent buzzwords are as follows:

1. *Delayering* may evolve an image of a cake, but there is nothing sweet about it. In plain English, it means managers are being fired. It's the latest manifestation of rightsizing and downsizing.
2. *Un-siloing* mangles the noun silo to make an important but simple point: Managers must cooperate across departments and functions, share resources and cross-sell products to boost the bottom line.
3. *Network optimization* refers to figuring out where to locate plants to manufacture products around the world.
4. *Process-flow analysis*, like many business buzzwords, is aimed at cutting costs. It refers to how many people spend time on a given effort, and at what cost.
5. A *volume-sensitive business* refers to one with massive fixed costs.
6. *Sox* (also *S–O* or *Sarbox*) refers to Sarbanes–Oxley, the 2002 governance reform act. If you want to stop something from going forward in a company these days, all you have to do is ask, "Will this pass Sox rules?" Sox makes CEOs halt in their tracks.
7. *Bucket* refers to a category or organizational unit, previously described as silos or baskets. Markets might also be referred to as buckets, such as the American and European buckets in terms of profitability for a prescription drug. An environmentally-minded manager might say that a particular product is "good for the conservation efficiency bucket."

Source: Excerpted from Carol Hymowitz, "Mind Your Language: To Do Business Today, Consider Delayering," *The Wall Street Journal*, March 27, 2006, p. B1; Christopher Rhoads, "Business Types Get a New Kick Out of the 'Bucket'," *The Wall Street Journal*, March 27, 2007, pp. A1, A16.

- *Use straightforward language and speak clearly.* When working with people who do not speak your language fluently, speak in an easy-to-understand manner. Look for signs of poor comprehension such as not asking any questions or nodding in agreement with everything you say. Minimize the use of idioms and analogies specific to your language. Particularly difficult for foreigners to interpret are sports analogies, such as "This should be a slam dunk" or "We pulled the hat trick."
- *Be alert to cultural differences in customs and behavior.* To minimize cross-cultural communication barriers, recognize that many subtle job-related differences in customs and behavior may exist. You need to search for these differences if you have regular contact with workers from another culture. For example, Asians may feel uncomfortable when asked to brag about themselves in the presence of others, even during a job interview. From their perspective, calling attention to oneself at the expense of another person is rude and unprofessional.
- *Be sensitive to differences in nonverbal communication.* Be alert to the possibility that a person from another culture may misinterpret your nonverbal signal. Hand gestures are especially troublesome. When communicating with people from another country, take caution in using the popular thumbs-up signal accompanied by a smile to indicate acceptance and contentment. The signal connotes acceptance and agreement in many cultures, but could be interpreted as a vulgarity in others. (It could be argued that the agreement signal is really verbal communication because it is a symbol.)

metacommunicate To communicate about a communication to help overcome barriers or resolve a problem.

- *Do not be diverted by style, accent, grammar, or personal appearance.* Although these superficial factors all relate to business success, they are difficult to interpret when judging a person from another culture. It is therefore better to judge the merits of the statement or behavior.[37] A brilliant individual from another culture may still be learning your language and may make basic mistakes in speaking your language.
- *Be attentive to individual differences in appearance.* A major cross-cultural insult is to confuse the identity of people because they are members of the same race or ethnic group. Research experiments suggest that people have difficulty seeing individual differences among people of another race because they code race first, such as thinking, "She has the lips of an African American." However, people can learn to search for more distinguishing features, such as a dimple or eye color.[38]

Engage in Metacommunication

A frequent response to a communication problem is to ignore the barrier by making no special effort to deal with the problem—a "take it or leave it" approach to communicating. Another possibility is to **metacommunicate**, or communicate about your communication to help overcome barriers or resolve a problem. If you as a manager faced heavy deadline pressures, you might say to a group member, "I might appear brusque today and tomorrow. Please don't take it personally. It's just that I have to make heavy demands on you because the group is facing a gruesome deadline." Metacommunicating also helps when you have reached a communication impasse with another person. You might say, for example, "I'm trying to get through to you, but you either don't react to me or you get angry. What can I do to improve our communication?"

HOW TO CONDUCT AN EFFECTIVE MEETING

Learning Objective 6
Describe how to conduct more effective meetings.

Much of workplace communication, including group decision making, takes place in meetings. When conducted poorly, meetings represent a substantial productivity drain, including wasted money. Most of the information presented in this chapter and in Chapter 5, which discussed decision making, applies to meetings. The following suggestions apply to those who conduct physical and electronic meetings, and some are also relevant for participants. By following these suggestions, you increase the meeting's effectiveness as a vehicle for collaborative effort and communication.

1. *Meet only for valid reasons.* Many meetings lead to no decisions because they lacked a valid purpose in the first place. Meetings are necessary only in situations that require coordinated effort and group decision making. Memos can be substituted for meetings when factual information needs to be disseminated and discussion is unimportant. Having clear objectives contributes to the validity of a meeting.[39]

---

37 David P. Tulin, "Enhance Your Multi-Cultural Communication Skills," *Managing Diversity*, Vol. 1 (1992), p. 5.
38 Siri Carpenter, "Why Do 'They All Look Alike'?" *Monitor on Psychology*, December 2000, p. 44.
39 Stuart R. Levine, "Make Meetings Less Dreaded," *HR Magazine*, January 2007, p. 107.

2. *Start and stop on time, and offer refreshments.* Meetings appear more professional and action-oriented when the leader starts and stops on time. If the leader waits for the last member to show up, much time is lost and late behavior is rewarded. Stopping the meeting on time shows respect for the members' time. Offering refreshments is another tactic for emphasizing the importance of the meeting, and also enhances satisfaction with the meeting.
3. *Keep comments brief and to the point.* A major challenge facing the meeting leader is to keep conversation on track. Verbal rambling by participants creates communication barriers because other people lose interest. An effective way for the leader to keep comments on target is to ask the contributor of a non sequitur, "In what way does your comment relate to the agenda?"
4. *Avoid electronic distractions.* Many people attending meetings pretend to be focused on the meeting but instead are doing other work on their laptops, or responding to information outside the meeting by using wireless e-mail devices. Get the group to agree not to be performing other work, as is mandated during executive meetings at Ford Motor Company. As a reward, offer briefer meetings with more accomplished.
5. *Capitalize on technology when appropriate.* Although electronic devices can be distracting at meetings they can also make a major contribution, as in group–decision making software. Web sites are now being used by boards of governors at several large companies. Often board members need to consult masses of information that previously required hauling oversized briefing binders to the meetings. For example, directors at the AIM Management Group Inc. have switched to running paperless meetings. All the information they need is stored on a Web site, and using a laptop computer members click on a specific page as needed.[40] (We assume that board members can be trusted not to go surfing during the meetings.) Or, if participants have keen vision the meeting leader can flash the Web pages on a giant screen.
6. *Encourage critical feedback and commentary.* Meetings are more likely to be fully productive when participants are encouraged to be candid with criticism and negative feedback. Openness helps prevent groupthink and also brings important problems to the attention of management.
7. *Strive for wide participation.* One justification for conducting a meeting is to obtain a variety of input. Although not everybody is equally qualified to voice a sound opinion, everyone should be heard. A key role for the meeting leader is to facilitate the meeting so that participation is widespread. Asking participants for their point of view is a good facilitation technique. A skillful leader may have to limit the contribution of domineering members and coax reticent members to voice their ideas. Asking participants to bring several questions to the meeting will often spur participation. If the meeting leader spends the entire time making a PowerPoint presentation,

---

40 Jaclyne Badal, "Goodbye Briefing Books: A Paperless Board Meeting? It's Starting to Happen," *The Wall Street Journal*, October 23, 2006, p. R11.

participation will be discouraged. The slides should supplement the meeting and be starting points for discussion.

8. *Solve small issues ahead of time with e-mail.* Meetings can be briefer and less mundane when small issues are resolved ahead of time. E-mail is particularly effective for resolving minor administrative issues, and also for collecting agenda items in advance.
9. *Consider "huddling" when quick action is needed.* A huddle is a fast-paced, action-oriented way to bring workers together into brief meetings to discuss critical performance issues. A department store manager might bring together five floor managers ten minutes before opening to say, "We have a line-up of about 500 customers waiting to get in because of our specials today. Is everybody ready for the rush of excitement? What problems do you anticipate?" The huddle is particularly important when it would be difficult for the workers to attend a long meeting.[41] See the accompanying Management in Action.
10. *Ensure that all follow-up action is assigned and recorded.* All too often, even after a decision has been reached, a meeting lacks tangible output. Distribute a memo summarizing who is responsible for taking what action and by what date.

management in action

The Three-Minute Huddle at UPS

How does UPS keep 220,000 drivers and package handlers on time? Wireless transmitters, reliable trucks, and a world-class logistics network are critical, of course. But managers have their own safeguard against slack. Every morning, and often several times per day, managers gather workers for a mandatory meeting that lasts precisely three minutes.

The talks start with company announcements, from benefits updates to bulletins about software upgrades on drivers' handhelds. The managers go over local information: traffic conditions or customer complaints. Every meeting ends with a safety tip.

The meetings ensure that workers are always kept in the loop, and the 180-second limit helps enforce system-wide punctuality. If drivers are late to start their routes because meetings run long, they'll earn overtime pay and deliver fewer packages—exactly what UPS strives to avoid. The practice has proven so successful that many hourly office workers now start their days with a three-minute huddle of their own.

Questions

1. What is your opinion of the value of a three-minute meeting for UPS?
2. What type of communication skills would a person need to develop in order to be effective in three-minute meetings?
3. As a UPS manager, what would you do with a driver who was consistently three minutes late for the three-minute meeting?

Source: Owen Thomas, "Secret 20: The Three-Minute Huddle," *Business 2.0,* April 2006, p. 94.

41 Pamela Babcock, "Sending the Message," *HR Magazine,* November 2003, p. 70.

ORGANIZATIONAL POLITICS AND INTERPERSONAL COMMUNICATION

Learning Objective 7

Describe how organizational (or office) politics affects interpersonal communication.

At various places in our study of management we mention political factors. For example, Chapter 1 describes political skill as essential to success as a manager, and Chapter 5 describes the role of political factors in decision making. Politics affects communication because so much interpersonal communication in organizations is politically motivated. Our communication is often shaped by a desire to gain personal advantage. As used here, **organizational politics** refers to informal approaches to gaining power or other advantage through means other than merit or luck. As managers rely more on personal influence and less on hierarchy, people tend to recognize the more positive aspects of organizational politics. For example, a team of management researchers defines political skill as "an interpersonal style that combines social awareness with the ability to communicate well. People who practice this skill behave in a disarmingly charming and engaging manner that inspires confidence, trust, and sincerity."[42]

organizational politics
Informal approaches to gaining power or other advantage through means other than merit or luck.

In this section we describe a sampling of political tactics, classified as relatively ethical versus relatively unethical. We also mention what managers can do to control politics. Exhibit 12-6 gives you an opportunity to think through your own political tendencies.

0191

Relatively Ethical Political Tactics

A political tactic might be considered relatively ethical if used to gain advantage or power that serves a constructive organizational purpose such as getting an influential executive on your side so you can implement a company wellness program. Five useful and relatively ethical tactics are described next.

1. *Develop power contacts.* After you have identified powerful people are in your network establish alliances with them. To use this tactic you may need to bring influential people into your network. Cultivating friendly, cooperative relationships with organizational members and outsiders can advance the cause of the manager or professional. These people can support your ideas or directly assist you with problem solving. Power contacts are also essential because they can recommend you for promotion or high-visibility assignments.
2. *Be courteous, pleasant, and positive.* Having good human relations skills creates many more friends than enemies and can help you be chosen for good team assignments and stay off the downsizing list. It is widely acknowledged by human resource specialists that courteous, pleasant, and positive people are the first to be hired and the last to be fired (assuming they are also technically qualified).

42 Gerald R. Ferris, Pamela L. Perrewé, William P. Anthony, and David C. Gilmore, "Political Skill at Work," *Organizational Dynamics*, Spring 2000, p. 25.

exhibit 12-6 The Positive Organizational Politics Questionnaire

Answer each question "mostly agree" or "mostly disagree," even if it is difficult for you to decide which alternative best describes your opinion.

	Mostly Agree	Mostly Disagree
1. Pleasing my boss is a major goal of mine.	____	____
2. I go out of my way to flatter important people.	____	____
3. I am most likely to do favors for people who can help me in return.	____	____
4. Given the opportunity, I would cultivate friendships with powerful people.	____	____
5. I will compliment a coworker even if I have to think hard about what might be praiseworthy.	____	____
6. If I thought my boss needed the help, and I had the expertise, I would show him or her how to use an electronic gadget for personal life.	____	____
7. I laugh heartily at my boss's humor, so long as I think he or she is at least a little funny.	____	____
8. I would not be too concerned about following a company dress code, so long as I looked neat.	____	____
9. If a customer sent me a compliment through e-mail, I would forward a copy to my boss and another influential person.	____	____
10. I smile only at people in the workplace whom I genuinely like.	____	____
11. An effective way to impress people is to tell them what they want to hear.	____	____
12. I would never publicly correct mistakes made by the boss.	____	____
13. I would be willing to use my personal contacts to gain a promotion or desirable transfer.	____	____
14. I think it is a good idea to send a congratulatory note to someone in the company who receives a promotion to an executive position.	____	____
15. I think office politics is only for losers.	____	____

Scoring and interpretation: Give yourself a plus 1 for each answer that agrees with the keyed answer. Each question that receives a score of plus 1 shows a tendency toward playing positive organizational politics. The scoring key is as follows:

1. Mostly agree
2. Mostly agree
3. Mostly agree
4. Mostly agree
5. Mostly agree
6. Mostly agree
7. Mostly agree
8. Mostly disagree
9. Mostly agree
10. Mostly disagree
11. Mostly agree
12. Mostly agree
13. Mostly agree
14. Mostly agree
15. Mostly disagree

- 1–6 Below-average tendency to play office politics
- 7–11 Average tendency to play office politics
- 12 and above Above-average tendency to play office politics; strong need for power

Skill Development: Thinking about your political tendencies in the workplace is important for your career because most successful leaders are moderately political. The ability to use politics effectively and ethically increases with importance in the executive suite. Most top players are effective office politicians. Yet being overly and blatantly political can lead to distrust, thereby damaging your career.

3. *Create a positive image.* A positive image can be created through such means as keeping your voice calm and well modulated, dressing fashionably, and matching your humor to others around you.[43] Speaking well is critical, and being courteous, pleasant, and positive also contributes to a positive image.
4. *Ask satisfied customers to contact your boss.* A favorable comment by a customer receives considerable weight because customer satisfaction is a top corporate priority. If a customer says something nice, the comment will carry more weight than one from a coworker or subordinate, because coworkers and subordinates might praise a person for political reasons. Customers' motivation, on the other hand, is assumed to be pure because they have little concern about pleasing suppliers.
5. *Be politically correct.* Political correctness involves being careful not to offend or slight anyone, and being extra civil and respectful.[44] An effective use of political correctness would be to say that "We need a ladder in our department because we have workers of different heights who need access to the top shelves." It would be politically incorrect to say, "We need ladders because we have some short workers who cannot reach the top shelves." Carried too far, political correctness can push a person in the direction of being too bland and imprecise in language. The ultra-politically correct person, for example, will almost never mention a person's race, sex, ethnicity, or health status when referring to another worker. Ultra-political correctness also involves using supposedly correct terms to describe people even if a given individual rejects the label. For example, many black people are correctly referred to as "black" rather than "African American" because they might be citizens of Africa, Haiti, England, etc. Also, the same people do not consider themselves to be African American.
6. *Send thank-you notes to large numbers of people.* One of the most basic political tactics, sending thank-you notes profusely, is simply an application of sound human relations. Many successful people take the time to send handwritten notes to employees and customers. Handwritten notes are warmer than e-mail messages, but both help create bonds with their recipients.

Relatively Unethical Political Tactics

In the ideal organization, each employee works harmoniously with work associates, all focused on achieving organizational goals rather than pursuing self-interest. Furthermore, everyone trusts each other. In reality not all organizations are ideal, and many people use negative political tactics to fight for political advantage. Downsizing can contribute to devious office politics because many people want to discredit others so that the other person is more likely to be "tapped" for termination. Here we describe four unethical political tactics.

---

43 "Office Politics a Positive," Gannett News Service, February 13, 2001.

44 Robin J. Ely, Debra Meyerson, and Martin N. Davidson, "Rethinking Political Correctness," *Harvard Business Review*, September 2006, p. 80.

1. *Backstabbing.* The despised yet widely practiced back stab requires that you pretend to be nice, but all the while plan someone's demise. A frequent form of backstabbing is to initiate a conversation with a rival, or someone you just dislike, about the weaknesses of a common boss. You encourage negative commentary and make careful mental notes of what the person says. When these comments are passed along to the manager, the other person appears disloyal and foolish.

   E-mail provides a medium for backstabbing. The sender of the message documents a mistake made by another individual and includes key people on the distribution list. A sample message sent by one manager to a rival began as follows: "Hi Ruth. Thanks for being so candid about why you think our corporate strategy is defective. I was wondering if you had any additional suggestions that you think would help the company compete successfully... ."

   A useful counterattack to the back stab is to ask an open-ended question to justify his or her actions, such as, "I'm not sure I understand why you sent that e-mail about my not supporting the corporate strategy. Can you explain why you did that, and what made you think I do not support corporate strategy?" You might also add, "Do you think this situation is serious enough to discuss with the boss?"
2. *Setting up another person to fail.* A highly devious and deceptive practice is to give another person an assignment with the hopes that he or she will fail and therefore be discredited. The person is usually told that he or she is being chosen to tackle this important assignment because of a proven capability to manage difficult tasks. (If the person does perform well, the "set-up" will backfire on the manager.) A typical example of setting a person up to fail is to assign a supervisor to a low-performing unit, staffed mostly with problem employees who distrust management.
3. *Playing territorial games.* Also referred to as *turf wars*, territorial games involve protecting and hoarding resources that give one power, such as information, the authority to make decisions, and relationships with key people. Organizational members also become territorial over physical spaces and ideas ("That was my idea"). A relationship is "hoarded" in such ways as not encouraging others to visit a key customer, or blocking a high performer from getting a promotion or transfer. For example, the manager might tell others that his star performer is mediocre to prevent the person from being considered a valuable transfer possibility. Other examples of territorial games include monopolizing time with clients, scheduling meetings so someone cannot attend, and shutting out coworkers from joining you on an important assignment. Not allowing group members to speak directly with your boss is another example of a territorial game because you are hoarding contacts with your boss.[45]
4. *Being unpredictable.* Some particularly devious executives behave unpredictably by design to keep people off guard. People are easier to control when they do

45 Annette Simmons, *Territorial Games: Understanding and Ending Turf Wars at Work* (New York: AMACOM, 1998); Graham Brown, Thomas B. Lawrence, and Sandra L. Robinson, "Territoriality in Organizations," *Academy of Management Review*, July 2005, pp. 577–594.

> not know whether you will be nice or nasty. In the words of business commentator Stanley Bing, "This quality of rampaging unpredictability is a well-known tool used by terrorists, authoritarian brainwashers, and those who wish to command and dominate others. It's used because it works better than straight-out intimidation, which can be anticipated and psychologically prepared for."[46]

Any political tactic can be considered unethical if it is used to advance oneself at the severe expense of others. Dick Grasso, the former chairman of the New York Stock Exchange, was considered to be unusually street smart in dealing with traders and the board of the exchange. He ingratiated himself to the board members he was supposed to regulate, and they reciprocated by giving him a compensation package, including retirement pay, of $140 million. When the extraordinary compensation was made public, Grasso was forced out of office.[47] His compensation disadvantaged others because some of the money he took for himself might have been used to pay higher salaries to NYSE workers or create more jobs. At one point, half the profits of the NYSE were paid to Grasso.

Exercising Control of Negative Organizational Politics

Carried to excess, organizational politics can damage productivity and morale and hurt the careers of innocent people. The productivity loss stems from managers and others devoting too much time to politics and not enough time to useful work. A survey of 150 executives indicated that about one day each week is spent handling office politics, which includes everything from rivalries to bickering.[48] Another problem is that when workers perceive too much office politics to be present, their performance may suffer, with this tendency being noticeable for older workers.[49] Just *being aware of the presence of organizational politics* can help a manager stay alert for its negative manifestations such as backstabbing. The politically aware manager carefully evaluates negative statements made by one group member about another.

Open communication can also constrain the impact of political behavior. For instance, open communication lets everyone know the basis for allocating resources, thus reducing the amount of politicking. If people know in advance how resources will be allocated, the effectiveness of kissing up to the boss will be reduced. *Avoiding favoritism* (giving the best rewards to the group member you like the most) is a powerful way of minimizing politics within a work group. If trying to be the boss's pet is not effective, people are more likely to focus on good job performance to get ahead. Annette Simmons recommends that managers *find a way to talk about territorial games.* Addressing the issues and bringing them out in the open might make group members aware that their territorial behavior is under close observation.[50]

---

46 Stanley Bing, "What Would Machiavelli Do?" *Fortune*, December 5, 1999, pp. 222–223.

47 Gary Weills, "The $140,000,000 Man," *Business Week*, September 15, 2003, pp. 84–92.

48 Survey reported in "Execs Regularly Must Soothe Staff," *Rochester Democrat and Chronicle*, December 31, 2000, p. 1G.

49 Darren C. Treadway et al., "The Role of Age in Perceptions of Politics—Job Performance Relationships: A Three-Study Constructive Replication," *Journal of Applied Psychology*, September 2005, pp. 872–881.

50 Simmons, *Territorial Games*, p. 218.

SUMMARY OF Key Points

1 Describe the steps in the communication process.

The communication process involves four basic elements, all of which are subject to interference, or noise. The process begins with a sender encoding a message and then transmitting it over a channel to a receiver, who decodes it. Feedback from receiver to sender is also essential. In successful communication, the receiver decodes the message, understands it, and then acts on it.

2 Recognize the major types of nonverbal communication in the workplace.

Six major modes of transmitting nonverbal messages are hand and body gestures; facial expressions and movements; posture; body placement; voice quality; and clothing, dress, and appearance. Nonverbal communication has been applied to help screen airline passengers as security risks.

3 Explain and illustrate the difference between formal and informal communication channels.

Formal channels follow the organization chart, and also include blogs. Management by walking around can also be considered a formal communication channel. Informal channels are the unofficial network of communications that supplement the formal pathways. Managers often use informal networks to accomplish goals as well as chance encounters. The grapevine is the major informal communication pathway, and it transmits rumors. Management can take steps to neutralize negative rumors by enhancing formal channels. Messages are transmitted in four directions: upward, downward, sideways, and diagonally.

An important output of both formal and informal communication channels is to transmit information to other workers to advance knowledge and learning throughout the organization. The learning organization creates and transfers knowledge, and knowledge management leverages knowledge to generate business value.

4 Identify major communication barriers in organizations.

Barriers exist at every step in the communication process. Among them are (1) low motivation and interest, (2) inappropriate language, (3) defensive communication, (4) insufficient nonverbal communication, (5) information overload, (6) poor communication skills, and (7) electronic communication problems.

5 Develop tactics for overcoming communication barriers.

To overcome communication barriers, you must (1) understand the receiver, (2) communicate assertively and directly, (3) use two-way communication and ask for clarification, (4) elicit verbal and nonverbal feedback, (5) enhance listening skills, (6) unite with a common vocabulary, (7) be sensitive to cultural differences, and (8) engage in metacommunication (communicate about the communications).

6 Describe how to conduct more effective meetings.

To improve communication effectiveness and the decision-making quality of meetings, follow these suggestions: (1) meet only for valid reasons; (2) start and stop on time, and offer refreshments, (3) keep comments brief and to the point; (4) avoid electronic distractions, (5) capitalize on technology when appropriate, (6) encourage critical feedback and commentary, (7) strive for wide participation; (8) solve small issues ahead of time with e-mail; (9) consider "huddling" when quick action is needed; and (10) ensure that follow-up action is assigned and recorded.

7 Describe how organizational (or office) politics affects interpersonal communication.

Politics is related to communication because so much interpersonal communication in organizations is politically motivated. Relatively ethical political tactics include (a) developing power contacts, (b) being courteous, pleasant, and positive, (c) creating a positive image, (d) asking satisfied customers to contact your boss, (e) being politically correct, and (f) sending thank-you notes to large numbers of people. Four relatively unethical political tactics are (a) backstabbing, (b) setting up another person to fail, (c) playing territorial games, and (d) being unpredictable. Used for a negative purpose, any political tactic can be unethical. Managers must take steps to control excessive negative politics. Open communication and avoiding favoritism can help.

KEY TERMS AND PHRASES

Communication, 409
Encoding, 410
Decoding, 410
Feedback, 410
Noise, 411
Nonverbal communication, 411
Formal communication channel, 413
Informal communication channel, 415
Grapevine, 416
Communication network, 418
Learning organization, 420
Knowledge management, 420
Defensive communication, 422
Information overload, 422
Informative confrontation, 425
Active listening, 427
Metacommunicate, 430
Organizational politics, 433

QUESTIONS

1. Employers continue to emphasize good communication skills as one of the most important qualifications for screening career-school and business graduates. What are some of the reasons for this requirement?
2. How might understanding the steps in the communication process help managers and professionals do a better job?
3. What kind of facial expression do you think might make a person appear intelligent?
4. Some top-level managers insist that employees use instant messaging (IM) to communicate with each other on the job. What do you think is their justification for the widespread use of IM?
5. Many telemarketers possess poor spoken communication skills, which makes them difficult to understand. What should telemarketing managers do about this problem?
6. For what reasons do executives spend an average of about 30 hours per week in meetings?
7. Many workers who have been laid off contend that if they had possessed better political skills they could have avoided losing their job. What are they talking about?

SKILL-BUILDING EXERCISE 12-A: Practicing Your Active Listening Skills

Before conducting the following role plays, review the suggestions for active listening in this chapter. The suggestion about reflecting the message back to the sender is particularly relevant because the role plays involve emotional topics.

The Elated Coworker. One student plays the role of a coworker who has just been offered a promotion to supervisor of another department. She will be receiving 10 percent higher pay and be able to travel overseas twice a year for the company. She is eager to describe full details of her good fortune to a coworker. Another student plays the role of the coworker to whom the first coworker wants to describe her good fortune. The second worker decides to listen intently to the first worker. Other class members will rate the second student on his or her listening ability.

The Discouraged Coworker. One student plays the role of a coworker who has just been placed on probation for poor performance. His boss thinks that his performance is below standard and that his attendance and punctuality are poor. He is afraid that if he tells his girlfriend, she will leave him. He is eager to tell his tale of woe to a coworker. Another student plays the role of a coworker he corners to discuss his problems. The second worker decided to listen intently to his problems but is pressed for time. Other class members will rate the second student on his or her listening ability.

When evaluating the active listening skills of the role players, consider using the following evaluating factors, on a scale of 1 (low) to 5 (high):

Evaluation Factor	Rating 1	2	3	4	5
1. Maintained eye contact					
2. Showed empathy					
3. Reflected back what the other person said					
4. Focused on other person instead of being distracted					
5. Asked questions					
6. Let other person speak until he or she was finished					
Total Points: ________________					

SKILL-BUILDING EXERCISE 12-B: Cross-Cultural Communication Skills

The information presented in the chapter about overcoming cross-cultural communication barriers will lead to cross-cultural skills development if practiced in the right setting. During the next 30 days, look for an opportunity to relate to a person from a given culture in the way described in this chapter. Observe the reaction of the other person to provide feedback on your cross-cultural effectiveness.

INTERNET SKILL-BUILDING EXERCISE: The Communication Component of Jobs

Search the Internet for a description of any three jobs that might possibly interest you now or in the future. In addition, the job must mention some type of communication component, such as "good presentation skills." Based on this brief sample of three jobs, reach a conclusion about the communication requirements of the type of work that interests you. An easy starting point might be to visit the "hotjobs" section of Yahoo!. If you are currently working, you might use a job description for that position.

Case Problem 12-A

Do We Need This Blogger?

Genève Ltd. is a manufacturer of upscale clothing and accessories for men and women. The company is headquartered in New York, and has worldwide distribution. Manufacturing is carried out in the United States, Italy, Spain, Lithuania, and most recently, China. Genève was founded in 1925, and has remained in business as an independent company.

As the demand for formal business attire diminished during the 1990s, Genève suffered a 35 percent decrease in sales. However, as the demand for formal attire on the job rebounded from 2002 forward, Genève has reestablished its sales volume. A few late-night shows featured guests who mentioned they were wearing suits with the Genève label, resulting in a surge in sales.

CEO Pauline Matthieu holds a 10 a.m. staff meeting most Monday mornings. Although she would like to have the meetings at 8 a.m., Matthieu recognizes that the commuters on the top executive team can rarely get to the office before 9:30 a.m. On this particular Monday, Matthieu is visibly upset. She tells her staff:

> *It's not my pattern to dig too deeply into operational matters. As you know, I'm interested primarily in strategy and merchandising. Yet, I'm ticked off today. You probably all know about Jimmy Kincaid, the production planner from our Vermont plant who has set up a blog on http://Blogger.com to hold his personal forum about Genève. What he has to say about our fashions and our company usually isn't too negative, but he has become an embarrassment.*
>
> *In his latest blog, Jimmy has superimposed the faces of apes on the models featured in a current ad. The male ape says that Genève fashions will never be sold at Wal-Mart or Target, and the female ape responds, 'Are you sure?'*

"I guess that is a little edgy," said Harry Overstreet, vice president of operations. "Can you give us another recent example of Jimmy's blogs that should be a concern to the company?"

"I have a print copy in my briefcase," replied Matthieu. "Here I will read it to you:"

> *The Genève label is still tops, but we're are slipping into some of the offshoring excesses of other companies. I saw a few undercover photos taken in one of our China factories, and the image does not do us proud. There are loads of Chinese women working in cramped quarters, the lighting is poor, and some of the girls working the cutting tools look to be adolescents.*
>
> *Maybe the cool Genève image has an ugly underbelly at times.*

Georgia Santelli, vice president of merchandising, commented, "Has any manager in our Vermont operation attempted to shut down this clown? I mean, he is a corporate menace."

Overstreet chimed in, "Wait a minute. Jimmy Kincaid may be a clown at times, yet he also says a lot of good things about Genève. He drops a lot of hints that create a buzz for our next season's offerings. One time he had mentioned something about seeing a new handbag in the design stages that will make thousands of women switch from the Coach bags."

Sam Cohen, the director of marketing, said the company is contemplating a policy on blogging, and that it has been discussed internally. He said, "Here let me dredge up the preliminary policy from my laptop. Pauline was in on one of the preliminary discussions, but we didn't do much with it."

Cohen projected the slides, containing some bulleted points on the conference room screen:

- At work, employees can use their blogs only for work-related matters.
- Employees cannot disclose confidential or proprietary information.
- Private issues must be kept private.
- Public statements cannot be defamatory, profane, libelous, harassing, or abusive.
- Employees can form links for their blogs to Genève only with permission from executive-level management.
- An employee's blog must contain the following disclaimer: "The views expressed on this blog are mine alone and do not necessarily reflect the views of Genève Ltd."
- A breach of the above blogging policy could result in discipline up to and including termination.

Case Problem 12-A

"I'm still ticked off at Jimmy, but before we take action, let's think through whether he has done something drastically wrong. We have to protect Genève brand equity, but we must be fair. Let's talk."

Discussion Questions

1. Even though the blogging policy has not yet been implemented, how well have Kincaid's actions conformed to the tentative policy?
2. What steps, if any, do you think top management should take to control Kincaid's blogs?
3. What relevance does this case have for the subject of interpersonal communication?

Source: The blogging policy ideas are adapted from "Myemployersucks.com: Why You Need a Blogging Policy," *Virginia Employment Law Letter*, http://www.HRhero.com.

Case Problem 12-B

B.S. Bingo at Violet Cow

Cindy Perrin is the brand manager for Violet Cow, a successful new energy drink manufactured and distributed by a medium-size food and beverage company. Violet Cow is still a small player in the beverage market but has been successfully marketed into supermarkets, convenience stores, service stations, and a scattering of restaurants. As the brand manager, Cindy looks out for the welfare of Violet Cow. She strives to make sure that the beverage gets enough resources from the company such as advertising dollars and incentives for supermarkets to distribute the brand.

Cindy holds weekly strategy meetings with four team members to make plans for building the Violet Cow brand, to receive feedback on progress, and to investigate any problems in manufacturing, marketing, or distribution. An outsider, such as a representative from manufacturing or the dietitian staff, is invited to most meetings.

Cindy's boss, Larry Tate, the vice president of noncarbonated beverages, was holding a progress meeting with her about the success of Violet Cow. Cindy said she was pleased with the progress, and that the market share she was taking from Coca Cola, Pepsi, and Cadbury Schweppes continued to increase. Cindy did comment, however, that she wished her meetings were more effective. When Larry asked for clarification, Cindy lamented:

"We have a creative staff, so they have to be granted leeway in how they behave. I can't rightfully expect them to be well disciplined all the time. Yet I wonder if they are going too far."

"How about a few specifics?" asked Larry.

"Two meetings ago, the team was playing B.S. Bingo (short for Business Speak Bingo). Jenny, one of the team members, passed out bingo cards filled with business jargon. The idea for the game was the first person to check off a row of terms used during the meeting was to jump up and say 'B.S. Bingo.' Pete won with a row with the five words, *synergy*, *strategize*, *rocket science*, *incent*, and *globalization*. We didn't conduct much serious work while the team laughed for about five minutes.

"Another problem is that I wonder exactly what the team members are doing with their laptops at the meeting. They look like they are typing away to take notes, but I have the distinct impression there is a little bit of surfing going on.

"We more or less agreed that cell phones should not be used during the meeting, but I get the impression several of our team members check their cell phones for messages periodically during the meetings. They are kind of sneaky about it. Richard, for example, puts his cell phone on his lap and glances down.

"It's the same thing with the PDAs. Quite often the team members place their PDAs on the table and glance at them regularly, even when I or somebody else is presenting.

"You would think Georgia (another team member) has an attention-deficit disorder. During a one-hour meeting, she'll leave at least twice. Or maybe she has a bladder problem. I'm not sure. We do drink a lot of Violet Cow around here.

"So I guess you could say, our meetings are not as productive as I would like. Yet if I come down too heavy on the team, they might not like the work environment."

Larry replied, "I agree that your meetings could be more disciplined, but I also agree that we don't want to hurt morale. Let's both think through this problem a little more."

Discussion Questions

1. What do you recommend Cindy do to have more disciplined meetings? (Or, should she do anything?)
2. Should Cindy conduct her business meeting with language that would make it very difficult to win at B.S. Bingo?
3. What stance should Cindy take about multitasking during the meetings?

chapter 13

Teams, Groups, and Teamwork

The conglomerate Siemens AG operates a range of businesses, including power, transportation, automation and controls, healthcare lighting, and building technology. Siemens has annual sales of approximately $90 billion, and locations in 190 countries. With 460,000 employees worldwide, including 70,000 in the United States, the 159-year old company is the world's eighth largest private employer. Siemens' German operations employ 165,000 and are costly to run, says Klaus Kleinfeld, the chief executive. Yet he insists they are not a drag on the overall corporation. Klienfeld chose to not renew his contract ending in September 2007 because of a corruption scandal about the possibility that executives at Siemens bribed foreign officials to win contracts. Kleinfeld was not accused of personal conduct or having been informed of events related to the bribes.

"The teams in Germany are among our most intelligent," says Kleinfeld. "They bring out products to world markets at a fast pace. You should never change a winning team." He said that customers from all over the world come to Siemens facilities in remote parts of Germany to learn about cutting-edge products. "Whether I have additional costs or not, doesn't matter as much as the speed to market and the quality of the design. We're not talking about a pure cost game."

Objectives

After studying this chapter and doing the exercises, you should be able to:

1 Identify various types of teams and groups, including self-managed work teams and project groups.

2 Describe the characteristics of effective groups and teams.

3 Describe the stages of group development.

4 Summarize managerial actions for building teamwork.

5 Explain the actions and attitudes of an effective team player.

6 Point to the potential contributions and problems of teams and groups.

7 Describe the positive and negative aspects of conflict and how team leaders and managers can resolve conflict.

Kleinfeld said strong leaders need to maintain their personal independence, but at the same time they must be team players, leveraging the team's resources and information. His leadership mantra is that "Nobody's perfect, but a team can be."[1]

The international CEO's exalted comments about the power of teams and teamwork illustrate the prominent role teams occupy in business. The heavy emphasis on teams and group decision making in the workplace increases the importance of understanding teams and other types of groups. (You will recall the discussion of group decision making in Chapter 5 and the mention of teams throughout the book.) We approach an additional understanding of teams, groups, and teamwork here by presenting a handful of key topics: types of groups and teams, characteristics of effective work groups; stages in the development of groups, building teamwork, and becoming a team player. We also describe the manager's role in resolving conflict that takes place within groups and between groups.

group
A collection of people who interact with one another, are working toward some common purpose, and perceive themselves to be a group.

team
A special type of group in which members have complementary skills and are committed to a common purpose, a set of performance goals, and an approach to the task.

TYPES OF TEAMS AND GROUPS

Learning Objective 1

Identify various types of terms and groups, including self-managed work teams and project groups.

A **group** is a collection of people who interact with each other, are working toward some common purpose, and perceive themselves to be a group. The head of a customer service team and her staff would be a group. In contrast, 12 people in an office elevator would not be a group because they are not engaged in collective effort. A **team** is a special type of group. Team members have complementary skills and are committed to a common purpose, a set of performance goals, and an approach to the task. **Teamwork** is characterized by understanding and commitment to group goals on the part of all team members.[2]

Some groups are formally sanctioned by management and the organization itself, while others are not. A **formal group** is deliberately formed by the organization to accomplish specific tasks and achieve goals. Examples of formal groups include departments, project groups, task forces, committees, and Six Sigma teams. In contrast, **informal groups** emerge over time through the interaction of workers. Although the goals of these groups are not explicitly stated, informal groups typically satisfy a social or recreational purpose. Members of a department who

PLAY VIDEO

TEAMS, GROUPS, AND TEAMWORK

Go to academic.cengage.com/management/dubrin and view the video. What are some norms that might be important to develop in a Cold Stone team? What might be some of the challenges in creating a global team?

1 Adapted from "Siemens CEO Klaus Kleinfeld: 'Nobody's Perfect, but a Team Can Be'" *Knowledge.wharton.upenn.edu*, April 20, 2006. The updated information is from Jack Ewing, "A Setback for German Reform: Ousted Siemens CEO Kleinfeld was Emblematic of a Nation's Turnaround," *Business Week*, May 7, 2007, p. 49.

2 Jon R. Katzenbach and Douglas K. Smith, "The Discipline of Teams," *Harvard Business Review*, March–April 1993, p. 113.

teamwork A situation characterized by understanding and commitment to group goals on the part of all team members.

formal group A group deliberately formed by the organization to accomplish specific tasks and achieve goals.

dine together occasionally would constitute an informal group. Yet the same group might also meet an important work purpose of discussing technical problems of mutual interest.

All workplace teams share the common element of people who possess a mix of skills, working together cooperatively. No matter what label the team carries, its broad purpose is to contribute to a collaborative workplace in which people help each other achieve constructive goals. Here we describe six types of work groups even though they have many similarities. The groups are self-managing work teams, project teams and task forces, cross-functional teams, crews, top management teams, and virtual teams.

Because of the widespread use of team, is it helpful for you to be aware of the skills and knowledge needed to function effectively on a team, particularly a self-managing work team. Exhibit 13-1 presents a representative listing of team skills as perceived by employers.

exhibit 13-1 Team Skills

A variety of skills are required to be an effective member of various types of teams. Several different business firms use a skill inventory to help guide team members toward the competencies they need to become high-performing team members. Review each team skill listed and rate your skill level using the following classification:

S = strong (capable and comfortable with effectively implementing the skill)
M = moderate (demonstrated skill in the past)
B = basic (minimum ability in this area)
N = not applicable (not relevant to the type of work I do or plan to do)

	Skill Level (S, M, B, or N)		Skill Level (S, M, B, or N)
Communication Skills		**Thought Process Skills**	
Speak effectively	________	Use sound judgment	________
Foster open communications	________	Analyze issues	________
Listen to others	________	Think "outside the box"	________
Deliver presentations	________	**Organizational Skills**	
Prepare written communication including PowerPoint	________	Know the business	________
Self-Management Skills	________	Use technical/functional expertise	________
Act with integrity	________	Use financial/quantitative data	________
Demonstrate adaptability	________	**Strategic Skills**	________
Engage in personal development	________	Recognize big picture impact	________
Strive for results	________	Promote corporate citizenship	________
Commitment to work	________	Focus on customer needs	________
Thought Process Skills		Commit to quality	________
Innovate solutions to problems	________	Manage profitability	________

Self-Managed Work Teams

A dominant trend in work group formation is to organize workers into teams with considerable authority to direct themselves. Many U.S. corporations use some form of team structure in their organizations, often a type of self-managed teams. Team structures are also prevalent in Canadian, European, and Asian industry. A **self-managed work team** is a formally recognized group of employees who are responsible for an entire work process or segment that delivers a product or service to an internal or external customer.[3] Two other terms for self-managed work are *self-directed work team*, and *work team*. Self-managed work groups originated as an outgrowth of job enrichment. Working in teams broadens the responsibility of team members.

Self-managed work teams usually have an internal leader who is usually designated as team leader. At the same time the team is likely to have an external leader to whom the team reports.[4] This individual is often a middle manager to whom a group of work teams report. So the self-managing work team is not totally independent.

The key purposes for establishing self-managed teams are to increase productivity, enhance quality, reduce cycle time (the amount of time required to complete a transaction), and respond more rapidly to a changing workplace. Self-managed work teams also present an opportunity to empower employees.

informal group
A group that emerges over time through the interaction of workers.

self-managed work team
A formally recognized group of employees who are responsible for an entire work process or segment that delivers a product or service to an internal or external customer.

Method of Operation

Members of the self-managed work team typically work together on an ongoing, day-by-day basis, thus differentiating it from a task force or committee. The work team often assumes total responsibility or "ownership" of a product or service. A work team might be assigned the responsibility for preparing a social networking Web site for a search engine company. At other times, the team takes on responsibility for a major chunk of a job, such as building a truck engine (but not the entire truck). The self-managed work team is taught to think in terms of customer requirements. The team member might ask, "How easy would it be for a left-handed person to use this tire jack?"

To promote the sense of ownership, management encourages workers to be generalists rather than specialists. Each team member learns a broad range of skills and switches job assignments periodically. Members of the self-directed work team frequently receive training in team skills. Cross training in different organizational functions helps members develop an overall perspective of how the firm operates. Exhibit 13-2 presents the distinguishing characteristics of a self-managing work team. Studying these characteristics will provide insight into work teams.

---

3 Richard S. Wellings, William C. Byham, and Jeanne M. Wilson, *Empowered Teams: Creating Self-Directed Work Groups That Improve Quality, Productivity, and Participation* (San Francisco: Jossey-Bass, 1991), p. 3.

4 Frederick P. Morgeson, "The External Leadership of Self-Managing Teams: Intervening in the Context of Novel and Disruptive Events," *Journal of Applied Psychology*, May 2005, p. 497.

exhibit 13-2 Characteristics of a Self-Managed Work Team

1. Through empowerment, team members share many management and leadership functions, such as making job assignments and giving pep talks.
2. Members plan, control, and improve their own work processes.
3. Members set their own goals and inspect their own work.
4. Members create their own schedules and review their group performance.
5. Members often prepare their own budgets and coordinate their work with other departments.
6. Members typically order materials, keep inventories, and deal with suppliers.
7. Members hire their own replacements or assume responsibility for disciplining their own members.
8. Members assume responsibility for the quality of their products and services, whether provided to internal or external customers.

Source: Adapted from Richard S. Wellings, William C. Byham, and Jeanne M. Wilson, *Empowered Teams: Creating Self-Directed Work Groups That Improve Quality, Productivity, and Participation* (San Francisco: Jossey-Bass, 1991), p. 3.

The level of responsibility for a product or service contributes to team members' pride in their work and team. At best, the team members feel as if they operate a small business, with the profits (or losses) directly attributable to their efforts. An entry-level worker, such as a data-entry clerk in a government agency, is less likely to experience such feelings.

Self-Managed Work Team Effectiveness

Self-managed work teams demonstrate a reasonably good record of improving productivity, quality, and customer service. About 50 percent of the time they result in productivity gains, yet effective teams can produce remarkable results. When self-management works, productivity gains of 10 to 20 percent are typical.[5] A specific example is a study of customer service workers in the telecommunications industry. The work groups organized into self-managing teams produced more sales volume and better customer service. Teams gained a 26 percent sales increase and a 6 percent service quality increase over work groups using the traditional production-line approach.[6]

Despite their potential contribution, self-managed work teams create challenges for managers. High-caliber employees are required for the team because they must be able to solve problems on their own and rely less on a supervisor. Many of the personal qualities required for team effectiveness are outlined in Exhibit 13-2. Effective contributors to a self-managed team must be multi-skilled, and not all employees are willing or able to develop new skills. Another challenge for the manager is that many prefer having more authority over the group than a self-managing team requires. A manager who becomes a team leader has much less authority over them group than he or she did as a unit manager.

5 The evidence is reviewed in Roy A. Cook and J. Larry Goff, "Coming of Age with Self-Managed Teams: Dealing with a Problem Employee," *Journal of Business and Psychology*, Spring 2002, pp. 487–488; Andrew Leigh and Michael Maynard, "Self-Managed Teams: How they Succeed or Fail," in Perseus Publishing's *Business: The Ultimate Resource* (Cambridge, MA: Perseus, 2002), p. 202.

6 Peter Venn and contributors, "Self-Managing Teams," *Business Potential*, http://www.businesspotential.com/self_manage_teams.htm, 2002. Accessed, January 10, 2007.

Project Teams and Task Forces

Project teams comprise the basic component of the matrix structure described in Chapter 8. A **project team** is a small group of employees working on a temporary basis in order to accomplish a particular goal. Being able to manage a project is a core competence for most managers.[7] One reason is that projects are so frequently used to manage change, such as launching a new product or introducing a new method of delivering service or manufacturing a large product including a new vehicle launch. Here we present additional details about project teams to help you understand this important type of work group.

project team
A small group of employees working on a temporary basis in order to accomplish a particular goal.

1. Project managers operate independently of the normal chain of command. They usually report to a member of top-level management, often an executive in charge of projects. This reporting relationship gives project members a feeling of being part of an elite group.
2. Project managers negotiate directly for resources with the heads of the line and staff departments whose members are assigned to a given project. For example, a project manager might borrow an architectural technician from the building design department. For the team member who likes job rotation, project teams offer the opportunity for different exciting projects from time to time.
3. Project managers act as coordinators of the people and material needed to complete the project's mission, making them accountable for the performance of the people assigned to the project. Project members therefore feel a sense of responsibility to their project leader and their team.
4. Members of the project team might be from the same functional area or from different areas, depending on the needs of the project. The members of a new-product development team, for example, are usually from different areas. A cross-functional team might therefore be regarded as a special type of project team. An example of a project team with members from the same functional area would be a group of financial specialists on assignment to revise the company pension program.
5. The life of the project ends when its objectives are accomplished, such as adding a wing to a hospital or building a prototype for a new sports car. In contrast, most departments are considered relatively stable.

Project teams are found in almost every large company. Being part of a project encourages identification with the project, which often leads to high morale and productivity. A frequently observed attitude is "we can get this important job done." From the standpoint of the organization, a project team offers flexibility. If the project proves not to be worthwhile the project can be disbanded quickly, without having committed enormous resources like renting a separate

7 Robert Buttrick, "Project Management," in Perseus Publishing's *Business: The Ultimate Resource* (Cambridge, MA: Perseus, 2002), p. 165.

task force
A problem-solving group of a temporary nature, usually working against a deadline.

cross-functional team
A group composed of workers from different specialties at the same organizational level who come together to accomplish a task.

building or hiring a large staff. If the new project is a big success, it can become the nucleus of a new division of the company or a major new product line.

One problem with project teams, as well as other temporary teams, is that people assigned to the project may be underutilized after the project is completed. Unless another project requires staffing, some of the project members may be laid off.

A **task force** is a problem-solving group of a temporary nature, usually working against a deadline. It functions much like a project except that is usually of smaller size and more focused on studying a particular problem or opportunity. The task force is often used to study a problem and then make recommendations to higher management. Representative task-force assignments include: investigating whether stock options are being used illegally and unethically in the company; finding a potential buyer for the company; making recommendations about improved promotional opportunities for minorities and women; and investigating whether the number of suppliers can be reduced. Being a member of a task force is good for your career because you are likely to make good contacts and be noticed if the task force produces useful results.

Cross-Functional Teams

A **cross-functional team** is a group composed of workers from different specialties, at the same organizational level who come together to accomplish a task. (A cross-functional team might be considered a type of project team or even a task force.) A cross-functional team blends the talents of team members from different specialties as they work on a task that requires such a mix. To perform well on a cross-functional team a person must think in terms of the good of the larger organization, rather than in terms of his or her own specialty. A typical application of a cross-functional team would be to develop a new product like a video mobile phone. Among the specialties needed on such a team would be computer science, engineering, manufacturing, industrial design, marketing, and finance. (The finance person would help guide the team toward producing a video mobile phone that could be sold at a profit.)

When members from different specialties work together, they take into account each other's perspectives when making their contribution. For example, if the manufacturing representative knows that a video mobile phone must sell for about one-fourth the price of a plasma screen TV, then he or she will have to build the device inexpensively. Using a cross-functional team for product development enhances communication across groups, thus saving time.

In addition to product development, cross-functional teams might be used to improve customer service, reduce costs, and improve the workings of a system such as online sales. Cross-functional teams are used widely in conglomerates like Siemens, and often include representatives from different companies within the larger organization.

A key success factor for cross-functional teams is that the team leader has both technical and process skills. The leader needs the technical background to understand he group task and to recognize the potential contribution of members from diverse specialties. At the same time the leader must have the interpersonal skills to facilitate a diverse group of people with limited zero, or even negative experience in working collectively.[8] The success of a cross-functional team requires collaboration among its members.

A major advantage of cross-functional teams is that they enhance communication across groups, thereby saving time. The cross-functional team also offers the advantage of a strong customer focus because the team orients itself toward satisfying a specific internal or external customer or group of customers. A challenge with these teams, however, is that they often breed conflict because of the different points of view.

The accompanying Management in Action illustrates how a cross-functional team can be used to develop products as well as enhance cooperation.

management in action

Hypertherm Chief Executive Organizes for Teamwork

Richard Couch is the chief executive of Hypertherm Inc., a closely held maker of metal-cutting equipment in Hanover, NH, with annual revenues of roughly $200 million. He has long promoted cooperation, with a company-wide profit-sharing plan that pays the same percent of salary to each employee.

As Hypertherm grew in the 1990s, Couch saw increasing friction between departments, such as engineering and marketing. So in 1997, he reorganized the company into cross-functional teams based on Hypertherm's five product lines. He forced the teams of researchers, engineers, marketers, and salespeople to sit together in closely bunched circles. He wanted the teams close to the shop floor, but retreated in face of safety rules requiring that manufacturing be shielded by a wall.

The plan met resistance at first. One engineer complained about "sitting next to this marketing guy. I don't have anything to say to him," Couch recalls. "I thought, precisely my point. Maybe you will actually say something to him." Some employees quit, he says, although the once-unhappy engineer is still at Hypertherm.

Today, Couch credits the reorganization with helping Hypertherm grow faster and more profitably. Instead of one product-development team, Hypertherm has five, which helps the company introduce new products faster. Couch says the new organization is also more efficient, because salespeople and marketers, who know customers best, are more involved in product development. The company recently paid $6.7 million in profit-sharing, equivalent to 26 percent of salaries, to its 612 employees.

Couch acknowledges that the team approach doesn't appeal to everyone. "The star can make more money going somewhere else," he says. But with attrition below 5 percent annually, Couch believes Hyperterm is doing a good job screening out non-team players before they are hired.

Questions

1. In what way did cross-functional teams fit the purposes of a Hypertherm?
2. How do you think the company screens out non-team players before they are hired?
3. What is the difference between a star and a team player?

Source: Scott Thurm, "Teamwork Raises Everyone's Game," *The Wall Street Journal,* November 7, 2005, p. B8.

8 Glenn Parker, "Team with Strangers: Success Strategies for Cross-Functional Teams," http://www.glennparker.com/Freebees/teaming-with-strangers.html. Material copyright © 1998 Glenn Parker.

Crews

crew
A group of specialists, each of whom has specific roles, perform brief events that are closely synchronized with one another, and repeat these events under different environmental conditions.

We are all familiar with common usage of the term *crew* in relation to such groups as those who operate airplanes, boats, and fire fighting equipment. The technical meaning of the term means virtually the same thing. A **crew** is a group of specialists each of who have specific roles, perform brief events that are close synchronized with each other, and repeat these events under different environmental conditions. A crew is identified by the technology it handles, such as an aircraft crew, or a deep-sea salvage operation. The crewmembers rarely rotate specialties, such as the flight attendant taking over for the chief pilot. (Special training and licensing would be required.) The following are several criteria of a group qualifying as a crew:[9]

- Clear roles and responsibilities
- Workflow well established before anyone joins the team
- Careful coordination required with other members in order to perform the task
- Group needs to be in a specific environment to complete its task
- Different people can join the group without interfering with its operation or mission

Because of the specialized roles they play, and the essential tasks they perform, much is expected of crews. The future of crews is promising. For example, computer-virus fighting crews would be a welcome addition to business and society. Also, some business firms establish their own crews to help cope with a natural disaster such as a flood, hurricane, or ice storm.

Top-Management Teams

The group of managers at the top of most organizations is referred to as a team, the management team, or the top-management team. Yet as Jon R. Katzenbach observes, few groups of top-level managers function as a team in the sense of the definition presented earlier in this chapter.[10] The CEO gets most of the publicity, along with credit and blame for what goes wrong. Nevertheless, groups of top-level managers are teams in the sense that they make most major decisions collaboratively with all members of the top-management group included. Michael Dell (Dell Computers) exemplifies a highly visible chairman who regularly consults with trusted advisors before making major decisions.

The term top-management team has another less frequently used meaning. A handful of companies are actually run by a committee of two or more top executives who claim to share power equally. In this way they are similar to a husband-and-wife team running a household. The co-CEO arrangement fits here, where two executives become a CEO team. Two successful applications of this approach are the Denihan Hospitality Group (DHG) that focuses on hotels and investments, and Primerica a consumer financial services subsidiary

9 Shelia Simsarian Webber and Richard J. Klimoski, "Crews: A Distinct Type of Work Team," *Journal of Business and Psychology*, Spring 2004, pp. 261–279.
10 Jon R. Katzenbach, "The Myth of the Top Management Team," *Harvard Business Review*, November–December 1997, pp. 82–99.

of Citigroup. In both cases the co-CEOs have separate responsibilities and see themselves as trusting their counterparts.[11] At Primerica responsibilities are shared by one executive specializing in marketing and sales and the other in administration and finance. At DHG, one executive focuses on hotels and the other on investment strategies.

Another approach to power sharing is to designate one executive as CEO and another as chairperson instead of combining the position as is the usual case. As a result the company has two top-level bosses, leading to confusion. In discussing the scandal about spying on board members that took place at Hewlett Packard in 2006, Jack and Suzy Welch believe that employees should have had one boss in CEO Mark Hurd. As a respected industry veteran, Hurd had established strategic goals for HP, and employees were motivated to attain them.

However, there was also another boss, chairwoman Patricia Dunn who was reaching out to selected employees with her own agenda and deploying company resources. "That meant HP was being run by two leaders, a dynamic which can lead to confusion, or worse, to employees shopping around for the answer they like best."[12]

Quite often the egos of the power-sharers are too big for the team arrangement to work well. Some observers are skeptical that a company can really be run well without one key executive having the final decision. Can you imagine your favorite athletic team having two head coaches, or your favorite band having two leaders?

Virtual Teams

Workplace teams are no longer tied to a physical location. A **virtual team** is a small group of people who conduct almost all of their collaborative work by electronic communication rather than in face-to-face meetings. E-mail, including IM, is the usual medium for sharing information and conducting meetings. Collaborative software (or groupware) is another widely used approach to conducting an electronic meeting. Using collaborative software, several people can edit a document at the same time, or in sequence, and also have access to a shared database. Videoconferencing is another technological advance that facilitates the virtual team. Electronic brainstorming, as described in Chapter 5, is well suited for a virtual team. A more advanced approach is to have a company Website (intranet) dedicated to the shared project. Members can update other members, and the status of the project is posted daily. A "virtual work space" of this type was shown at Shell Chemical to be more effective than sending hundreds of e-mail messages back and forth to each other.[13]

virtual team
A small group of people who conduct almost all of their collaborative work by electronic communication rather than in face-to-face meetings.

The trend toward forming cross-cultural teams from geographically dispersed units of a firm increases the application of virtual teams. Strategic alliances in which geographically dispersed companies work with each other depend on virtual teams in many regards. The field technician in Iceland who

---

11 "Co-CEOs Brooke Barrett and Patrick Denihan," http://www.denihan.com, July 1, 2005; "Trust of Primerica co-CEOs Seals Relationship," http://ww4.primerica.com, accessed January 10, 2007.

12 Jack and Suzy Welch, "A Dangerous Division of Labor," *Business Week*, November 6, 2006, p. 122.

13 Ann Majchrak, Avrind Malhotra, Jeffrey Stamps, and Jessical Lipnack, "Can Absence Make a Team Grow Stronger?" *Harvard Business* Review, May 2004, pp. 134–135.

holds an electronic with her counterparts in South Africa, Mexico, and California realizes a significant cost savings over bringing them all together in one physical location. IBM makes some use of virtual teams in selling information technology systems, partially because so many IBM field personnel work from their homes, vehicles, and hotel rooms. Meeting electronically does not cure all the problems of geographically dispersed teams from different cultures. For example, the manager or team leader must often confront the problem of different attitudes toward hierarchy and authority, such as workers from many cultures not feeling comfortable with the flat structure of a team.[14]

Virtual teams are sometimes the answer to the challenge of hiring workers with essential skills who do not want to relocate. The company can accommodate these workers by creating virtual teams, with perhaps one or two members working in company headquarters. A similar application of virtual teams is to integrate employees after a merger. Instead of relocating several employees from the acquired company, a virtual team is formed. In one merger, the company's legal division became virtual teams.

Trust is a crucial component of virtual teams. Managers must trust people to perform well without direct supervision. Team members develop trust in their coworkers without the benefit of face-to-face meetings. Managers face the same challenge as that for assembling self-managed work teams: self-reliant and talented employees must be selected for the team. Getting team members to feel that they are part of a team is another challenge that can sometimes be met by an in-person meeting about twice per year. Frequent electronic communication also contributes to team spirit.

Virtual teams are inadvisable in industries such as manufacturing, health care, and restaurants. Any type of work that is sequential or integrated would create problems for a virtual team, including project work that emphasizes face-to-face interaction.[15]

CHARACTERISTICS OF EFFECTIVE WORK GROUPS

Learning Objective 2

Describe the characteristics of effective groups and teams.

Groups, like individuals, possess characteristics that contribute to their uniqueness and effectiveness. As shown in Exhibit 13-3, these characteristics can be grouped into nine categories. Our description of work group effectiveness follows this framework.[16]

14 Jeanne Brett, Kristin Behfar, and Mary C. Kern, "Managing Multicultural Teams," *Harvard Business Review*, November 2006, pp. 87–88.

15 Carla Johnson, "Managing Virtual Teams," *HR Magazine*, June 2002, p. 70; Cristina B. Gibson, and Susan G. Cohen (eds.), *Virtual Teams That Work: Creating Conditions for Virtual Team Effectiveness* (San Francisco: Jossey-Bass, 2003).

16 Michael A. Campion, Ellen M. Papper, and Gina Medsker, "Relations between Work Team Characteristics and Effectiveness: A Replication and Extension," *Personnel Psychology*, Summer 1996, p. 431; Bradley L. Kirkman and Benson Rosen, "Powering Up Teams," *Organizational Dynamics*, Winter 2000, pp. 48–52; Stanley M. Gulley, Kara A. Incalcaterra, Aparna Joshi, and J. Matthew Beaubien, "A Meta-Analysis of Team Efficacy, Potency, and Performance: Interdependence and Level of Analysis as Moderators of Observed Relationships," *Journal of Applied Psychology*, October 2002, pp. 819–832; Scott W. Lester, Bruce M. Meglino, and M. Audrey Korsgaard, "The Antecedents and Consequences of Group Potency: A Longitudinal Investigation of Newly Formed Work Groups," *The Academy of Management Journal*, April 2002, pp. 352–368; Vanessa Urch Druskat and Steven B. Wolff, "Building the Emotional Intelligence of Groups," *Harvard Business Review*, March 2001, pp. 80–90; Claus W. Langred, "Too Much of a Good Thing? Negative Effects of High Trust and Individual Autonomy in Self-Managing Work Teams," *Academy of Management Journal*, June 2004, pp. 385–399.

exhibit 13-3 Work-Group Characteristics Related to Effectiveness

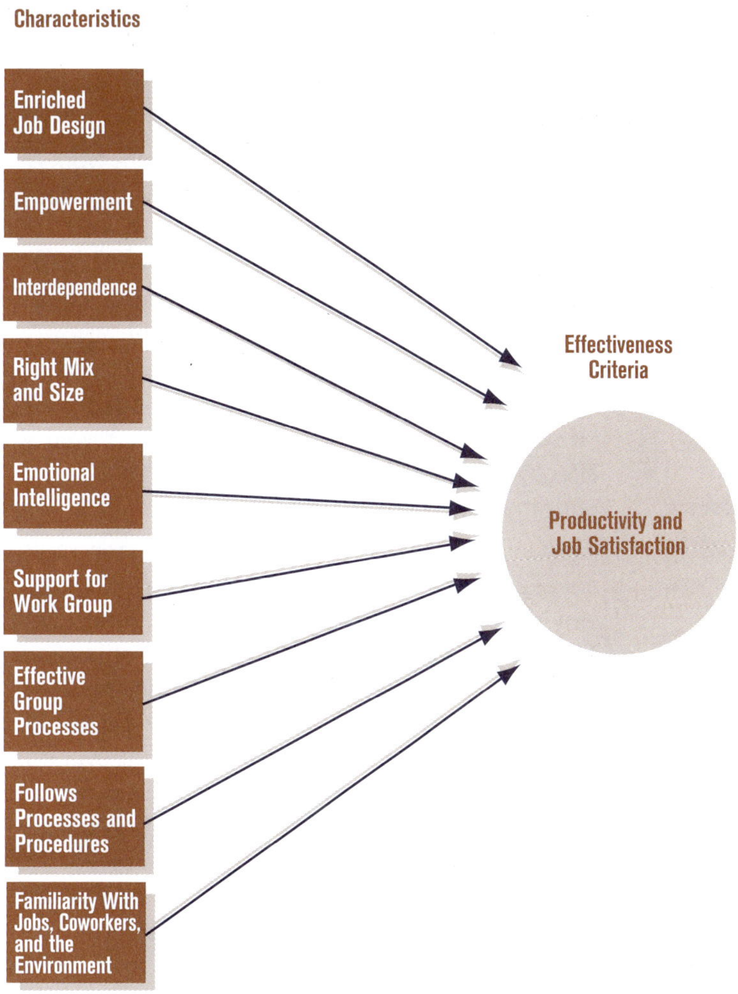

Sources: Michael A. Campion, Ellen M. Papper, and Gina Medsker, "Relations between Work Team Characteristics and Effectiveness: A Replication and Extension," *Personnel Psychology*, Summer 1996, p. 431; Stanley M. Gulley, Kara A. Incalcaterra, Aparna Joshi, and J. Matthew Beaubien, "A Meta-Analysis of Team Efficacy, Potency, and Performance: Interdependence and Level of Analysis as Moderators of Observed Relationships," *Journal of Applied Psychology*, October 2002, pp. 819–832; Vanessa Urch Druskat and Steven B. Wolff, "Building the Emotional Intelligence of Groups," *Harvard Business Review*, March 2001, pp. 80–90; Claus W. Langred, "Too Much of a Good Thing? Negative Effects of High Trust and Individual Autonomy in Self-Managing Work Teams," *Academy of Management Journal*, June 2004, pp. 385–399.

1. *Enriched job design.* Effective work groups follow the principles of job design embodied in job enrichment and the job characteristics model described in Chapter 7. For example, task significance and task identity are both strong. Group members therefore perceive their work as having high intrinsic motivation.
2. *A feeling of empowerment.* An effective group or team believes in its authority to solve a variety of problems without first obtaining approval from management. Empowered teams share four experiences: potency, meaningfulness, autonomy, and impact. Potency refers to teams members believing in themselves

and exhibiting a confident, can-do attitude. (*Team efficacy* is another useful term for potency.) Teams with a sense of meaningfulness collectively commit to their mission and see their goals as valuable and worthwhile. Autonomy refers to the freedom, discretion, and control that teams experience (the same as in job enrichment). A team experiences impact when members see the effect of their work on other interested parties such as customers and coworkers (the same as task significance).[17]

3. *Interdependent tasks and rewards.* Effective work groups are characterized by several types of group member dependencies on one another. Such groups show task interdependence in the sense that members interact and depend on one another to accomplish work. Goal interdependence refers to the linking of individual goals to the group's goals. Unless the task requires interdependence, such as building a motorcycle, a team is not needed. A member of a sales team might establish a compensation goal for herself, but she can realize this goal only if the other team members achieve similar success. Interdependent feedback and rewards also contribute to group effectiveness. Individual feedback and rewards should be linked to group performance to encourage good team play.
4. *Right mix and size.* A variety of factors relating to the mix of group members are associated with effective work groups. The diversity of group members' experience, knowledge, and education generally improves problem solving. Teams with members who have diverse educational backgrounds are likely to benefit from the different information that stems from the diversity.[18] For example, a person who majored in fine arts could make design suggestion that engineers and business majors might overlook. Cultural diversity tends to enhance creativity by bringing various viewpoints into play. However, only when each team member enjoys high quality interactions can the full benefits of diversity be realized. The interactions relate to both the task itself (such as talking about improving a motorcycle starter) and social interactions (such as chatting about children during a break).[19]

   Groups should be large enough to accomplish the work, but when groups become too large, confusion and poor coordination may result. Also, larger groups tend to be less cohesive. Cross-functional teams, work teams, committees, and task forces tend to be most productive with seven to ten members. The rule of thumb at Amazon is that product development teams should be small enough to be fed on two large pizzas.[20] (We assume no team members are super-size or super-hungry.)

   Another important composition factor is the quality of the group or team members. Bright people with constructive personality characteristics contribute the most to team effectiveness. A study involving 652 employees composing 51 work teams found that teams with members higher in mental

---

17 Kirkman and Rosen, "Powering Up Teams," pp. 48–52.

18 Kristin B. Dahlin, Laurie B. Weingart, and Pamela J. Hinds, "Team Diversity and Information Use," *Academy of Management Journal*, December 2005, pp. 1107–1123.

19 Priscilla M. Ellsass and Laura M. Graves, "Demographic Diversity in Decision-Making Group: The Experience of Women and People of Color," *Academy of Management Review*, October 1997, p. 968.

20 Robert D. Hof, "Jeff Bezos' Risky Bet," *Business Week*, November 13, 2006, p. 58.

ability, conscientiousness, extraversion, and emotional stability received higher supervisor ratings for team performance.[21] (Put winners on your team and you are more likely to have a winning team.)

5. *Emotional intelligence.* The group itself should have high emotional intelligence in the sense of being able to build relationships both inside and outside the team, and make constructive use of its emotion. Norms that establish mutual trust among group members contribute to an emotionally intelligent group.[22] A potential problem, however, is that when group members trust each other too much, they neglect to monitor each others' work and may not catch errors and unethical behavior.[23]
6. *Support for the work group.* One of the most important characteristics of an effective work group is the support it receives from the organization. Key support factors include giving the group the information it needs, coaching group members, providing the right technology, and receiving recognition and other rewards. Training quite often facilitates work group effectiveness. The training content typically includes group decision making, interpersonal skills, technical knowledge, and the team philosophy. Managerial support in the form of investing resources and believing in group effort fosters effectiveness.
7. *Effective processes within the group.* Many processes (activities) take place within the group that influence effectiveness. One is the belief that the group can do the job, reflecting high team spirit and potency. Effectiveness is also enhanced when workers provide social support to each other through such means as helping each other have positive interactions. Workload sharing is another process characteristic related to effectiveness. Communication and cooperation within the work group also contributes to effectiveness. Collectively, the right amount of these process characteristics contributes to cohesiveness, or a group that pulls together. Without cohesiveness, a group will fail to achieve synergy.
8. *Follows processes and procedures.* Teams that can be trusted to follow work processes and procedures tend to perform better. Adhering to such processes and procedures is also associated with high-quality output. Although following processes and procedures might appear to be a routine expectation, many problems are created by workers who fail to do so. For example, a group might show a productivity dip if workers on a project fail to back up computer files and a computer virus or worm attacks.
9. *Familiarity with jobs, coworkers, and the environment.* Another important set of factors related to work group effectiveness is familiarity. It refers to the specific knowledge group members have of their jobs, coworkers, and the environment. Familiarity essentially refers to experience, and for many types of job experience—at least to the point of proficiency—is an asset. The contribution

---

21 Murray R. Barrick et al., "Relating Member Ability and Personality to Work-Team Processes and Team Effectiveness," *Journal of Applied Psychology*, June 1998, pp. 377–391.

22 Vanessa Urch Druskat and Steven B. Wolff, "Building the Emotional Intelligence of Groups," *Harvard Business Review*, March 2001, pp. 80–90.

23 Claus W. Langred, "Too Much of a Good Thing? Negative Effects of High Trust and Individual Autonomy in Self-Managing Work Teams," *Academy of Management Journal*, June 2004, pp. 385–399.

of familiarity is evident also when new members join an athletic team. Quite often the team loses momentum during the adjustment period.

Effective leadership should supplement the characteristics of an effective work group. Team leaders must emphasize coaching more than controlling. The group as an entity should be coached, not only individual members. An example would talking with the group about communicating more freely with each other. Frederick P. Morgeson, in a study conducted in three organizations, found that supportive coaching was associated with being perceived as effective by team members. However, coaching in the form of the manager jumping in with suggestions was associated with effectiveness when the team was facing an urgent problem.[24]

Effective work groups are found in most successful organizations, and many of these groups have all nine major characteristics in place. An example of a highly effective work team is the group of engineers and designers that developed the RAZR, the cell phone that revived Motorola to become a stylish technology powerhouse. The highly cohesive group conducted their work in an exurban (nice setting beyond the suburbs) setting, an hour's drive from company headquarters. The challenge facing the group was to create the thinnest phone ever released, and to do it in one year. Top-management gave the team all the staff and money necessary to develop the stylish new phone. Conflict in the group was typically over design and engineering issues rather than personalities. The RAZR was ready for production later than planned but getting it right was more important than the deadline. Within two years, 50 million RAZRs were shipped and team members were rewarded with a boatload of stock options.[25]

STAGES OF GROUP DEVELOPMENT

Learning Objective 3

Describe the stages of group development.

To understand the nature of work groups, one must understand what the group is doing (the content) and how it proceeds (the process). A key group process is how a group develops over time. To make this information meaningful, relate it to any group to which you belonged for at least one month. Understanding the stages of group development can lead to more effective group leadership or membership. We describe the five group stages next.[26] (See Exhibit 13-4.)

Stage 1: Forming. At the outset, members are eager to learn what tasks they will be performing, how they can benefit from group membership, and what constitutes acceptable behavior. Members often inquire about rules they must follow. Confusion, caution, and being cordial toward each other typically characterize the initial phase of group development.

24 Frederick P. Morgeson, "The External Leadership of Self-Managing Teams: Intervening in the Context of Novel and Disruptive Events," *Journal of Applied Psychology*, May 2005, pp. 497–508.

25 Adam Lashinsky, "Razr's Edge," *Fortune*, June 12, 2006, pp. 124–132.

26 J. Steven Heinen and Eugene Jacobsen, "A Model of Task Group Development in Complex Organizations and a Strategy for Implementation," *Academy of Management Review*, October 1976, pp. 98–111.

exhibit 13-4 The Stages of Group Development

Most groups follow a predictable sequence of stages.

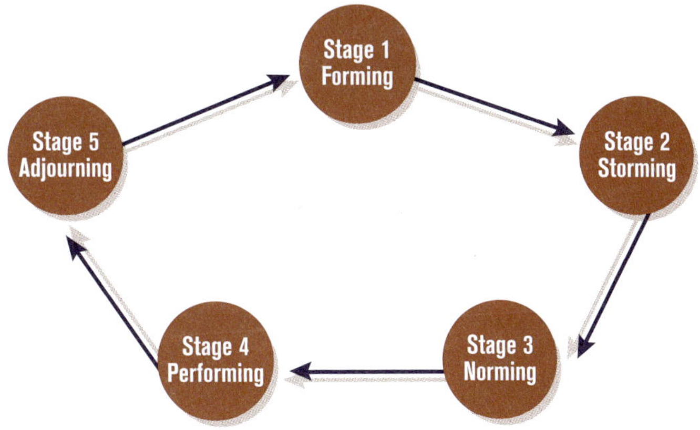

Stage 2: Storming. During this "shakedown" period, individual styles often come into conflict. Hostility, infighting, tension, and confrontation occur at this stage. Members may argue to clarify expectations about their contributions. Coalitions and cliques may form within the group, and one or two members may be targeted for exclusion. Subgroups may form to push an agenda of interest to them. (Despite the frequency of storming, many workplace groups work willingly with one another from the outset, thus skipping Stage 2.)

Stage 3: Norming. Overcoming resistance and establishing group norms (standards of conduct) follow the storm. Cohesiveness and commitment begin to develop. The group starts to come together as a coordinated unit, and harmony prevails. Norms stem from three sources: The group itself quickly establishes limits for members, often by effective use of glares and nods. For example, the team member who responds sarcastically to the group leader's suggestions might receive disapproving glances from other members. Norms may also be imposed that are derived from the larger organization and professional codes, such as that used by accountants and financial planners. A third source of norms might be an influential team member who inspires the group to elevate its performance or behavior. A team member might say, "Why stop at having the best safety record in this division. Let's be number one in the entire company."

Stage 4: Performing. When the group reaches the performing stage, it is ready to focus on accomplishing its key tasks. Issues concerning interpersonal relations and task assignment are put aside as the group becomes a well-functioning unit. Internal motivation and creativity are likely to emerge as the group performs. At their best, members feel they are working "for the cause," much like a political campaign team or a team bringing a breakthrough product to market.

Stage 5: Adjourning. Temporary work groups disband after accomplishing their task. Those same group members, however, developed important relationships and understandings they can take with them should they be part of the same team in the future. The link between adjourning and forming shown in Exhibit 13-4 indicates that many groups do reassemble after one project is completed. The link between Stages 4 and 5 would not apply for a group that disbanded and never worked together again.

Helping the group move past the first three stages into performing poses a key managerial challenge. At times, leaders may need to challenge group members to spend less time on process issues and more time on task—getting the job done!

MANAGERIAL ACTIONS FOR BUILDING TEAMWORK

Learning Objective 4

Summarize managerial actions for building teamwork.

Given the importance of teams, managers may need to invest time in building teamwork. Here we highlight managerial actions and organizational practices that facilitate teamwork.[27] We use the term managerial practices to include team leader practices because many groups and teams do not use the title team leader for the person in charge. A department manager, for example, might be able to build teamwork. Good teamwork enhances, but does not guarantee, a successful team. For example, a group with excellent teamwork might be working on improving a service no longer valued by the company or customers. No matter what the output of the team, it will probably be ignored.

Gordon Bethune, the CEO who helped rebuild Continental Airlines from "worst to first" offers a good starting point for building teamwork. He maintains that the entire team must agree on what constitutes success. Every team member has to say: "Yes, that's it."[28] Another early step is to help team members believe they have an urgent, constructive purpose. A demanding performance challenge helps create and sustain the team. Rewards should stem from meeting the challenge.

Competing against a common enemy is often used to build team spirit. It is preferable that the adversary is external, such as an independent diner competing against franchised family restaurants. A primary strategy for teamwork promotes the attitude that working together effectively is an expected norm. The team leader can communicate the norm of teamwork by making frequent use of words and phrases that support teamwork. Emphasizing the words team members or teammates, and deemphasizing the words subordinates and employees, helps communicate the teamwork norm.

Using the consensus decision-making style provides another way to reinforce teamwork. A sophisticated approach to enhancing teamwork, it feeds team members valid facts and information that motivate them to work together. New information prompts the team to redefine and enrich its understanding of the challenge it is facing, thereby focusing on a common purpose. A subtle yet potent method of building teamwork emphasizes the use of language that fosters cohesion and commitment. In-group jargon bonds a

27 Katzenbach and Smith, "The Discipline of Teams," p. 112; Regina Fazio Maruca (ed.), "Unit of One: What Makes Teams Work?" *Fast Company*, November 2000, pp. 109–14; "Build Teamwork by Showing Employees You Respect Them," *Manager's Edge*, April 2002, p. 1.

28 Shelia M. Puffer, "Continental Airlines' CEO Gordon Bethune on Teams and New Product Development," *Academy of Management Executive*, August 1999, p. 30.

team and sets the group apart from others. For example, a team of computer experts says "Give me a core dump" to mean "Tell me your thoughts."

micromanagement
Supervising group members too closely and second-guessing their decisions.

To foster teamwork, the manager should minimize **micromanagement**, or supervising group members too closely and second-guessing their decisions. Micromanagement can hamper a spirit of teamwork because team members do not feel in control of their own work. Also, morale suffers when the manager is more concerned about the format of a document than its purpose.[29] A high-impact strategy for encouraging teamwork rewards the team as well as individuals. The most convincing team incentive is to calculate compensation partially on the basis of team results. Managers might also apply positive reinforcement whenever the group or individuals engage in behavior that supports teamwork. For example, team members who took the initiative to have an information-sharing session can be singled out and praised for this activity.

The manager can publish a team book containing a one-page biography of each team member. The biography can include a photo, a list of hobbies, personal interests, and family information. As team members look through the book, they become better acquainted with each other, leading to feelings of closeness. An emerging approach to enhancing teamwork is to encourage team members to supplement e-mail communication with phone calls and face-to-face meetings.

Showing respect for team members is a general technique for building teamwork. Respect can be demonstrated in such ways as asking rather than demanding something be done, For example, "Jeremy could you investigate our developing a Web site for the team?" Giving team members your undivided attention when they come to you with a problem is another demonstration of respect. Making positive comments about other team members, and not talking behind their back is another way of showing respect.

Another option available to organizations for enhancing teamwork comes through experiential learning such as sending members to outdoor training. NASA invests two weeks every several years in wilderness training to develop teamwork among astronauts because accomplishing their mission and surviving depends on high-level teamwork.[30] In outdoor training, participants acquire leadership and teamwork skills by confronting physical challenges and exceeding their self-imposed limitations. In rope activities, which are typical of outdoor training, participants attached to a secure pulley with ropes climb ladders and jump off to another spot. Another form of outdoor training for elite teams, a day at an auto-racing track, provides team members with an opportunity to drive at racecar speeds in some kind of cooperative venture. Yet another approach to team building requires the group to prepare a seven-course meal. All of these challenges require teamwork rather than individual effort, hence their contribution to team development.

Building teamwork within a virtual team creates additional challenges because members rarely meet face-to-face thereby having less opportunity to build the chemistry often found within traditional teams. A study involving

29 Jared Sandberg, "Bosses Who Fiddle With Employees' Work Risk Ire, Low Morale," *The Wall Street Journal*, April 25, 2006, p. B1.
30 Robert Levine, "The New Right Stuff," *Fortune*, June 12, 2006, pp. 116–118.

15 European and U.S. multinational companies observed that certain factors helped build teamwork in virtual teams. Several of the success factors are as follows: First, invest in an online resource where team members can readily learn about each other. Second, to capitalize on familiarity, choose a few team members who have worked together previously. Third, create an online site where team members can exchange ideas, collaborate, and encourage and inspire each other. Fourth, when establishing the team, rely on volunteers as much as possible. Volunteers are more likely to enjoy being virtual team members, and will therefore be willing to cooperate with each other.[31]

Outdoor training generally offers the most favorable outcomes when the trainer helps the team members comprehend the link between such training and on-the-job behavior. Reviewing what has been learned is a key step in this direction. Still, the manager should not impose outdoor training on the growing number of workers who dislike the idea or fear bodily damage. Also, dissent is growing about outdoor activities that require athletic ability because less physically capable team members feel excluded.[32]

Effective managers pick and choose from strategies as appropriate to build teamwork. Relying too heavily on one tactic, such as establishing a mission statement or outdoor training, limits the development of sustained teamwork.

BEING AN EFFECTIVE TEAM PLAYER

Learning Objective 5

Explain the actions and attitudes of effective team players.

Being an effective team player makes collaborative effort possible. Being an effective team player also affects managerial perceptions because they value such behavior among employees and job applicants. Here we describe a number of skills, actions, and attitudes contributing to effective team play. For convenience, five are classified as task-related, and five as people-related. In reviewing these attributes, remember that all team situations do not have identical requirements.

Task-Related Actions and Attitudes

Task-related actions and attitudes focus on group or teamwork goals rather than on interpersonal relationships. An effective team player is likely to behave and think in the following ways:

1. *Possesses and shares technical expertise.* Most people are chosen to join a particular work team on the basis of their technical or functional expertise. Glenn Parker believes that using technical expertise to outstanding advantage requires a willingness and ability to share that expertise. It is also necessary for the technical expert to be able to communicate with team members in other disciplines who lack the same technical background.[33]

31 Lynda Gratton, "Working Together...When Apart," *The Wall Street Journal*, June 16–17, 2007, p. R4.

32 Duff McDonald, "Why We All Hate Offsites," *Business 2.0*, May 2006, p. 79; Jared Sandberg, "Can Spending a Day Stuck to a Velcro Wall Help Build a Team?" *The Wall Street Journal*, December 26, 2006, p. B1.

33 Glenn M. Parker, *Cross-Functional Teams: Working with Allies, Enemies, & Other Strangers* (San Francisco: Jossey-Bass Publishers, 1994), p. 3.

2. *Assumes responsibility for problems.* The outstanding team player assumes responsibility for problems. If he or she notices a free-floating problem (not yet assigned to a specific person), the team member says, "I'll do it." The task should be one suited for independent rather than coordinated activity, such as conducting research.
3. *Is willing to commit to team goals.* The exceptional team player will commit to team goals even if his or her personal goals cannot be achieved for now. For instance, the team member seeking visibility will be enthusiastic about pursuing team goals even if not much visibility will be gained.
4. *Is able to see the big picture.* As described in Chapter 1, a basic management skill is to think conceptually. Exceptionally good team players exhibit this same skill. In team efforts, discussion can get bogged down in small details. As a result, the team might temporarily lose sight of what it is trying to accomplish. The team player (or team leader) who can help the group focus on its broader purpose plays a vital role.
5. *Is willing to ask tough questions.* A **tough question** helps the group achieve insight into the nature of the problem it faces, what it might be doing wrong, and whether progress is sufficient. Tough questions can also be asked to help the group see the big picture. Asking tough questions helps the group avoid groupthink. Here is a representative tough question asked by a team member: "I've been to all our meetings so far. What specifically have we accomplished?"
6. *Is willing to try something new.* An effective team player experiments with new ideas even if the old method works relatively well. Trying something new leads to a spirit of inventiveness that helps keep the group vibrant. In one of the Harley-Davidson work teams, several of the workers designed a device to guide the brush in painting Harley's trademark striping. Although the more experienced manufacturing technicians had been successful with the hand-painting method, in the spirit of teamwork they were willing to try the new technique.

tough question
A question that helps the group achieve insight into the nature of the problem, what it might be doing wrong, and whether progress is sufficient.

People-Related Actions and Attitudes

Outstanding team players cultivate a conscious awareness of their interpersonal relations within the group. They recognize that effective interpersonal relationships are important for task accomplishment. An outstanding team player is likely to do or think the following:

1. *Trust team members.* The cornerstone attitude of the outstanding team player is to trust team members. If you do not believe that the other team members have your best interests at heart, it will be difficult to share opinions and ideas. Trusting team members includes believing that their ideas are technically sound and rational until proven otherwise. Another manifestation of trust is taking a risk by trying out a team member's unproven ideas. (As cautioned above, however, do not trust teammates to the point that you never monitor their work.)

2. *Share credit.* A not-to-be-overlooked tactic for emphasizing teamwork is to share credit for your accomplishments with the team. Sharing credit is authentic because other members of the team usually have contributed to the success of a project. Related to sharing credit, Steve Covey, best-selling author and consultant, says that teamwork is fostered when you don't worry about who gets the credit.[34] To the strong team player, getting the group task accomplished is more important than receiving individual recognition.
3. *Recognize the interests and achievements of others.* A fundamental tactic for establishing yourself as a solid team player is to recognize the interests and achievements of others. Let others know that you care about their interests by such means as asking, "How do my ideas fit into what you have planned?" Recognizing the achievements of others can be done by complimenting their tangible accomplishments.
4. *Listen actively and share information.* The skilled team player listens actively both inside and outside of meetings. An active listener strives to grasp both the facts and feelings behind what is being said. Information sharing helps other team members do their job well and also communicates concern for their welfare. Information sharing can take many forms, such as bringing in news clips and magazine articles, sending teammates links to useful Web sites, and recommending relevant books.
5. *Give and receive criticism.* The strong team player offers constructive criticism when needed, but does so diplomatically. A high-performance team demands sincere and tactful criticism among members. In addition to criticizing others in a helpful manner, the strong team player benefits from criticism directed toward him or her. A high-performing team involves give and take, including criticism of each other's ideas. The willingness to accept constructive criticism is often referred to as self-awareness. The self-aware team player insightfully processes personal feedback to improve effectiveness.
6. *Don't rain on another team member's parade.* Pointing out the flaws in another person's accomplishments, or drawing attention to your own achievements when somebody else is receiving credit, creates disharmony within the group. When a teammate is in the spotlight, allow him or her to enjoy the moment without displaying petty jealousy.

POTENTIAL CONTRIBUTIONS AND PROBLEMS OF TEAMS AND GROUPS

Learning Objective 6

Point to the potential contributions and problems of teams and groups.

Given that teams and groups are such an integral part of how organizations function, it is easy not to look critically at their contribution. However, researchers, writers, and managerial workers themselves assess the contributions of groups, both the upside and downside, especially with teams.

34 Steven Covey, "Team Up for a Superstar Office," *USA Weekend*, September 4–6, 1998, p. 10.

Potential Contributions of Teams and Groups

Teams and groups make a contribution to the extent that they produce results beyond what could be achieved without a high degree of collaboration among workers. Considerable case history evidence supports the contribution of teams over independent effort. The previous discussion of self-managed work teams presented examples of this evidence. Another perspective on the importance of teams is **lift-outs**—the practice of recruiting an entire high-functioning team from another organization. The company doing the recruiting believes that the team is more important for attaining its goals than an individual star. It is also believed that the recruited team can get up to speed rapidly in the new setting. An imported team might also help the company enter a new market or line of business quickly.[35]

lift-outs (in relation to teams) The practice of recruiting an entire high-functioning team from another organization.

Lift-outs have been frequent in such industries as financial services, law, and information technology. Now professional services firms, such as management consulting and accounting firms are hiring more teams. Despite the increase in lift-outs, the concept can raise legal issues and might be considered unethical. Is it fair to decimate a competitor by hiring one of its key teams? Or, is it just part of competitive business?

Teams tend to be the most useful as a form of organization under the following conditions:[36]

- When work processes cut across functional lines (as in new-product development)
- When speed is important (keeping the number of team meetings to a minimum)
- When the organization faces a complex and rapidly changing environment (as in developing toys and video games for the next holiday season)
- When innovation and learning have high priority (entering a new market or field)
- When the tasks to be accomplished require integration of highly interdependent performers (gathering inputs for a strategic plan).

When these conditions do not exist, the organization is better off assigning the task to more traditional groups, or to individuals working alone. Remember that a team is essentially a supergroup.

Potential Problems of Teams and Groups

Although the collaborative workplace enjoys popularity, many concerns accompany the use of teams and groups. In Chapter 5, discussing problem solving and decision making, we described two problems with groups: time

---

35 Boris Groysberg and Robin Abrahams, "Lift Outs: How to Acquire a High-Functioning Team," *Harvard Business Review*, December 2006, pp. 133–140; Jena McGregor, "I Can't Believe They Took the Whole Team," *Business Week*, December 18, 2006, pp. 120–122.

36 Russ Forrester and Allan B. Drexler, "A Model for Team-Based Performance," *Academy of Management Executive*, August 1999, p. 47.

group polarization
A situation in which post-discussion attitudes tend to be more extreme than pre-discussion attitudes.

social loafing
Freeloading, or shirking individual responsibility, when a person is placed in a group setting and removed from individual accountability.

wasting and groupthink. Here we look at other problems: group polarization, social loafing, limited accountability, and career retardation.

Group Polarization

During group problem solving, or group discussion in general, members often shift their attitudes. Sometimes the group moves toward taking greater risks, called the risky shift. At other times the group moves toward a more conservative position. The general term for moving in either direction is **group polarization**, a situation in which post-discussion attitudes tend to be more extreme than pre-discussion attitudes.[37] For example, as a result of group discussion members of an executive team become more cautious about entering a new market.

Group discussion facilitates polarization for several reasons. Discovering that others share our opinions may reinforce and strengthen our position. Listening to persuasive arguments may also strengthen our convictions. The "devil-made-me-do-it" attitude is another contributor to polarization. If responsibility is diffused, a person will feel less responsible—and guilty—about taking an extreme position.

Group polarization has a practical implication for managers who rely on group decision making. Workers who enter into group decision making with a stand on an issue may develop more extreme post-decision positions. For example, a team of employees who were seeking more generous benefits may decide as a group that the company should become an industry leader in employee benefits.

Social Loafing

An unfortunate by-product of group and team effort happens when an under-motivated person squeezes by without contributing a fair share. **Social loafing** is freeloading, or shirking individual responsibility, when a person is placed in a group setting and removed from individual accountability. Readers who have worked on group projects for courses may have encountered this widely observed dysfunction of collective effort.

Two motivational explanations of social loafing have been offered. First, some people believe that because they are part of a team, they can "hide in the crowd." Second, group members typically believe that others are likely to withhold effort when working in a group. As a consequence they withhold effort themselves to avoid being played for a sucker.

As one approach to minimizing the effects of social loafing, a manager may ask group members to contribute to the evaluation of each other. Concerns about being evaluated as a freeloader by peers would prompt some people to work harder.

Limited Accountability

A curious problem about workplace teams is that they are often given credit for accomplishment, but they rarely blamed for failures. Instead, individual

37 Gregory Moorhead and Ricky W. Griffin, *Organizational Behavior: Managing People and Organizations*, 4th ed. (Boston: Houghton Mifflin, 1995), pp. 52–62.

team members are blamed for team failures, and group escapes the blame. Support for this argument comes from two complicated studies involving graduate business students who were assigned to a variety of group task, and had the opportunity to assign credit and blame after the tasks were completed.

Another way of interpreting these results is that teams develop a positive halo, and they are perceived as being able to attain high performance.[38] So when the team does fail, observers (including the manager) look for individuals to blame.

Career Retardation

A final concern about teams arises from focusing too much on group or team effort, rather than individual effort, which can retard a person's career. Some managers classify workers as team players versus leaders. (The perception is somewhat misleading because most effective leaders and managers are also good team players.) Yet it is true that a person who tries too hard to be a good team player might become a conformist and not seek individual recognition. People who do break away from the team and become higher-level managers are typically those known for independent thought and outstanding accomplishment.

For those who want to advance beyond being a team member, or team leader, it is important to be recognized for outstanding performance. As a team member, for example, volunteer to take on leadership roles such as chairing a team meeting or coordinating a special project. Bring a dossier of your individual accomplishments to your performance review. Every team has a most valuable player (MVP) who is still a good team player.

RESOLVING CONFLICT WITHIN TEAMS AND GROUPS

Learning Objective 7

Describe the positive and negative aspects of conflict and how team leaders and managers can resolve conflict.

Although harmony and collaboration are an important goal of groups and teams, some disagreement and dispute is inevitable. **Conflict** is the simultaneous arousal of two or more incompatible motives. It is often accompanied by tension and frustration. Whenever two or more people in the group compete for the same resource, conflict occurs. Two team members, for example, might both want to take the team's one allocated seat on the corporate jet on business trips they are taking on the same day. Conflict can also be considered a hostile or antagonistic relationship between two people.

conflict
The simultaneous arousal of two or more incompatible motives.

Another reason conflict often occurs in groups is the existence of different factions within a group, often because group members are from different units within the company. Also, after a merger of acquisition various groups may be composed of people from the acquired company and the company that made the acquisition.[39] A purpose of the group might be

38 Charles E. Naquin and Renee O. Tynan, "The Team Halo Effect: Why Teams Are Not Blamed for Their Failures," *Journal of Applied Psychology*, April 2003, pp. 332–340.

39 Jiato Li and Donald C. Hambrick, "Factional Groups: A New Vantage on Demographic Faultlines, Conflict, and Disintegration in Work Teams," *Academy of Management Journal*, October 2005, p. 794.

task conflict Conflict that focuses on substantive, issue-related differences, related to the work itself.

relationship conflict Conflict that focuses on personalized, individually oriented issues.

to help smooth the integration of two large firms such as Procter & Gamble and Gillette.

Here we look at three aspects of conflict particularly relevant to managers and team leaders of small groups: task versus relationship conflict, consequences of conflict, and methods of conflict resolution.

Task Versus Relationship Conflict

Some conflicts within the group deal mostly with disagreements over how work should be done. They are referred to as task or *cognitive* conflicts because they deal mostly with the work itself rather than emotions and relationships. Two group members, for example, might argue over whether it is better to use their limited advertising budget to buy space on the outside of a bus versus on the Internet. **Task conflict** focuses on substantive, issue-related differences, related to the work itself. These issues are tangible and concrete and can be deal with more intellectually than emotionally.

Other conflicts within the group are more people-oriented. They occur because people have personality clashes, are rude to each other, or simply view many problems and situations from a different frame of reference. **Relationship conflict** focuses on personalized, individually oriented issues. The conflict relates to subjective issues that are dealt with more emotionally than intellectually.[40] One symptom that relationship conflict exists within the group is when, during a meeting, two people say to each other frequently, "Please let me finish. I'm still speaking."

Task conflict in moderate doses can be functional because it requires teams to engage in activities that foster team effectiveness. Team members engaged in moderate task conflict would critically examine alternative solutions and incorporate different points of view into their goals or mission statement. Because frank communication and different points of view are encouraged, task conflict can encourage innovative thinking. In contrast, relationship (or affective) conflict undermines group effectiveness by blocking constructive activities and processes. By such means as directing anger toward individuals and blaming each other for mistakes, relationship conflict leads to cynicism and distrust.

An analysis of many studies cautions that both task conflict and relationship conflict can be equally disruptive. A little conflict may be beneficial, but this advantage quickly breaks down as conflict intensifies.[41] The underlying explanation is that most people take differences of opinion personally whether the issue is strictly the task, or their personal characteristics.

40 Allen C. Amason, Wayne A. Hockwater, Kenneth R. Thompson, and Allison W. Harrison, "Conflict: An Important Dimension in Successful Management Teams," *Organizational Dynamics*, Autumn 1995, pp. 2–30; Carsten K. W. De Dreu and Laurie R. Weingart, "Task Versus Relationship Conflict, Team Performance, and Team Member Satisfaction: A Meta-Analysis," *Journal of Applied Psychology*, August 2003, pp. 741–749.

41 De Dreu and Weingart, "Task Versus Relationship Conflict," p. 746.

Consequences of Conflict

Conflict results in both positive and negative consequences. The right amount of conflict may enhance job performance, but too much or too little conflict lowers performance. If the manager observes that job performance is suffering because of too much conflict, he or she should reduce it. If performance is low because employees are too placid, the manager might profitably increase conflict. For example, the manager might establish a prize for top performance in the group.

Positive Consequences of Conflict

Many managers and scholars believe that job conflict can have positive consequences. The right amount of conflict is usually quite low—somewhat like fat in your diet. Because a touch of conflict is beneficial, it is dysfunctional for a team to fear conflict.[42] With the right amount of conflict in the workplace, one or more of the following outcomes can be anticipated.

1. *Increased creativity.* Talents and abilities surface in response to conflict. People become inventive when they are placed in intense competition with others.
2. *Increased effort.* Constructive amounts of conflict spur people to new heights of performance. People become so motivated to win the conflict that they may surprise themselves and their superiors with their work output.
3. *Increased diagnostic information.* Conflict can provide valuable information about problem areas in the department or organization. When leaders learn of conflict, they may conduct investigations that will lead to the prevention of similar problems.
4. *Increased group cohesion.* When one group in a firm is in conflict with another, group members may become more cohesive. They perceive themselves to be facing a common enemy.

Negative Consequences of Conflict

When the wrong amount or type of conflict exists, job performance may suffer. Some types of conflict have worse consequences than others. A particularly bad form of conflict is one that forces a person to choose between two undesirable alternatives. Negative consequences of conflict include the following:

1. *Poor physical and mental health.* Intense conflict is a source of stress. A person under prolonged and intense conflict may suffer stress-related disorders. Many acts of workplace violence stems from highly stressed employees or ex-employees who experienced conflict with supervisors or coworkers.
2. *Wasted resources.* Employees and groups in conflict frequently waste time, money, and other resources while fighting their battles. One executive

42 Patrick M. Lencioni, *The Five Dysfunctions of a Team* (San Francisco: Jossey-Bass, 2002).

took a personal dislike to one of his managers and therefore ignored his cost-saving recommendations.

3. *Sidetracked goals.* In extreme forms of conflict, the parties involved may neglect the pursuit of important goals. Instead, they focus on winning their conflicts. A goal displacement of this type took place within an information technology group. The rival factions spent so much time squabbling over which new hardware and software to purchase that they neglected some of their tasks.
4. *Heightened self-interest.* Conflict within the group often results in extreme demonstrations of self-interest at the expense of the group and the larger organization. Individuals or groups place their personal interests over those of the rest of the firm or customers. One common result of this type of self-interest is hogging resources. A team member might attempt to convince the team leader to place him on an important customer trouble-shooting assignment even though he knows his rival on the team is better qualified.

Methods of Conflict Resolution

Managers spend as much as 20 percent of their work time dealing with conflict. A leader who learns to manage conflict effectively can increase his or her productivity. In addition, being able to resolve conflict enhances one's stature as a leader. Employees expect their boss to be able to resolve conflicts. Here we describe the five basic styles or methods of resolving conflict: forcing, accommodation, sharing, collaboration, and avoiding. An effective manager will choose the best approach for the situation.

Forcing

The forcing, or competitive, style is based on the desire to win one's own concerns at the expense of the other party, or to dominate. Autocratic leaders such as Al Dunlap, formerly of Scott Paper and Sunbeam Corp., chose to resolve conflict in this way. Dunlap's bullying style of resolving conflict, combined with his extensive job cutting, led many employees to cheer when he was fired as CEO of Sunbeam. A person with a forcing style is likely to engage in win-lose ("I win, you lose") power struggles, resulting in poor teamwork. Steve Jobs, the legendary leader of Apple Inc., also relies on forcing to resolve conflict such as in questions about design issues.

Accommodation

The accommodative style favors appeasement, or satisfying the other's concerns without taking care of one's own. People with this orientation may be generous or self-sacrificing just to maintain a relationship. An irate customer might be accommodated with a full refund "just to shut him (or her) up." The intent of such accommodation might also be to retain the customer's loyalty.

Sharing

The sharing style is midway between domination and appeasement. Sharers prefer moderate but incomplete satisfaction for both parties. The result is compromise. The term *splitting the difference* reflects this orientation. The sharing style of conflict resolution is commonly used in such activities as purchasing a house or car. Within the work group, sharing might take the form of each team member receiving the same percentage salary increase rather than haggle over dividing the pool of money available for increases.

Collaboration

In contrast to the sharing style, collaboration reflects an interest in fully satisfying the desire of both parties. It is based on an underlying win-win philosophy, the belief that after conflict has been resolved both sides should gain something of value. For example, a small-company president might offer the management team more stock options if they are willing to take a pay cut to help the firm through rough times. If the firm succeeds, both parties have scored a victory.

All parties benefit from collaboration, or a win-win approach to resolving conflict. In addition, compliance with the solution occurs readily, and the relationship between those in conflict improves.

A conflict-resolution technique built into the collaboration style is *confrontation and problem solving*. Its purpose is to identify the real problem and then arrive at a solution that genuinely solves it. First the parties are brought together and the real problem is confronted.

Another collaborative approach involves asking what action can break an impasse. When a conflict reaches a point where progress has reached a standstill, one of the parties asks, "What would you like me to do?" The other side often reacts with astonishment and then the first party asks, "If I could do anything to make this situation okay in your eyes, what would that be?"[43] Frequently the desired action—such as "Treat me with more respect"—can be implemented.

An example of win-win conflict resolution took place between PN Hoffman, a condominium developer and the First Congregational Church of Christ in Washington DC. The developer planned to build 140 condominiums on a street where one of the Washington oldest churches had existed since the end of the Civil War. As part of the deal, PN Hoffman agreed to build a $17 million sanctuary for the church with eight floors of apartments above, along with balconies, a swimming pool, and a fitness center. The church planned to occupy the first two floors and continue serving breakfast and dinner to several hundred homeless people. A PN manager said he recognized that some home buyers might not care to live above a homeless service center, but other potential buyers would be "fully aware of the urban lifestyle."[44] PN Hoffman won because they could

43 James A. Autry, *Love & Profit* (New York: Morrow, 1991).

44 Paul Schwartzman, "Million-Dollar Condos with a Soup Kitchen Below," *Washington Post*, http://www.washingtonpost.com, December 27, 2006.

go ahead with their development, and the Church won because it could still function intact and add a new sanctuary. Was this an example of conflict resolution made in heaven?

Avoiding

The avoider combines uncooperativeness and unassertiveness. He or she is indifferent to the concerns of either party. The person may actually be withdrawing from conflict or relying upon fate. Managers sometimes use the avoiding style to stay out of a conflict between team members. The members are left to resolve their own differences.

Experience and research suggest that the cooperative approaches to resolving conflict (sharing and collaboration) work more effectively than the competitive approaches (forcing and accommodation). For example, a study conducted with 61 self-managing teams involved 489 employees from the production department of a leading electronics manufacturer. A cooperative (focus on mutual benefits or win-win) approach to conflict resolution led to confidence in skills for dealing with conflict. The heightened confidence in dealing with conflict, in turn, led to more effective performance as evaluated by managers.[45]

Resolving Conflicts Between Two Group Members

A high-level managerial skill is to help two or more group members resolve conflict between or among them. Much of the time a manager invests in conflict resolution is geared toward assisting others resolve their conflict. The most useful approach is to get the parties in conflict to engage in confrontation and problem solving. The manager sits down with the two sides, and encourages them to talk to each other about the problem, not talk directly to him or her. This approach is preferable to inviting each side to speak with the manager alone, because it encourages each side to attempt to convince the manager that he or she is right. An abbreviated example follows:

Manager: I've brought you two together to see if you can overcome the problems you have about sharing the workload during a period in which one of you is overloaded.

Melissa: I'm glad you did, Luke never wants to help me, even when I'm drowning in customer requests.

Luke: I would be glad to help Melissa, if she ever agreed to help me. If she has any downtime, she runs to the break room so she can chat on her cell phone.

Melissa: Look who's talking. I have seen you napping in your SUV when you have a little down time.

Manager: I'm beginning to see what's going on here. Both of you are antagonistic toward each other, and look for little faults to pick. With a little more respect on both sides, I think you would be more willing to help each other out.

---

45 Steve Alper, Dean Tjosvold, and Kenneth S. Law, "Conflict Management, Efficacy, and Performance in Organizational Teams," *Personnel Psychology*, Autumn 2000, pp. 625–642.

Luke: Actually, Melissa's not too bad. And I know she can perform well when she wants to. Next time I see her needing help, I'll pitch in.

Melissa: I know that the name "Luke" can sound like a tough guy, but our Luke really has a warm heart. I'm open to starting with a fresh slate. Maybe Luke can ask me politely the next time he needs help.

Conflict specialist Patrick S. Nugent believes that being able to intervene in the conflicts of group members is a management skill that grows in importance. Such competencies are useful in an emerging form of management based less on traditional hierarchy and more on developing self-managing subordinates and teams.[46]

46 Patrick S. Nugent, "Managing Conflict: Third-Party Interventions for Managers," *Academy of Management Executive*, February 2002, p. 152.

SUMMARY OF Key Points

1 Identify various types of teams and groups, including self-managed work teams and project groups.

Formal groups are deliberately formed by the organization, whereas informal groups emerge over time through worker interaction. Representative types of work teams include self-managed work teams, project teams, task forces, cross-functional teams, crews, top-management teams, and virtual teams.

2 Describe the characteristics of effective groups and teams.

Effective work group characteristics are well documented. Member jobs are enriched, and workers feel empowered to solve problems. Group members operate interdependently in terms of tasks and rewards. Culturally diverse members enjoy task and social interaction. The right size of the group as well as the intelligence and personality of group members and the emotional intelligence of the group as a whole are all crucial factors. The work group requires good support from management. Effective group processes include team spirit, workload sharing, and communication and cooperation. Following work processes and procedures also aids effectiveness, as does familiarity with jobs and coworkers.

3 Describe the stages of group development.

Groups usually go through predictable stages: forming, storming, norming, performing, and adjourning. A key managerial challenge is to get the group to the performing stage.

4 Summarize managerial actions for building teamwork.

Managers and leaders can enhance teamwork through many behaviors, attitudes, and organizational actions, including the following: get agreement on what success means for the group; give the team an urgent, constructive purpose; compete against a common adversary; use a consensus decision-making style; use in-group jargon; minimize micromanagement; keep the group small; create physical structures for interaction including idea sharing by computer; reward the team as well as individuals; publish a team book with details about members; supplement e-mail with conversations; give special consideration to building teamwork in a virtual team; and support outdoor training but with caution about dislike for the process and possible physical injuries.

5 Explain the actions and attitudes of an effective team player.

Task-related actions and attitudes of effective team players include: sharing technical expertise; assuming responsibility for problems; committing to team goals; seeing the big picture; asking tough questions; and trying something new. People-related actions and attitudes include trusting team members; sharing credit; recognizing others; listening and information sharing; giving and receiving criticism; and not downplaying the success of others.

6 Point to the potential contributions and problems of teams and groups.

Teams and groups make a contribution when they lead to results that could not be achieved without collaboration. Evidence indicates that collective effort leads to enhanced productivity.

Lift-outs of competitive teams suggests that teams are productive. Groups and teams also have potential problems. Group polarization (taking extreme positions) may occur, and members may engage in social loafing (freeloading). Groups too often escape blame for their mistakes, with individuals being blamed instead. Also, focusing too much on group or team effort instead of attaining individual recognition can retard a person's career.

7 Describe the positive and negative aspects of conflict and how team leaders and managers can resolve conflict.

Although harmony and collaboration are important goals of groups and teams, some conflict is inevitable. Task or cognitive conflict focuses on substantive, issue-related differences. Relationship or affective conflict focuses on personalized, individually oriented issues that are dealt with more emotionally than intellectually. Task conflict in small doses leads to such positive outcomes as creative problem solving. Positive consequences of conflict also include increased effort, obtaining diagnostic information, and increased group cohesion. Negative consequences of conflict include wasting resources and heightened self-interest.

Five major modes of conflict management have been identified: forcing, accommodation, sharing, collaboration, and avoiding. Each style is based on a combination of satisfying one's own concerns (assertiveness) and satisfying the concerns of others (cooperativeness). Confrontation and problem solving is a widely applicable collaborative technique of resolving conflict. Managers often need to resolve conflict between and among group members, with confrontation and problem solving being useful.

KEY TERMS AND PHRASES

Group, 445
Team, 445
Teamwork, 446
Formal group, 446
Informal group, 447
Self-managed work team, 447
Project team, 449
Task force, 450
Cross-functional team, 450
Crew, 452
Virtual team, 453
Micromanagement, 461
Tough question, 463
Lift-outs (in relation to teams), 465
Group polarization, 466
Social loafing, 466
Conflict, 467
Task conflict, 468
Relationship conflict, 468

QUESTIONS

1. In what way is participating on a sports team, musical band, or orchestra good preparation for being a member of a work group on the job?
2. Why is experience working on a cross-functional team particularly valuable for a person who aspires to a career in management?
3. In what ways is being a member of a virtual team much like being a telecommuter?
4. In what way does the position of a project manager resemble that of a general manager, including a CEO?
5. Give an example of a tough question a manager might ask a team.
6. Provide two examples of interdependent (or collaborative) tasks in the workplace for which teams are well suited.
7. Describe an example of conflict you have witnessed as a team member, at work, for a class project, or a sports team. How might this conflict have been resolved?

SKILL-BUILDING EXERCISE 13-A: Housing for the Homeless

Organize the class into teams of about six people. Each team takes on the assignment of formulating plans for building temporary shelters for the homeless. The task will take about one hour and can be done inside or outside of class. The dwellings you plan to build, for example, might be two-room cottages with electricity and indoor plumbing. During the time allotted to the task, formulate plans for going ahead with Housing for the Homeless. Consider dividing up work by assigning certain roles to each team member. Sketch out tentative answers to the following questions:

1. How will you obtain funding for your venture?
2. Which homeless people will you help?
3. Where will your shelters be located?
4. Who will do the actual construction?

After your plan is completed, evaluate the quality of the teamwork that took place within the group. Specify which teamwork skills were evident and which ones did not surface. Search the chapter for techniques you might use to improve teamwork. The skills used to accomplish the house-for-the-homeless task could relate to the team skills presented in Self-Assessment Quiz 13–1 or some team skill not mentioned in this chapter. Here is a sampling of the many different skills that might be relevant in this exercise:

- ☐ Speaks effectively
- ☐ Listens to others
- ☐ Innovates solutions to problems
- ☐ Thinks outside the box
- ☐ Displays a high level of cooperation and collaboration
- ☐ Provides knowledge of the task
- ☐ Sees the big picture
- ☐ Focuses on deadlines

SKILL-BUILDING EXERCISE 13-B: The Scavenger Hunt

The class organizes into groups to conduct a 35-minute scavenger hunt on school premises. Your instructor might give you five items to scavenge, or you might use the following list. The group must return in 35-minutes with as much of the task accomplished as possible. All groups that return with the five items are winners. During debriefing session, answer these two questions: (1) What did we learn about teamwork? (2) Which personal characteristics of the team members contributed to the success, or failure, of the group.

Possible Items for Your Scavenger Hunt

1. A roll of dental floss.
2. A fountain pen.
3. A man's tie.
4. A book with "group" or "teamwork" in the title.
5. A piece of wood (but not ripped off furniture or the like).

INTERNET SKILL-BUILDING EXERCISE: Productivity of Teams and Groups

The U.S. Department of Labor regularly publishes information about the productivity of workers. Yet there is much less information published about the productivity of teams and work groups. Conduct an Internet search to find two sources of information on team or workgroup productivity. You might begin by consulting the U.S. Department of Labor, Bureau of Labor Statistics Web site (http://www.bls.gov) but you will most likely have to search further. Compare your findings with those of a few classmates. If you cannot find any evidence about group productivity in general, at least find a case history of any successful work group.

Case Problem 13-A

The Adam Aircraft Work Group/Team

Joe Wilding scanned the skies over Oshkosh, Wisconsin, looking for the A700 jet aircraft he'd help build. Wilding and his colleagues at Adam Aircraft had decided just six weeks earlier to sprint and finish their plan in time for Oshkosh's big summer air show.

In the aviation world, the A700's appearance would be one of the biggest surprise debuts ever. No one at the Oshkosh show expected Adam Aircraft Industry, a Colorado startup, to arrive with its jet. The company had announced the aircraft—its second product—only a year ago.

The plane had taken to the skies for its inaugural test flight just four days before. It had flown for a grand total of 15 hours since then, and was still a work in progress. The cabin wasn't pressurized, so the pilots had to wear oxygen masks in the cockpit. There were no seats or carpeting in the cabin. The landing gear stayed down, since the hydraulic system to retract it hadn't been installed yet.

Adam Aircraft's A700 was just one entrant in a race to build the first of a new generation of small jets. Also called "light business jets" or "personal jets," these planes hold fewer than eight passengers. They use newer, more fuel-efficient turbofan engineers to slash the operating costs of the current generation of gas-guzzling private planes. The A700 costs about $2.25 million, less than half many planes bought for personal use.

At a banquet dinner, Rick Adam had batted the idea around with a few of his employees: What if they tried to finish the A700 in time for a cameo at the air show at Oshkosh? Adam felt good about the company's momentum. Earlier in his career, he had been chief information officer at Goldman Sachs, and then started a software company, New Era of Networks. As a Captain in the U.S. Air Force, Adam had worked on the mission-control computers for lunar missions 8 through 14.

When Adam returned to his office the day after the banquet, he called a meeting. "There were about 10 of us," recalled Dennis Olcott, the vice president of design engineering. The question was the feasibility of getting the A700 flying in time for Oshkosh. What would it take? Would be a distraction from getting the A500 (the company's other plane) certified by the FAA?

The conceptual design for the A700 had been completed earlier in the year. In the spring, the team had started building a few random parts for the new plane. But the only pieces that were done by June, says Olcott, were "a lot of wing, most of the pieces for the tail, the landing gear, and one-half the fuselage shell." Only about 15 percent of the plan's exterior was finished.

The group started to give the A700 a green light, and work started immediately. The plane would look like an elongated version of the A500, with twin turbofans on the back of the fuselage, instead of at the front and back of the cabin.

The team was able to move fast because they did almost everything in-house. The engineers and the quality assurance manager sit in one big room at headquarters, with Rick Adam in the middle. In addition, the A700 shared more than 80 percent of its components with its predecessor. The manufacturing department already had experience assembling those parts on the three A500s they had already put together.

The carbon composite construction would make the A700 lighter than jets made from aluminum, but more important Olcott said, it let the team work faster. "We can build our own tools for making exterior panels extremely fast, and change them quickly. Our process takes a week and a half to build a tool. Aluminum tooling is bigger and heavier, and it can take months to have it made. You also wind up with more parts, which have to be riveted together, which takes a long time."

The streamlined process also meant the plan was a vivid presence for the team. "There was visible progress every day, and it was just incredible," Olcott said. "Parts would be glued together, or the plane would be painted, or the engines put on. One day it was standing on its own landing gear."

"Everyone in the whole company knew what out goal was, and everyone chipped in," says Wilding. In the engineering department, there's a large window that overlooks the shop floor. "We could see in an instant what the status was. The airplane itself became the motivator."

A month after the initial A700 meeting, the company's chief test pilot began conducting slow-speed taxi tests. "We've never built an airplane that fast before," says Wilding. "I don't know if anybody's build an airplane that fast before." During the first airborne test of the plane, the electrical generators did not function and had to be fixed the next morning.

Case Problem 13-A

The A700's presence so surprised the crowd at the Oshkosh show that Adam put a sign on the nose asserting that, yes the airplane really did fly to the show from Denver. After the show, the team continued its work, treating the first A700 as a kind of airborne proof-of-concept, using it to make small adjustments to the design before they begin building planes for customers. The A700 received FAA certification in May 2005. Mike Leahy, a chiropractor from Colorado whose patients include Denver Broncos, bought the first plane in November 2005. By May 2006, Adam Aircraft had orders for 350 A700 and A500 twin piston aircraft, valued at more than $700 million.

Management is proud of the finished product, as stated on http://www.adamaircraft.com: "The A700 AdamJet is revolutionizing the value proposition in the Very Light Jet (VLJ) business jet class by delivering exceptional performance and comfort at a fraction of the ownership course. Modern airframe design and materials, coupled with highly efficient turbofan engines, usher in a new era of business jet travel."

Discussion Questions

1. In what way did the speed factor enhance group performance?
2. Which characteristics of an effective work group does the Adam Aircraft team display?
3. In what way might the task of building a personal jet have contributed to being a high-performing work group?

Source: Scott Kirsner, "Some Magnificent Men and their Flying Machines," *Fast Company*, November 2003, pp. 100–108; Kelly Yamanouchi, "Pops Go to Company, Pilot," *DenverPost.com*, November 15, 2005; "Ramping Up," http://www.redcoatpublishing.com/features/f_09_05_Cover.asp; "Adam Aircraft," http://www.compositiesworld.com/hpc/issues, ©2007 Ray Publishing.

Case Problem 13-B

Home Rehab Day at Tymco

Fifteen years ago Maria Cortez was working as a freelance writer of technical manuals for a variety of companies. The manuals supported a number of products including household appliances, alarm systems, lawnmowers, and tractors. Soon Cortez's freelance activity became more than she could handle, so she subcontracted work to one other freelancer, and then another, and then another. Two years later, Cortez founded Tymco, and the firm has grown steadily. The company now provides technical manuals, training and development, and foreign language translation and interpreting.

Tymco now employs 75 full-time employees, as well as about 45 freelancers who help the company with peak loads as well as specialized services. For example, one freelancer translates software into Japanese. Another free-lancer specializes in preparing user guides for digital cameras and digital video cameras.

Cortez recently became concerned that the unit heads and other key personnel in the company were not working particularly well as a team. She explained to Tim Atkins, a training specialist on the staff, "We all work for a company called Tymco, yet we function like independent units and freelancers. I notice that our staff members hardly even have lunch together. I've arranged a couple of group dinners, but other than having a nice meal no team spirit seems to develop.

"I think that if we had better teamwork, our units could help each other. We might even be able to cross-sell better. I'll give you an example. A person in the technical manual group might have an assignment to prepare a manual for an appliance. He or she should immediately mention that Tymco has another group that could do the foreign language translations for the manual. A lot of manuals for U.S. distribution are written in English, Spanish, and French."

Atkins replied, "Look, I've been eager to run a team development activity that has worked well for dozens of companies, and it is so simple. We first designate who you think should be included in the group that requires the most development as a team. You choose one work day for the team building activity. It involves targeting an old house badly in need of repair in a poor neighborhood. Abandoned houses don't count. We need a house with a family living in it. Working with churches in the neighborhood, it's easy to find a suitable house and a family willing to be helped.

"About a week before the team-building date, a handy person and I visit the house to get some idea of the type of work that needs to be done. We then purchase all the needed supplies such as paint, roofing shingles, and wood. We also round up the ladders, paint brushes, and tools. Our team descends on the house about 7 the morning of the rehabilitation.

"On team building day, the group descends on the house and starts the rehab process. Two days is usually needed. If we start the job on Friday, it could be finished on Saturday. In this way the group would receive one day off from work, and the members would contribute one day of their time."

Cortez was so enthused about Atkins' idea that she agreed on the spot on Friday, May 19 as the team building day. She suggested that the day be called Tymco Home Rehab. Cortez made up a list of ten key employees, including her, to participate in the team building activity.

Friday morning at 7, the first of five different cars and trucks filled with Tymco staff members, ladders, tools, and home-building supplies arrived at 47 Blodgett Street. Teena Jones, supervisor of technical manuals, shouted to the group, "We can't get anywhere until we start getting rid of the debris around the house and in the hallway. So let's get shoveling. The dumpster is on the way."

"Grab a few people and do what you want," responded Larry Boudreau, supervisor of technical documentation. "If we don't patch up that torn apart roof first, nothing else will matter. I need two warm bodies who aren't acrophobic [afraid of heights] to help me." Two other staffers agreed to agreed to work with Boudreau, while the seven other staff members including Cortez formed the clean-up brigade.

"Carpentry is my thing," said Mary Benito from translations services. "Let's get out the hammers, saws, nails, and screws and start repairing this broken porch first. I want us to be ready for painting the house by noon tomorrow."

"Do what you want Mary," said Dale Jenkins, a technical training team leader. "I'm good at home plumbing, and the toilets and sinks here are leaking more

Case Problem 13-B

than the Titanic. I need a skill pair of hands to help me. Any volunteer?"

Cortez said, "While you folks are shoveling debris and fixing, I'll run out and get us the food for snacks and lunch, and I'll order pizza for a supper break."

"That's the most sensible idea I've heard today," commented Larry Boudreau.

The Tymco team building participants had supper together at 5 that evening, and went home at 8 to return at 7 the next morning. By 1 p.m., painting the house began will all ten people on the team participating. By 7:30, the house at 47 Blodgett Street was painted. The family, who were staying with neighbors, came by to cheer and weep with joy.

The Tymco team members exchanged smiles, hi-fives, and hugs. "We can all go home now feeling that we've accomplished something really important as a team. And we can come back to the office on Monday morning knowing that we can work well as a team despite a few bumps and bruises."

"Good comment, Mary," said Ian Graham from the technical manual group. "Yet, I'm not so sure that replacing shingles on an old roof has made me a better team player."

Case Questions

1. What evidence was presented in this case that the staff members from different units at Tymco might have become better acquainted with each other.
2. What should Maria Cortez do next to improve the chances that the home rehab day results in genuine team development?
3. What evidence is presented in this case that the home rehab day did give a boost to team spirit?
4. How valid is Graham's comment about replacing shingles having no particular impact on becoming a better team player?

Source: The company described in the above case has chosen to remain anonymous.

chapter 14

Information Technology and e-Commerce

Objectives

After studying this chapter and doing the exercises, you should be able to:

1 Summarize the demands information technology places on the manager's job.

2 Describe positive and negative consequences of information technology for the manager.

3 Discuss the impact of the Internet on customer and other external relationships.

4 Explain the effects of the Internet on internal company operations.

5 Pinpoint factors associated with success in e-commerce.

Jerry Driggs, chief operation officer of Little Earth, took four months one winter to move his business onto the NetSuite system. (The system features a *dashboard*—software that presents corporate information such as sales data and customer service requests on a PC in colorful graphics, similar to an automobile speedometer.) Little Earth sells funky eco-fashion products, such as a handbag made with recycled license plates. Today half of the company's 50 employees use the system to manage their production, sales, and financial operations. "Once you see it is so intuitive, you wonder how we ran the business before," says Driggs.

In fact, Driggs ran the business by the seat of his pants, and it showed. Because the company had no system to measure its production requirements or level of raw materials, much of which came from China, it took about six weeks to make and ship a handbag. And Little Earth constantly struggled with cash problems because Driggs would often buy more trim pieces than he needed. "You used to see dollars sitting on the shelves," he says. Now, using NetSuite, Driggs can monitor his purchase orders and inventory levels, and the system even alerts him when he is running low on closures and other parts. The result: Little Earth has slashed its shipping time to three days. "All those things that used to drive us crazy are literally at out fingertips," says Driggs.[1]

The story about the fashion company CEO relying on dashboard software to help operate his business efficiently illustrates how information technology has become incorporated in the manager's job. This chapter highlights how information technology, including e-commerce, influences the manager's job. Although e-commerce is part of information technology, it is described separately here because of its profound impact on both the manager's job and the conduct of the business. Your present knowledge of information technology, including computers, provides the necessary technical background for understanding this chapter.

INFORMATION TECHNOLOGY AND THE MANAGER'S JOB

Learning Objective 1

Summarize the demands information technology places on the manager's job.

Information technology changes the work methods of workers in a wide variety of jobs. For example, office workers are rarely out of touch with their computers, and associates in auto supply stores use computerized databases to search for the availability of replacement parts. Managerial workers also feel the profound influence of information technology. In this section we look at the heavy demand information technology places on managers, as well as the specific impact of wireless devices.

Increased Demands Placed on Managers

From the perspective of work methods, the landscape of a manager's job looks substantially different. Instead of handing work to an office assistant, the manager now types, sends, and receives his or her own messages, and makes appointments on a palm-sized computer. Our concern here, however, is with the broader implications of the changes created by information technology. Management today must build an organization that constantly transforms itself because information technology increases competition. For instance, Mark Kolko, the CEO of a supplier of industrial motors, said there is no such thing as a loyal customer anymore because other vendors can be found so readily through the Internet.[2]

PLAY VIDEO

INFORMATION TECHNOLOGY AND E-COMMERCE

"Go to academic.cengage.com/management/dubrin and view the video. What other types of information technology systems might be useful to Peet's?"

Managers must develop and respond continuously to new technologies, new types of businesses, and new people in the form of employees and customers. Information technology itself changes so rapidly that managers must adapt themselves to the changes, and help others adapt. For example, managers expect and prepare for productivity dips while workers adapt to a new companywide software system.

1 Spencer E. Ante with Jena McGregor, "Giving the Boss the Big Picture," *Business Week*, February 13, 2006, pp. 50–51.
2 Interview with Mark Kolko, CEO of Power Equipment Co., Rochester, New York, October 14, 2006.

Another general issue with technology, including information technology, is how the development and spread of the new technology increases the importance of innovating to remain competitive. The continuous development of technology decreases product life cycles, creating more pressure on managers and workers involved in the development and manufacture of products.

Information and communications technology is at the center of the technological revolution. This technology is used in most business firms and provides an integral part of many systems, such as inventory control. Information technology makes globalization more practical because it allows ready access to employees all over the world at nominal cost. The same technology makes it feasible to customize many industrial products by combining special features with standard features, such as a Dell computer to meet your personal preferences.

The sampling of technological changes just mentioned illustrates why information technology pushes managers into a continuous learning mode. Even if the manager is not an expert on how to use information technology to customize mass-produced products, the manager still requires a working understanding of the process. Otherwise, he or she will seem foolish when asked questions.

The Wireless Environment, Including Wi-Fi

A specific, direct consequence of information technology comes from managers' use of wireless communication devices to facilitate their work from different locations. For almost a century, managers used wired telephones to stay in touch with the office. In the modern environment, a rapidly evolving number of devices give managers more constant access to the office and to customers. Cell phones, personal digital assistants (such as the BlackBerry), and laptop computers are standard in the manager's tool kit.

Many managers use laptop computers away from the office for the same purposes they would use a desktop computer when in the office. Managers who travel find laptops particularly convenient for preparing daily reports as well as processing e-mail and conducting Internet searches while on the road. The growing availability of Wi-Fi has enhanced the value of laptop computers because the Internet can be accessed even when an electric outlet is not available. (*Wi-Fi* refers to wireless fidelity, a high-speed, high-capacity network built on radio signals.) Most business-oriented hotels and restaurants now offer Wi-Fi networks, as do Internet cafés. A current limitation to Wi-Fi is that hackers can penetrate these networks easier than they can cell phones and wired Internet access.

To use most mobile devices effectively, the manager must be able to tolerate a miniaturized keyboard and have sharp vision. Also note that not every manager finds these devices comfortable or productive. For example, many managers and professionals still prefer paper-based desk planners over personal digital assistants. And many managers can wait until they return to the office to obtain information through e-mail and the Internet so they can enjoy the comforts of a large monitor.

THE POSITIVE AND NEGATIVE CONSEQUENCES OF INFORMATION TECHNOLOGY

Learning Objective 2

Describe the positive and negative consequences of information technology for the manager.

Information technology is integrated into the everyday work of first-level and middle-level managers and staff professionals. Top-level managers also rely on PCs and laptops to conduct their work. Furthermore, executives who depend on office assistants to access their e-mail, or open Web pages, are extremely rare. The vast majority of executives are information tech-savvy. Here we look at both the advantages and disadvantages of information technology as part of the manager's job.

Positive Consequences of Information Technology for the Manager

An information technology revolution that did not help managers, other workers, and organizations perform better would not last. The following description of the positive consequences of IT emphasizes its benefits to managerial work. Exhibit 14-1 outlines these potential advantages.

Improved Productivity and Teamwork

A major justification for installing information technology is its capability for improving productivity. Information technology facilitated much of the slimming down of organizations. A reduction in staffing leads to increased productivity, providing that the sales volume remains constant or improves. For example, most banks found they could reduce the number of branches and consolidate customer service into centralized call centers. From the perspective of the job seeker, a negative side to improved productivity has been slow job growth.

Small business owners can increase their productivity in many ways by exploiting information technology. An advanced application of IT is using online services to find sources of investment capital. The business owner posts a message to which potential investors (venture capitalists) respond.

exhibit 14-1 Positive Consequences of Information Technology for the Manager

Information technology can help the manager work smarter.

1. Improved productivity and teamwork
2. Increased competitive advantage
3. Enhanced business models
4. Improved customer service and supplier relationships
5. Enhanced communication and coordination, including the Virtual Office
6. Quick access to vast information (e.g. dashboard)
7. Enhanced analysis of data and decision making
8. Greater empowerment and flatter organizations
9. Time-saving through employee self-service
10. Monitoring work and employee surveillance

Finding investors online can be quicker than extensive letter writing and telephone-calling campaigns.

Information technology enhances teamwork by allowing team members to maintain frequent contact with each other through e-mail and pagers. Even if the group cannot hold an in-person meeting, team members can give electronic feedback to each other's ideas. Furthermore, with extensive use of IT, teammates can work in geographically dispersed locations. (The virtual office will be described later.)

Increased Competitive Advantage

Effective use of information technology can give a firm a competitive advantage. Information technology enables companies to conduct business in ways that would be impossible without such technology. For example, it would be difficult to buy and sell used cars throughout the country without using the Internet, such as done through eBay. The alternative would be to use a combination of toll-free telephone numbers along with faxing photos of the vehicles. Today, not using modern information technology makes a company noncompetitive. Imagine how embarrassing it would be for a company to have neither a Web site nor e-mail for interacting with customers and suppliers. Today, even low-tech establishments like restaurants and sub shops often have Web sites and e-mail addresses.

Enhanced Business Models

A *business model* refers to a company's general plan for earning money, such as Victoria's Secrets selling merchandise through toll-free telephone numbers, by mail, physical stores, and online. By using information technology, Victoria's Secrets has expanded its method of distribution. Information technology assists not only in direct selling but also in maintaining inventory and targeting expensive catalogs to the right potential buyers. Business strategy expert James Champy cites the Dell model as being dependent on information technology: Build to order while reducing costs substantially and creating a direct path to the consumer. This model would not work without information technology. The Internet enables a tech-savvy company like Dell to extend the model even further, smoothly interacting with suppliers and providing new channels to customers.[3] Note that an enhanced business model is another way of gaining competitive advantage.

Improved Customer Service and Supplier Relationships

Advances in information technology, including networking, can lead to improved customer service and smoother working relationships with suppliers. Customer service improves when service representatives can immediately access information to resolve a customer problem. USAA, a large financial services firm, provides a model for the industry in terms of prompt service. The company sells insurance directly to the public, without the use of external sales representatives or insurance agents. Policyholders can call an 800 number to receive immediate answers to complex questions such as

3 James Champy, "Technology Doesn't Matter—but Only at Harvard," *Fast Company*, December 2003, p. 119.

how much rates will increase if a 16-year-old family member becomes a licensed driver.

Supplier relationships can be more productive when suppliers and purchasers are part of the same network. Large retailers such as Wal-Mart authorize some of their suppliers to ship and stock goods based on electronic messages sent from point of purchase to the suppliers' computers. When inventory gets low on a fast-moving item, supplies are replenished automatically without a retail store official having to make a phone call or send a letter.

Another development to improve customer services is the **extranet**, a secure section of a Web site that only visitors with a password can enter. Many financial services firms use an extranet to allow customers to manage accounts and trade stocks online. The extranet is also used to share inventory or customer information with suppliers, send information to vendors, and sell products and services.

Enhanced Communication and Coordination, Including the Virtual Office

Nowhere is the impact of information technology on the manager's job more visible than in communication and coordination. By relying on information technology, managers can be in frequent contact with group members without being physically present. They can also be part of the **virtual office**, in which employees work together as if they were part of a single office despite being physically separated. Highly coordinated virtual office members form a virtual team. Such teams are groups of geographically separated coworkers who are assembled using information technology to accomplish a task.

Virtual teams rarely meet face-to-face. They are sometimes established as temporary structures to accomplish a specific task such as developing a companywide mentoring program. At other times virtual teams assume an ongoing responsibility such as providing input for the future direction of the organization. Geographically dispersed workers, such as those working in different countries or in different parts of the same country, are sometimes assigned to virtual teams.

The virtual office and virtual teams conduct much of the work through virtual meetings, a gathering of participants in scattered locations using videoconferencing or e-mail. A videoconference enables people to see and hear each other through real-time video. Virtual meetings can accommodate from 4 to 200 people. Large firms often establish their own videoconferencing centers, whereas smaller firms typically rent a center as needed. Videoconferencing can enhance productivity by reducing travel costs and time, and also appeals to workers who fear flying and dislike going through airport security.

Frequent electronic contact with company employees, customers, and suppliers enhances coordination. The alternative is for the manager to communicate primarily when back at the office. A high-tech manager is never away from the office—even if he or she would like to be!

Virtual teams, virtual meetings, and other means of communicating via information technology have created the necessity for **e-leadership**, or providing leadership to people when their work is mediated by information

extranet
A secure section of a Web site that only visitors with a password can enter.

virtual office
Employees who work together as if they were part of a single office despite being physically separated.

e-leadership
Providing leadership to people when their work is mediated by information technology.

technology. Instead of a warm smile and a handshake, the leader might send a congratulatory note by e-mail. Or the leader might set up a chat room to obtain input from workers about a controversial or complex issue. The general idea is that the e-leader relies heavily on information technology to build and maintain relationships with group members.[4]

intranet (or company intranet) A Web site for company use only.

Quick Access to Vast Information

Information technology gives managers quick access to vast amounts of information. A careful library researcher could always access vast amounts of business-related information. Advances in information technology, however, allow for fingertip access if the manager has the right computer search skills. For example, a sales manager might want a targeted list of prospects for her company's new pool tables. She uses an electronic database to locate sporting goods stores in her region, ranking them by revenue and zip code to streamline her sales strategy.

A major contributor to accessing information quickly is the company **intranet**, a Web site for company use only. Workers at all levels can use the intranet for critical information such as inventory levels, new product development, and sales. According to WiseGeek.com, executives make regular use of an intranet for such purposes as accessing bottom-line information like quarterly profit/loss reports, company stock reports, profiles of key employees and customers, and meeting minutes.[5] Google uses an intranet to collect employee suggestions for improving the company's products and services. Employees from all departments are expected to regularly submit ideas to advance the company.

The Web-based dashboard described in the chapter opener might be classified as a type of intranet. The essential idea behind a dashboard is that it places all the computerized data the manager, business owner, or corporate professional might need in one place. Instead of a batch of reports to integrate, the dashboard generates key data in an easy-to-read, constantly updated dashboard-style readout. For a dashboard to be highly valuable, the manager must first identify the company's critical drivers (or success factors). These typically include revenue and sales data, and marketing data such as new sales leads. Other drivers include customer satisfaction, and worker productivity and satisfaction. Lewis Farsedakis, the owner of the cosmetics firm Blinc Inc., says, "The dashboard [supplied by NetSuite] enables me to measure the business results on a daily basis. It also enables me to catch business problems as they emerge, as opposed to later."[6]

Although dashboards have a scientific, slick appearance they provide useful readouts only if they are based on accurate data. For example, is someone who clicked on your Web site to receive product information truly a sales lead? Or is a sales lead someone who has received the production information and has requested that a representative visit his or her company?

---

4 Bruce J. Avolio and Surinder S. Kahai, "Adding the 'E' to E-Leadership: How It May Impact Your Leadership," *Organizational Dynamics*, No. 4, 2003, pp. 325–326.

5 "What is an Intranet?" http://www.wiseGEEK.com, accessed October 17, 2006.

6 The information about dashboards and the quote are from Mark Henricks, "Dashing Looks," *Entrepreneur*, August 2006, p. 60.

Enhanced Analysis of Data and Decision Making

Closely related to gathering a wider array of information, information technology allows for better analysis of data and decision making. Managers at business firms of all sizes now analyze data better to improve efficiency. A before-and-after example follows:

The office manager of a large medical practice in Birmingham, Michigan, observed that during December, January, February, and the first half of March many patients cancelled their appointments. As a result, revenue for the medical group was down during these months. The medical staff as well as the office manager accepted these cancellations as a reality of medical practice. The office manager then decided to conduct a computerized statistical analysis of which patients in particular had the most cancellations. It was found that, in general, older patients as well as others with mobility problems had the highest number of cancellations during the most severe part of winter. The partial solution to the cancellation problem was for a member of the office staff to telephone older patients and those with mobility problems in advance and encourage them to visit the office along with the suggestion of having a family member or friend drive them to the office. The outreach program, based on an analysis of patient data, reduced wintertime cancellations 40 percent.

Another way in which information technology helps managers make better decisions is through gathering multiple inputs on an online document before taking action. A **wiki** is a password-protected Web page that allows for the collaboration of multiple users. Each contributor can add ideas to the document or plan, plus make suggestions for improving the suggestions of other contributors. Visualize a manager posting on the company wiki a proposal for reducing retirement costs. He suggests reducing the pension of every retiree by $60 per month. One of the collaborators on the document writes, "You better not rush into this. The negative publicity for our company could be enormous." Several other collaborators agree with the comment about the bad publicity, so the manager decides to look for another way to reduce costs.

The two main benefits of wikis are boosting group productivity, and serving as a business knowledge base where information is stored and readily accessed. Informative, a Brisbane, California-based marketing company, found that using as wiki reduced the amount of group e-mails and intranet traffic required to accomplish projects.[7]

Greater Empowerment and Flatter Organizations

wiki
A password-protected Web page that allows for collaboration of multiple users.

The widespread use of information technology gives more workers access to information they need for decision making. As a result, more workers can be empowered to make decisions. Fewer layers of management are needed to act as information conduits. Instead, workers at lower levels access information directly through computer networks. Information technology therefore

7 Amanda C. Kooser, "Get Wiki with It: Boost Group Productivity—and Cut Down on e-Mails—with Wiki," *Entrepreneur*, April 2005, p. 28.

provides line employees with the documents they need to perform their jobs more effectively and make decisions on their own.

Time Saving Through Employee Self-service

Another important way in which information technology benefits managers is when employees are able to serve themselves in some areas rather than requiring managerial or staff assistance. Managers are freed from the need to supervise routine activities. Also, from the standpoint of top management, fewer managers and staff support need to be hired.

A notable example of information technology–based employee self-service is the electronic travel and expense reporting (T&E) system used at Cisco Systems Inc. Employees submit expense reports through an intranet and browser. When an employee logs on to the system, it registers charges from his or her corporate American Express card. The employee then adds out-of-pocket expenses and the system generates a travel and expense report. Within four days, the employee receives the reimbursement by direct deposit to his or her bank. Expense reports submitted by paper took 21 days for reimbursement at Cisco.

Another advantage to the company is that the system can spot discrepancies and send the e-form back to the employee for clarification. A suspicious form can be routed for audit approval. However, after all the proper information is in place, the system can generate the credit card payments to American Express and cash reimbursements to the employee. By automating the process, Cisco auditors boosted the number of claims they can review annually from 19,000 to 35,000. The firm saves money by paying off credit card debt faster. Additionally, the cost of processing an expense report went from upwards of $25 down to $3.

Cisco now uses many of the same self-service techniques to improve its internal travel reservation system. Jennifer Loftin, manager of T&E automation, says, "It's letting managers and employees focus on high-value activities."[8]

Monitoring Work and Employee Surveillance

Automation in the workplace not only changes how employees labor, it changes the ability of management to measure and monitor the work, and the workers. In many jobs—especially in manufacturing and the more mechanical service industries—employees are increasingly held to standards derived from metering or measuring the work. Management also has new responsibilities and tools to oversee employee behavior in the wired workplace. Closer monitoring of work might be perceived as an advantage of information technology from the perspective of some managers. However, some workers and managers as well might perceive such surveillance to be a *negative* feature of information technology. The topic of computer-aided monitoring of work will be reintroduced in Chapter 15 about controls. One example of technology-based employee surveillance will therefore suffice for now:

---

8 Samuel Greengard, "Technology Finally Advances HR," *Workforce*, January 2000, pp. 38–39.

An employee called in sick to Scott McDonald, CEO of Monument Security in Sacramento, California. The CEO decided to investigate. He had already informed his staff of 400 security guards and patrol drivers that he was installing Xora, a software program that tracks workers' whereabouts through surveillance technology on their company cell phones. A Web-based "geo-fence" around work territories would alert the boss if workers strayed or even drove too fast. (The technology also enabled McDonald to route workers more efficiently.) So when McDonald logged on, the program told him exactly where the worker was—and it wasn't in bed with the sniffles. "How come you're eastbound on 80 heading to Reno right now if you're sick?" asked the boss. There was a long silence—the sound of a job ending—followed by "You got me."[9]

What is your opinion of the fairness of using Xora to track the whereabouts of workers? Also, does a worker have the right for an occasional "mental health day" at Reno, Nevada?

Negative Consequences of Information Technology

Information technology continues to make extraordinary contributions to organizational productivity. Nevertheless, the same exciting technology produces some unintended negative consequences. Even when these negative consequences do not affect the manager directly, he or she usually plays a major role in dealing with the consequences. For example, if extensive use of information technology deteriorates customer service, the manager faces angry customers and discouraged employees. Awareness of these potential problems can help managers prevent them from occurring.

1. *Wasting time at the computer.* One subtle problem occurs when managers or other employees become **computer goof-offs.** They spend so much time attempting new computer routines and accessing information of questionable value that they neglect key aspects of their jobs. Some managers, for example, would prefer to surf the Internet for low-value information than to confront an employee about a discipline problem. Lost productivity is a major problem as workers surf the Internet for nonwork reasons. According to an Accountemps survey of senior executives, workers spend an average of 56 minutes per day with nonwork-related Internet use.[10] A related problem is bandwith waste, as workers download complex graphics and videos (especially with the popularity of YouTube). Legal liability may surface when workers transfer or display sexually explicit content because such material may be interpreted as creating a hostile work environment. E-mail and Internet-born viruses may work their way into the company's information technology system as a by-product of surfing.

computer goof-offs Employees who spend so much time attempting new computer routines and accessing information of questionable value that they neglect key aspects of their job.

2. *Repetitive-motion disorders.* As was described in Chapter 7, information technology contributes to repetitive motion disorders found in the workplace. In addition to well-designed workplaces, improved technology may decrease

9 Kristina Dell and Lisa Takeuchi Cullen, "Snooping Bosses," *Time,* September 11, 2006, p. 62.

10 Survey cited in "Workers Dawdle on Net an Hour a Day, Firm Says," *Rochester (NY), Democrat and Chronicle,* August 22, 2005, p. 10D.

repetitive-motion disorders. Voice recognition systems enable computer users to dictate commands into word processors, thereby cutting back on keyboarding. The software is cumbersome at present because it has to be adapted to an individual user's speech patterns, including pronunciation and accents. Dictation software now allows for continuous speech, rather than pauses between words as in the past. But watch out for the "Wreck a nice beach" problem. (Repeat "Wreck a nice beach" a few times until you get the joke.)

3. *Deterioration of customer* service. A problem of considerable magnitude comes from the deterioration in customer service that sometimes accompanies information technology. Many banks, for example, force customers with a service problem to call a toll-free number rather than allowing them to deal with a branch representative. A voice-response system instructs the customer to punch in lengthy account numbers and make choices from a complicated menu. The process is time-consuming and impersonal, and difficult for customers unfamiliar with information technology. A related problem occurs when highly automated customer-service operations appear unfriendly and detached. An extensive investigation into self-service technologies uncovered several areas of customer discontent. Self-service machines were often broken, Web sites were down, personal identification numbers failed to work, and items were not shipped as promised.[11] (The same study also found many positive features of employee self-service such as being able to order goods 24/7.)
4. *Dealing with baffled consumers.* Another challenge for managers in dealing with consumers in the information age is that some electronic products are baffling to use for many people. As a result these customers become dissatisfied customers, and the manager may have to deal with angry customers and poor sales of a particular product. A case in point are advanced digital cameras that come with a 125-page operator's manual—not including the software guide. Analysts attribute some of the blame to falling electronics prices, which leaves less money to spend on after-sales service. The problem for managers is that many consumers may finally be getting fed up. People are embracing the latest gadgets with less enthusiasm than for previous generations of technology, partly because the new consumer electronics are difficult to comprehend. A small industry of information technology technicians who make house calls has arisen to help baffled consumers. One such national chain is Geeks on Wheels. However, there is a limit to how many baffled customers are willing to pay an outside firm to help them work their information technology gadget.
5. *Wired managerial workers.* As implied in the discussion of wireless communication, information technology results in wired managerial workers. Being electronically connected to the office at all times leads many managers and professionals to complain that their employers expect them to be always available for consultation. Many managers, for example, are expected to bring pagers, laptop computers, and cell phones on vacation so they can

11 Mary Jo Bitner, Amy L. Ostrom, and Matthew L. Meuter, "Implementing Successful Self-Service Technologies," *Academy of Management Executive,* November 2002, p. 110.

respond to inquiries from the office and customers. The spreading use of Wi-Fi intensifies the problem because there are more opportunities to remain linked to the office. Another contributor to mobile computing, and keeping managers connected to the office, are key fobs that enable employees get beyond corporate firewalls from anywhere. The devices establish a private network for access to e-mail and intranets.[12] A problem noted with devices such as a BlackBerry is that managers sometimes make decisions too quickly because instant communication lends itself to superficial thinking. Instead of reflecting on a problem, the manager dashes back an answer to a problem.[13]

6. *The encouragement of nonproductive multitasking.* A major negative consequence of information technology is that it encourages inappropriate multitasking. Using several electronic devices at once often interferes with a person's ability to concentrate carefully on the major problem at hand. Computerized information encourages multitasking to the point that may managers feel they are wasting time unless they are attempting two tasks at once, such as talking on a cell phone and accessing e-mail at the same time. The problem is that diminished concentration often leads to poorer-quality work. "Multitasking doesn't look to be one of the great strengths of human cognition," according to James C. Johnston, a research psychologist at NASA. "It's almost inevitable that each individual task will be slower and of lower quality."[14] Another way to understand the potential hazards of multitasking is to personalize the problem. If you were a passenger in an airplane going through a storm would you want the pilot to be chatting on the cell phone or reading e-mail while commandeering the plane?

THE IMPACT OF THE INTERNET ON CUSTOMERS AND OTHER EXTERNAL RELATIONSHIPS

Learning Objective 3

Discuss the impact of the Internet on customer and other external relationships.

The Internet profoundly affects how business is conducted. Developments of similar magnitude include electricity, the railroad, and the interstate highway system. As a consequence, the Internet also influences managerial work, especially the technical problem-solver role of a manager who might be contributing ideas about such work as marketing, purchasing, and information systems. Even when managers are not directly involved in such specialized activities, they are still concerned with making decisions about the Internet. Here we look at six ways in which the Internet affects external relationships: e-commerce marketing, e-commerce purchasing, changing of intermediaries, enhanced globalization, integrating the old and new economies, and living with increased visibility.

12 Robert D. Hof, "The Future of Tech: The Power of Us," *Business Week*, June 20, 2005, p. 90.

13 Bill Husted, "Execs Embrace, Lament Always Being in Touch," *The Atlanta Journal Constitution*, http://www.ajc.com, June 9, 2006.

14 Quoted in Jared Sandberg, "Cubicle Culture: Yes, Sell All my Stocks. No, the 3:15 from JFK. And Get Me Mr. Sister," *The Wall Street Journal*, September 12, 2006, p. B1.

The Marketing Side of e-Commerce

The biggest impact on business comes from selling many goods and services to other businesses and consumers over the Internet. Eighty percent of business conducted on the Net today takes place between firms (B2B, or business-to-business) rather than with individual consumers. Business-to-business sales online are running about $800 billion per year, whereas e-tailing sales are approximately $130 billion. Online shopping, however, still accounts for only about 5 percent of all retail sales. According to Shop.org, retail sales in general are growing about 3 percent per year, where online growth is in double digits.[15] Michael Dell is one of many influential business executives who believe that online business will continue to grow.[16]

The influence of the Internet on marketing is far greater than on sales conducted online because many consumers first research a product online and then make a purchase at a store. A specific example of the interrelationship between online and offline selling might occur in this manner: A person reads a print ad about a Web site, visits the Web site to learn about a specific product, and then visits the store to make the purchase.

E-commerce affects managerial work in two major ways. First, the manager must be familiar with e-commerce to suggest strategies for marketing over the Internet and resolving problems. Second, managers who formerly worked directly with salespeople (such as coaching and motivating) may have fewer subordinates. One Web specialist might replace 50 face-to-face salespeople. The manager, with fewer people to supervise, would spend more time developing business strategy and perhaps interacting with a few major customers. Exhibit 14-2 presents some technical details managers need to know in working with e-commerce.

exhibit 14-2 How to Make Your Web Site Pop

Allan Gorman, director of Bandspa, a marketing and branding consultant firm in Montclair, New Jersey, offers the following five tips for companies trying to make a splash on the Web:

1. *Wow them from the first page.* First impressions mean everything on the Web, so your site's front page must shine in order to be effective. A company's front page, for example, should forgo bandwidth-heavy graphics and instead feature a bulleted list of services and a simple, readily accessible way to contact the owner for an estimate or additional information. Subsequent pages can showcase your portfolio, testimonials from satisfied customers, and links to free e-newsletters.
2. *Make it user friendly.* Ease of use equates to both a pleasant visiting experience and marketing effectiveness. Use clear language, useful links, and navigation bars to steer customers in the right direction.
3. *Make them eager to return soon.* Attracting visitors is important, but persuading them to return is even more important. Create long-term customers by incorporating relevant, self-assessment tests, surveys, and other tools with related products and services

(Continued)

15 Data reported in Mindy Fetterman, "Retailers' Online Business Burgeons: Travel is Biggest Part of Growing Internet Sales," *USA Today* syndicated story, May 24, 2006; James Mehring, "Cash Registers are Ringing Online," *Business Week*, March 5, 2007, p. 24.

16 "Michael Dell: Still Betting on the Future of Online Commerce and Supply Chain Effectiveness," *Knowledge @Wharton*, http://knowledge.wharton.upenn.edu/, September 6, 2006.

exhibit 14-2 How to Make Your Web Site Pop *(Continued)*

that your business provides. This ensures an educational and interactive experience for the customer and is an effective marketing tool for your business. Start with a simple biweekly newsletter, a blog, or a chat forum on a topic of interest to your customers.

4. *Get back to basics.* Browse through a few sites and you'll quickly discover that accessing information can be a challenge. To make sure your visitors don't get turned off by poor navigation, broken links, and irrelevant information, be sure to give them a clear explanation of your product or service, making sure to highlight exactly what makes your firm and its offerings unique.
5. *Give 'em the royal tour.* When designing your site, put yourself in your customers' shoes. What do they want to see or know? What format suitably presents this information? How can you keep them interested and make the experience fun?

Source: Bridget McCrea, "Make Your Website Pop," *Black Enterprise,* November 2005, p. 70.

A largely unanticipated positive consequence of e-commerce is that many firms are beginning to generate more revenue from small, niche products. According to *Wired* Editor-in-Chief Chris Anderson, the Internet continues to cut the cost of finding and distributing products. As a result, the Internet facilitates the creation of new markets for obscure books, movies, and similar products that never made it to local stores and theaters. These products lie at the long, tailing-off part of the demand curve as depicted by the normal curve. Most physical retailers need to conserve their available space for products that sell well. Today niche products can be stocked efficiently in warehouses or superstores and sold to anyone throughout the world via the Internet.[17] In the past, only a few customers would order by mail, and this service was not always available. Keep in mind, however, that hit products still make up for a large percentage of Internet sales, even if *misses* are getting more play. For example, industry data suggest that misses will not outsell hits at Netflix and Amazon for another decade. Also, hits are still the driving force in the music business.[18]

The Purchasing Side of e-Commerce

An important consequence of e-commerce is that it sometimes enables companies to purchase more efficiently than they could by speaking to sales representatives or purchasing through catalogs over the telephone. Many companies assume that both customers and suppliers prefer to conduct business with them over the Internet. For example, a company cannot stay on the General Electric–approved supplier list unless the company is willing to accept orders and inquiries online.

Companies realize smaller transaction costs and a time saving by purchasing over the Web. As a result, product prices tend to be lower than when purchasing

17 Chris Anderson, *The Long Tail: Why the Future of Business is Selling Less of More* (New York: Hyperion, 2006).

18 Lee Gomes, "Many Companies Still Cling to Big Hits To Drive Earnings," *The Wall Street Journal,* August 2, 2006, p. B1; Gomes, "It May Be a Long Time Before the Long Tail Is Wagging the Web," *The Wall Street Journal,* July 26, 2006, p. B1.

through sales representatives or catalogs. The purchaser can also ask questions online about products and services. A good starting point for any company wanting to purchase over the Internet would be to visit http://www.yahoo.com/business. The manager or professional can quickly locate companies that offer the product or service he or she needs, and then make inquiries.

Purchasing over the Internet saves time because purchasing agents spend less time talking to and being entertained by sales representatives. Nevertheless, e-commerce has not completely eliminated the human touch in business. Many big deals are still made over lunch and on the golf course, and executives tend to purchase from people they like. Furthermore, many well-established companies that have worked hard to develop their brand names refuse to join buyer exchanges. The established companies are concerned that online buying through an exchange or open market often results in the lowest bidder (sometimes an unknown supplier) getting the sale. Business is conducted with customers online, but not through the medium of a large buyer exchange. A company with a good reputation would prefer that customers stay loyal to them based on high product quality and after-sale service.

Changing of Intermediaries

The Internet has made it easier for buyers and sellers to deal directly with each other. As a result, many business firms that acted as intermediaries between buyers and sellers have been forced out of business, or have had to redefine themselves. Among the intermediaries affected are travel agents, many retailers, food brokers, and independent sales representatives. For example, airlines are now selling only about 50 percent of their tickets through outside agents. Included in this figure are online travel agencies not directly owned by airlines, further reducing the share of sales for the traditional agency. Most travel agencies that have survived offer services such as arranging complex business trips and vacations where knowledge of the hotels and best airline service is important.

The Internet has badly squeezed music retailers, in terms of both paid legal purchases such as iTunes and illegal downloading or file sharing. Of enormous significance to music publishers, the popular social network MySpace began a program in 2006 to enable its members to sell their own tunes directly on the site, circumventing music publishers entirely. MySpace says it hosts Web pages for more than 3 million recording artists with bands of many different sizes.[19]

Although the Internet may be forcing out some intermediaries, others have been created, such as a broker that promises to obtain you the best price for airline tickets. An example of a Web-based intermediary is an online auction for business that locates suppliers who are willing to supply what a company needs at the price the company is willing to pay. Many companies now sell through eBay as well as Amazon.com Inc. and Yahoo Inc. Another Internet-based intermediary is an eBay store that takes care of preparing your offerings for sale on eBay, and also handles the shipping.

---

19 Alex Veiga, "MySpace Intrudes on Music's Middlemen: Website to Enable Members to Sell Own Tunes Directly," The Associated Press, September 4, 2006.

The Enhancement of Globalization

The Internet is a driving force in globalization for several reasons. E-mail allows for rapid communication with business partners throughout the world. Being in rapid contact with partners in other countries, such as a company's call center in a country 7,000 miles away, helps bring about a feeling of closeness. Companies throughout the world can trade more readily with each other because so much buying and selling takes place over the Internet.

The Internet facilitates globalization in part because more and more countries throughout the world have developed their telecommunications infrastructure. A case in point is China, which has surpassed the United States in Internet use. According to research conducted by Sohu.com, Chinese Internet users number about 150 million, and possibly up to 200 million. The United States had 154 million active Internet users in January 2006—about one half the population.[20] The vast majority of Web users in China are individuals, not companies. However, still plenty of business firms are included among the online Chinese, thereby contributing to globalization. It is therefore easier for a company like Hewlett-Packard to be in frequent contact with its Chinese subcontractors to review such issues as delivery dates and product quality.

Integrating the New Economy with the Old Economy

Managers at all levels face the challenge of how to integrate the traditional way of doing business (the old economy) with e-business (the new economy). In Net-speak, it is the difference between bricks and clicks. During the initial surge of e-businesses, many Internet-based companies regarded traditional business firms as virtually obsolete. Many predicted that establishments like shopping malls, automobile dealers, and companies that sold hard-copy greeting cards would soon go the way of the dinosaurs. Furthermore, they thought companies that acted as brokers between business firms and suppliers would soon be vaporized (tough talk for being run out of business). By early 2000, that prediction turned into a realization that the vast majority of companies relying strictly on the Internet for sales could not earn a profit, and continue to sustain enormous losses. Today, approximately 50 percent of Web-based businesses earn a profit.

Well-established companies that integrated e-commerce into their marketing and internal operations became the biggest beneficiaries of the Internet revolution. Also, the well-established companies suffer from less business swings. Traditional retailers such as Wal-Mart, Target, Best Buy, and Macy's are attracting more shoppers with enhanced Web sites including easy-to-use search capabilities.[21] Also, virtually every large industrial firm has its own Web site.

At Staples, customers can purchase from Staples' catalog, retail stores, or Web site. Each of these channels is designed to serve as a sales pitch and backup for the others. In terms of channels, there is no effort to sway the

20 Chinese and U.S. data from Natalie Pace, "China Surpasses U.S. In Internet Use," http://www.Forbes.com, April 3, 2006.
21 Mylene Mangalindan, "Web Sales Boom Could Leave Amazon Behind," *The Wall Street Journal*, January 21, 2005, p. C1.

customers one way or another. "Whatever makes their life easier," comments Paul Gaffney, the company's chief information officer.[22]

Living with Increased Visibility

An unanticipated consequence of the Internet is a different kind of visibility than in the past to which companies must adjust. People who like or dislike the organization can disseminate this information over the Internet, including the placement of personal blogs. Several current Web sites encourage consumers to voice their complaints. Negative comments on the Web can be dismissed as the work of jealous people or kooks, but the exposure carries the potential to badly hurt the corporate image. Companies recognize the need for risk and damage control in a variety of scenarios. For example, management at several large companies purchases a set of potential negative domain names, such as http://www.companyname.sucks.org. In this way, the critics will not be able to launch such a site.

To counteract the downside of increased visibility, management must work extra hard to create fans and to deal openly with the issues that make people dislike you. Suppose a company subcontracts the manufacture of a clothing line to a company that hires prison labor at low wages under punitive working conditions. The company addresses the issue by setting higher standards for subcontractors to minimize negative publicity over the Internet.[23] Another hope is that only a handful of consumers with an ax to grind will bother visiting a negative Web site about your company.

The accompanying Management in Action illustrates the workings of a successful e-business in a basic industry.

management in action

Using e-Commerce to Turn Surplus Steel into Gold

In early 2003, Scott Shapiro, an independent steel broker, was trolling for leads online when he came across an auction site called SteelSalvor. The site provided a way for steel importers or insurance companies to find buyers for their damaged or surplus steel, potentially putting middlemen such as Shapiro out of business. "As a steel broker, I hated it—in capital letters—what the guy was doing," said Shapiro. "But as a businessperson, I thought it was a brilliant idea."

Shapiro promptly flew to Houston to meet with the site's owner, Scott Dawson. Dawson had worked inspecting and selling rejected steel for a marine insurance adjuster before he came up with the idea of putting the surplus steel on a virtual auction block instead. About $5 billion of steel is orphaned in U.S. ports each year, much of it damaged during shipping. Importers and their insurance companies, on the hook for the value of the steel in its pristine state, must then scramble

(Continued)

22 Tim Hanrahan, "When Worlds Collide," *The Wall Street Journal,* April 28, 2003, p. R4.
23 Esther Dyson, "Mirror, Mirror, on the Wall," *Harvard Business Review,* September–October 1997, pp. 24–25.

management in action (Continued)

Using e-Commerce to Turn Surplus Steel into Gold

to find local salvage buyers. With $100,000 from investors and his own savings, Dawson figured he could put the whole process on the Web.

Shapiro impressed Dawson with ideas to lure new sellers and a hefty Rolodex filled with potential steel buyers. The two men quickly realized they could make great partners. Since then, what had been just another struggling e-marketplace has become a fast-growing and profitable partnership. SteelSalvor collects a 5 percent fee on every sale that meets or exceeds the seller's minimum price. Annual revenues are about $15 million, based on about 20 auctions a month. SteelSalvor signs up about four new bidders a day. With only four employees, and little overhead, "Everything we do is geared toward making a profit," says Shapiro. "You don't grow for growth's sake."

Sellers can auction anything from a 20-ton coil of sheet steel to entire truckloads. SteelSalvor sends e-mails with details about sales to a list of 6,300 registered bidders, most of whom are brokers or smaller manufacturers. Buyers must pay cash, usually via wire transfer. SteelSalvor's roster of regular sellers includes manufacturers such as Honda, which sells odd lots every month, and Ryerson Tull, which auctions off slow-moving inventory. "SteelSalvor has been saving us a lot of legwork," says Katie Jorgenson, a claims manager with Cargill's steel trading unit. "Their site provides a very good vehicle for customers to gather around. It creates a competitive environment."

Much of SteelSalvor's rapid growth is the result of the 49-year-old Shapiro's won't-take-no-for-an-answer attitude. It took 13 months of phone calls, for instance, before Honda agreed to a trial auction. Shapiro's next frontier is Europe, where he's working with insurance companies on a separate European site.

Questions

1. What contribution does SteelSalvor make to the steel industry?
2. In what way is SteelSalvor's approach to e-commerce an improvement of doing all the buy and selling over the telephone?

Source: Michael Arndt, "An eBay for Steel: Turning Surplus Steel into Gold," *Business Week Small Biz*, Fall 2005, p. 30; http://www.steelsalvor.com.

THE EFFECTS OF THE INTERNET ON INTERNAL OPERATIONS

Learning Objective 4

Explain the effects of the Internet on internal company operations.

Working in an Internet environment affects internal operations as well as relationships with outsiders. Doing business on the Internet is far more complicated than simply taking orders over an electronic catalog. E-commerce often brings about changes in the way in which a company operates. Here we look at several issues influenced by the Internet environment: more effective work processes, a squeeze on profits and pressure toward cost control, dealing with instability and chaos, and data mining.

More Effective Work Processes

The Internet ushered in a new era and transforms the way in which businesses operate internally. Using the Internet, many companies changed their methods of distributing goods, of collaborating inside the company, and of dealing with suppliers. Technology companies pioneered this use of the Internet to develop more effective work processes and overhaul their operations. In general, the flattening of the business playing field (see the section in Chapter 2 about the *flat world*) has encouraged more effective work processes for companies to stay competitive in a global economy. Information technology makes it is easier to send work offshore and keep a project going 24/7. The Internet and workflow software have reduced the importance of geography. For example, radiologists in Los Angeles might send CAT-scans of the brain to Barcelona, Spain, for diagnosis and interpretation of images.[24]

Here we look at several examples of how the impact of information technology, including the Internet, has improved work processes and operations.

The Ordering and Production of PCs

Ingram Micro, the biggest PC distributor, teamed up with Solectron, a major contract manufacturer of high-technology equipment. Ingram custom-makes PCs inexpensively for brand-name computer companies. Instead of the PC companies handling orders and manufacturing, Ingram and Solectron perform the task for them. The Web-based system speeds up communication and decreases assembly times. The PC companies continue to design and market their products, and handle quality assurance. The difference in operations comes from their alliance with Ingram, which functions as a virtual company.[25] The Web-based system enhances productivity because products are shipped more rapidly.

Exhibit 14-3 presents a step-by-step analysis of the Web-based process for customizing an order for a PC.

Unifying Knob Production at Nissan

Nissan Motor Company faced a problem with its automobile knobs. Because of the difficulty of getting engineers across three worldwide divisions to collaborate smoothly, each division designed its own knob. With 3 million cars sold every year, a lot of money is tied up in knobs. Nissan management decided it needed to improve its operational and manufacturing practices in a highly competitive business environment. So, beginning in 2003, Nissan employed a wide array of Microsoft® technology tools. Now, all divisions integrate their activities. Executives stay in touch wherever they are via personal computers or smart phones using Microsoft software, something that could not be done previously because of incompatible networks. Nissan saved approximately $135 million in a three-year period, shortened its time-to-market cycle, and improved work processes and customer service.[26] And, yes the production of knobs is uniform, saving some money on every Nissan vehicle.

---

24 Silviya Svejenova, "Quo Vadis, Europe?" *Academy of Management Perspectives*, May 2006, p. 83.

25 Steve Hamm and Marcia Stepanek, "From Reengineering to E-Engineering," *Business Week e.biz*, March 22, 1999, p. 16.

26 "Business Impact in Manufacturing: The Pace of Change," http://www.microsoft.com/net/business/industry, August 8, 2006.

exhibit 14-3 The Internet Supply Chain

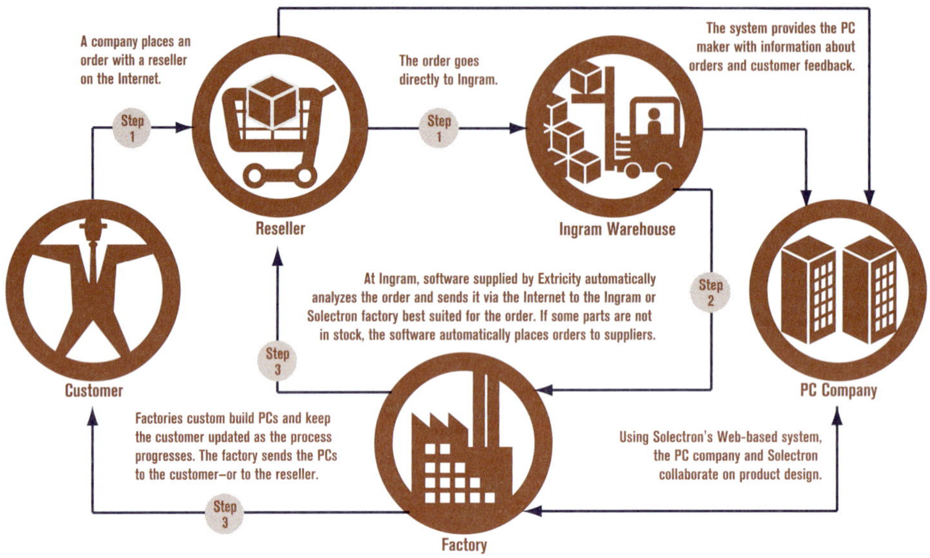

Source: Solectron Corp., Ingram Micro Inc., and Extricity Inc.

Work Streamlining at a Wine Maker

work streamlining Eliminating as much low-value work as possible and concentrating on activities that add value for customers or clients.

A major contribution of information technology has been **work streamlining,** the elimination of as much low-value work as possible and concentrating on activities that add value for customers or clients. Streamlining thus minimizes waste and helps perform work more efficiently. You are probably quite familiar with streamlining research by accessing databases from your computer rather than visiting a physical library. An industrial example took place at Trinchero Family Estates, the winery that produces Sutter Hill and other popular brands of wines. Because the wine is low priced, production efficiency receives high priority.

Company management wanted to track the processing of grapes from harvesting to bottling to selling. So Trinchero specialists set up an online system, fed by bar codes on everything from barrels of grapes to bottles of wine. The payoff was a reduction in the cost of handling raw materials by 3 percent. Furthermore, the company avoided spending $100,000 on a system to comply with new bioterrorism rules.[27] The company could now document when and who was handling the grapes. According to the Bioterrorism Response Act of 2002, every U.S. food processing company except farms and restaurants must be able to account for every link in the supply chain.

Squeeze on Profits and Pressure Toward Cost Control

The changing flow of information created by the Internet tipped the balance of power from sellers to buyers. In the past, sellers had almost all the

27 Heather Green, "The Web Smart 50," *Business Week*, November 21, 2005, p. 94.

information about profit margins and manufacturer's true costs. Industrial buyers and individual consumers can now use the Web to uncover information about costs that puts them on the same level as professionals. Many prospective car purchasers today walk into dealers' offices with copies of factory invoices showing the true dealer cost of a given car model. The dealer can no longer claim, "We are giving you this car at $50 over dealer cost," unless it is true.

data mining
The extraction of useful analyses from the raw mass of business transactions and other information.

Given that the buyer knows so much about costs, the seller must offer products with lower profit margins than in the past. The manager is therefore responsible for controlling costs in any sensible way possible including reducing turnover, minimizing expenditures, and using the Internet for purchasing!

Data Mining

Data mining is yet another useful application of information technology to business, yet also is linked to the Internet because some of the databases are accessed over the Internet. However, companies develop some of their own databases, and others are purchased in CD format. The term **data mining** describes the extraction of useful analyses from the raw mass of business transactions and other information. Data mining derives its name from the similarities between searching for valuable business information in a large database, and mining a mountain to find valuable ore.[28] Insurance companies use data mining to help price insurance policies, particularly automobile policies. For example, a revamped pricing model used by Allstate Corp. considers data such as the driver's credit history, allowing the company to predict more accurately how many claims a driver is likely to file. The underlying human factor here might be that someone with a good credit record tends to be responsible about both paying bills on time and driving safely. Data mining by an insurance company can therefore lead to lower premiums for some drivers, and higher premiums for others.

Data mining helps deliver answers to such questions as "Which customers are most likely to respond to my next promotional mailing, and why?" and "Which job candidates are likely to stay with the company a long time, and why?" Two major outputs of data mining are as follows:

- *Automated prediction of trends and behavior.* Questions that traditionally required extensive hands-on analysis can now be answered directly from the data in rapid fashion. Predictive marketing is a key example. Data on previous promotional mailings can be used to identify the targets most likely to maximize return on investment in future mailings. A certain age group within a particular zip code, for example, might be the most receptive to purchasing smoked meats through the mail.

---

28 This section is based closely on Kurt Thearling, "An Introduction to Data Mining," http://www.thearling.com/text/dmwhite/dmwhite.htm, accessed April 2, 2004.

- *Automated discovery of previously unknown patterns.* Data mining tools rifle though databases and identify previously hidden patterns. An example of pattern discovery is the analysis of retail sales data to identify seemingly unrelated products that are often purchased together, such as laser cartridges and video games.

The technique underlying data mining is modeling. In brief, modeling refers to building a model (or general framework) in one situation and where you know the answer and then applying the model to a situation where the answer is yet unknown. You might know how your customers behaved in one situation—such as whether they were receptive to caller ID—and use that model to estimate who might purchase a satellite television service.

SUCCESS FACTORS IN E-COMMERCE

Learning Objective 5

Pinpoint factors associated with success in e-business.

To help synthesize the vast amounts of information about the impact of the Internet, here we list six factors that contribute to success in e-business. Factors that contribute to success in any type of business, such as offering high-quality products that customers want, also apply.[29]

1. *Develop an excellent call center to allow for the human touch.* Despite conducting business over the Internet, many customers want to follow up with telephone calls. Several online investment brokers found that telephone traffic actually increases after online trading is initiated. Many customers want to follow up online inquiries with human beings. Customers often seek the type of clarification that is difficult to obtain by asking questions online.
2. *Keep customers informed about order progress.* The online transaction is not completed until the customer receives the order and is satisfied. If the company experiences shipping delays, it should notify the customer. The problem of delays is especially relevant for complex products such as industrial machinery or custom-made computer servers.
3. *Constantly monitor and update the e-business system.* "There's nothing more annoying to a customer than going through the buying process and not being able to close the transaction," says Sam Taylor of onlineretailpartners.com. "It's very tiring for them to have to re-input the information."[30] Many order systems turn out to be much more complex than their developers realize, and executing an order can be complicated and time-consuming.

29 Adrienne Carter, "Telling the Risky From the Reliable," *Business Week*, August 1, 2005, p. 57; Rosabeth Moss Kanter, "The Ten Deadly Sins of Wanna-Dots," *Harvard Business Review*, January 2001, p. 91; Jennifer Reingold, "What We Have Learned in the New Economy," *Fast Company*, March 2004, pp. 57–58; Beckey Bright, "How Do You Say 'Web'," *The Wall Street Journal*, May 23, 2005, p. R11; Brian Gow and Ben Elgin, "Click Fraud: The Dark Side of Online Advertising," *Business Week*, October 2, 2006, pp. 46–56; Loretta Chao, "What Happens When an e-Bay Steal Is a Fake?" *The Wall Street Journal*, June 26, 2006, p. D1; Joël-Denis Bellavance, «Les Criminels Menacent la Cyberéconomie,» [Criminals Threaten the Cybereconomy] http://www.cyberpress.ca, le 16 octobre, 2006.

30 "Three Overlooked Keys to E-Commerce Success," *What's Working Online*, Special Issue of *Business Week*, 2001, p. 6.

4. *Mix bricks and clicks.* The most successful players in e-tailing give customers the opportunity to purchase online, in stores, and by telephone. Among the many successful companies that offer multiple channels for customers to make purchases are Gateway Computer, Macy's, Panasonic, and Lands End (now a division of Sears).
5. *Develop a global presence.* Customers throughout the world like to shop on American Web sites, which provides a unique opportunity for U.S. companies. Although the U.S. firm must adapt to local tastes and laws, back-office, distribution, and marketing functions translate well overseas. Web veterans suggest that the best way to perform well in foreign markets is to bring in experienced local partners who know the nuances of the market and can work through local rules and regulations. One key regulation is to obtain a local domain name, such as one ending in ".co.uk" for Britain. Several surveys indicate that up to 80 percent of Europeans shop first at Web sites with local domains. So how about CarloRossi.co.fr for selling low-price California wine in France?
6. *Protect customers against fraud.* At the retail level in particular, crime and fraud are rampant on the Internet. To maintain a good reputation and to prevent losing valuable customers, companies need to protect their customers against identity threat. A given customer may now know which Web site led to identify theft, but might become discouraged about making future purchases on the Web. As a consequence, all companies engaged in e-commerce need to protect customers as much as possible through secure Web sites. Another common type of fraud found on the Internet is offering for sale counterfeits (or knockoffs) of luxury brands. The problem is more pronounced on the Internet because prospective purchasers see only a photograph of the merchandise, and even the photo might not be of the product at hand. Auction sites on eBay, Yahoo!, and Amazon cannot be blamed for fake merchandise offered on their sites because they only put buyers and sellers together. However, a person who learns he or she has purchased a fake Gucci wallet on eBay may not want to make another purchase on that site. (eBay as well as other auction sites are aware of this fraud, and try hard to screen out criminals.) Click fraud, or fake hits on your Web site as described in Chapter 3, is another type of Internet fraud, but only directed at companies that advertise on Web sites.

Despite the many positive changes brought about by the Internet revolution, some of its promises fell short. The vast majority of consumers prefer to shop in physically real stores, most automobile dealers don't pay much attention to auto prices listed on the Internet, and personal contacts still dominate high-level business. The Internet supplements and enhances traditional business activity but does not replace the practice of management and personal relationships.

SUMMARY OF Key Points

1 Summarize the demands information technology places on the manager's job.

Management must build an organization that constantly transforms itself as information technology increases competition. To remain competitive requires innovation. Information and communications technology is at the center of the technological revolution and also makes globalization more practical because of ready access to employees everywhere. In general, information technology places managers in a continuous learning mode. Wireless communication devices facilitate work from different locations.

2 Describe the positive and negative consequences of information technology for the manager.

Information technology helps the manager work smarter in such ways as improved productivity and teamwork, gaining competitive advantage, enhanced business models, improved customer service and supplier relationships, enhanced communication including the virtual office, quick access to vast information, enhanced analysis of data and decision making, greater empowerment and flatter organizations, time saved through employee self-service, and monitoring work and employee surveillance.

Negative consequences of information technology include wasting time at the computer, repetitive-motion disorder, deterioration of customer service, dealing with baffled customers, wired managerial workers, and the encouragement of nonproductive multitasking.

3 Discuss the impact of the Internet on customer and other external relationships.

The biggest impact of the Internet on business comes from selling many goods and services to other businesses over the Internet. Eighty percent of business conducted on the Net today occurs between firms (B2B). The manager must be familiar with e-commerce to help develop strategy, and the manager may work with a reduced staff because of online selling. E-commerce sometimes enables companies to purchase more efficiently than they could through other channels. Managers face the major challenge of how to integrate the traditional way of doing business (the old economy) with e-business (the new economy). Relying strictly on Internet sales is rarely profitable. Well-established companies that integrate e-commerce into their marketing and internal operations have benefited the most from the Net revolution.

Using the Internet, many companies changed their methods of distributing goods, of collaborating inside the company, and of dealing with suppliers. Buyers' power makes it more difficult to charge higher prices, forcing companies to more carefully control costs. Some intermediaries, such as travel agents, have changed because of the Internet. Globalization is enhanced because of the Internet. Companies also experience increased visibility, particularly from angry consumers.

4 Explain the effects of the Internet on internal company operations.

The Internet affects companies in a number of ways, beginning with more effective work processes as encouraged by the flattening of the business playing field through global competition. Information technology facilitates changing the method of distributing goods, and work streamlining. The Internet also squeezes profits and exerts pressure toward cost control, and facilitates data mining. Two outputs of data mining are automated prediction of trends and behavior, and automated discovery of unknown patterns.

5 Pinpoint factors associated with success in e-commerce.

Successful e-businesses provide an excellent call center to allow for the human touch and keep customers informed about order progress. The e-business system requires constant monitoring and updating. Other strategies e-businesses can employ include mixing bricks and clicks, developing a global perspective, and protecting customers against fraud.

KEY TERMS AND PHRASES

Extranet, 486
Virtual office, 486
e-leadership, 486
Intranet (or company intranet), 487
Wiki, 488
Computer goof-off, 490
Work streamlining, 500
Data mining, 501

QUESTIONS

1. What do you regard as the most important way in which a manager can use information technology?
2. What is it about using a BlackBerry (or another brand of personal digital assistant) that so many managers believe increases their productivity?
3. Walk through almost any office, laboratory, or factory today, and you will see most of the workers seated in front of a computer. What did workers do before the advent of computers?
4. Propose a new model for restaurants (other than the quick service type) that will capitalize on automation and information technology.
5. A growing number of managers believe that in order to work on difficult business problems, they must refrain from looking at e-mail for certain blocks of time during the day. In what ways might checking e-mail frequently interfere with problem solving?
6. Many retailing experts predict that retail stores will never die because online shopping cannot replace the experience of visiting a store. What aspects of visiting a store make it preferable to shopping online for so many people?
7. You may have noticed that one of the most frequently offered product categories online is pharmaceuticals. However, the number of physical pharmacies, such as those at CVS, Rite Aid, and Wal-Mart continue to grow. Why do so many consumers continue to choose to purchase pharmaceuticals offline?

SKILL-BUILDING EXERCISE 14-A: Cost Reduction through Information Technology

Work in small groups to identify ten tangible ways that a manager can use information technology to reduce costs. For each item on your list, explain precisely the way in which information technology will reduce costs. Take into account all types of information technology, from a desktop printer to the Internet. A team leader from each group might present the team's findings to the rest of the class.

SKILL-BUILDING EXERCISE 14-B: Thinking about Data Mining

As implied in the text, data mining boils down to making sense of bits of information embedded in a large mass of information. No matter how exquisite the software performing the data mining, the manager or professional has to have good intuition about the potential value of information or patterns of information. To get you in the right mind-set for data mining, do the following puzzlers.

- You are a manager in an insurance company. Your data mining software notes that people under 30 purchase less sun-blocking lotion, buy more cigarettes, and are more likely to let their auto inspection stickers expire. What sense do you make of these data that could help your insurance company?
- You are a human resources professional. Your data mining software indicates that employees who purchase American flags, watch professional football on TV, and own an SUV tend to stay longer with the company. What implications might this information have for staffing your company?
- You are a marketing specialist at a music company. Your data mining software indicates that people who purchase toothpaste with fluoride, own an umbrella, and give money to charity are more likely to pay to download music. What value for your company might you extract from this information?

INTERNET SKILL-BUILDING EXERCISE: E-Commerce Fraud

Many people, including Bill Gates, the cofounder of Microsoft, are worried that Internet fraud, scam, and spam could severely damage the future effectiveness of the Internet. For example, in 2006, a private citizen in Rochester, New York, placed for sale on eBay the city's ferry although he had no involvement with the ferry. (He did receive a bid of $29.8 million from one jokester.) Working individually or as part of a team, find ten apparent e-mail or Web site frauds. Divide your search between Web sites, including online auctions, and e-mail offerings. For Web sites, attempt to identify the person or organization behind the fraud. What prompted you or your group to conclude that the particular offerings were frauds? Should any level of government be taking action about these apparent frauds?

Case Problem 14-A

Tesco PLC Mines Data to Combat Wal-Mart

When Wal-Mart Stores Inc. entered the British market in 1999 by buying Asda, a chain of stores in England, they expected to dominate. Instead, Wal-Mart's largest non-American operation has been struggling recently, and its top British rival is thriving.

That rival is Tesco PLC, Britain's largest retailer. Its big weapon is information about its customers. Tesco has signed up 12 million Britons for its Clubcard program, giving cardholders discounts in exchange for their name, address, and other personal information. The Clubcard has helped boost Tesco's market share in groceries to 31 percent, nearly double the 16 percent held by Wal-Mart's Asda chain.

The data let Tesco tailor promotions to individual shoppers and figure out quickly how new initiatives are working. After Tesco introduced Asian herbs, cooking oil, and other ethnic foods in neighborhoods with many Indians and Pakistanis, the data showed the new products were also popular with affluent white customers. The company quickly expanded the rollout.

Tesco's computers often turn up counterintuitive results. Shoppers who buy diapers for the first time at a Tesco store can expect to receive coupons by mail for baby wipes, toys—and beer. Tesco's analysis showed that new fathers tend to buy more beer because they are home with the baby and can't go to the pub.

The data-driven strategy puts Tesco at the vanguard in retailing as traditional advertising loses effectiveness. Procter & Gamble, Coca-Cola Co., and Kimberly-Clark are among the consumer-products companies that buy analyses based on Tesco data.

The British retailer is increasingly battling Wal-Mart around the globe. It plans to open a chain of small stores on the West Coast of the United States, its first foray onto Wal-Mart's home turf. Wal-Mart wants to expand in Central Europe, where Tesco has a firm foothold.

Tesco has used its knowledge of shoppers to fight Wal-Mart's core appeal: low prices. After Wal-Mart bought Asda, Tesco searched its database and singled out shoppers who buy the cheapest available item. They were most likely to be tempted by Asda, Tesco figured. Tesco then identified 300 items that these price-sensitive shoppers bought regularly. One was Tesco Value Brand Margarine. Tesco lowered the price of the margarine, along with other products with similar profiles. As a result, shoppers didn't defect to Asda, says Clive Humby, chairman of a British research firm that is majority-owned by Tesco and analyzes customer data for the retailer.

One of the company's private labels is the "Tesco Finest" line that includes duck pâté and cashmere sweaters. The idea for the finest line came a few years ago when Clubcard data showed that higher-spending customers weren't buying wine, cheese, and fruit from Tesco. The retailer upgraded its offerings in those categories.

Discussion Questions

1. What has this case description got to do with data mining?
2. How ethical is Tesco in making use of information about its customers?
3. Advise Tesco management on how they could make even more profitable use of customer data.
4. Wal-Mart has great information technology of its own, so why are they not able to out-compete Tesco in England?

Source: Cecile Rohwedder, "Stores of Knowledge: No. 1 Retailer in Britain Uses 'Clubcard' to Thwart Wal-Mart," *The Wall Street Journal*, June 6, 2006, pp. A1, A16.

Case Problem 14-B

Down the Tubes at utube

YouTube's enormous popularity has created a big headache for another "utube"—a Toledo, Ohio, company that sells used machines that makes tubes. Universal Tube & Rollform Equipment Corp.'s Web site, http://www.utube.com, was inaccessible for most of the week, overwhelmed by millions of people looking for the popular online video site. The confusion took off during the summer of 2006, said Ralph Girkins, Universal Tube's president.

The company with just 17 employees got 68 million hits on its site in August 2006, making it one of the most popular manufacturing websites. The site shut down just before Google Inc. announced plans to buy YouTube for $1.65 billion. A move to a new server didn't help, but a few days later Universal Tube's site was back up after the company added more capacity.

"We couldn't work on it, couldn't do anything," Girkins said one day after the site was back up and running. At least 50 customers called during the week to point out the problem, he said. He hasn't figured out yet how much it has cost to get the site running. "Just get me going. I don't care," Girkins said. "If I miss a $300,000 sale because of a Web site problem, it doesn't make any sense not to fix it."

Universal Tube, based in suburban Perrysburg and founded in 1985, has about $12 million in annual sales. The company is looking to sell the Web address and find a new home for its Web site even though the company uses the http://www.utube.com name to advertise to customers overseas, Girkins said.

"We know we can't keep it," he said. "It's going to be a never-ending problem."

Discussion Questions

1. What would you advise Universal Tube to do about the conflict with YouTube versus utube?
2. Utube preceded YouTube, so should Google (the owner of YouTube) be sued for damages done to Universal Tube?
3. Is there any way in which utube might be able to capitalize on the confusion by YouTube visitors?
4. What does this case tell us about the hazards of e-commerce?

Source: Keith Regan, "You Tube Sued Over Domain Name," *E-Commerce Times*, March 5, 2007; Justin Mann, "UTube Sues You Tube," *TechSpot*, November 2, 2006; John Seewer, "You Tube Causes Headache for Another 'utube'," Associated Press, October 13, 2006.

chapter 15

Essentials of Control

Objectives

After studying this chapter and doing the exercises, you should be able to:

1 Explain how controlling relates to the other management functions.

2 Understand the different types and strategies of control.

3 Describe the steps in the control process.

4 Explain the use of nonbudgetary control techniques.

5 Have an awareness of the various types of budgets, and the use of budgets and financial ratios for control.

6 Explain how managers and business owners manage cash flow and control costs, and use nontraditional measures of financial performance.

7 Describe how an information system contributes to control.

8 Specify several characteristics of effective controls.

Ever since taking a $1 million business improvement loan in 1997, Sophie and Roman Shor, owners of Roman Jewelers in Flemington, NJ, had struggled. Sure, the loan let them renovate their store. But it also saddled them with $12,500-a-month payments. The Shors were forced to keeping tapping into a line of credit to pay their other bills. "It created a lot of stress," says Sophie, vice-president of the 35-employee, $5 million company. "We were always borrowing from the bank, but it was important that we pay our vendors on time."

After four years of this, the husband-and-wife team finally consulted a financial planner. By improving their accounts receivable and taking control of their debt, they were able to sharply increase their cash flow and get back on track. The Shors have since expanded to a second location, completed the renovations of the original store, and added more profitable, higher-end jewelry lines. "Cash flow is the most important thing in business," says CEO Roman Shor. "Without it, you can't function. But when you have it, you can purchase the most modern technology and get the best employees."[1]

The story about the jewelry store owners and operators illustrates the importance of managing cash and cost control. After the couple better managed their cash and kept costs under control, the business turned profitable. The control

1 Virginia Munger Kahn, "Beating the Cash Crunch," *Business Week Small Biz*, Spring 2005, p.79.

function of management involves measuring performance and then taking corrective action if goals are not being achieved.

Controls make many positive contributions to the organization. Controlling aligns the actions of workers with the interests of the firm. Without the controlling functions, managers cannot know whether people are carrying out their jobs properly. As seen by the National Oceanic and Atmospheric Administration, management controls are used daily by managers and employees to accomplish the identified objectives of the organization.[2] Controls enable managers to gauge whether the firm is attaining its goals. Controls often make an important contribution to employee motivation. Achieving the performance standards set in a control system leads to recognition and other deserved rewards. Accurate control measurements give the well-motivated, competent worker an opportunity to be noticed for good work.

In this chapter we emphasize the types and strategies of controls, the control process, budgets and controls, how managers manage cash flow and cut costs, and the use of information systems in control. Finally, we describe characteristics of effective controls.

CONTROLLING AND THE OTHER MANAGEMENT FUNCTIONS

Learning Objective 1

Explain how controlling relates to the other management functions.

Controlling, sometimes referred to as the terminal management function, takes place after the other functions have been completed. Controlling is most closely associated with planning, because planning establishes goals and the methods for achieving them. Controlling investigates whether planning was successful.

The links between controlling and other major management functions are illustrated in Exhibit 15-1. Controlling helps measure how well planning, organizing, and leading have been performed. The controlling function also measures the effectiveness of the control system. On occasion, the control measures are inappropriate. For example, suppose one measure of sales performance is the volume of sales. Such a measure might encourage a sales representative to push easier to sell products instead of helping the company establish a few new products. Spending more time developing a market for the new products would probably boost the sales representative's effectiveness. More will be said about effective control measures later.

PLAY VIDEO

ESSENTIALS OF CONTROL

"Go to academic.cengage.com/management/dubrin and view the video. How has Honda used quality to promote its production? How does Honda ensure quality?"

The planning and decision-making tools and techniques described in Chapter 6 can be used as tools and techniques of control as well. For example, a Gantt chart keeps track of how well target dates for a project are being met. Keeping track is a control activity. If an event falls behind schedule, a project manager usually takes corrective action.

2 "Management Controls Overview," *National Oceanic & Atmospheric Administration, U.S. Department of Commerce*, http://www.corporateservices.noaa.gov, October 20, 2005.

exhibit 15-1 **The Links Between Controlling and the Other Management Functions**

The control function is extremely important because it helps managers evaluate whether all four major management functions have been implemented.

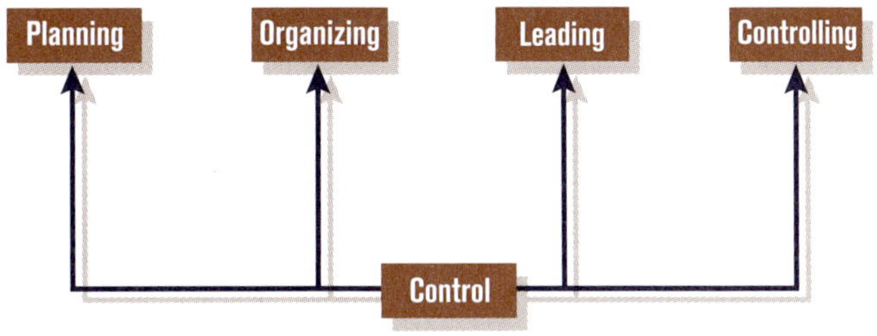

TYPES AND STRATEGIES OF CONTROL

Learning Objective 2

Understand the different types and strategies of control.

Controls can be classified according to the time at which the control is applied to the activity—before, during, or after. Another way of describing controls relates to the source of the control—external versus internal.

The Time Element in Controls

A **preventive control** (or precontrol) takes place prior to the performance of an activity. A preventive control prevents problems that result from deviation from performance standards. Preventive controls are generally the most cost-effective. A manufacturer that specifies quality standards for purchased parts establishes a preventive control. By purchasing high-quality parts, the manufacturer prevents many instances of machine failure. Preventive controls are also used in human resource management. Standards for hiring employees are preventive controls. For example, a company may require that all job candidates are nonsmokers. This preventive control helps decrease lost productivity due to smoking breaks outside the building and smoking-related illnesses.

Concurrent controls monitor activities while they are carried out. A typical concurrent control takes place when a supervisor observes performance, spots a deviation from standard, and immediately makes a constructive suggestion. For example, suppose a telemarketing manager overhears a telemarketing specialist fail to ask a customer for an order. On the spot, the manager would coach the telemarketer about how to close an order.

Feedback controls (or postcontrols) evaluate an activity after it is performed. Feedback controls measure history by pointing out what went wrong in the past. The process of applying the control may provide guidelines for future corrective action. Financial statements are a form of feedback control. If a financial report indicates that one company in a conglomerate lost money, top-level managers can then confer with company (or division) managers to see how to improve the situation.

Exhibit 15-2 summarizes the three types of time-based controls. Most firms use a combination of preventive, concurrent, and feedback controls. An important part of a manager's job is choosing controls appropriate to the situation.

preventive control
A control that takes place prior to the performance of an activity.

concurrent control
A type of control that monitors activities while they are carried out.

feedback control
A control that evaluates an activity after it is performed.

exhibit 15-2 Three Types of Time-Based Controls

Controlling can take place before, during, or after an event or process. Preventive controls usually offer the biggest payoff to the organization.

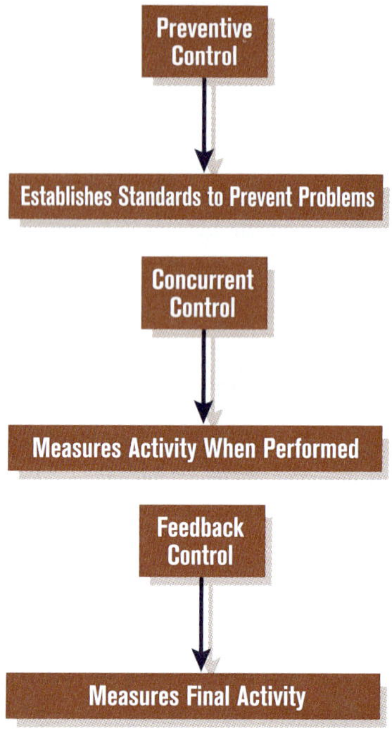

External Versus Internal Controls

Controls can be classified according to their underlying strategy. **External control strategy** is based on the belief that employees are motivated primarily by external rewards and need to be controlled by their managers. An effective external control system involves three steps. First, the objectives and performance standards need to be relatively difficult in order to gain optimum effort of team members and leave little leeway in performance. Second, the objectives and measures must be set in such a way that people cannot manipulate or distort them. For instance, top-level management should make its own investigation of customer satisfaction rather than take the word of field personnel. Third, rewards must be directly and openly tied to performance.

external control strategy An approach to control based on the belief that employees are motivated primarily by external rewards and need to be controlled by their managers.

An external control strategy produces several different effects. On the positive side, employees may channel considerable energy into achieving objectives. Employees do so because they know that good performance leads to a reward. A tightly structured control system translates into a high degree of control over employee behavior.

External control can create problems, however. Employees may work toward achieving performance standards, but they may not develop a commitment to the firm. They may reach standards but not be truly productive. Reaching standards without being productive is sometimes referred to as "looking good on paper." Suppose the marketing and sales director of a telecommunications company establishes as a performance standard a high number of customers processed. To achieve this standard, the customer service manager instructs the customer service representatives, "Take care of as many calls as you can. And minimize the time customers are kept on hold." As a result, the customer service reps spend brief amounts of time on the phone attempting to resolve problems with most customers. Instead of customers being happy with customer service, many of them are dissatisfied with the abrupt treatment. The standard of taking care of more customers is met, yet at the same time customer service deteriorates.

internal control strategy
An approach to control based on the belief that employees can be motivated by building their commitment to organizational goals.

Internal control strategy is based on the belief that employees can be motivated by building their commitment to organizational goals. Self-managed work teams and other forms of empowerment rely on an internal control strategy. Management may impose the controls but the employees are committed to them. Toyota Corp. provides an instructive example of employees being committed to controls, especially in the form of high quality and cleanliness. Adhering to high quality is part of the Toyota culture, so the majority of Toyota manufacturing workers enjoy meeting the quality standards imposed by management.

Building an effective internal control system requires three steps. First, group members must participate in setting goals. These goals are later used as performance standards for control purposes. Second, the performance standards (control measures) must be used for problem solving rather than for punishment or blame. When deviations from performance are noted, superiors and subordinates work together to solve the underlying problem. Third, although rewards should be tied to performance, they should not be tied to only one or two measures. An internal control strategy calls for evaluation of an employee's total contribution, not one or two quantitative aspects of performance.

An internal control system is not necessarily good, and an external control system is not necessarily bad. Internal controls work satisfactorily for a high-caliber, well-motivated workforce. External controls compensate for the fact that not everybody is capable of controlling their own performance (or self-leadership), or is committed to organizational goals. If applied with good judgment and sensitivity, external control systems work quite well. The effective use of controls thus follows a contingency, or "if…, then…," approach to management.

STEPS IN THE CONTROL PROCESS

Learning Objective 3
Describe the steps in the control process.

The steps in the control process follow the logic of planning: (1) performance standards are set, (2) performance is measured, (3) performance is compared to standards, and (4) corrective action is taken if needed. The following discussion describes these steps and highlights the potential problems associated with each one. Exhibit 15-3 presents an overview of controlling.

exhibit 15-3 Steps in the Controlling Process

Controlling begins with setting meaningful standards that are accepted by the people doing the measuring and those being measured.

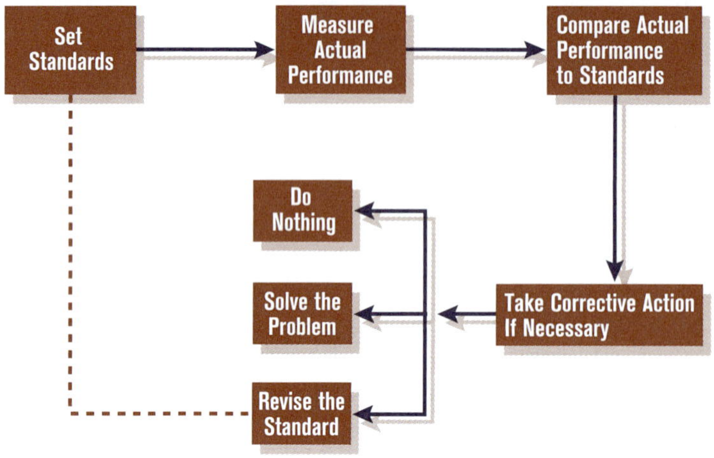

Setting Appropriate Performance Standards

standard A unit of measurement used to evaluate results.

A control system begins with a set of performance standards that are realistic and acceptable to the people involved. A **standard** is a unit of measurement used to evaluate results. Standards can be quantitative, such as cost of sales, profits, or time to complete an activity. Standards can also be qualitative, such as a viewer's perception of the visual appeal of an advertisement. Laws are often the basis for standards because performance must comply with laws and regulations such as those relating to disposal of toxins, fair employment practices, and safety. An effective standard shares the same characteristics as an effective objective (see Chapter 4). Exhibit 15-4 presents two of the

exhibit 15-4 Two Performance Standards Established for a Customer-Service Operation

The performance standards shown here give customer-service representatives precise targets for meeting organizational objectives. Performance evaluation is based on how well customer-service representatives, individually and as a group, meet these standards.

CSR Objectives	Distinguished Performance (4 points)	Above-Standard Performance (3 Points)	Standard Performance (2 Points)	Below-Standard Performance (1 Point)
Customer Satisfaction	89% or higher overall customer satisfaction	86%–88% overall customer satisfaction	83%–85% overall customer satisfaction	<83% overall customer satisfaction
Calls Answered in 30 Seconds	Group consistently answers 80% or more of calls within 30 seconds.	Group consistently answers 75%–79% of calls within 30 seconds.	Group consistently answers 70%–74% of calls within 30 seconds.	Group consistently answers <70% of calls within 30 seconds.

performance standards established for a customer service representative unit within a telecommunications company.

Historical information about comparable situations often provides the basis for setting initial standards. Assume a manufacturer wants to establish a standard for the percentage of machines returned to the dealer for repair. If the return rate for other machines with similar components is 3 percent, the new standard might be a return rate of no more than 3 percent.

At times, profit-and-loss considerations dictate performance standards. A case in point is the occupancy-rate standard for a hotel. Assume break-even analysis reveals that the average occupancy rate must be 75 percent for the hotel to cover costs. Hotel management must then set an occupancy rate of at least 75 percent as a standard.

Measuring Actual Performance

To implement the control system, performance must be measured. Performance evaluations are one of the major ways of measuring performance. Supervisors often make direct observations of performance to implement a control system. A simple example would be observing to make sure a sales associate always asks a customer, "Is there anything else I could show you now?" A more elaborate performance measure would be a ten-page report on the status of a major project submitted to top-level management. The aspects of performance that accountants measure include manufacturing costs, profits, and cash flow (a statement of cash receipts and payments). Measurement of performance is much more complex than it would seem on the surface. The list that follows presents three important conditions for effective performance measurement:[3]

1. *Agree on the specific aspects of performance to be measured.* Top-level managers in a hotel chain might think that occupancy rate is the best measure of performance. Middle-level managers might disagree by saying, "Don't place so much emphasis on occupancy rate. If we try to give good customer service, the occupancy rate will take care of itself. Therefore, let's try to measure customer service."
2. *Agree on the accuracy of measurement needed.* In some instances, precise measurement of performance is possible. Sales volume, for example, can be measured in terms of customer billing and accounts paid. The absolute number or percentage of customer returns is another precise measurement. In other instances, precise measurement of performance may not be possible. Assume top-level managers of the hotel chain buy the idea of measuring customer service. Quantitative measures of customer satisfaction—including the ratings that guests submit on questionnaires and the number of formal complaints—are available. However, many measurements would have to be subjective, such as the observation of the behavior of guests, including their spontaneous comments about service. These qualitative measures of performance might be more relevant than the quantitative measures.

3 Richard O. Mason and E. Burton Swanson, "Measurement for Management Decision: A Perspective," *California Management Review,* Spring 1979, pp. 70–81.

deviation
In a control system, the size of the discrepancy between performance standards and actual results.

3. *Agree on who will use the measurements.* In most firms, managers at higher levels have the authority to review performance measures of people below them in the hierarchy. Few people at lower levels object to this practice. In a team-based organization, peers might be allowed to see each other's performance measurements. Another issue centers on the level of staff access to control reports. Line managers sometimes believe that too many staff members make judgments about their performance.

Comparing Actual Performance to Standards

After establishing standards and taking performance measurements, the next step is to actually compare performance to standards. Key aspects of comparing performance to standards include measuring the deviation and communicating information about it.

Deviation in a control system indicates the size of the discrepancy between performance standards and actual results. It is important to agree beforehand how much deviation from the standard is a basis for corrective action. When using quantitative measures, statistical analysis can determine how much of a deviation is significant. Recall the 75 percent occupancy rate standard in the hotel example. A deviation of plus or minus 3 percent may not be considered meaningful but rather caused by random events. Deviations of 4 percent or more, however, would be considered significant. Taking corrective action only in the case of significant deviations applies the exception principle.

Sometimes a deviation as small as 1 percent from the standard can have a big influence on company welfare. If a business unit fails by 1 percent to reach $100 million in sales, the firm has $1 million less money than anticipated. At other times, deviations as high as 10 percent might not be significant. A claims department might be 10 percent behind schedule in processing insurance claims. However, the claims manager might not be upset, knowing that all the claims will eventually be processed.

When statistical limits are not available, it takes wisdom and experience to diagnose a random deviation. Sometimes factors beyond a person's influence lead to a one-time deviation from performance. In such a case, the manager might ignore the deviation. For example, a person might turn in poor performance one month because he or she faced a family crisis.

For the control system to work, the results of the comparison between actual performance and standards must be communicated to the right people. These people include the employees themselves and their immediate managers. At times, the results should also be communicated to top-level managers and selected staff specialists. They need to know about events such as exceptional deviations from safety and health standards. For example, nuclear power plants are equipped with elaborate devices to measure radiation levels. When a specified radiation level is reached or exceeded, several key people are notified automatically.

Taking Corrective Action

An evaluation of the discrepancy between actual performance and a standard presents a manager with three courses of action: do nothing, solve the problem, or revise the standard. Each of these alternatives may be appropriate, depending on the results of the evaluation.

Do Nothing

The purpose of the control system is to determine whether the plans are working. No corrective action is required if the evaluation reveals that events are proceeding according to plan. Doing nothing, however, does not mean abdicating, or giving up, responsibility. A manager might take the opportunity to compliment employees for having achieved their objectives (thus increasing employee motivation), but do nothing about their approach to reaching objectives because performance measurements show it to be effective.

Solve the Problem

The big payoff from the controlling process concerns the correction of deviations from substandard performance. If a manager decides that a deviation is significant (nonrandom), he or she starts problem solving. Typically the manager meets with the team member to discuss the nature of the problem. Other knowledgeable parties might participate in the problem-solving process. At times, a significant deviation from a performance standard demands a drastic solution. A severe shortfall in cash, for example, might force a retailer to sell existing inventory at a loss.

Sometimes a manager can correct the deviation from a performance standard without overhauling current operations. An office manager in a group dental practice used a control model to measure the percentage of professional time allotted to patient care. The analysis revealed that non-billed time exceeded 10 percent—an unacceptable deviation. The corrective action involved two steps. First, workers scanned dental records to find patients overdue for cleaning and checkups. Second, the office manager telephoned these people and asked whether they would like to schedule an appointment for cleaning and a checkup. The successful telemarketing campaign filled virtually all the slack time within ten days.

Revise the Standard

Deviations from standard are sometimes attributable to errors in planning rather than to performance problems. Corrective action is thus not warranted because the true problem is an unrealistic performance standard. Consider an analogy to the classroom: If 90 percent of the students fail a test, the real problem could be an unrealistically difficult test.

Standards often must be revised because of changes in the external environment. As more and more companies shifted to e-commerce, standards of hotel occupancy rates had to be lowered. The reason is that business travel decreased as more business was conducted over the Internet rather than in person. The use of videoconferences to substitute for in-person meetings also bit into hotel occupancy. Planning for a new task can also create a need for revised standards. Performance quotas may be based on "guesstimates" that prove to be unrealistically difficult or overly easy to reach. A performance standard is too difficult if no employee can meet it. A performance standard may be too easy if all employees can exceed it. As Exhibit 15-3 shows, revising standards means repeating the control cycle.

NONBUDGETARY CONTROL TECHNIQUES

Learning Objective 4

Explain the use of nonbudgetary control techniques.

One way of classifying control techniques is to divide them into those based on budgets versus those not based on budgets. In this section we describe nonbudgetary techniques, and classify them into two types. **Qualitative control techniques** are methods based on human judgments about performance that result in a verbal rather than a numerical evaluation. For example, customer service might be rated as "outstanding." Even using a 1-to-5 rating scale could be interpreted as a qualitative technique because the rating is based on an overall human judgment. **Quantitative control techniques** are methods based on numerical measures of performance, such as lines of computer code produced per hour.

quantitative control technique A method of controlling based on numerical measures of performance.

Exhibits 15-5 and 15-6 summarize qualitative and quantitative control techniques, respectively. The purpose in listing them is primarily to alert you to their existence. Chapter 6 provided details about four of the quantitative control techniques described in Exhibit 15-6. When interpreting the results of an audit, it is necessary to evaluate carefully the processes used to provide the information. A key factor to investigate is the political motivation of the people conducting the audit. Are the auditors going out of their way to please management? Are they out to make management look bad? Or are they motivated only to be objective and professional?

The auditing process has come under considerable scrutiny in recent years because of many reported cases of unethical and illegal reporting of financial

exhibit 15-5 Qualitative Control Techniques

The competence and ethics of people collecting information for qualitative controls influence the effectiveness of these controls.

Technique	Definition	Key Features
External audit	Verification of financial records by external agency or individual	Conducted by an outside agency, such as a CPA firm
Internal audit	Verification of financial records by an internal group of personnel	Wide in scope, including evaluation of control system
Management audit	Use of auditing techniques to evaluate the overall effectiveness of management	Examines wide range of management practices, policies, and procedures
Personal observation	Manager's firsthand observations of how the well plans are carried out	Natural part of manager's job
Performance appraisal	Formal method or system of measuring, evaluating, and reviewing employee performance	Points out areas of deficiency and areas for corrective action; manager and group member jointly solve the problem

exhibit 15-6 Quantitative Control Techniques Used in Production and Operations

Quantitative control techniques are widely accepted because they appear precise and objective.

Technique	Definition	Purpose
Gantt chart	Chart depicting planned and actual progress of work on a project	Describes progress on a project
PERT	Method of scheduling activities and events using time estimates	Measures how well the project is meeting the schedule
Break-even analysis	Ratio of fixed costs to price minus variable costs	Measures organization's performance and gives basis for corrective action
Economic-order quantity (EOQ)	Inventory level that minimizes ordering and carrying costs	Avoids having too much or too little inventory
Variance analysis	Major control device in manufacturing	Establishes standard costs for materials, labor, and overhead, and then measures deviations from these costs

information by business firms. The auditors are dependent on the client for their fees, and also the same firm that audits a company's books might be selling consulting services to them. Auditors, being human, suffer from an unconscious bias to see what they want to see and not displease the clients they serve.[4] It is sometimes difficult to be objective because of our unconscious tendencies to survive by not biting the hand that feeds us.

Another problem is that sometimes auditors ask managers whose books they are investigating if they (the managers) suspect fraud. If the managers say no, the auditors are less likely to dig deeply because there is less apparent risk.[5] The Sarbanes-Oxley Act of 2002 includes provisions for making auditors more independent, and puts the accounting industry under tightened federal oversight.

qualitative control technique A method of controlling based on human judgments about performance that result in a verbal rather than numerical evaluation.

budget A spending plan expressed in numerical terms for a future period of time.

BUDGETS AND BUDGETARY CONTROL TECHNIQUES

Learning Objective 5

Have an awareness of the various types of budgets, and the use of budgets and financial ratios for control.

When people hear the word *budget,* they typically think of tight restrictions placed on the use of money. The car-rental agency name Budget Rent-A-Car was chosen because of popular thinking that the adjective *budget* means conservative spending. In management, a budget does place restrictions on the use of money, but the allotted amounts can be quite generous. A **budget** is a plan, expressed in numerical terms, for allocating resources. The numerical terms typically refer to money, but they could also refer to such things as the amount of energy or the number of laser cartridges used. A budget typically involves cash outflow and inflow.

4 Jonathan Weil, "Behind Wave of Corporate Fraud, A Change in How Auditors Work," *The Wall Street Journal,* March 25, 2004, p. A1.

5 Max H. Bazerman, George Lowenstein, and Don A. Moore, "Why Good Accountants Do Bad Audits," *Harvard Business Review,* November 2002, pp. 96–102.

Virtually every manager assumes some budget responsibility, because a budget outlines a plan for allocating resources. Without budgets, keeping track of how much money is spent in comparison to how much money is available would be nearly impossible. Here we look at different types of budgets and how to use budgets for control. We also describe four other topics closely tied in with budgeting and control: managing cash flow and cost cutting, the balanced scorecard, activity-based accounting, and the measurement of intellectual capital. Readers familiar with accounting and finance will find much of this information a review.

Types of Budgets

Budgets can be classified in many ways. For example, budgets are sometimes described as either fixed or flexible. A *fixed budget* allocates expenditures based on a one-time allocation of resources. The organizational unit receives a fixed sum of money that must last for the budget period. A *flexible budget* allows for variation in the use of resources on the basis of activity. Under a flexible budget, an e-commerce department would receive an increased information technology budget if the department increased the scope of its program. Any type of budget can be classified as fixed or flexible.

Many different types of budgets help control costs in profit and nonprofit firms. Exhibit 15-7 presents a tabular summary of eight commonly used budgets. Most other budgets are variations of these basic types. Exhibit 15-8 provides an example of one of the revenue-and-expense budget.

exhibit 15-7 Budgets Commonly Used in Organizations

Type of Budget and Definition	Notable Characteristic
Master budget—consolidates budgets of various units.	Purpose is to forecast financial statements for entire company.
Cash budget—forecast of cash receipts and payments.	Important control measure because it reflects a firm's ability to meet cash obligations, and invest in new opportunities.
Cash flow budget—prediction of a business firm's cash inflow and outflow over a specified time.	Primary purpose is to predict the firm's capacity to take in more cash than it dispenses.
Revenue-and-expense budget—describes in currency amounts plan for revenues and operating expenses.	Most widely used budget, such as a sales budget to forecast sales and estimate expenses.
Production budget—a detailed plan that identifies the products and services needed to match sales forecast and inventory requirements.	Follows the sales forecast and can be considered a production schedule.
Materials purchase/usage budget—identifies the raw materials and parts that must be purchased to meet production demands.	When accurate leads to smooth production. Can be used in retailing to purchase merchandise.
Human-resource budget—provides a schedule to identify human-resource needs for future and the compensation requirements.	Needed to satisfy sales and production demands, and predicts whether hiring or layoffs will be required.
Capital expenditure budget—a plan for spending money on assets used to produce goods or services.	Are usually regarded as major expenditures and are tied to long-range plans.

exhibit 15-8 **March Revenue-and-Expense Budget for Nightclub and Restaurant**

Item	Budget	Actual	Over	Under
Revenues	$40,000	$42,500	$2,500	
Beginning inventory	3,500	3,500		
Purchases	19,250	19,000		$250
End inventory	3,000	3,000		
Cost of goods sold	19,750	19,500		
Gross profit	20,250	23,000	2,750	
Salaries expense	10,500	10,500		
Rent and utilities expense	1,500	1,500		
Miscellaneous expense	100	250	150	
Maintenance expense	650	650		
Total operating expenses	12,750	12,900	150	
Net income before tax	7,500	10,100	2,600	
Taxes (40%)	3,000	4,040		$1.040
Net income	$4,500	$6,060		

Budget summary: Revenues and Net Income exceed budget by $2,500 and $1,560, respectively.

Note: Data analyzed according to Generally Accepted Accounting Principles by Jose L. Cruzet of Florida National College.

Suggestions for Preparing a Budget

Although budgets give the appearance of being factual, objective documents, judgment and political tactics all enter into budget preparation. When preparing a budget, a manager can impress higher-ups if he or she tracks variables with care and makes sound assumptions. In contrast, if the manager allocates resources poorly or permits too much flab, he or she will lose credibility. Here are several recommendations for preparing a sensible budget:[6]

- *Leave wiggle room.* Optimistic projections with little basis in reality will come back to haunt you. Budget conservatively for income and liberally for expenses. Using this approach, you will be impressive if you constrain costs and generate more revenue than you anticipated.
- *Research the competition.* Do some fact-finding to determine how your competitors at other firms arrive at their budget estimates. For example, find out how others adjust for inflation or an industry slump. Managers who submit the best budgets show comparisons to the competition and explain how they can outperform and why.

6 The first three suggestions are from "Master the Art of Budget Projection," Working*SMART*, March 1999, p. 6; the one is from Edward Low Foundation, "How to Prepare a Cash Budget," *eSmallOffice* (http://www.esmalloffice.com/), Copyright © 1999–2006.

- *Embrace reality.* Study the facts carefully, and take a historical perspective in arriving at the correct estimates for any given financial period. For example, if your industry traditionally experiences high turnover, factor high turnover costs into your budget forecast.
- *Do not neglect intuition.* Future sales are contingent on many factors including the competition, the local economic climates, and your own internal operations and capacity. Past experience is important but so is intuition. Estimates must be based on reality and yet contain a little creativity, and optimism if warranted.

Budgets and Financial Ratios as Control Devices

The control process relies on the use of budgets and financial ratios as measures of performance. To the extent that managers stay within budget or meet their financial ratios they perform according to standard.

Budgets and the Control Process

Budgets are a natural part of controlling. Planned expenditures are compared to actual expenditures, and corrective action is taken if the deviation is significant. Exhibit 15-8 shows a budget used as a control device. The nightclub and restaurant owner operates with a monthly budget. The owner planned for revenues of $40,000 in March. Actual revenues were $42,500, a positive deviation. The discrepancy is not large enough, however, for the owner to change the anticipated revenues for April. Expenses were $150 over budget, a negative deviation the owner regards as insignificant. In short, the performance against budget looks good. The owner will take no corrective action on the basis of March performance.

Financial Ratios and the Control Process

A more advanced method of using budgets for control is to use financial ratio guidelines for performance. Four such ratios are presented here.

Gross profit margin. One commonly used ratio is **gross profit margin,** expressed as the difference between sales and the cost of goods sold, divided by sales:

$$\text{Gross profit margin} = \frac{\text{Sales} - \text{Cost of goods sold}}{\text{Sales}}$$

This ratio measures the total money available to cover operating expenses and to make a profit. If performance deviates significantly from a predetermined performance standard, corrective action must be taken.

Assume the nightclub owner needs to earn a 30 percent gross profit margin. For March, the figures are as follows:

gross profit margin A financial ratio expressed as the difference between sales and the cost of goods sold, divided by sales.

$$\text{Gross profit margin} = \frac{\$42{,}500 - \$19{,}500}{\$42{,}500} = \frac{\$23{,}000}{\$42{,}500} = 0.54 \text{ or } 54\%$$

The night club owner is quite pleased with the gross profit margin of 54 percent, and will take no corrective action. However, for the next budgeting cycle, the owner might raise expectations.

Profit margin. One could argue that the gross profit margin presents an overly optimistic picture of how well the business is performing. Another widely used financial ratio is the **profit margin,** or return on sales. Profit margin measures profits earned per dollar of sales as well as the efficiency of the operation. In the business press, the profit margin is usually referred to as simply the margin and calculated as profits divided by sales.

$$\text{Profit margin} = \frac{\text{Net income}}{\text{Sales}} = \frac{\$6{,}060}{\$42{,}500} = 0.14 \text{ or } 14\%$$

A profit margin of 14 percent would be healthy for most businesses. It also appears to present a more realistic assessment of how well the nightclub in question performs as a business.

Return on equity. The **return on equity** is an indicator of how much a firm is earning on its investment. It is the ratio between net income and the owner's equity, or

$$\text{Return on equity} = \frac{\text{Net income}}{\text{Owner's equity}}$$

Assume that the owner of the nightclub and restaurant invested $400,000 in the restaurant, and that the net income for the year is $72,500. The return on equity is $72,500/$400,000 = 0.181 or 18.1 percent. The owner should be satisfied, because few investments offer such a high return on equity.

Revenue per employee. A simple financial ratio that is widely used by business managers is **revenue per employee,** expressed as

$$\text{Revenue per employee} = \frac{\text{Number of Employee}}{\text{Total revenues}}$$

A company with 100 employees that generated $20 million in sales would have revenue per employee of $200,000. According to the 2006 SHRM Human Capital Benchmarking Study, the median revenue per employee for publicly owned for profit organizations is $210,673. The variation among industries and companies is considerable. At the high end, the figure for utilities is $374,932; at the low end, the figure for health-care services is $103,166.[7] Revenue per employee is often used to measure the productivity of the firm. Top management at Cisco Systems, for example, uses revenue per employee as their primary productivity measure.

The ratios presented above offer a traditional view of the financial health of an organization because they emphasize earning a profit. Many start-ups in the telecommunications, information technology, and biotechnology fields with revenues far below their expenses pay salaries and other expenses out of investor capital. Dozens of other companies do not pay their bills at all because they lacked the necessary cash. Without cash to pay bills and profits to pay investors, most companies eventually fail. Ratios such as profit margin and return on equity are therefore still relevant in today's economy.

profit margin
A financial ratio measuring return on sales, or net income divided by sales.

return on equity
A financial ratio measuring how much a firm is earning on its investment, expressed as net income divided by owner's equity.

revenue per employee
A financial ratio measuring how much revenue is generated by each employee, expressed as number of employees divided by total revenues.

7 Study reported in Karen M. Kroll, "Repurposing Metrics for HR," *HR Magazine,* July 2006, p. 67.

economic value added (EVA) Measures how much more (or less) a company earns in profits than the minimum amount its investors expect it to earn.

Other Measures of Financial Health

Several other measures of financial success in addition to financial ratios are widely used by managers. The purpose of most of these measures is to portray the company in a favorable light, so as to impress investors. Economic value added, however, is a conservative measure of a company's financial performance.

Economic value added (EVA). A measure of financial health that works much like a financial ratio is **economic value added (EVA)**. EVA refers to how much more (or less) the company earns in profits than the minimum amount its investors expect it to earn. The index can also be regarded as a measure of the company's efficiency in using resources, or its true economic profit. The minimum amount also known as the cost of capital represents what the company must pay the investors to use their capital. Cost of capital is also calculated as the overall percentage cost of the funds used to finance a firm's assets. If the sole source of financing were junk (high risk) bonds that paid investors 10 percent, the cost of capital would be 10 percent. All earnings beyond the minimum are regarded as excess earnings.

For example, assume that investors give their company $2 million to invest and the investor's minimum desired return is 10 percent, or $200,000 per year. The company earns $300,000 per year. The EVA is $100,000 as follows:

Earnings:	$300,000
Cost of capital:	$200,000 (10% × $2 million capital)
Excess earnings:	$100,000

To put the matter quite simply, if you could earn 5 percent on your investment just by purchasing CDs in a bank, why invest that money in a business that does not return much more than 5 percent? Investors expect higher excess earnings when they invest in a risky venture, such as a company with unproven technology entering a new industry. An example might be manufacturing electronic communication systems for space stations. Investors willing to settle for lower excess earnings usually invest in a company with proven technology in a stable industry, such as construction supplies. EVA is a frequently used control measure because it focuses on creating shareholder value.

EBITDA = revenue – expenses (excluding tax and interest, depreciation, amortization.)

Earnings before interest, taxes, depreciation, and amortization (EBITDA). A rough measure of the success of a company is how much it earns after deducting all expenses but taxes, depreciation, and amortization. **EBITDA is earnings before interest, taxes, depreciation, and amortization.** Capital-intensive business firms often report EBITDA to give investors an inkling of available cash before debt payments, taxes, depreciation, and amortization charges.[8] EBITDA has become a well established measure of the financial success of telecommunications, cable, and media companies.[9] As you can see, EBITDA paints an optimistic picture of a company's financial health because it excludes

8 Richard McCaffrey, "The Limits of EBITDA (News—Telecom Sector)," *The Motley Fool* (http://www.fool.com), Copyright © 1995–2006.
9 "Calculating EBITDA," in Perseus Publishing's *Business: The Ultimate Resource* (Cambridge, MA: Perseus, 2002), p. 677.

important costs. For example, the United Refining Company at one time reported quarterly net income of $6.1 million and EBITDA of $20.1 million. Imagine how profitable many businesses would be if they did not have to pay taxes.

Pro forma earnings. Another way of "putting lipstick on a pig" is to report earnings that exclude nonrecurring items such as restructuring and merger costs. **Pro forma** is a financial statement that excludes write-downs or goodwill and other one-time charges not relevant to future earnings. A large depreciation cost might also be excluded, such as a computer company having to downgrade the value of a warehouse full of desktops that are now powerful enough to run Microsoft's latest operating system.

Pro forma is also referred to as "earnings excluding bad-stuff." The use of pro forma earnings has been criticized because it does not follow Generally Accepted Accounting Principles (GAAP). In its early days when Amazon.com was struggling to produce a profit, company management published pro forma earnings. Eventually Amazon.com did produce a profit, and management no longer emphasized pro forma earnings—so in this case the pro forma statement made sense.

Net debt. Yet another measure of the financial health of an organization is how much money it owes after taking into account how much money is on hand to eliminate the debt if necessary. **Net debt** refers to a company's debt minus the cash and cash equivalents it has on hand.[10] The net debt calculation might be considered a cosmetic device to make corporate debt appear slimmer. Yet, informing the public that debt could be lowered immediately, if necessary, seems like a reasonable assertion.

pro forma
A financial statement that excludes write-downs or goodwill and other one-time charges not relevant to future earnings.

net debt
A company's debt minus the cash and cash equivalents it has on hand.

cash flow
Amount of net cash generated by a business during a specific period.

MANAGING CASH FLOW AND COST CUTTING

In addition to developing and monitoring the cash budget, many managers pay special attention to keeping cash on hand to prevent overreliance on borrowing and being perceived by investors as a firm in financial trouble. Both cash flow and controlling, or cutting, costs help meet these objectives. We look at these two major business processes separately.

Learning Objective 6

Explain how managers and business owners manage cash flow and control costs, and use nontraditional measures of financial performance.

Managing Cash Flow

Cash is so vital to keep almost any type of organization running that cash has been analyzed in many ways. **Cash flow** is the amount of net cash generated by a business during a specific period. Although this definition appears straightforward, many other definitions of cash flow add to its complexity. For example, cash flow can also be described as the excess of cash revenues over cash outlays. Another complexity is that cash flow is calculated in many ways. A useful and readily understandable approach is to divide a corporation's cash flow statement into three sections, each

10 Shawn Young, "Talking Up 'Net Debt' Allows Some Firms To Take a Load Off," *The Wall Street Journal*, July 28, 2003, p. C1.

specifying a different source of cash, with a fourth section that combines the first three.[11]

1. *Cash provided by (or used in) operating activities.* This section indicates how much cash a business uses (a loss), thereby containing clues to the health of earnings. Cash from operating activities is the heart of cash flow and includes subsections: net income, provision for uncollectible money owed to the company, tax benefit from stock options, receivables, inventories, and accounts payable. When most people think of cash flow, they are referring to cash generated by earnings.
2. *Cash provided by (or used in) financing activities.* This section records cash from or paid to outsiders such as banks or stockholders.
3. *Cash provided by (or used in) investing activities.* Recorded here is the cash used to buy or received from selling stock, assets, and businesses, plus capital expenditures.
4. *Summary.* This revealing section lists cash at the beginning and end of the specific period, plus the change in cash position.

A subtle problem with the four types of cash flow listed above is that accounting firms do not always agree with managers as to the definition of *cash*. Of course, money deposited in a bank or in the cash registers or safes is cash, but what about money invested in short-term money market funds, certificates of deposit, or bonds? Are these investments really the equivalent of cash? The Big Four accounting firms are strict about what they count as cash equivalents. Short-term or highly liquid investments are generally classified as cash.[12]

Firms with large cash flows make attractive takeover targets because acquiring firms are likely to use the cash to pay off the cost of the acquisition. A company that does not want to be taken over might deliberately lower its cash flow by taking on a lot of debt. A large cash flow for a business owner contributes to peace of mind because the owner can keep operating without borrowing during a business downturn. During turbulent times having cash in the bank gives managers a feeling of tranquility. With stocks and other investments being so volatile in recent years, "cash is royalty" is truer than ever. Cash on hand is a key measure of financial well-being.

Cash flow analysis is well accepted because it provides a more accurate picture of financial health than sales volume. A company frequently makes a sale but then does not receive payment for a minimum of 30 days. Cash flow analysis provides an important tool because it is less subject to distortion than is a statement of revenues. Many managers use the questionable accounting practice of classifying as "revenue" goods in the hands of distributors, which have not yet been sold, and contracts for which no money has yet been exchanged.

---

11 Anne Tergesen, "The Ins and Outs of Cash Flow," *Business Week,* January 22, 2001.
12 Steven D. Jones, "Firms Ponder What Constitutes Cash," *The Wall Street Journal,* July 27, 2006, p. C3.

Cash flow analysis helps keep managers focused on the importance of managing cash. Paying suppliers too quickly wastes money as does paying too slowly. The latter may lead to penalties or higher prices because the supplier needs to compensate for late payments. Taking steps to receive prompt payment from customers is an essential part of cash management.

free cash flow
A refinement of cash flow that measures the cash from operations minus capital expenditures.

A refinement of cash flow is **free cash flow**, or the cash from operations minus capital expenditures. The capital expenditures in this context are the investments necessary to maintain or expand the company's fixed assets. Free cash flow therefore takes into account the idea that managers should be thinking of needed expenditures such as purchasing a modern call center before they brag about how much cash is on hand. Similarly, if you were a home owner before calculating how much cash you have available, set aside a reserve for the inevitable replacement of your roof or furnace.

Cash flow is sometimes drained by unprofitable customers. The astute manager checks to see if each customer is making a positive contribution to cash flow, as illustrated in the accompanying Management in Action.

Cost Cutting to Improve Financial Health

The ideal way to improve cash flow is to generate more revenue than expenses. However, generating more revenue can be an enormous challenge. Many companies therefore trim costs to improve cash flow. Even when revenues are increasing, some firms reduce costs to remain more

management in action

Analyzing Unprofitable Customers

Phyllis Rothschild, a director for Mercer Management Consulting, says sales averages or bottom-line numbers often hide subtle profitability problems, such as big customer whose many service requests drain the sales team, or a customer that always expects rush delivery on low-margin products.

Rothschild says Mercer worked with a European consumer products company that was selling a slew of custom products to a $5 million customer. To meet the customer's demand, the company relied on four factories and a mixing plant that was used for distribution. When executives tallied the shipping and service costs, they realized they were losing $700,000 a year on the account.

More rigorous accounting showed that the consumer-products company was losing money on other customers too. That prompted a reorganization. The company closed a high-cost factory, dropped some customers, and renegotiated pricing terms with others.

Rothschild suggests managers watch for troubling signs, such as customers that grow more needy or an influx of competitors in the field, which could increase pressure on the sales team. When that happens, she says, managers can't be afraid to act. "It's okay to not try to be everything to everybody," she says.

Source: Jaclyne Badal, "A Reality Check for the Sales Staff: Firms Crack Down on Deals That Generate Revenue While Racking Up Losses," *The Wall Street Journal*, October 16, 2006, p. B3.

competitive. As you may have noticed, the less cash you spend, the more you have on hand. A caution about cost cutting is that it can lead to low morale, lower-quality goods and services, and foster the image of being a cheap company. For example, using old newspapers as packing material is environmentally friendly and saves money but does not fit with a high-quality image.

How do managers know when it is time to cut costs? Obviously, when a firm has low cash flow or is losing money, costs need to be cut pronto. In addition, managers can use ratios as rules of thumbs. Eastman Kodak Company looks carefully at selling, general, and administrative (SG&A) expenses as a percentage of sales to know when cost cutting is required. At one point, Kodak had SG&A costs at 18.9 percent of sales. To become more competitive as it planned to enter the consumer inkjet business, the company established a goal of 15 percent of sales for selling, general, and administrative expenses. During the same time period, Dell Computer had SG&A costs as 10 percent of sales. One of the many ways Kodak reduced these costs was through a reduction in advertising expenses.[13]

Cutting costs by demanding lower prices from suppliers is widely practiced, yet can backfire. For example, in 2006, parts maker Collins & Aikman Corp. halted deliveries to Ford Motor Co. As a result Ford had to temporarily shut down production at an assembly plant in Mexico. The dispute between Ford and Collins & Aikman stemmed from a pricing dispute over instrument panels, carpeting, and other interior parts totaling millions of dollars.[14]

Exhibit 15-9 presents a variety of measures companies use to reduce costs. We caution again about managers resorting to cost-cutting measures that make the company appear cheap. The situation is worsened when everybody but top-level managers and selected professionals is expected to trim costs. At Credit Suisse, for example, hundreds of investment bankers every year receive seven-figure bonuses. At the same time associates who prepare deal books are not permitted to print out color PowerPoint slides because the bank needs to pinch pennies.[15] Cynicism can mount, as illustrated by the following fictitious lodging standard for business travel:[16]

> *All employees are encouraged to stay with relatives and friends while on business travel. If weather permits, public areas such as parks should be used as temporary lodging sites. Bus terminals, train stations, and office lobbies may provide shelter in periods of inclement weather.*

---

13 Mike Dickinson, "Kodak Zeroes In On SG&A Costs on Final Leg of Its Transition," *Rochester Business Journal*, November 3, 2006, pp. 1, 8, 11.

14 Jeffrey McCracken, "Ford Gets Cut Off by a Top Supplier As Detroit Squeezes Parts Maker," *The Wall Street Journal*, October 18, 2006, p. A1.

15 Daniel Gross, "Pinching the Penny Pinchers," *Slate* (http://www.slate.com), September 25, 2006.

16 "Work Place Notices: New Corporate Cost-Cutting Policy," http://www.home.att.net/~angry_old_man/, accessed January 14, 2007.

exhibit 15-9 A Variety of Ways to Cut Costs

Saving money can greatly affect profit levels, so managers look for many ways to trim costs that do not damage productivity or morale. Annual savings range from a few hundred dollars to millions, depending on the measures used.

TECHNIQUES FOCUSED MOSTLY ON PEOPLE

- Minimize business travel by using e-mail, telephone, or videoconferencing when possible.
- Have business travelers fly coach instead of first class, and stay at budget hotels and motels.
- Establish per diem rates for meal allowances instead of an open-ended travel account substantiated by receipts.
- Keep offices, factories, and laboratories at the coolest or warmest temperature that does not lower morale or productivity, or damage equipment. Encourage employees to wear warm clothing in cold months, and light clothing in warm months.
- Establish a telecommuting program to reduce the demand for office space.
- Place frequent business travelers on hoteling status, whereby they do not have a permanent office or cubicle when in the office.
- Ask employees to conduct bimonthly brainstorming sessions to find ways to reduce costs. Offer rewards for the best savings.
- Keep on the payroll only those employees who contribute to the goals of the firm. Hire consultants and subcontractors instead of keeping on the payroll those employees whose skills are needed only occasionally.
- Establish a cadre of retired employees who can serve as temporary workers during peak periods.
- Drop customers who cost you money because of their constant demands for service despite modest purchases.
- Eliminate free coffee and food except for special occasions such as training or Saturday morning meetings.
- Automate wherever possible to reduce payroll costs so long as the automation does not drive away business, such as in many call centers that rely heavily on menus driven by voice-recognition.

TECHNIQUES FOCUSED MOSTLY ON MATERIAL AND EQUIPMENT

- Use remanufactured parts wherever feasible. As a general rule, 70 percent of the cost to build something new is in the materials, and 30 percent in the labor. Salvaging and rebuilding typically gets the material costs down to 40 percent.[17]
- Compare prices on the Internet before committing to a purchase.
- Substitute e-mail messages for postal mail whenever possible.
- To save on telephone bills, use Internet phones.
- Instead of owning advanced hardware and software, use information technology on demand to provide for information technology requirements.
- Lease equipment when it is less expensive than owning.
- Demand an immediate 5 percent price cut from all suppliers. (Asking for more is likely to lead to resistance and lower-quality supplies.)
- Hold a sale of surplus and obsolete equipment. At the same time sell the equipment over an Internet auction site.
- Centralize buying for a multilocation company, and ask managers to cart some supplies with them after a visit to headquarters.
- Subcontract manufacturing and services that can be done less expensively by other firms.
- Sell the corporate jet and limousines, and ask executives to fly on commercial airlines and drive their own vehicles for business (or take the bus or train).
- Try eBay and other auction sites when making purchases, or use a reverse auction in which suppliers bid on providing you the equipment or supplies you need.
- Trim box sizes for regular shipments to save on postage costs and possibly for other shippers such as FedEx, UPS, and DHL.

TECHNIQUES FOCUSED MOSTLY ON MONEY MANAGEMENT

- Centralize purchasing to obtain better prices on bulk purchases, as done by Home Depot and many other large, geographically dispersed firms.
- Ask suppliers for discounts on early payments. If the discounts are not granted, pay all bills including taxes, utilities, and suppliers as late as possible without incurring a fee. In this way you rather than someone else is earning a return on the money.
- For small businesses, share office expenses, including support services, with several other firms by renting a large office space together and dividing it into offices for each firm.
- Use activity-based costing to help trim costs that do not add value for customers.
- Consolidate advertising and marketing with one agency to earn volume discounts.
- Use a "sweep" checking account that places your unused balances in a relatively high-paying money market account overnight.

17 Brian Hindo, "Everything Old is New Again," *Business Week*, September 25, 2006, p. 65.

NONTRADITIONAL MEASURES OF FINANCIAL PERFORMANCE

As managers continue to look for ways to measure the financial performance of the units they manage, several nontraditional measures of financial performance have emerged. Three such indicators are the balanced scorecard, activity-based costing, and the measurement of intellectual capital.

The Balanced Scorecard

Many researchers and managers have abandoned their exclusive reliance on financial ratios and related indices to measure the health of a firm. Budgets reveal important, but incomplete, information. Managers continue to look for ways to overcome the limited view of performance sometimes created by budgets. An accounting professor and a technology consultant worked with hundreds of companies to devise a **balanced scorecard**—a management system that enables organizations to clarify their vision and strategy and translate them into action.[18] Managers using the balanced scorecard do not rely on short-term financial measures as the only indicators of a company's performance. The balanced scorecard is a strategic approach and performance management system that helps an organization set goals and measure performance from four perspectives that are vital to all businesses, as outlined in Exhibit 15-10.

The balanced scorecard follows a strategy to the extent that it directs the company effort toward achieving the four goals of financial health, customer satisfaction, business processes, and learning and growth. Internal business processes are the mechanisms through which performance expectations are achieved. An example of an internal business process would be whether products and services are built to meet customer requirements. Compensation is based on achieving all the factors included in the balanced scorecard. Many managers attend seminars given by the Balanced Scorecard Institute to guide them in using the balanced scorecard approach.

balanced scorecard
A set of measures to provide a quick but comprehensive view of the business.

activity-based costing (ABC)
An accounting procedure that allocates the costs of producing a product or service to the activities performed and the resources used.

Robert S. Kaplan and David P. Norton report that business firms such as Mobil North American Marketing and Refining, and Brown and Root Engineering Services have imbedded the balanced scorecard into their management systems. As a result, these firms achieved breakthrough performance within two years.[19]

Activity-Based Costing

Concerns that conventional methods of measuring financial performance may be misleading prompt the use of another approach to understanding the true costs involved in conducting business. **Activity-based costing (ABC)** is an accounting procedure that allocates the costs of producing a product

18 Robert S. Kaplan and David P. Norton, "Using the Balanced Scorecard as a Strategic Management System," *Harvard Business Review*, January–February 1996, pp. 75–77; Kaplan and Norton, "Clarifying and Communicating Vision and Strategy into Action: The BSC Framework," http://www.valuebasedmanagement.net, September 27, 2006.

19 Robert S. Kaplan and David P. Norton, "The Balanced Scorecard," in *Business: The Ultimate Resource* (Cambridge, MA: Perseus, 2002), p. 303.

exhibit 15-10 The Official Model for the Balanced Scorecard

The balanced scorecard suggests that we view the organization from *four* perspectives, and to develop metrics, collect data, and analyze it relative to each of these perspectives:

- The Learning and Growth Perspective
- The Business Process Perspective
- The Customer Perspective
- The Financial Perspective

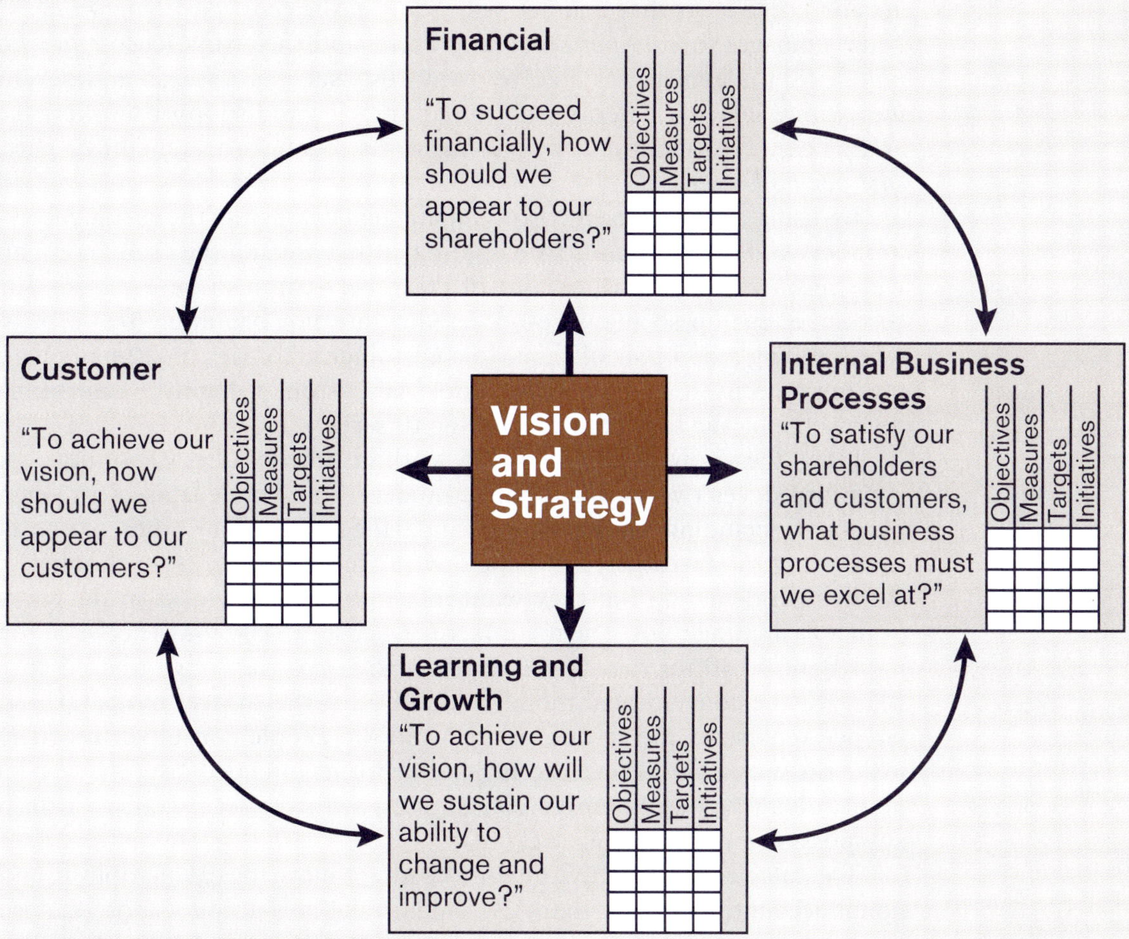

Source: "The Balanced Scorecard Institute," http://www.balancedscorecard.org.

or service to the activities performed and the resources used. An activity-based costing system offers managers a more strategic approach to their business because it presents a comprehensive view of all the costs involved in making a product or service and getting it to market.[20] Among these costs would be research and development, marketing, and delivery. In contrast,

20 Robin Cooper and Robert S. Kaplan, "The Promise—and Peril—of Integrated Cost Systems," *Harvard Business Review*, July-August 1998, p. 111.

a more traditional cost system might focus most on costs such as labor, parts, and administrative overhead. Some ABC systems rank activities by the degree to which they add value to the organization or its outputs. For example, at UPS the trucker driver might add more value to the service than the fuel, truck maintenance, or human resource support.

Activity-based costing is used in both the public and private sectors. For example, many combat activities within the Department of Defense have been using cost-per-unit measures for a long time. Among these applications are Air Force units that manage with the measure *cost per flying hour*. The Navy manages in *cost per streaming hour*, and the Army in *cost per tank mile*.[21] All three measures involve many costs such as research and development time, salaries, deterioration of equipment, and support workers back at the base. Treating military personnel for stress disorders might be part of *cost per tank mile*.

By using activity-based costing, managers can assess the productivity of products and business units by assigning costs based on the use of company-wide resources. The profitability of customers can also be assessed: Some customers use up so many resources they are not profitable to keep. Is it worth selling a $35 pair of shoes to a customer who tries on 20 pairs before making a decision? Similarly, an industrial customer might be unprofitable because he or she takes too much time to serve.

How does activity-based costing work in practice? Let's assume a company introduces two new cell phone models. One phone is used for general purposes, including taking photos and video clips. The other phone is a waterproof model targeted at people who are so attached to technology, or are in such demand, that they want a cell phone that works in the shower or in a swimming pool. The manufacturing cost is $100 for the conventional model and $130 for the shower model. However, the activity-based cost is $125 for the conventional model and $400 for the shower model. The difference represents the resources used and the people consulted in order to make the shower model as safe as possible for its intended use. The wet-look model also requires extensive consultation with the legal staff to iron out any possible product liability claims.

The calculations in activity-based costing follow the calculations in traditional accounting, except that ABC might take into account more materials and processes in determining costs. As shown in Exhibit 15-11, the average unit cost is calculated by dividing the total cost of production by the total number of units of output produced. You will find many good uses in your career for this handy formula.

Measurement of Intellectual Capital

Activity-based costing is but one advance in measuring the financial performance of a firm. A more radical approach regards employee brainpower as a major contributor to the wealth of an organization. This approach makes

---

21 "Activity-Based Costing Concept Paper: Accounting for Operational Readiness," http://www.dod.mil/comptroller/icenter, accessed January 15, 2007.

exhibit 15-11 Measuring Unit Costs with Activity-Based Costing

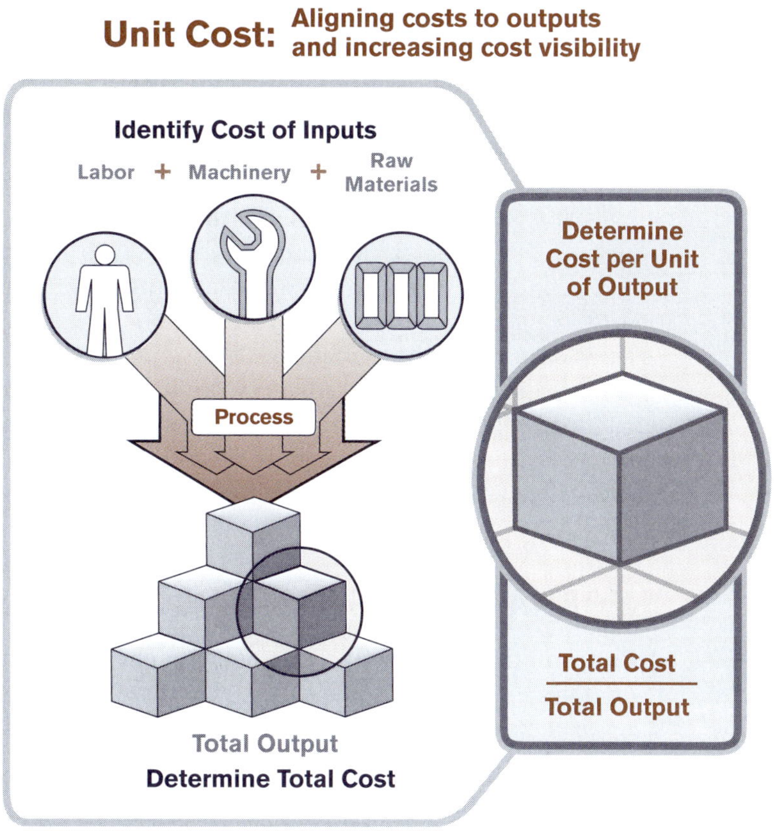

Source: "Accounting for Operational Readiness," http://www.dod.mil/comptroller/icenter/learn/abconcept.htm, accessed January 15, 2007.

some attempt to measure **intellectual capital**, which is the value of useful ideas and the people who generate them. In brief, intellectual capital is knowledge and also the basis for knowledge management. If you are smart and talented, you are probably worth more to a company than its new business jet. Components of intellectual capital include employee knowledge, patents, and research.

A Columbia University study estimates that investing in intangible assets like research and development and employee education and training yields a return eight times greater than an equal investment in new plants and equipment. The reason is that new machinery only allows for incremental improvements. In contrast, research and development and employee education lead to innovations that bring competitive advantage.[22]

intellectual capital
The value of useful ideas and the people who generate them.

The difficult part of using intellectual capital to measure value, for example, comes in trying to attach a reliable value to a group of programmers and

22 "Intellectual Capital: How Top Performing Companies are Measuring the Intangible," http://www.best-in-class.com/research/bestpracticespotlights/intellectual_capital_20.htm, accessed July 9, 2004.

the software they produce. In traditional accounting methods, a fleet of company trucks would receive a higher valuation than the company's software. Intellectual assets are found throughout a firm. An office assistant who has a good feel for customer preference is also a valuable asset, even if difficult to measure. Setting such valuation raises a number of issues because the company does not own the office assistant who can leave at will.

Robert Howell, a professor of finance and accounting, believes that the real assets of a knowledge-intensive company are the know-how of its workforce, intellectual property (such as its patents), brand equity, and relationships with employees, customers, and suppliers. As a starting point as to how these might be valued, Howell says, "At a minimum, I would book as assets such costs as recruitment and training and development, and amortize them over some sort of employment life. Why aren't they as much of an asset as some piece of machinery?"[23]

If you are a manager, and you want to help your company preserve intellectual capital, it is important to keep smart people happy and satisfied. The many human resource initiatives described in Chapter 9 would be helpful, as well as day-by-day effective leadership.

INFORMATION SYSTEMS AND CONTROL

Learning Objective 7

Describe how information system contributes to control.

An **information system (IS)**, or **management information system (MIS)**, is a formal system for providing management with information useful or necessary for making decisions. A managerial control based on valid information makes an effective IS an indispensable part of any control system. The next sections describe how an information system can be used to control, and the electronic monitoring of work.

Control Information Supplied by an Information System

information system (or management information system)
A formal system for providing management with information useful or necessary for making decisions.

The control information that can be generated by an information system is virtually unlimited. Exhibit 15-12 shows a sampling of what an IS keeps track of. A company-specific example is Southland Corp., which owns and franchises the 7-Eleven convenience stores. Its computerized information system tracks inventory and forecasts sales. The system can precisely track 2,300 items and help individual stores stock the right number of items such as Slurpees and low-fat turkey breast on pita. Another advantage of the information system is that it can help analyze sales trends on such factors as time of day, weather, and socioeconomic level of the neighborhood. A computer information system of this type can help the individual store manager and owner cope with the major problems of overstocking perishable items and understocking hot items—such as beer, soft drinks, and snacks in response to a major sports event on television.

23 Quoted in Thomas A. Stewart, "Accounting Gets Radical," *Fortune*, April 16, 2001, p. 192, Much of the discussion of intellectual capital is based on the entire article, pp. 184–194.

exhibit 15-12 Examples of Control Information Supplied by Information Systems

Information systems can:

- Report on sales of products by territory, sales representative, and customer category
- Supply inventory-level information by region, plant, and department
- Describe magazine subscribers by age, income, occupational level, and ZIP code
- Report turnover rates by age, sex, job title, and salary level
- Supply information about budget deviations by location, department, and manager
- Automatically compile financial ratios and compare them to industry standards
- Automatically compile production and operation control indexes and compare them from plant to plant
- Print out a summary of overdue accounts according to customer, and goods or services purchased
- Report hospital-bed occupancy rates according to diagnosis, sex, and age of patient
- Report when sudden increases in absenteeism occur, suggesting that employee stress levels are unacceptably high
- Calculate, by subsidiary, the return on investment of cash surpluses
- Using the Internet, make price comparisons for goods and services
- Estimate how baby boomers are likely to retire within the next five years, thereby providing clues to upcoming recruiting needs

Computer-Aided Monitoring of Work

Information systems are widely used for **computer-aided monitoring of work.** In this type of monitoring, a computer-based system gathers data about the work habits and productivity of employees. Computer-based systems are also used to uncover instances of employees leaking sensitive information, including trade secrets, to outsiders. For example, using software designed for the purpose, a security manager at a pharmaceutical company detected that an employee had sent confidential drug-manufacturing information outside the company.[24] Employee monitoring systems capitalize on the networking of computer terminals to monitor the work of employees who use computer terminals in their jobs or who operate complex machine tools. Once the monitoring software is installed, the central computer processes information from each terminal and records the employee's efficiency and effectiveness.

computer-aided monitoring of work
A computer-based system to monitor the work habits and productivity of employees.

A contributing factor to electronic monitoring of work is that an increased number of employees conduct their work far from their manager's gaze, including at home and in hotel rooms. Also, in the face of global competition and tight budgets, managers are forced to boost worker productivity. Another boost to the use of electronic monitoring is that electronic evidence plays an important role in lawsuits and regulator investigations including insider trading.

Office workers, including those in frequent telephone contact with the public, are the most likely to be monitored. Word-processing specialists are measured by such factors as words keyed per minute, the number of breaks

24 Phred Dvorak and Vauhini Vara, "At Many Companies, Hunt for Leakers Expands Arsenal of Monitoring Tactics," *The Wall Street Journal*, September 11, 2006, p. B1.

taken, and the duration of each break. The reservation center for JetBlue Airways consists of 700 reservation agents who work from home, using computers and phone systems provided by the company. JetBlue management is able to attain exceptional productivity with the assistance of software that enables it to track each agent's telephone activity. When an agent receives a call, the telephone system logs data such as the duration of the call, who hangs up first, and whether the agent is immediately available to answer another call. Also, to monitor quality, every month a supervisor listens to about ten calls, recorded at random, for each worker supervised.[25]

A general guideline is that high-technology monitoring tools can be applied best with workers who perform discrete, measurable tasks during prescribed hours, such as employees in call centers, finance departments, and insurance claims. Monitoring workers whose jobs primarily involve thinking is much more difficult. For example, a chemist might be looking out the window with his feet on the desk—yet at the same time developing an idea for a drug that will prevent high blood pressure.

The results of computer-aided monitoring of work are often used to take harsh action against employees who violate company rules. A survey about electronic monitoring and surveillance involving 526 companies indicated that 25 percent of the organizations surveyed fired workers for misusing the Internet; 25 percent terminated employees for e-mail abuse, and 6 percent were fired for misusing office phones. Over 80 percent of the companies surveyed inform employees that the surveillance will take place, and also post policies about e-mail and Internet use.[26]

The major advantage of an electronic monitoring system is the close supervision it allows managers. Some employees welcome computerized monitoring because it supplements arbitrary judgments by supervisors about their productivity. Computerized work-monitoring systems have substantial disadvantages, however. Many argue that these systems invade employee privacy and violate their dignity. As a result, many lawsuits are being filed against companies. Moreover, electronic monitoring often contributes to low levels of job satisfaction, absenteeism, high turnover, and job stress.

Another concern about electronic monitoring is that executives are usually not monitored even though they are in a better position than other workers to commit fraud such as stealing company money and selling trade secrets. A notable exception about not monitoring executives is that a former CEO of Boeing Corp. was fired when he was caught sending explicit e-mails to his mistress at the company. The basis of his firing was his use of language that would have embarrassed the company—a violation of Boeing's code of conduct.[27]

A study with young workers provides some understanding of when electronic monitoring will be the best accepted. Seasonal high school and college students were surveyed about their reaction to being monitored in their work at

25 The information about JetBlue and the few preceding statements are from Riva Richmond, "It's 10 a.m. Do You Know Where Your Workers Are?" *The Wall Street Journal*, January 12, 2004, pp. R1, R4.

26 Survey results reported in Javad Heydary, "Companies Step Up Electronic Monitoring of Employees," *Ecommerce Times* (http://www.ecommercetimes.com), July 21, 2005.

27 Jared Sandberg, "Monitoring of Workers Is Boss's Right but Why Not Include Top Brass?" *The Wall Street Journal*, May 18, 2005, p. B1.

a summer amusement water park. In one condition of the study, lifeguards were told in advance that they would be monitored to maintain safety standards and to reduce insurance costs. The lifeguards were even told when the detectives with their video cameras would be on the scene. In the other condition, a group of private detectives posed as customers of the water park, and surreptitiously videotaped ticket agents, good service, and gift shop employees. The workers had more favorable attitudes toward the surveillance when they were given advance notice of the system.[28] (Would you have predicted these results?)

An important recommendation to managers about electronic monitoring of workers is to establish an Acceptable Usage Policy and an employee monitoring policy. The usage policy defines appropriate as well as inappropriate use of corporate resources, including the use of telecommunication devices. For example, setting up an eBay business with your employer's desktop is out of bounds. The monitoring policy explains exactly where and when inappropriate Internet access is blocked, and when the company monitors telephone, computer, and Internet usage.[29]

CHARACTERISTICS OF EFFECTIVE CONTROLS

Learning Objective 8

Specify several characteristics of effective controls.

An effective control system improves job performance and productivity by helping workers correct problems. A system that achieves these outcomes possesses distinct characteristics. The greater the number of the following characteristics a given control system contains, the better the system will be at providing management with useful information and improved performance:

1. *The controls must be accepted.* For control systems to increase productivity, employees must cooperate with the system. If employees are more intent on beating the system than on improving performance, controls will not achieve their ultimate purpose. For example, the true purpose of a time-recording system is to ensure that employees work a full day. If workers are intent on circumventing the system through such means as having friends punch in and out for them, the time-recording system will not increase productivity.
2. *The control measures must be appropriate and meaningful.* People tend to resist control measures that they believe do not relate to performance in a meaningful way. The number of visitors to a Web site is sometimes used as a performance measure for the developers of the site. A glitzy Web site might attract a lot of business because it is recommended by network members to each other, yet the visitors may not necessarily purchase from the merchants advertising on the site. For the Web site to continue to generate ad revenues, a more meaningful performance measure is the number of visitors who click on the advertisers' links and make a purchase. So a less glitzy site that attracted fewer but more serious buyers would indicate that the Web site developer is doing a better job.

28 Audra D. Hovorka-Mead, William H. Ross Jr., Tracy Whipple, and Michella B. Renchin, "Watching the Detectives: Seasonal Student Employee Reactions to Electronic Monitoring With and Without Advance Notification." *Personnel Psychology*, Summer 2002, pp. 329–362.

29 Gary S. Millefsky, "Employee Monitoring Facts Every CIO Should Know," http://www.SearchCIO.com, July 25, 2006, p. 3.

3. *An effective control measure provides diagnostic information.* If controls are to improve performance, they must help people correct deviations from performance. A sales manager might be told that he or she was performing well in all categories except selling to small-business owners. This information might prompt the manager to determine what services the company sells that would have more appeal to small businesses.
4. *Effective controls allow for self-feedback and self-control.* A self-administering control system saves considerable time. Employees can do much of their own controlling if the system permits them access to their own feedback. An example is a system whereby clients complain directly to the employee instead of going to management.
5. *Effective control systems provide timely information.* Controls lead to positive changes in behavior if the control information is available quickly. It is more helpful to give workers daily rather than monthly estimates of their performance against quota. Given day-by-day feedback, an employee can make quick adjustments. If feedback is withheld until the end of a month or a quarter, the employee may be too discouraged to make improvements.
6. *Control measures are more effective when employees have control over the results measured.* People rebel when held responsible for performance deviations beyond their control. For example, a resort hotel manager's profits might fall below expectations because of a factor beyond his or her control such as a sudden shift in weather that results in cancellations.
7. *Effective control measures do not contradict each other.* Employees are sometimes asked to achieve two contradictory sets of standards. As a result, they resist the control system. Employees told to increase both quantity and quality, for example, may experience confusion and chaos. A compromise approach would be to improve quality with the aim of increasing net quantity in the long run. Care taken in doing something right the first time results in less rework. With less time spent on error correction, eventually the quantity of goods produced increases.
8. *Effective controls allow for random variations from standard.* If a control allows for random variations that do not differ significantly from the standard, then it is more effective. An ineffective way of using a control system is to quickly take action at the first deviation from acceptable performance. A one-time deviation may not indicate a genuine problem. It could simply be a random or insignificant variation that may not be repeated for years. For example, would you take action if a team member exceeded a $3,000 travel expense allowance by $2.78?
9. *Effective controls are cost-effective.* Control systems should result in satisfactory returns on investment. In many instances they don't because the costs of control are too high. Having recognized this fact, some fast-service restaurants allow employees to eat all the food they want during working hours. The cost of trying to control illicit eating is simply too high. (This policy provides the added benefit of building worker morale.)

In short, the intelligent and sensible use of controls enhances organizational and individual effectiveness without creating morale problems and resentment. Managers must control and lead at the same time.

SUMMARY OF
Key Points

1 Explain how controlling relates to the other management functions.

Controlling is used to evaluate whether the manager is effective in good job planning, organizing, and leading. Controls can also be used to evaluate control systems.

2 Understand the different types and strategies of control.

Controls can be classified according to the time when they are applied. Preventive controls are applied prior to the performance of an activity. Concurrent controls monitor activities while they are being carried out. Feedback controls evaluate and prompt corrective action after activity performance.

Controls can also be classified according to their underlying strategy. An external control strategy is based on the assumption that employees are motivated primarily by external rewards and need to be controlled by their managers. An internal control strategy assumes that managers can motivate employees by building commitment to organizational goals.

3 Describe the steps in the control process.

The steps in the controlling process include setting standards, measuring actual performance, comparing actual performance to standards, and taking corrective action if necessary. To measure performance, agreement must be reached on the aspects of performance to be measured, the degree of accuracy needed, and who will use the measurements.

The three courses of action open to a manager are to do nothing, to solve the problem, or to revise the standard. Taking corrective action on significant deviations only is called the exception principle.

4 Explain the use of nonbudgetary control techniques.

Nonbudgetary control techniques can be qualitative or quantitative. Qualitative techniques include audits, personal observation, and performance evaluation. The auditing process has come under considerable scrutiny in recent years because of many cases of unethical and illegal reporting of financial information by business firms. Quantitative techniques include Gantt charts, PERT, and economic-order quantity.

5 Have an awareness of the various types of budgets, and the use of budgets and financial ratios for control.

A budget is a spending plan for a future period of time, expressed in numerical terms. A fixed budget allocates expenditures based on a one-time allocation of resources. A flexible budget allows variation in the use of resources based on the level of activity. Seven types of budgets are summarized in Exhibit 15-7 for reference purposes. Budgets function as a natural part of controlling. Managers use budgets to compare planned expenditures to actual expenditures, and they take corrective action if the deviation is significant.

Three key financial ratios are gross profit margin, profit margin, return on equity, and revenue per employee. Other ways of measuring financial performance are economic value added (EVA); EBITDA (revenue – expenses) (excluding tax and interest, depreciation, etc.); pro forma earnings; and net debt.

6 Explain how managers and business owners manage cash flow and control costs, and use nontraditional measures of financial performance.

Closely tied in with the cash budget is the special attention managers pay to cash flow. Cash flow measures how much actual cash is available for conducting business. The three sections of a cash-flow statement are cash provided by (or used in) operating activities, financing activities, and investing activities. A firm that writes off many income deductions will have a bigger cash flow. Many companies trim costs to improve cash flow. Too much cost cutting can lead to low morale, low quality, and a company image of cheapness.

Many researchers and managers no longer rely exclusively on financial ratios and related indices to measure the health of a firm. Instead, they use a balanced scorecard that measures the various aspects of an organization's performance, and is also a management system for implementing vision and strategy. Activity-based costing offers another approach to measuring financial performance that goes beyond traditional measures. The method focuses on the activities performed and the resources used to deliver a product or service. Another approach to determining a firm's wealth measures intellectual capital or the brainpower of a firm.

7. Describe how an information system contributes to control.

An information system (IS), or management information system (MIS), is a formal system for providing management with information useful or necessary for making decisions. The IS provides considerable information used for control. Information systems are also used for the electronic monitoring of the work habits and productivity of employees. Although the method helps managers monitor employee performance, it has met with considerable criticism. Electronic monitoring works best when its results are used for constructive feedback.

8 Specify several characteristics of effective controls.

An effective control system results in improved job performance and productivity because it helps people correct problems. An effective control measure is accepted by workers, appropriate, provides diagnostic information, allows for self-feedback and self-control, and provides timely information. It also allows employees some control over the behavior measured, does not embody contradictory measures, allows for random variation, and is cost-effective.

KEY TERMS AND PHRASES

Preventive control, 511
Concurrent control, 511
Feedback control, 511
External control strategy, 512
Internal control strategy, 513
Standard, 514
Deviation, 516
Quantitative control technique, 518
Qualitative control technique, 518
Budget, 519
Gross profit margin, 522
Profit margin, 523
Return on equity, 523
Revenue per employee, 523
Economic value added (EVA), 524
Earnings before interest, taxes, depreciation, and amortization (EBITDA), 524
Pro forma, 525
Net debt, 525
Cash flow, 525
Free cash flow, 527
Balanced scorecard, 530
Activity-based costing (ABC), 530
Intellectual capital, 533
Information system (or management information system), 534
Computer-aided monitoring of work, 535

QUESTIONS

1. Provide an example of how feedback from customers can be used as part of a control system.
2. Tony works full-time as a computer-repair technician who makes onsite repairs for individuals and small businesses. He says his gross profit margin is 94 percent because last year his total revenues were $100,000 and his expenses were $6,000. "I'm actually doing better than Microsoft. They talk about gross profit margins of 80 percent," says Tony. What is wrong with Tony's estimate of his gross profit margin?
3. How does EVA give a company a more accurate picture of its profitability than does profit margin?
4. How can you apply cash flow analysis to better control your personal finances?
5. What type of intellectual capital do you think you provide, or will be providing, an employer?
6. Explain whether you think the work of managers should be electronically monitored?
7. In several companies, a performance standard for maintenance technicians is to have relatively few demands for service from the manufacturing department. Explain the logic behind this performance standard.

SKILL-BUILDING EXERCISE 15-A: Constructive and Destructive Cost Cutting

Using in-person interviews, telephone conversations, or e-mails obtained, do some live research on cost cutting with several people. Ask your respondents for examples of useful, or constructive, cost cutting they have observed on the job. You might include yourself as an interviewee for this exercise. Do the same for useless, or destructive, cost cutting. Look for patterns. What type of cost-cutting measures is likely to be well accepted by workers? What type of cost-cutting measures is likely to be resisted by workers?

SKILL-BUILDING EXERCISE 15-B: Financial Ratios

Jessica Albanese invested a $50,000 inheritance as equity in a franchise print and copy shop. Similar to well-established national franchises, the shop also offers desktop publishing, digital printing, and computer graphics services. Jessica's revenue-and-expense statement for her first year of operation follows:

Item	Financial Result
Revenues	$255,675
Beginning inventory	15,500
Purchases	88,000
End inventory	14,200
Cost of goods sold	89,300
Gross profit	166,375
Salaries expense	47,000
Rents and utilities expense	6,500
Miscellaneous expense	1,100
Maintenance expense	750
Total operating expenses	55,350
Net income before taxes	111,025
Taxes (40%)	44,410
Net income	66,615

Working individually or in small groups, compute the following ratios: gross profit margin, profit margin (return on sales), and return on equity. Groups might compare answers. Discuss whether you think that Jessica is operating a worthwhile business.

INTERNET SKILL-BUILDING EXERCISE: Computing Financial Ratios of Public Companies

Here is an opportunity to financially analyze one of your favorite companies. Go to http://www.hoovers.com and search for the company in question, such as "Memorex." Use the financial information given in Hoover's, including the section on additional financial information. Compute as many of the financial ratios presented in this chapter as you can with the information available. Based on your analyses, what is your opinion of the financial health of the company that you investigated. What recommendations can you make to management?

Case Problem 15-A

The Cash Squeeze at ModernFurnCo

ModernFurnCo is a manufacturer of office and home furniture for a niche market, cramped office and home space in the metropolitan New York market. The 20-person company builds some furniture to display in its Soho district showroom, yet the bulk of its sales are custom designed. A typical customer demand would be to design furniture that would fit in an alcove in an old office building or home. Customers are willing to pay a premium for ModernFurnCo furniture because it enables them to have more usable space, and to feel much less cramped in an office that might be as small as 450 square feet.

Sales slowed down after the attacks of September 11, but have progressed steadily since January 2002. The company attained $6 million in gross revenues for the first time in 2008, and sales have continued to progress since that time. Because of the custom design of the furniture for tight space, ModernCo does not face major competition from discount office furniture stores like Office Depot, Staple, and Office Max. However, there are still hundreds of office and home furniture stores in the area.

Company founder Connie Hoi was asked how she felt about her company's success in the highly competitive New York metropolitan market. "I was feeling great until yesterday," replied Hoi. "I was so proud of our continued growth, and the amount of sales. But then I had a meeting with the accountant to whom we outsource our accounting, taxes, and payroll.

"He told me that despite our high sales and good profit margins, we are facing a cash crisis. Great sales, but not enough money to pay our bills including all our payroll expenses."

Asked what seemed to be the cause of the cash crunch, Hoi replied, "Our home customers are paying us right on time, because no furniture leaves our showroom without a payment in cash, check, or credit card for furniture delivered to a home. The trouble is with our business customers. Enough of them are taking so long to pay that I don't have enough cash on hand to operate the business. So I have had to borrow too much money for the business. Interest payments are taking big chunks out of our profits."

In discussing her plans to improve the cash flow at the company, Hoi said, "I'm hesitant to put too much pressure on our customers. If we irritate a customer, we might not get repeat business. Also, some of our customers suffer from the same problem we do: some of their customers are slow payers or no-payers.

"I know we have to do something. I would hate to see ModernFurnCo go bankrupt despite wonderful sales."

Discussion Questions

1. What do you recommend that Hoi do to improve the company's cash flow?
2. What approach should Hoi take to getting bills paid from delinquent customers?
3. How might the conflict resolution skills described in Chapter 12 help Hoi?

Case Problem 15-B

Microsoft Counts Calories for Employees

Steve Ballmer hates it when Microsoft loses. But for the screamingly competitive CEO, there is one glaring exception: the 61,000 pounds that have vanished from the bodies of 2,152 Microsoft Corp. employees since 2002.

The company did not simply add tips on the low-cal life to in-house newsletter *MicroNews,* or pop for some Jenny Craig. Instead, Microsoft created a weight management benefit (employees already get free medical coverage). The software giant picks up 80 percent of the tab—up to $6,000—for a comprehensive clinical weight-loss program. Cecily Hall, Microsoft's director of U.S. benefits, says that the company has already realized a one-to-one return on investment since the program began. "These people are coming off of prescription drugs, they're seeing their primary care physician less, and not having as much hospitalization," says Hall.

Microsoft's weight management benefits include up to a year's worth of sessions with a personal trainer, behavior and nutritional counseling, support groups, and medical supervision. Its war against weight started in 2002, about the same time Ballmer, then all puff and jowl, lost a fast 50 and turned taut and lean. His newly restructured physique was the inspiration of Redmond, and soon 800 Microsofties were forgoing the logger-man portions in the cafeteria and subbing diet sodas for the free pop.

Today the program is open to all employees who are obese, or who are clinically overweight and have at least two other diseases such as hypertension and depression. A little over a year ago, Strohm Armstrong, 44, weighed 295 pounds, suffered from high blood pressure, and was on his way to Type 3 diabetes. He thought he would never see a day past 70. But after worsening back problems in the fall of 2005, the 5-foot-7-inch technical writer signed on and soon found himself in a special workout facility with private changing rooms to avoid locker room embarrassment.

Now, after a year of eating 2,000 calories a day, Armstrong has lost 116 pounds and is down to a hard body 179. The back pain, high blood pressure, and threat of diabetes are gone. He runs 5K races, exercises at least five times a week, has a few chicken wings at the bar instead of a few dozen, and knows eating is often more about emotions than hunger.

Discussion Questions

1. In what way does this story about Microsoft relate to cost control?
2. In what way does this story relate to monitoring of employee behavior?
3. What do you advise Microsoft managers, including Steve Ballmer, do about employees who feel that the company is encroaching on their civil rights?
4. Explain whether you think Microsoft employees in the weight-loss program should receive a financial bonus or salary increase for having attained their weight-loss goals.
5. What other areas for controlling unhealthy behavior do you suggest that Microsoft attempt to control?

Source: Michelle Conlin, "More Micro, Less Soft: The Software Giant Is Leading the Private Sector in Doing Something About Obese Employees," *Business Week,* November 27, 2006.

chapter 16

Managing Ineffective Performers

Objectives

After studying this chapter and doing the exercises, you should be able to:

1. Identify factors contributing to poor performance.
2. Describe the control model for managing ineffective performers.
3. Know what is required to coach and constructively criticize employees.
4. Understand how to discipline employees.
5. Develop an approach to dealing with difficult people, including cynics.
6. Explain the recommended approach to terminating employees.

Valerie Frederickson, a human resources consultant in Silicon Valley, had a delicate problem: Her office administrator was smart and well-spoken, but after two months of the job, she didn't seem to like the work. "We needed to have her do things like data entry and clean the refrigerator, and she wanted to plan events for us," Frederickson says.

So Frederickson decided to let the administrator go—gently. She gave the woman a small amount of severance pay, helped her get a new job and assured her that the firing wasn't personal. "I told her, 'I like you a lot, and I think of you like a little sister, but I don't want you working here any more. I would like to give you the type of work you seem to want. But we just don't have what you are looking for in our department. The job we have requires the most basic type of help, like entering data and tidying up the place.'"

Frederickson went on to explain to the office administrator that she had many skills and talents that were not being used effectively on the job. "You want to do more higher level work than the position calls for. You want to plan events, yet we have lots of basic work that needs to be performed regularly. I hope we didn't oversell you on the job when you were hired."

The office administrator thought over Frederickson's comment and admitted that the job was a poor fit for her needs. "I thought

ineffective job performance Job performance that lowers productivity below an acceptable standard.

maybe I could grow the job into something that fit my needs, but I guess I was wrong. I never had a chance to be a true office administrator. Instead, the job calls for someone who does grunt work everyday.

"I'll try to find a better fit for me in my next job."[1]

The incident about the office administrator who wasn't a good fit for the job illustrates how dealing with substandard performance is another key part of a manager's job, even if it might be the most uncomfortable. The human resources manager in question handled the situation well even though terminating an employee is the last resort in managing poor performance.

Managerial control requires dealing constructively with **ineffective job performance**, defined as performance that does not meet standards for the position. Ineffective performers are also referred to as problem employees because they create problems for management.

Ineffective performers lower organizational performance directly by not accomplishing their fair share of work. They also lower organizational productivity indirectly. Poor performers decrease the productivity of their superiors by consuming managerial time. Additionally, the productivity of coworkers is often decreased because coworkers must take over some of the ineffective performer's tasks.

The consequences of ineffective performance are enormous, yet difficult to calculate precisely. For example, one set of factors contributing to poor performance is employee deviancy. It includes behaviors such as stealing, cheating, substance abuse, and lack of regard for cost control or quality.[2] In this chapter we address ineffective performance as a control problem for which the manager can take corrective actions. However, control of performance might also involve effective leading, motivating, and staffing.

FACTORS CONTRIBUTING TO INEFFECTIVE PERFORMANCE

Learning Objective 1

Identify factors contributing to poor performance.

Employees are or become ineffective performers for many different reasons. The cause of poor performance can be rooted in the person, the job, the manager, or the company. At times, the employee's personal traits and behaviors create so much disturbance that he or she is perceived as ineffective. Performance is sometimes classified as ineffective, or substandard, because of an arbitrary standard set by management, such as the rank and yank system mentioned in Chapter 9.

Exhibit 16-1 lists a variety of factors that can contribute to ineffective performance, divided into four categories: personal, or related to the job, manager, or company. Usually, the true cause of ineffective performance is a combination

1 The first 65 words are from Phred Dvorak, "Firing Good Workers Who Are a Bad Fit," *The Wall Street Journal*, May 1, 2006, p. B5.

2 Barrie E. Litzky, Kimberly A. Eddleston, and Deborah L. Kidder, "The Good, the Bad, and the Misguided," *Academy of Management Perspectives*, February 2006, p. 91.

of several factors. Assume that an employee is late for work so frequently that his or her performance becomes substandard. The contributing factors in this situation could be the worker's disrespect for work rules, an unchallenging job, and an unduly harsh supervisor. One factor may be more important than others, but they are all contributors.

The following list expands on how the factors listed in Exhibit 16-1 are related to ineffective performance:

The Employee

- *Insufficient mental ability and education.* The employee lacks the problem-solving ability necessary to do the job, such as not being able to understand the software used to run a machine. Poor communication skills are included here such as not being able to read instructions or speak clearly to customers and coworkers. Insufficient mental ability and education of the U.S. workforce available for basic jobs has become a major challenge for managers.
- *Insufficient job knowledge.* The employee is a substandard performer because he or she comes to the job with insufficient training or experience. The employee might be smart enough to learn but lacks the skills to perform

exhibit 16-1 Factors Contributing to Ineffective Performance

Dozens of factors can lower job performance. The factors listed contribute to the majority of ineffective performance.

Factors Related to the Employee

Insufficient mental ability and education
Insufficient job knowledge
Job stress or burnout
Low motivation and loafing
Excessive absenteeism and tardiness
Emotional problem or personality disorder
Alcoholism and drug addiction
Tobacco addiction or withdrawal symptoms
Conducting outside business on the job
Family, personal, and financial problems
Physical limitations
Preoccupying office romance
Fear of traveling
Poor organizational citizenship behavior

Factors Related to the Job

Ergonomics problems and cumulative trauma disorder
Repetitive, physically demanding job, including heavy travel
Built-in conflict
Night-shift work assignments
Substandard industrial hygiene
A "sick" building

Factors Related to the Manager

Inadequate communication about job responsibilities
Inadequate feedback about job performance
Inappropriate leadership style
Negative and untrusting attitude
Bullying or intimidating manager

Factors Related to the Organization

Organizational culture that tolerates poor performance
Poor ethical climate
Counterproductive work environment
Negative work group influences
Intentional threats to job security
Violence or threats of violence
Sexual harassment
A compensation/reward structure that encourages deviant behavior

the job today. Insufficient job knowledge includes technological obsolescence in which the employee does not keep up with the state of the art in his or her field. He or she avoids using new ideas and techniques and becomes ineffective.

- *Job stress and burnout.* Severe short-term stress leads to errors in concentration and judgment. As a result of prolonged job stress, an employee may become apathetic, negative, and impatient. He or she can no longer generate the energy to perform effectively.
- *Low motivation and loafing.* An employee who is poorly motivated will often not sustain enough effort to accomplish the amount of work required to meet standards. Closely related to low motivation is goofing off and loafing. Many employees spend too much time surfing the Internet or engaging in some other diversionary activity, such as making personal phone calls and running personal errands during working hours.
- *Excessive absenteeism and tardiness.* The employee is often not at work for a variety of personal or health reasons. Lost time leads to low productivity, costing employers an estimated 15 percent of payroll expenses.[3]
- *Emotional problem or personality disorder.* The employee may have emotional outbursts, periods of depression, or other abnormal behaviors that interfere with human relationships and work concentration. Cynical behavior may lower the performance of an entire work group if the negative attitude spreads to others.
- *Alcoholism and drug addiction.* The employee cannot think clearly because his or her mental or physical condition has been temporarily or permanently impaired by alcohol or other drugs. Attendance is also likely to suffer. A national U.S. survey indicated that 3.1 percent of employed adults use illicit drugs on the job although 14.1 percent of workforce members are illicit drug users off the job.[4] (Illicit drugs in this study included marijuana, cocaine, and four psychotherapeutic drugs.) Managers must be aware that not every drug user is impaired because many workers develop tolerance to drugs, including prescription drugs.
- *Tobacco addiction or withdrawal symptoms.* The employee who smokes is often fatigued and takes so many cigarette breaks that his or her work is disrupted. Sick leave may also increase. Even workers who stop smoking may suffer performance problems for a while. However, as smokers drop the habit, they may become more productive. According to one estimate, the cumulative lost time due to smoking breaks can add up to one day per week.[5]
- *Conducting outside business on the job.* The employee may be an "office entrepreneur" who sells merchandise to coworkers or spends time on the phone and e-mail, working on investments or other outside interests. Operating an

---

3 Sarah Fister Gale, "Sickened by the Cost of Absenteeism, Companies Look for Solutions," *Workforce Management*, September 2003, p. 72.

4 Michael R. Frone, "Prevalence and Distribution of Illicit Drug Use in the Workforce and in the Workplace: Findings and Implications from a U.S. National Survey," *Journal of Applied Psychology*, July 2006, pp. 856–869.

5 Mark Schoeff Jr., "Smoke-Free Marriott Moves to Help Workers Kick Habit," *Workforce Management*, January 15, 2007, p. 6.

eBay business or other online auction site during working hours is a notable distraction. Time spent on these activities lowers productivity.

- *Family, personal, and financial problems.* The employee is unable to work at full capacity because of preoccupation with an off-the-job problem, such as a marital dispute, conflict with children, a broken romance, or indebtedness. In reference to financially troubled employees, E. Thomas Gorman, professor emeritus at Virginia Tech, says, "They are absent more frequently and waste time at work dealing with financial matters—on the telephone with creditors, trying to get a loan from their 401(k)."[6]
- *Physical limitations.* Job performance decreases as a result of injury or illness. For example, in the United States, lower-back problems account for approximately eight million lost workdays a year and is a major source of worker compensation claims.[7]
- *Preoccupying office romance.* For many people, a new romance is an energizing force that creates positive stress, resulting in a surge in energy directed toward work. For others, an office romance becomes a preoccupation that detracts from concentration. Time spent together in conversation and long lunch breaks can lower productivity.
- *Fear of traveling, especially flying.* In an era of worldwide terrorism, some employees refuse to travel for business, particularly by airplane, because of their perception of the potential danger. Others are hesitant to visit tall office towers. Yet to meet the full requirements of the job, many employees are required to visit remote locations.[8]
- *Poor organizational citizenship behavior.* A subtle cause of low performance is that some employees will not inconvenience themselves to provide assistance not strictly related to their job descriptions. As such, they are poor organizational citizens. **Organizational citizenship behavior** is employee behavior that is discretionary and typically not recognized or rewarded but which nevertheless helps the organization. A small example would be taking it on your own to repair a broken chair that might create an accident. An analysis of 49 different groups found that workers low on organizational citizenship behavior were more likely to engage in counterproductive workplace behaviors.[9] The latter include any activities that harm the organization, such as wasting resources and stealing money.

organizational citizenship behavior
Employee behavior that is discretionary and typically not recognized or rewarded but that nevertheless helps the organization.

The Job

- *Ergonomics problems and repetitive motion disorder.* If equipment or furniture used on the job contributes to fatigue, discomfort, or injury, performance problems result. For example, if an employee develops neck pain and

6 Quoted in Eilene Zimmerman, "Financial Education Courses Can Be a Valuable Asset in Employers' EAP Portfolios," *Workforce Management*, May 8, 2006, p. 52.

7 Joseph J. Martocchio, David A. Harrison, and Howard Berkson, "Connections Between Lower Back Pain, Interventions, and Absence from Work: A Time-Based Meta-Analysis," *Personnel Psychology*, Autumn 2000, p. 496.

8 Clarence T. Pollard, "Fear of Flying," *HR Magazine*, January 2002, pp. 81–84.

9 Reeshad S. Dalal, "A Meta-Analysis of the Relationship Between Organizational Citizenship Behavior and Counterproductive Work Behavior," *Journal of Applied Psychology*, November 2005, pp. 1241–1255.

eyestrain from working at a poorly designed computer configuration, performance will suffer. As described in Chapter 7 about job design, repetitive motion disorder, including carpal tunnel syndrome, is a major problem stemming from poorly designed or poorly utilized computer equipment.

- *Repetitive, physically demanding job.* A repetitive, physically demanding job can cause the employee to become bored and fatigued, leading to lowered performance. Many workers report feeling burned out from working for package-delivery services because of the constant heavy physical demands, leading to mental stress. The problem has become more acute as online shopping increases, particularly during the holiday season.
- *Built-in conflict.* The nature of the job involves so much conflict that job stress lowers performance. The position of collection agent for a consumer-loan company might fit this category. So would a telemarketer who receives such a high percentage of rejections, including slammed-down telephone receivers.
- *Night-shift work assignments.* Employees assigned to all-night shifts suffer many more mental lapses and productivity losses than those assigned to daytime or evening shifts. A major problem is that night-shift work interrupts the natural rhythms of the body.
- *Substandard industrial hygiene.* Excessive noise, fumes, uncomfortable temperatures, inadequate lighting, high humidity, and fear of injury or contamination engender poor performance.
- *A "sick" building.* In some office buildings, a diverse range of airborne particles, vapors, and gases pollute the indoor environment. As described on the Web site "Doctor Fungus," the problems include the transmission of standard infectious diseases such as tuberculosis, and carbon monoxide poisoning related to recirculation of exhaust fumes. The result can be headaches, nausea, and respiratory infections. Performance suffers and absenteeism increases.[10]

The Manager

- *Inadequate communication about job responsibilities.* The employee performs poorly because he or she lacks a clear picture of what the manager expects.
- *Inadequate feedback about job performance.* The employee makes a large number of errors because he or she does not receive the feedback—early enough or at all—to prevent them.
- *Inappropriate leadership style.* The employee performs poorly because the manager's leadership style is inappropriate to the employee's needs. For example, an immature employee's manager gives him or her too much freedom and the result is poor performance. This employee needs closer supervision. Related to leadership style is the problem of some managers unwittingly setting up a group member to fail. The manager perceives

10 "Sick Building Syndrome," http://www.doctorfungus.org, January 22, 2007, p. 1.

a given group member as mediocre, and that person lives down to the manager's expectations, perhaps because the group member loses some self-confidence.[11]

- *Negative and untrusting attitude.* Some managers believe that employees cannot be trusted to behave ethically or in the best interest of the company. As a result, these managers will often exert too much control, leading some employees to retaliate by such means as personally slowing down production. Also, when managers expect the worse from employees, the employees live down to the manager's expectations.[12]
- *Bullying or intimidating manager.* Many employees perceive that they are intimidated and bullied by their managers to the point that they cannot work effectively. Bullying and intimidation go far beyond being firm and setting high standards. They include such behaviors as publicly insulting group members, frequent yelling, and insensitivity toward personal requests, such as time off to handle a severe personal problem. One study showed that one in six Americans report they have been abused in the workplace. However, coworkers and customers as well as managers can be bullies. Eleven states have proposed legislation that would ask employers to correct and prevent bullying abuses, and give victims the right to sue for limited damages.[13]

The Organization

- *Organizational culture that tolerates poor performance.* Suppose an organization has a history of not imposing sanctions on employees who perform poorly. When managers demand better performance, many employees may not respond to the new challenge.
- *Poor ethical climate.* An unethical climate sets the tone for employees engaging in deviant behavior that can produce poor performance, as suggested by a study of working business graduates. Among these behaviors are working on personal matters during work time, and intentionally slowing down the work pace.[14]
- *Counterproductive work environment.* The employee lacks the proper tools, support, budget, or authority to accomplish the job. An example would be a telecommuter whose company-provided computer is plagued with viruses, and the company hesitates taking care of the problem.
- *Negative work group influences.* Group pressures restrain good performance or the work group penalizes a high-performance worker. Similarly,

---

11 Barrie E. Litzky, Kimberly A. Eddleston, and Deborah L. Kidder, "The Good, the Bad, and the Misguided: How Managers Inadvertently Encourage Deviant Behaviors," *Academy of Management Perspectives*, February 2006, p. 95.

12 Jean-François Manzoni and Jean-Louis Barsoux, "The Set-Up-to-Fail Syndrome," *Harvard Business Review*, March–April 1998, pp. 101–113.

13 Harvey A. Hornstein, *Brutal Bosses and Their Prey* (New York: GP Putnam's Sons, 1996); Carolyn Said, "Bullying Bosses Could Be Busted: Movement Against Worst Workplace Abusers Gains Momentum with Proposed Laws," *San Francisco Chronicle*, http://www.SFGate.com, January 22, 2007.

14 Dane K. Peterson, "Deviant Workplace Behavior and the Organization's Ethical Climate," *Journal of Business and Psychology*, Fall 2002, pp. 47–61.

peer-group social pressure may cause an employee to take overly long lunch breaks, neglecting job responsibilities. A study conducted in 20 organizations showed that antisocial behaviors such as lying, spreading rumors, loafing, and absenteeism were more frequent when coworkers exhibited the same behavior.[15]

- *Intentional threats to job security.* Suppose a company might make excessive work demands on an employee in the context of a veiled threat that the job will be eliminated unless the extra work is done. Performance suffers as the worker becomes fearful and anxious.
- *Violence or the threat of violence.* Employees witness violent behavior in the workplace, such as physical assaults, knifings, shootings, or threats of violence. Many employees not directly affected are nevertheless distracted and fearful, leading to lowered productivity.
- *Sexual harassment.* The employee who is sexually harassed usually experiences enough stress to decrease concentration and performance in general. Sometimes an employee who files a sexual harassment complaint is retaliated against in the form of being excluded from meetings he or she previously attended. The consequent feelings of alienation might lower job performance. (The U.S. Supreme Court has ruled against this type of retaliation.[16]) In situations where the manager is the harasser, resentment toward the manager may lead to lowered performance. The person who commits sexual harassment and is under investigation for or charged with the act is likely to experience stress and preoccupation about the charges. One consultant observes that the gossip and distraction stemming from an explosive sexual-harassment case can cause a temporary 20 percent dip in productivity.[17]
- *A compensation/reward structure that encourages deviant behavior.* A compensation/reward structure, similar to an ineffective control standard, might encourage workers to perform in counterproductive ways. Too much of compensation based on commissions might encourage some sales workers to engage in counterproductive practices. Studies of sales representatives in a variety of industries whose income was over 80 percent based on commissions found evidence of workplace deviance, including undercharging for services, lying about meeting quotas, and padding expense accounts. For example, automobile service technicians who work for commission might be encouraged to recommend unnecessary repairs ultimately leading to a poor reputation for the service center.[18]

You are invited to take the self-quiz in Exhibit 16-2 to ponder tendencies of your own that could ultimately contribute to substandard performance. Many sports figures, elected officials, and business executives experience the problems pinpointed in the questionnaire.

---

15 Sandra L. Robinson and Anne M. O'Leary-Kelly, "Monkey See, Monkey Do: The Influence of Work Groups on the Antisocial Behavior of Employees," *Academy of Management Journal*, December 1998, pp. 658–672.

16 Todd Heneman, "After High Court Ruling, Firms May Want to Take Long Look at Anti-Harassment Strategies," *Workforce Management*, July 31, 2006, p. 33.

17 Cited in Sheila Anne Feeney, "Love Hurts," *Workforce Management*, February 2004, p. 37.

18 Litzky, Eddleston, and Kidder, "The Good, the Bad, and the Misguided," pp. 93–94.

exhibit 16-2 The Self-Sabotage Questionnaire

Directions: Indicate how accurately each of the following statements describes or characterizes you, using a five-point scale: (0) very inaccurately, (1) inaccurately, (2) midway between inaccurately and accurately, (3) accurately, (4) very accurately. Consider discussing some of the questions with a family member, close friend, or work associate. Another person's feedback may prove helpful in providing accurate answers to some of the questions.

	Answer
1. Other people have said that I am my worst enemy.	_______
2. If I don't do a perfect job, I feel worthless.	_______
3. I am my own harshest critic.	_______
4. When engaged in a sport or other competitive activity, I find a way to blow a substantial lead right near the end.	_______
5. When I make a mistake, I can usually identify another person to blame.	_______
6. I have a strong tendency to procrastinate.	_______
7. I have trouble focusing on what is really important to me.	_______
8. I have trouble taking criticism, even from friends.	_______
9. My fear of seeming stupid often prevents me from asking questions or offering my opinion.	_______
10. I tend to expect the worst in most situations.	_______
11. Many times I have rejected people who treat me well.	_______
12. When I have an important project to complete, I usually get sidetracked, and then miss the deadline.	_______
13. I choose work assignments that lead to disappointments even when better options are clearly available.	_______
14. I frequently misplace things such as my keys, then get very angry at myself.	_______
15. I am concerned that if I take on much more responsibility, people will expect too much from me.	_______
16. I avoid situations, such as competitive sports, where people can find out how good or bad I really am.	_______
17. People describe me as the "office (or class) clown."	_______
18. I have an insatiable demand for money and power.	_______
19. When negotiating with others, I hate to grant any concessions.	_______
20. I seek revenge for even the smallest hurts.	_______
21. I have a giant-size ego.	_______
22. When I receive a compliment or other form of recognition, I usually feel I don't deserve it.	_______
23. To be honest, I choose to suffer.	_______
24. I regularly enter into conflict with people who try to help me.	_______
25. I'm a loser.	_______
Total score	_______

Scoring and interpretation: Add your answers to all the questions to obtain your total score. Your total score provides an approximate index of your tendencies toward being self-sabotaging or self-defeating.

0–25: You appear to have few tendencies toward self-sabotage. If this interpretation is supported by your own positive feelings toward your life and yourself, you are in good shape with respect to self-defeating

(Continued)

exhibit 16-2 The Self-Sabotage Questionnaire *(Continued)*

behavior tendencies. However, stay alert to potential self-sabotaging tendencies that could develop at later stages in your career.

26–50: You may have some mild tendencies toward self-sabotage. It could be that you do things occasionally that defeat your own purposes. A person in this category, for example, might write an angry e-mail memo to an executive, expressing disagreement with a decision that adversely affects his or her operation. Review actions you have taken during the past six months to decide if any of them have been self-sabotaging.

51–75: You show signs of engaging in self-sabotage. You probably have thoughts, and carry out actions, that could be blocking you from achieving important work and personal goals. People whose scores place them in this category characteristically engage in negative self-talk that lowers their self-confidence and makes them appear weak and indecisive to others. For example, "I'm usually not good at learning new things." People in this range frequently experience another problem. They sometimes sabotage their chances of succeeding on a project just to prove that their negative self-assessment is correct.

76–100: You most likely have a strong tendency toward self-sabotage. (Sometimes it is possible to obtain a high score on a test like this because you are going through an unusually stressful period in your life.) You might discuss your tendencies toward undermining your own achievements with a mental health professional.

THE CONTROL MODEL FOR MANAGING INEFFECTIVE PERFORMERS

Learning Objective 2

Describe the control model for managing ineffective performers.

The approach to improving ineffective performance presented here follows the logic of the control process shown in Exhibit 16-3. Problem identification and problem solving lie at the core of this approach. The control process for managing ineffective performers is divided into the eight steps illustrated in Exhibit 16-3, and should usually be followed in sequence. This section will describe each of these steps in detail. Another key method of improving ineffective performance—employee discipline—receives separate attention later in the chapter.

Two cautions are in order in using the control model for improving ineffective performance. First, the model may need slight modification to follow company procedures. Company policy, for example, might establish certain procedures about documenting poor performance and reporting it immediately to higher levels of management. Second, the control process is not designed to deal with mental illness. An employee who suddenly begins to neglect the job because of a sudden change in personality should be referred immediately to a human resource specialist. The specialist, in turn, will make an appropriate referral to a mental-health professional.

Define Performance Standards

Penalizing employees for not achieving performance standards without first carefully communicating those standards is unfair. Therefore, the first step in the control model for managing ineffective performers is to clearly define what is expected of employees. Performance standards are commonly established by such means as job descriptions, work goals, production quotas, and formal discussions of what is to be accomplished in a position.

exhibit 16-3 **The Control Model for Managing Ineffective Performers**

The most systematic and effective method for bringing ineffective performance up to standard is to follow the control process, referred to in this application as the control model.

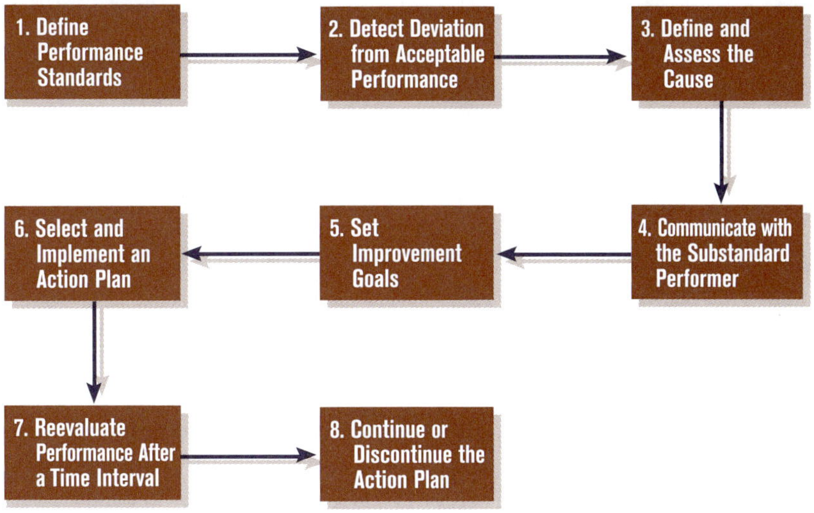

Detect Deviation from Acceptable Performance

Detection is the process of noting when an employee's performance deviates from an acceptable standard. Managers use the various control measures described in Chapter 15 to detect deviations from acceptable performance. For performance to be considered ineffective or poor, it must deviate significantly from the norm.

At times, quantitative measures can be used to define ineffective performance. For some jobs, ineffective performance might begin at 30 percent below standard. For other jobs, the cutoff point could be 20 or 50 percent, or any other percentage of deviation that fits the situation. What percentage of deviation from standard do you think would be acceptable for a commercial airline pilot? For a bank teller?

Personal observation plays a key role in detecting ineffective performance. One reason that observation is so important is that it is a concurrent control. By the time quantitative indicators of poor performance have been collected, substantial damage may have been done. Assume a bank manager observes that one of the loan officers is taking unduly long lunch hours on Fridays. Upon return, the officer appears to be under the influence of alcohol. Eventually, this unacceptable behavior will show up in quantitative indicators of performance. However, it might take a year to collect these data.

Define and Assess the Cause

At this stage, the manager attempts to diagnose the real cause of the problem. Following the logic of Exhibit 16-1, the primary contributor to the problem could be a personal factor or a factor related to the job, the manager, or the organization. A discussion with the employee (the next step in the control mode) may be necessary to reveal the major cause of the problem. For example, an office assistant was absent so frequently that her performance suffered. She claimed that photocopying made her sick. The supervisor investigated further and called in the company health and safety expert. A medical examination confirmed that the office assistant was allergic to the trace fumes from the toner in the large-volume photocopier. After the office assistant was reassigned, her attendance became satisfactory.

Communicate with the Substandard Performer

After detecting unacceptable performance or behavior, the manager must communicate concern to the worker. At times, a simple discussion will suffice. At other times, a more sensitive form of feedback may be necessary. **Confrontation** means dealing with a controversial or emotional topic directly. Confrontation is necessary whenever the employee does not readily admit to experiencing a problem.

Managers often avoid confrontation for several reasons. They may have limited skill in criticizing employees. Or, they may prefer not to deal with the anger and resentment that confrontation is likely to trigger. A third reason is the manager not wanting to make the employee feel uncomfortable. Another concern about confrontation is that the rights of the employee might be violated if he or she is suffering from a problem covered by the Americans with Disabilities Act, such as alcoholism. In reality, the law allows employers to confront employees with disabilities, and to hold those with an alcohol problem to the same performance standards of other employees.[19]

A recommended confrontation technique is to communicate an attitude of concern about the confronted person's welfare. To use this technique, confront the person in a sincere and thoughtful manner. Using the words *care* and *concern* can be helpful. For instance, a manager might begin by saying: "The reason I'm bringing up this problem is that I care about your work. You have a good record with the company, and I'm concerned that your performance has slipped way below its former level."

confrontation
Dealing with a controversial or emotional topic directly.

improvement goal
A goal that, if attained, will correct unacceptable deviation from a performance standard.

Set Improvement Goals

The fifth step in the control model is to set improvement goals. An **improvement goal** is one that, if attained, will correct an unacceptable deviation from a performance standard. The goals should be documented on paper or electronically. Improvement goals should have the same characteristics as other objectives (see Chapter 4). Above all, improvement goals should specify the behavior or result that is required. Vague improvement goals are not likely to cause changes in performance.

An example of a specific improvement goal is "During this month, nine of your ten customer service reports must be in on time." This specific goal is likely to be more effective than a general improvement goal, such as "Become more prompt in submitting customer service reports."

19 Saundra Jackson, Ruhal Dooley, and Diance Lacy, "Substance Abuse, Ethics, Intermittent Leave," *HR Magazine*, July 2003, p. 41.

If the ineffective performer expresses an interest in improvement, joint goal setting is advisable. By providing input into goal setting, the substandard performer stands a good chance of becoming committed to improvement. At times, managers need to impose improvement goals on substandard performers, especially in cases involving a motivation problem. If substandard employees were interested in setting improvement goals, they would not have a motivation problem.

Select and Implement an Action Plan

The setting of improvement goals leads logically to the selection and implementation of action plans to attain those goals. Much of the art of remedying ineffective performance is contained in this step. Unless appropriate action plans are developed, no real improvement is likely to take place. Many attempts at improving substandard performance fail because the problem is discussed and then dropped. Thus the employee has no concrete method of making the necessary improvements.

Types of Action Plans

An action plan for improvement can include almost any sensible approach tailored to the specific problem. An action plan could be formulated to deal with every cause of ineffective performance listed in Exhibit 16-1.

Action plans for improving ineffective performance can be divided into two types. One type is within the power of the manager to develop and implement. Plans of this type include coaching, encouraging, and offering small incentives for improvement. The other type of action plan is offered by the organization or purchased on the outside, and include training programs, stress-management programs, and stays at alcoholism-treatment centers. Exhibit 16-4 lists a selection of feasible corrective actions.

exhibit 16-4 Corrective Actions for Ineffective Performers

When attempting to bring ineffective performers up to standard or beyond, managers can either take action by themselves or refer employees to a company program designed to help them with performance problems.

Managerial Actions and Techniques

- **Coaching.** The manager points out specifically what the performer could be doing better or should stop doing. In daily interaction with the team members, the manager makes suggestions for improvement. Coaching is the most widely used technique for performance improvement.
- **Closer supervision.** The manager works more closely with the subordinate, offering frequent guidance and feedback.
- **Reassignment or transfer.** The manager reassigns the ineffective performer to a position that he or she can handle better.
- **Motivational techniques.** The manager attempts to improve employee motivation by using positive reinforcement or some other motivational technique.
- **Corrective discipline.** The manager informs the employee that his or her behavior is unacceptable and that corrections must be made if the worker is to

(Continued)

exhibit 16-4 Corrective Actions for Ineffective Performers *(Continued)*

remain employed by the firm. The employee is counseled as part of corrective discipline.

- **Lower performance standards.** If performance standards have been too high, the manager lowers expectations of the team member. Consultation with higher management would probably be necessary before implementing this step.
- **Job rotation.** If ineffective performance results from staleness or burnout, changing to a different job of comparable responsibility may prove helpful.

Organizational Programs

- **Employee assistance programs (EAPs).** The employee is referred to a counseling service specializing in rehabilitating employees whose personal problems interfere with work.
- **Wellness programs.** The organization encourages employees to participate in specialized programs that help them stay physically and mentally healthy. By doing so, employees may prevent or cope with health problems—such as heart disease or an eating disorder—that interfere with job performance or lead to absenteeism. The wellness program usually includes stress management.
- **Career counseling and outplacement.** The employee receives professional assistance in solving a career problem, including being counseled on finding a job outside the firm.
- **Job redesign.** Specialists in human resource management and industrial engineering redesign job elements that could be causing poor performance. For example, the job is changed so that the employee has less direct contact with others, leading to reduced conflict.
- **Training and development programs.** The employee is assigned to a training or development program linked directly to his or her performance deficiency. For example, a reserved sales representative receives assertiveness training.
- **Business (or executive) coaching.** The company hires a personal coach who helps the professional or managerial worker with such problems as poor interpersonal relationships, resolving conflict, and ineffective approach to problem solving.
- **Anger-management program.** The company sends a worker whose anger results in poor performance to an anger-management workshop, where the workers learn how to control anger and express it in constructive ways. The problem is that anger creates a less cohesive workplace and damages morale. Anger also interferes with focused attention, therefore impairing judgment and decreasing reaction time.[20]

employee assistance program (EAP) An organization-sponsored service to help employees deal with personal and job-related problems that hinder performance.

When attempting to improve ineffective performance resulting from a variety of personal problems, the preferred action plan for many managers is to refer the troubled worker to an **employee assistance program (EAP)**. The EAP is an organization-sponsored service to help employees deal with personal and job-related problems that interfere with job performance. Professionals who specialize in dealing with particular problems staff an employee assistance program. Many companies that do not have an EAP of their own refer employees to such a program that serves firms in the area. Employee assistance programs offer extensive services to employees. For example, three of the services offered by the EAP associated with the Federal Occupational Health are as follows:

- Seven-day, 24-hour telephone access for employees and family members to professional counselors for assessment, consultation, referral, and crisis management.

20 Linda Wasmer Andrews, "When It's Time For Anger Management," *HR Magazine*, June 2005, p. 132.

- Professional assessment of issues related to mental health, substance abuse, and workplace and other challenges in living.
- Face-to-face short-term, focused counseling for individuals, couples, and families.[21]

Employees and their families use assistance programs to cope with a variety of personal and family problems and illnesses. Among them are alcoholism and other substance abuse, financial and legal difficulties, emotional problems, chronic illness such as AIDS or cancer, compulsive gambling, and weight control. Employees also use EAPs to deal with job-related concerns such as work stress, chronic job dissatisfaction, and sexual harassment.

When supervisors refer employees to the EAP, workplace problems should be the focus. The supervisor should not say, "I am encouraging you to go to the EAP. The EAP can help you with any personal problems you may have." Say instead, "I encourage you to go to the EAP. The EAP may be able to help you solve your workplace problems."[22] The second approach usually creates less defensiveness than the first.

The accompanying Management in Action provides details about the operations of a modern employee assistance program, this one offered by a state government.

Implementation of the Action Plan

After the action plan is chosen, it must be implemented. As shown in Exhibit 16-3, implementation begins in Step 6 and continues through Step 8. The manager utilizes the approaches listed under "Managerial Actions and Techniques" in Exhibit 16-4. Human resources specialists outside the manager's department usually implement organizational programs.

An important part of effective implementation is continuation of the remedial program. Given the many pressures facing a manager, it is easy to forget the substandard performer who needs close supervision or a motivational boost. Often, a brief conversation is all that is needed.

Reevaluate Performance After a Time Interval

Step 7 in the controlling process helps ensure that the process is working. In this step the manager measures the employee's current performance. If the remedial process is working, the team member's performance will move up toward standard. The greater the performance problem, the more frequent the reevaluations of performance should be. In instances of behavior problems, such as alcoholism, weekly performance checks are advisable.

Formal and Informal Reviews

A reevaluation of performance can be formal or informal. A formal progress review takes the form of a performance-evaluation session. It might include written documentation of the employee's progress and samples of

21 "Documenting the Value of Employee Assistance Programs," *Federal Occupational Health Program Support Center*, http://www.foh.dhhs.gov, September 2003.

22 Jonathan A. Segal, "I'm Depressed—Accommodate Me!" *HR Magazine*, February 2001, p. 148.

management in action

The State of Tennessee Employee Assistance Program

TENNESSEE.GOV The Official Web Site of the State of Tennessee

Department of Finance & Administration
Dave Goetz, Commissioner

Tennessee.gov Home | search Tennessee.gov | A to Z Directory | Policies Survey | Help | Site Map | Contact

Search F&A

Division Home
Insurance Administration
At this site
Free Seminars
Orientation
Supervisor Training
Alcohol and Depression
Screening
Self-Assesments
Newsletters and Other
Resources
Megellan Health Services
Rocking and Rolling
Through Changes Registration

Employee Assistance Program

What is an Employee Assistance Program?
An employee assistance program, or EAP, is a counseling service for employees and their eligible dependents who may be experiencing personal or work place problems. You can reach the EAP by calling 1-800-308-4934 any time of day, any day of the year. Everyone has problems from time to time. Usually, we work them out. But sometimes problems persist, becoming serious enough to affect us both off and on the job. At such times, an EAP counselor may be able to help.

Why Does Your Employer Offer an EAP?
First, it's smart business. If you're doing well and day-to-day problems aren't a distraction, you are more likely to be alert, motivated and concentrating on your job. This means we have a more productive organization. Second, it costs more to hire and train a new employee than it does to help and keep a current employee. And third, we care about our employees. It's that simple.

What Types of Problems Does EAP Handle?
The EAP handles a wide range of problems. These include problems related to:

- Emotional
- Family
- Marital
- Stress
- Financial
- Substance Abuse
- Legal
- Work Place
- Elder Care

What Other Services are Available?

- Consultation
- Referrals
- Noon-hour Seminars
- Orientation sessions for employees and supervisors

Call 615-741-1925 or 1-800-253-9981 for more information about these services.

Will the Counselor Keep my Problem Confidential?
Yes. Absolutely. Confidentiality is a requirement and a guarantee we make to all employees. Without it, the EAP wouldn't work. Every counselor knows this rule. No information goes anywhere without your request and written permission. Remember, too, counselors are specially trained in EAP work. They handle delicate issues, and they have the knowledge and skills to assist you toward solving your problems.

When Can I Schedule an Appointment?
Appointments are scheduled during the regular work day. Some evening times are available upon request. With approval, you may use work time to see an EAP counselor. Over 500 counseling sites are available throughout the state.

What is an EAP Counselor?
An EAP counselor is someone educated, trained and experienced in helping employees and their eligible dependents solve their problems or referring them to professionals or organizations in the community who can. EAP counselors typically are experienced in dealing with problems in substance abuse, behavioral health, relationships, work place and numerous social, financial and legal situations that plague all of us at one time or another.

How Much Will the EAP Cost Me?
Nothing. What's more, you are encouraged to use EAP services whenever you need help or information to best handle your job or family responsibilities. EAP services are offered at no cost to all full-time state and higher education employees and their eligible dependents, regardless of whether they participate in the State's Group Insurance Program. Also, local education (K-12) and local government employees who participate in any of the State's medical insurance plans and their covered dependents may also use EAP services. EAP counseling is available for problems that can be resolved in a short period of time. You may receive up to six sessions per problem episode. Referrals are made for problems requiring more time.

his or her work. Formal reviews are particularly important when the employee has been advised that dismissal is pending unless improvements are made. Reviews are critical to avoid lawsuits over a dismissal.

The first level of informal review consists of checking on whether the employee has started the action plan. For example, suppose a reserved sales representative agreed to attend an assertiveness-training program. One week later, the manager could ask the rep, "Have you signed up for or started the training program yet?"

The next level of informal review is a discussion of the employee's progress. The manager can ask casual questions such as, "How much progress have you made in accounting for the missing inventory?" Or the manager might ask, "Have you learned how to use the new diagnostic equipment yet?"

Positive Reinforcement and Punishment

If the employee makes progress toward reaching the improvement goal, positive reinforcement is appropriate. Rewarding an employee for progress is the most effective way of sustaining that progress. The reward might be praise, encouragement, or longer intervals between review sessions. The longer time between reviews may be rewarding because the employee will feel that he or she is "back to normal."

Giving rewards for making improvement generally proves more effective than giving punishments for not making improvement. Yet if the problem employee does not respond to positive motivators, some form of organizational punishment is necessary. More will be said about punishment in the discussion about employee discipline.

Continue or Discontinue the Action Plan

Step 8 in the control model for managing ineffective performers is making the decision whether to continue or discontinue the action plan. This step can be considered the feedback component of the control process. If the performance review indicates the employee is not meeting improvement goals, the action plan is continued. If the review indicates goal achievement, the action plan is discontinued.

An important part of using the control model to manage ineffective performers is realizing that positive changes may not be permanent. Performance is most likely to revert to an unacceptable level when the employee is faced with heavy job pressures. For instance, suppose an employee and a manager formulated an action plan to improve the employee's work habits. The employee's performance improved as a result. When the employee is under pressure, however, his or her work may once again become badly disorganized. The manager should then repeat the last five steps of the process, beginning with confrontation.

COACHING AND CONSTRUCTIVE CRITICISM

Learning Objective 3

Know what is required to coach and constructively criticize employees.

coaching
A method for helping employees perform better, which usually occurs on the spot and involves informal discussion and suggestions.

Most performance improvement takes place as a result of a manager dealing directly with the worker not meeting standards. The usual vehicle for bringing about this improvement is **coaching**. It is a method for helping employees perform better, which usually occurs on the spot and involves informal discussion and suggestions. Workplace coaching is much like coaching on the athletic field or in the performing arts. Coaching involves considerable **constructive criticism**, a form of criticism designed to help people improve. To be a good coach, and to criticize constructively, requires considerable skill.

Business psychologists James Waldroop and Timothy Butler point out that good coaching is simply good management. Coaching requires the same skills that contribute to effective management, such as keen observation skills, sound judgment, and an ability to take appropriate action. Coaching and effective management share the goal of making the most of human resources.[23] The following suggestions will help you improve your coaching skill if practiced carefully:

constructive criticism
A form of criticism designed to help improve performance or behavior.

1. *Focus feedback on what is wrong with the work and behavior rather than the employee's attitude and personality.* When the feedback attacks a person's self-image, he or she is likely to become hostile. A defensive person is more likely to focus on getting even rather than getting better. Another way to upset the person being coached is to exaggerate the nature of the poor performance, such as saying, "You've committed the same mistake 100 times," when you have only observed the mistake four times.
2. *Be timely with negative feedback.* Negative feedback should be given close in time to the incident of poor performance. If you observe a worker being rude to a customer, do not wait until the annual performance evaluation to share you observation. Schedule a coaching session as soon as feasible. The worker might be rude to many more customers until he or she receives your criticism.[24]
3. *Listen actively and empathize.* An essential component of coaching employees requires careful listening to both their presentation of facts and feelings. Your listening will encourage the employee to talk. As the employee talks about his or her problem, you may develop a better understanding of how to improve performance. As you listen actively, the opportunity to show empathy will arise naturally. Suppose the employee blames being behind schedule on the servers being down so frequently. You might show empathy by saying, "Yes, I know it is frustrating to have a computer breakdown when faced with a deadline. Yet we all have to deal with this problem."
4. *Ask good questions.* An effective workplace coach asks questions that help people understand their needs for improvement. Start the coaching question by asking a question, thereby encouraging the person being coached to be an active participant immediately. Consultant Marilyn J. Darling says that effective coaching is based on asking good questions. She notes that the simpler the question, the better.

- What are you trying to accomplish?
- How will you know if you have succeeded?
- What obstacles do you believe are stopping you?
- How can I help you succeed?[25]

These questions contribute to active listening because they are open-ended. An open-ended question requests that the person provide details rather than a Yes or No response. "What obstacles do you believe are stopping you?" is open-ended because the worker must point to obstacles to answer the question. A closed question on the same topic would be "Are there any obstacles stopping you?" Such a question fails to promote dialog.

23 James Waldroop and Timothy Butler, "The Executive as Coach," *Harvard Business Review*, November–December 1996, p. 111.
24 John Reh, "How to Give Negative Feedback Properly," http://www.management.about.com, accessed January 19, 2007.
25 Marilyn J. Darling, "Coaching Helps People Through Difficult Times," *HR Magazine*, November 1994, p. 72.

5. *Engage in joint problem solving.* Work together to resolve the performance problem. One reason joint problem solving is effective is that it conveys a helpful and constructive attitude on the part of the manager. Another is that the employee often needs the superior's assistance in overcoming work problems. The manager is in a better position to address certain problems than is the employee.
6. *Offer constructive advice.* Constructive advice can be useful to the employee with performance problems. A recommended way of giving advice is first to ask an insightful question. You might ask the employee, "Could the real cause of your problem be poor work habits?" If the employee agrees, you can then offer some specific advice about improving work habits. As part of giving advice it is more effective to suggest that a person do something rather than try to do something. For example, it is more persuasive to say, "Be at our staff meetings on time," than to say "Try to be at our staff meetings on time." "Trying" something gives a person an excuse not to succeed.

    An especially effective aspect of constructive advice is to help the person who is performing poorly understand the link between the negative act and attaining key goals such as increased revenue and productivity.[26] Suppose a store manager typically neglects to respond to questions asked by customers using the "Contact Us" function. His or her manager/coach might point out, "Customers who are ignored will soon ignore us, leading to the loss of some important customers, along with some important sales. We need every customer we can get or keep."
7. *Give the poor performer an opportunity to observe and model someone who exhibits acceptable performance.* A simple example of modeling would be for the manager to show the employee how to operate a piece of equipment properly. A more complex example of modeling would be to have the poor performer observe an effective employee making a sale or conducting a job interview. In each case, the ineffective performer should be given opportunities to repeat the activity.
8. *Obtain a commitment to change.* Ineffective performers frequently agree to make improvements but are not really committed to change. At the end of a session, discuss the employee's true interest in changing. One clue that commitment may be lacking is when the employee too readily accepts everything you say about the need for change. Another clue is agreement about the need for change but with no display of emotion. In either case, further discussion is warranted.
9. *When feasible, conduct some coaching sessions outside of the performance evaluation.* The coaching experience should focus on development and improvement, whereas the performance review is likely to be perceived by the ineffective performer as a time for judging his or her performance.

---

26 Gary P. Latham, Joan Almost, Sara Mann, and Celia Moore, "New Developments in Performance Management," *Organizational Dynamics*, Vol. 34, No. 1 (2005), p. 85.

Despite this perception, performance evaluations should include an aspect of development.

10. *Applaud good results.* Effective coaches on the playing field and in the workplace are cheerleaders. They give encouragement and positive reinforcement by applauding good results. Some effective coaches shout in joy when a poor performer achieves standard performance; others clap their hands in applause.

EMPLOYEE DISCIPLINE

Learning Objective 4

Understand how to discipline employees.

Up to this point, the chapter emphasized positive approaches to improving substandard performance. At times, however, using the control model requires a manager to discipline employees in an attempt to keep performance at an acceptable level. It is also part of an effective manager's role to be willing to take harsh and unpopular action when the situation requires such behavior. **Discipline**, in a general sense, is punishment used to correct or train. In organizations, discipline can be divided into two types.

Summary discipline is the immediate discharge of an employee because of a serious offense. The employee is fired on the spot for rule violations, such as stealing, fighting, or selling illegal drugs on company premises. In unionized firms, the company and the union have a written agreement specifying which offenses are subject to summary discipline.

Corrective discipline allows employees to correct their behavior before punishment is applied. Employees are told that their behavior is unacceptable and that they must make corrections if they want to remain with the firm. The manager and the employee share the responsibility for solving the performance problem. The controlling process for managing ineffective performers includes corrective discipline. Steps 4 through 7 in Exhibit 16-3 are based on corrective discipline.

discipline
Punishment used to correct or train.

summary discipline
The immediate discharge of an employee because of a serious offense.

corrective discipline
A type of discipline that allows employees to correct their behavior before punishment is applied.

The group or team sometimes assumes some of the disciplinary activity that was formerly the manager's sole responsibility. Sharing responsibility for discipline reflects the empowerment of teams to carry out managerial functions. An experiment conducted with 231 members of 41 work groups indicated that managers and group consensus decisions (the group as a whole) show similarities in what they consider to be fair discipline for the same offense. For example, both managers and the group as an entity might recommend a one-week suspension for one employee harassing another. The same study also concluded that groups are capable of making valid and fair decisions about poor performance of group members.[27]

Taking disciplinary action is often thought of in relation to lower-ranking employees. Managers, professionals, and other salaried employees, however, may also need to be disciplined, such as in backdating stock options for themselves and harassing employees.

27 Robert C. Liden et al., "Management of Poor Performance: A Comparison of Manager, Group Member, and Group Disciplinary Decisions," *Journal of Applied Psychology*, December 1999, p. 846.

progressive discipline The step-by-step application of corrective discipline.

The paragraphs that follow will describe three other aspects of discipline. First, we describe the most widely used type of corrective discipline, progressive discipline. Second, we explain the rules for applying discipline. Third, we examine the positive consequences of punishment, to the organization.

Progressive Discipline

Progressive discipline is the step-by-step application of corrective discipline, as shown in Exhibit 16-5. Progressive discipline alerts the employee that a performance problem exists, such as not properly documenting claims on an expense report. The manager confronts and then coaches the poor performer about the performance problem. If the employee's performance does not improve, the employee is informed in writing that improvements must be made. The written notice often includes a clear statement of what will happen if performance does not improve. The "or else" could be a disciplinary layoff or suspension. If the notice is ignored and the disciplinary action does not lead to improvement, the employee may be discharged. Many firms codify the specific steps in progressive discipline. At the University of Arizona, for example, the *written warning* describes the type of problem or problems, the corrections that will be required, and the right of the employee to appeal the written warning.[28]

Progressive discipline, an old concept, continues to be widely used for two key reasons. First, it provides the documentation necessary to avoid

exhibit 16-5 Steps in Progressive Discipline

Progressive discipline is a standard practice that remains important because it gives the worker a chance to improve, and it documents poor performance. Should discharge be necessary, it would be more difficult for the employee to claim unfair treatment and wrongful discharge.

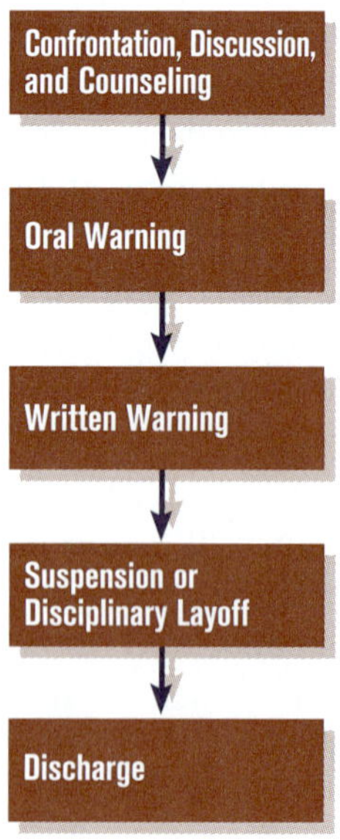

28 "Corrective Discipline and Discharge," *Human Resources*, http://www.hr.arizona.edu/05, 2005.

legal liability for firing poorly performing employees. Second, many labor-management agreements require progressive discipline because of the inherent fairness of the step-by-step procedure. Employees are not harshly punished for first offenses that fall outside the realm of summary discipline.

Rules for Applying Discipline

This chapter discussed discipline as it relates to the correction of ineffective performance. However, discipline is more frequently used to deal with infractions of policy and rules. The employee in these situations may not necessarily be a poor performer. The administration of discipline, whether for poor performance or infractions, should adhere to certain time-tested rules. Before applying these rules, a manager in a unionized firm must make sure they are compatible with the employee discipline clauses in the written union agreement.

The red-hot-stove rule offers an old-fashioned but still valid principle in administering discipline. According to the *red-hot-stove rule*, employee discipline should be the immediate result of inappropriate behavior, just as a burn is the result of touching a very hot stove. The employee should receive a warning (the red metal), and the punishment should be immediate, consistent, and impersonal. A manager should keep this rule and those that follow in mind when disciplining employees. Several of these suggestions incorporate the red-hot-stove rule.

1. *All employees should be notified of what punishments will be applied for what infractions.* For example, paralegals might be told that discussing the details of client cases with outsiders, a violation of company policy, will result in discharge.
2. *Discipline should be applied immediately after the infraction is committed.* As soon as is practical after learning of a rule violation, the manager should confront the employee and apply discipline.
3. *The punishment should fit the undesirable behavior.* If the punishment is too light, the offender will not take it seriously. If, on the other hand, it is too severe, it may create anxiety and actually diminish performance.
4. *Managers should be consistent in the application of discipline for each infraction.* Every employee who violates a certain rule should receive the same punishment. Furthermore, managers throughout the organization should impose the same punishment for the same rule violation.
5. *Disciplinary remedies should be applied impersonally to offenders.* "Impersonal" in this context implies that everybody who is a known rule violator should be punished. Managers should not play favorites.
6. *Documentation of the performance or behavior that led to punishment is required.* Justification for the discipline must be documented in substantial detail. Documentation is essential for defending the company's action in the event of an appeal by the employee or the union or in the case of a lawsuit.

7. *When the discipline is over, return to usual work relations.* The manager should not hold a grudge or treat the rule violator as an outcast. How the person who violated the rule is treated could become a self-fulfilling prophecy. Treating the person, who was disciplined, as an outcast may make that person feel alienated, causing his or her performance to deteriorate. If the person is treated as someone who is expected not to commit mistakes, he or she will most likely try to live up to that expectation.

You will know that the effort you invest in corrective or progressive discipline is successful when the worker you have disciplined has returned to acceptable performance. In contrast, your efforts in progressive discipline have not been successful when the worker does not improve or his or her performance deteriorates. If progressive discipline proceeds in the spirit of coaching, it is more likely to be successful. In contrast, if progressive discipline results in a legalistic battle with each side fighting for its rights, changes in performance are unlikely.

Positive Consequences of Punishment

Conventional wisdom is that punishment should be avoided in the workplace or used only as a last resort because of its negative side effects. Workers who are punished may become anxious, fearful, revengeful, and even violent. Evidence, however, suggests that punishment perceived in certain ways can actually benefit the organization.[29]

A key factor in whether punishment is beneficial is the employee's *belief in a just world*, or that people get the rewards and punishments they deserve. Employees who believe in a just world are likely to accept punishment when they violate rules or perform poorly because they believe they deserve to be punished. As a consequence, they do not complain about punishment, and might even spread the word that the organization is fair.

When employees observe that another employee has been punished justly (fairly), they will often rally on the side of management. The employees may think that the offending employee deserved the punishment. In some instances, other employees may desire that a rule violator be punished because it fits their sense of justice.

Just punishment also informs employees that certain types of misconduct will not be tolerated, as documented in an interview study conducted with 77 managers from different organizations. Many managers therefore regard punishment as an opportunity to promote vicarious learning (in this sense, learning through others).[30] For example, if one employee receives a ten-day suspension for racial harassment, other employees learn that the organization takes racial harassment seriously.

---

29 Gail A. Ball, Linda Klebe Treviño, and Harry P. Sims Jr., "Just and Unjust Punishment: Influence on Subordinate Performance and Citizenship," *Academy of Management Journal*, April 1994, pp. 300–301.

30 Kenneth B. Butterfield, Linda Klebe Treviño, and Gail A. Ball, "Punishment from the Manager's Perspective: A Grounded Investigation and Inductive Model," *Academy of Management Journal*, December 1996, p. 1493.

DEALING WITH DIFFICULT PEOPLE, INCLUDING CYNICS

Learning Objective 5

Develop an approach to dealing with difficult people, including cynics.

Although to this point, the chapter focused on dealing with substandard performers, another group of employees may perform adequately yet be annoying and waste managers' time as well as that of coworkers. At times their performance slips below standard because they divert their energy from accomplishing work. A person in this category is often referred to as a **difficult person**, an individual whose personal characteristics disturb other people. Difficult people are such a drain on productivity and personal well-being that they are the subject of study in both the business press and in research journals.

difficult person
An individual whose personal characteristics disturb other people.

Three Types of Difficult People

Difficult people have been placed into many different categories or types. Among them are whiners and complainers, know-it-alls, office bullies, pessimists, poor team players, back stabbers, and saboteurs. People who whistle in the office are considered difficult by many, yet a few people find the whistling to be soothing. A common feature of difficult people is that they focus on their own needs and agenda, such as wanting to control and manipulate others. For example, the office bully who insults and intimidates others is attempting to control them. Here we focus on three of the most frequently found types of difficult employees: the disgruntled, the passive-aggressive, and the uncivil. Later we highlight cynics because of their unusual nature.

Disgruntled workers are angry and often see themselves as victims. They justify their feelings by blaming work associates, including supervisors, coworkers, and customers. Typically, they isolate themselves from those around them.[31] Extremely disgruntled employees with low emotional stability may engage in workplace violence. The passive-aggressive worker, on the other hand, expresses anger and hostility by such means as neglecting to take care of an emergency or sitting silently in a meeting without making a contribution.

Uncivil workers are growing rapidly as standards for civility in society continue to lower. A survey of 2,000 respondents indicated that nearly four out of five people believe that lack of respect and courtesy is a serious problem that appears to be getting worse. Representative examples of uncivil behavior include dealing with your request while talking on the phone with another person, processing e-mail while talking to you, insulting you in public, and barging past you from the other direction as you exit a door. According to workplace-behavior researchers Christine M. Pearson and Christine L. Porath, because of being treated uncivilly, many workers decrease work effort, time on the job, productivity, and performance.[32]

---

31 Paul Falcone, "Welcome Back Disgruntled Workers," *HR Magazine*, February 2001, p. 133.

32 Except for the examples, the information about incivility is from Christine Pearson and Christine L. Porath, "On the Nature, Consequences and Remedies of Workplace Incivility: No Time for 'Nice'? Think Again," *Academy of Management Executive*, February 2005, pp. 7–18.

Tactics for Dealing with Difficult People

Much of the advice about dealing with difficult people centers on certain tactics, as described next. It will often be necessary to use a combination of these tactics to help a difficult person become more cooperative. The more the difficult behavior is an ingrained personality pattern, the more difficult it will be to change. In contrast, it is easier to change difficult behavior that stems from the pressures of a given situation. For example, a worker might be sulking because he was not appointed as team leader, rather than being a long-term passive-aggressive personality.

The list that follows describes a variety of tactics for dealing with a variety of difficult people. Pick and choose from them as needed to fit the situation. Despite the many categories of difficult people, the approach to dealing with them is about the same for each type. The medical analogy is that the same antibiotic works successfully for a wide variety of infections.

- *Give feedback about the difficult behavior and stay focused on the issues at hand.* Providing timely feedback about the problems the difficult person is creating is essential to bring abut change. Do not react specifically to the problem-maker's antics, but instead stay focused on work issues. Describe the behavior you want changed, and explain why the behavior is disruptive. Pause for a moment, then wait for a response. Acknowledge what the person says, then state what needs to be changed, such as "Please stop giving customers an exasperated look and a loud exhale when they make a special request." Ask how the difficult person will make the change, and then get a commitment to change. (Notice the good coaching technique.)
- *Use tact and diplomacy.* Team members who irritate you rarely do annoying things on purpose. Tactful actions on your part can sometimes take care of these problems without your having to go through the controlling process. For example, if a coworker is engaging in a tirade about how terrible the company is, you might say, "I am really interested in your observations, but I will not attain my goals today if I don't get out these e-mails by 5 this afternoon." When subtlety does not work, you may have to confront the person. Incorporate tact and diplomacy into the confrontation. For example, as you confront a team member, point out one of his or her strengths.
- *Use humor.* Nonhostile humor can often be used to help a difficult person understand how his or her behavior annoys or blocks others. The humor should point to the person's unacceptable behavior but not belittle him or her. You might say to a subordinate who is overdue on a report: "I know we are striving for zero defects in our company. But if you wait until your report is perfect before submitting it, we may not need it anymore." Your humor may help the team member realize that timeliness is an important factor in the quality of a report.
- *Give recognition and attention.* Difficult people, like misbehaving children, are sometimes crying out for attention. Give them recognition and attention, and their difficult behavior will sometimes cease. For example, in a staff meeting, mention the person's recent contributions to the department.

If the negative behavior is a product of a deeper-rooted problem, recognition and attention by themselves will not work. The employee may have to be referred for professional counseling.

- *Listen and then confront or respond.* When discussing the problem with the difficult person, allow the individual a full expression of feelings. Next, acknowledge your awareness of the situation, and confront the person about how you size up the situation. Finally, specify what you would like changed, such as: "Please stop complaining so much about factors beyond our control." Avoid judging the person ("You shouldn't be like that") or generalizing ("You always act this way").[33]
- *Stand fast and do not make unwarranted concessions.* A variety of difficult people, but particularly bullies, expect you to sacrifice your position or standards, such as breaking the rules just for them. If a person insults you, don't laugh it off or sidestep the remarks. Instead, say, "That's not called for. I cannot let your lack of professionalism pass unnoticed." If you are not intimidated, and do not appear insecure, the difficult person is less likely to keep pushing for the advantage.[34]
- *Boost the difficult worker's self-confidence.* Many workers who complain and make excuses frequently or exhibit other forms of difficult behavior are suffering from low self-confidence. They may not stay focused on work because of fear of failure. Assign these employees an easy task, so they can succeed and begin to build self-confidence. Then move up the scale with a more difficult task. Administer praise and recognition after each success.[35]
- *If the difficult person is your boss, defend yourself without a defensive tone.* A difficult person with formal authority over you will sometimes attack you in a mean-spirited way. Assume that your boss finds a mistake in your work, and then says to you, "You're totally screwing up." You can defend yourself without a defensive tone by saying, "It is true that I made a mistake, and I appreciate constructive feedback to minimize errors in the future." Defend yourself by acknowledging the error, but refuse to be incorrectly labeled as a screw-up.[36]

Dealing with Cynical Behavior

Many employees carry extremely negative attitudes toward their employers, and these negative attitudes often take the form of cynicism. Much of the cynicism appears to be a reaction to top-level management actions, such as boosting their own compensation substantially while laying off lower-ranking workers to save money. Hiring so many contract and temporary workers at the expense of offering full-time employment also leads to cynicism. Cynics are classified as difficult people because they express their cynicism more negatively and persistently than do others.

---

33 Sam Deep and Lyle Sussman, *What to Say to Get What You Want* (Reading, MA: Addison-Wesley, 1991).
34 "Fighting off Bullies," WorkingSMART, September 1997, p. 1; http://www.kickbully.com/2004.
35 "How to Deal with 'Problem' Workers," *Positive Leadership*, Sample Issue 2004, p. 6.
36 Nando Pelusi, "Dealing with Difficult People," *Psychology Today*, September/October 2006, p. 69.

termination The process of firing an employee because of poor job performance, unacceptable behavior, or interpersonal problems.

Cynicism is usually expressed by finding something negative about even the best intentions of others. An investigation into the topic concludes that workplace cynicism is shown on any of three dimensions:

- *A belief that the organization lacks integrity* (The cynic might say, "Our advertising is a pack of lies.")
- *A negative affect toward the organization* (Cynics frequently make such comments as "This company is the pits," or "Who in his right mind would join this company today?")
- *Tendencies toward disparaging and critical behaviors directed at the organization that are consistent with these beliefs* (The cynic might use a competitor's consumer product and brag about it.)[37]

Managers may not want to suppress dissent, but too much cynicism in the workplace can lower the morale of others and interfere with recruiting positive people. Cynicism can also be distracting enough to harm productivity. One promising approach to dealing with cynics is to ignore cynical comments, and move on to another subject. If the cynic is seeking attention by being cynical, the lack of response will defeat the purpose of the sarcastic comments.

Cynical commentary can sometimes be reduced by demanding evidence to support harsh comments. Ask for the facts behind the opinion. A cynic might say, "I doubt there will be any money in the bonus pool this year. As usual, top management is taking care of itself first and leaving little money for the rest of us." You might respond, "I seriously doubt top management is going to deny us raises. Where did you get your information?" As in dealing with most difficult people, changing the individual substantially is unlikely. However, you can work toward enough improvement to bring about a more positive working relationship.

TERMINATION

Learning Objective 6

Explain the recommended approach to terminating employees.

When corrective actions fail to improve ineffective performance, an employee is likely to be terminated. The company may also assist the person in finding new employment. Termination is considered part of the control process because it is a corrective action. It can also be considered part of the organizing function because it involves placing people.

Termination is the process of firing an employee because of poor job performance, unacceptable behavior, or interpersonal problems. Termination is regarded as the last alternative. It represents a failure in staffing and in managing ineffective performers. Nevertheless, to maintain discipline and control costs, a firm is often forced to terminate nonproductive employees. When substandard performers are discharged, it communicates the message

37 James W. Dean Jr., Pamela Brandes, and Ravi Dharwadkar, "Organizational Cynicism," *Academy of Management Review*, April 1998, pp. 341–352.

that adequate performance must be maintained. Thus, a firing can also be valuable because it may increase the productivity of employees who are not fired.

Termination usually takes place only after the substandard performer has been offered the types of help described throughout this chapter. In general, every feasible alternative—such as retraining and counseling—should be attempted before termination. A manager must also accumulate substantial written documentation of substandard performance. Appropriate documentation includes performance evaluations, special memos to the file about performance problems, e-mail messages written to the employee about his or her performance, and statements describing the help offered the employee.

good cause
A legally justifiable or good business reason for firing an employee.

wrongful discharge
The firing of an employee for arbitrary or unfair reasons.

Employees must be fired for **good cause**, a legally justifiable or good business reason. For example, it is easy to fire an employee who is caught taking bribes from a vendor or because management decides to close a unit of the company. Without documentation of substandard performance, the employer can be accused of **wrongful discharge**, the firing of an employee for arbitrary or unfair reasons. Many employers face wrongful discharge suits. Court rulings in the last 20 years increasingly prohibited the termination of employees when good faith, fair dealing, and implied contracts were at issue.

To minimize major errors in firing an employee, also follow these guidelines:

- *Never fire an employee when you are angry.* Words said in anger may be too harsh, and could also reveal a prejudice, such as, "I'm getting rid of you, Harry, because we need some fresh young thinkers in this department."
- *Never fire anyone based on second-party information.* For your own legal protection you should have first-hand knowledge and evidence of the employee's unsatisfactory, immoral, or illegal behavior. For example, a frequent reason for firing a worker today is based on *charges* of sexual harassment by one person. Managers need to collect solid evidence before firing an employee stemming from only charges or accusations.
- *Be direct and clear in your language.* Inform the employee explicitly that he or she is being fired and why. Yet ease the blow with a few reassuring phrases such as, "I am sorry this job did not work out for you. Good luck in your next job."[38]

---

38 Steve Lauer and B. Jack Gebhardt, *Now Hiring* (New York: AMACOM, 1997).

SUMMARY OF Key Points

1 Identify factors contributing to poor performance.

Job performance is ineffective when productivity falls below a standard considered acceptable at a given time. Ineffective performers consume considerable managerial time. The causes of poor job performance can be rooted in the employee, the job, the manager, or the organization. Usually, ineffective performance is caused by a combination of several factors.

2 Describe the control model for managing ineffective performers.

The approach to improving ineffective performance presented in this chapter is a controlling process. It consists of eight steps that should be followed in sequence: (1) define performance standards, (2) detect deviation from acceptable performance, (3) define and assess the cause, (4) confront the substandard performer, (5) set improvement goals, (6) select and implement an action plan for improvement, (7) reevaluate performance after a time interval, and (8) continue or discontinue the action plan.

Corrective actions for ineffective performers are divided into managerial actions and techniques, and organizational programs. Managerial actions include coaching, close supervision and corrective discipline. Organizational programs include employee assistance programs (EAPs), counseling, outplacement, job redesign, and anger-management programs.

3 Know what is required to coach and constructively criticize employees.

Coaching and constructive criticism are useful approaches to managing poor performers. Coaching consists of giving advice and encouragement. Most coaching includes constructive criticism. Skill is required to coach ineffective performers and criticize them constructively. Among the components of good coaching are to offer advice and applaud good results.

4 Understand how to discipline employees.

The controlling process may also call for discipline. Summary discipline is the immediate discharge of an employee who commits a serious offense. Corrective discipline gives employees a chance to correct their behavior before punishment is applied. Both the manager and the employee share the responsibility for solving the performance problem. Corrective discipline involves counseling.

The major type of corrective discipline is called progressive discipline. It represents a step-by-step application of corrective discipline. The manager confronts the ineffective performer about the problem and then coaches him or her. If the employee's performance does not improve, the employee is given a written warning. If this fails, the employee is suspended or given a disciplinary layoff. The next step is discharge.

The red-hot-stove rule refers to administering discipline right away. The situation should include a warning; consistent, impersonal punishment should be administered immediately after the infraction is committed.

Punishment can help an organization because many employees believe that a rule violator should be punished. Also, punishment emphasizes that certain types of misconduct will not be tolerated.

5 Develop an approach to dealing with difficult people, including cynics.

Difficult people exist in many different types, including the disgruntled, passive-aggressive workers, uncivil people, and cynics. When dealing with difficult people, give feedback about the behavior and stay focused on the issue at hand. Use tact and diplomacy, and humor, while giving recognition and attention. Listen to the difficult person and confront the person about your evaluation of the situation. Do not make unwarranted concessions. Boost the difficult person's self-confidence by starting with an easy task to perform. If your boss is the difficult person, defend yourself without using a defensive tone. One approach to dealing with cynics is to ignore cynical comments. However, the cynic might also be challenged to support the basis for his or her cynicism.

6 Explain the recommended approach to terminating employees.

Termination should take place only after the substandard performer has been offered the type of help built into the control model. Documentation of poor performance is required. Coworkers should be offered a performance-based explanation of why the substandard performer was terminated. Never fire anyone based on second-hand information.

KEY TERMS AND PHRASES

Ineffective job performance, 546
Organizational citizenship behavior, 549
Confrontation, 556
Improvement goal, 556
Employee assistance program (EAP), 558
Coaching, 562
Constructive criticism, 563
Discipline, 565
Summary discipline, 565
Corrective discipline, 565
Progressive discipline, 566
Difficult person, 569
Termination, 572
Good cause, 573
Wrongful discharge, 573

QUESTIONS

1. What problems might be created by assuming that the bottom 10 percent, or bottom 5 percent, of the company workforce contains ineffective performers?
2. What is the link between managing ineffective performers and organizational productivity?
3. How can a person avoid becoming a substandard performer?
4. Visualize the work of an athletic coach, such as the coach of a basketball or soccer team. How might the coach apply the control model for managing ineffective performers to improve team performance?
5. Why should management be willing to rehabilitate employees through an employee assistance program when so many workers have been downsized in recent years?
6. What types of uncivil behavior have you observed in the workplace or in the classroom?
7. In what type of job might being a difficult person not be much of a liability?

SKILL-BUILDING EXERCISE 16-A: Managing Ineffective Performance Role Play

Imagine that you are the team leader, and one of the team members frequently fails to show up when a critical task has to be performed. He or she usually has an excuse, such as having to perform a task for higher-level management that demands his or her attention, having to attend a funeral, or having a medical appointment. You and the other team members are concerned that this team member is a social loafer. One person plays the role of the teammate with excuses; one person plays the role of the team leader; and three or four other students play the role of the rest of the team members. At your meeting today, you intend to confront the errant team member, and develop a plan for improvement. Being a self-managed team, all team members will contribute to dealing with the problem member. Run the session for about 10 to 15 minutes.

SKILL-BUILDING EXERCISE 16-B: Web-based Instructions on Bully Busting

Concerns about office bullies have led to the publication of many books, articles, and Web sites dealing with the topic. One Web site, http://www.kickbully.com/main.html, offers a specific set of instructions for dealing with workplace bullies. The program moves in a series of interesting steps, much like a PowerPoint presentation, but with more detailed and specific instructions. After you complete this module, compare it to the control model for managing ineffective performers.
Happy bullybusting!

INTERNET SKILL-BUILDING EXERCISE: Can This Employee Be Salvaged?

To learn more about when employee termination is advisable or inadvisable, visit the Business Resource Center's Web site at http://www.morebusiness.com. Check out their free interactive questionnaire (choose Templates, Business Checklists), which asks a manager 29 questions to determine whether salvaging an ineffective performer is feasible. The site also offers guidelines on wrongful discharge to managers and future managers. You might ask the 29 questions about an ineffective performer you observed in action, including a present or former coworker. Readers with supervisory experience might answer the questions about a present or former direct report.

Case Problem 16-A

Coach Fred Zweiger

Fred Zweiger is a vice president and investment consultant at a large branch of a leading financial services firm. Zweiger's main responsibility is managing the portfolios of clients with over $250,000 in assets. Reporting to Zweiger are two office assistants, and his administrative assistant Maria Mehani. Maria's main responsibilities are to take care of administrative tasks in relation to clients, such as making sure they complete the correct paperwork or computer forms, and arranging meetings between clients and Fred.

Each client is supposed to have one face-to-face meeting with Fred each year to discuss his or her investment portfolio. Maria telephones the clients to encourage them to visit the office for the meetings. Relatively little contact with clients is conducted over e-mail, to minimize the security risk of account numbers or social security numbers beings stolen by hackers.

Maria has worked as Fred's assistant for three years. He has been generally satisfied with her performance, yet believes that if Maria reached out more to clients she would help establish better client relationships, thus encouraging more investments by clients. Fred has also noticed that several clients have mentioned that Maria continues to spell their names incorrectly, and needs several reminders on address changes. As a result of these needs for improvement, Fred decides to hold a coaching session with Maria.

Later that afternoon, Fred drops by Maria's desk about 25 feet outside his office. He explains that he would like to have a staff-development meeting with her on Thursday at 4 p.m., right after the U.S. stock markets close. Maria responds with a smile, "Are you going to develop me to become a financial consultant? Or are you going to fire me?"

"Somewhere in between," responded Fed with a smile. "I'll see you Thursday." A partial transcript of the meeting is presented next.

Fred: Thanks for being here on time. It was a great day on Wall Street, so I'm in a good mood to talk about your development. Specifically I want to talk about your development into a more helpful administrative assistant to me.

Maria: I thought that I was already pretty helpful. I do whatever is required in my job description. Also, I stay late many times without overtime pay just to take care of office details.

Fred: Maria, I am not accusing you of doing a poor job. I just think you could do a better job. You need more oomph, more push, more caring, and more warmth in what you are doing.

Maria: More oomph, push, caring, and warmth. I don't know what you're talking about. I like my job but I wasn't hired to be a cheerleader.

Fred: If you don't know what I'm talking about, it only proves that I'm right. You're missing out on the subtle things needed to be an outstanding administrative assistant to an investment consultant.

Maria: I feel like I'm being accused of not doing things that are not even in my job description. I was never told this job required oomph and warmth toward clients.

Fred: But it is part of your job to serve our clients in the best way you can. You need to show them more concern and interest when they telephone you, or come into the office to see me. You should act like everyone is our most important client. To make matters worse, I've heard lots of complaints that you don't spell some of the clients' names correctly on the envelopes you mail them.

Maria: What do you mean by "lots of complaints"? Is that two, three, four, or one hundred?

Fred: I haven't kept a log, but I think you are making way too many mistakes with our clients' names. A few of our clients with long Indian last names have complained the most. Just be a little more careful with the names. The big change I want is for you to make more of an impact on our clients. Form stronger bonds with them.

Maria: How do you recommend I make that big change with all the other responsibilities I have?

Fred: You figure it out. Maybe study a book about charisma or go to a human relations seminar. I'll pay for it. That's all I have to say on the subject for now.

Maria: I'll talk to you later Fred. I am not very happy about our meeting today.

Discussion Questions

1. What is Fred doing wrong from a coaching standpoint?
2. What is Fred doing right from a coaching standpoint?
3. What suggestions would you offer Maria so she can develop warmer and closer relationships with clients?
4. What is your evaluation of Maria's willingness to develop her job-relevant skills?

Case Problem 16-B

Caustic Charlie of the Claims Department

Charlie O'Shea is one of five claims examiners in a regional office of a large casualty and property insurance company. The branch is still thriving despite the insurer selling many policies online, and billing conducted by a centralized office. The sales group sells policies and services already existing business, such as consulting with managers and business owners about upgrading their policies. The sales representatives also answer questions about policies, such as questions about whether the policy owner is covered against a terrorist attack.

Charlie works with four other examiners, as well as his supervisor Melissa Benson. The essential job of the claims examiner is to visit the site of a client with a demand for reimbursement for damages, such as a fire, flood, or industrial accident. The claims examiner then files a report with a recommendation for payment that is reviewed by the examiner's supervisor. Also, the home office reviews estimated payments beyond $17,500. Charlie has held his position for five years. He has received satisfactory performance evaluations, particularly for the accuracy and promptness of his insurance-claim reports.

Charlie has frequent negative interactions with his coworkers who resent many of his suggestions and criticisms. Jim, a senior claims analyst, says his nickname for Charlie is "Mr. Pit Bull," although he has not shared this nickname with him. Asked why he refers to Charlie as a pit bull, he replied, "It's not that Charlie physically attacks people, but it's that he's so negative about so many things. I'll give you two recent examples:

"Charlie asked me to show him a sample claims report for mud damage. I e-mailed him a report. Two days later he sent me back the report, underlining six words or phrases he said were wrong. He didn't even thank me for the report.

"I came back from a two-day trip to inspect a building damaged by a runaway truck. When I returned to the office, Charlie asked me why it took me two days to investigate a simple claim."

Sharon, a junior claims examiner, says that at his best, Charlie is a charming coworker. Yet at his worst, he grates on people's nerves. "Here's what I'm talking about. Last week I came to work wearing a blue skirt and a red blouse, on a day the vice president of claims was coming to visit our office. Charlie tells me that a person should never wear a red-and-blue combination for a special event. Not only is Charlie critical, his criticisms are sometimes way off base.

"Another time he told me that I should not waste my time studying for advanced certification in claims because it's a waste of time. He said that no manager in the company really cares about certification. Either you can do your job or you can't."

A human resource specialist from the home office asked Melissa Benson how she was handling Charlie's personality clashes with coworkers as well as with her personally. Melissa said that she was mildly concerned about Charlie's personality problems, but that Charlie still gets his work done. Yet Melissa did mention that several clients indicated that Charlie surprised them with some of his criticisms of their operation. He told one tool-and-die shop owner that a well-managed firm never has a serious accident. That was the company's first claim in 50 years of being insured by us.

"When he's snippy with me, I just shrug it off unless it gets too personal. Then I tell Charlie that he's gone too far. Like a week ago he told me that I don't do a good job of getting enough resources for our branch. That if I were a strong branch manager, we would have our offices refurbished by now. I told Charlie that our conversation was now over."

The human resources director said to Melissa, "I think you and I should talk about effective ways of dealing with Charlie and his problems."

Discussion Questions

1. What do you recommend that Melissa Benson do to improve Charlie's interpersonal relationships in the office?
2. What is your evaluation of Melissa's approach to dealing with Charlie so far?
3. What do you recommend that Charlie's coworkers do to develop more harmonious relationships with him?

chapter 17

Enhancing Personal Productivity and Managing Stress

Objectives

After studying this chapter and doing the exercises, you should be able to:

1 Identify techniques for improving work habits and time management.

2 Explain why people procrastinate, and identify techniques for reducing procrastination.

3 Understand the nature of stress and burnout, including their consequences.

4 Explain how stress can be managed effectively.

Like many Americans, Maris Friedman finds it hard to completely chill out on vacation. A senior manager for PricewaterhouseCoopers in Los Angeles, Friedman says it usually takes her a few days to decompress, and she finds herself checking her office e-mail daily. To discourage such behavior, the accounting giant shuts down its U.S. operations between Christmas and New Year's giving virtually all employee the time off with pay. Friedman calls the hiatus "fantastic. No one's e-mail, there are no phone calls, no nothing [she means either *nothing* or *no anything*]."

Worried about employee burnout and turnover, some employers are forcing workers to take the vacation time they are entitled to. Determined to take some of the labor out of Labor Day and other holidays, employers are encouraging these workaholics to switch off their cell phones and log out of e-mail while they are away.

Some employers go even a step further—giving weaker performance reviews or lower pay raises to those who don't make use of their allotted time. The 400 employees of the American Management Association, for example, risk being dinged for poor time management, said Manny Avramidis, head of human resources for the New York–based training group.[1]

1 Molly Selvin, "All Work and No Play? No Way," *Los Angeles Times* (http://latimes.com), September 4, 2006.

The information about some companies urging workers to take true vacations away from the office illustrates the recognition that overwork can cause stress and burnout, leading to lower productivity and morale in the long run. In this chapter, we describe methods for both improving productivity and managing stress, because the two are as interlocked as nutrition and health. If you are well organized, you will avoid much of the negative stress that stems from feeling that your work and life are out of control. If your level of stress is about right, you will be able to concentrate better on your work and be more productive.

The emphasis in this final chapter of the book is about managing yourself rather than managing other people or managing a business. Unless you have your work under control, and effectively manage stress, it is unlikely you can be an effective manager or leader.

IMPROVING YOUR WORK HABITS AND TIME MANAGEMENT

Learning Objective 1

Identify techniques for improving work habits and time management.

High personal productivity leads to positive outcomes such as higher income, more responsibility, and recognition. Furthermore, in an era of work streamlining and downsizings based on company consolidations, the demand for high productivity among managerial workers has never been higher. Productivity enhancers, such as daily planners, sell at record rates. High job productivity also allows you to devote more worry-free time to your personal life. In addition, high productivity helps reduce the stress experienced when a person's job is out of control. The new thrust in time management is to help people lead a better life. Don Wetmore, president of The Productivity Institute, says, "Time management is the foundation for creating balance in our lives in vital areas, such as health and family."[2]

Here we describe improving productivity by improving work habits and time management. In the next section, productivity improvement is approached from the perspective of reducing procrastination. Improving your work habits and time management is much like applying scientific management to boost personal productivity.

Develop a Mission, Goals, and a Strong Work Ethic

A major starting point in becoming a better organized and more productive person is to have a purpose and values that propel you toward being productive. In the words of Steven Covey, without a personal mission statement, you have nothing to plan and act for.[3] Assume that a person says, "My mission in life is to become an outstanding office supervisor and a caring, constructive spouse and parent." The mission serves as a compass to direct that person's activities (such as getting done on time) to developing a reputation that will lead to promotion to supervisor. Goals are more specific than mission statements, and

2 Quoted in Kathryn Tyler, "Beat the Clock," *HR Magazine*, November 2003, p. 103.

3 Cited in Ed Brown, "The 'Natural Laws' of Saving Time," *Fortune*, February 1, 1999, p. 138.

work ethic
A firm belief in the dignity and value of work.

support the mission statement, but the effect is the same. For example, the person in question might set a goal one day to respond to 75 different customer inquiries that have accumulated on the Internet by the end of the day. Accomplishing that amount of work today would be one more step toward being promoted to supervisor.

Closely related to establishing goals is to have a strong **work ethic**—a firm belief in the dignity and value of work. Developing a strong work ethic may lead to even higher productivity than goal-setting alone. For example, one might set the goal of earning a high income. It would lead to some good work habits, but not necessarily to a high commitment to quality. A person with a strong work ethic believes in quality, is highly motivated, and minimizes time-wasting activities.

Clean Up Your Work Area and Sort Out Your Tasks

People sometimes become inefficient because their work area is messy. They waste time looking for things and neglect important papers. According to the consultancy the Delphi Group, 15 percent of all paper handled in business is lost, and 30 percent of employee time is invested in searching for lost documents.[4] Electronic documents can also be lost, even if not as readily.

So to get started on improving personal productivity, clean up your work area and sort out what tasks you need to accomplish. "Getting Things Done" is a popular system for improving productivity that hits on many of the principles described in this chapter. The starting point for uncluttering your life is to collect everything you must do that is unfinished or undecided. After that you begin sorting out the tasks and assigning priorities in terms of their accomplishment[5] (as described below).

Get rid of as much clutter as possible, including personal souvenirs. Cleaning up your work area includes your briefcase, your file of telephone numbers, your hard drive, and your e-mail files. Having loads of e-mail messages stacked in your Inbox, Sent, and Deleted files can easily lead to overlooking important new messages. Weeding out your mailing list is also important. Ask to be removed from the distribution of paper and e-mail that is of no value. Rebel against being spammed. Many people begin their workday by immediately deleting unwanted e-mail messages. Deleting these messages is a bigger task for people who work at home or at smaller firms that lack elaborate protections against spam.

Katsuaki Watanabe, the chief executive officer of Toyota Motor Corp., presents the anti-clutter argument. He says, "I am told that a CEO should worry about big-picture stuff and shouldn't be concerned about minute details. I am obsessed with details. I will be an irritant, and I am persistent. I am going to grumble if the shop floor is cluttered or too greasy."[6]

4 Study cited in Jane M. Von Bergen, "Getting Organized at the Office," *The Philadelphia Inquirer*, http://www.philly.com, March 31, 2006.

5 Paul Keegan, "The Master of Getting Things Done," *Business 2.0*, July 2007, p. 77.

6 Norihiko Shirouzu, "As Rivals Catch Up, Toyota CEO Spurs Big Efficiency Drive," *The Wall Street Journal*, December 9–10, 2006, p. A6.

Recognize that the issue of avoiding clutter is controversial. Many workers believe that working in the midst of a mess is effective so long as you are organized—being able to find what you need within the mess. For example, the popular book *A Perfect Mess* advises people to not be organized because when you are superorganized, you have less flexibility to respond to spur-of-the-moment opportunities.[7] Another problem cited with avoiding clutter by filing away papers is that many people work by the principle "out of sight, out of mind." If something is put into a drawer or other file, it will be neglected.[8]

Prepare a To-Do List and Assign Priorities

A to-do list lies at the heart of every time-management system, and is a building block for planning because it records what needs to be accomplished. A survey of small-company executives revealed that about 95 percent keep a list of things to do. The vast majority has between 6 and 20 items on their list. Less than one percent accomplish everything on the list everyday.[9]

In addition to writing down tasks you need to do, assign priorities to them. A simple categorization, such as top priority versus low priority, works well for most people. In general, take care of top-priority tasks before low-priority ones. There are so many things to do on any job that some very low-priority items may never get done. Keep your to-do list on a desk calendar or a large tablet or in your computer. Setting deadlines for accomplishment is also helpful in directing your efforts, so long as the deadlines are real rather than arbitrary. A real deadline would be one imposed by your boss or law, or one that is necessary to attain so you can start on another project by a particular date.

A word-processing file may suffice, but more advanced software for work scheduling is also available, such as Microsoft Outlook. Small slips of paper in various locations tend to be distracting and often get misplaced. Plan the next day's activities at the end of each workday, thereby giving yourself a fresh plan of attack for the next day, including discharging today's unfinished work.

Many workers use daily or weekly planners to serve as a to-do list. A planner typically divides the day into 15-minute chunks and leaves room for the daily to-do list. Some planning systems are linked to a person's mission, thus giving an extra impetus to accomplishing tasks. No matter how elaborate the system that incorporates the humble to-do list, it will not boost productivity unless the items are referred to frequently, perhaps daily. An exception is that some well-organized people plan their to-do list in their head. As they move through the day, they keep working the list.

Taking care of a small, easy-to-do task first—such as sharpening pencils—has a hidden value. It tends to be relaxing because it gives you the emotional lift of having accomplished at least one item on your list. Also, accomplishing small tasks helps reduce stress.

---

7 Eric Abrahamson and David H. Freedman, *A Perfect Mess: The Hidden Benefits of Disorder* (New York: Little Brown and Company, 2006).

8 Rhonda Abrams, "Getting Organized Helps Us Refocus Energy," Gannet News Service, January 22, 2007.

9 Mark Hendricks, "Just 'To-Do' It," *Entrepreneur*, August 2004, p. 71.

Streamline Your Work

A work habit and time-management principle especially designed for the modern organization is work streamlining—eliminating as much low-value work as possible and concentrating on activities that add value for customers or clients. To streamline work, justify whether every work procedure, memo, report, meeting, or ceremonial activity contributes value to the firm. The number of group luncheon meetings away from the office might be cut in half, giving staff members more time during the day to conduct urgent work.

Masterfoods analyzed who was communicating with whom in order to understand how its product development, packaging, and process-development staff spent their time. A surprising finding was that too much time was being spent in collaboration. The manager of research and development said, "When we looked at the data, it turned out it was hard to do business internally. People had to talk to 30 or 40 other people just to get their jobs done, which took away from their time to work on new ideas." Masterfoods then redesigned the workflow of the packaging group to eliminate many of the extraneous steps that consumed so much time.[10]

The accompanying Management in Action presents another example of this highly important principle of work streamlining.

management in action

Cummins Inc. Searches to Jettison Unnecessary Work

The last place most people would look to for help reducing their workload is their employer. But that's exactly where John L. Williams got help last year, cutting back his workday to a manageable length. Overloaded with unplanned phone calls and reports, Williams, an account executive at Cummings Inc., an engine manufacturer based in Columbus, Indiana, had been taking work and toiling as late as 2 a.m. on his laptop.

An annual survey of 6,700 employees in 2004 showed a drop in employee satisfaction with workloads, says Janet Dunn, Cummins' director of diversity development. So, two Tennessee work teams met with WFD Consulting to figure out how to jettison low-value tasks.

Luckily for Williams, Cummins had embarked on a pilot project to eliminate unnecessary work. Now he is getting more core job duties done at the office—and getting to bed earlier. Team members began meeting biweekly to identify and cut out redundant work, Dunn says.

They reduced unplanned phone calls and the number of sales-history and analysis reports they had to generate for sales people, by referring requests to online resources. Customer-help teams also organized to back each other up on service calls, to avoid any one employee getting backed up with complex jobs. Such changes helped enable Williams, who works in a pricing unit, and more than 30 others to get more done during the workday, he says. Cummins plans to expand the pilot to other teams.

(Continued)

10 Michael Mandel, "The Real Reasons You're Working So hard... and What You Can Do About It," *Business Week*, October 3, 2005, p. 66.

management in action (Continued)

Cummins Inc. Searches to Jettison Unnecessary Work

Questions

1. Why might unplanned phone calls be considered a low-value task?
2. In what way does Cummins make good use of information technology to reduce low-value tasks?
3. Why should Cummins care if Williams has to work until 2 a.m. to get his job done? He's not being paid overtime.

Source: Sue Shellenbarger, "Talking Back the Weekend: Companies Help Employees Cut Back on Overwork," *The Wall Street Journal*, May 18, 2006, p. D1. Reprinted with permission through the Copyright Clearance Center.

Work at a Steady, Rapid Pace

Although a dramatic show of energy (as in "pulling an all-nighter") is impressive, the steady worker tends to be more productive in the long run. The spurt employee creates many problems for management; the student who works in spurts is in turmoil at examination time or when papers are due. Managers who expend the same amount of effort day-by-day tend to stay in control of their jobs. When a sudden problem or a good opportunity comes to their attention, they can fit it into their schedule. Working at a steady pace often means always working rapidly. To be competitive, most organizations require that work be accomplished rapidly.

An important exception about working rapidly all the time is that some decisions require careful deliberation and should not be rushed. A team of researchers studied for 19 months the decision making of an Internet start-up. Making decisions too rapidly resulted in many errors in purchasing software and hiring people.[11]

The recommendations about working rapidly yet making major decisions deliberately are compatible. After you take enough time to make a major decision, work rapidly to accomplish the tasks necessary to implement the decision. A manager might carefully weigh the evidence about the value of outsourcing some operations to Africa. After the decision is made, the manager and his or her staff work rapidly to make the outsourcing a reality.

Minimize Time Wasters and Interruptions

An important strategy for improving personal productivity is to minimize time wasters. Each minute invested in productive work can save you from working extra hours. A major time waster is interruptions from others. One of the

11 Leslie A. Perlow, Gerardo A. Okhuysen, and Nelson P. Repenning, "The Speed Trap: Exploring the Relationship Between Decision Making and Temporal Context," *Academy of Management Journal*, October 2002, pp. 931–955.

benefits of telecommuting is that interruptions from other workers are minimized. When doing intellectually demanding work, getting the appropriate flow of thought is difficult. When interrupted, people lose momentum and must launch themselves again. The definition of what constitutes an *interruption* is tricky. A coworker asking you to participate in a basketball pool is certainly an interruption, but socializing with him or her might strengthen your network. Some executives feel that a demand from a customer should never be classified as an interruption. A sudden demand from a boss might also not be classified as an interruption.

A contingency perspective on interruptions is that most of them are harmful to work, but some are helpful. For example, if somebody walks into your cubicle while you are attempting to calculate a gross profit margin—that your boss wants in ten minutes—the interruption is dysfunctional. Yet at another time, chatting with an intruder could result in some useful information sharing that is functional. A scientific analysis of the positive and negative consequences of four different types of interruptions is presented in Exhibit 17-1.

Exhibit 17-2 presents a list of significant ways to reduce wasted time. Many of the other suggestions in this chapter can also help you save time directly or indirectly.

exhibit 17-1 **Four Types of Interruptions and their Positive and Negative Consequences**

Type of Interruption	Negative Consequences for Person Being Interrupted	Positive Consequences for Person Being Interrupted
Intrusion (unexpected encounter)	Not enough time to accomplish the task leading to stress; disruption in concentration	Informal feedback and information sharing that otherwise might not be available
Break (planned or spontaneous recess from work)	Procrastination and/or significant amounts of time spent relearning essential details of work being performed	Alleviation of fatigue or distress; more job satisfaction; time for ideas to incubate; refreshed approach to task
Distraction (secondary activity that disrupts concentration)	Mediocre performance when work is complex and demanding, and requires full attention	Enhanced performance when the distraction increases stimulation levels on routine tasks
Discrepancy (inconsistency between what you expected and what is really happening)	Strong negative emotional reaction (such as from finding out that you have been working on improving a product that management has decided to drop)	Recognition of the need for change and triggering person into action

Source: Adapted and abridged from Quintus R. Jett and Jennifer M. George, "Work Interrupted: A Closer Look at the Role of Interruptions in Organizational Life," *Academy of Management Review*, July 2003, p. 497.

exhibit 17-2 Ways to Prevent and Overcome Time Wasting

Wasted time is a major productivity drain, so it pays to search for time wasters in your work activities. The following list suggests remedies for some of the major time wasters in the workplace.

1. Use a time log for two weeks to track time wasters.
2. Minimize daydreaming on the job by forcing yourself to concentrate.
3. Avoid the computer as a diversion from work, such as sending jokes back and forth to network members, including people on your buddy list; playing video games; and checking out recreational and shopping Web sites during working hours.
4. Batch tasks together such as responding to e-mail messages or returning phone calls. For example, in most jobs it is possible to be productive by reserving two or three 15-minute periods per day for taking care of e-mail correspondence. Checking e-mail too frequently, such as every five minutes, is a major time waster unless necessary for your job.
5. Socialize on the job just enough to build your network. Chatting with coworkers is a major productivity drain and one of the reasons so many managers work at home part of the time when they have analytical work to get done.
6. Be prepared for meetings, such as having a clear agenda and sorting through the documents you will be referring to. Make sure electronic equipment is in working order before attempting to use it during the meeting.
7. Keep track of important names, places, and things, to avoid wasting time searching for them.
8. Set a time limit for tasks after you have done them once or twice.
9. Prepare a computer template for letters and computer documents that you send frequently. (The template is essentially a form letter, especially with respect to the salutation and return address.)
10. Avoid perfectionism, which leads you to keep redoing a project. Let go and move on to another project.
11. Make use of bits of time; for instance, five minutes between appointments. Invest those five minutes in sending a business e-mail, or revise your to-do list. (Note the exception to the batch principle.)
12. Sort out your mail over a wastebasket or recycling bin. Dispose immediately of mail you have no need to open now or later. You save time by having less accumulated mail to sort through.
13. Decrease grabbing for your cell phone at every conceivable moment, such as when you exit the building. Some of the time devoted to chatting on the cell phone could be invested in planning your work or searching for creative ideas. Many managers and corporate professionals consult their personal digital assistant for business instead of social purposes on the way to or back from lunch.
14. Minimize procrastination, the number-one time waster for most people.

Source: Suggestions 4, 5, and 6 are based on Stephen R. Covey with Hyrum Smith, "What If You Could Chop an Hour from Your Day for Things That Matter Most?" *USA Weekend*, January 22–24, 1999, pp. 4–5.

Concentrate on One Task at a Time

Productive managers develop their capacity to concentrate on the problem facing them at the moment, however engulfed they are with other obligations. Intense concentration leads to sharpened judgment and analysis and also decreases the chances of making major errors. Another useful by-product of concentration is reduced absentmindedness. The person who concentrates on the task at hand allows less chance of forgetting what he or she intended.

To assist their concentration levels on the task at hand, some people use performance cues, or items to concentrate on when under pressure.[12] For

12 Shane Murphy, *The Achievement Zone: Eight Skills for Winning All the Time from the Playing Field to the Boardroom* (New York: G. P. Putnam's Sons, 1996).

example, when facing a difficult customer, your performance cue might be a smile. Say to yourself, "I must smile now." Smiling is effective because it helps reduce the difficult customer's hostility. Another performance cue might be taking notes when major points come up in your conversation with a group member. Taking notes forces you to concentrate intently on the message sender. Your performance cue is, "When she says something of special importance, I will jot down the idea on paper."

Multitasking has become a typical mode of operation for many workers. However, multitasking is best reserved for routine tasks such as discarding unwanted e-mail messages and cleaning your desk at the same time. As described in Chapter 14, multitasking on important tasks may lead to serious errors, and many forms of multitasking may be perceived as rude by other workers who do not engage in the same behavior. *Surfer's voice* is a term to describe the habit of half-heartedly conversing with someone on the telephone while simultaneously surfing the Web, reading e-mail messages, or exchanging instant messages.[13]

The case for concentrating on one important task at a time is strongly stated by time-management guru Stephanie Winston: "Successful CEOs do not multitask. They concentrate intensely on one think at a time.... How can you do your best work if you are constantly distracted?"[14] An exception is that there are some successful CEOs who routinely consult their BlackBerry while talking to employees or customers. People of this nature are often referred to as "CrackBerrys." (The analogy is being addicted to crack cocaine.)

In contrast to the problems just stated, multitasking for routine tasks can lead to productivity gain. A growing form of multitasking is to work with two computer monitors. You use one monitor to go about your regular work, and the other monitor for e-mail. In this way you do not have to constantly minimize and maximize your document to access e-mail.[15] However, if you are working on a document that requires full attention, it is hazardous to continually glance at the e-mail monitor. For example, if you analyzing tax data for the company, do not keep looking at your second monitor.

Concentrate on High-Output Tasks

Many people interpret time-management techniques as a way of becoming a tidy perfectionist who never lets a detail slip by. In contrast, a major time-management principle is that to become more productive on the job or in school, concentrate on tasks in which superior performance could have a large payoff. For a manager, a high-output task would be to develop a strategic plan for the department, or finding ways to obtain a high return on investment for surplus cash. For a student, a high-output task would be to think of a creative idea for an independent study project. Expending your work effort on high-output items is analogous to looking for a good return

13 Dennis K. Berman, "Technology Has Us So Plugged Into Data, We Have Turned Off," *The Wall Street Journal*, November 10, 2003, p. B1.

14 Quoted in Anne Fisher, "Get Organized at Work—Painlessly," *Fortune*, January 10, 2005, p. 30.

15 Lee Gomes, "Want to Simplify? Add a Monitor," *The Wall Street Journal*, July 24, 2006, p. R11.

on investment for your money. The high-output strategy also follows the Pareto principle, described in Chapter 6.

A new twist on high-output tasks is that they usually involve some risk because they are a departure from the typical way of doing business. The risk taker works perhaps fewer hours than many other workers, but courageously pushes for new ideas like a replacement for the standard lightbulb if working for General Electric. Many people are hesitant to take such risks because they fear failure, standing out, or being rejected.[16]

Do Creative and Routine Tasks at Different Times

Similar to concentrating on high-output tasks, to improve productivity, organize your work so you do not shift between creative and routine tasks. For many people it is best to work first on creative tasks because they require more mental energy than routine tasks. A minority of people prefer to get minor paperwork and e-mail chores out of the way so they can get to the pleasure of doing creative tasks. Whichever order you choose, it is important not to interrupt creative (or high-output) tasks with routine activities such as deleting spam or rearranging the desk.

It is also helpful to tackle creative tasks when you are typically at your best. For many people, their mentally best time is the morning; for others the afternoon is best. The reason for selecting your high-energy time for creative work is that creativity requires considerable mental energy. Routine work can then be performed when you are not at your best mentally.

Stay in Control of Paperwork, E-Mail, and Voice Mail

No organization today can accomplish its mission unless paperwork, including the electronic variety, receives appropriate attention. If you handle paperwork improperly, your job may get out of control. Once your job is out of control, the stress level will increase greatly. Invest a small amount of time in paperwork and electronic mail every day. Avoid becoming a paper shuffler or frequently rereading e-mail messages. The ideal is to handle a piece of paper or an e-mail message only once. When you pick up a hard-copy memo or read an electronic one, take some action: throw it away or delete it, route it to someone else, write a short response to the sender, or flag it for action later. Loose ends of time can be used to take care of the flagged memos.

A recommended method for efficiently dealing with paper memos and letters is to place them into stacking bins on the floor labeled "To Read," "To File," and "To Do."[17] E-mail messages could be placed into folders with the same labels.

Staying in control of voice mail messages is also important to stay productive. Stacked up voice mail messages will often detract from your ability to concentrate on other work. Not returning voice mail messages promptly also creates the problem of perceived rudeness and poor customer service.

16 Seth Godin, "A Brief History of Hard Work, Adjusted for Risk," *Fast Company*, April 2003, p. 64.
17 Lisa Kanarek, "Clean Sweep," *Entrepreneur*, June 2006, p. 44.

Disciplining yourself to answer voice mail messages in batches, as mentioned in Exhibit 17-2, will help you manage these messages productively.

Make Effective Use of Office Technology

Many managerial workers boost their productivity by making effective use of office technology. Yet the productivity gains are not inevitable. Just because a person can receive rapidly transmitted e-mail messages from all over the world, search the Internet on a cell phone, and produce exquisite pie charts, increased sales and decreased costs do not always follow. Boosting your personal productivity is contingent upon choosing equipment that truly adds to productivity and does not drain too much time for purposes of learning, consulting with the tech center, or bringing it back and forth to the repair shop. A specific example of making effective use of office technology to help you become more efficient would be to use desktop search to help you find documents quickly.

A major reason many workers do not achieve productivity gains with information technology is that they do not invest the time saved in other productive activity. If sending a batch of e-mail messages instead of postal mail saves you two hours, you will only experience a productivity gain if the two hours are then invested in a task with a tangible output, such as searching for a lower-cost supplier. Another problem is that electronic communication systems like IM encourage diverting your attention away from the task at hand.

Office technology devices are attractive and intriguing. It is also important to know when simple mechanical or handwritten procedures are faster than office technology. For example, the simple 3×5 index card remains a powerful low- technology way of preparing and executing a to-do list. Managers and professionals who move from one location to another may find it a time waster to access a computer just to check their daily list. Even a palm-size computer can be more disruptive than simply glancing at an index card attached to a pocket calendar. A complaint some people have about large $81/2 \times 11$ planners is they are cumbersome to lug around unless you are carrying an attaché case.

Finally, keep in mind that our imagination and focus are the major contributors to productivity; office technology offers only a valuable assist. Donald Trump leaves the only computer in his office unplugged, and Bill Clinton wrote his best-selling book by hand in a converted barn. (Trump and Clinton, however, hire people to do their computer work, so they are not really avoiding office technology.)

Practice the Mental State of Peak Performance

To achieve maximum potential productivity, one must transcend ordinary levels of concentration and devotion to duty. That occurs in **peak performance**, a mental state in which maximum results are achieved with minimum effort. Peak performers remain mentally calm and physically at ease when challenged by difficult problems. They focus intensely and stay involved, much like they would be in playing the best tennis games of their lives. Peak performance also involves

peak performance
A mental state in which maximum results are achieved with minimum effort.

careful planning for the task to be accomplished, including obtaining input from others. For example, if you had an upcoming meeting with a major customer, you might research the type of information that would be important to that customer. You may have experienced the state of peak performance when totally involved with a problem or task. At that moment, nothing else seems to exist.

To achieve peak performance, you must continually work toward being mentally calm and physically at ease. Concentrate intensely, but not so much that you choke. In addition to frequent practice, peak performance can be achieved through visualization. In visualization you develop a mental image of how you would act and feel at the point of peak performance. For example, imagine yourself making a flawless presentation to top-level management about the contributions of your department. Psychologist Charles Garfield observed that people who achieve peak performance typically have an important mission in life—such as building a top-quality company.[18]

Take Naps or Meditate

A productivity-booster is to take a nap of about 15 to 30 minutes designed to recharge the individual. A major reason that productivity-enhancing naps are important is because so many workers, including managers, are sleep deprived.[19] Naps of 30 minutes or more may create grogginess and lower productivity. Well-placed naps actually enhance rather than diminish productivity, and they are also an excellent stress reducer. According to one researcher, "The remarkable aspect of napping in advance of an extended period of work is that the benefits of the nap, even one of only 25 minutes duration, can be evident in performance hours afterward."[20]

Napping for purposes of boosting productivity has surged in Japan in recent years, as a way of Japanese workers gaining a mental edge. Nap salons have surfaced in Japan's major cities, where office workers can take a brief lunchtime nap on a daybed for the equivalent of about $4.50. Department stores and catalogs sell desk pillows, and some companies now permit in-office napping.[21]

Naps can also prevent industrial disasters by overcoming grogginess before it leads to an accident such as the *Exxon Valdez* oil spill. Naps are also an effective way of decreasing incidences of driving home from work drowsy.

The organizational nap taker must use discretion in napping so as not to be perceived as sleeping on the job. Toward this end, some workers nap in their cars or in a storeroom during lunch break. In companies where the organization accepts such behavior, some employees nap with their heads resting on their desks or worktables during breaks. Many workers continue to nap under their desks.

---

18 Ingrid Lorch-Bacci, "Achieving Peak Performance: The Hidden Dimension," *Executive Management Forum*, January 1991, pp. 1–4; Don Straits, "Peak Performers: In Search of the Best," pp. 1–2, http://www.careerbuilder.com, accessed March 10, 2006.

19 Charles A. Czeisler, "Sleep Deficit: The Performance Killer," *Harvard Business Review*, October 2006, pp. 53–59.

20 Donald J. McNerney, "Napping at Work: You Snooze, You Win!" *HRfocus*, March 1995, p. 3.

21 Anthony Faiola, "Nation of Workaholics Sleeps on the Job," http://www.washingtonpost.com, June 21, 2006, p. A1.

Closely related to the productivity-boosting value of napping is *transcendental meditation* or simply *meditation*. The process physically changes neurological connections between parts of the brain and allows for a deep state of relaxation. Workers who meditate before and after work often find that they can think more clearly about job challenges. A frequently used form of meditation is to get in a physically relaxed state, and keep repeating a word or mantra. Yoga is essentially another form of meditation. Meditation, like striving for peak performance and napping, helps you concentrate and focus, thereby boosting your productivity, assuming that you have the right talent and skills to perform well.[22]

Work Smarter, Not Harder

A comprehensive time-management principle is to plan your activities carefully, and discharge them in an imaginative way rather than simply working furiously. Several of the time-management suggestions already presented facilitate working smarter, not harder, such as streamlining your work and concentrating on high-output tasks. A working-smart approach requires that you spend a few minutes carefully planning how to implement your task. An example of working smarter would be the placement of an online or newspaper ad to fill a job vacancy. If you list the qualifications precisely, you can decrease the flood of completely unqualified candidates even though most candidates will still be unqualified.

Another example of working smarter, not harder is to use new technology that fosters collaboration. (As pointed out earlier, however, too much collaboration can slow you down.) A company intranet that allows you to find out what colleagues in other parts of the company are working on will enable you to spend less time in duplicated effort.[23] For example, if you are developing a list of cost-savings suggestion for customer service, and you learn that Kim in Portland, Oregon, is also developing such a list, you can share suggestions.

Build Flexibility into Your System

A time-management system must allow some room for flexibility. How else could you handle unanticipated problems? If you work 50 hours per week, build in a few hours for taking care of emergencies. If your plan is too tight, delegate some tasks to others or work more hours. Perhaps you can find a quicker way to accomplish several of your tasks. As with other forms of planning, do not let your to-do list become a straightjacket that prevents you from capitalizing on new opportunities. Marissa Mayer, V.P. search products and user experience at Google, notes that her workday changes so rapidly, she may have to revamp the to-do list she prepared the night before. She once said, "This morning I had my list of what I thought I was going to do today, but now I'm doing entirely different things."[24] Mayer would then develop a new to-do list rapidly to take care of tasks for the changed day.

Suppose an item on today's to-do list is to download the latest antivirus program. A customer calls unexpectedly wanting to place a $150,000 order.

---

22 Mark Henricks, "A Head Start," *Entrepreneur*, July 2003, pp. 73–74.

23 Mandel, "The Real Reasons You're Working So Hard," p. 62.

24 Quoted in "How I Work," *Fortune*, March 20, 2006, p. 68.

procrastination The delaying of action for no good reason.

Do not reply, "Let me call you back after I have finished checking for new antivirus programs." Finally, to avoid staleness and stress, your schedule must allow sufficient time for rest and relaxation.

UNDERSTANDING AND REDUCING PROCRASTINATION

Learning Objective 2

Explain why people procrastinate, and identify techniques for reducing procrastination.

The number-one time waster for most people is **procrastination,** the delaying of action for no good reason. Reducing procrastination pays substantial dividends in increased productivity, especially because speed can give a company a competitive advantage. Procrastination also needs to be taken seriously because such tendencies can doom a person to low performance. Exhibit 17-3 gives you an opportunity to think about your own tendencies toward procrastination, so get to it without delay. Here we consider why people procrastinate, and what can be done about the problem.

Why People Procrastinate

People procrastinate for many different reasons, with some of them being deep-rooted emotional problems, and others more superficial and related directly to the work. Here we look at seven major reasons for procrastination.

exhibit 17-3 Procrastination Tendencies

Circle yes or no for each item:

1. I usually do my best work under the pressure of deadlines.	Yes	No
2. Before starting a project, I go through such rituals as sharpening every pencil, straightening up my desk more than once, and discarding bent paper clips.	Yes	No
3. I crave the excitement of the "last-minute rush."	Yes	No
4. I often think that if I delay something, it will go away, or the person who asked for it will forget about it.	Yes	No
5. I extensively research something before taking action, such as obtaining five different estimates before getting the brakes repaired on my car.	Yes	No
6. I have a great deal of difficulty getting started on most projects, even those I enjoy.	Yes	No
7. I keep waiting for the right time to do something, such as getting started on an important report.	Yes	No
8. I often underestimate the time needed to do a project, and say to myself, "I can do this quickly, so I'll wait until next week."	Yes	No
9. It is difficult for me to finish most projects or activities.	Yes	No
10. I have several favorite diversions or distractions that I use to keep me from doing something unpleasant.	Yes	No

Total yes responses ___

The more yes responses, the more likely it is that you have a serious procrastination problem. A score of 8, 9, or 10 strongly suggests that procrastination lowers your productivity.

1. Some people fear failure or other negative consequences. As long as a person delays doing something of significance, he or she cannot be regarded as having performed poorly on the project. Other negative consequences include looking foolish in the eyes of others or developing a bad reputation. For instance, if a manager delays making an oral presentation, nobody will know whether he or she is an ineffective speaker. Fear of failure can be—but is not always—a deep-rooted personality problem that will make it difficult to overcome procrastination by the suggestions presented in the following section. To use a baseball analogy, "If I don't get up to bat, I can't strike out."[25]
2. Procrastination may stem from a desire to avoid uncomfortable, overwhelming, or tedious tasks. Many people delay preparing their income tax forms for this reason.
3. People frequently put off tasks that do not appear to offer a meaningful reward. Suppose you decide that your computer files need a thorough updating. Even though you know it should be done, having a completely updated directory might not be a particularly meaningful reward to you.
4. Some people dislike being controlled. When a procrastinator does not do things on time, he or she has successfully rebelled against being controlled by another person's time schedule.
5. People sometimes are assigned tasks they perceive to be useless or needless, such as checking someone else's work. Rather than proceed with the trivial task, the individual procrastinates.
6. A curious reason for procrastination is to achieve the stimulation and excitement that stems from rushing to meet a deadline. For example, some people enjoy fighting their way through traffic or running through an airline terminal so they can make an appointment or airplane flight barely on time. They appear to enjoy the rush of adrenaline, endorphins, and other hormones associated with hurrying.
7. Procrastination is sometimes a symptom of a negative emotional state such as self-defeating behavior (see Exhibit 16-2 about self-sabotage) or depression. The procrastinator may want to fail as a form of self-punishment, or may be so depressed that he or she just cannot get started on an important task. In such cases, mental-health counseling may be required.

Approaches to Reducing and Controlling Procrastination

Procrastination often becomes a strong habit that is difficult to change. Nevertheless, the following strategies and tactics can be helpful in overcoming procrastination:

1. *Break the task down into smaller units.* By splitting a large task into smaller units, you can make a job appear less overwhelming. This approach is useful, of course, only if the task can be done in small pieces, such as a small-business owner preparing tax returns by working on one category of

---

25 Steven Berglas, "Chronic Time Abuse," *Harvard Business Review*, June 2004, pp. 96–97.

expenses at a time: "Friday I document telephone and Internet expenses; Saturday I'll work on travel and entertainment."

2. *Make a commitment to others.* Your tendency to procrastinate on an important assignment may be reduced if you publicly state that you will get the job done by a certain time. You might feel embarrassed if you fail to meet your deadline.
3. *Reward yourself for achieving milestones.* A potent technique for overcoming any counterproductive behavior pattern is to give yourself a reward for progress toward overcoming the problem. Make your reward commensurate with the magnitude of the accomplishment.
4. *Calculate the cost of procrastination.* You can sometimes reduce procrastination by calculating its cost. Remind yourself, for example, that you might lose out on obtaining a high-paying job you really want if your résumé and cover letter are not ready on time. The cost of procrastination would include the difference in the salary between the job you do find and the one you really wanted. Another cost would be the loss of potential job satisfaction.
5. *Post encouraging notes in your work and living area.* Encourage yourself to get something done by a particular time, via small notes, perhaps even using a digital camera to create computer wallpaper. For example, "The plan for recycling laser print cartridges is due September 15, and YOU CAN DO IT!!!!!"
6. *Counterattack.* Another way of combating procrastination is to force yourself to do something uncomfortable or frightening. After you begin, you are likely to find that the task is not as onerous as you thought. Assume you have been delaying learning a foreign language even though you know it will help your career. You remember how burdensome it was studying another language in school. You grit your teeth and remove the cellophane from the CD for the target language. After listening for five minutes, you discover that beginning to study a foreign language again is not nearly as bad as you imagined.
7. *Post a progress chart in your work area.* The time and activity charts presented in Chapter 6 can be applied to combating procrastination. As you chart your progress in achieving each step in a large project, each on-time accomplishment will serve as a reward, and each missed deadline will be self-punishing. The constant reminder of what needs to be accomplished by what date will sometimes prod you to minimize delays. Exhibit 17-4 presents a basic version of a chart for combating procrastination. The time and activity chart is helpful because it fits into the more general solution to procrastination—get organized.

THE NATURE OF STRESS AND BURNOUT

Learning Objective 3

Understand the nature of stress and burnout, including their consequences.

Job stress and its related condition, job burnout, contribute to poor physical and mental health. Employee stress is a source of discomfort and a major concern to managers and stockholders. According to the Attitudes in the American Workplace Gallup Poll, worker stress costs $300 billion annually due to lost productivity, increased workers' compensation claims, and

exhibit 17-4 **A Time and Activity Chart to Combat Procrastination**

Charting key tasks and their deadlines, along with your performance in meeting the deadlines, can sometimes help overcome procrastination.

	Deadlines for Task Accomplishment					
Task to Be Accomplished	**Jan 1**	**Jan 31**	**Feb 15**	**Feb 28**	**Mar 15**	**Mar 31**
Expense reports	Did it					
Real-estate estimates		Blew it				
Web site installed			One day late			
Replace broken furniture				Made it		
Plan office picnic					On time	
Collect delinquent account						Blew it

healthcare costs.[26] Also, an estimated 45 percent of unwanted job turnover is stress related. Another survey indicated that 50 percent of employees miss one to two days of work per year due to stress, and 46 percent admitted that they come to work one to four days per year even when they are too stressed to be effective.[27]

In order to effectively prevent and control stress, you first need to understand the nature and cause of these conditions. A good starting point in understanding stress symptoms is to take the self-quiz presented in Exhibit 17-5.

As used here, **stress** is the mental and physical condition that results from a perceived threat that cannot be dealt with readily. Stress is therefore an internal response to a state of activation. The stressed person is physically and mentally aroused. Stress ordinarily occurs in a threatening or negative situation, such as being fired. However, stress can also be caused by a positive situation, such as receiving a major promotion.

A person experiencing stress displays certain symptoms indicating that he or she is trying to cope with a stressor (any force creating the stress reaction). These symptoms can include a host of physiological, emotional, and behavioral reactions.

Physiological symptoms of stress include increased heart rate, blood pressure, breathing rate, pupil size, and perspiration. If these physiological symptoms are severe or persist over a prolonged period, the result can be a stress-related disorder, such as a heart attack, hypertension, migraine headache, ulcer, colitis, or allergy. Stress also leads to a chemical imbalance that adversely affects the body's immune system. People experiencing emotional stress may experience difficulty shaking a common cold or recovering from

stress
The mental and physical condition that results from a perceived threat that cannot be dealt with readily.

26 Survey results presented in "Research: the High Cost of Stress," http://www.themoreproductiveworkplace.com, accessed January 28, 2007.

27 Survey results reported in Kathryn Tyler, "Stress Management," *HR Magazine*, September 2006, p. 81.

exhibit 17-5 The Stress Questionnaire

Here is a brief questionnaire to give a rough estimate of whether you are facing too much stress. Apply each question to the last six months of your life. Check the appropriate column.

Mostly Yes	Mostly No	
☐	☐	1. Have you been feeling uncomfortably tense lately?
☐	☐	2. Do you frequently argue with people close to you?
☐	☐	3. Is your romantic life very unsatisfactory?
☐	☐	4. Do you have trouble sleeping?
☐	☐	5. Do you feel lethargic about life?
☐	☐	6. Do many people annoy or irritate you?
☐	☐	7. Do you have constant cravings for candy and other sweets?
☐	☐	8. Is your consumption of cigarettes or alcohol way up?
☐	☐	9. Are you becoming addicted to soft drinks, coffee, or tea?
☐	☐	10. Do you find it difficult to concentrate on your work?
☐	☐	11. Do you frequently grind your teeth?
☐	☐	12. Are you increasingly forgetful about little things, such as answering an e-mail or mailing a letter?
☐	☐	13. Are you increasingly forgetful about big things, such as appointments and major errands?
☐	☐	14. Are you making far too many trips to the lavatory?
☐	☐	15. Have people commented lately that you do not look well?
☐	☐	16. Do you get into verbal fights with others too frequently?
☐	☐	17. Have you been involved in more than one breakup with a friend lately?
☐	☐	18. Do you have more than your share of tension headaches?
☐	☐	19. Do you feel nauseated much too often?
☐	☐	20. Do you feel light-headed or dizzy almost every day?
☐	☐	21. Do you have churning sensations in your stomach far too often?
☐	☐	22. Are you in a big hurry all the time?
☐	☐	23. Are far too many things bothering you these days?
☐	☐	24. Do you hurry through activities even when you are not rushed for time?
☐	☐	25. Do you often feel that you are in the panic mode?

Scoring

0–6	Mostly Yes answers: You seem to be experiencing a normal amount of stress.
7–16	Mostly Yes answers: Your stress level seems high. Become involved in some kind of stress-management activity, such as the activities described in this chapter.
17–25	Mostly Yes answers: Your stress level appears to be much too high. Seek the help of a mental-health professional or visit your family physician (or do both).

sexually transmitted disease. In general, any disorder classified as psychosomatic is precipitated by emotional stress.

Emotional symptoms of stress include anxiety, tension, depression, discouragement, boredom, prolonged fatigue, feelings of hopelessness, and various kinds of defensive thinking. Note that anxiety is a general sense of dread, fear, or worry for no immediate reason, and is a symptom of stress. Behavioral symptoms include nervous habits, such as facial twitching, and sudden decreases in job performance due to forgetfulness and errors in concentration or judgment. Increased use of alcohol and other drugs may also occur. Procrastination is another potential symptom of negative stress.

Stress has both negative and positive consequences. **Hindrance stressors** are those stressful events and thoughts that have a negative effect on motivation and performance. In contrast, **challenge stressors** have a positive direct effect on motivation and performance.[28]

hindrance stressors
Stress events and thoughts that have a negative effect on motivation and performance.

challenge stressors
Sources of stress that have a positive direct effect on motivation and performance.

People require the right amount of stress to keep them mentally and physically alert. Managers create challenge stressors by challenging workers, and being passionate about work.[29] If the stress is particularly uncomfortable or distasteful, however, it will lower job performance—particularly on complex, demanding jobs. An example of a stressor that will lower job performance for most people is a bullying, abrasive manager who wants to see the employee fail.

A person's perception of something (or somebody) usually determines whether it acts as a challenge or hindrance stressor. For example, one person might perceive an inspection by top-level managers to be so frightening that he is irritable toward team members. Another manager might welcome the visit as a chance to proudly display her department's high-quality performance. An extensive review of research about job stress concludes that stress is less likely to lower performance when employees have high levels of self-esteem and commitment to the organization.[30]

After prolonged exposure to job stress, a person runs the risk of feeling burned out—a drained, used-up feeling. **Job burnout** is a pattern of emotional, physical, and mental exhaustion in response to chronic job stressors. Cynicism, apathy, and indifference are the major behavioral symptoms of the burned-out worker. Hopelessness is another key symptom of burnout, with the worker often feeling that nothing he or she does makes a difference, and is not accomplishing much of value. Correspondingly, burnout involves losing a sense of the basic purpose and fulfillment of your work.[31] Supervisors are more at risk for burnout than other workers because they deal primarily with the demands of other people.

job burnout
A pattern of emotional, physical, and mental exhaustion in response to chronic job stressors.

A study with firefighters suggested that being emotionally exhausted leads to lowered motivation.[32] Two studies conducted in a variety of organizations showed that burnout in the form of emotional exhaustion leads to lowered job

---

28 Jeffery A. Lepine, Nathan P. Podsakoff, and Marcie A. Lepine, "A Meta-Analytic Test of the Challenge-Stressor-Hindrance Stressor Framework: An Explanation for Inconsistent Relationships Among Stressors and Performance," *Academy of Management Journal*, October 2005, pp. 764–775.

29 Peg Gamse, "Stress for Success," *HR Magazine*, July 2003, p. 102.

30 Steve M. Jex, *Stress and Job Performance: Theory, Research, and Implications for Managerial Practice* (Thousand Oaks, CA: Sage, 1998).

31 Lin Grensing-Pophal, "HR, Heal Thyself," *HR Magazine*, March 1999, p. 84.

32 Jonathon R. B. Halbesleben and Wm. Matthew Bowler, "Emotional Exhaustion: The Mediating Role of Motivation," *Journal of Applied Psychology*, January 2007, pp. 93–106.

performance, less organizational citizenship behavior, and an intention to quit.[33] Have you ever experienced the phenomenon of being so exhausted that your motivation suffered?

Absence of ample positive feedback and other rewards is strongly associated with job burnout. As a consequence of not knowing how well they are doing and not receiving recognition, employees often become discouraged and emotionally exhausted. The result is often—but certainly not always—job burnout.

Factors Contributing to Stress and Burnout

Factors within a person, as well as adverse organizational conditions, can cause or contribute to stress and burnout. Personal-life stress and work stress also influence each other. Work stress can create problems—and therefore stress—at home. And stress stemming from personal problems can lead to problems—and therefore stress—at work. Because stress is additive, if you have considerable personal stress you, will more susceptible to job stress, and vice versa.

Factors Within the Individual

Hostile, aggressive, and impatient people find ways of turning almost any job into a stressful experience. Such individuals are labeled Type A, in contrast to their more easygoing Type B counterparts. In addition to being angry, the outstanding trait of Type A people is their strong sense of time urgency, known as "hurry sickness." This sense of urgency compels them to achieve more and more in less and less time. Angry, aggressive (usually male) Type A people are more likely than Type Bs to experience cardiovascular disorders. In one study, Type A behavior was measured among 250 police workers and firefighters. A seven-year follow-up indicated that Type A people were more likely to have experienced cardiovascular disorders, including a fatal heart attack.[34]

Although Type A behavior is associated with coronary heart disease, only some features of the Type A personality pattern may be related to cardiac disorders. The adverse health effects generally stem from hostility, anger, cynicism, and suspiciousness in contrast to impatience, ambition, and drive. Recognize also that not every hard-driving, impatient person is correctly classified as Type A. Managers who love their work and enjoy other people are not particularly prone to heart disease. An example of a 30-year-old Type A manager loaded with hostility, and at high risk for heart attack, follows:

> *When business associates fail to follow straightforward directions or miss deadlines on projects, Matt Sicinski gets angry, really angry. "My feet get cold,*

---

33 Russell Cropanzano, Deborah E. Rupp, and Zinta S. Byrne, "The Relationship of Emotional Exhaustion to Work Attitudes, Job Performance, and Organizational Citizenship Behaviors," *Journal of Applied Psychology*, February 2003, pp. 160–169.

34 John Schaubroeck, Daniel C. Ganster, and Barbara E. Kemmer, "Job Complexity, 'Type A' Behavior, and Cardiovascular Disorder: A Prospective Study," *Academy of Management Journal*, April 1994, pp. 426–439; Updated research conforming these results is reported in Ron Winslow, "Choose Your Neurosis: Some Type-A Traits are Riskier than Others," *The Wall Street Journal*, October 22, 2003, p. D1.

and I get a throbbing in my head," says Mr. Sicinski, who works for a company that runs drug studies for the pharmaceutical industry. "I can feel every muscle in my body tense up." Sometimes in the middle of a conversation, he puts the phone on mute, he says, and starts "cursing somebody up one side and down the other." He is on a combination of drugs to control his blood pressure, with limited success, he says.[35]

locus of control The way in which people look at causation in their lives.

Another notable personality characteristic related to job stress is **locus of control**, the way in which people look at causation in their lives. People who believe that they have more control over their actions than do external events are less stress prone. For example, a 50-year-old person with an internal locus of control might lose his job and say, "I don't care if a lot of age discrimination in business exists. I have many needed skills and many employers will want me. Age will not be an issue for me in finding suitable employment." This man's internal locus of control will help him ward off stress related to job loss. A 50-year-old with an external locus of control will experience high stress because the person believes that he or she is helpless in the face of job discrimination. A study with 5,185 managers from 24 geopolitical entities around the world found a strong association between having an internal locus of control and both psychological and physical well-being. In this study, having low *well-being* is the same as having stress symptoms.[36]

People who have high expectations are likely to experience job burnout at some point in their careers, because they may not receive as many rewards as they are seeking. People who need constant excitement also face a high risk of job burnout, because they bore easily and quickly.

Adverse Organizational Conditions

Under ideal conditions, workers experience just enough stress to prompt them to respond creatively and energetically to their jobs. Unfortunately, high stress levels created by adverse organizational conditions lead to many negative symptoms. A major contributor to job stress is work overload. Demands on white-collar workers appear to be at an all-time high, as companies attempt to increase work output and decrease staffing at the same time.

A specific overload demand relates to information overload, as many managers and professionals are so bombarded with simultaneous and competing messages that they suffer from *attention deficit trait.* The brain becomes overloaded leading to symptoms of distractibility, inner frenzy, and impatience. According to Edward M. Hallowell, people with this trait struggle to stay organized, set priorities, and manage time.[37] In short, their brains are so loaded they become spastic. (If you are suffering from attention deficit trait, follow the suggestions about personal productivity and stress management presented in this chapter.)

---

35 Winslow, "Choose Your Neurosis," p. D1.

36 Paul E. Spector and 29 other contributors, "Locus of Control, and Well-Being at Work: How Generalizable are Western Findings?" *Academy of Management Journal*, April 2002, pp. 453–466.

37 Edward M. Hallowell, "Why Smart People Underperform," *Harvard Business Review*, January 2005, pp. 54–62.

job demand–job control model A model demonstrating the relationship between high or low job demands and high or low job control. It shows that workers experience the most stress when the demands of the job are high yet they have little control over the activity.

emotional labor The process of regulating both feelings and expressions to meet organizational goals.

Extreme conflict with other workers, including office politics or with management, is also a stressor. According to a survey of 1,000 employees, the major source of job stress is annoying and abusive coworkers.[38] Another annoyance is short lead times—too little notice to get complex assignments accomplished. A powerful stressor today is job insecurity due to the many mergers and downsizings. Worrying about having one's job outsourced to another region, country, or a subcontractor is also a stressor.

According to the **job demand–job control model,** workers experience the most stress when the demands of the job are high, yet they have little control over the activity.[39] (See Exhibit 17-6.) A customer-service representative with limited authority who has to deal with a major error by the firm would fit this category. In contrast, when job demands are high and the worker has high control, the worker will be energized, motivated, and creative. A branch manager in a successful business might fit this scenario.

Interactions with customers can be a major stressor. Stressful events include customers losing control, using profanity, badgering employees, harassing employees, and lying. Part of the problem is that the sales associate often feels helpless when placed in conflict with a customer. The sales associate is told that "the customer is always right." Furthermore, the store manager usually sides with the customer in a dispute with the sales associate.

Another aspect of adverse customer interaction is the stressor of having to control the expression of emotion to please or avoid displeasing a customer. Imagine having to smile at a customer who belittles you or makes unwanted sexual advances. **Emotional labor** is the process of regulating both feelings and expressions to meet organizational goals.[40] Regulation involves both surface acting and deep acting. Surface acting means faking expressions such as smiling, whereas deep acting involves controlling feelings such as suppressing anger toward a customer you perceive to be annoying or hostile. Faking feelings often leads to the emotional exhaustion component of burnout.

Sales workers and customer-service representatives experience considerable emotional labor among all workers because so often they have to fake

exhibit 17-6 The Job Demand–Job Control Model

A worker is likely to experience the most job stress when he or she exercises low control over a job with high demands.

	Low Job Demands	High Job Demands
Low Control	Passive Job	High-Strain Job
High Control	Low-Strain Job	Active Job

38 Survey reported in "Stress Buster," *Manager's Edge*, February 2007, p. 7.

39 Marilyn L. Fox, Deborah J. Dwyer, and Daniel C. Ganster, "Effects of Stressful Job Demands and Control on Physiological and Attitudinal Outcomes in a Hospital Setting," *Academy of Management Journal*, April 1993, pp. 290–292.

40 Alicia A. Grandey, "Emotion Regulation in the Workplace: A New Way to Conceptualize Emotional Labor," *Journal of Occupational Health Psychology*, Vol. 5, No. 1 (2000), pp. 95–110.

facial expressions and feelings, so as to please customers. The supervisor often dictates the type of emotional display (or display rules). Call center workers are expected to calm down angry callers—a behavior that often requires the suppression of negative feelings. In addition, they are supposed to end calls on a positive note, perhaps with a sale.[41]

Readers with acting experience may be interested in knowing that workers who faked their emotions were observed to have done a better job interacting with customers than workers who simply faked facial expressions. "Getting into the role" helps you interact well with customers. Also, emotional exhaustion was more likely to occur when workers engaged in surface acting.

Engaging in emotional labor for prolonged periods of time can lead to job dissatisfaction, stress, and burnout. A contributing cause is that faking expressions and emotion takes a physiological toll. Workers who engage in emotional labor may also develop cardiovascular problems and weakened immune systems.[42]

work–family conflict
A major stressor that represents a combination of individual and organizational factors contributing to stress.

Work–family conflict is a major stressor that represents a combination of individual and organizational factors contributing to stress. It occurs when the individual has to perform multiple roles: worker, spouse, and often parent. The stress comes about because of the difficulty of attempting to fill two roles at the same time, such as having to manage a restaurant on New Year's Eve, while your spouse insists you celebrate the event together. Dual-earner couples are particularly susceptible to work–family conflict because of the demands on their time.

Another major contributor to work–family conflict is that because of information technology, the boundaries between work and family life are often blurred. A Lexmark study of knowledge workers found that 92 percent of respondents admit they initiate or receive work-related communications outside of work. Another information technology–based source of work–family conflict is that people bring home into work, such as doing online shopping during working hours, and sending e-mails back and forth to family and friends. In the words of Jared Sandberg of *The Wall Street Journal*, "Work and life aren't so much balanced as they are stirred into a stew that often satisfies neither quarter."[43] Some wired executives even ski with a cell phone built into their ski helmet, which could create conflict with other family members. (Crashing into a tree or other skiers might be considered another form of work–family conflict.)

The more time invested in the job, the greater the exposure to work–family conflict, and the greater the stress. A confusing aspect of work–family conflict is that it works in both directions. Work responsibilities can create conflict with home responsibilities, and family responsibilities can create conflict with work. The conflict in both directions creates stress.[44] Imagine yourself as a marathon

41 Steffanie L. Wilk and Lisa M. Moynihan, "Display Rule 'Regulators': The Relationship between Supervisors and Worker Emotional Exhaustion," *Journal of Applied Psychology*, September 2005, pp. 917–927.

42 Grandey, "When 'The Show Must Go On': Surface Acting and Deep Acting as Determinants of Emotional Exhaustion and Peer-Rated Service Delivery," *Academy of Management Journal*, February 2003, pp. 86–96.

43 The survey results and the quote are from Jared Sandberg, "Back to the Future: Mixing Work, Home Is a Very Old Dilemma," *The Wall Street Journal*, December 12, 2006, p. B1.

44 Leslie B. Hammer, Talya N. Bauer, and Alicia A. Grandey, "Work-Family Conflict and Work-Related Withdrawal Behaviors," *Journal of Business and Psychology*, Spring 2003, pp. 419–434.

runner, who runs a weekend marathon. You are too exhausted to go on a business trip on Monday, so you become stressed about dealing with this conflict.

Although work–family conflict is widespread, some new research suggests that being committed to the marital and parental role might actually enhance the work performance of managers. The study was conducted with 346 managers from 314 organizations throughout the United States, attending a leadership development program. Using both questionnaires and ratings of work performance, it was found that family commitment and marital commitment did not interfere with work. Furthermore, being committed to the parental role was associated with improved work performance. One explanation for the findings offered by the researchers is that when you have a committed marital partner, he or she helps you in your work. Another possibility is that being committed to marriage and family is a motivational force for performing well.[45]

Many companies have implemented programs, such as flexible working hours and telecommuting, to help employees deal with work–family conflict. Ernst & Young, the professional services firm, is often cited for its initiatives that encourage staff members to resolve work–family conflict. The firm's Flexible Work Arrangement Program includes reduced work schedules, telework, and compressed work weeks. Approximately 10 percent of Ernst & Young's U.S. workers are engaged in the formal program, yet all 23,000 U.S. employees are allowed to work flexibly on a daily basis.

The company encourages employees to create flexible schedules that satisfy the demands of work and personal life. Some employees work full time from January to March, then a reduced schedule the rest of the year. Another group within the flexible work program leave early to pick up children from school, then work from home later. Employees who participate in the flexible program are considered first-class citizens, and have a good promotion rate.[46]

STRESS-MANAGEMENT TECHNIQUES

Learning Objective 4

Explain how stress can be managed effectively.

Everybody experiences stress, so how you manage stress can be the key to your well-being. A survey conducted by Mental Health America found that people frequently deal with chronic stress by watching television, skipping exercise, and neglecting to eat healthy food.[47] Constructive techniques for managing job stress on your own can be divided into three categories: control, symptom management, and escape.[48] Companies often provide services, such as employee-wellness programs, that give you the opportunity to implement some of these techniques.

45 Laura M. Graves, Patricia J. Ohlott, and Marion N. Ruderman, "Commitment to Family Roles: Effects on Managers' Attitudes and Performance," *Journal of Applied Psychology*, January 2007, pp. 44–56.

46 "Emergent Company Profiles: Ernst & Yong," http://www.spherion.com, 2005–2007; Chuck Salter, "Solving the Real Productivity Crisis," *Fast Company*, January 2004, p. 37.

47 Survey reported in Christine Gorman, "6 Lessons for Handling Stress," *Time*, January 29, 2007, p. 80.

48 Janina Latack, "Coping with Job Stress: Measures and Future Direction for Scale Development," *Journal of Applied Psychology*, August 1986, pp. 522–526; David Antonioni, "Two Strategies for Responding to Stressors: Managing Conflict and Clarifying Work Expectations," *Journal of Business and Psychology*, Winter 1996, pp. 287–295; Gail Dutton, "Cutting Edge Stressbusters," *HRfocus*, September 1998, pp. 11–12.

Methods for Control and Reduction of Stress

The five control techniques described next consist of both actions and mental evaluations that help people take charge in stressful situations.

1. *Get social support.* Few people can go it alone when experiencing prolonged stress. Receiving social support—encouragement, understanding, and friendship—from other people is an important strategy for coping successfully with job stress.
2. *Improve your work habits.* You can use the techniques described for improving your personal productivity to reduce stress. People typically experience stress when they feel themselves losing control of their work assignments. Conscientious employees are especially prone to negative stress when they cannot get their work under control.
3. *Develop positive self-talk.* Stress-resistant people are basically optimistic and cheerful. This kind of positivism can be learned by switching to positive self-talk instead of thinking many negative thoughts.
4. *Hug the right people.* Hugging is seriously regarded as vital for physical and mental well-being. People who do not receive enough quality touching may suffer from low self-esteem, ill health, depression, and loneliness. Conversely, quality touching may help people cope better with job stress. The hugging, however, has to represent loving and caring.
5. *Demand less than perfection from yourself.* By demanding less than 100 percent performance from yourself, you will fail less frequently in your own perceptions. Not measuring up to one's own unrealistically high standards creates a considerable amount of stress. Few humans can operate with zero defects or ever achieve Six Sigma perfection!
6. *Strive to not neglect aspects of life outside of work.* There is a big difference between a negative type of workaholic and a person who simply works hard and long to attain constructive goals. A negative workaholic usually becomes anxious when not working.[49] When a person neglects other aspects of life outside of work, such as spending time with family, friends, and physical exercise, the person is more likely to suffer from stress symptoms such as irritability and lack of focus.

Symptom Management

This category of stress management refers to tactics that address the symptoms related to job stress. Dozens of symptom-management techniques have been developed, including the following:

1. *Make frequent use of relaxation techniques, including meditation.* Learning to relax reduces the adverse effects of stress. The **relaxation response** is a general-purpose method of learning to relax by yourself, and is a form of meditation. The key ingredient of this technique is to make yourself quiet and comfortable. At the same time, think of the word *one* (or any simple

relaxation response
A general-purpose method of learning to relax by yourself.

49 Dana Mattioli, "When Devotion to Work Becomes Job Obsession," *The Wall Street Journal*, January 23, 2007, p. B8.

chant or prayer) with every breath for about ten minutes. The technique slows you down both physiologically and emotionally. An extremely easy relaxation method is to visualize being in an unusually pleasant situation, such as floating on a cloud, walking by a lake, or lying on a comfortable beach. Choose any fantasy that you find relaxing.

2. *Get appropriate physical exercise.* Physical exercise helps dissipate some of the tension created by job stress, and it also helps the body ward off future stress-related disorders. A physically fit, well-rested person can usually tolerate more frustration than can a physically run-down, tired person. One way in which exercise helps combat stress is that it releases endorphins. These morphine-like chemicals are produced in the brain and act as painkillers and antidepressants. Workers who travel frequently particularly need physical exercise because travel can damage the body, producing such symptoms as muscle cramps and even blood clots from long airplane trips. More information about the benefits of physical exercise is presented in Exhibit 17-7.
3. *Try to cure hurry sickness.* People with hurry sickness should learn how to relax and enjoy the present for its own sake. Specific tactics include having at least one idle period every day; eating nutritious, not overly seasoned foods to help decrease nervousness; and finding enrichment in an area of life not related to work.

Removal of the Stressor

Methods of removing the stressor are actions and reappraisals of situations that provide the stressed individual some escape from the stressor. Eliminating

exhibit 17-7 The Benefits of Physical Exercise

- Increases energy and reduces feelings of frequent fatigue
- Reduces feelings of tension, anxiety, and depression
- Improves sleep
- Improves concentration
- Enhances self-esteem and self-confidence
- Helps you lose weight or maintain a healthy weight
- Reduces the risk of heart disease, or improves cardiac function if you have had a heart attack or bypass; reduces harmful cholesterol and raises level of HDL (good) cholesterol in as little as eight weeks
- Reduces the risk of colon cancer
- Lowers pulse rate thereby decreasing high blood pressure and the risk of stroke
- Controls blood sugar levels if you have, or are at risk for, diabetes
- Improves bone density and lowers the risk of osteoporosis and fractures as you get older
- Improves muscle tone so you feel better and look better

Source: The American Heart Association, the American College of Sports Medicine, Shape Up America!, The American Academy of Family Physicians, and National Cattlemen's Beef Association. As compiled by Shari Roan, "The Theory of Inactivity," The Los Angeles Times, March 9, 1998; Tara Parker-Pope, "Doctors' Orders: Ways to Work Exercise Into a Busy Day," *The Wall Street Journal*, January 9, 2007, p. D1; Tedd Mitchell, "To Balance Cholesterol: Exercise," *USA Weekend*, February 17–19, 2006, p. 10.

the stressor is the most effective escape technique. For example, if a manager is experiencing stress because of serious understaffing in his or her department, that manager should negotiate to receive authorization to hire additional help. Mentally blocking out a stressful thought is another escape technique, but it may not work in the long run.

freeze-frame technique
A scientifically based method of stress reduction that emphasizes reappraisal, along with some symptom management.

A scientifically based method of stress reduction that emphasizes reappraisal, along with some symptom management, is the **freeze-frame technique**, developed by the HeartMath Institute. The method proceeds as follows:[50]

Step 1. Recognize the stressful feeling and freeze-frame it. See your problem as a still photo, not a movie. Stop the inner conversation about it.

Step 2. Make a sincere effort to *shift your focus* away from the racing mind or disturbed emotions in the area around your heart. Pretend you are breathing through your heart to help focus energy in this area. Stay focused there for ten seconds or more.

Step 3. Recall a positive fun feeling or time you've had in your life and visualize experiencing it again.

Step 4. Using your intuition, common sense, and sincerity, *ask your heart what would be a more efficient response* to the situation—one that will minimize future stress.

Step 5. Listen to what your heart says in answer to your question. Here you are using an in-house source of commonsense solutions.

You may hear nothing, but at least you will feel calmer. You may receive confirmation of something you already know. Equally important, you may gain a perspective shift and see the problem in a different way. Although we may not have control over the event, we do have control over how we perceive it.

A strategic method of escaping stress is to identify your work skills, and then find work to match those skills. Assessing your skills and preferences can help you understand why you find some tasks or roles more stressful than others.[51] For example, many people enter the computer or information technology field without having appropriate skills and interest for that type of work. When they are asked to perform such tasks as coding for nine hours in one day, they become stressed out, because they lack the right aptitude and interest for such work.

Given that you could probably locate five million articles, books, and Internet comments on the subject of job stress, we have not mentioned every possible approach to managing stress. To prevent information overload, study Exhibit 17-8 to get a few more ideas on reducing stress, and reinforce a few suggestions made already.

50 Bruce Cryer, Rollin McCraty, and Doc Childre, "Pulling the Plug On Stress," *Harvard Business Review*, July 2003, pp. 102–107; http://www.HeartMath.com, 2003.

51 William Atkinson, "When Stress Won't Go Away," *HR Magazine*, December 2000, pp. 108–109.

exhibit 17-8 Stress Busters

- Take a nap when facing heavy pressures. Napping is regarded as one of the most effective techniques for reducing and preventing stress (as well as enhancing personal productivity). Rest helps because negative events tend to be perceived as less frustrating when you have enough sleep.
- Give in to your emotions. If you are angry, disgusted, or confused, admit your feelings to yourself. Suppressing your emotions adds to stress.
- Take a brief break from the stressful situation and do something small and constructive like washing your car, emptying a wastebasket, or getting a haircut.
- Get a massage because it can loosen tight muscles, improve your blood circulation, and calm you down.
- Get help with a stressful task from a coworker, boss, or friend.
- Concentrate on reading, surfing the Internet, a sport, or a hobby. Contrary to common sense, concentration is at the heart of stress reduction.
- Have a quiet place at home and have a brief idle period there every day.
- Take a leisurely day off from your routine.
- Finish something you have started, however small. Accomplishing almost anything reduces some stress.
- Stop to smell the flowers, make friends with a young child or elderly person, or play with a kitten or puppy.
- Strive to do a good job, but not a perfect job.
- Work with your hands, doing a pleasant task.
- Find somebody or something that makes you laugh, and have a good laugh.
- Minimize drinking caffeinated or alcoholic beverages. Drink fruit juice or water instead.
- Simplify your life by getting rid of unessential activities and possessions. Less mental and physical clutter will help you gain more control of your life, leading to less stress. But don't cut back so much that an impoverished life creates new stress.

SUMMARY OF Key Points

1 Identify techniques for improving work habits and time management.

One way of increasing your personal productivity is to improve your work habits and time-management skills: develop a mission, goals, and a strong work ethic. Clean up your work area and sort out your tasks. Prepare a to-do list and assign priorities. Also, streamline your work; work at a steady, rapid pace; minimize times wasters and interruptions; and concentrate on one task at a time. Concentrate on high-output tasks; do creative and routine work at different times; and stay in control of paperwork, e-mail, and voice mail. Making effective use of office technology is essential. Practice the mental state of peak performance, take naps or meditate; work smarter, not harder; and build flexibility into your system.

2 Explain why people procrastinate and identify techniques for reducing procrastination.

Avoid procrastinating by understanding why you procrastinate and taking remedial action, including the following: break the task down into smaller units, make a commitment to others, reward yourself for achieving milestones, calculate the cost of procrastination, post encouraging notes in your work and living area, counterattack against an uncomfortable task, and post a progress chart.

3 Understand the nature of stress and burnout, including their consequences.

Stress is the mental and physical condition that results from a perceived threat that cannot be dealt with readily. Hindrance stressors are negative, whereas challenge stressors are positive. Job burnout is a pattern of emotional, physical, and mental exhaustion in response to chronic job stressors. Hopelessness is another key symptom of burnout. Key stress symptoms include tension, anxiety, and poor concentration and judgment. Job stress is caused by factors within the individual such as Type A behavior and an external locus of control. A variety of adverse organizational conditions, including work overload and low control over a demanding job, and work–family conflict, contribute to stress. People with high expectations are candidates for burnout. Limited rewards and lack of feedback from the organization contribute to burnout.

4 Explain how stress can be managed effectively.

Methods of preventing and controlling stress and burnout can be divided into three categories: attempts to control stressful situations, symptom management, and removal of the stressor. Specific tactics include getting social support, improving your work habits, using relaxation techniques, getting appropriate physical exercise, eliminating the stressor, and using the freeze-frame technique.

KEY TERMS AND PHRASES

Work ethic, 581
Peak performance, 589
Procrastination, 592
Stress, 595
Hindrance stressors, 596
Challenge stressors, 596
Job burnout, 596
Locus of control, 599
Job demand-job control model, 600
Emotional labor, 600
Work–family conflict, 601
Relaxation response, 603
Freeze-frame technique, 605

QUESTIONS

1. What is your mission in life? If you do not have a mission, how might you develop one?
2. How can an employee be well organized yet unproductive?
3. With so much of most tasks being computerized, why bother studying about improving personal productivity?
4. How can a person determine whether answering e-mail is an important part of the job or a productivity drain?
5. Why might a self-employed person, or contract worker, be more likely than a salaried worker to obtain a quick financial return from improving work habits and time management?
6. Why are good work habits and time management so effective in reducing job stress?
7. Assume you are the human resource director for a large, diversified company and you want to develop a tentative policy about employee napping to boost productivity and reduce stress. Perhaps you might want to call in a few other managers to help you refine the policy. Plan for such possibilities as (a) how many members of a department or team are allowed to nap at the same time, (b) if you have a formal napping room, who is allowed to nap in the room at the same time, and (c) the priority napping has in relation to taking care of urgent tasks.

SKILL-BUILDING EXERCISE 17-A: Getting Uncluttered

Many time-management experts believe that a major contributor to low productivity is that people's lives are too cluttered with material possessions. If you have less clutter around you, your concentration and focus will improve. A specific recommendation is to throw out one object everyday, including old newspapers, magazines, and e-mail messages. (Selling some of your clutter in a garage sale or on eBay might be an extra incentive.) Beginning today, throw out something everyday from your living quarters or work area. Anything you discard counts, from a few pencils stubs to an obsolete CPU. By the end of two weeks, see how much progress you have made in reducing clutter. Of more significance, analyze whether your efforts at becoming uncluttered are enhancing your ability to accomplish work. Also, has this exercise made you feel better, including the feeling of less stress?

SKILL-BUILDING EXERCISE 17-B: Good and Bad Ways to Reduce Stress

The purpose of this exercise is to help participants understand the difference between constructive and less constructive ways of reducing stress. The materials needed for the exercise are a whiteboard, a blackboard, an overhead projector, or a computerized method of projecting information on a screen.

For ten minutes, participants suggest as many techniques as possible for managing or reducing stress that they are willing to share with class members. (Some class members might have ways of reducing stress they would prefer to keep private.) Participants speak one at a time. As each new technique is suggested, the audience shouts either

"Good" or "Bad." Based on majority opinion, the moderator places the technique in the Good or Bad column.

A good technique is defined roughly as one that produces almost all benefits. A bad technique is one that produces short-lived benefits such as a "high," followed by negative side effects. (An example would be getting drunk to escape a major problem.) For some or all of the techniques, people should justify their classification as Good or Bad.

After the techniques are listed for all to see, the class discusses any conclusions about the difference between good and bad techniques. The group also discusses why knowing the difference is important.

Source: The idea for part of this exercise is from Robert E. Epstein, "Stress Busters: 11 Quick, Fun Games to Tame the Beast," *Psychology Today*, March/April 2000, p. 34.

INTERNET SKILL-BUILDING EXERCISE: Boosting and Lowering Productivity on the Internet

Gather into small teams or work individually to identify ten ways in which the Internet can increase personal productivity either on the job or at home. Also identify several ways in which the Internet can decrease personal productivity. To supplement your own thinking, you might search the Internet for ideas on how the Internet is supposed to boost productivity. Also, look for negative comments about the ability of the Internet to boost productivity. If you have been using the Internet for several years, comment on whether you think the Internet is becoming a more useful productivity tool or method.

Case Problem 17-A

Hard Charger Turned Soccer Mom

I was an extremely shy, awkward kid. I'm 5-foot-10, and I've had the feeling of being 5-foot-10 since I was ten years old. It wasn't until I got to college that I developed a lot of self-confidence. I went to an obscure but wonderful small college, Lynchburg College, in Virginia, much to my parents' chagrin. My mother had gone to Purdue, my dad to Carnegie Mellon. They wanted me to go to a school with a big name. But I had a lot of support at college.

I have worked since I was 15, so early on I had a sense of how to support myself. My parents had rough times financially. I was the oldest of three girls. We weren't poor, but we went without the nicest clothes; we didn't go on elaborate vacations or buy brand-new cars. I thought I'd really made it when I got to college and was able to buy Pepperidge Farm instead of day-old bread. My first job after college was at Chevy Chase Savings Bank in Washington, as a management trainee.

The day my son, Will, was born, I worked all day and then drove myself to the hospital in Wilmington, Delaware, at 2 a.m. This was eight years ago—I was working for a bank in Wilmington and commuting to our home in Chevy Chase, Md., on the weekends. My husband drove up and joined me at the hospital. I was in labor for several hours, then they gave me an epidural. I couldn't feel anything. I was just waiting around for the baby to be born. So I kept on working. I had colleagues sending me faxes at the hospital. Doctors were walking into my room handing me documents I had to sign for work. The baby was born that afternoon. I took the minimum maternity leave of six weeks.

It took six months before I realized—time out! I can't be that hard-charging work-all-the-time person anymore. Before I had the baby, I was known as a straight-A student who knew all the answers and intimidated my peers. I set aggressive deadlines. I micromanaged people.

After having Will, I became a more balanced person. When you come home to a baby who demands your full attention, you stop thinking about all the issues at work. You give your brain a time out. Because I reduced my hours after having Will, I was forced to delegate more. I learned to listen, and I'm a better executive now. Had my son not come along, I doubt I would be in the position I'm in today.

The most difficult time was that first year after the baby was born. I was torn between my responsibilities on the job and my devotion to my child. My supervisor at the company I used to work for once called me at 10 on a Saturday night and told me I had to come to the office immediately. The company was in the midst of a merger. I had worked that day at home, even though my son and I were sick with the flu. My husband was out of the country on a business trip. I knew no one in town, except the people I worked with. So I told my supervisor, "No can do," but he insisted. When I asked if I could bring my son, he said it would not be appropriate. I felt under so much pressure. I knew the security officer in my building well enough, so I said, "Issac, can you take care of the baby?" I left him there, went to work and after about an hour realized the absurdity of the situation. By then it was almost midnight, and I just left.

I've really learned to put up boundaries since then. My average day used to be from 7 a.m. to 10 p.m. Now I'll work from 7 or 8 a.m. to 7 or 8 p.m. Then I'll spend time reading to Will, have dinner, put him to bed. Once he's asleep, I'll go back to my e-mail a little bit. But I don't work weekends like I used to. I'm a soccer mom now.

Discussion Questions

1. What kind of conflicts and stress was the case heroine facing?
2. Has this woman really achieved an effective work/life balance?
3. What suggestions can you make the case heroine to create an even more effective work/life balance?
4. How should this woman have dealt with the late-night request by her boss?

Source: Reprinted with permission from, As Told to Julia Lawlor, "A New Sense of Time," *The New York Times* (http://nytimes.com), March 27, 2005.

Case Problem 17-B

"Nick, You Have Let Us Down Again"

So often in high school and career school, Nicholas Ragu begged for an extension on his papers and other major assignments. "I was all set to complete this assignment," he would plea, "but then my grandmother who lives out of town became suddenly ill, and I had to drop the report for awhile." Or Nick's car would be towed away, so he had to spend the day retrieving his vehicle instead of finishing his assignment. Nick delayed so long ordering his cap and gown for graduation that he had to make special last-minute arrangements so he could attend the ceremony.

Three out of four years, Nick was late preparing his income tax form. Once he filed for an extension and was late for the extended deadline. To pay the fine, Nick asked his father for the money. When Dad demanded to know why Nick couldn't file his income tax form on time, Nick replied, "I had so many things going, I just couldn't get to the taxes."

Jeanne Tobin, a family friend of the Ragus, was the vice president of marketing for a company that organizes trade shows for business firms. Her company needed a trade-show assistant, and Nick with his interest in business, good interpersonal skills, and high energy seemed to be a reasonable fit. Yet Tobin told Nick, "I am a little hesitant to make you a job offer because you have a reputation of always being behind schedule. I remember when you were an adolescent. The newspaper had to fire you from your paper route because you delivered the papers late so often."

"Jeanne, have no fear," replied Nick. "You are talking about Nick of the past. Nick of the present is an on-time guy who's put procrastination behind him. Please give me a chance to prove I can be an asset for your company."

Jeanne did give Nick one more chance by hiring him for the position. Nick would be responsible for a variety of tasks, including booking hotel arrangements for trade shows, making sure flyers and e-mail announcements were sent out on time, and arranging for equipment needs of the exhibitors.

For the first six months, Nick was given light responsibilities so he could learn the business and phase his way into the full responsibilities of his position. One of his responsibilities was to order a thousand key rings as a trade-show trinket. Four days before the trade show, the trinkets had not arrived. The key rings were shipped special delivery at the last moment, resulting in an extra shipping payment that could not be passed on to the client. Nick explained to Jeanne, "I guess I had a misunderstanding about the time needed for getting the key rings ready for us. But don't worry, it won't happen again."

Nick's first big assignment was a trade show for a manufactured (prefabricated) homebuilder's association. The trade show was held in Tampa, Florida. One of Nick's responsibilities was to make sure that all the booths that needed one had projectors available for PowerPoint presentations. During the first day of the show, five of the booths did not have a working projector in place. Nick explained to Jeanne, "Oh no. I let one thing slip through the cracks. I didn't get around yet to seeing if all the projectors worked. If I have to work until midnight, all the projectors will be working by tomorrow."

During the first day of the show, the president of the manufactured homebuilder's association complained to Jeanne that attendance was down about 25 percent from the previous year. When the president did a little digging to find out why attendance was down, he found out that many would-be attendees said that they did not hear about the time and place of the convention until it was too late to get ready.

Jeanne confronted Nick about the delayed notices. Nick said, "I let the date slip a little on the announcements because I assumed the builders all knew about the date. They had preliminary information months ago. Besides, I had so much to do for this show that I had to set my priorities. There is only so much you can do at once."

Jeanne retorted, "Nick, you have let us down again. Because of your negligence, we may lose one of our most important clients. I want you to think seriously about finding another type of job—one where getting working done on time isn't important."

Discussion Questions

1. In what way does Nick display self-defeating behavior?
2. What advice can you offer Nick to help him with his procrastination?
3. Explain whether you think Jeanne should fire Nick.
4. How is Nick likely to interpret the phrase "I want you to think seriously about finding another type of job . . ."

Glossary

360-degree feedback A performance appraisal in which a person is evaluated by a sampling of all the people with whom he or she interacts.

A

achievement need The need that refers to finding joy in accomplishment for its own sake.

action plan The specific steps necessary to achieve a goal or an objective.

active listening Listening for full meaning, without making premature judgments or interpretations.

activity In the PERT method, the physical and mental effort required to complete an event.

activity-based costing (ABC) An accounting procedure that allocates the costs of producing a product or service to the activities performed and the resources used.

administrative management The use of management principles in the structuring and managing of an organization.

affiliation need A desire to have close relationships with others and to be a loyal employee or friend.

affirmative action An employment practice that complies with antidiscrimination law and correcting past discriminatory practices.

anchoring In the decision making process, placing too much value on the first information received and ignoring later information.

authority The formal right to get people to do things or the formal right to control resources.

autocratic leader A task-oriented leader who retains most of the authority for himself or herself and is not generally concerned with group members' attitudes toward decisions.

B

balance of trade The difference between exports and imports in both goods and services.

balanced scorecard A set of measures to provide a quick but comprehensive view of the business.

behavior modification A way of changing behavior by rewarding the right responses and punishing or ignoring the wrong responses.

behavior In performance evaluation, what people actually do on the job.

behavioral approach to management An approach to management that emphasizes improving management through an understanding of the psychological makeup of people.

behavioral interviewing A style of interviewing in which the interviewer asks questions whose answers reveal behaviors that would be either strengths or weaknesses in a given position.

bounded rationality The observation that people's limited mental abilities, combined with external influences over which they have little or no control, prevent them from making entirely rational decisions.

brainstorming A group method of solving problems, gathering information, and stimulating creative thinking. The basic technique is to generate numerous ideas through unrestrained and spontaneous participation by group members.

break-even analysis A method of determining the relationship between total costs and total revenues at various levels of production or sales activity.

budget A spending plan expressed in numerical terms for a future period of time.

bureaucracy A rational, systematic, and precise form of organization in which rules, regulations, and techniques of control are specifically defined.

C

carpal tunnel syndrome The most frequent cumulative trauma disorder which occurs when frequent wrist bending results in swelling, leading to a pinched nerve.

cash flow Amount of net cash generated by a business during a specific period.

centralization The extent to which authority is retained at the top of the organization.

challenge stressors Sources of stress that have a positive direct effect on motivation and performance.

charisma The ability to lead or influence others based on personal charm, magnetism, inspiration, and emotion.

c-level manager A recent term to describe top-level managers because they usually have *chief* in their title.

coaching A method for helping employees perform better, which usually occurs on the spot and involves informal discussion and suggestions.

coalition A specific arrangement of parties working together to combine their power, thus exerting influence on another individual or group.

communication network A pattern or flow of messages that traces the communication from start to finish.

communication The process of exchanging information by the use of words, letters, symbols, or nonverbal behavior.

compressed workweek A full-time work schedule that allows 40 hours of work in less than five days.

computer goof-off Employees who spend so much time attempting new computer routines and accessing information of questionable value that they neglect key aspects of their job.

computer-aided monitoring of work A computer-based system to monitor the work habits and productivity of employees.

concurrent control A type of control that monitors activities while they are carried out.

conflict of interest A situation that occurs when one's judgment or objective is compromised.

conflict The simultaneous arousal of two or more incompatible motives.

confrontation Dealing with a controversial or emotional topic directly.

constructive criticism A form of criticism designed to help improve performance or behavior.

contingency approach to management A perspective on management that emphasizes that no single way to manage people or work is best in every situation. It encourages managers to study individual and situational differences before deciding on a course of action.

contingency plan An alternative plan to be used if the original plan cannot be implemented or a crisis develops.

contingent workers Part-time or temporary employees who are not members of the employer's permanent workforce.

corporate social performance The extent to which a firm responds to the demands of its stakeholders for behaving in a socially responsible manner.

corporate social responsibility The idea that firms have an obligation to society beyond their economic obligations to owners or stockholders and beyond those prescribed by law or contract.

corrective discipline A type of discipline that allows employees to correct their behavior before punishment is applied.

creativity The process of developing novel ideas that can be put into action.

crew A group of specialists, each of whom has specific roles, perform brief events that are closely synchronized with one another, and repeat these events under different environmental conditions.

critical path The path through the PERT network that includes the most time-consuming sequence of events and activities.

cross-functional team A group composed of workers from different specialties at the same organizational level who come together toaccomplish a task.

cultural sensitivity Awareness of local and national customs and their importance in effective interpersonal relationships.

culture shock A group of physical and psychological symptoms that may develop when a person is abruptly placed in a foreign culture.

cumulative trauma disorders Injuries caused by repetitive motions over prolonged periods of time.

D

data mining The extraction of useful analyses from the raw mass of business transactions and other information.

data-driven management An attitude and approach to management rather than a specific technique that stems from data-based decision making.

decentralization The extent to which authority is passed down to lower levels in an organization.

decision tree A graphic illustration of the alternative solutions available to solve a problem.

decision A choice among alternatives.

decision-making style A manager's typical pattern of making decisions.

decisiveness The extent to which a person makes up his or her mind promptly and prudently.

decoding The communication stage in which the receiver interprets the message and translates it into meaningful information.

defensive communication The tendency to receive-messages in a way thatprotects self-esteem.

deficiency needs Lower-order needs that must be satisfied to ensure a person's existence, security, and requirements for human contact.

delegation Assigning formal authority and responsibility for accomplishing a specific task to another person.

departmentalization The process of subdividing work into departments.

development A form of personal improvement that usually consists of enhancing knowledge and skills of a complex and unstructured nature.

deviation In a control system, the size of the discrepancy between performance standards and actual results.

difficult person An individual whose personal characteristics disturb other people.

discipline Punishment used to correct or train.

diversity training Training that attempts to bring about workplace harmony by teaching people how to get along better with diverse work associates.

diversity A mixture of people with different group identities within the same work environment.

downsizing The slimming down of operations to focus resources and boost profits or decrease expenses.

E

earnings before interest, taxes, depreciation, and amortization (EBITDA) A well-established formula to measure the financial success of telecommunications, cable, and media companies.

economic order quantity (EOQ) The inventory level that minimizes both administrative costs and carrying costs.

economic value added (EVA) Measures how much more (or less) a company earns in profits than the minimum amount its investors expect it to earn.

e-leadership Providing leadership to people when their work is mediated by information technology.

e-learning A Web-based form of computer-based training.

emotional intelligence The ability to connect with people and understand their emotions.

emotional labor The process of regulating both feelings and expressions to meet organizational goals.

employee assistance program (EAP) An organization-sponsored service to help employees deal with personal and job-related problems that hinder performance.

employee benefit Any noncash payment given to workers as part of compensation for their employment.

employee network groups A group composed of employees throughout the company who affiliate on the basis of group characteristics such as race, ethnicity, gender, sexual orientation, or physical ability status.

employee orientation program A formal activity designed to acquaint new employees with the organization.

empowerment The process by which managers share power with group members, thereby enhancing employees' feelings of personal effectiveness.

encoding The process of organizing ideas into a series of symbols designed to communicate with the receiver.

entrepreneur A person who founds and operates an innovative business.

entropy A concept of the systems approach to management that states that an organization will die without continuous input from the outside environment.

ergonomics The science of fitting the worker to the job.

ethically centered management An approach to management that emphasizes that the high quality of an end product takes precedence over its scheduled completion.

ethics The study of moral obligation, or separating right from wrong.

event In the PERT method, a point of decision or the accomplishment of a task.

evidence-based management An approach to management whereby managers translate principles based on best evidence into management practices.

expectancy theory of motivation The belief that people will expend effort if they expect the effort to lead to performance and the performance to lead to a reward.

expected time The time that will be used on the PERT diagram as the needed period for the completion of an activity.

expected value The average return on a particular decision being made a large number of times.

external control strategy An approach to control based on the belief that employees are motivated primarily by external rewards and need to be controlled by their managers.

extranet A secure section of a Web site that only visitors with a password can enter.

F

feedback control A control that evaluates an activity after it is performed.

feedback The communication stage in which the receiver responds to the sender's message.

first in First Out (FIFO) Selling an item first that has been in inventory the longest.

first-level managers Managers who supervise operatives (also known as first-line managers or supervisors).

flat organization structure A form of organization with relatively few layers of management, making it less bureaucratic.

flexible benefit package A compensation plan that allows employees to select a group of benefits tailored to their preferences.

flow experience The ultimate involvement in work or a condition of heightened focus, productivity, and happiness.

forced rankings An offshoot of evaluating employees against a performance standard in which employees are measured against one another.

formal communication channel The official pathways for sending information inside and outside an organization.

formal group A group deliberately formed by the organization to accomplish specific tasks and achieve goals.

free cash flow A refinement of cash flow that measures the cash from operations minus capital expenditures.

freeze-frame technique A scientifically based method of stress reduction that emphasizes reappraisal, along with some symptom management.

functional departmentalization An arrangement that defines departments by the function each one performs, such as accounting or purchasing.

G

gainsharing A formal program allowing employees to participate financially in the productivity gains they have achieved.

gantt chart A chart that depicts the planned and actual progress of work during the life of the project.

geographic departmentalization An arrangement of departments according to the geographic area or territory served.

global leadership skills The ability to effectively lead people of other cultures.

global start-up A small firm that comes into existence by serving an international market.

goal An overall condition one is trying to achieve, or a conscious intention to act.

good cause A legally justifiable or good business reason for firing an employee.

grapevine The informal means by which information is transmitted in organizations.

gross profit margin A financial ratio expressed as the difference between sales and the cost of goods sold, divided by sales.

group decisions The process of several people contributing to a final decision.

group polarization A situation in which post-discussion attitudes tend to be more extreme than pre-discussion attitudes.

group A collection of people who interact with one another, are working toward some common purpose, and perceive themselves to be a group.

groupthink A psychological drive for consensus at any cost.

growth needs Higher-order needs that are concerned with personal development and reaching one's potential.

H

hawthorne effect The phenomenon in which people behave differently in response to perceived attention from evaluators.

heuristics A rule of thumb used in decision making.

high-performance work system A way of organizing work so that front-line workers participate in decisions that have an impact on their jobs and the wider organization.

hindrance stressors Stress events and thoughts that have a negative effect on motivation and performance.

homeshoring Moving customer service into workers' homes as a form of telecommuting.

horizontal structure The arrangement of work by teams that are responsible for accomplishing a process.

I

improvement goal A goal that, if attained, will correct unacceptable deviation from a performance standard.

ineffective job performance Job performance that lowers productivity below an acceptable standard.

informal communication channel An unofficial network that supplements the formal channels in an organization.

informal group A group that emerges over time through the interaction of workers.

informal learning Any learning in which the learning process is not determined or designed by the organization.

informal organization structure A set of unofficial relationships that emerge to take care of events and transactions not covered by the formal structure.

information overload A condition in which an individual receives so much information that he or she becomes overwhelmed.

information system (or management information system) A formal system for providing management with information useful or necessary for making decisions.

informative confrontation A technique of inquiring about discrepancies, conflicts, and mixed messages.

intellectual capital The value of useful ideas and the people who generate them.

internal control strategy An approach to control based on the belief that employees can be motivated by building their commitment to organizational goals.

intranet (or company intranet) A Web site for company use only.

intuition An experience-based way of knowing or reasoning in which weighing and balancing evidence are done unconsciously and automatically.

J

job burnout A pattern of emotional, physical, and mental exhaustion in response to chronic job stressors.

job characteristics model A method of job enrichment that focuses on the task and interpersonal dimensions of a job.

job crafting The physical and mental changes individuals make in the task or relationship aspects of their job.

job demand-job control model A model demonstrating the relationship between high or low job demands and high or low job control. It shows that workers experience the most stress when the demands of the job are high yet they have little control over the activity.

job description A written statement of the key features of a job along with the activities required to perform it effectively.

job design The process of laying out job responsibilities and duties and describing how they are to be performed.

job embeddedness A theory of turnover suggesting that a combination of many factors influences whether employees stay with a firm.

job enlargement Increasing the number and variety of tasks within a job.

job enrichment An approach to including more challenge and responsibility in jobs to make them more appealing to employees.

job evaluation The process of rank-ordering jobs based on job content, to demonstrate the worth of one job in comparison to another.

job involvement The degree to which individuals identify psychologically with their work.

job rotation A temporary switching of job assignments.

job sharing A work arrangement in which two people who work part-time share one job.

job specialization The degree to which a job holder performs only a limited number of tasks.

job specification A statement of the personal characteristics needed to perform the job.

judgmental forecast A qualitative forecasting method based on a collection of subjective opinions.

just-in-time (JIT) system A system to minimize inventory and move it into the plant exactly when needed.

K

knowledge management The ways and means by which a company leverages its knowledge resources to generate business value.

L

last in First Out (LIFO) Selling an item first that was received last in inventory.

lateral thinking A thinking process that spreads out to find many alternative solutions to a problem.

law of effect The underlying principle of behavior modification stating that behavior leading to positive consequences tends to be repeated and that behavior leading to negative consequences tends not to be repeated.

leadership Grid A visual representation of different combinations of a leader's degree of concern for task-related issues.

leadership style The typical pattern of behavior that a leader uses to influence his or her employees to achieve organizational goals.

leadership The ability to inspire confidence and support among the people who are needed to achieve organizational goals.

learning organization An organization that is skilled at creating, acquiring, and transferring knowledge.

lift-outs (in relation to teams) The practice of recruiting an entire high-functioning team from another organization.

locus of control The way in which people look at causation in their lives.

M

management by objectives (MBO) A systematic application of goal setting and planning to help individuals and firms be more productive.

management The process of using organizational resources to achieve organizational objectives through planning, organizing and staffing, leading, and controlling.

manager A person responsible for the work performance of group members.

maslow's need hierarchy The motivation theory that arranges human needs into a pyramid-shaped model with basic physiological needs at the bottom and self-actualizing needs at the top.

matrix organization A project structure superimposed on a functional structure.

mentor A more experienced person who develops a protégé's abilities through tutoring, coaching, guidance, and emotional support.

metacommunicate To communicate about a communication to help overcome barriers or resolve a problem.

micromanagement Supervising group members too closely and second-guessing their decisions.

middle-level managers Managers who are neither executives nor first-level supervisors, but who serve as a link between the two groups.

milestone chart An extension of the Gantt chart that provides a listing of the subactivities that must be completed to accomplish the major activities listed on the vertical axis.

mission The firm's purpose and where it fits into the world.

modified work schedule Any formal departure from the traditional hours of work, excluding shift work and staggered work hours.

moral intensity The magnitude of an unethical act.

moral laxity A slippage in moral behavior because other issues seem more important at the time.

motivation The expenditure of effort to accomplish results.

multicultural worker An individual who is aware of and values other cultures.

multiculturalism The ability to work effectively and conduct business with people from different cultures.

multinational corporation (MNC) A firm with operating units in two or more countries in addition to its own.

N

need A deficit within an individual, such as a craving for water or affection.

net debt A company's debt minus the cash and cash equivalents it has on hand.

noise In communication, unwanted interference that can distort or block a message.

nominal group technique (NGT) A group decision making technique that follows a highly structured format.

nonprogrammed decision A decision that is difficult because of its complexity and the fact that the person faces it infrequently.

nonverbal communication The transmission of messages by means other than words.

O

offshoring Global outsourcing.

open-book company A firm in which every employee is trained,empowered, and motivated to understand and pursue the company's business goals.

operating plans The means through which strategic plans alter the destiny of the firm.

operational planning Planning that requires specific procedures and actions at lower levels in an organization.

organization structure The arrangement of people and tasks to accomplish organizational goals.

organizational citizenship behavior Employee behavior that is discretionary and typically not recognized or rewarded but that nevertheless helps the organization.

organizational culture (or corporate culture) The system of shared values and beliefs that actively influence the behavior of organization members.

organizational politics Informal approaches to gaining power or other advantage through means other than merit or luck.

outsourcing The practice of hiring an individual or another company outside the organization to perform work.

P

$P = M \times A$ An expression of the relationship between motivation and performance, where P refers to performance, M to motivation, and A to ability.

pareto diagram A bar graph that ranks types of output variations by frequency of occurrence.

participative leader A leader who shares decision making with group leaders.

peak performance A mental state in which maximum results are achieved with minimum effort.

performance evaluation (or appraisal) A formal system for measuring, evaluating, and reviewing performance.

policies General guidelines to follow in making decisions and taking action.

power motivation A strong desire to control others and resources or get them to do things on your behalf.

power The ability or potential to influence decisions and control resources.

preventive control A control that takes place prior to the performance of an activity.

pro forma A financial statement that excludes write-downs or goodwill and other one-time charges not relevant to future earnings.

problem A discrepancy between ideal and actual conditions.

procedures A customary method for handling an activity. It guides action rather than thinking.

procrastinate To delay in taking action without a valid reason.

procrastination The delaying of action for no good reason.

product–service departmentalization The arrangement of departments according to the products or services they provide.

profit margin A financial ratio measuring return on sales, or net income divided by sales.

profit-sharing plan A method of giving workers supplemental income based on the profitability of the entire firm or a selected unit.

program evaluation and review technique (PERT) A network model used to track the planning activities required to complete a large-scale, nonrepetitive project. It depicts all of the interrelated events that must take place.

programmed decision A decision that is repetitive, or routine, and made according to a specific procedure.

progressive discipline The step-by-step application of corrective discipline.

project organization A temporary group of specialists working under one manager to accomplish a fixed objective.

project team A small group of employees working on a temporary basis in order to accomplish a particular goal.

pygmalion effect The idea that people live up to the expectations set for them.

Q

qualitative control technique A method of controlling based on human judgments about performance that result in a verbal rather than numerical evaluation.

quantitative approach to management A perspective on management that emphasizes use of a group of methods in managerial decision making, based on the scientific method.

quantitative control technique A method of controlling based on numerical measures of performance.

R

realistic job preview A complete disclosure of the potential negative features of a job to a job candidate.

recognition need The desire to be acknowledged for one's contributions and efforts and to feel important.

recruitment The process of attracting job candidates with the right characteristics and skills to fill job openings.

reengineering The radical redesign of work to achieve substantial improvements in performance.

reference check An inquiry to a second party about a job candidate's suitability for employment.

relationship conflict Conflict that focuses on personalized, individually oriented issues.

relaxation response A general-purpose method of learning to relax by yourself.

results In performance evaluation, what people accomplish, or the objectives they attain.

return on equity A financial ratio measuring how much a firm is earning on its investment, expressed as net income divided by owner's equity.

revenue per employee A financial ratio measuring how much revenue is generated by each employee, expressed as number of employees divided by total revenues.

role An expected set of activities or behaviors stemming from a job.

rule A specific course of action or conduct that must be followed. It is the simplest type of plan.

S

satisficing decision A decision that meets the minimum standards of satisfaction.

scientific management The application of scientific methods to increase individual workers' productivity.

self-leadership The process of influencing oneself.

self-managed work team A formally recognized group of employees who are responsible for an entire work process or segment that delivers a product or service to an internal or external customer.

shadowing Directly observing the work activities of the mentor by following the manager around for a stated period of time, such as one day per month.

situational leadership II (SLII) An explanation of leadership that matches leadership style to the readiness of group members.

six Sigma A data-driven method for achieving near-perfect quality with an emphasis on preventing problems.

small-business owner An individual who owns and operates a small business.

social loafing Freeloading, or shirking individual responsibility, when a person is placed in a group setting and removed from individual accountability.

socialization The process of coming to understand the values, norms, and customs essential for adapting to the organization.

span of control The number of workers reporting directly to a manager.

stack-ranking A ranking system that requires managers to rank each employee within each unit, and distribute raises and bonuses accordingly.

stakeholder viewpoint The viewpoint on social responsibility contending that firms must hold themselves responsible for the quality of life of the many groups affected by the firm's actions.

standard A unit of measurement used to evaluate results.

stockholder viewpoint The traditional perspective on social responsibility that a business organization is responsible only to its owners and stockholders.

strategic human resource planning The process of anticipating and providing for the movement of people into, within, and out of an organization to support the firm's business strategy.

strategic planning A firm's overall master plan that shapes its destiny.

strategy The organization's plan, or comprehensive program, for achieving its vision, mission, and goals in its environment.

stress The mental and physical condition that results from a perceived threat that cannot be dealt with readily.

subculture A pocket in which the organizational culture differs from the dominant culture, as well as other pockets of the subculture.

summary discipline The immediate discharge of an employee because of a serious offense.

superordinate goals An overarching goal that captures the imagination.

SWOT analysis A method of considering the strengths, weaknesses, opportunities, and threats in a given situation.

synergy A concept of the systems approach to management that states that the whole organization working together will produce more than the parts working independently.

systems perspective A way of viewing aspects of an organization as an interrelated system.

T

tactical planning Planning that translates a firm's strategic plans into specific goals by organizational unit.

task conflict Conflict that focuses on substantive, issue-related differences, related to the work itself.

task force A problem-solving group of a temporary nature, usually working against a deadline.

team leader A manager who coordinates the work of a small group of people, while acting as a facilitator and catalyst.

team A special type of group in which members have complementary skills and are committed to a common purpose, a set of performance goals, and an approach to the task.

teamwork A situation characterized by understanding and commitment to group goals on the part of all team members.

telecommuting An arrangement with one's employer to use a computer to perform work at home or in a satellite office.

termination The process of firing an employee because of poor job performance, unacceptable behavior, or interpersonal problems.

time-series analysis An analysis of a sequence of observations that have taken place at regular intervals over a period of time (hourly, weekly, monthly, and so forth).

top-level managers Managers at the top one or two levels in an organization.

tough question A question that helps the group achieve insight into the nature of the problem, what it might be doing wrong, and whether progress is sufficient.

training Any procedure intended to foster and enhance learning among employees, particularly directed at acquiring job skills.

traits Stable aspects of people, closely related to personality.

transformational leader A leader who helps organizations and people make positive changes in the way they do things.

transnational corporation A special type of MNC that operates worldwide without having one national headquarters.

two-factor theory of work motivation The theory contending that there are two different sets of job factors. One set can satisfy and motivate people, and the other set can only prevent dissatisfaction.

U

unity of command The classical management principle stating that each subordinate receives assigned duties from one superior only and is accountable to that superior.

V

variable pay When the amount of money a worker receives is partially dependent on his or her performance.

vertical thinking An analytical, logical process that results in few answers.

virtual office Employees who work together as if they were part of a single office despite being physically separated.

virtual team A small group of people who conduct almost all of their collaborative work by electronic communication rather than in face-to-face meetings.

virtuous circle The relationship between social and financial performance where corporate social performance and corporate financial performance feed and reinforce each other.

vision An idealized picture of the future of an organization.

W

whistle blower An employee who discloses organizational wrongdoing to parties who can take action.

wiki A password-protected Web page that allows for collaboration of multiple users.

work ethic A firm belief in the dignity and value of work.

work streamlining Eliminating as much low-value work as possible and concentrating on activities that add value for customers or clients.

work–family conflict A major stressor that represents a combination of individual and organizational factors contributing to stress.

wrongful discharge The firing of an employee for arbitrary or unfair reasons.

Index

A

B

C

Q

R

S